Herbert Marcuse and the Crisis of Marxism

Herbert Marcuse and the Crisis of Marxism

Douglas Kellner

Department of Philosophy
University of Texas at Austin

UNIVERSITY OF CALIFORNIA PRESS
Berkeley • Los Angeles

© Douglas Kellner 1984

First published 1984 by
UNIVERSITY OF CALIFORNIA PRESS
Berkeley and Los Angeles
California

ISBN 0 520 05176 9 (hard case)
ISBN 0 520 05295 1 (paper case)

Filmsetting by Vantage Photosetting Co. Ltd
Eastleigh and London

Printed in United States of America by
Edwards Brothers inc., Ann Arbor, Michigan

Library of Congress Cataloging in Publication Data

Kellner, Douglas, 1943–
  Herbert Marcuse and the crisis of Marxism.

  Bibliography: p.
  Includes index.
  1. Marcuse, Herbert, 1898–   2. Philosophy,
Marxist.   3. Fascism.   4. Communism.   I. Title.
B945. M2984K44   1984   335. 4' 1   84–69
ISBN 0-520-05176-9 (cloth)
      0-520-05295-1 (paper)

In remembrance of Herbert Marcuse, 1898–1979

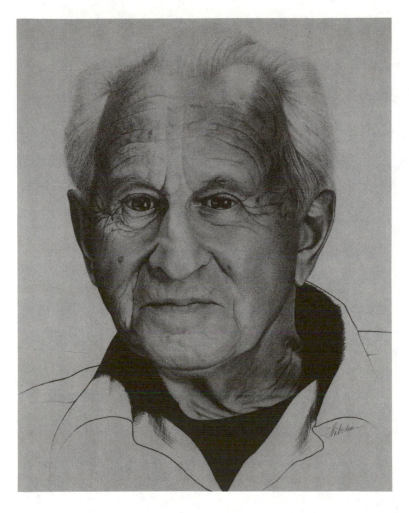

Contents

Acknowledgements

During the period from 1970 to 1983 when I conceived and wrote this book many people contributed ideas and criticisms of earlier drafts. I am grateful to Betsy Tenenbaum, Christian Dunis, Joan Ifland, Klaus Böhme, Paige Mitchell, Russ Scarboro and Tony Wheedon for friendship and discussion during my sojourn in Paris where I conceived the book and wrote the first draft. For interesting discussions of Marcuse and critical theory that helped in the development of the book, I would like to thank Stanley Aronowitz, Ernst Bloch, Jürgen Habermas, Martin Jay, Leo Lowenthal and Henry Pachter. In Austin, many people read and criticized chapters of the book, including Carolyn Appleton, Dan Davison, Charles Guignon, James Schmidt, Thomas Seung, Deborah Slavin, Jack Schierenbeck and Robert Solomon. Andrew Arato and Paul Breines offered suggestions for revision that were extremely useful. For reading the entire manuscript and offering many cogent criticisms, I am indebted to Robert Antonio, Stephen Bronner and Judith Burton. Thanks to Daniel Thibodeau for his portrait of Marcuse included in the book and to Judith Burton for her photograph of it. Finally, Herbert Marcuse generously set aside time for discussion and responded to many questions during trips to California in 1977 and 1978 when I interviewed him. I would like to dedicate the book to him and to the spirit of critical thinking that he promoted.

DOUGLAS KELLNER

Author's Notes

I have used the following abbreviations for Marcuse's major books, followed by the pagination in the edition cited below:

S1	*Schriften* 1 (Frankfurt: Suhrkamp, 1978).
R&R	*Reason and Revolution* (Boston: Beacon Press Paperback, 1960).
E&C	*Eros and Civilization* (Beacon Press Paperback, 1966).
SM	*Soviet Marxism* (New York: Vintage Press Paperback, 1961).
ODM	*One-Dimensional Man* (Beacon Press Paperback, 1964).
CPT	*A Critique of Pure Tolerance* (Beacon Press Paperback, 1965).
EL	*An Essay in Liberation* (Beacon Press Paperback, 1969).
5L	*Five Lectures* (Beacon Press Paperback, 1970).
SCP	*Studies in Critical Philosophy* (Beacon Press Paperback, 1973).
CR&R	*Counterrevolution and Revolt* (Beacon Press Paperback, 1972).
AD	*The Aesthetic Dimension* (Beacon Press, 1978).

The text is divided into chapters, sections, and sometimes subsections designated by numbers: 3.4, for instance, refers to Chapter 3, Section 4. This system has proved useful for cross-reference. I usually follow the published English translations of Marcuse's German writings, although I sometimes modify existing translations. The bibliography contains the most extensive list yet compiled of Marcuse's writings and interviews, as well as a list of books consulted and cited in this text.

Introduction: Herbert Marcuse and the Crisis of Contemporary Civilization

During the 1960s, Herbert Marcuse was more widely discussed than any other living philosopher. His criticisms of advanced industrial society and defence of radical politics achieved world-wide impact, and he was acclaimed 'father of the New Left'.[1] Almost alone among contemporary philosophers, Marcuse's ideas became topics of debate not only in scholarly journals, but in the popular press as well. For instance, an author in the *Saturday Evening Post* wrote that: 'Like rock 'n' roll and some of the mind-expanding drugs and those movies in which beginning-middle-end come in reverse or spiral or other or no patterns, Marcuse is a stimulant to fantasy and action, not the architect of a system. He is a writer of anthems and manifestos, not the organiser of reality. Thoughtful students are temporary people, bound for elsewhere – an elsewhere that they cannot clearly define. Marcuse tells them that this voyage is freedom, and that in the world to come the perpetual student will be the whole man.'[2] Summing up this phenomenon, Paul Breines writes:

Almost overnight the unknown dialectician became, in *Fortune*'s phrase, the 'improbable guru of surrealist politics' and simultaneously evoked the wrath of authorities and authoritarians everywhere. Indeed, it is one of the unique achievements of Marcuse's work that it has unified California's right-wing elders, *Pravda*, liberals such as Irving Howe and Nathan Glazer, the French Communist Party, and, most recently, the Pope in a single chorus of reprobation against the supposed pied piper who has corrupted the minds, morals and manners of the young.[3]

Although his popularity waned in the 1970s, after his death in 1979 many major newspapers, magazines and journals contained reflections on Marcuse.

Why Marcuse?

A most curious phenomenon: a relatively unknown German-American philosopher becomes a media celebrity and international hero for youth in revolt. How did this happen? Why did Marcuse become the most talked about and controversial intellectual of the day? In retrospect, Marcuse's ideas fit remarkably well into the cultural and political milieu of the 1960s. His uncompromising critique of advanced industrial society articulated the anger and disgust felt by a generation of young people outraged by the Vietnam war, the oppression of blacks and other minorities, and the continued existence of poverty alongside the wealth of the consumer society. Widespread revolt erupted against the oppressive conformity of complacent middle-class life, fuelled by the belief that the price of entry into the affluent society involved 'selling out' to corporate society and submission to alienated labour. Rebellion against bureaucracy and the socio-economic apparatus spread as individuals recoiled from becoming cogs in the machine, or faceless members of an impersonal, technocratic society. Many perceived the university to be a factory for processing servants of the corporation and the bureaucratic machine, with professors as purveyors of the kind of 'one-dimensional', conformist thinking that Marcuse so sharply criticized.

Marcuse's critique of contemporary society was radical in the sense that it penetrated to the roots of current alienation and revolt in the existing system of production, consumption and social control. Ambiguity in his own theory as to whether the primary source of oppression was advanced industrial society and its 'technological rationality', or the capitalist mode of production, led both counterculture enemies of the 'machine' and radical opponents of capitalism to see Marcuse as their spokesperson and ally. Most importantly, Marcuse provided alternatives to existing society. Once again, ambiguities in Marcuse's thought enhanced his popularity. Counterculture advocates of play, free love, flower power and personal liberation could find powerful articulations of their values in Marcuse's writings. And the New Left found a sharp critique of capitalism and an uncompromising defence of a type of democratic and libertarian socialism quite congenial to their radicalism. Marcuse thus legitimated liberation and revolutionary struggles. Unlike most in his generation, he enthusiastically embraced both the New Left and youth revolts. He never claimed to be a leader, or even spokesperson for these movements, but it is clear that the struggles of the 1960s excited him tremendously and rejuvenated his thought.

Marcuse tirelessly propagated his critiques of contemporary society and demands for radical social change through numerous writings, lectures, conferences and travels throughout the Western world. The 1960s finally provided a movement with which he could identify after decades of political isolation. His enthusiasm for the various New Left and Third World political movements endeared him to his young admirers and, as Marshall Berman testifies, he was able to generate personal appeal and charisma:

> One Friday evening a few years ago, I was standing in the midst of a noisy, happy crowd of students in an auditorium at Brandeis, waiting for a concert to begin, when word suddenly came up the line: Marcuse's here!' At once there was a hush, and people divided themselves up to clear a path. A tall, erect, vividly forceful man passed down the aisle, smiling here and there to friends, radiant yet curiously aloof, rather like an aristocrat who was a popular hero as well, perhaps Egmont in the streets of Brussels. The students held their breaths and gazed at him with awe. After he had got to his seat, they relaxed again, flux and chaos returned, but only for a moment, till everyone could find his place; it was as if Marcuse's very presence had given a structure to events.[4]

Marcuse was also a very exciting teacher who attracted a group of devoted followers before his rise to international fame,[5] and then gained a wide audience for his ideas through his writings, travels and media exposure. Although it is unlikely that many people who responded to his ideas and politics actually studied his writings seriously, there is no doubt that his thought was absorbed into the political culture of the 1960s and had world-wide impact.[6] True, he suffered the inevitable media eclipse when his works were no longer the fashion of the day. Moreover, he lost a social base for his theory with the split of the New Left into warring factions – many of whom explicitly repudiated Marcusean politics for Old Left sects or terrorist cadres – and with the splintering of the 1960s counterculture into diverse fads and cults in the 1970s.

In addition to discussing why Marcuse emerged as an international cultural hero and subject of controversy, we face today the task of appropriating and evaluating Marcuse's challenging body of writings in order to appraise his theoretical and political legacy. For these tasks the media phenomenon 'Marcuse' provides an obstacle to comprehending Herbert Marcuse the theorist, who bequeathed literally thousands of pages of difficult and fascinating texts to posterity. In fact the polemics, mystifications and simplifications of Marcuse's works in its world-wide reception have frequently obscured his important contributions to contemporary thought. To counter widespread misinterpretations, I shall trace the development of Marcuse's life-work and shall provide analyses and criticisms that will help initiate a process, barely begun, of evaluating Marcuse's legacy. By examining the entirety of Marcuse's published work and the socio-cultural situation to which it responds, the adequacy of his thought can be assessed in terms of (1) his contributions to philosophy and social theory; (2) his political project calling for radical social transformation; and (3) his vision of an alternative society and human liberation.

In respect of these issues, Marcuse's work is quite impressive. His writings respond to and interpret the most significant historical and intellectual events of the century. In the 1920s he perceived the tendencies towards alienation and dehumanization in advanced industrial society, while in the 1930s he made clear the dangers of fascism. Marcuse was also alert to important intellectual trends and developments, producing one of the first major interpretations and critiques of Martin Heidegger's *Being and Time*. Here he attempted the first synthesis of Marxism and phenomenological existentialism. In 1932 Marcuse recognized the importance of Marx's recently published *Economic and Philosophical Manuscripts of 1844* and began revising interpretations of Marxism from the vantage point of Marx's early works. Marcuse was also a major Hegel scholar and contributed to the Hegel renaissance in the 1930s and 1940s, while after the Second World War he was an influential exponent of a synthesis of Freud and Marx. From the time of his arrival in the

United States in 1934, Marcuse helped transmit the best of European radical thought and developed penetrating critiques of advanced industrial society.

Not only was Marcuse a transmitter of a tradition of radical thought which was rediscovered by many in the 1960s, but he was an original contributor to this tradition. During the post-war period, Marcuse trenchantly criticized both Soviet Marxism and US capitalism, calling attention to new forms of domination, repression and social control in advanced industrial societies. He accompanied his social critique with a theory of liberation and defence of his own version of utopian socialism. Marcuse was one of the few contemporary thinkers to attempt a fusion of philosophy and politics and became a major figure in contemporary history both through his work in philosophy and social theory and through his concern with radical politics. From his first published essays, Marcuse sought the unity of theory and practice which he believed was the mark of genuine Marxism, and sought to reinvigorate and reconstruct Marxian theory during an era when Marxism was degenerating into sterile orthodoxy.

Marcuse and the crisis of Marxism

A central focus of my study will be Marcuse's many-sided responses to what has been called the 'crisis of Marxism'.[7] From the late 1920s until his death, Marcuse attempted to re-examine and develop the Marxian project in order to make it more relevant to the particular situation and problems of the present age. Contrary to many previous interpretations which present Marcuse as a pre-Marxist, a non-Marxist or even an anti-Marxist thinker,[8] I shall try to show that his work is an extremely critical, speculative and idiosyncratic version of Marxism. We shall discover that even in works where Marx is never mentioned, such as *Eros and Civilization*, or in those where traditional Marxism is radically questioned, such as *One-Dimensional Man*, Marcuse is using Marxian concepts and methods to expand the Marxian theory, to overcome its limitations and to question aspects that he believes should be revised or rejected. On the whole, Marcuse's version of Marxism consists of a series of revisions and renewals of Marxian theory that provides a theoretical project seeking to comprehend and transform contemporary society.

What distinguishes Marcuse's life-work are his heroic and often desperate attempts both to reconstruct the Marxian theory and to criticize its limitations and shortcomings. To Marcuse, Marxism had neither absorbed the most advanced currents of contemporary thought, nor kept pace with changes in contemporary society. Moreover, he believed that it had lost its efficacy as a theory of social change and emancipatory politics, and thus required new perspectives and ideas to restore its liberating promises and hopes. Despite the perceived problems and deficiencies in Marxism, Marcuse committed himself deeply to the Marxian project and identified with it from his first published essays until his death in 1979. He struggled with what he perceived as the mixture of truth and historical obsolescence of primary Marxian categories and theories, and tried to preserve its emancipatory possibilities in the face of its failure as a theory of radical politics. Marxism's theoretical and political deficiencies led Marcuse to bring into Marxism what he saw as the most progressive and important tendencies of classical and modern thought. This led to revision – and even rejection – of certain features of orthodox Marxism and to the production of a new synthesis that would be more adequate to developments in contemporary society and would restore Marxism as a total, integrative revolutionary project for the modern epoch. Thus Marcuse's work is solidly within Marxism, yet it goes beyond its traditional versions. His reconstruction of Marxism therefore produces a series of tensions between Marcuse's thought and orthodox Marxism, while his own multi-dimensional appropriations and revisions of Marxism render his theory full of conflicting tendencies and surprising developments.

Marcuse's dilemma was that although for a previous generation of leftist radicals Marxism was the unquestioned foundation for revolutionary politics, during his lifetime history and the development of contemporary society raised fundamental questions concerning the continued validity and relevance of the Marxian theory. Traditional Marxism claimed to provide a theory and method that allows its initiates to analyse and to understand the world. Marxism indicates both 'what is to be done' and provides concrete political instructions to unite theory and practice. Marxian theory presents itself as part of the historical process, claiming that its concepts articulate the movement and direction of history; it asserts that history will in turn confirm both the truth and practical usefulness of the theory. Marcuse's problem is that instead of confirming Marxism, the historical process during his life seemed to refute, or to put into question, crucial elements of the Marxian theory.

Marcuse came of age during the collapse of the Second International in the face of the outbreak of the First World War.[9] Although the working class and its socialist parties were supposed to oppose nationalism, militarism and war, the dominant working-class mass parties were carried along by nationalist-militarist sentiment and overwhelmingly elected to support the war effort in their respective countries. Consequently, rather than resisting the 1914 war in the name of the Socialist International and working-class solidarity, the socialist parties, for the most part, participated in the imperialist war. Many saw this as the betrayal of proletarian internationalism that led to a splintering of the socialist movement into warring parties and factions, which greatly weakened the Second International and tarnished its image as a revolutionary movement. Although there was seemingly a confirmation of Marxism in the Russian Revolution of 1917, the failure of the German and European revolutions created an anomaly for Marxian theory: although socialist revolution was supposed to happen in the most developed industrialized-capitalist countries of the West, the revolution took place instead in quasi-feudal, semi-asiatic and underdeveloped Russia.

Furthermore, the construction of socialism in the Soviet Union did not follow the Marxian scenario, calling for socialist democracy, a classless society and workers' self-management, which together would eliminate alienated labour and provide the conditions for social justice and equality, as well as making possible the liberation and development of the individual. In Marcuse's view, this process of emancipation did not take place: the state, instead of withering away, constituted a new ruling class and party bureaucracy that soon fell prey to Stalin's repressive and autocratic rule. Although Marcuse followed the Russian Revolution with great enthusiasm, he soon became suspicious of the Soviet domination of the German Communist Party and the Communist International.[10] And though he remained firmly committed to the socialist project, he was deeply disturbed by Communist Party dictatorship, Stalinist trials and prison camps, and the Soviet pact with Hitler and Nazi Germany. Thus it was impossible for Marcuse to join the Communist Party, and he suffered a political identity crisis that was to lead him to a life-long search for new forces and strategies for revolution in the advanced capitalist countries.[11]

The triumph of fascism in central and southern Europe and the barbarism of the Second World War seemed to refute the optimistic elements in the Marxian theory of history that saw inexorable progress towards socialism as the direction of history. Instead of socialism, a pseudo-revolutionary fascist movement gained power, and the working class suffered fascist domination while again being sacrificed in a murderous war. The regressive nature of fascism put in question the Marxian theory of history and revolution, since it appeared that history was not progressing towards democratic socialism and the liberation of the working class.

After the Second World War the unparalleled affluence and stabilization of the economy in advanced capitalist societies rendered problematic certain aspects of the Marxian theory of capitalist crisis and collapse. Moreover, Marcuse began to believe that the integration of the working class robbed traditional Marxian theory of its revolutionary agent. The Cold War stimulated the economy and ideologically mobilized Western society against the Red Enemy – Communism. Consequently, what for Marcuse had been the theory and image of liberation – Marxian socialism – became equivalent to the 'foreign ideology of Communism' and was identified with the Soviet Union. This situation made it dangerous for a Marxian radical to call for socialist revolution, especially in the United States, where Marcuse chose to live. Indeed, McCarthyism led to a widespread suppression of Marxian radicals – and even critical liberals! – in government, universities and the entertainment industries.

In sum, Marxism seemed to have lost its moorings, no longer possessing its integrative practical and theoretical vision which could chart the course of historical development and give concrete political directives. For many, Marxism was impoverished because in its party versions it was cut off from the more advanced elements of social theory, philosophy and modern art, all of which appealed to Marcuse, yet were denounced as 'bourgeois ideology' by many orthodox Marxists. Marxian theory had become a dogma, serving as a legitimating ideology for the practice of Communist, Social Democratic and various sectarian groups. As a theory, Marxism failed to keep pace with the development of modern history and culture and had instead become a closed system that degenerated into a fossilized orthodoxy, legitimizing Communist state and party practice.[12]

Yet despite its problems, Marcuse held on to the Marxian theory and defended its continued theoretical importance and political relevance. In a 1978 BBC interview, after discussing Marcuse's criticisms of Marxism's shortcomings and attempts to reconstruct Marxism, his interviewer, Bryan Magee, asked: 'You have catalogued a formidable list of defects in Marxist theory ... What many people will be asking themselves is: all this being so, why did you and the other members of the Frankfurt School remain, or even want to remain, Marxists? What's the point of hanging on to a theory so riddled with error? Why not try to liberate your thought-categories from it altogether, and look at reality afresh?' Marcuse replied:

Easy answer: because I do not believe that the theory, as such, has been falsified. What has happened is that some of the concepts of Marxian theory, as I said before, have had to be re-examined; but this is not something from outside brought into Marxist theory, it is something which Marxist theory itself, as an historical and dialectical theory, demands. It would be relatively easy for me to enumerate, or give you a catalogue of, those decisive concepts of Marx which have been corroborated by the development of capitalism; the concentration of economic power, the fusion of economic and political power, the increasing intervention of the state into the economy, the decline in the rate of profit, the need for engaging in a neo-imperialist policy in order to create markets and the opportunity of enlarged accumulation of capital, and so on. This is a formidable catalogue – and it speaks a lot for Marxian theory.[13]

These remarks indicate that Marcuse himself defines his project in terms of appropriating the method and 'decisive concepts' of Marxism while criticizing those elements that are outmoded or historically obsolescent. Unlike mechanical Marxists, Marcuse uses Marxism to think creatively and to analyse contemporary problems and historical situations. For Marcuse, Marxism is a method of analysis and instrument of critique and social transformation and is not a dogma or system of absolute knowledge.

Reading Marcuse

Previous books on Marcuse have failed to present Marcuse's complex relations to Marxism and to show how he both criticizes and develops Marxian theory in response to changing historical conditions. The heated political situation in which Marcuse became the most widely discussed thinker of the day exposed his work to sharp polemics that frequently present a distorted version of his thought. Critics of all political persuasions tried to 'refute' Marcuse and to demonstrate the failings of his theory. These works generally do not investigate the origins and genesis of his work, nor do they adequately interpret Marcuse's work in relation to Marxism and critical theory.[14] Moreover, many of the books and studies published in the late 1960s and early 1970s focus on a stage of Marcuse's thought which he himself was attempting to go beyond.[15] Although some useful critical analyses appeared of stages of Marcuse's project (such as studies in the Habermas *Festschrift*) or of aspects of his theory (such as studies of his relation to Freud), most interpretations failed to present the full range of his thought and its characteristic tensions and ambivalences.[16]

As I shall show in the following chapters, some critics interpret Marcuse as an 'essentialist', while others present him as a 'historicist'. Some dismiss his alleged bleak pessimism, whereas others criticize him for starry-eyed utopianism. Marcuse is sometimes called an old-fashioned rationalist and at other times a blatant irrationalist. He has been attacked both as a dogmatic Marxist and as an anti-Marxist. These conflicting characterizations fail to capture the tension within Marcuse's thought and his life-long attempt to overcome dichotomies between essentialism and historicism, materialism and idealism, and a series of dualities that he believes have plagued traditional and contemporary thought. In order to counter one-sided or distorted interpretations, I shall attempt to analyse in detail the complex syntheses, ambiguities, tensions and modifications of Marcuse's thought. This project requires a historical-genetic approach which traces the developments and revisions of his thought rather than a structural reading that takes Marcuse's works as a systematic totality.

My study will allow us to discern both the ruptures and novel departures, as well as the continuity in Marcuse's thinking and the theoretical constants and perspectives at the core of his work.

For example, although a constant theme in Marcuse's work has been the concern for liberation and revolution, these concepts are historical categories for him that are related to specific social contexts and take on different form and content in different situations. In the successive stages of his work Marcuse stresses liberation *from* various socio-historical forces and proposes different strategies and goals *for* social transformation. Through this historical-genetic perspective, Marcuse's thought can be read as a philosophical articulation and explanation of the major historical and political transformations in this century of revolution and counter-revolution. Consequently, a reading of each of his major texts will be provided that will focus on the issues and problems in Marcuse's thought within its historical and theoretical context.

In the spirit of his advocacy of critical thinking, I shall develop detailed evaluations of Marcuse's works which will address the success or failure of his attempts to provide new theories to help us understand and transform contemporary society. In this way his work can be evaluated in terms of his various attempts to realize his project's own self-professed intentions. We shall see how internal limitations of his project, as well as historical obstacles, drive Marcuse constantly to revise and develop his theory. To illuminate the itinerary of Marcuse's work as it goes through a series of stages of development that appropriate Marxian and non-Marxian ideas, we must examine how his various writings meet, or fail to meet, the demands he himself sets for his work. This procedure will enable us to perceive how Marcuse deepens and expands the Marxian theory, infusing it with elements from traditions which confront issues and problems that Marxism had tended to ignore. The result is a version of Marxism that enriches the Marxian theory through the production of a compelling and comprehensive body of writings comparable in scope to the monumental work of Lukács, Bloch and Sartre.

Since Marcuse's project represents a series of responses to changing historical conditions and crises, an adequate interpretation of his thought requires a combination of biography, intellectual history, textual exegesis, philosophical and political analysis, polemical debate and critical evaluation of both its theoretical and political dimensions. Previous studies of Marcuse's thought have been vitiated by their failure to situate his works adequately within their historical, political and intellectual contexts and have failed to show how the various stages and works fit into Marcuse's evolving synthesis. To overcome this problem I shall interpret Marcuse's writings in relation to their historical context and shall demonstrate how history and various theoretical and practical critiques reveal the limitations of his theories and drive Marcuse to revise his positions. This study therefore seeks to provide comprehensive interpretations and criticisms of the entirety of Marcuse's work in order to help produce critical discussion of his legacy to contemporary philosophy and social theory.

1

Origins: Politics, Art and Philosophy in the Young Marcuse

In 1922 Marcuse summarized his early life in the 'Lebenslauf' (biography) required as part of a German doctoral dissertation:

> I was born on July 19, 1898 in Berlin, the son of the businessman Carl Marcuse and his wife Gertrud, born Kreslawsky. I attended the Mommsen Gymnasium and from 1911 the Kaiserin-Augusta Gymnasium in Charlottenburg until my summons to military service in 1916. After completing my final examination (*Reifeprüfung*), I entered Reserve Division 18 (*Train-Ers.-Abtg. 18*) but remained in the homeland on account of my poor eye-sight and was transferred to the Zeppelen Reserves (*Luftschiffer-Ers.-Abtg. 1*) where I received permission and the opportunity to visit lectures. After my release in the Winter of 1918, I studied regularly for four semesters in Berlin and four semesters in Freiburg, first Germanistik, and then modern German literary history as my main subject (*Hauptfach*) and philosophy and political economy as subsidiaries (*Nebenfach*).[1]

Marcuse has always insisted that his childhood and upbringing was that of a typical German upper-middle-class youth.[2] He claims that his Jewish family was well integrated into German society and that he never felt any acute alienation because of his Jewish origins.[3] While it is tempting to try to find clues to the later man and thinker in his early biography, Marcuse himself implicitly warns against such a procedure in his last book, *The Aesthetic Dimension*: 'What is true of the classics of socialism is true also of great artists. They break through the class limitations of their family background, environment. Marxist theory is not family research.'[4]

In various interviews Marcuse has claimed that his political education did not really begin until he was drafted into the German army and experienced the German Revolution in Berlin in 1918.[5] Consequently, section 1 will discuss his 'road to Marx', which Marcuse told me was the most significant development in his early life.[6] After his decisive early political experiences Marcuse turned to study German literature, and section 2 will examine Marcuse's doctoral dissertation, *The German Artist-Novel* (*Der deutsche Künstlerroman*) which contains striking anticipations of his later theories. Section 3 discusses Marcuse's study with the philosopher Martin Heidegger, whose impact on Marcuse's early writings will be the topic of Chapter 2. Since many of Marcuse's early concerns and ideas continued to shape his later works, I shall in effect be laying bare the hitherto relatively unknown source of Marcuse's later writings. Although I shall stress the shifts and discontinuities in his later works, it should be emphasized that there is a strong continuity and set of basic ideas in Marcuse's thought which are first evident in his early views of politics, art and philosophy. In this chapter I shall therefore uncover his early political experiences, studies and texts, which played an important role in shaping his later thought and writings.

1.1   Marcuse's road to Marx

Marcuse claims that he first became actively interested in politics and socialism when he was stationed in Berlin during the First World War. The agitation of socialist radicals against the war and the increasing opposition of prominent Social Democrats raised fundamental political issues that were especially pressing to those who were fighting the war. Massive strikes and the beginnings of the workers' councils movement dramatized the political issues, and Marcuse became involved in these struggles.[7] In 1917 he joined the Social Democratic Party (SPD) as a protest against the war and the society that produced it.[8] It is significant that, myths to the contrary, Marcuse did not join the radical Spartacus faction of Rosa Luxemburg and Karl Leibknecht (although he came to sympathize with it), nor did he join the Independent Social Democratic Party (USPD) which had formed in April 1917 to break with the SPD war policy.[9] The previously apolitical eighteen year-old youth had probably not understood adequately the political options open in 1917 and, as noted, Marcuse himself claims that his political education began in earnest only with the German Revolution of 1918 and its aftermath. Hence his joining the majority socialist party (SPD) was not the result of any well thought-out political theory; rather, it was the protest of a young man from an upper-middle-class background who was just beginning his political involvement.

The year 1918 was a crucial one for modern German history, and it deeply influenced Herbert Marcuse. In January, a general strike was instigated in Berlin by the revolutionary shop stewards of the metal workers' union, which dramatized the Spartacus programme of the mass strike, workers' control, and revolutionary struggle.[10] Although the strike failed, the rapid deterioration of the German military situation raised the spectre of social revolution. In October 1918, rebellions by sailors in Kiel set off a series of insurrections by soldiers and workers all over Germany. These upheavals led to the establishment of a socialist 'councils republic' in Bavaria and forced the abdication of the Kaiser.[11] The November Revolution which swept through Germany was especially intense in Berlin.[12] At the time when military revolt was spreading from Kiel and Hamburg to Berlin, Marcuse joined a soldiers' council in Reinickerndorf, a northern working-class suburb of Berlin. He likes to tell of how his first disillusionment with the revolution came when the soldiers elected their old officers to positions of authority, suggesting to him that the change might not be so radical after all.[13] It seems that the officers were almost automatically re-elected, as the younger soldiers, lacking in administrative experience and self-confidence, looked to their officers to get them home from the war as soon as possible.[14]

Marcuse's engagement in the tumultuous political activity occurring in late 1918 during the German Revolution decisively shaped his political views. At a meeting of over 3,000 delegates of the Greater Berlin workers' and soldiers' councils, the political alternatives were debated by prominent socialists of all tendencies. Friedrich Ebert of the Social Democrats urged an end to socialist disunity and disorder, and called for the development of a constitutional republic under Social Democratic leadership. Karl Leibknecht of the Spartacus League argued that counterrevolution was threatening, and that the time was right to carry out a revolutionary insurrection aimed at establishing a socialist republic. Marcuse listened carefully to these debates and was increasingly drawn to the Spartacus position, attending meetings, rallies and demonstrations at which Spartacus leaders spoke. At the time he was part of a civilian security force (*Sicherheitswehr*), mobilized at the urging of Ernst Daumig and the council communists, and supported by the soldiers' councils, that was to defend the revolution against counter-revolutionary attacks. In November 1918 Marcuse found himself standing in Berlin Alexanderplatz under orders to fire at snipers who shot periodically at demonstrators and at those involved in the revolutionary movement.[15]

After his discharge from the army in December 1918, Marcuse quit the Social Democratic Party in protest against their actions and policies.[16] The SPD was increasingly compromising and making conciliatory gestures towards the old Prussian-bourgeois establishment, while it supported and perhaps instigated repression of the Left. The Social Democratic President Ebert believed that the SPD government needed the collaboration of General Wilhelm Gröner and other members of the general staff for an orderly troop disengagement. Gröner agreed to cooperate with the SPD government on condition that the officers could keep their ranks and military privileges under the new government. Ebert agreed and thus allowed the Prussian military establishment to maintain its former hierarchy. The SPD also moved to disband the revolutionary naval units which the radicals wanted to keep intact and to preserve the bourgeois judiciary apparatus. Furthermore, the much touted socialization programmes allegedly supported by the Social Democrats were never carried out.[17]

As the SPD moved towards alliances with the ruling powers of the German bourgeoisie, Marcuse moved to the Left and was now attracted to revolutionary politics. He became a bitter opponent of the Social Democrats after the 'arrest' and murder of Liebknecht and Luxemburg, in which, it was believed, the SPD government was implicated. In 1967, Marcuse told students in Berlin:

> Let me say something personal. If you mean by revisionism the German Social Democratic Party, I can only say to you that from the time of my own political education, that is since 1919, I have opposed this party. In 1917 to 1918 I was a member of the Social

Democratic Party, I resigned from it after the murder of Rosa Luxemburg and Karl Liebknecht, and from then on I have criticized this party's politics. Not because it believed that it could work within the framework of the established order – for we all do this, we all make use of even the most minute possibilities in order to transform the established order from inside it – that is not why I fought the SPD. The reason was rather that it worked in alliance with reactionary, destructive, and repressive forces.[18]

During this period Marcuse began to study Marx seriously.[19] Although he had read socialist pamphlets during the war, the intense political activity had made comprehensive study of Marxism impossible. He stressed that his experiences of the war and the German Revolution led him to a thorough study of Marxism in order to grasp more clearly the dynamics of capitalism and imperialism, as well as the failure of the German Revolution. He was also determined to understand his inability to identify with the major Left parties, the Social Democrats and the Communists. Marcuse began reading Marx and other socialist classics to learn the Marxian theory of revolution and concept of socialism.[20]

Although, like most radicals of his generation, Marcuse was excited by the Russian Revolution, he did not join the Communist Party (KPD) although he often voted Communist as a 'protest'.[21] It was no doubt difficult for a young man of Marcuse's class and background to identify himself with the working-class politics of the KPD. Although Georg Lukács and Karl Korsch joined the Communist Party, they were older than Marcuse, and based their decision on political experiences and knowledge of Marxism unavailable to the young Marcuse. It seems that after the turmoil of the war and the German Revolution, Marcuse was unable to make any clear political commitments. He did, however, already see himself on the Left politically and would remain there the rest of his life. When asked why he failed to join any Communist organization at the time, he responded in a 1972 interview:

I didn't join any, and if you ask me why I must confess to my shame that I can give you no answer. I simply don't know. By 1919, when I went from Berlin to Freiburg, life in Freiburg was completely unpolitical. Then when I came back to Berlin the communist party was already split. I detected foreign influence –

Russian influence – which I didn't consider exactly beneficial, and that may be one of the reasons why I didn't join. Nevertheless I became more and more politicized during this period. It was evident that fascism was coming, and that led me to an intensive study of Marx and Hegel. Freud came somewhat later. All this I did with the aim of understanding just why, at a time when the conditions for an authentic revolution were present, the revolution had collapsed or been defeated, the old forces had come back to power, and the whole business was beginning all over again in degenerate form.[22]

By 1919 Marcuse's brief period of political activity was over. He decided to return to his studies, interrupted by the war, and entered Humboldt University in Berlin where he took courses for the next four semesters in 1919–20. Marcuse was too young and inexperienced to pursue the career of a professional revolutionary, and gravitated naturally towards his former interests. After two years of study of traditional curricula in Berlin, he transferred to Freiburg, where he concentrated in German literature, and took courses in philosophy and political economy, his two minor fields. Here he carried out a systematic study of German literature, and wrote and defended his doctoral dissertation on *Der deutsche Künstlerroman* (*The German Artist-Novel*) which was accepted in 1922.[23] As a teenager, Marcuse loved both classical and modernist literature, and his choice of a degree in literary studies indicates that his interest in literature was stronger than his interest in politics and philosophy.[24]

1.2 The German artist-novel

Marcuse wrote his dissertation under the direction of Philip Witkop (1880–1942), a literature professor who had published articles on a wide range of German poetry and who himself was attracted to neo-romanticism and the aesthetic modernism of the Stefan George circle.[25] The method, structure and themes of Marcuse's dissertation are heavily influenced by Hegel's aesthetics and the theory of hermeneutics developed by Wilhelm Dilthey.[26] Following the method of the cultural sciences dominant at the time, Marcuse situated German literature in the context of German history and, like Hegel, delineated a progression and development of literary forms emerging out of interaction and sometimes conflict with each other. Like Dilthey and the hermeneuticists, he attempted through 'empathy' (*Einfühlung*) to identify with the artist or novel under investigation and to bring back to life the position and views therein.

In fact, *The German Artist-Novel* contains a Hegelian structure and rhythm that prefigures his later appropriation of Hegel's dialectical method: in each chapter, after sympathetically examining and portraying a type of artist-novel and artistic life, Marcuse discloses the contradictions and deficiencies in the novels or writers under consideration. He then shows how the problems with various forms and types of novel give rise to competing positions – which in turn contain their own contradictions and deficiencies and give rise to further developments. Marcuse especially valorizes the syntheses of Goethe, Keller and Mann for their ability to overcome the tensions and contradictions within the problematic of the German artist-novel. Thus Marcuse's procedure is similar to Hegel's dialectic in *The Phenomenology of Spirit*, even though there is no textual evidence in his dissertation that he had actually studied the *Phenomenology*. In any case, Marcuse learned to think and write dialectically in his doctoral dissertation before he had fully appropriated materialist dialectics.

Many of the themes and categories used in *The German Artist-Novel*, as well as its Hegelian methodology, were influenced by Georg Lukács's *Theory of the Novel* and his earlier work, *Soul and Form*.[27] Like Lukács in *Soul and Form*, Marcuse thematizes conflicts between demands of the ideal and the real, and between art and life. Following Lukács in *The Theory of the Novel*, Marcuse assumes an earlier state of harmony and reconciliation of artists and the surrounding world which, when sundered, produces an alienation of the individual that Lukács calls 'transcendental homelessness'.[28] He also follows Lukács in providing an historicized typology of the artist-novel, utilizing many of Lukács's distinctions and categories while adopting his philosophico-historical approach.[29]

Marcuse begins by situating the artist-novel within broader literary categories. Like Lukács, and following Hegel, Marcuse distinguishes between the novel and epic poetry, arguing that the epic expresses the collective life of an entire people, while the novel expresses the alienation of the individual artist from social life (*S1*, pp. 9ff).[30] The novel articulates individual longing and striving for a higher, more authentic mode of existence.[31] The artist-novel centres on characters who are torn between the artistic calling and the demands of everyday life. It presupposes a 'prosaic reality' (Hegel) and a world lacking in meaning and harmony (*S1*, p. 10). The artist-novel arises when the artist becomes possible as a distinct social type and when the life forms of the artist (*Künstlertum*) do not correspond with those of humanity (*Menschentum*).

The hero of the artist-novel 'does not find fulfilment in the life-forms of his environment with all its limitations. His essence and longing cannot be contained in them and he stands alone against everyday reality ... He somehow seeks a solution, a new unity, for his opposition is so powerful that he cannot stand it for very long without destroying his artistic being and his humanity' (*S1*, p. 16). The problem underlying the artist-novel is therefore the alienation of the individual, and especially the artist, from bourgeois society, and the subsequent fragmentation of life and lack of a harmonious community. In Marcuse's dramatic formulation, the artist-novel constitutes 'the struggle of the German people for a new society' (*S1*, p. 333).

Following standard interpretations, Marcuse assumes that Greek culture in the 'age of epic poetry' (prior to the appearance of Socrates) was a harmonious totality 'where life was itself art and mythology life, the public property of the people' (*S1*, p. 10).[32] Marcuse also postulates an heroic epoch at the origins of Germanic culture, where, in the integrated society of Norse warriors, 'the perfect unity of art and life' spoke through the ancient bards (*S1*, p. 11).[33] The original unity is torn asunder with the collapse of feudal culture, the foundation of the bourgeois city, and the Thirty Years War. At this time, a historical epoch of division and conflict emerges in which the individual confronts a world 'utterly devalued, impoverished, brutal and hostile which offers no fulfilment' (*S1*, p. 14).[34] Such an alienated world makes possible, however, 'the eruption of self-conscious subjectivity' (*S1*, p. 13) and the yearning for the overcoming of alienation. The artist objectifies his feelings and strivings, and desires their realization in the world. This leads the artist to try to shape reality according to his ideals and to overcome artistic alienation (*S1*, p. 16) – or to seek refuge in a world of beautiful illusion (*S1*, p. 17).

This notion of art previews later works such as *Eros and Civilization* and *The Aesthetic Dimension*, where Marcuse develops a theory of art as a revelation of utopian images of fulfilment and happiness that rejects the alienated world. His dissertation also centres on analysis of the sources of alienation and ways of overcoming it through the quest for liberation and a harmonious community – themes that would later become central to Marcuse's thought. There is anticipation too of his later position in which alienated outsiders and the 'Great Refusal' are important forces of opposition. Marcuse writes that at the dawn of bourgeois society there arose a

> travelling community of musicians and mimes, but in particular young clerics and students who broke out of 'the monastic cells and discipline of the cloister schools and leaped forth into a joyful life, wandering from land to land' (Winterfeld . . .). However, this insolent assault was battered to pieces by the resistance of feudal and ecclesiastical restrictions. Although some of these vagrants . . . enjoyed princely and spiritual protection, on the whole, they were total outcasts, permanently excluded; for them, there is no place in the life-forms of the surrounding world. Too proud, too wild in their ecstatic pursuit of freedom to seek compromise or conciliation, their lives vanish into the mists of restless vagrancy, of dissolute wandering (*S1*, p. 13).

Here Marcuse reveals sympathy for non-integrated outsiders as harbingers of emancipation.[35] From these wandering minstrels arose the first European artist types, who, in opposition to their society, cultivated their aesthetic sensibilities, while producing 'perhaps the first self-conscious artist whose vagrancy and opposition to the social environment was often seized and stressed as artistic necessity' (*S1*, p. 13).

After setting out this critical-historical framework, Marcuse offers a series of detailed, often fascinating, interpretations of the historical development of the German artist-novel.[36] He classifies the artist-novels in terms of a distinction between the poles of the 'realistic-objective' and the 'subjective-romantic', which in turn are related to the two main cultural tendencies of the time, a rationalistic Enlightenment and a subjectivistic pietism (*S1*, pp. 15ff). His own writing style follows these two tendencies, moving from sober, objective discussion of the novels to poetic flights of romantic lyricism. The subjective-romantic current tends to submit empirical existence to aesthetic ideals that generally cannot be realized, and thus often leads to a rejection of everyday life for art. This position was initiated by *Sturm und Drang* writers like Heinse, and to some extent Moritz.[37] It was the position also of the Romantics, French symbolism and aesthetes of the art-for-art's-sake tendency (*l'art pour l'art*). The subjective-romantic orientation creates a 'poeticized reality, a dreamlike world' in which there is perfect harmony, unity and beauty denied in everyday life.[38] The more objective-realistic tendency corresponds to later Romantics like Brentano, E. T. A. Hoffman and Eichendorff, as well as to the politicized writers of the Young Germany movement and social novel schools.[39] The 'objective-realist' novel, at least in its politicized versions, contains a 'demand for the radical restructuring of life-forms, which came to be formulated in practical terms as demands for social and political reform' (*S1*, pp. 174ff).

Contrary to some interpretations, Marcuse's *The German Artist-Novel* should not be read as an affirmation of Romanticism.[40] Throughout the book, there are critiques of Romanticism, and Marcuse praises in particular Goethe, Gottfried Keller and Thomas Mann for overcoming their early Romanticism and reaching an accommodation with their respective societies while attaining an epical, objective-realist prose style. After describing the early work of Goethe, such as *The Sorrows of Young Werther*, which was so typical of Sturm und Drang and so beloved by the Romantics, Marcuse turns to Goethe's *Theatralische Sendung* and *Wilhelm Meister*, claiming that 'the decisive progress over *Werther* is clear' (*S1*, p. 69). He then criticizes excessive Romantic subjectivism and idealism:

> Werther was trapped in his extreme subjectivism and absolute inwardness and could not transcend the split between idea and reality, self and world, and his only return to unity was through death, the extinction of empirical being. The Wilhelm Meister of the *Theatralische Sendung* has so far overcome the artistic subjectivism that he grasps full development in reality, in the environment, as necessary for the artist: from the bourgeois confines of his home city, from the inwardness of his youth, he travels with the theatre group from place to place, becomes acquainted with people and things, workers and nobility, factory and castle, village and city; in opposition to Jarno, he programmatically

emphasizes his resolution to plunge into the rich life and to create out of its fullness (*S1*, pp. 69ff).

Marcuse then discusses Goethe's *Wilhelm Meister*, where his hero progresses further towards overcoming artistic subjectivism and alienation through integrating himself into society and nature. Goethe's artist-hero experiences the 'unity of art and nature' (*S1*, p. 71) and manages to overcome his artistic alienation through integrating himself into society and common humanity. For Wilhelm Meister, 'the highest affirmation of life conditions the deepest personal resignation. In the ideal of "Humanity" it finds its proper form: the world's "limitations and inner laws are freely recognized. Henceforth, education (*Bildung*) enters in place of subjectivism (*Selbstigkeit*)"' (*S1*, p. 72). Goethe affirms the classical concept of Humanitas, of shaping one's personality according to an ideal of humanity. This requires his artist-hero to integrate himself within society and everyday life to create a 'harmonious personality' (*S1*, p. 72) and demands 'sacrifice and renunciation': the artist must renounce his one-sided obsession with art and 'through the reconciliation of the artist the opposition between artistic life and everyday life is overcome' (*S1*, p. 72).

Marcuse presents sympathetically Goethe's ideal of the integrated artist who attains a respectable profession within society and overcomes all the conflicts between art and life by serving humanity (see *S1*, pp. 74–84). In this way Goethe resolves the problems of the artist-novel and passes beyond its problematic to the *Bildungsroman* (the novel of education).[41] Throughout the next chapters Marcuse uses Goethe to criticize Romanticism (*S1*, pp. 104, 111, 119, *passim*) which returned to the problematic of the artist-novel and championed art over life, the artist over common humanity. Throughout the study, Marcuse criticizes Romantic idealist fantasies, ineffectual strivings, and the various failures of Romantic artists. He criticizes the Romantic tendency to withdraw from everyday reality and to create ideal fantasy worlds, as well as the Romantic belief that the artist is the highest form of human reality. He praises the efforts of late Romantics to return to history and everyday life: 'Bretano, E. T. A. Hoffmann, Eichendorff and Arnim share the knowledge that the artist can find no fulfilment through pure devotion to an ideal world. Besides the yearning for the ideal, there enters a yearning for life, for reality . . . real life has again become a value: in it the artist again sees meaning and goal' (*S1*, p. 122). Whereas Bretano and E. T. A. Hoffmann were not able to overcome their artistic alienation and find a home in the world, Marcuse believes that Eichendorff and Arnim did find reconciliation with everyday life, which made possible an 'overflowing affirmation of life' and the full development of their personalities (*S1*, p. 144).

In Marcuse's view, 'the brightest affirmation of life, the restoration and recovery of reality, the rooting of the artist in an immediate and present this-sidedness (*Diesseitigkeit*) . . . finds its fulfilment in Gottfried Keller' (*S1*, p. 210) whose novel *Der grüne Heinrich* Marcuse believes is the greatest German artist novel.[42] '*Grüne Heinrich* emerges as the genuine antipode to the subjective and romantic artist-novel: in opposition to the great symbol of Romanticism he posits a new realism . . . closely connected with the philosophy of Feuerbach who opposes Romanticism and German idealism. . . . A clear sunshine and the brilliance of a warm summer day radiates over the people in the novel' (*S1*, p. 210).

Keller's 'sensuous pantheism' obtains a unity of art and life and integrates the artist into 'a common and ordered form of life' (*S1*, p. 211). Marcuse traces Keller's development towards a peaceful and happy accommodation with his environment and the development of an epic-realist prose style that celebrates life in its totality. He defends Keller against charges that he ends up with a conservative celebration of bourgeois forms of life: 'The bourgeois life of Heinrich is only a symbol for the epic renunciation and integration and in no way is the unconditional recognition that the behaviour and values of a single social group (*Standes*) be accorded normative validity' (*S1*, p. 230). In fact, the peace, harmony, affirmation and celebration of life in Keller's novel anticipates Marcuse's later defence of hedonism and the social ideal of reconciliation and harmony. It is very likely, in fact, that his study of the German artist-novel helped shape his later ideal of liberation and vision of utopian socialism.

Although Marcuse enthusiastically projects an ideal of the integration of art and life and overcoming alienation through integration in a harmonious community, he is aware that the development of bourgeois society created new forms of alienation which were reflected in the artist-novel. In his dissertation he often discusses artistic revolts as conscious rejections of bourgeois society and capitalism that were destroying previous forms of life and were creating new obstacles to overcoming artistic alienation. For example, he writes:

The revolution of 1830, in which the Romantics proclaim the complete liberation of the artistic subjectivity, the capturing of beautiful reality, was followed very soon after by an absolute disenchantment. The bourgeoisie had taken over social leadership and a narrow, business-oriented, money-grubbing bourgeois society, totally concerned with practical interests, became entangled in a dry materialism. A rapid technification and industrialization of the spiritual and economic life begins; in this period, there was a powerful rise of the press . . . and the penetration of the business-principle in literature (*S1*, p. 248).

Marcuse sees social change prefigured in artistic subcultures and in the productions of artists and intellectuals. For example, in a section discussing the effects of the French revolutions of 1830 and 1848 on German literature, Marcuse points to the anticipation of these revolutions in the French 'bohemian' subculture and utopian socialism (*S1*, pp. 174ff).[43] He describes the French bohemian literary circle as 'the first attempt to carry through an authentic artistic form-of-life' and praises Saint-Simon, Fourier and Enfantin for creating 'great systems for a new social order' (*S1*, p. 179). In a passage prefiguring his own later political position, Marcuse writes: 'Far beyond the economic meaning of these systems, one saw in them a way to total revolutionizing of the fragmented forms of life, a revolutionizing that was a burning longing, a so bitter necessity for these groups' (*S1*, pp. 179–80). Marcuse then describes the effects of the July 1830 revolution: 'The French upheaval was the decisive experience for the young German artistic generation: the first great attempt was made there radically to transform the forms-of-life. There arose an incandescent longing of the oppressed youth to carry through this transformation in practice, directly on the grounds of the current reality; yes, to fight with weapons in their hands' (*S1*, p. 180). In this situation, 'art was placed in the service of life, submitted to the tendencies of the day; the artist became a man of practice, a political and social fighter' (*S1*, p. 181).

Marcuse describes enthusiastically the writers in the Young Germany movement who hoped to serve as 'the arousers of the people', with 'a call to struggle for necessary social transformation' (*S1*, p. 183). For them, 'art itself became a weapon, it would be a service to the revolutionary tendencies' (*S1*, p. 183). The revolution of 1830 soon gave way to reaction on a European scale and a new 'technical age' began: 'The powerful boom of commerce, of industry and technology, the conquests of natural science and economics led to an almost undisputed triumph of practical-material interests, which soon dominated the entirety of life' (*S1*, p. 193). But industrial society also gave birth to the proletariat and socialism, and to a new wave of revolutions in 1848 which 'appeared to open a new way' (*S1*, p. 195). Now 'the people were awake, they had arisen – from them it appeared that something new should originate. Now the artists believed that they had found cohorts of struggle and attained union: they entered the side of the revolutionary people, accompanied their striving and suffering, participated in their attacks on the old forms of life' (*S1*, p. 195). These struggles too went down in defeat, and the artistic *avant-garde* suffered disappointment and new alienation.

Artistic responses to the triumph of capitalist industrialization and the bourgeoisie included the development of the doctrine of 'art for art's sake' (*l'art pour l'art*) and artistic subcultures that again championed art over life, the artist over the bourgeois. Marcuse presents with great penetration literary bohemia, Flaubert, Zola and the French religion of art. He examines a series of novels in which artists renounce everything for the pursuit of their artistic calling and emphasizes the suffering, misery and frequent collapse of these artists. In so doing, he presents a strong critique of the 'aesthete' as a social type and the 'art-for-art's-sake' ideology. He claims that in the 'dandyism' of Oscar Wilde, the pursuit of sensual pleasures in Huysman's *Against Nature*, and in the aestheticism of various other French and Italian writers, 'something always remains unfulfilled: their humanity' (*S1*, p. 294). Marcuse comments:

> those who seek only aesthetic charms . . . who are forced to become constantly conscious spectators of their own life can never step out of their own ego-centricity ('I can only talk of myself' says Stelio Effrena in *Fire!*). For them, every human activity and togetherness is prohibited. They can only live as 'artist', as 'creator of beautiful things' (Oscar Wilde). . . . Life only has meaning and value when it is seen through the medium of art, is transformed into art' (*S1*, p. 294).

Origins: Politics, Art and Philosophy 27

Marcuse portrays critically the 'hysterical amorality' that emerges from this aesthetic ideal and highlights the tragedies of the artists in novels by Flaubert, Zola, Ibsen and others who try to live out such ideals.

It is striking that in every chapter one finds previews of his later ideas. His writing on *Sturm und Drang* and Goethe praises the emancipatory aspects of 'the feeling for nature' and 'experience of love' (*S1*, pp. 42ff). In his discussion of the French bohemian culture he quotes Gautier in an interesting anticipation of his later philosophical hedonism: '"joy appears to me as the end of life and the only thing useful in the world. God too wanted it: he made women, perfumes, light, beautiful flowers, good wines, curly hair, lips, and angora cats; he did not say to his angels: Have Virtue, but: Make Love"' (*S1*, p. 179). While Marcuse is sympathetic towards Romanticism and the aesthetics of German idealism, he also indicates attachment to the classics of realism and the materialism of Feuerbach (*S1*, pp. 210, 214).[44] His colourful portrayals of the German artist's quest for community prefigure his later concept of a non-repressive civilization in *Eros and Civilization* and his defence of utopian socialism in the 1960s. His presentation of the demand that ideas should shape reality previews his later appropriation of Hegel's idealism and his book *Reason and Revolution*.[45] The Romantic demand for a 'Kingdom of Beauty and Love' (*S1*, pp. 87ff) anticipates his emphasis on the importance of the aesthetic-erotic dimension for an emancipated existence (see, especially, Marcuse's sympathetic discussions of *Sturm und Drang* writers, the Romantics, and 'art for art's sake').

Marcuse's sympathetic portrayal of the variety of artistic tendencies, types of novels and writers is in part a result of his use of the method of 'empathy' (*Einfühlung*) practised by Wilhelm Dilthey and others in the German hermeneutical and 'cultural history' traditions.[46] Through empathy with each novelist, type of novel and the novel itself, the hermeneutical cultural historian presents the German artist-novels, for instance, not merely as a typology of artistic forms but also as forms-of-life, ways of living. Marcuse seems to identify with each artistic form or way of life in turn, almost as if he himself were debating which course of life he should follow. Should he escape from mundane everyday life for a life of cultivated aesthetic pleasures, as did certain *Sturm und Drang* and Romantic writers that he discusses? Or should he turn from illusory aesthetic concerns to practical everyday affairs and come to terms with

everyday life? Should he devote himself to the vocation of revolution? Or should he try to attain a balance between art, everyday life
and politics, as did Goethe, Keller and Mann? I suspect that
Marcuse was himself debating these options, which helps explain
the remarkable sympathy that he seemed to have for every artistic
type examined. In fact, to various degrees, Marcuse would himself
live out these different, and conflicting, options in the 1920s. Hence
I would suggest that the most interesting aspects of Marcuse's
dissertation result both from his having mastered the *Einfühlung*
method of the German cultural sciences and from his personal
involvement in the project.

The final chapter on Thomas Mann ends his study on a note of
ambiguity that I think reveals some of the contradictions on Marcuse's own situation and his attitude towards his class and bourgeois
society. Although Marcuse seems to sympathize both with the
alienated artists who oppose a cold, heartless world and with those
artists who are able to find sustenance and support in their environment, he concludes by acknowledging the possibility of reconciliation of the artistic life with bourgeois society, as was accomplished
by some of the characters in Thomas Mann's novels – and as Mann
himself seemed to achieve and advocate during the period in which
Marcuse was writing his dissertation. Accommodation with the
bourgeois world is possible, Mann suggests, through pursuing writing as a bourgeois profession, exemplifying the values of conscienti-
ousness, professionalism and creativity (*S1*, pp. 322ff).[47] If the
writer can become an educator and ethical force within bourgeois
society, he has overcome his alienation and is once more an
integrated member of society. Then he can quell his 'demonic Eros'
and 'dionysian powers' and can fit into everyday life (*S1*, pp. 326ff).
Hence it appears that Mann has solved the essential problem of the
artist-novel and has brought it to conclusion: 'the artistic existence
and bourgeois society are no longer two life-forms, two essentially
opposed unities, but the artist is integrated into the bourgeois
world, art and life are united, with the result that the problematic of
the artist-novel is no longer acute' (*S1*, p. 329).

Marcuse's discussion of Mann's *Death in Venice* foreshadows his
later adherence to the Freudian instinct theory and shows the
precariousness of Thomas Mann's solution to the problems of the
artist-novel. In the beginning of *Death in Venice*, Mann's artist-
hero Gustav von Aschenbach is exemplary of the ideal of the artist

who is both integrated in bourgeois society as a professional writer and educator, and who overcomes Romantic, subjectivist and anti-bourgeois tendencies to become an 'objective, bourgeois artist' (*S1*, p. 325). Von Aschenbach's achievement is a result of moral rigourism, a constant struggle to overcome Romanticism, lyricism, cynicism, irony and other traits of the conscious artistic personality. Von Aschenbach struggles for objective form in his work and stability and order in his life. He succeeds in his quest and is a well integrated member of bourgeois society who is officially recognized as a great artist and educator. Von Aschenbach, however, succumbs to demonic drives from within which force him to flee his quiet artistic residence and to travel to, eventually, Venice. There he succumbs further to 'dionysian powers' and temptations, and pursuing an overpowering attraction for a beautiful young Polish boy, he collapses.

Following Mann's novel, Marcuse describes how von Aschenbach falls prey to 'demonic powers' that break through his bourgeois exterior and throw him into a whirlpool of passion that shatters his carefully constructed persona and morality. Marcuse's description of these 'dark primordial powers' anticipates his appropriation of Freud's instinct theory: 'incorrigible, innate, nature – they designate a sphere that is beyond the resolution of the will' and that is both creative and destructive (*S1*, pp. 327ff). While von Aschenbach's inability to master these instinctual forces seems to put in question the viability of Mann's ideal of the integration of the artist in bourgeois society, Marcuse seems to think that *Death in Venice* represents a catharsis for Mann: he was able thereby to free himself from the demonic powers and artistic alienation so often portrayed in his early work and was able to attain in *Death in Venice* an 'objective epic' style that achieved a 'Homeric mania and beauty' (*S1*, pp. 328–9). In Marcuse's reading,

Death in Venice is the as yet final exorcism (*Beschwörung*) of the darkness, the discord, the abyss: what now follows is completely the product of the new integration and rootedness. From the feeling of ethical and social responsibility and posture, Mann wrote *Friedrich and the Great Coalition* (1914) and *Reflections of an Unpolitical Person* (1918), as well as the idylls 'Man and Dog' and 'Kindchen's Song' (1917) which are the purest emanation of the 'reborn contentment' ('*wiedergeborenen Unbefangenheit*'): a

thankful, conscious, self-immersion in the simplest appearances
of the newly won life, in the happiness and peace of community.
The artist has returned to bourgeois life, is connected to life anew.
The struggle that the artist-novel has fought since the l'art pour
l'art period is once again brought together in Thomas Mann's
work: the sacrificial artistry of l'art pour l'art, the artistic life of
knowledge and striving, aestheticism – and at the end stands a
victory, an overcoming (*S1*, p. 329).

Just as it appears that Thomas Mann emerges as the hero of his long
study, Marcuse raises some perplexing questions: 'The question
must be posed: is this victory, this overcoming, rooted in that pure
epic world-feeling which alone can reveal in the artist-novel the
totality and unity of things? Can it bring about the inner resolution
of oppositions?' (*S1*, p. 329). Marcuse comments:

> The epical basic-experience of the harmony and beauty of the
> world, of the necessity and appropriateness of everything, even
> the smallest appearances, of the supraindividual interconnected-
> ness of all that is essential, the loving affirmation and grasp of
> Being: that is an eternal fundamental experience (*ewiges
> Urerlebnis*) that transcends all temporal and spatial conditions,
> that is bound to no determinate form-of-life, that is given as a
> possibility to all and everyone. But the living and artistic working
> out of this experience – the epical life and shaping of art –
> demands always and everywhere a presupposition: the presence
> of an organic and meaningful (*sinnhaltigen*) form-of-life, unified
> and carrying its own values – a 'community' (*Gemeinschaft*) in
> the most extreme and deepest sense. It alone is the solid and
> fruitful ground out of which the great epics arose, in which the
> resigned (*entsagend*) artist can perform a proper and fulfilling
> accommodation (*Einordnung*) (*S1*, pp. 329–30).

Goethe found such a community in the Rococo society of Weimar,
and Keller found it in the Swiss democratic city-state, but what
about Mann? Marcuse suggests that the bourgeois society of
Mann's novels is too individualistic, egotistical, and too limited (*S1*,
pp. 330–1). Hence, although he ends his chapter on Mann with
renewed praise, he concludes the study by remarking: 'for the
German artist-novel, the community is not something given, but

something given up and something to strive for (*Aufgegebenes*). Beyond the literary historical problem, a piece of human history is visible: the struggle of the German people for a new community' (*S1*, p. 333).

Since the term *Aufgegebenes* signifies both 'something given up' and 'something to strive for', the implication is that a community does not yet exist to which artistic individuals can freely give themselves, but remains something to be striven for, a task yet to be accomplished. Thus, it seems that Marcuse does not acquiesce in Mann's resignation and acceptance of bourgeois society. However, his sympathetic portrayal of Mann presents ambivalences in his own situation, and suggests that he was attracted to Mann's solution. It also shows that his ideal society – later sketched out in *Eros and Civilization* and subsequent writings and anticipated in his doctoral dissertation – was something still to be fought for and won. Such a utopian ideal would make accommodation with bourgeois society impossible, and indeed, in his first published essays, Marcuse would call for its overthrow and would support socialist revolution.[48]

Lukács's self-criticism in his 1962 preface to *The Theory of the Novel* can be applied to Marcuse's *The German Artist-Novel*.[49] Their overly literary histories were both too far removed from the socio-economic context. Although, as I have noted, Marcuse often provides discussions of social history and its effect on literature, his analysis is sketchy and inadequate, and does not provide sufficient mediation of the literature and society. Hence he provides no real social history of the German artist-novel and no detailed account of the rise of capitalism and its impact on society and culture beyond the brief sketch cited. In sum, Marcuse has yet to appropriate the Marxist concept of ideology, or theory of historical materialism, and his work really did not transcend the bounds of the German cultural history school.

Neither Lukács nor Marcuse in their early literary studies could solve the problem of the contradictions between art and life which so deeply concerned the European intelligentsia. In *Soul and Form*, Lukács presents a series of meditations which pose the question of whether aesthetics or ethics are of primary importance for human life.[50] He portrays the inability of the aesthetic life to provide secure, lasting happiness in the face of death, an unstable society, the attractions and demands of other people, and political-historical contingencies. The early Lukács sought an ethical rather than an aesthetic solution to the problems of existence. Soon after, he yearned for a social solution in *The Theory of the Novel*, portraying the harmonious city-states (polis) of Greece as the ideal of an integrated society in which there is no alienation. Significantly, most of the novels analysed by the early Lukács and by Marcuse in his dissertation were critical in various ways of bourgeois society, and they might have enabled both to see the radical potential in bourgeois art to turn the individual against an alienating society in order to seek individual authenticity and social alternatives. Moreover, their attraction to socialism was nourished by their aesthetic studies, which may have led them to view socialism as an ethical and political ideal that could solve the cultural problems with which they were concerned in their early work. In fact, Lukács was to interpret socialism explicitly as his hoped-for social alternative in essays published after his conversion to Marxism in 1918, some of which were collected in *History and Class Consciousness*.[51]

Lukács temporarily put aside his studies of aesthetics when he made his commitment to political activism at the time of the Hungarian Revolution and only returned to centre his work on aesthetic concerns in the 1930s when he considered himself a failure in politics.[52] Marcuse, on the other hand, turned away from his political involvement to the study of literature, yet after completing his dissertation he did not pursue an academic career but instead decided to return to Berlin to undertake a short-lived business venture. It was not until much later, in fact, that both Lukács and Marcuse were able to synthesize their interests in aesthetics and politics, and thus reconciled their interests in art and revolution.

1.3 Heidegger and philosophy

In 1922 Marcuse returned to Berlin and worked for several years in an antiquarian and book-dealer publishing firm. He lived at the time in an apartment in Charlottenburg with his wife Sophie, a former student of mathematics and statistics whom he met in Freiburg and married in 1924. His father had survived the economic crisis of 1923 through good property investments and helped Marcuse buy a partnership in the firm of the antiquarian book dealer and publisher, S. Martin Fraenkel, where he worked primarily as a catalogue researcher and bibliographer.[53] Here he prepared his first publication, a Schiller bibliography which appeared in 1925 and which Marcuse insists was 'just a job' and 'unimportant' for his intellectual development.[54] In it, he updated the standard Schiller bibliographies with sparsely annotated factual notes on the various Schiller texts and editions. Marcuse later claimed that it was not until he was working on *Eros and Civilization* that Schiller took on a crucial importance for him, but I suspect once again that his early literary studies influenced him deeply and returned to play a decisive role in his later work. Then, in Marcuse's words, 'I read *Sein und Zeit* when it came out in 1927 and after having read it, I decided to go back to Freiburg (where I had received my PhD in 1922) in order to work with Heidegger. I stayed in Freiburg and worked with Heidegger until December 1932, when I left Germany a few days before Hitler's ascent to power'.[55]

Martin Heidegger was at the time one of the most influential German philosophers. His work *Being and Time* presented a synthesis of Edmund Husserl's phenomenology and what was soon to be called 'existentialism' with elements of classical philosophy.[56] Although Marcuse attended the lectures of both Husserl and Heidegger in Freiburg, he found Heidegger 'more exciting', despite his admiration for Husserl's attempt to make a 'new beginning'.[57] Heidegger's work blended the concern for the authenticity of the individual championed by Kierkegaard and Nietzsche with Husserl's demand that philosophy turn to 'the things themselves', to concrete phenomena and experience.[58] Husserl proposed that philosophers put aside their abstract categories and theories, and return to a study of experience and consciousness that is not distorted by philosophical blinders and preconceptions. Husserl developed the method of 'phenomenology' in order to provide a radically new starting point, method of inquiry and foundation for philosophy.[59] Heidegger associated with Husserl and published *Being and Time* in his journal.[60]

Heidegger's book applied the phenomenological method to a wealth of phenomena like the work world, the social world, the individual experience of death, anxiety and conscience, questions of choice and commitment, and 'historicity'. Moreover, he developed these themes in a philosophical problematic addressed to traditional philosophical problems, and reinterpreted philosophers like Aristotle, Descartes, Kant and Hegel, as well as more recent philosophers like Dilthey, Scheler and Husserl. To many readers, Heidegger appeared to give new answers to fundamental philosophical questions and to have effected a philosophical revolution.[61] Heidegger was reportedly a truly exciting teacher and Marcuse was impressed with his serious philosophizing, his method of reading texts, and his seemingly radical, new philosophy. A letter from Marcuse to friends in Berlin provides a vivid picture of Heidegger and discloses Marcuse's views of both Heidegger and Husserl in 1929:

> Concerning Heidegger: It is hard to imagine a greater difference than between the shy and obstinate lecturer (*Privatdozent*) who eight years ago talked out of the window in a small lecture hall compared to the successor of Husserl who lectures in an over-flowing auditorium with at least six hundred listeners (mostly women) in brilliant lectures with unshakeable certainty, talking with that pleasant tremor in his voice which so excites the women, dressed in a sports suit that almost looks like a chauffeur's uniform, darkly tanned, with the pathos of a teacher who feels himself completely to be an educator, a prophet and pathfinder and whom one indeed believes to be so. The ethical tendencies found in *Being and Time* – which aim at philosophy becoming practical – really seem to achieve a breakthrough in Heidegger himself, although, to be sure, in a way that is somewhat alienating. He is all in all too rhetorical, too preachy, too primitive. He is reminiscent of Guardini, whom he is similar to in behaviour. In the large lecture on German Idealism and the philosophical problems of the present he has so far treated the dominant tendencies of contemporary philosophy as anthropological tendencies and metaphysics . . .
>
> He does not really have disciples in the genuine sense. The girls are especially bad. Many have already come with him from Marburg. They are completely drilled in his philosophy, know sufficient Aristotle – in order to be able to use the right vocabulary at an appropriate moment – but have certainly not noticed that Heidegger himself has changed since the Marburg period and his early Freiburg period. There is still little to say about this transformation because it is not yet completed. At its centre stands the new Kant-interpretation, which will appear shortly . . . Perhaps one can provisionally characterize the direction of this

change as a tendency to transcendental metaphysics. Plato and Kant, ontology and transcendental philosophy will stand at its centre. Anyway, that's what we expect. Overall impression: he is a fine fellow, a lively personality, a genuine teacher, a true philosopher (if all this really belongs to philosophy) and that is today more than enough . . .

Concerning Husserl, we are attending his seminar on empathy (*Einfühlung*). Unfortunately, a complete decline is evident here. He jabbers away without interruption, still only recognizes transcendental phenomenology, the pure I as the 'Urmonad' and naturally takes great care with how this Urmonad comes to other I's![62]

Marcuse recollects that

during this time, let's say from 1928 to 1932, there were relatively few reservations and relatively few criticisms on my part. I would rather say on our part, because Heidegger at that time was not a personal problem, not even philosophically, but a problem of a large part of the generation that studied in Germany after the First World War. We saw in Heidegger what we had first seen in Husserl, a new beginning, the first radical attempt to put philosophy on really concrete foundations – philosophy concerned with the human existence, the human condition, and not with merely abstract ideas and principles. That certainly I shared with a relatively large number of my generation, and, needless to say, the disappointment with this philosophy eventually came – I think it began in the early 30s. But we re-examined Heidegger thoroughly only after his association with Nazism had become known.[63]

It should be noted that not all radicals of Marcuse's generation shared this fascination with Heidegger. Brecht, Benjamin and their circle perceived immediately the dangers of the seductive power and reactionary content of Heidegger's philosophy, as we learn from a letter which Benjamin sent to his friend Scholem in 1930: 'There was a plan afoot here to establish this summer a very small critical reading circle, led by Brecht and myself, to destroy Heidegger. But unfortunately Brecht, who is not doing well at all, will have to go out of town soon, and I won't take it on by myself'.[64] This quote shows that Heidegger was already a controversial figure and that radicals were both attracted to and repelled by his philosophy, a division that continues to this day. The complexity and difficulty of Heidegger's works enable those influenced by Heidegger to find profound philosophical truths and those hostile to his philosophy to find mystification and reactionary pedantry, masquerading as new truths and a new approach to philosophy.[65]

Unlike other Heideggerians, Marcuse was interested in Marxism, and contributed articles to the Social Democratic journal *Die Gesellschaft*, edited by Rudolf Hilferding.[66] During the late 1920s Marcuse sought to merge Marxism and Heidegger's phenomenological existentialism into a 'concrete philosophy', stressing radical action, authenticity and revolutionary social transformation. In retrospect, he notes,

I first, like all the others, believed there could be some combination between existentialism and Marxism, precisely because of their insistence on concrete analysis of the actual human existence, human beings, and their world. But I soon realized that Heidegger's concreteness was to a great extent a phony, a false concreteness, and that in fact his philosophy was just as abstract and just as removed from reality, even avoiding reality, as the philosophies which at that time had dominated German universities, namely a rather dry brand of neo-Kantianism, neo-Hegelianism, neo-Idealism, but also positivism.[67]

When asked how Heidegger responded to the attempt to integrate his philosophy with a Marxian social philosophy, Marcuse answers, 'He didn't respond. You know as far as I can say, it is today still open to question whether Heidegger ever really read Marx, whether Heidegger ever read Lukács, as Lucien Goldman maintains. I tend not to believe it. He may have had a look at Marx after or during the Second World War, but I don't think that he in any way studied Marx'.[68]

By the end of the 1920s, the three pillars of what would eventually emerge as Marcuse's later synthesis were present: politics, aesthetics and philosophy. We have noted how Marcuse turned from political activism to a study of literature and then to a study of philosophy. This move from concern with art to philosophy indicates some scepticism on Marcuse's part as to the power of art as a cognitive source of knowledge and as an instrument of personal liberation and social change. Whereas Ernst Bloch, Walter Benjamin, the early Lukács and T. W. Adorno privileged art as a source of knowledge and liberation,[69] Marcuse turned instead to a serious and productive study of philosophy. Although Marcuse focused, in his dissertation on *The German Artist-Novel,* on the role of art in dealing with the fundamental questions of human life, in his work from about 1928 until *Eros and Civilization* (1955), he turned his attention to philosophy and social theory as fundamental sources of knowledge and social change. Consequently it was not until the 1950s, with his work on *Eros and Civilization,* that he would bring aesthetics into his theory in systematic fashion, although the preliminary work for this move was done in the period that we have just examined. Thus only in his post-Second World War work would Marcuse achieve the union of philosophy, politics, psychology and aesthetics that would be the distinguishing feature of his critical theory.

2

Phenomenological Marxism?

Marcuse's first published essay, 'Contributions to a Phenomenology of Historical Materialism',[1] proposes a synthesis between Marxism and Heidegger's phenomenological existentialism. His goal is to produce a 'concrete philosophy' capable of dealing with the central problems of the day. This remarkable philosophical debut anticipates later attempts to create a 'phenomenological' or 'existential' Marxism, and historically situates Marcuse within a current of 'critical Marxism' that sought to reconstruct Marxism in order to provide an alternative to the 'revisionism' of the dominant trends of the Second International and the dogmatism of Soviet Marxism.[2] The essay articulates an activist, practice-oriented interpretation of Marxism that has continued to shape Marcuse's later writings, and contains one of the first and best interpretations and critiques of Heidegger's influential *Being and Time.*

It has been argued that Marcuse's early writings represent a false start in an untenable project that he quickly abandoned.[3] His attempt to merge phenomenology and Marxism has been called a 'mechanical juxtaposition' which failed to unify these tendencies coherently.[4] According to others, his early writings are 'generally considered uncertain, confused, and incomplete'.[5] Such dismissive positions, however, fail to illuminate Marcuse's serious attempt to grapple with problems brought about by the crisis of capitalism and crisis of Marxism that are still with us today. Marcuse attempts to overcome both the limitations of Marxism and the dominant trends of academic philosophy in order to create a new 'concrete philosophy' capable of serving as an instrument of radical social change. This enterprise would define Marcuse's entire intellectual project. Consequently his early essays sketch the outlines of his theoretical project and contain important constitutive elements of his thought that would continue to shape his later works.

2.1 Marxism and revolutionary practice

Marcuse's first published essay indicates that he saw Marxism primarily as a theory of revolutionary practice. Marxism, he writes, 'is not a scientific theory, a system of truth whose significance lies alone in its correctness as a knowledge, but is a theory of social activity and historical action. Marxism is the theory of proletarian revolution and the revolutionary critique of bourgeois society'.[6] Together with Lukács and Korsch, Marcuse is resisting the tendency of leading Marxists of the Second International and Soviet Marxists to interpret Marxism as a theory of 'scientific socialism', which is to be judged according to criteria of scientific rigour.[7] Marcuse does not, however, advocate a strictly voluntaristic concept of radical action, arguing instead that 'Marxism is science in so far as the revolutionary action that it wants to liberate and establish requires insight into its historical necessity and truth'.[8] But he stresses above all 'the inseparable unity of theory and praxis, science and action, which every Marxian investigation must preserve as the highest guide'.[9] We see here that Marcuse has not yet begun the critique of science that will be one of the distinctive features of his version of critical Marxism; at this point he conceives of science and theory as integral components of social practice.[10]

The question of revolutionary practice is decisively raised, Marcuse suggests, only when 'activity is posited as the crucial realization of the human essence and, at the same time, when this realization appears precisely as a *factual* impossibility i.e. in a revolutionary situation'.[11] If an examination of the concrete historical situation shows that free development of human powers and potentialities is not possible in a society in which 'personal powers are transformed into objective forces', then 'one's own activity becomes an alien power that stands over against one'.[12] Dominated by alien forces, the individual is 'robbed of the real content of life' (i.e. freedom, individuality, pleasure, etc.) and is reduced to the form of an 'abstract individual'. This picture portrays the 'existence of capitalist society that reveals the "reality of an inhuman existence" (*The Holy Family*) behind its economic and ideological forms'.[13] Marcuse argues that capitalist society obstructs and suppresses free human activity and calls for 'radical action' as a 'counter-movement' against the forms of alienated existence.[14] In his theory of radical action, Marcuse grounds his early perspectives on revolution in a contradiction between the human need for free, self-realizing activity and an inhuman capitalist society which dominates and alienates the human individual – a position that would often return in his later writings.

Marcuse is building here on Lukács's theory of reification, which describes how capitalist society objectifies and alienates individuals.[15] In a famous analysis in *History and Class Consciousness*, Lukács describes how commodity fetishism, the capitalist labour system, the market, bureaucracy and mass media – as well as science and technology – tend to promote conformist modes of thought and behaviour which eradicate individuality and freedom. 'Reification' in Lukács's theory also appears as the 'phenomenal form of bourgeois society' and as a corresponding 'reified' consciousness that perceives a specific socio-historical form of existence as 'natural' and 'eternal', and consequently resistant to change.[16] Reification thus describes the peculiar form of objectivity in capitalist society and is related to what the Frankfurt School would later criticize as technological rationality, one-dimensional thought, and instrumental reason.[17] But at this point in Marcuse's development, 'reification' in his usage refers more to a process of dehumanization and alienation produced by the material conditions of capitalist society than to the form of bourgeois society and objectivity.[18]

Lukács's analysis of reification set the programme and framework for Marcuse's critique of capitalist – and later socialist – societies throughout his work. Marcuse told me that he read *History and Class Consciousness* when it was first published and found it superior to the dominant varieties of orthodox Marxism.[19] He admired its revival of the neglected aspects of Marxism, such as the Hegelian dialectic, the emphasis on consciousness and the subjective factors of revolution, and its attempt to develop a Marxian philosophy. Although he never shared Lukács's celebration of the Communist Party and enthusiastic embrace of Leninism, Marcuse continued to believe that the Korsch–Lukács interpretations of Hegelian Marxism represented the most advanced and revolutionary current of Marxism which most strongly influenced his own appropriation of Marx.[20]

2.1.1 *The radical act*

The concept of the *radical act* stands as the centre of Marcuse's theory. For Marcuse – and here we see for the first time indications of his synthesis between Heidegger and Marx – the radical act is *existential*: it aims at an alteration of the roots of existence; it intends to bring forth a fundamental change in human existence. Marcuse recalls Marx's famous aphorism: 'To be radical is to seize something by the roots. The root of man, however, is man himself'.[21] Marcuse claims that at the bottom of every revolutionary project is a radical decision to change fundamentally the basic conditions of human existence. The radical act strives simultaneously to transform the circumstances of both one's own way of life and one's social situation so as to create new forms of existence. In Marx's words, quoted by Marcuse, 'The coinciding of the alteration of circumstances and human activity can only be conceived and rationally understood as revolutionary praxis'.[22] An act that merely alters the circumstances of the body politic, without at the same time effecting a change in ways of human existing, is not radical. The Russian Revolution was seen by Marcuse and others at the time as 'radical, since it both modified social-political-economic conditions and the way people worked, thought and lived. Further, the radical act is *demanded by an intolerable social reality* and is therefore a compelling *imperative*. It is an historical act demanded by one's being in a specific historical situation that is intolerable. Marcuse argues,

> The radical act is according to its essence *necessary* (*Not-wendig*) for the actor as well as for the environment in which it is done. Through its happening it turns toward (*wendet*) the need (*Not*), changes something that has become absolutely intolerable, and puts in its place what is itself necessary (*Notwendige*), that which alone can abolish (*aufheben*) what is intolerable.[23]

This passage contains a rather unorthodox concept of 'necessity' which Marcuse uses in his early writings. When he speaks of 'necessity' or 'historical necessity', he does not intend necessary causal connection (nor logical necessity), but rather plays on the German roots of *Not-wendig*: a historical situation, on this account, contains a need (*Not*) which individuals turn to (*wendet*) to abolish, bringing about an abolition of what is absolutely intolerable;[24] as, for example, a need for radical change in Russia in 1917 demanded radical action to replace intolerable conditions. Marcuse is rejecting an 'objectivism' which posits inexorable, deterministic laws of history characteristic of dominant versions of Marxism.[25] In discussing 'historical necessity', Marcuse injects a subjective element of need as a consciousness of an intolerable state of affairs which can lead to action to overcome it. Thus Marcuse roots his notion of 'historical necessity' in a subject–object dialectic rather than in an objectivist theory of history.[26] In another early article criticizing the Marxism of Max Adler, Marcuse notes the problems of postulating objective laws of society: 'The danger in Adler's interpretation of Marxism lies in the transformations of the theory of proletarian revolution to a scientific society, which deflects and isolates Marxism from the concrete affliction of the historical situation, thus devaluating radical practice.'[27]

For Marcuse, the necessity of the radical act is demanded by an *immanent necessity*: the historical situation itself demands resolute action. For instance, the intolerable conditions in Russia during the First World War demanded a revolutionary solution. The radical act is therefore a fundamentally *historical* act rooted in the exigencies of a concrete historical situation:

> One can only act radically when one must act from necessity, and only in knowledge can human existence be certain of necessity. In the interrogated historical situation, the class is the decisive historical unity and the knowledge of the unique historical social necessity is the achievement of 'class consciousness'. In class consciousness, the summoned class becomes mature as the bearer of historical action. When the revolutionary situation is given, only the class that is conscious of its historical situation can seize it.[28]

Although Marcuse has not really developed a theory of revolution at this point, it is clear from his early articles that he is committed to the Marxian theory of class struggle.[29] In his early essays, Marcuse does maintain that individuals can carry out radical acts (see the discussion in 2.3), but he does not conceive of revolution without a class-conscious and revolutionary proletariat. He states that 'the history of the past years is full of such botched-up (*verfuschten*) revolutionary situations',[30] alluding to the failure of revolutionary struggles in the industrialized capitalist countries during the recent past, but he has not yet begun the critique of the Marxian theory of the proletariat as the subject of revolution that would be a distinguishing feature of his later theory.

The thrust of Marcuse's early essays is towards a radical activism that runs counter to the trend towards resignation and 'inwardness' (*Innerlichkeit*) that was prevalent in sectors of German society in the 1920s. In an audacious interpretation of Heidegger's *Being and Time*, Marcuse attempts to reconstruct Heidegger's concepts of 'resoluteness' and 'authenticity' and to merge them with Marxian concepts of revolutionary practice in his concept of radical action. This initial attempt to merge Marxism and phenomenological existentialism – a project later undertaken by a variety of European and American intellectuals – is fraught with difficulties and raises questions concerning whether such a synthesis between, in many ways, incompatible philosophical doctrines is useful. I do not however, believe that Marcuse's early essays should be dismissed as merely an early, and unsuccessful, attempt to synthesize Marxism and phenomenological existentialism, which other thinkers would later take up in different historical situations. For I believe that his early essays contain a critique of Heidegger, phenomenology and existentialism that is still cogent and compelling.[31] Marcuse's criticism of these philosophies – unlike many other Marxian 'ideology critiques' – has the advantage of understanding the doctrines that he was criticizing. Whereas, from a Marxian point of view, his deep immersion in Heidegger's philosophy was to lead him astray into an ahistorical 'existential ontology, and subjectivism, it also enabled him to criticize these tendencies from within. Indeed, throughout his career Marcuse has been extremely effective at critique of ideology – an enterprise that began with his critical confrontation with one of the dominant creators of the 'German Ideology' of the day, Martin Heidegger.

2.1.2 *Authenticity and revolution*

Marcuse claims that Heidegger's *Being and Time* is important for his project 'because it appears to us that in this book a turning point in the history of philosophy is reached: the point where bourgeois philosophy dissolves itself from within and makes the way clear for a new "concrete" science'.[32] Marcuse believes that Heidegger's problematic is important because its concept of authenticity contributes to a theory of radical action. In Marcuse's reading, Heidegger's analysis of inauthenticity discloses some of the obstacles to radical action by suggesting how society comes to dominate the individual – an issue that would later lead him to appropriate Freud. Moreover, Marcuse believes that Heidegger's philosophical starting point – being-in-the-world – overcomes the subject–object dichotomy endemic to previous bourgeois philosophy, which begins with the consciousness of the subject and describes its attempt to gain knowledge of a world standing over and against the wordless subject.[33] Heidegger rejects this dualistic standpoint, which is the source of all the endless debates about knowledge and reality that plague modern philosophy; Marcuse and others believe that Heidegger therefore provides a promising new start in philosophy. Furthermore, Marcuse thinks that Heidegger's concept of 'historicity' explicates a process of historical movement that at once overcomes the subject–object dichotomy and the endless debate between idealism and materialism over the nature of reality by positing a single, unitary process of movement that encompasses subject and object, material conditions and consciousness, facts and values. This new, seemingly concrete and historical, approach provides, so Marcuse believes, access to concrete social and human affairs, which would henceforth be the subject matter of philosophy. For Marcuse, Heidegger seems to have concretized the phenomenological method and, unlike Husserl, to have developed a phenomenology of everyday human existence.

Marcuse begins his merger of Marx and Heidegger by assimilating Heidegger's categories of inauthenticity and 'fallenness' to Marxian categories of alienation and reification. Heidegger argues that all individuals in a society fall under the dictatorship of *das Man* (the public, the others) and exist in a condition of not-being-a-self (inauthenticity).[34] On Heidegger's account, the individual is dominated by powerful social forces, conforms to standard modes of behaviour, and thereby falls into inauthenticity, where one loses one's individuality and autonomy, failing to develop one's powers of creativity, will, responsibility, etc. For Marcuse, Heidegger's analysis reinforces the impression, nurtured by his study of Marxism, that the established society is totally corrupt; it also helps explain why revolutionary consciousness failed to develop in a situation in which 'inauthentic' individuals were dominated by society and incapable of 'resolute' revolutionary action.

Heidegger's way of overcoming an alienated-inauthentic existence is a project of individual authenticity, which requires what
seems like a radical act to carry out a process of self-transformation.
He claims that even within a state of inauthenticity one has a
potentiality (*Sein-können*) for authenticity. Heidegger argues that
everyday experiences of anxiety, one's impending death, guilt and a
call of conscience can bring the individual to reject the everyday
world and prepare one for the choice of authenticity.[35] This transformation from inauthentic to authentic existence requires what
Heidegger calls *resoluteness*: a decision to modify one's inauthentic
existence by embarking on a project of self-transformation through
choosing authentic possibilities from the heritage.

Heidegger bases his concept of authentic choice on a distinction
between tradition and heritage. The *heritage* is the ensemble of past
possibilities for authentic existence, whereas *tradition* is how these
possibilities have been interpreted, handed down to us, and incorporated in the modern world. Heidegger calls for a 'destruction of
tradition', and a novel re-appropriation of past possibilities from
the heritage that would utilize past possibilities (say Hölderlin or
Lenin) against their traditional interpretation and embodiment in
today's society. Consequently, the repetition (*Wiederholung*) of
possibilities from the heritage involves a 'disavowal' (*Widerruf*) of
the tradition and a novel re-appropriation (*Erwiderung*) of the
possibilities that, in Marcuse's words, 'must necessarily come into
conflict with today, and can be won only as a counterthrust against
what is factically existing today'.[36]

A revolutionary, on this analysis, could engage in a repetition of
Lenin as his or her authentic project that would adapt Lenin's ideas
and praxis to current historical situations, rejecting (*Widerruf*) what
is no longer applicable to the specific features of the current
situation, while retaining what is of continuing validity, and thus
responding (*Erwiderung*) to Lenin with a novel re-appropriation.
Marcuse's Marxian interpretation of the Heideggarian concepts of
Wiederholung-Widerruf-Erwiderung shatters Heidegger's individualistic and ontological framework by translating his concepts
into a Marxian theory of radical action, aiming at the transformation of bourgeois society. In his interpretation, Heidegger's 'disavowal of that which works itself out today as the past' requires an
overthrow of those outworn historical possibilities (capitalism) that
continue to constitute the present in a destructive fashion, i.e. the
contradictions of monopoly capital which lead to imperialism,

economic crisis and war. The radical acts thus requires a dialectic of appropriation-rejection not only towards self-chosen past possibilities for authentic existence (as in Heidegger's 'repetition'), but towards the totality of the historical situation into which the heritage has developed 'today'. In this way, the radical act is an act of dialectical negation that attacks the surpassed and obsolete historical possibilities, while it preserves and projects the liberating alternatives.

Marcuse draws revolutionary implications from Heidegger's existential analysis and assimilates the project of authenticity that strives to overcome the 'fallenness' of social existence to the Marxian theory of revolution. Marcuse saw in both Heidegger and Marx a radical social critique, combined with an impulse for radical action to overcome 'intolerable situations'. Bringing together Marxian and Heideggerian categories, he made an effort to create what Sartre would call an 'anthropology of revolution'.[37] In Marcuse's words:

> Since this development is itself only achived through (historical) activity, 'the future' (*das Kommende*) will constantly be a 'negation of the present state of affairs'. Let us remember, as *Heidegger* indicates, that the resoluteness for authenticity which is conscious of its fate is only possible as a 'disavowal' (*Widerruf*) of the past, whose domination constantly stands opposed as fallenness. This is, in the Marxian breakthrough to practical concretion, the theory of revolution. Because what exists necessarily becomes fallenness at a certain point of historical development, in which all forms of existence turn inauthentic, the historical action that makes authentic existence again possible is necessarily revolutionary action.[38]

At this point, after formulating what he believes is a kinship between Marx and Heidegger, Marcuse summarizes his appreciation of Heidegger:[39]

> in so far as Heidegger recognized the historical thrownness of the human being and its historical determination and rootedness in the destiny of the community, he has driven his radical research to the furthest point that bourgeois philosophy has reached up to now – and can in general reach. He has shown that theoretical ways of behaving are 'derivative' founded in practical concern

(*Besorgen*) and has thus exhibited praxis as the field of decisions. He has determined the moment of decision, the resoluteness in the historical situation, and resoluteness itself as a taking-up-in-oneself of historical fate. He has contraposed the bourgeois concepts of freedom and determinism with a being-free and being-able-to-choose what is necessary, as genuine being-able-to-seize prescribed possibilities. And he has set up history as the single authority in this 'loyalty to one's own existence'. But here the radical impulse has reached its end.[40]

Marcuse now begins his critique of Heidegger. In Heidegger's terminology, Marcuse argues that what his ontological analysis requires is an ontic concretion; i.e. what is needed now is a turning to and describing of the 'decisive facts of today in their historical concretion' – a particularly urgent task, Marcuse believes, because the 'threatening current human situation demands reflection'. Whereas Heidegger is concerned with universal ways of being and asks 'what is authentic existence and how is it possible?', explicating the ontological conditions of the possibility of authenticity, Marcuse wants to know, 'what is authentic existence concretely?' – that is, how is authentic existence possible today?[42] This type of questioning would have to go beyond Heidegger's ontological analysis of inauthenticity and show what is obstructing authentic existence in the current situation. It would analyse the current forms of inauthenticity and bondage in the existing society. These questions would in turn require a historically specific analysis of the current social situation, its tendency towards domination and alienation and a disclosure of authentic, liberating possibilities – the type of analysis found in Marx and in Marcuse's later writings.

For Marcuse, one of the many problems with Heidegger's abstract ontological analysis is that it does not provide any concrete guidlines for action in the present situation. Heidegger's theory of fallenness and inauthenticity claims to be universal and valid for all historical situations, so that specific features of today's problems are excluded in principle from the Heideggerian ontological analysis. There were important reasons central to his philosophical project and personal world-view that prohibited Heidegger himself from extending his criticisms of social behaviour to a concrete criticism of his own German bourgeois society. According to Heidegger's ontological analysis in *Being and Time*, all societies in all historical periods exhibit the features of fallenness and inauthenticity, which Heidegger did not believe could be changed; thus he was pessimistic about the possibility of radical social change. In this view a socialist revolution, for example, could only create new forms of domination and alienation that would themselves enslave the individual and require yet another project of overcoming. Since Heidegger's analysis does not allow for the possibility of revolutionary change that would overcome 'fallenness' with a new social structure, the most he can recommend is individual self-transformation. Marcuse rejects this individualistic solution: 'Heidegger's attempt to refer the decisive resoluteness back to the position of the isolated individual instead of driving one forward to the resoluteness of action must be rejected. This action is more than a "modifying" of past experience; it is a restructuring of all spheres of public life'.[43]

This notion of overthrowing the current system and restructuring public life goes beyond Heidegger and indicates that on Marcuse's own analysis of the radical act, Heidegger's authentic individual is not really radical. For we have seen that a radical act, on Marcuse's account, must transform the self and the conditions of existence, whereas for Heidegger, the authentic individual is basically concerned with his or her own personal authenticity and not with changing society. The bourgeoisie can tolerate and even perform Heidegger's move towards authenticity because it leaves their interests and domination unchanged, and consequently risks nothing. Marcuse, against Heidegger here, wants the radical act to be a *public act* that 'restructures all spheres of public life' – a move that runs counter to Heidegger's quietism. Marcuse thus resists both the stoical resignation of certain German intelligentsia and the project of cultivating one's individuality urged by others, choosing instead the Marxist notion of revolutionary praxis.

Heidegger, on the other hand, scorned the public act, being firmly convinced that one must do 'the one thing necessary without occupying oneself with the idle chatter and agitation of intelligent and enterprising men'.[44] The 'one thing necessary' for Heidegger was 'rational and critical destruction of the philosophical and theological traditions', which was 'something apart from and perhaps outside of the expectations of the agitation of the day'.[45] Heidegger's letters from the 1920s reveal scorn for social and institutional practices, including philosophy congresses, the proliferation of philosophy journals, the study of foreign cultures, and the 'agitation and idle chatter' of the issues of the day.[46] This avoidance of current socio-political problems, and the withdrawal into strictly intellectual concerns, marks a crisis in the German intelligentsia that was to have dire historical effects. Heidegger and his contemporaries were in a state of political disorientation brought about by the German collapse after the First World War and the economic-political uncertainty of the Weimar Republic. There was a general fear of catastrophe (which was indeed soon to come), and it seemed that after the Russian Revolution and the Spartacus uprising in Germany the upheaval would come from the Left. Thus, while some German intellectuals were drawn to Marxian ideas, the prospects of proletarian revolution frightened others who either actively opposed it or turned from history to purely academic concerns.

Consequently, although Heidegger sometimes sounded highly radical with his critique of inauthenticity, his call for resoluteness and self-transformation, and his project of a 'destruction' of the philosophical tradition, in fact his theory was really conservative; thus, German students could follow Heidegger and be 'authentic' while still conforming to the dominant social powers. This pseudo-radicalism was very dangerous, for it led to a repression of the real problems of social life, and a refusal of social-political involvement. The mystification of socio-economic conditions was particularly striking in Heidegger's theory of authenticity and historicity, which contained an abstract reflection on the ontology of human historicity, while relegating the real problems of history to 'ontic history' that was evidently not worth the philosopher's time. Such a retreat of the German intelligentsia from the public arena left an intellectual-moral vacuum which the Nazis and their allies filled. Indeed the Nazi seizure of power clearly revealed the danger and deficiencies in the Heideggerian project. One was supposed to be resolute in order to be authentic, but what was one to resolve upon? Heidegger provided no answer,[47] and in fact his own resolve in support of fascism clearly revealed the moral-political vacuum at the heart of his philosophy.[48] Refusing, in *Being and Time*, to advocate any definite social, moral or political values, Heidegger fell into the grips of the nihilism which Nietzsche had warned was to be the fate of Western civilization. Such nihilism played into the hands of fascism, and Heidegger's capitulation showed the bankruptcy of his philosophy.[49]

2.2 Heidegger, historicity and historical materialism

Although Heidegger's individualistic and ontological perspectives were to shape Marcuse's thought and play a role in his later writings, from the beginning Marcuse attempted to ground Heidegger's theories of authenticity, historicity and society in a Marxian historical materialist foundation. Against Heidegger's theory of the *Mitwelt* (i.e. environmental-social world), Marcuse argues that the world in which the individual finds himself is not constituted by any abstract 'worldhood', as in Heidegger's theory, but is rather a definite socio-historical world with a particular material constitution. Likewise, the individual is not human being in general (*Dasein überhaupt*) but is a living, hungry creature, in a historically specific environment, constituted by a particular society, with a specific *mode of production*: 'The mode of production of society, which expresses its existential needs, is the constitutive historical basis . . . from which its historical movement unfolds'.[50] Here Marcuse calls attention to the central role of the mode of production in constituting society à la Marx: 'This we call the material conditions of historicity; these are . . . the ultimate determinates of human being'.[51] These material conditions involve human and social needs, relations of production and reproduction to satisfy them, class domination, and ideological systems which together in their totality constitute the individual's human life-world. Marcuse's analysis of the materially constituted human life-world follows the argument in Marx's *The German Ideology* and carried out a Marxian reconstruction of Heidegger's analysis, driving Heidegger's social ontology and anthropology to a material foundation. He concretizes Heidegger's notion that care is the defining attribute of human being, suggesting that one's primary care is for one's material needs, which are satisfied in production and reproduction – again marxizing Heidegger.[52]

The thrust of Marcuse's interpretation is that Heidegger overlooks the material constituents of history (needs, classes, economics and historical specificity), suggesting that Heidegger's concept of history at best manifests a *pseudo-concreteness*.[53] Heidegger himself makes a distinction between his concept of 'historicity' and 'ontic history', which banishes the real content of history, real historical crises and problems, from his pure ontological perspective. This flight from concrete history into an ontological realm of Being reveals the dangers of the Heideggerian ontological perspective which at the time had Marcuse at least partially under its seductive sway. Perhaps, in his early essays, Marcuse thought that he could de-mystify Heidegger much as Marx had concretized and reconstructed Hegel. This seems to be an impulse behind Marcuse's project, a motive that is especially visible in Marcuse's attempt to create a dialectical phenomenology that would, supposedly, liberate phenomenology from the Husserlian-Heideggerian tendencies towards an abstract ontology.

To put this project in the proper historical perspective, however, it should be kept in mind that Marcuse does not merely intend to improve phenomenology; he also wants to revitalize Marxism, which in the hands of the official Marxists was degenerating into a sterile scientistic orthodoxy used as an instrument of Soviet or Social Democratic political interests. Hence Marcuse believed that the confrontation between Marxism and phenomenology would reciprocally correct and complement what he believed were pernicious tendencies in both orthodoxies. This enterprise, although fraught with many of the same difficulties as his attempt to merge Heidegger's concept of authenticity into a Marxist concept of revolution, has been historically a more fruitful tendency. Indeed, Sartre and the leftist French phenomenologists, Kosik and the Eastern European praxis philosophers, Paci and the Italian phenomenological Marxists, accompanied by some Americans, have repeated Marcuse's project in post-Second World War attempts to create a new philosophical synthesis of varying aspects of Marxism, phenomenology and existentialism.[54]

In the following pages I shall set forth Marcuse's presentation of the Marxian dialectical method and Heideggerian-Husserlian phenomenology, and I shall show how Marcuse's essay contains an implicit critique of phenomenology which I shall spell out more explicitly than Marcuse himself does in his first essay. We shall see also, however, that Marcuse develops a critique of dominant versions of Marxism and is struggling to develop his own methodological and philosophical perspectives – a struggle that would occupy him his entire life.

2.2.1 *Dialectics and phenomenology*

For Marcuse, the method by which Marxists attempt to grasp the movement, development and transformations of history is the *dialectical method*, as formulated by Hegel, Marx, Engels and Lenin. This method sees 'every developing form in the river of movement' and perceives its object as historical: 'it considers its object as being in a state of becoming and passing away, as necessarily arising from a determinate historical situation, related to human existence rooted in this situation; dialectics can understand its object only within the context of this situation'.[55] Dialectical categories analyse the constitutives of human existence and describe historical development.

Marcuse explicates his understanding of dialectics by citing a famous passage from Engels, who writes that dialectics exemplifies 'The great fundamental thought that the world is not to be conceived as a complex of ready-made things, but as a complex of *processes*, in which the seemingly stable things, not less than their images (*Gedankenabbilder*) in our heads, the concepts, pass through an uninterrupted transformation of becoming and passing away'.[56] Marcuse then cites Lenin, who defines four fundamental characteristics of the dialectical method:

> Dialectical logic demands that we go further. In order to really know an object, one must grasp and investigate all sides of the object, all its relations and 'mediations' . . . Second, dialectical logic requires that the object be taken in its development, in its 'self-movement' . . . in its transformation. Third, the whole of human praxis must enter into the 'definition' of the object, as well as the critique of its truth, since as a practical determination the object is bound together with what is necessary to man. Fourth, the dialectical logic teaches that 'there is no abstract truth'; truth is always concrete.[57]

Marcuse believes that the dialectical method grasps the immanent necessity of historical movement by showing how later forms of development are found in the earlier situation, and by showing how a negation of what exists produces historical development. Marxists apply this method to the analysis of social, economic and ideological objects, grounded in Marx's theory of the mode of production. Dialectical analysis is a guide to revolutionary praxis, for it shows what features of a given social-economic-historical situation should be negated in order to liberate more progressive tendencies and forms – thus dialectics preserve the unity of theory and praxis. After providing this interpretation of the dialectical method, Marcuse inquires whether 'the dialectical method is really the corresponding mode of access to its object, and how wide its realm of validity is'.[58] In other words, does the dialectical method provide a proper mode of access to the whole of human historicity? Since phenomenology is another method that is supposed to provide access to concrete human existence, Marcuse proposes to inquire whether methodological insights will result from a comparison between phenomenology and dialectics. His analysis, I shall argue, shows the unquestionable superiority of dialectics over phenomenology, both as a mode of access to the object and in terms of the wealth of disclosures of the object.

Phenomenology wants the questions and the access to the subject matter of investigation to come only from the 'things themselves', and it wants to bring its object 'completely in view'.[59] Marcuse begins his critique of phenomenology with the idea that since the object of phenomenology stands in history, phenomenology must become dialectical to grasp historical change and development. This will entail a radical departure from Husserlian phenomenology, which aims, through the intuition of essences (*Wesenschau*) at grasping the atemporal, eternal, unchanging essence. An historical phenomenology would also complement Heidegger's phenomenological ontology, which conceptualizes universal, essential structures of human being.

Historicizing phenomenology is necessary, Marcuse believes, because any method that stays on the *a priori* (transcendental) level of essence and universality cannot deal with concrete, historical movement and change. Thus, since change is fundamental to historical being, phenomenology does not adequately grasp fully and concretely the phenomenon of history: 'therefore the investigation of its object fails to bring the phenomenon completely in view'.[60] Further, phenomenology is supposed to penetrate to the phenomenon's ultimate concretion; hence it should, as an investigation of a historical object, 'allow the concrete historical situation, the concrete "material conditions" to enter into the analysis'.[61] Because the existing phenomenological theories do not do this, they lack 'necessary fullness and clarity'.[62] Marcuse then argues for another mode of historical analysis to overcome the deficiencies of phenomenological-ontological analysis:

It is exactly this ability to attain concreteness that is the achievement of the dialectical method. The issue is to come correctly to the particular concrete historical situation of the object at any moment. The static, free-floating abstraction will become concrete when it is again integrated with the human existence that it 'belongs' with. The genuine dialectic first fulfils the demand of an ultimate concretion and will be justified in regard to the mode of being of human existence when out of knowledge of the concrete historical situation it also draws consequences for the decisive sphere of human existence: Praxis . . . In so far as it addresses in its analysis the present human existence, it forces one to take a practical position with one's whole existence and, accordingly, to *act* in one's historical situation.[63]

Marcuse not only indicates the superior concreteness of the dialectical method, but if we look back to the four requirements for a philosophical methodology, set forth on pages 22–3, we shall see that Husserl's and Heidegger's phenomenology fails to fulfil any of these requirements. As we have seen, the Husserlian-Heideggerian phenomenological method does not allow us to grasp the object from all sides, in all of its connections and mediations, for it conceives its object in abstraction from its historical context, and it overlooks the social-material constituents that are found in the object. For example, a phenomenological analysis of a factory 'brackets' from its social-historical existence and conceives of it, in Husserl's terms, as an intentional object of an act of consciousness, in which the 'phenomenological reduction' excludes its social-material constituents and grasps the 'giveness' of the factory as an 'object of perception', a thing with the qualities of extension, colour, solidity, etc. But does the example not show how the phenomenological reduction to an object's 'essence' is highly abstract and impoverished?[64] For when I look at a factory in its concrete presence I see a place of business, a place of work, a place where consumer items are produced; I see the private property of a capitalist or corporation; I see an assembly line and working conditions that slowly destroy its workers; I see a profit-mad industry polluting the environment; perhaps I see a strike, or a factory occupation, or workers being dismissed due to automation, or bankruptcy and closure. I see a configuration and use of technology, a type of architecture, and if I am walking through the countryside perhaps I suddenly encounter an annoying intrusion. These material-social constituents of the factory are just as 'real' to me as its outline, colour, weight, dimensions, etc. A philosophical method that aims at concretion and fullness must take these social-material condition into its analysis.

I might note that Marcuse does not distinguish between Husserl's and Heidegger's phenomenological method. His thematic explication of phenomenology sometimes seems to refer to Husserl's phenomenology, but his actual critique deals with Heidegger's phenomenology of existence in *Being and Time*. Thus Marcuse fails to raise the complex and difficult problem of the relation between Husserl's and Heidegger's phenomenology, and offers a critique which refers indiscriminately to both of the, at the time, most important representatives of the phenomenological movement.[65]

As opposed to Husserl's more abstract phenomenology, Heidegger's phenomenology in *Being and Time* begins to take into account constituents of the work world, social world and everyday life, but his ontological analysis, in Marcuse's view, also fails to grasp material conditions and historical constituents of phenomena. For Marcuse, Heidegger's phenomenology is capable of, at best, providing an ontology of history and is not capable of conceptualizing historical development or change. Consequently, the dimension of real history is lacking in phenomenology.

Moreover, the phenomenology current at the time was not intimately connected with human practice and did not provide practical directives for action and change, because it did not consider the specific features of an historical situation which should be transformed or eliminated. In fact, Husserl's phenomenology falls prey to a rigid fact-value, descriptive-normative distinction, excluding from analysis normative claims in the interests of carrying through a purely objective scientific description of 'essences'. Indeed, Husserl tends to reify values into Platonic essences when he touches on problems of values or ethical issues.[66] Heidegger too explicitly claims to exclude normative concerns and values from *Being and Time*. Thus Marcuse finds phenomenology to be lacking a theory of human action and social practice geared towards existing problems and social change. The lack of a materialist theory of history, society and social transformation in phenomenology thus led him to Marxism to provide crucial aspects of a 'concrete philosophy' which he found missing in phenomenology.

One could argue that the failure of Marcuse's attempt to synthesize phenomenology with Marxism lies in the limits of the
phenomenological movement of the day. That is, when Marcuse
published his first essays, the two main proponents of phenomenology were Husserl, who was in the transcendental idealism stage of
his complex development, and Heidegger, whose phenomenology
of everyday life in *Being and Time* was being displaced by his work
in speculative metaphysics. Later, Husserl, in *The Crisis of European Sciences*, would return phenomenology to the 'human life-
world' and contemporary problems, and French phenomenology in
the 1930s and 1940s would similarly attempt to develop a concrete
philosophy. Thus perhaps Marcuse's rather sharp critique of
phenomenology was due to the fact that phenomenology was in
particularly idealist and metaphysical stage of development at the
time that he published his first essays.

Despite its problems, Marcuse believed that a more concrete
version of phenomenology could supplement and complement
Marxism. Hence, having carried out a critique of phenomenology
and argued that Marxian dialectics could help overcome its deficiencies, Marcuse then critically examines Marxian dialectics and
shows in turn how phenomenology could help overcome some of its
deficiencies. He stated that:

> If we demand, on one hand, that the phenomenology of human
> existence begun by Heidegger advance to a dialectical concretion
> and fulfil itself in a phenomenology of concrete human existence
> and the current historically demanded concrete act, so, on the
> other hand, the dialectical method of knowledge must become
> phenomenological and achieve concretion in the other direction
> as well through a full comprehension (*Erfassung*) of its object ...
> Only a unification of both methods – a dialectical phenomenolo-
> gy that is a method of continuous and radical concretion – is able
> to grasp appropriately the historicity of human existence'.[67]

Marcuse anticipates the later project, alluded to earlier, of developing a dialectical phenomenology or 'phenomenological Marxism'.
He argues that the dialectical method must in turn 'become
phenomenological' and must go beyond the historical givens of the
situation to ask 'whether there dwells within an integral meaning
that endures through all historicity'.[68] The implication is that where-

as traditional phenomenology cannot grasp change, development and process, dialectics overlooks the abiding, enduring, universal aspects of human existence. A dialectical phenomenology, Marcuse argues, aims at 'the being of historical human existence and to be sure as much in its essential structures as its concrete forms and configurations'.[69] It encompasses all of the regions of meaning created by the human being (i.e. it is a phenomenology of culture, and what Dilthey calls 'cultural history', *Geistesgeschichte*). Marcuse therefore seems to be inserting into dialectics some notion of phenomenological essence and hermeneutics that it is the task of a dialectical phenomenology to work out and clarify.

The 'dialectical basic science' is to be, Marcuse writes, a 'science of the essence of historicity in general, of its structures, laws of movement, and possible existential forms of historical human being'.[70] He believes that the truths concerning the essence of historicity are 'universally valid' and distinguishes between these universal truths concerning the essential structures of existence and 'dialectical knowledge', which is concerned with the changing facts of history (this distinction corresponds to Heidegger's distinction between the ontological and the ontic). Marcuse seems to believe that phenomenology is a more suitable method than dialectics for discovering and grounding the universally valid propositions which grasp the essence of historicity, and that phenomenology therefore conceives, secures and founds the basic presuppositions of historical materialism. The task of phenomenology, then, would be to distinguish enduring truths from the transitory truths of history, to distinguish the permanent from the changing. As opposed to the universally valid truths of phenomenology, 'all other dialectical knowledge-claims concern truths that are ordered in a determinate, concrete historicity; only through a phenomenology of this historicity can they be found and established',[71]

This statement is a bit perplexing, for Marxism prides itself – and Marcuse usually follows this belief – on being both a science of concrete history and a theory that provides fundamental concepts for historical analysis. In Marcuse's words: 'Every dialectic presupposes a thematizing of historicity in which the authentic dialectical basic knowledge-claims are rooted and which determines the further progression of the investigation. *Marx* designated this realm of basic knowledge of the structures of historicity as historical materialism'.[72] This passage would seem to indicate that Marxism does thematize the basic structures of history; if it did so adequately, it is not clear what phenomenology could contribute. In fact, Marcuse's analysis of Marx and Engels' *German Ideology* in the essay we are analysing seems to indicate that Marx does provide an acceptable theory of the fundamental structures of history. Marcuse was one of the first to call attention to the importance of the recently published *German Ideology*, and he uses its ideas in a philosophical problematic that conceptualizes the basic structures of history, society and human nature.[73] Why, then, does Marcuse think that phenomenology can correct historical materialism?

Although Marxism corrects phenomenology in crucial ways, Marcuse believes that phenomenology in turn would help overcome some of the methodological and epistemological deficiencies that Marcuse found in the dominant versions of Marxism.[74] Marcuse believed that Marxism was solidifying into a rigid orthodoxy, dogmatically committed to metaphysical materialism and economic reductionism, both of which maintained the primacy of matter (or economics) and the secondary, or derivative, status of ideas, consciousness and culture. Moreover, Marxists who stress laws of history devalue human practice and the significance of human action as revolutionary practice. Further, Marxists who stress the primacy of class tend to neglect the individual and its needs and potentialities. The result is what Marcuse sees as a philosophical crisis which requires a reconstruction of historical materialism. He believes that a materialist version of phenomenology and existentialism could help in this enterprise. In the next section, we shall examine several reasons for Marcuse's belief that phenomenology might correct or complement Marxian dialectics – an analysis that will help explain his motivation in attempting to develop a phenomenology of historical materialism. Then, in section 2.3, we shall see what elements of existentialism Marcuse wants to bring into Marxism in order to provide a 'concrete philosophy'.

2.2.2 *Towards a reconstruction of historical materialism*

After the deaths of Marx and Engels, the dominant currents of the official Marxian movement were hostile to philosophy and conceived of Marxism as a theory of scientific socialism, or an instrument of political practice. The result was that the Marxian theory was ossifying into a rigid orthodoxy which was serving as a legitimating ideology for the political practice of Marxian parties or governments. As a response to this theoretically sterile Marxism, Lukács and Korsch attempted to provide a philosophical dimension to Marxism by emphasizing and articulating its Hegelian-dialectical roots.[75] At the same time, Max Adler and other Austro-Marxists were trying to establish a Kantian foundation for Marxism,[76] while others discerned a kinship between Marxism and positivism.[77] In this situation Marcuse thought that phenomenological existential-ism would provide a philosophical dimension needed to revitalize the Marxian theory and to enable it to expand its problematic to encompass concrete problems of human existence, subjectivity and culture, closed off to more traditional versions of Marxism.

Marcuse seemed to believe that the basic presuppositions of Marxism should be articulated, developed and defended in order to provide a 'foundation' for Marxism. This very issue shows how Marxism in the 1920s was not only the ideology of left-wing political movements, but also became an affair for intellectuals, who wanted to defend it against other theories and to participate in the Marxian enterprise. They saw that 'orthodox' Marxism either relied on unexamined or questionable premises and frequently sought supplementary support for the Marxian theory in other philosophers such as Hegel, Kant, and, in Marcuse's case, Heidegger and phenomenology. Marcuse's position in the attempts of radical intellectuals to expand and strengthen the Marxian theory is interesting. On the one hand, he was one of the first to call attention to the writings of the early Marx as a source of the basic presuppositions of Marxism, but he seemed to think, on the other hand, that it needed a phenomenological-existential foundation which he believed Heidegger could provide.[78]

Marcuse seemed to believe that there is a normative dimension to the Marxian claims that under capitalism people are alienated, exploited and dehumanized, and that the goal of revolutionary practice is to overcome all forms of alienation to achieve 'a life worthy of a human being'. This critique presupposes that certain institutions and forms of practice are alienating and dehumanizing, that overcoming alienation is necessary for human liberation and well-being, and that the goal of the process of transformation is a state of being more fully human. Now Marcuse seemed to think that it is important to have a normative concept of non-alienated human being, and that phenomenology could describe and secure its essential structures – from which standpoint one could criticize certain forms of alienated practice and alienated social structures that repress or mutilate human beings. In another essay, Marcuse writes:

> In that unique transcendence of historical processes, contexts become visible which render problematic the taking of the historical stages as the final giveness. Neither the current historical situation as facticity, nor the continuous historical development as a causal connection without gaps constitutes the full reality of historical processes; rather, these factical states of affairs constitute themselves in a reality whose fundamental structures lie at the foundation of all factical realizations in history. All historical situations are as factical realizations only historical transformations of such basic structures that will be realized in every order of life in various ways. The way of the realization of human living-with-one-another in capitalist society, for example, is a realization of the basic structures of human being-with-one-another in general – not in some formal-abstract sense, but as highly concrete basic structures. Truth and falsity would then lie in the relation of factual realization of such basic structures: an order of life would be true when it fulfilled, false when it concealed or repressed them.[79]

This passage was written in the context of a critique of Karl Mannheim's *Ideology and Utopia*, which suggests that Marcuse believed a phenomenological Marxism could overcome the dilemma of historical relativism.[80] Mannheim had argued that Marxism is an ideology which merely reflects the historical situation of a given class and thus has but a relative historical validity. Marcuse wished to defend the validity-claims (*Geltungsanspruch*) of Marxism against its sociological devaluation, and to establish that there were criteria of validity which surpassed the realm of historical change. This point of view is consistent with the Hegelian-Marxian distinction between appearance and essence, and the claim that it is the task of theory to describe the essential structures and processes that underlie the less essential, derivative and changing appearances. Marcuse seemed to believe that phenomenology could ground and explicate these fundamental structures, which then would provide criteria that could determine the historical validity of Marxism or a given form of historical practice; i.e., that a given form of practice could be justified as a striving to overcome alienated forms of practice and to aim at the realization of essential aspects of human being that the theory had validated. Marcuse was in fact to adopt a similar approach using the Hegelian and Marxian philosophies in his work with the Frankfurt Institute for Social Research on the critical theory of society. However, in his post-1934 work with the Institute for Social Research, concepts of human *needs* and *potentialities* and historical *tendencies* would replace the early attempt to grasp *ontological structures*. The crucial development in his thought is his appropriation of the Marxian anthropology and the concept of labour and its alienation under capitalism found in Marx's early writings – which we shall examine in Chapter 3.

Perhaps Marcuse's most compelling reason for developing a phenomenology of historical materialism lies in his life-long aversion to crude materialism and economic reductionism. In a discussion of Marxist materialism, Marcuse argues that the claim that all human products, institutions, ideas, etc. are rooted in relations and forces of production is not a 'value-priority'. Rather:

> With this claim no ontic-temporal priority is meant, such that first pure production and reproduction existed and then 'cultural' and 'spiritual' object regions and ways of behaving came. Rather – one must hold fast to this often overlooked basic proposition – existence as a being-in-the-world is always at the same time already 'material' and 'spiritual', 'economical' and 'ideological' (these terms serve only to indicate traditionally differentiated regions). Thus, in the historical movement of the particular human existence the ideological region is already co-reproduced (*mit-reproduziert*).[31]

In this passage Marcuse attempts to avoid a crude, mechanistic materialism which holds that spiritual or intellectual products are but epiphenomena of the material base, mere reflections of economic phenomena or relations, contingent superstructures that have no autonomy or causal efficacy of their own. This form of reductionistic materialism was widespread in his day and Marcuse clearly opposed it.[32] In the passage cited, Marcuse puts into question the validity of the traditional opposites of 'material' and 'spiritual', 'economic' and 'ideological' to indicate that these notions are unclear and are in need of further clarification. He then argues that what are traditionally separated into two different realms of being are actually reproduced together in the same historical process and are thus 'equiprimordial' (to use Heidegger's term). The point at issue here comes out in another passage which seems to put into question what was then taken as the 'fundamental thesis' of 'dialectical materialism' (*Diamat*):

> The old question of which has objective priority, which 'was there first', Spirit or Matter, Consciousness or Being, is not to be decided by the dialectical phenomenology and is already in its formulation meaningless. What is always given is only human being as historical being-in-the-world, that is *both* spirit and matter, consciousness and being; thus only on the basis of this evident giveness can one make statements about the founding relationship that dominates the phenomena. Every deflection from this giveness to an absolutizing of one of its parts is dogmatism and a procedure that flouts all dialectics, for it begins its dialectical investigation with a rigid abstraction, a *primum absolutum*.[83]

On the basis of the last two passages quoted, I suggest that aversion to crude 'dialectical materialism' provided another strong motive for Marcuse to develop a dialectical phenomenology. This aim was shared by Lukács and Korsch, and later by Sartre.[84] These thinkers all accepted the Marxist critique of capitalism and bourgeois society, the theory of revolution, and much of the theory of history, but opposed the then current dogma of dialectical materialism because it lent itself to crude mechanistic-reductionistic interpretations, and produced inadequate concepts of human nature, society, culture and history. Marcuse seemed to believe that a dialectical phenomenology could bracket the question of the priority of matter and thus avoid a materialist metaphysical domatism. The question of the priority of matter over spirit, or being over consciousness, is dismissed as a pseudo-problem by a phenomenology that focuses solely on describing the givens of experience without raising metaphysical dilemmas. Apparently, Marcuse thought that he could use a basic phenomenological procedure of bracketing certain metaphysical questions and undercutting dualisms to avoid committing himself on what Marxists were claiming as the 'fundamental question of philosophy'.[85] This phenomenological way of avoiding commitment to a mechanistic materialism of the sort that dominated Second and Third International Marxism was a compelling motive for Marcuse's attempt to mediate between Marxism and phenomenology. There is no question that many orthodox Marxists, both then and now, adhere unambiguously to the priority of being over consciousness, of matter over idea, and thus maintain a 'dialectical materialism' as the foundation of their world-view which Marcuse could not accept.[86]

A final possible motivation for Marcuse's turn to phenomenological existentialism as a mode of new philosophical sustenance for Marxism is his commitment to a concern with the concrete problems of human existence and with the situation of the existing individual (an enduring legacy in Marcuse's writings from his early interest in phenomenological existentialism). Orthodox Marxism, at the time of Marcuse's early writings (and even today in some of the more sterile regions of Marxist theory and practice) neglected the problems of the existing individual and often saw individuals as functions of a class or group with no special interest or importance as individuals. Marcuse maintained, against this trend, a strong belief in the importance of the human individual, and seemed to believe in his early writings that Heidegger's seeming concern with the unique individual was an important focus that should be incorporated into Marxism.[87] This tendency is clearly expressed in Marcuse's second essay, 'On Concrete Philosophy', which represents Marcuse's proposals for the sort of philosophy needed to supplement the current forms of 'historical materialism'.

2.3 'On Concrete Philosophy'

In 'On Concrete Philosophy' Marcuse attempts to synthesize Marxism and phenomenological existentialism into a 'concrete philosophy' and shifts from Marxist to phenomenological-existentialist positions in the spirit of dialectical mediation.[88] In his first published essays Marcuse sought a 'concrete philosophy' that would deal with the urgent problems of the existing individual and current society. The concrete philosophy would be 'radical' in the sense of going to the roots of the phenomena at issue.[89] This meant for Marcuse concern with the material conditions of existence, with the production and reproduction of everyday life. The quest for the concrete would eventually lead him towards inquiry into the nature of labour, needs, sexuality, consciousness, art and, especially, into the nature and dynamics of contemporary social organization. Concrete philosophy for Marcuse also meant concern for history, inquiry into the dynamics of historical movement and change. The drive towards the concrete involved concern with historical specificity, with the unique configurations and characteristics of the current society whose vicissitudes would be a major focus of Marcuse's life-work.

'On Concrete Philosophy' was written in the last days of the Weimar Republic during severe and continuing economic, political and social crises that were to lead eventually to the triumph of fascism. Marcuse argues that the crisis is a crisis of capitalism, resulting in a crisis of the totality of existence. Hence, whereas Heidegger and his contemporaries in the existentialist and idealist traditions were describing the crisis in mystifying metaphysical terms, Marcuse was calling attention to the social-economic factors of capitalism-in-crisis that were the foundation of the problems of the time. In this situation, he argued, science and philosophy are in a position to secure 'knowledge of this crisis, its causes and their solution'.[90] Consequently, 'philosophy stands under the immense demand to make this knowledge concrete, to confront the threatened existence with its truths'.[91] Since the suffering of contemporary individuals is determined by 'the structure of capitalist society', a concrete philosophy concerned with the real problems of the existing individual must describe the structures of capitalism that have caused human suffering and the crisis of everyday life, and should engage philosophy in the struggle against capitalism.

Marcuse's claim that capitalism is responsible for the major problems of the present age is closely connected to Lukács's theory of reificiation and critique of capitalism. The Lukácsian aspects of his theory come out in the following passage:

> The historical situation in which 'today's' existence stands, and in regard to which this investigation was begun, is determined in its structure through the structure of capitalist society in the stage of 'high capitalism' (organized capitalism, imperialism). These concepts do not merely signify here political or economic facts, but refer to the existential determinants of contemporary existence.

In capitalist society, a determinate mode of human existence has become, in its own fashion, reality. Out of the system of the economy, all regions are caught up in a process of 'reification' which dissolves all the forms of life and unities-of-meaning (*Sinneseinheiten*) which were once bound together with the concrete personhood of human beings. Capitalism created forces which stand between and above persons, which, once present, subject all forms and values of the person and community under its domination. The ways of being-with-one-another (*Miteinander-sein*) are emptied of every essential content and become 'alien' laws regulated from outside: the social relations (*Mitmenschen*) are primarily economic subjects or objects, professional colleagues, citizens, members of the same 'society'; the essential relationships of friendship, love and every genuinely personal, communal association remain limited to the small spheres of life that are still left alone by the business-principle (*Geschäftigkeit*). At the same time, an externally driven individuality (which in no way contradicts a well-defined collectivism of the economy!) separates the individual person from its 'activity', which is 'imposed' on it and performed without in fact being able to accomplish the fulfilment of itself.[92]

For Lukács, in *History and Class Consciousness*, the proletariat offers a solution to the reification of life under capitalism by becoming the subject-object of history – with a little help from the Marxian theory and the Party. That is, Lukács believed that the proletariat could become a revolutionary subject which could break through capitalist reification and create a new, more rational and human society. Although Marcuse has not yet reached the point where he will question the Marxian orthodoxy of the Proletariat-as-Revolutionary-Subject, it is significant that even at this stage, it is in effect 'concrete philosophy' which is assigned the role that Lukács ascribed to the proletariat. For concrete philosophy is at once to provide knowledge of the existing society and to become a force in its transformation. This requires a radical break with the abstractness and contemplative stance of traditional philosophy and a reconstruction of philosophy towards 'practical philosophy'.

In 'On Concrete Philosophy' Marcuse combines the existentialist concern for the concrete situation of the existing individual with the Marxian focus on social and historical problems and revolutionary

praxis. His enterprise represents a critique of the German existentialist tendency to withdraw from history and society in order to
cultivate subjectivity far from the social issues and struggles of the
day. Marcuse's essay suggests that this is an evasion which abandons
the existing individual to the real powers of society and history. The
concrete philosophy, on the other hand, confronts real problems of
contemporary society, searches for the causes of suffering, and
points the way to the abolition of human misery and bondage. It
seeks to engage the individual in the liberating activity of changing
both one's life and the constitutive social conditions.

In order to engage the philosopher in the decisive struggles and
issues of the day, the concrete philosophy must *become public*.[93]
This involves real concern with social problems and taking a stand
on contemporary issues. Philosophy thus commits itself to a 'drive
towards actuality', placing itself under a duty to be engaged in social
practice: 'The noblest desire of all philosophizing is the unity of
theory and practice', translating philosophy into practice, realizing
philosophy. Interestingly, the example of philosophy becoming
concrete, historical and public that Marcuse cites is the proto-
existentialist Kierkegaard, who is usually pictured as a paradigm of
inwardness solely cultivating his relation to God and his individual
sensibility, while advocating an ideal of 'the single one'.[94] Marcuse,
however, points out that at a decisive point in Kierkegaard's life he
stepped out of his isolation and struggled against the tendencies of
his day, which he believed were the source of its spiritual crisis:

He went, in the Socratic sense of this activity, into the street:
wrote article after article in a daily newspaper, gave out pamphlets, pressed his entire struggle in the decisiveness of the
historical moment. This struggle in the public domain . . . directed
in all acuteness towards a concrete movement of contemporary
man, aimed at a 'true' change of existence, and his attacks and
demands directed themselves steadily towards concrete ways and
tasks of this existence, holding the possibilities of achievement of
the moment in full view. Only when one conceives how much
Kierkegaard, in the fulfilment of his concrete philosophizing,
came upon the urgent nowness of a real decision, upon a true
movement and transformation of contemporary existence, only
then can one understand the sharpness of his attack, the agita-
tional violence of his public performance, the sought clash with

the representative personalities of the public, the revolutionary concretion of his demands.[95]

Marcuse seems to want to drive intellectuals into the public sphere, into a serious concern with problems of the day. Refusing the resignation and withdrawal from public life typical of the German intellectuals of the Weimar Republic (which was soon to have such disastrous results), Marcuse exhorts philosophers to engage in socio-political action. To the existentialist, he concedes the importance of the concerns of the existing individual, the needs of human subjectivity and the drive towards authenticity. But he argues that a real change of inauthentic existence pre-supposes a transformed society. The subject of history is not the 'single one', he argues, but 'the historical unity is continually a unity of being-with-one-another of "social" being – it is constantly a "society"'.[96] Certainly philosophy should respect and cultivate the authenticity of the individual, but the 'single one' and its inwardness does not stand outside of history and society; instead, every individual is a social individual, living in and conditioned by a social-historical situation. Hence, gaining authenticity does not mean stepping outside or beyond social existence and history; rather, social existence is 'the reality of existence itself and only through it can the single one in truth be addressed and encountered'.[97]

Marcuse introduces here a dialectic of liberation and revolution that characterizes his life-long philosophical project as a whole. Concrete philosophy aims at a social practice that will at the same time liberate the individual and revolutionize society. Since the individual is always a social individual and since one's possibilities for thought and action are prescribed by the given social-historical situation, the individual project of liberation necessarily presupposes a project of social revolution. Philosophy that involves itself with contemporary problems is aware of the duty to seize upon the current problems of existence. 'Hence the public act stands necessarily at the end of every genuine concrete philosophy. The trial and defence of Socrates; Plato's political effort in Syracuse; Kierkegaard's struggle with the state church'.[98]

In this chapter I have been trying to indicate what Marcuse appropriated from Heidegger and Marx for his own project; how and why he thought Marxism and phenomenological existentialism could be united; and what I take to be an implicit, and powerful, critique of Heidegger and phenomenology in his first essay. I shall offer some critical remarks on Marcuse's early writings at the end of Chapter 3. First, I shall discuss the impact of Marcuse's deeper study of Hegel and his enthusiastic appropriation of the newly published *1844 Manuscripts* of Marx on his evolving theory.

3

Studies in the Marxian Philosophy

In the early 1930s Marcuse began an in-depth study of Hegel and wrote a series of articles on Hegelian and Marxian dialectics while preparing a dissertation under Heidegger on *Hegel's Ontology and the Theory of Historicity*.[1] Marcuse never really explained why he involved himself in such intensive work on Hegel – a project that would be at the centre of his philosophical inquiries, in different contexts, for the next decade. Perhaps Marcuse thought that Hegel's dynamic and historical ontology provided a corrective to Heidegger's more static and ahistorical ontology, which was not really able to conceptualize movement and change.[2] Since Hegel was a great philosopher in the classical tradition of German Idealism – in whom Heidegger was also interested – Marcuse was able to do his post-doctorate work on Hegel while working with Heidegger.[3] Moreover, Hegel was an important source of Marx's theory, and Marcuse could thus continue work on his appropriation of Marxism through deepening his grasp of Hegel's philosophy and dialectical method.[4] The result of his study of Hegel was a version of Hegelian Marxism that would be a characteristic feature of Marcuse's own work.

There was a tension in Marcuse's appropriation of Hegel – indeed, at the heart of his theoretical labours during this period – between the current of Hegelian Marxism initiated by Lukács and Korsch and the ontology of Heidegger and German Idealism. Marcuse told me that he believed that Korsch and Lukács represented the 'most authentic' current of Marxism.[5] As we have seen, his definition of Marxism in his first essay as a theory of proletarian revolution and revolutionary critique of bourgeois society closely followed Lukács, and the problematic of his first essays was deeply influenced by *History and Class Consciousness*.[6] Although Marcuse does not accept Lukács's notion of the party, or 'class consciousness', both Marcuse and Lukács stress the unity of theory and practice as distinguishing features of Marxism, and both have a somewhat apocalyptic notion of total revolution. Crucially, each stresses the fundamental importance of the Marxian dialectic and its Hegelian roots.[7]

Yet while working with Heidegger, Marcuse focused on Hegel's ontology, and through his studies came to gain a life-long respect for ontological inquiry. Although there is a somewhat mystical quest for the 'meaning of Being' in Heidegger's understanding of ontology, there is also a notion of ontology in Heidegger's *Being and Time* as the attempt to lay bare 'the fundamental structures of human existence'.[8] It was this structural-categorical concept of ontology that preoccupied Marcuse, and in his early philosophical studies he searched for the fundamental structures of human existence, society and history, which he believed were necessary to provide an adequate foundation for social theory. In his early ontological studies, Marcuse mixed Hegel, Marx and Heidegger in an uneasy synthesis and criticized other ontologies and social theories from this perspective. His blend of German Idealism and Marxism was rather unique for a German academic philosopher, as there were few professional philosophers who were concerned with the question of Marxism and philosophy at the time.[9]

3.1 Philosophy and social theory

In an essay on Max Adler's Marxism, Marcuse defines philosophy as 'the scientific expression of a specific human basic orientation (*Grundhaltung*) and, to be sure, a basic orientation of being and entities'.[10] As such, it is a privileged mode of perception and discourse 'in which a historical-social situation can often be more clearly and deeply expressed than in the rigid and reified practical spheres of life' – and, the essay suggests, than the social sciences.[11] This 'basic orientation', Marcuse claimed, was frequently oppositional and set the philosophical subject against the existing capitalist society: 'In many regions of scientific research, there exists a basic orientation that no longer has any thing to do with the familiar forms-of-life of capitalist society, and which, moreover, has already anticipated a good piece (*gutes Stück*) of historical development'.[12] Marcuse presents here a concept of philosophy as critical, oppositional and anticipatory that would guide his intellectual endeavours throughout his life.[13]

In his book on *Hegel's Ontology*, Marcuse cites Hegel's doctrine that 'philosophy arises from necessity (*Not*), from a need (*Bedürfnis*) of human life in a specific historical situation: that of division' – a situation of suffering, conflict and alienation.[14] Philosophy is directed to analyse and overcome oppositions, so as to create a more harmonious and less divided and conflictual way of being-in-the-world. Marcuse thus combines the Hegelian-Hiedeggerian notion that philosophy emerges from existential needs and concerns with Marx's notion that the task of philosophy is to transform the world.

Marcuse's essays in this period exhibit a sometimes tortuous and not very successful attempt to overcome traditional philosophy and to move towards a new philosophy that seeks to conceptualize real historical movement and to act as a practical lever of individual emancipation and social transformation. He is inspired by the attempts of Lukács and Korsch to investigate the relations between Marxism and philosophy, and during his entire life he would defend the importance of philosophy for social theory and would contribute to developing a Marxist philosophy. For instance, in an article on the relation between philosophy and social theory, Marcuse calls attention to Korsch's work *Marxism and Philosophy*, and approves of Korsch's struggle against tendencies in Marxism that would dismiss philosophy as mere ideology.[15] Marcuse agrees with Korsch that this is not merely a theoretical error, but one that destroys the unity of theory and practice. Such a dismissal of philosophy robs practice of the guiding light of theory and excludes the dimension of ideological struggle from revolutionary theory and practice. Against all tendencies that purge Marxism of philosophy, Marcuse replies – following Korsch – that the critique of ideology and philosophy is an indispensable aspect of revolutionary struggle: 'theoretical critique and practical transformation' are 'inextricably interconnected actions'.[16] This is so because genuine philosophy is not merely an instrument of critique, but itself contains a revolutionary drive towards its realization which requires a transformation of reality'.[17] Marcuse argues that the Marxian notion of 'the realization of philosophy' signifies the abolition of philosophy's abstract

and contemplative nature and realization of its inner drive towards
a unity of theory and practice – a goal best reached through
'revolutionary practice'.[18]

Lukács and Korsch's attempts to develop the Marxian philosophy
would occupy Marcuse for many years to follow. Their immediate
impact is evident in his defence of the importance of philosophy for
social theory and practice – a position that would guide Marcuse's
work throughout his life. In the period under inquiry, this project
took the form of work on the foundation of the Hegelian-Marxian
philosophies and dialectical method, and criticisms of current forms
of social theory and philosophy from a Hegelian standpoint. Many
of the thirteen essays published between 1928 and 1933 criticize
contemporary interpretations of Marxism which Marcuse believes
deflect it from its revolutionary goals and undermine its philosophical foundation. For example, he criticizes the sociological interpretation of Marx by Mannheim which reduces Marxism to a historically surpassed ideology.[19] He attacks the neo-Kantian tendency towards a 'transcendental Marxism' that would articulate an '*a priori*'
of social theory and objective laws of society,[20] and he criticizes
misinterpretations of Hegel and the dialectic.[21] Other essays contain critiques of academic German social theories and philosophies
that Marcuse believes rest on dubious philosophical assumptions.[22]
Let us now examine in some detail the most important of Marcuse's
studies in Marxian philosophy.

3.2 Dialectics and historicity

In a two-part essay, 'On the Problem of the Dialectic', published in
Die Gesellschaft, Marcuse analyses the philosophical concept of
dialectics in Plato, Kant, Hegel and Marx. His aim is to criticize the
Kantian concept of dialectics set forth in a survey of *The Dialectic in
Contemporary Society* by Siegfried Marck.[23] For Marck, 'critical
dialectics', rooted in the philosophy of Kant, maintains itself in the
tension between the ego and existence (*Ich und Ist*) and value and
existence (the ought and the is). Such a 'critical dialectics', Marcuse
objects, posits an *a priori* dualism between these regions and claims
that the human fate is to live out this tension. What Marcuse
calls 'concrete dialectics', on the other hand, does not posit a
subject–object dualism, but conceives of dialectics as a historical

process that encompasses all realms of human and social existence. It analyses the contradictions and conflicts which generate historical movement. A tendency to merge dialectics and history is evident in Marcuse's claim that the movement of history exhibits a dialectical structure; consequently, dialectics provides the proper method both to investigate and interpret history and society. In Marcuse's view dialectics is especially oriented towards human existence and generates values and ideals from analysis of the concrete human situation, rather than positing external values or maintaining a rigid distinction between facts and values. Hence, 'concrete dialectics as an objective value-free science is an absurdity'.[24]

In the second part of the article, Marcuse summarizes his theses on Hegel's ontology, which are developed in his book on the topic.[25] He argues that Hegel's ontology, as set out in the early writings, the *Phenomenology of Spirit* and *Logic*, 'produces for Hegel the actual basis of the dialectic'.[26] For Marcuse, the category of *life* is the conceptual key to Hegel's dialectic and articulates the movement of social-historical life. In his view, the categories of 'movement' and 'life', which comprise the essence of historicity for Hegel, were developed most adequately by Dilthey in his *Lebensphilosophie* (philosophy of life).[27] Marcuse's explication of the dialectical category of 'negation' in terms of human practice is especially interesting and significant as a key to his philosophical mind-set.[28] The basic modality of practice is the 'truly creative and transformative' *negation* of objects and social-material conditions of life. Human life, he argues, goes beyond, or transcends, its 'determinations ... by overcoming its own immediate present situation and driving itself forward from its current possibilities to a higher situation'.[29] He claims that Hegel's analysis of desire and labour in *The Phenomenology of Mind* shows the 'essential *action* character of "negation"' as labour becomes conscious of its creative nature, its ability to modify and transform itself and its environment.[30]

We find here the roots of Marcuse's notion of 'negation in the dialectic' which will play an important role in his later theory. The theory of negation, though, does not signify an absolute negation, but rather a *determinate negation* that preserves any useful or liberating potentials of a situation being negated, while eliminating obsolete or repressive aspects. Marcuse's notion of dialectical negation is thus connected with the Hegelian concept of *Aufhebung* which at once negates, preserves and raises to a higher level. Marx is praised for his transformative application of the Hegelian dialectical categories and method to a study of the contemporary historical situation:

Marx exposed again the original concept of history and the essential character of historical life, but not – and this *separates his work decisively not only from Hegel but from all philosophy –* for a philosophical determination of life within all being. Instead Marx attempts the analysis of the contemporary historical situation of this life for the purpose of a revolutionary upheaval. Consequently, Marx describes the process of reification and its negation in the expressly delimited historical form that is decisive for the revolutionary situation; i.e. the reification of life in capitalist commodity production.[31]

Hegelian and Marxian dialectics is thus appraised by Marcuse as the appropriate method to study history, society and human existence, since its categories describe the very structure and movement of these domains. Though Marcuse seems to believe that the dialectical method and its categories best conceptualize historical reality – rather than the scientific method – he stresses that the dialectical method is integrally connected to revolutionary practice and that its categories describe the activity of transforming the world. Moreover, although he does not mention Marx in his dissertation on *Hegel's Ontology,* he concludes 'On the Problem of Dialectic' by affirming that Marx has the most adequate dialectical method and the best theory of historicity:

When Marx stood the Hegelian dialectic on its feet, this was no mere correction of a part of Hegelian philosophy, no mere emphasis or appropriation of method, no materialist reinterpretation, but the return of the dialectic to its proper domain and, hence, the scientific discovery of the true dimension of history which now, since the dialectic had been rediscovered, could be grasped in its basic structure. Marx was the first to grasp the true historicity of human existence, using the only approach appropriate for this purpose. In a much deeper sense, Marx is the heir of German Idealism because this philosophy was only able to become authentic again on the way to and through the historicity of human existence.[32]

Throughout his early articles, Marcuse utilizes an Hegelian concept of historicity – influenced by Heidegger – which is the focus of his book on *Hegel's Ontology*. In the introduction he writes: 'The intention of this work is the attempt to provide access for ascertaining the basic characteristics of historicity. Historicity is the title for that which characterizes history as "history" and delimits it from regions like "nature" and "economy".'[33] Marcuse believes that Dilthey has gone furthest in presenting the fundamental characteristics of historicity in recent times, but that his categories of 'life', 'spirit' and history as the unity of 'I and world' contain undefined ontological presuppositions.[34] These presuppositions derive, Marcuse claims, from the philosophy of Hegel: 'Hegel's ontology is the foundation and ground of the being of historicity worked out by Dilthey and consequently is the ground and foundation of the tradition in which the philosophical questions concerning historicity presently move'.[35] Therefore a detailed conceptual clarification of Hegel's ontology is necessary to elucidate the concept of historicity. Marcuse's interpretation is distinguished by a new interpretation of Hegel's logic and early writings; he claims that they, and not the later *Philosophy of History, Philosophy of Right*, or Hegel's system, contain the genuine presuppositions of Hegel's theory of history and, in fact, unfold the basic presuppositions of his philosophy.[36]

Marcuse's first book on Hegel is an extremely technical, systematic work in the style of German academic philosophy. He concludes the introduction with a special thanks to Martin Heidegger, under whom he wrote it: 'What this work contributes to the unfolding and clarification of the problems, it owes thanks to the philosophical work of Martin Heidegger. This should be stated right at the beginning, rather than through particular citations'.[37] Although Marcuse occasionally asks Heideggerian questions concerning the meaning of the being of an entity and finds Heideggerian categories operative in Hegel, such as being-in-the-world, on the whole the work tends to interpret Hegel from a 'philosophy of life' perspective and thus makes Dilthey, rather than Heidegger or 'existential philosophy', Hegel's true heir.[38] Marx is never mentioned, and Marcuse's situating of Hegel in the *Lebensphilosophie* tradition – rather than Marxism – later led Lukács to attack Marcuse's study as one of a group of *Lebensphilosophie* interpretations of Hegel which tried to appropriate Hegel for an irrationalist tradition and sever the Hegel–Marx relation[39] – which would in fact, be the central focus of

Marcuse's later interpretation of Hegel in *Reason and Revolution*. Marcuse's systematic interpretation of the basic categories of Hegel's ontology is probably of primary interest today to Hegel scholars, some of whom believe that it is Marcuse's best book.[40] He provides detailed textual and analytical clarifications of Hegel's concept of historicity, which is interpreted in terms of Hegel's concepts of life, movement, essence, spirit, concept (*Begriff*) and reality (*Wirklichkeit*). The most interesting anticipation of his later philosophy is the section on 'The Movement of Essence in its "Two-Dimensionality"' (pp. 79ff); here Marcuse shows that the origin of his theory of one-dimensional thought is a reading of Hegel's distinction between 'appearance' and 'essence' – an issue we shall return to in our discussions of *Reason and Revolution* and *One-Dimensional Man*.[41] Despite the abstract nature of the treatise, Adorno believed that the book disclosed a move away from Heidegger: 'he is tending to move from concern with the meaning of being to disclosure of entities; from fundamental ontology to history-philosophy; from historicity to history'.[42] This is a strange reading of Marcuse's first Hegel book, since he rarely mentions concrete history but stays on the level of pure ontology. Adorno's subsequent critique is provocative, however, arguing that Marcuse's quest to develop a unitary concept of historicity, enveloping subjectivity and objectivity, as well as a set of other dualisms, suppresses the fact that Hegel's basic presupposition is 'absolute subjectivity' and not 'life', as Marcuse claims.[43] Adorno claims that Hegel's philosophy is at bottom really 'idealism' and falls prey to all its traditional deficiencies.[44] His review discloses that Marcuse is more sympathetic towards Hegel and German Idealism than Adorno, bringing to light Adorno's early desire to carry through a sharp critique of Hegelian Idealism.[45]

It should be made clear that there is a major difference between Marcuse's interpretation of Hegel in *Hegel's Ontology* and his later interpretation in *Reason and Revolution*.[46] In *Reason and Revolution* Marcuse stresses the relation of Hegel to Marx and the importance of the Hegelian concepts of freedom, reason and critical dialectics, while in *Hegel's Ontology* he is interested in the ontological features of Hegel's philosophy and totally excludes the historical-political dimension that plays such an important role in his later interpretation of Hegel.[47] This is not surprising, since the work was written as a '*Habilitations-Dissertation*' under Heidegger, designed to gain Marcuse employment in the German university world that required such a treatise for promotion to the rank of *Dozent.* Since Marcuse was to drop his early reading of Hegel and the ontological concern with 'historicity' in his work with the Frankfurt Institute for Social Research and subsequent writing, we can forgo a more detailed discussion of Marcuse's early essays on historicity and dialectics in order to focus on two topics that were to remain important themes in his later writings: his appropriation of the early Marx's anthropology, critique of capitalism and theory of revolution, combined with his own development of a philosophical concept of labour.

3.3 Marx's *Economic and Philosophical Manuscripts*

Marcuse's review article on Marx's *Economic-Philosophical Manuscripts* is one of the most important of his early essays.[48] His interpretation begins a tendency to reinterpret Marx in the light of his early writings and continues efforts to develop the philosophical foundations of Marxism. Marcuse's study, which remains one of the best interpretations of the early Marx, portrays the synthesis of philosophy, political economy and revolutionary social theory as the distinguishing feature of Marxism. It contains a provocative discussion of the young Marx, whose early writings would have a powerful impact on contemporary thought and would decisively shape Marcuse's own theoretical enterprise.

The publication of Marx's *Manuscripts,* written in Paris in 1844 and first published in 1932, has been called one of the great philosophical events of the century.[49] Marcuse was evidently sensitive to important new theoretical works, for just as he had written one of the first interpretations of Heidegger's *Being and Time,* he also published one of the first comprehensive interpretations of Marx's *Manuscripts.* Marcuse later tells how the *Manuscripts* 'liberated' him from Heidegger and turned him closer to Marx:

During this entire period, I had already read Marx and continued to study Marx; then arrived the publication of the *Economic-Philosophical Manuscripts.* That was probably the turning point. Here was, in a certain sense, a new Marx, who was truly concrete and at the same time went beyond the rigid practical and theoretical Marxism of the parties. And from then on the problem of Heidegger versus Marx was no longer really a problem for me.[50]

Marcuse must have felt an affinity for the doctrine in Marx's *Manuscripts*, as the theory of alienation, the humanism which undercut both philosophical idealism and materialism, and the broad philosophical perspectives found there corresponded with his own emerging theory. Marx's early writings provided powerful support for Marcuse's own enterprise, which could inspire him to develop the full philosophical-revolutionary import of Marxism which he thought was being distorted and covered over by the leading Marx interpreters and tendencies of the day. His enthusiasm and belief in the importance of Marx's *Manuscripts* for a correct interpretation of the Marxian project is disclosed in the opening paragraph of his essay:

> The publication of Marx's *Economic-Philosophical Manuscripts* from the year 1844 is a decisive event in the history of Marx-research. These *Manuscripts* put the discussion of the origins and original meaning of historical materialism, indeed the whole theory of 'scientific socialism', on a new basis; they also make possible a more fruitful and productive posing of the question of the actual connection between Marx and Hegel. (*SCP*, p. 3)

Marcuse's argument is that the 1844 *Manuscripts* disclose the 'original meaning of Marx's fundamental categories; thus it could become necessary to revise the current interpretation of the later working out of the critique through reference to its origin' (*SCP*, p. 3). Marcuse announces the important project of revising the interpretation of Marxism on the basis of the writings of the early Marx.[51] These 'revisionist' projects represent attempts to develop an interpretation of Marxism critical of the various orthodoxies. The 'Marxist–Leninist' establishment long remained quiet on the issue of the relation of the *Manuscripts* to Marx's later writings, assigning them a minimal importance in the Marxian corpus; eventually, however, they were forced to engage in heated polemics against those who would found their Marxism on the early Marx. The standard 'orthodox' argument is that the early 'philosophical-humanist' Marx was an opening stage which Marx completely abandoned in his later critique of political economy.[52] The early

Marx, however, has also been used as a weapon to criticize bureaucratic Communism and to affirm a more emancipatory notion of Marxism and socialism than is found in most contemporary 'socialist' societies.[53] Hence, the 1844 *Manuscripts* have had a wide and varied impact and have been the subject of much intense polemic.[54]

Marcuse characterizes Marx's *Manuscripts* as 'a philosophical critique and foundation for political economy in the sense of a theory of revolution' (*SCP*, p. 3). Marx's critique of political economy is philosophical in that its fundamental categories 'develop out of a critical confrontation with the categories of Hegelian philosophy (i.e. labour, objectification, alienation, sublation, property)' (*SCP*, p. 4). Moreover, Marx's dialectical method was developed by thinking through problems at the root of Hegel's philosophy and was not, Marcuse suggests, merely an abstraction of dialectics from Hegel's philosophy. Most important, the Marxian theory of alienation and its revolutionary abolition rests on a philosophical conception of human nature that is the basis of an argument that human beings are alienated in capitalist society, which must be eliminated to liberate the individual. Thus, 'the revolutionary critique of political economy itself has a philosophical foundation, just as, conversely, the philosophy underlying it already contains revolutionary praxis' (*SCP*, pp. 4–5). Marcuse claims that the Hegelian dialectical categories and method, as well as the theory of alienation and its overcoming, remain operative throughout the succeeding stages of Marx's thought, even in the later, more specifically economic, writings.[55]

Marcuse therefore rejects the 'cleavage thesis', which claims that the early works of Marxism are 'philosophical' in opposition to the later 'scientific' works, and stresses instead the *continuity* of Marxism via the *interconnection* of philosophy, political economy and revolutionary practice throughout Marx's writings. Marcuse argues that Marx's critique of political economy is at once a demonstration of the deficiencies of the early theories of capitalism in classical political economy (i.e. Adam Smith, Ricardo, Say, etc.) and a critique of capitalist society and what it does to human beings.[56] In opposition to these theories, Marx lays the foundation for a 'new science' that becomes a 'science of the necessary conditions of the communist revolution' (*SCP*, p. 5). This revolution is not only an economic transformation, but is also a 'revolution of the whole history of the human species and the determination of its essential being' (*SCP*, p. 5). The critique of political economy is therefore not merely one science that stands beside others, but is 'the scientific expression for a problematic that involves the human being in its entirety' (*SCP*, p. 5). In Marcuse's reading, Marx rejects the academic division of the sciences into separate disciplines and endeavours to found a 'new human science' that serves as a superordinate, unifying discipline which aims at human liberation and the creation of a new social order.

The target of the critique of political economy is the 'total "alienation" and "devaluation" of human reality as it is found in capitalist society' (*SCP*, p. 5). It is exactly this phenomenon that is covered over by bourgeois political economy. The basis of human alienation in capitalist society is the *alienation of labour*, which is the fundamental concept of the new science that Marx develops. While bourgeois social sciences neglect alienated labour, for Marx the alienation of labour is the fundamental fact of capitalist society from which such other categories of political economy as production, exploitation, profits and wages can be interpreted and criticized.[57]

Marx's achievement was to take the philosophical concept of alienation developed by Hegel and others and give it a concrete material foundation by analysing alienation in contemporary capitalist society. For Marx, the alienation of labour is not only the cornerstone of political economy, but contains a fundamental anthropological dimension, for it designates 'not only an economic fact, but an alienation of human being, a degeneration of life, a devaluation and loss of human reality' (*SCP*, pp. 7–8). This phenomenon of alienation is an historical event, indeed 'a decisive event in human history', the abolition of which will 'revolutionize the whole history of the human species' (*SCP*, p. 9). Bourgeois political economy is criticized by Marx because it lacks this anthropological-historical and critical dimension: 'Because bourgeois political economy does not have human beings and their history in its conceptual scheme, it is in the deepest sense not a "human science", but is a non-human science of an inhuman world of things and commodities' (*SCP*, p. 9). In this view, bourgeois political economy fails to grasp its essential object, the human being who is the subject of labour and foundation of economic activity. Marx, however, provides both a historical theory of human nature and its development as well as an analysis of what capitalism does to human beings. Marcuse points out that consideration of the importance of Marx's philosophical anthropology refutes attempts to interpret or impugn Marxism as a reductionistic economism that sees the human being solely as an economic animal (*SCP*, p. 9).

For Marx, alienated labour is an historical phenomenon produced by concrete socio-economic conditions. 'Alienation' does not refer to a timeless metaphysical condition, nor does Marx identify alienation with 'objectification' or 'externalization', as do some Hegelians and existentialists.[58] For Marx, objectification refers to an essential aspect of labour (making objective human powers, making objects), whereas alienation is a form of objectification that takes place under certain socio-economic conditions that are to be abolished in order to produce non-alienated labour. Consequently, for both Marx and Marcuse, although the activity of objectification is a ground for the possibility of alienation, 'alienation' itself is historically constituted by the capitalist mode of production and can only be overcome when capitalism is abolished.

3.3.1 *Marx's anthropology, theory of alienation and critique of capitalism*

Marcuse argues that the whole Marxian critique of political economy and theory of revolution is founded on a certain conception of human nature and its essential powers (*SCP*, pp. 8ff). The intention of the critique is to show that essential human needs and powers are being repressed and distorted in capitalist society; consequently, the theory of alienation provides a justification of revolutionary social transformation on the grounds of capitalism's oppressive and destructive effects on human life. The analysis aims at not merely another philosophical theory of human nature, but at characterizing the contemporary human situation, which is evaluated in the light of its failure to satisfy essential human needs and to develop human potentialities.

Marcuse shows how Marx's theory of human nature and alienation developed in a critical dialogue with Hegel, Feuerbach and the 'young Hegelians'. As a correction against interpretations that exaggerate the Feuerbachian roots of Marx's early anthropology, Marcuse argues that Marx derives essential aspects of his theory from Hegel's analysis of labour, objectification and alienation and that therefore 'Marx's theory has its roots in the centre of Hegel's philosophical problematic' (*SCP*, p. 13).[59] Specifically, Marcuse believes that Marx begins with a materialist reconstruction of Hegel's concepts of labour and spirit (*Geist*), which are concretized in terms of Feuerbach's 'naturalism'. However, Marx then proceeds to interpret human sensuousness and needs stressed by Feuerbach in terms of practical social activity which develops human nature and constitutes the human-social world (i.e. praxis).

The concept of labour is central to Marx's anthropology because it develops essential human *potentialities* and fulfils basic *needs*.[60] Marx stresses the primacy of human agency, the creative ability to produce objects and to recognize one's self and one's humanity objectified in the human-social world. Labour is thus an activity in which basic human powers are manifest: it develops one's faculties of reason and intelligence, it exercises bodily capabilities, it is social and communal activity, and it exemplifies human creativity and freedom. Human needs and potentialities are a product, in Marx's view, of the entirety of previous history, and consequently Marx argues that human nature is essentially *historical* (pp. 24ff). Against tendencies to interpret human nature as universal and unchanging, Marx stresses the constitutive power of historically specific modes of production. The human world, in this view, is a historical world; to cite Marx, 'History is the true natural history of the human being, its act of origin, the creation of the human being through human labour' (*SCP*, p. 24).

In this regard, it is important to point out that although Marcuse uses the language of ontology and 'essence', he rejects concepts of a fixed, universal and ahistorical concept of the human essence. He argues that

To play off essence (the determinants of 'the' human being) and facticity (the given concrete historical situation) against each other is to miss completely the new standpoint that Marx had already assumed at the outset of his investigations. For Marx, essence and facticity, the situation of essential history and the situation of factual history, are no longer separate regions or levels independent of each other: the historical experience of the human being is *taken up into the definition of the human essence*. We are no longer dealing with an abstract human essence, which remains equally valid at every stage of concrete history, but with an essence that can be defined in *history* and *only* in history. (*SCP*, p. 28)[61]

Consequently, although there are ontological-essentialist tendencies in Marcuse's work, they are always interpreted in a theoretical framework that attempts to undercut previous dichotomies between essentialism and historicism, thus offering a new philosophical framework and theory. Admittedly, Marcuse does not adequately clarify this project and sometimes uses the language of traditional ontology (see *SCP*, pp. 35–9). Although he often engages in ontological generalization, he then calls for situating his ontological categories in a concrete historical situation. For example, after generalizing Hegel's master–slave categories into a universal framework to discuss the dynamics of domination (*SCP*, pp. 37ff), he states: 'After the possibility of alienated labour has been shown to have its roots in the essence of the human being, the limits of philosophical description have been reached and the discovery of the real origin of alienation becomes a matter for historical analysis' (*SCP*, pp. 37–8).

A major error in attempts to interpret Marcuse's philosophy has been to reduce his thought to philosophical problematics – idealist or materialist, essentialist or historicist – the limitations of which Marcuse himself was trying to overcome.[62] Marcuse thought at this point that Heidegger, too, had overcome these philosophical dualisms, but soon perceived that Heidegger fell into traditional essentialist-idealist traps and that the early Marx provided the most powerful alternative to previous philosophical dualisms. It is also a mistake to claim that Marcuse's, or Marx's, anthropology is 'reductionist' and falls prey to a 'metaphysics of labour' which reduces essential human activity to labour and greatly exaggerates its constitutive role in human life.[63] In fact, Marx and Marcuse refer to human beings not as productive, labouring beings in any narrow or solely economic sense, but as many-sided beings with a wealth of needs and powers that are at once individual, social and historical.[64] The Marxian concept of the production and reproduction of everyday life includes sex, communication, symbolic interaction and exchange, and many other human activities. Far from being reductionist, the anthropology of the early Marx provides a concept of a many-sided human being, from which standpoint the one-sidedness and restrictions of capitalist society can be criticized. Hence the Marxian concept of human being and its alienation is not measuring and condemning capitalism from the standpoint of a fixed, ahistorical and identical human essence which is then shown to be in contradiction with activity in capitalist society. Rather, Marx argues, and Marcuse assents, that human life under capitalism is fatally deprived of free, creative activity and thus suppresses fundamental human potentialities and distorts fundamental human needs (*SCP*, pp. 26ff). Crucially, the Marxian theory of labour and its alienation leads to, and provides the justification for, a theory of socialism and revolution.

3.3.2 Humanism, revolution and socialism

In Marcuse's interpretation of Marx's *Economic-Philosophical Manuscripts*, the central fact that grounds and justifies revolution is the contradiction between one's essential human needs and powers and the historical conditions of capitalist society. As noted this contradiction involves the opposition between free, many-sided, creative activity and alienated labour. Marcuse concludes that:

> If essence and existence stand opposed to each other, and if their union as their actual realization is the authentic free *task* of human praxis, then where the factical conditions have progressed to the complete *perversion* of the human essence, the *radical abolition* of this factical condition is the definitive task. It is precisely the unceasing focus on the human essence that becomes the inexorable impulse for the founding of the radical revolution. For the actual situation of capitalism is characterized not only by an economic or political crisis, but by a catastrophe of the human essence – this insight condemns to failure from the outset mere economic or political *reform* and unconditionally demands the catastrophic abolition of the actual conditions through *total revolution.*(*SCP*, p. 29)

It is here that Marcuse most dramatically departs from the traditional Marxian concept of revolution. Indeed, in many of his works, Marcuse will move away from analysis of the contradictions in the political-economic system and class struggles to focus on repression of individuals, which generates refusal and revolt. Marcuse posits dormant, emancipatory powers in human nature striving for realization and expression as the foundation of revolt and struggle, and he finds a Marxian basis for such a position in the *Economic-Philosophical Manuscripts* – while later he will seek a similar guarantee of revolutionary potentiality in human nature through Freud's instinct theory and 'authentic art'.

Marcuse continues to argue – as expressed in the above passage – that the capitalist system of alienation, exploitation and oppression is literally 'catastropic' for human beings and that only total revolution could overcome the contradiction between human beings and capitalist society. Total revolution is required, Marcuse believes, both because alienated labour affects the totality of life and because the entire system of labour and leisure under capitalism is alienating and oppressive. Economic and political reform alone will not eliminate the evils of capitalism, thus total revolution is necessary. Following Rosa Luxemburg's concept of revolution, Marcuse still envisages revolution as a 'catastrophic upheaval' that will overthrow and transform the existing society in its entirety.[65] Marcuse's later work will attempt to justify this position and will later make his ultra-radical ideas the centre of heated controversy.

In his essay on Marx's *Manuscripts*, Marcuse analyses the role of alienated labour, private property, money, commodities, class domination and reification in capitalist society – ideas that would crucially influence his own theory of advanced capitalism.[66] He was also impressed by the vision of human emancipation in Marx's *Manuscripts*, one of the sources of Marcuse's later theory of liberation, which envisages the image of an emancipated human being in a non-repressive society – a vision of liberation that would be shared by many in the New Left and countercultures of the 1960s. Developing Marx's reflections on Communism and humanism in his early works, Marcuse stresses the gratification of needs, the cultivation of the senses, the aesthetic-erotic components in a non-repressive civilization, and a new sensibility and consciousness as necessary components of a liberated society.[67] Marcuse is thus one of the few Marxists to take seriously Marx's early vision of an emancipated sensibility and the total revolution that would involve developing new human needs and powers, a new sensibility, new human relationships, new institutions, and a new labour system – in short, a totally new society – all dedicated to the fulfilment and realization of many-sided human beings. In this way Marcuse appropriates and developes the revolutionary-socialist content in the much discussed Marxian humanism.

Marcuse also takes seriously Marx's vision that all antagonisms, conflicts and contradictions found in capitalist societies would be overcome in an emancipated socialist society. The Marcusian themes of reconciliation and harmony thus have their origins (or at least Marxian roots) in Marx's *Manuscripts*. Marx believed that with the socialist revolution the antagonisms between human potentialities and actual existence would be abolished through the abolition of alienated labour, private property and class domination. Socialism would make possible labour as a 'universal and free appropriation' of the world that would make possible a 'many-sided development and expression' of human nature (*SCP*, pp. 33–4).

Marcuse's stress on 'total revolution' and a radical restructuring of society as a whole shows that those Marxist-Leninist critics are wrong who complain that Marcuse is merely advocating an 'anthropological revolution',[68] for we have seen that revolution for Marcuse requires both a change of human activity and consciousness, combined with the transformation of socio-economic conditions and institutions. Marcuse's reading of Marx's *Economic-Philosophical Manuscripts*, however, provides a philosophical reading of Marx clearly at odds with the dominant tendencies of 'scientific Marxism'. He continues the attempt, begun by Lukács and Korsch, to develop a version of 'critical Marxism' that emphasizes subjectivity, needs, emancipation and Hegelian dialectics as providing the method and categories of social transformation. Since Marx's *Manuscripts* were first published in 1932, he felt that they confirmed the interpretation of Marxism developed by Lukács and Korsch (who had not seen Marx's *Manuscripts)* and thus provided textual support in Marx for a version of critical Marxism.

Although Marcuse's interpretation of Marx's *Manuscripts* is excellent, his own understanding of capitalism, revolution and socialism is too dependent on Marx's early writings, and he has not yet appropriated adequately Marx's later studies of capitalism and politics. Marcuse is thus too caught up in the philosophical problematic of the early Marx and German Idealism and has not yet achieved a solid enough grasp of the Marxian theories of society and history. His theory of revolution is too focused on human nature and its alienation and not enough on the socio-economic causes of alienation, or the contradictions of capitalism and class struggle which generate revolutionary struggle and consciousness. After 1933, in his work with the Institute for Social Research, he would study the later Marx and would correctly argue in *Reason and Revolution*: 'Under all aspects, however, Marx's early writings are mere preliminary stages to his mature theory, stages that should not be overemphasized'.[59] And in his work following the Second World War, Marcuse would develop his own controversial critiques of Marxism and his own theory of capitalist society, socialism and political change.

Hence, Marcuse has not yet developed the sort of socio-economic analysis that he proposes in his early essays. Although from the beginning he calls for philosophy to become concrete, to be directed towards a practice which would change the world and help create new forms of social life, which would lead philosophers to become radical and perform 'public acts', and which would develop a theory of the present situation that would serve as a 'lever of revolution', Marcuse's own work has not yet fulfilled these requirements. Moreover, he was still too much under the infuence of Heidegger and had not yet escaped from certain philosophical premises of German Idealism, especially its exaggeration of the constitutive role of human subjectivity and tendencies towards idealist ontology. These influences are visible in his last published essay during his pre-Institute period.

3.4 The philosophical foundation of the concept of labour

In 'On the Philosophical Foundation of the Concept of Labour',[70] Marcuse develops in his own way Marx's notion that labour is the fundamental human activity in which one develops or fails to develop one's human potentialities. Marcuse seeks to construct a concept of labour that will clarify its centrality in the constitution of human experience and social theory. Motivating this effort was his view that the bourgeois and Marxian standpoints prevailing at the time proceeded from a flawed concept of labour which often suppressed entirely its philosophical-anthropological dimension. Against interpretations which solely posit labour as economic activity, Marcuse sought to reconstruct the foundations of political economy by outlining an ontology of human experience grounded in a philosophical-anthropological account of the key concept, labour. He considered this enterprise consistent with Marx's standpoint regarding the relationship of philosophy and political economy – a standpoint which, Marcuse also believed, had been neglected by later Marxists.

As with most of his writings, the essay on labour is a critical dialogue with Marxism in the specific sense of aiming to avert its degeneration into rigid orthodoxy. In particular, Marcuse attempts to restore to its proper status the role labour had played not only in Marx's early writings but in the corpus of his work. It is notable that the neglect of this concept prevailed to the point where even Lukács and Korsch, who had preceded Marcuse by a decade in reformulating Marxism's Hegelian-philosophical dimension, gave it little attention. However, with the publication in 1932 of the *Economic and Philosophic Manuscripts* of 1844, it became obvious that Marx had founded his whole project upon a complex, two-pronged disagreement with both Hegel and British political economy over precisely the concept of labour. Marcuse sought to develop that contention by elaborating a concept of labour that would avoid the reduction of labour to mere economic activity presupposed by both 'orthodox' Marxist and bourgeois theory.

The concept of labour that Marcuse criticizes posits labour as economic activity aimed at the satisfaction of needs interpreted on a biological, ahistorical model, taking coercive 'wage-labour' as the paradigm. Against this, Marcuse argues that labour is not merely an economic, but an ontological concept: 'a concept that conceptualizes the being of human existence itself and as such'.[71] What must be shown is that economic activity is rooted in the practice through which the human species constitutes its social-historical world and its own unique way of life. Marcuse thus develops an *ontology of labour* that exhibits the central constitutive features of the concept of labour and a *dialectic* that develops the interplay between labour's subjective (i.e. the creation of the human self) and objective moments (i.e. the constitution of the human world).[72] It becomes clear, however, that what is at stake in the essay is not only a dialogue between philosophy and political economy concerning the nature and function of labour, but also the question of the *liberation of labour*.[73]

The essay on the concept of labour has a curious position in Marcuse's corpus. It is a culmination of Marcuse's first attempt to develop a synthesis between Marxism and bourgeois philosophy and clearly shows the deficiencies of Marcuse's early theoretical efforts. The essay reveals the influence of Heidegger, which comes out in the overly ontological and subjectivistic emphasis in Marcuse's analysis of labour. It is, however, the last essay Marcuse wrote before the rise of fascism and his break with Heidegger.

Although the essay was published after the essay on the early Marx, it is more Heideggerian, and clearly exposes some of the weaknesses of Marcuse's early problematic before his work with the Frankfurt Institute for Social Research. Specifically, I want to make clear those aspects of Heidegger's influence which Marcuse had not yet overcome in order to reveal the main deficiencies in Marcuse's early work. I shall, however, also be concerned to indicate what is of enduring interest and importance in Marcuse's essay on labour and in his early work in general, so as to provide a balanced interpretation of its strengths and weaknesses.

The tendency in Marcuse's early essays towards excessive ontological generalization comes out of his claim that labour follows 'the law of the object' and that it therefore inevitably contains 'externalization' and 'alienation', and is ontologically a 'burden'.[74] The analysis is faulty because it eternalizes alienation and does not allow for creative, non-alienated labour.[75] In this regard, Stefan Breuer has argued that Marcuse's early ontology of labour reproduces recurrent features of labour under capitalism which are projected into a universal Concept, thus falling prey to what I call 'the fallacy of ontological generalization'.[76] Indeed, the features Marcuse ascribes to labour – externalization, alienation, being-a-burden, constant and enforced activity – describe features of wage-labour under capitalism and not necessarily universal features of human labour. Against Marcuse, one could argue that it was capitalism that made production the centre of life and which forced labour in the form of wage-labour on individuals, first for survival and then as a means of success and advancement, while generating a 'work ethic' that imposed labour on individuals as a moral duty. Moreover, capitalism unleashed Promethean forces of production and incessant growth, thereby helping engender a personality-structure and values consistent with the needs of the capitalist system. If this is the case, then Marcuse is simply projecting features of labour under capitalism on to his ontological concept of labour and is overlooking the fact that labour in precapitalist societies often partook of features of play, communal ritual and festival, or was often only seasonal and intermittent, and thus was not a constant task or function, as Marcuse's analysis implies.[77]

Moreover, Marcuse excludes labour from the realm of freedom and authentic individuality by – following Marx in *Capital III* – severing human activity into two realms: a realm of freedom which contains possibilities for creation of an authentic self, and a realm of necessity in which labour is in bondage to the domain of material production.[78] Marcuse also falls prey here to a Heideggerian tendency to subjectivize the self, limiting its essential activities to self-constitution and not constitution of a world. The realm of material production is dismissed as a realm of mere bondage, submission to natural necessity. The philosophical roots of the claim that labour in the realm of necessity is intrinsically unfree is a desire, central to Heidegger, German Idealism and existentialism, for an unconditioned freedom of the self.[79] Marcuse counterposes to the idealist-Heideggerian notion of the primal, absolute freedom of the self, the claim that the labour system is a fetter on individual's free self-activity. But the unfortunate consequence of Marcuse's correction of the idealist doctrine of total freedom is to separate the realm of freedom and necessity into two ontological realms, and to exclude labour from the realm of freedom. Furthermore, Marcuse assigns a central role to Heidegger's concept of authenticity and assumes a Nietzschean 'hierarchy or order' (*Rangordnung*) in which labour in the 'realm of necessity' is excluded from activity that develops the potentialities of the self.[80] Consequently, Marcuse seems to exclude material production and reproduction from the authentic possibilities of the self, assigning it as inferior status as a mere condition of being-a-self that is not in itself an activity in which the self can develop and fulfill itself.

In the essay on labour, the primary weakness of Marcuse's early project are apparent: excessive ontological generalization and often extreme subjectivism. These tendencies derive from the influence of Heidegger and German Idealism and would at least temporarily be displaced by his work with the Institute for Social Research. In general, his early essays have a tentative, preliminary nature: they are beginnings which attempt to develop a new 'concrete philosophy' that will both overcome the limitations of traditional academic philosophy and orthodox Marxism. Although Marcuse's early essays are suggestive and attempt to develop new philosophical perspectives, they are fettered by their overly ontological and individualistic perspectives. On the other hand, precisely their attempt to overcome the limitations of traditional philosophical and Marxian theories and their emphasis on the existing individual provides an impetus to reconstruct Marxism which has often lacked philosophical depth and rigour and which has neglected the individual and subjectivity. In other words, the limitations of his early essays should be weighed against the theoretical and practical tendency of orthodox Marxism to reduce individuals to functions of abstract universals (such as historical progress, revolutionary class, counter-revolutionary class and the like, as well as to characterize labour in strictly economic terms). That tendency, which influenced broad sections of the Western Left, made serious Marxist theorizing on the issue of the individual and the liberation of labour impossible. In contrast, Marcuse's emphatic focus on the subject of labour, despite the flaws suggested, had its merits. Indeed, the subjective moment, operative throughout Marcuse's writings, poses a challenge to Marxism to develop an adequate theory of subjectivity.

In this regard, it is important to note that Habermas's recent critique of Marxism and 'classical' critical theory revolves around his rejection of the centrality of labour, which is replaced (in status) by the category of symbolic interaction; the Marxian critique of political economy, in turn, is displaced by communication theory.[81] Marcuse never really addresses himself to Habermas's theses.[82] He does, however, implicitly indicate the outlines of a critical response in the first section of *Counterrevolution and Revolt*, where the concept of labour is vigorously reassserted as the core of critical theory. This enterprise is rooted in the early studies of labour and anthropology that we have just investigated, which are, despite their deficiencies which Marcuse would in part overcome, an important element of his later critical theory.

The essay on labour marks a turning point in Marcuse's career – one that separates his 1928–1933 attempts to mediate Marxism with Heidegger's phenomenological existentialism from his later work with the Institute for Social Research. During this early period, the Heideggerian influence is pronounced, and accounts for its most serious deficiencies. However, shortly following publication of the essay on labour, Marcuse broke with Heidegger. Such Heideggarian concepts as 'historicity' and 'authenticity', which play a central role in Marcuse's early work, were discarded in favour of historically specific Marxian categories. Among the results of this turn is that Marcuse extensively revised his 1933 analysis of labour. The relevant chapters of *Reason and Revolution* contain a major statement of his revised position, and Marcuse has occupied himself with the problem of labour in all of his later major works.[33]

After this examination of the early Marcuse, we shall turn to an inquiry into Marcuse's work with the Institute of Social Research in developing a critical theory of society.

4

Critical Theory and the Critique of Fascism

In 1932, as the Nazis came to power, the situation in Freiburg became precarious for Marcuse. As he remembers it: 'Because of the political situation I desperately wanted to join the Institute. At the end of 1932 it was perfectly clear that I would never be able to qualify for a professorship (*mich habilitieren können*) under the Nazi regime'.[1] Consequently, Marcuse corresponded with the Institute for Social Research in Frankfurt, asking if he could work with them. They invited him for an interview, and the Institute appointed him to a position.[2] This was fortunate, for in 1933 Heidegger joined the Nazi party and began making speeches for them.[3] Husserl had sent the Kurator of Frankfurt University, Kurt Riezler, a letter of support, and the Institute considered petitioning the University to accept Marcuse's Hegel '*Habilitation-Dissertation*' – which was already published as a book – so that he could be appointed a university professor. In fact, however, Marcuse never actually worked with the Institute in Frankfurt, since they, anticipating fascist suppression, had set up a branch office in Geneva, to which Marcuse was assigned.[4] Henceforth, despite later philosophical and political differences, Marcuse would strongly identify with what is now often called the 'Frankfurt School', and would make important contributions to their projects.

Marcuse's move in 1932 from the provincial philosophy department of Freiburg, dominated by Husserl and Heidegger, to association with the neo-Marxist Institute for Social Research played a crucial role in his development. Although Heideggerian influences are discernible in many of his later works, Marcuse abandoned the project of producing a synthesis of phenomenological existentialism and Marxism. Both Heidegger's 'political turn' in support of Nazism, and the relentless opposition of the Institute to Heidegger's philosophy, drove Marcuse to break with Heidegger and to commit himself to a version of Hegelian Marxism which the Institute was in the process of producing. The Director of the Institute, Max Horkheimer, loathed Heidegger's oracular ontology, while his colleague Theodor Adorno, who had just finished a critical study of Kierkegaard, was writing a critique of Husserlian and Heideggerian phenomenology.[5] For the next decade, Marcuse involved himself in the Institute's work and became one of its most important members.

Marcuse's previous studies of the Hegelian and Marxian dialectic had prepared him for work on the Institute's project of developing a dialectical social theory. However, in his collaboration with the Institute, there are important changes from his earlier writings. Methodologically, he no longer interprets Hegel and Marx as producers of an ontology of society and history, but uses their method and ideas for developing a critical theory of society.[6] Marcuse accepts the Institute's position that the Marxian critique of political economy is the centre and foundation for critical social theory. Accordingly, he switches his focus from 'concrete philosophy' and ontological analysis of such themes as 'historicity' to the development of a radical social theory rooted in the Marxian critique of political economy and historical materialism oriented towards the crucial social problems of the day. There is also a political change: Marcuse abandons concepts of the 'radical act' and a 'catastrophic total revolution' for the milder terms 'liberation' and 'transformation'. Part of this toning down of his revolutionary language was dictated by the decision made by the Institute that while in exile, they would adopt 'Aesopian language' to disguise their politics. Marcuse's shift in his political language, however, can also be attributed to the growing influence on him of Horkheimer and his associates. In view of the triumph of fascism, Stalinist tyranny and the concomitant failure of the proletariat in the West to emerge as a revolutionary agent, the Institute began to question central features of the Marxian theory.

Marcuse joined the Institute not long after Max Horkheimer took over its directorship and they began shifting their focus from empirical research and historical studies to development of an interdisciplinary social theory.[7] Horkheimer's role in the Institute's affairs during the 1930s was crucial, as he was in charge of its research projects, journal, political-theoretical orientation and overall direction.[8] Moreover, he assumed the role of philosophical and spiritual mentor for the Institute during the troubled period when German fascism forced the emigration of its members throughout Western Europe and to the United States. Horkheimer was trained as a philosopher and had broad intellectual interests. He pursued a Hegelian-Marxian direction in the attempt to develop a 'critical theory of society'. Alfred Schmidt argues that 'Horkheimer was one of the most important founders of a "philosophically" directed interpretation of Marx, that was indeed quite different from the currently dominant tendencies' (i.e. in Marx-interpretation).[9] He rejected both the orthodoxy of the Second International and Soviet Marxism, as well as current attempts to bind Marxism with neo-Kantian, positivist, humanist or existentialist philosophical currents. In Schmidt's words: 'for him a truly productive, progressive appropriation of dialectical materialism was necessarily bound up with a precise analysis of the historical as well as the substantive importance of Hegel and Marx'.[10] Horkheimer took as fundamental Marx's statement that 'Dialectic is unquestionably the last word in philosophy', and he believed that one had to liberate the dialectic from the 'mystical shell' it had assumed in Hegel.[11]

During Horkheimer's directorship, the Institute developed 'the critical theory of society'. Their work combined theoretical construction and social criticism with empirical and theoretical research. In addition to their focus on social psychology and mass culture, the major difference in the Institute's orientation under Horkheimer was a rehabilitation of the role of philosophy in social theory.[12] As Korsch pointed out in *Marxism and Philosophy*, the ruling Marxian orthodoxies tended towards positivistic materialism and oriented theory and practice towards politics and economics, thus suppressing the philosophical components in the Marxian theory.[13] Horkheimer, Adorno and Marcuse, however, were all professional philosophers who argued for the importance of philosophy in social theory. This approach was, of course, congenial to Marcuse, who, in his pre-Institute work, had just finished a study of Hegel's ontology and had been working on a synthesis of philosophy and social theory in the service of radical social change.

Horkheimer and his colleagues published their studies in a remarkable journal, *Zeitschrift für Sozialforschung*.[14] In a foreword to the first issue, Horkheimer indicates that the Institute's investigations would strive to develop a 'theory of the contemporary society as a whole'.[15] They intended to engage in historical investigations, to deal with current problems, to develop a general and comprehensive theory of contemporary society, to inquire into the 'future development of the historical process', and to provide instruments for social transformation.[16] In later articles, Horkheimer and Marcuse developed the programme of social research in terms of a 'critical theory of society'.[17]

The Frankfurt Institute's work was interrupted in 1933 by the rise of fascism. They had anticipated the fascist takeover by depositing their endowment in Holland and by establishing a branch office in Geneva. In the following years, the Institute suffered the uncertainties of exile, trying to set up research centres in Paris, London and New York. Marcuse went first to Geneva in 1933, then to Paris, and finally arrived in New York in July 1934, where he remained for some years in the Institute's branch located at Columbia University. Then Marcuse moved to Washington in 1942, working first with the Office of War Information and then with the Office of Strategic Services. He remained in government service for almost a decade, publishing during this time only a review article on Sartre's *Being and Nothingness* and a couple of book reviews. Marcuse became a US citizen in 1940 and remained so after the war, when many of his colleagues returned to Germany.

One can hardly exaggerate the importance of the Institute for Social Research in Marcuse's development. Under its influence, he broke with Heidegger and worked collectively with the members of the Institute on its projects. During Marcuse's first years of collaboration, the Institute was concerned with providing a theoretical explanation of the roots and causes of fascism. In this context, Marcuse wrote a series of essays in the 1930s which analysed the cultural forces and tendencies that contributed to the triumph of fascism in Germany.[18] He and his associates were certain that 'the fascist state was the fascist society, and that totalitarian violence and totalitarian reason came from the structure of the existing society' (*N*, p. xii). They accepted the orthodox Marxian theory that fascism was a product of capitalist society: its economic system, institutions, ideology and culture. The Institute assumed 'the task of identifying the tendencies that linked the liberal past with its totalitarian abolition' (*N*, p. xii). They perceived the roots of fascism in: (a) capitalist socio-economic crises that were given a totalitarian solution in order to protect the capitalist relations of production and to secure the continued control of the ruling class; (b) institutions such as the bourgeois family and repressive socialization processes which create authoritarian personalities who conform to and accept socially imposed domination; and (c) culture and ideologies that defend, or transfigure, the existing society while mystifying social relations of domination.[19] Let us now examine Marcuse's contributions to this programme, and then note some deficiencies in Marcuse's and the Frankfurt School's analysis of fascism.

4.1 Liberalism, capitalism and fascism

Marcuse's 1934 essay 'The Struggle Against Liberalism in the Totalitarian View of the State' marks the turning point in his work away from Heidegger, phenomenological existentialism and primarily philosophical analysis, towards development of an explicitly Marxian social theory and critique of ideology. As Marcuse later recalls, his essay was a response to 'a speech by Hitler, the speech at the industrial club in Düsseldorf; it became known, and Horkheimer called the colleagues together, pointed to a newspaper article and asked what was so significant about this speech that we should make it the object of a more or less independent study. We discussed it and made the decision'.[20] Marcuse's argument is that the totalitarian state and its ideology respond to a new era of monopoly capitalism and provide a defence of capitalism against crises engendered by its market system and protection against opposition to the system (i.e. the working-class parties).[21] Fascism was not seen, in this interpretation, as a monstrous rupture with the liberal past; rather, Marcuse demonstrates continuities between liberalism and fascism and shows how liberalism's unquestioned allegiance to the capitalist economic system prepared the way for the fascist-totalitarian order and with it the abolition of liberalism itself.

Marcuse follows the standard Marxian interpretation of liberalism as the ideology of capitalism: liberalism 'was the social and economic theory of European industrial capitalism in the period when the actual economic bearer of capitalism was the individual capitalist, the private entrepreneur' (*N*, p. 9). The pillar of liberal ideology was 'free ownership and control of private property, and the politically and legally guaranteed security of these rights'. (*N*, p. 9). The freedom of the economic subject to dispose of one's property and labour as one wished, the foundation of all freedom in liberalism, was the one freedom that liberalism would not compromise. Marcuse notes that during the era of liberal capitalism, powerful intervention by the state was permitted if the security of private property required it, 'especially if the threat came from the proletariat' (*N*, p. 9). Even if liberalism proclaimed 'pacifist-humanitarian' aims, it did not prevent or oppose the fighting of nationalistic wars, or embarking on imperialist adventures. Moreover, the liberal-bourgeois state did not hesitate to curtail or drop its political freedoms (speech, press, assembly, etc.) if the situation demanded. But the one freedom that liberalism would not compromise was 'free enterprise', freedom of capital-accumulation.

Although both liberalism and fascism successively defended the capitalist mode of production, Marcuse argues that their basic differences are produced by the transition from competitive capitalism, based on the enterprise of the individual entrepreneur, to monopoly capitalism, which concentrates economic power in the hands of a small corporate-political elite. The fascist invective against merchants (*Händlertum*), as well as against individual competition and greed for money, served the interests of monopoly capitalism, which had displaced this strata of the bourgeoisie and competitive form of capitalism with a less individualistic, less competitive and less anarchical form – which required, in turn, the totalitarian state to protect its interests. In Marcuse's view, fascism contributed to the stabilization of capitalism and only attacked those aspects of liberalism and capitalism that were already rendered obsolete by the requirements of monopoly capitalism.

Marcuse attempts to show how both liberalism and fascism share a belief in natural law, contain irrational ideological elements, and vehemently oppose Marxism. He begins here the sort of Marxian 'critique of ideology' for which he would eventually become famous. Marcuse analyses the three constitutive components of the totalitarian ideology – 'universalism', 'naturalism' and 'political existentialism' – and shows how this ideology opposes the Marxian social theory and, by mystifying socio-economic conditions, protects the existing capitalist society against demands for radical social change. *Universalism* maintains a 'priority and primacy of the whole over its "members" (parts)' (*N*, p. 19), claiming that the whole is a living, organic unity and that the destiny of its members is to serve the whole, to fulfil themselves through participation. In this conception, Marcuse believes, the social totality 'is programmatically mystified' (*N*, p. 7), for its real foundation is not an abstract 'nation' or 'people', but is rather the socio-economic system.

The fascist 'folk-community' is idealized by *naturalism*, which fetishizes natural properties of the folk, blood, soil, the homeland, racial purity and *der Führer* – who supposedly embodies these qualities – into objects of almost religious devotion (*N*, pp. 23ff). Class conflicts are veiled by an ideology of the nation's 'destiny' and individuals are urged to submit to poverty and to die for their country as their highest duty. Marcuse comments:

> Heroism, the ethic of poverty as the 'pedestal' of politics: here the struggle against the materialist world-view reveals itself in its final meaning, that of 'bringing to heel' instincts that rebel against the falling standard of living. A functional change in ideology, characteristic of certain stages of social development, has taken place. This ideology exhibits the status quo, but with a radical transvaluation of values: unhappiness is turned into grace, misery into blessing, poverty to destiny. Vice versa, striving for happiness and material improvement becomes sin and injustice. (*N*, p. 29)

The ideology of 'heroic-folkish realism' was supported by *political existentialism* which champions the 'existential' as something beyond the normative, outside the sphere of conventional morality.[22] The amorality of the existential was coupled with an anthropological activism, a glorification of action for action's sake, and contempt for theory and knowledge, resulting in a 'radical devaluation of the logos' (*N*, p. 34). 'Authentic praxis' was not proposed as a rational choice of a course of action, but a '"setting off in a direction", "taking sides" by virtue of a mandate of destiny ... It is really secondary to decide in favour of something I have come to know"' (*N*, pp. 33–4). Existential man acts, but he knows not why he acts. He sets off on a course of action, but he knows not where. He is to be resolved, but upon what he does not know – until the totalitarian state arrives to fill this moral vacuum. The total politicization of existence in the totalitarian state defined the 'existential' as political (the destiny of the folk, war, duty to the nation, etc.) and directed the activism into a total mobilization dictated by a '"mandate" issued to existence by the "folk"' (*N*, p. 35). In this situation, *political* relationships become the existential ones, and the individual is now sacrificed to domination by the total state (*N*, p. 31f).

The totalitarian state, Marcuse argues, is in fact the abolition of existentialism, for it abolishes the individuality, freedom and subjectivity that were the foundation of existentialist anthropology (i.e. in Heidegger's *Sein und Zeit*). Marcuse suggests that existentialism, like liberalism, prepared the way for its own abolition by supporting the totalitarian state. As the state takes over total responsibility for life, it becomes 'the only source and object of every individual's duties' (*N*, p. 38). The individual's privacy and subjectivity are abolished and one's freedom 'lies precisely in obligation to the folk and the state' (*N*, p. 39). Marcuse interprets this surrender of existentialism's previous individualism as a 'process of politicizing and deprivatizing that annihilates individual existence' (*N*, p. 39). Existentialism has betrayed itself by sacrificing the individual which it, like liberalism, was to protect and champion: 'Existentialism collapses the moment its political theory is realized. The total-authoritarian state for which it longed gives the lie to all its truths. Existentialism accompanies its debacle with a self-abasement unique in the history of ideas bringing its own history to end as a satyr play' (*N*, p. 40).[23]

The analysis of the connection of existentialism with fascism sharpens Marcuse's earlier critique of Heideggerian existentialism, stressing that existentialism's betrayal of its emancipatory tendencies is rooted in the inherent deficiencies of its abstract ontological position and its failure to produce a progressive moral and political doctrine, thus creating an ideological vacuum which fascism was ready to fill. The attempt of existentialism to regain the 'full concretion of the historical subject in opposition to the abstract "logical" subject of rationalism' (*N*, p. 32) shipwrecked on its failure to criticize the concrete conditions of existence. For Heidegger and his followers:

avoided looking more carefully at the historical situation, with regard to its material facticity, of the subject to which it addressed itself. At this point concretion stopped, and philosophy remained content to talk of the nation's 'link with destiny', of the 'heritage' that each individual has to adopt, and of the community of the 'generation', while the other dimensions of facticity were treated under such categories as 'they' (*das Man*), or 'idle talk' (*Gerede*), and relegated in this way to 'inauthentic' existence. Philosophy did not go on to ask about the nature of this heritage, about the people's mode of being, and about the real powers and forces that *are* history. It thus renounces every possibility of comprehending the facticity of historical situations and distinguishing between them. (*N*, p. 32)

Marcuse's continued ambivalence towards existentialism is clear from a close reading of this passage (*N*, pp. 32–42). He still seems to believe that Heidegger's attempt to regain 'the full concretion of the historical subject in opposition to the abstract "logical" subject of rationalism' is a progressive development that falls short of its promise by failing to analyse more fully the concrete material conditions which constitute the subject and provide its field of activity (*N*, p. 32f). Although Marcuse sharpens his critique of Heidegger's existentialism, his criticism does not really represent a radical departure from his former position, for he had already developed strong criticisms of Heidegger along the lines of the paragraph just cited.[24] Moreover, he continues to believe that the radical individualism promoted by existentialism constitutes a valuable philosophical heritage. On this issue, he stresses the betrayal by Heidegger of existentialism's philosophical promises rather than the inherent deficiencies of existentialism, which he continues to see, perhaps with some justification, as a progressive alternative to some forms of idealism, rationalism and vulgar Marxism.[25] Hence, whereas his break with Heidegger is now quite definite, it tends to take, in the essay under question, a quite bitter, personal tone, and perhaps unfairly identifies Heidegger's philosophy with Nazi ideologues, which he classifies together under the label 'political existentialism'.

Marcuse's continued sympathy for 'good existentialism' is expressed in a little known review of Karl Jaspers's *Philosophy*, where he favourably contrasts Jaspers's version of existentialism with Heidegger.[26] He begins by presenting Jaspers's notion that the 'basic questions' of philosophy (i.e. the Question of Being, or Problem of Knowledge) have no real answers and that philosophers should turn from such empty pseudo-questions and concern themselves with problems of individual existence.[27] He then explicates Jaspers's notion of 'existence' as a sphere of subjectivity and absolute selfhood that constitutes the individual's freedom.[28] For Jaspers, individual freedom confronts social-historical necessity, which it utilizes as material for its self-realization; the interaction of self and society constitutes its *historicity*; historical self-development takes place through *communication*.[29] Philosophy, for Jaspers, takes the forms of *world-orientation, existence-illumination* and *transcendence*, while he conceives of metaphysics as the deciphering of symbols.[30] After setting forth the central categories of Jaspers's philosophy, Marcuse concludes by noting the emancipatory elements of Jaspers's concept of philosophy as shipwreck and sharply contrasts Heidegger's and Jaspers's 'existence-philosophy':

> Roughly characterized, Heidegger's efforts tend toward a transcendental-ontological problematic (*Fragestellung*) (indicating and interpreting the meaning of 'Being'), in which the 'existential analytic' is only preparatory. For Jaspers, on the other hand, '*existence-illumination*' stands and remains in the centre of philosophizing; in it, the 'world-orientation' that preceded it is fulfilled, and in turn leads to a 'metaphysics' which succeeds it. It follows, therefore, that the categories of existence with Heidegger are purely ontologically intended, whereas they receive an '*ethical*' sense for Jaspers – which finds a clear expression in the inner method of existence-illumination as 'appeal' and 'awakening'.[31]

Marcuse states that Jaspers's work should not be too quickly dismissed as an 'ethical world-view', for it contains a radically new concept of philosophy directed towards concrete problems of existence – a conception rooted in the enterprises of Kierkegaard and Nietzsche. Both Heidegger and Jaspers, however, fail to address themselves adequately to real problems of the day: 'Existence-philosophy halts it concretizing of the concept of historicity exactly where the really dangerous problems begin', i.e. social critique or, more specifically, critique of fascism. Thus the existentialist concept of 'historicity' is really 'ahistorical':

> all talk of historicity remains abstract and unbinding as long as it fails to accentuate the really concrete 'material' situation in which

the philosophizing existence actually lives, and as long as it fails to consider the actual possibilities and realities from the standpoint of its factical structure.[32]

Marcuse has not yet complete broken with existentialism, which he still seems to believe provides important elements of a 'concrete philosophy', and in fact traces of existentialist individualism, activism and ethical concerns reappear in his later work.[33] A major point of departure, however, is Marcuse's more favourable turn to the tradition of critical rationalism, signified by his positive citations of Kant in the essay on the totalitarian state.[34] Marcuse now, for the first time, favourably quotes Kant's concepts of autonomy, moral freedom and responsibility (*N*, p. 38); Kant's defence of 'inalienable human rights' (*N*, p. 41); and Kant's notion of the autonomy of philosophy and its critical mission (*N*, p. 42). We see here an operation that will distinguish Marcuse's work with the Institute for Social Research: a return to the heritage of idealism and rationalism to criticize current forms of irrationalism, using the earlier forms of bourgeois philosophy to criticize the later decadent forms (in Heidegger, fascism, etc.)[35] Marcuse now explicitly champions rationalist social theory against irrationalist theories:

A theory of society is *rationalist* when the practice it enjoins is subject to the idea of autonomous reason, i.e. to the human faculty of comprehending, through conceptual thought, the true, the good and the right. Within society, every action and every determination of goals as well as the social organization as a whole has to legitimate itself before the decisive judgment of reason and everything, in order to subsist as a fact or goal, stands in need of rational justification ... The rationalist theory of society is therefore essentially *critical*; it subjects society to the idea of a theoretical and practical, positive and negative critique. (*N*, pp. 14–15)

Marcuse's return to the rationalist heritage of social theory represents, in part, a defensive manoeuvre against fascist irrationalism. This posture determined much of the work of the Institute for Social Research during its exile period, although they would later differentiate between different forms of reason and would later develop powerful critiques of Western rationalism.[36] During the 1930s, however, a type of critical rationalism dominates Marcuse's thought

– both in his efforts to construct a critical theory of society and in his critique of irrationalist ideologies and fascist society. Within these projects, *reason*, and its ability to gain knowledge and translate its concepts into reality through social practice, stands at the centre of his enterprise. The essay on the totalitarian state also discloses a clear commitment to Marxism and presents his first self-conscious exercise in the Marxian critique of ideology. Hence Marcuse's analyses of fascism, critiques of liberalism and existentialism, and presentation of his own positions follow a rather orthodox Marxian line – indeed, I shall argue in section 4.1.2 that the deficiencies of Marcuse's theory of fascism result in part from his too narrow reliance on the Comintern theory of fascism and the orthodox Marxian notion of the critique of ideology.

In the conclusion to his essay on the totalitarian state, Marcuse suggests that the fascist total politicalization of life can be reversed, and the progressive, liberating forces in the 'positing of man as a primarily historical, political and politically acting being' (*N*, p. 33) can be set in motion by a mobilized mass society, *if* the people become critical and ask: What are we acting for? What are the ends of our society? Does the community which we are to serve really promote human happiness and secure the possibility of a fulfilled human existence? Marcuse is arguing here that activism and the politicalization of a people can be used for the liberation and betterment of human life, as well as its slavery and degeneration. He also sees the recognition of 'freedom as an eminently political concept' as an improvement over the liberal attempts to privatize freedom: 'Real freedom for individual existence ... is possible only in a specifically structured polis, a "rationally" organized society' (*N*, p. 39). He then argues that freedom is bound up with obligation and raises the question of content: freedom for what and obligation to what? Marcuse answers:

The political identification of freedom and obligation is more than an empty phrase only if the community to which the free individual is a priori obligated secures the possibility of a fulfilled existence worthy of a human being or if the community can be directed towards such a possibility. The question that the identity of freedom and political obligation (an identity which as such deserves to be recognized) impels one to ask, rather than dispenses one from asking, is this: What is this community like, to which I am to obligate myself? Can it sustain human happiness and dignity? (*N*, p. 40).

Although Marcuse discerned progressive, liberating forces in opposition to fascist society, coexisting with the repressive-regressive forces, his essay ends on a note of pessimism and uncertainty. The philosophical betrayal by existentialism was seen as the betrayal of the whole German philosophical tradition. Moreover, he believed that the fate of Marxism and the labour movement, which represented for him the authentic heir to German philosophy and the progressive counterforce to fascism, was uncertain:

> Existentialism, which at one time understood itself to be the heir of German Idealism, has given up the greatest intellectual heritage of German history. It was not with Hegel's death but only now that the Fall of the Titans of German philosophy occurs. At that time, in the nineteenth century, its decisive achievements were preserved in a new form in scientific social theory and the critique of political economy. Today the fate of the labour movement, in which the heritage of this philosophy was preserved, is clouded with uncertainty. (*N*, p. 42)

In other essays, Marcuse argues that not only liberalism, but also bourgeois culture, the family and ideologies of authority contributed to the rise of fascism. Here Marcuse stresses the ideological, mystifying and conformist elements of bourgeois culture, while playing down their critical and emancipatory moments which were emphasized in his earlier study of German literature and which would again become a central focus in his later theory of culture.

4.1.1 *Bourgeois culture, authority and the family*

Marcuse's essay on the 'Affirmative Character of Culture' analyses the historical function of bourgeois culture and seeks to show how it at first contributed to the rise of fascism, and then was in turn vitiated by the totalitarian state. Although the essay contains some themes, concerning the function of art and the nature of the aesthetic dimension, which would later be a major focus of his work (see section 10.4) I shall limit my focus here to a discussion of the ideological function played by bourgeois culture and its role in helping make fascism possible. I shall discuss his aesthetics in more detail in Chapters 6 and 10.

By 'affirmative culture' Marcuse means the 'culture of the bourgeois epoch'. Affirmative culture projected its spiritual realm as a higher, more sublime and valuable realm than the everyday world and claimed its values were essential to the individual's well-being (*N*, pp. 95ff.). Since the time of the Greeks, 'culture' has been separated from the everyday world, and affirmed as a superior realm of Truth, Goodness and Beauty, where one could find the most stable and lasting happiness. In the bourgeois era the values of culture were allegedly accessible to each individual and offered a 'realm of apparent unity and apparent freedom in which the antagonistic relations of existence were supposed to be stabilized and pacified. Culture affirms and concels the new conditions of social life' (*N*, p. 96) and helps stabilize and preserve bourgeois society and its system of production.

Bourgeois culture serves an escapist function by allowing the individual to transcend the toil and tribulation of the everyday world into a higher spiritual realm which provides a refuge from the suffering and uncertainty in everyday life. Moreover, bourgeois culture provides a *veil* that covers social antagonisms and contradictions. It has a *mystifying* function that transfigures existence by overcoming suffering through a sublime world of art. This mystification of social conditions and misery is systematically carried out in bourgeois society through 'cultural education'. By participating in the world of art, the individual is to assimilate ideal values and to create an inner harmony undisturbed by the turmoil of existence. Bourgeois culture thus demands a new type of personality: the *great soul* (*N*, p. 103), as opposed to the universal man of the Renaissance who sought happiness in worldly action, in gaining power, and in achieving worldly success and sensual experience. In contrast, the spiritualized personality of bourgeois culture seeks ideal values in an ethical personality (Kant), aesthetic sensibility (German Idealism) and the higher spiritual salvation that renounces worldly happiness by seeking solace in a more refined spiritual world.[37]

Marcuse claims that bourgeois society's idealist culture contains both repressive and compensatory functions. Escape into a world of ideal beauty represses both the individual's claim for happiness and instinctual need for sensual gratification. Bourgeois culture contains a hierarchical ordering of body and soul in which the body is held to be inferior, animal, and to be dominated by the soul. Since release of sensuality would supposedly be subversive to the demands of the capitalist economy for a disciplined, hard-working labour force, bourgeois society condemns sensuality, either subjecting it to the domination of reason, or directing the soul to subliminate sensuality into bourgeois love, which is refined, exclusive and monogamous (*N*, pp. 110–2). Bourgeois society offers some compensation for instinctual renunciation and toil through the tranquillizing balm of its culture, which idealizes love and provides escape into a higher spiritual world. But this spiritualized culture 'uses the soul as a protest against reification only to succumb to it in the end' (*N*, p. 105). For bourgeois culture isolates its victims in their cultivated subjectivity, and it submits them to the domination of the unchallenged, repressive powers that rule the real world (*N*, pp. 103ff).

Although bourgeois culture mystifies social reality and induces the individual to escape from the problems of social existence into the sphere of subjectivity, it nonetheless preserves a sphere of individuality and freedom where the individual could find some degree of liberation (*N*, pp. 98f, 114ff). But the new situation of monopoly capitalism and its product, the fascist state, could not even tolerate this sphere of private life which was a source of potential opposition and subversion. The labour process demanded increased discipline and regimentation, and required ' "total mobilization", through which the individual must be subjected in all spheres of his existence to the discipline of the authoritarian state' (*N*, p. 124). Further, the fascist ideology had its own 'ideal values' of heroism, self-sacrifice, poverty and submission, as well as its notions of folk, race, blood and soil, which could not tolerate any competition from the idealist-humanist bourgeois culture. Thus the requirements of the capitalist labour system and the totalitarian state demanded an abolition of the individualistic, humanistic elements in bourgeois culture which were potentially subversive. Although some elements of bourgeois culture are sacrificed, culture is still 'to provide a new defence for old forms of existence. The basic function of culture remains the same' (*N*, p. 125), i.e. bourgeois culture and fascist culture both serve to preserve the capitalist order. Both make the same demand on the individual: 'renunciation and subjection to the status quo, made bearable by the real appearance of gratification' (*N*, p. 124). Bourgeois culture offers, Marcuse claims, the pleasures of its internal, spiritual values, while fascist culture offers the gratification of its external values of participation in 'folk-culture', sacrifice for the nation, heroic duty, parades, youth camps and mobilizations. Moreover, Marcuse believes that bourgeois culture helped prepare the way for its own abolition in fascist society by teaching submission and deflecting individuals from demanding material well-being and social change: 'That individuals freed for over four hundred years march with so little trouble in the communal columns of the authoritarian state is due in no small measure to affirmative culture' (*N*, p. 125).

In his essay on 'affirmative culture', Marcuse defends mind and reason over romantic 'soul culture', arguing that 'idealist inwardness' and fascist 'heroic outwardness' present a 'united front against the mind' which serves the interests of preserving the status quo (*N*, p. 126). Marcuse claims that the bourgeoisie, for the most part, manifested a 'deep contempt for the mind' (*N*, p. 126), distrusting intellectual activity. For the bourgeoisie,

> the mind was always somewhat suspect. It is more tangible, more demanding and nearer to reality than the soul. Its critical lucidity and rationality and its contradiction of irrational facticity are difficult to hide and to silence. Hegel goes poorly with an authoritarian state: he was for the mind, while the moderns are for the soul and for feeling . . . An individual full of soul is more compliant, acquiesces more humbly to fate, and is better at obeying authority. (*N*, pp. 126–7).

Consequently, in the fascist state, 'the intensive education to inner freedom that has been in progress since Luther is now, when inner freedom abolishes itself by turning into outer unfreedom, bearing its choicest fruit' (*N*, p. 127).

The submission of the German people to fascism and their complacent acceptance of totalitarian authority raised the question of what factors were responsible for developing a personality who would accept and obey even the most irrational, destructive authorities. The members of the Institute for Social Research conclude that the bourgeois family and its patriarchial structure played an important role in preparing the individual for the frightful submission to authority in fascist society. In a group project on 'Authority and the Family', they studied the historical role of the family in reproducing the institutions, social practices and ideology of bourgeois society. They investigated the psychological factors involved in the acceptance of authority and produced studies of authority and the family in different countries, which included a critical evaluation of the various literature on the family in these countries. The results were published in *Studien über Autorität und Familie.*[38]

Marcuse contributed to an essay on 'Freedom and Authority'[39] that traced the ideas of freedom and authority through the reformation, Kant, Hegel, the counterrevolution and Marx, to recent totalitarian theories of authority. In the essay he is concerned to show the dichotomy in the bourgeois concept of freedom which split the individual into two spheres: an inner realm of freedom (autonomy) and an external realm of submission and bondage (authority). The inner freedom of Protestantism and Kant, Hegel's deification of the State, and the irrational and traditionalistic doctrine of authority of the counterrevolution (Burke, de Maistre, F. J. Stahl) all contribute, Marcuse argues, to preparing the way for the totalitarian theory of authority. Marcuse's critique of the ideas that promoted the acceptance of the totalitarian theory and practice of authority is acute, and shows his ability to demonstrate connections and consequences of ideas that are often overlooked or ignored in standard intellectual history.

In a study of 'Authority and the Family in German Sociology to 1933', Marcuse attacks the sociological theories that provided a justification for the defence of the bourgeois family. He criticizes 'naturalistic' theories which 'interpret the family as a "natural", "eternal" formation on the basis of the society, which receives a normative validation by virtue of its naturalness'.[40] This 'naturalizing' of the family justifies it as an eternal and unchangeable social form that plays a necessary role in social life. He then shows how the defence of the family as the moral foundation and basic transmitter of social norms 'stands in service of the defence of the bourgeoisie against the growing threat from its own ranks and from the socialist tendencies', by arguing that the dominant theories of the family celebrate it as the reservoir of social values, the 'spring of authority and piety', and the principle of constancy against change.[41] These ideological theories reveal the family to be an institution that above all prepares the individual to accept authority and to conform to the existing society. The patriarchal structure of the family aids in this regard, giving the father unquestioned authority over his wife and child.

Male domination is justified in the theories Marcuse attacks by virtue of 'social inequality as a natural law'.[42] Such theories both defend the domination of the male and the domination of the ruling class on the grounds of 'natural superiority'. Theorists of the patriarchal family believe that maintenance of respect for the father's absolute authority is necessary for the preservation of civilization. Marcuse cites the view of Riehl, a defender of patriarchal authority:

In the home alone can our people still achieve the spirit of authority and piety. In the home, one can learn how discipline (*Zucht*) and freedom go together, how the individual must sacrifice himself for a higher moral, total personality – the family. And in the life of the state, although it is built on another Idea than the family, the fruits of the home schooling will be 'harvested'.[43]

Marcuse comments: 'The insight into the significance of authority leads to an enthusiastic defence of the old patriarchism. Riehl rejoices at the sound thrashing that the farmer bestows on his wife – yes, he even sees in the old German custom of sacrificing a servant at the burial of his master a "profound conception" of the idea of the "complete house"'.[44]

Other theories of the family which Marcuse examines reveal the economic roots of the family and its role in preserving the capitalistic economy. All the dominant sociological theories agree in celebrating the family as a fundamental transmitter of respect for authority and teacher of submission. Only one theorist discussed, Müller-Lyer, saw the family as a 'transitional stage' (*Durchgangstufe*). Hence, Marcuse concludes that the sociological theories of the family provide a 'familiar apology for the existing order of power through theological, philosophical and economic constructions of all types, diffused in part in the scholarly world, in part in the thoughts of the masses. The old naive affirmation of power is here idealistically embroidered. The existing power relationships receive here their ideology'.[45]

While Marcuse shows how ideologies of authority and the family contribute to legitimating authoritarian institutions and practices, other Institute studies analyse the social-psychological function of the family in preparing individuals to accept social authority. Horkheimer, for example, characterizes the family as the 'germ cell of bourgeois culture' and stresses the role of the family in 'the educating of authority-oriented personalities'.[46] In Horkheimer's view:

> The family has a very special place among the relationships which through conscious and unconscious mechanisms influence the psychic character of the vast majority of men. The processes that go on within the family shape the child from his tenderest years and play a decisive role in the development of his capabilities. The growing child experiences the influence of reality according as the latter is reflected in the mirror of the family circle. The family, as one of the most important formative agencies, sees to it that the kind of human character emerges which social life requires, and gives this human being in great measure the indispensable adaptability for a specific authority-oriented conduct on which the existence of the bourgeois order largely depends.[47]

Consequently, although Horkheimer indicates that the family has become less significant than previously as an instrument of socialization, he claims that it remains an important institution for the production of 'authoritarian personalities' who are inclined to submit to dominant authorities, however irrational.

Although the Institute members, according to Marcuse, believed that Wilhelm Reich moved too fast from objective socio-economic conditions to subjective conditions in his analysis of authority, and that he exaggerated the role of sexual repression in forming authoritarian personalities,[48] there are some interesting connections and differences between Reich's analysis of authority, family and fascism compared with those of the Institute. In his book, *The Mass Psychology of Fascism*, Reich argues that the authoritarian family is of crucial importance for the authoritarian state because the family *'becomes the factory in which the state's structure and ideology are moulded'*.[49] Crucial for Reich is the repression of childhood sexuality, which, in his view, creates children who are docile, fearful of authority, and in general anxious and submissive. Reich claims that

morality's aim is to produce acquiescent subjects who, despite distress and humiliation, are adjusted to the authoritarian order.

Thus the family is the authoritarian state in miniature, to which the child must learn to adapt himself as a preparation for the general social adjustment required of him later. *Man's authoritarian structure – this must be clearly established – is basically produced by the embedding of sexual inhibitions and fear in the living substance of sexual impulses.*[50]

Reich interprets the Führer-cult, the Nazi symbolism of the swastika, the goose-step, Nazi sadism, mass mobilizations, the race theory, militarism and imperialist adventures in terms of substitute sexual gratifications, which fascism provides for a repressed and anxious nation. He interprets fascism as 'organized mysticism' that is able to prey on the nation's fears and needs, and is able to create personality types who surrender to authority. Since the suppression of sexuality in the authoritarian family is crucial in providing fascist personality types, Reich believes that a liberation of sexuality and the creation of non-hierarchical democratic structures in the family, workplace and society at large would create personalities resistant to fascism.[51]

The Frankfurt School had no such panacea, and it was not until the publication of Erich Fromm's *Escape from Freedom* in 1941, after he had loosened his ties with the Frankfurt School, that any of the Institute members tried to answer Reich.[52] Fromm argues that the anxiety which Reich claims is a result of sexual repression is really a product of Germany's whole historical development. He singles out the factors of Protestantism and capitalism as crucial in producing a fearful, alienated individual who seeks a cure for his/her problems in fascism. Fromm claims that release from feudal bondage and ties has left the modern individual alone and insecure. Protestantism, with its emphasis on individual sin and salvation, increases anxiety and guilt, while capitalism both produces a possessive individualism and subjects the individual to the contingencies of intense economic competition, economic crises and fear of unemployment, as well as the miseries of imperialist wars. The result is a tendency to 'escape from freedom' and to submit to authorities who offer security and a sense of power. Fromm describes this personality type as sado-masochistic, arguing that the German institutions of the state, church, family and military cultivate authoritarian personalities who submit to fascism. He stipulates that analysis of fascism has to take account of both economic and psychological factors, and explains the appeal of fascism in terms of German nationalism, which makes it possible to identify with a powerful nation, and the race theory, which makes possible identification with a superior race. Fromm analyses fascism's special appeal to the lower-middle class and its attraction to other classes. The basic mechanism is, in his view, a fear and insecurity that induces submission and then a feeling of power as one identifies with fascism, leading to an explosive situation that encourages militarism, anti-semitism and eventually war.[53]

Fromm is able to provide a strong critique of Reich and an interesting, although flawed, account of fascism, but his analysis lacks some of the deeper insights of Ernst Bloch, Walter Benjamin and others. In the following discussion, I shall argue that the deficiencies in Marcuse's analysis of fascism are rooted in weaknesses of the Institute's approach to fascism, and I shall provide an alternative account rooted in the theories of Bloch, Benjamin and some more recent work.

4.1.2   *Critique of the Frankfurt School theory of fascism*

Marcuse's critiques of liberalism, fascist ideology, bourgeois culture and theories of the family and authority are penetrating and often brilliant, but I do not think that he and his Frankfurt Institute colleagues provide an adequate theory of fascism that can account for its triumph and power.

First, Marcuse is operating with too narrow a concept of ideology and lacks a theory of an ideological apparatus and ideological transmission.[54] His attack on fascist ideology is limited to analysing and criticizing written pronouncements by fascist ideologues. As far as it goes, the analysis is strong, but Marcuse does not discuss how fascist ideology is transmitted through the mass media of communication and popular culture, or how fascism uses radio, newspapers, pamphlets, film, drama, literature, posters, mass demonstrations and a whole cultural-ideological apparatus to transmit its ideology.[55] Consequently, his 'critique of ideology' does not explain how the ideas he analyses were disseminated and received by the German people and why they were effective.

In this regard Marcuse fails to discern the specific needs to which fascist ideology addresses itself, and consequently fails to see *fascism as a cultural synthesis* which also contains anti-capitalist and utopian moments.[56] Ernst Bloch, for instance, analyses those aspects of fascist ideology and its appeal, arguing that the Left's neglect of needs for mass participation, security, rootedness and aesthetics, coupled with fascism's ability to provide for them, helps to explain the failure of the Left in Germany and the triumph of fascism.[57] In *Heritage of These Times*, Bloch analyses the elements of revolt, mass mobilization and the aestheticizing of politics and everyday life in fascism that contributed to its successes.[58] Bloch sees fascism as part of a tradition of 'romantic anti-capitalism', arguing that fascism evolved out of a cultural tradition that was often not congenial to capitalism. In fact, for Bloch, fascism's success as a mass movement should be seen in terms of its efficacy as a synthesizing force which unites heterodox, sometimes conflicting, cultural and ideological tendencies. This interpretation accurately characterizes the national socialist movement, which was both socialist and nationalist in its original ideology, and which contained both a Left and a Right wing. Indeed, the Right wing of national socialism was eventually triumphant and, with its alliance with monopoly capital, was able to solidify power and to dispose of its own Left wing, as well as to eliminate the other Left parties. But emergent fascism contained many contradictory elements which it successfully fused into a cultural synthesis that was able to attract and mobilize a mass movement. Paradoxically, fascism was able to utilize a tradition hostile to capitalist modernity for the preservation of capitalism, producing what Bloch calls a 'false utopia'. Whereas Marcuse argues for the continuity between liberal and fascist ideologies, attacking both as rationalizations for capitalist domination, Bloch examines those elements in the fascist cultural synthesis that can be turned against fascism and used by the Left. Wilhelm Reich, too, calls attention to the people's needs that fascism was addressing, and urges the communist movement to take account of these needs by providing a cultural and political practice that would meet them.[59]

Furthermore, Marcuse and the Frankfurt School's analysis of fascism neglects what has been called the 'fascist public sphere',[60] as well as an analysis of fascist politics. The problem here, in part, is an underdeveloped concept of politics in the Institute's analyses. Contrary to popular myth, the Institute for Social Research engaged in many economic studies and published numerous fine articles on economics in their journal.[61] But, like many economistic Marxists, for the most part they failed to perceive the new primacy of politics in fascism, and failed to analyse the mechanisms of fascist politics and the fascist public sphere. Certain theorists on the fringes of the Frankfurt School did, however, contribute to this project.

Walter Benjamin, for example, emphasizes the 'aestheticization of politics',[62] and Benjamin, Bloch, Reich and Sigfried Kracauer analyse how fascism used symbolism, myths and a cultural apparatus as instruments of political mobilization. Kracauer, in his analysis of the 'mass ornament', shows how fascist festivals, parades and demonstrations attracted mass participation.[63] Marcuse neglects these aspects of fascist culture, limiting himself to analysing the ideological pronouncements in official fascist texts and their intellectual precursors. Marcuse's approach here is too textual and not socio-historical enough. Part of the problem is his exile in 1933, which made it impossible to examine fascism first hand. But the deeper reason for the limitations to his ideology-critique approach to fascism is his excessive dependence on orthodox Marxist explanations of fascism, which see it as a product of monopoly capitalism: its economy, institutions, culture and ideology.

Thus, although Reich, Bloch, and perhaps Benjamin, were more openly committed to the communist movement than were the Institute members, the Institute's analysis is more in line with orthodox Marxian theories of fascism than are the more heretical theories of Benjamin, Bloch and Reich. Most Institute analyses of fascism agree with orthodox Marxism that fascism is simply a product of capitalism in crisis. Marcuse writes in the foreword to *Negations*:

> if there was one matter about which the author of these essays and his friends were *not* uncertain, it was the understanding that the fascist state was fascist society, and that totalitarian violence and totalitarian reason came from the structure of existing society, which was in the act of overcoming its liberal past and incorporating its historical negation.[64]

In a famous aphorism, Horkheimer writes, 'he who does not wish to speak of capitalism, should also be silent about fascism.'[65] There were bitter arguments within the School between Franz Neumann, who saw fascism as a product of monopoly capitalism, stressing the continuity between fascism and capitalism, and Friedrich Pollock, who in his analysis of monopoly state capitalism argued that fascism be perceived as a 'new order'.[66] However, the Frankfurt Institute analysis ignored certain cultural features of fascism and the fascist public sphere, and thus could neither adequately explain fascism's success, nor account for the complexity of the fascist synthesis.

The triumph of fascism put in question central aspects of Marxian theory and intensified the 'crisis of Marxism' during the 1930s. The barbaric regression to blood and soil ideologies, terroristic state practices, violent warfare and the horrors of the holocaust raised serious doubts about the optimistic elements in the Marxian theory of history which forecast historical progress through the elimination of capitalism and the construction of socialism. Fascism preserved capitalism in an ever more repressive and brutal form and helped destroy socialist and communist working-class organizations. In such a situation, it was impossible to perceive a defeated proletariat as a 'revolutionary class', and it was difficult to conceive of the collapse of capitalism and the inevitability of socialism.

Fascism had a major impact on the Institute's programme and theory by driving the Institute members into exile and by decisively shaping their theoretical concerns, their language and their attitudes towards politics and society. The conditions of life in exile forced them to abandon more overtly Marxian formulations of their project, for they were dependent on support, in part, from American universities and foundations. Hence they adopted code words for Marxian concepts: critical theory stood for their version of Marxism; Hegel and Freud were often used as fronts for Marx's ideas, especially by Marcuse; and 'emancipation' and 'democracy' often stood for revolution and socialism. The result of the conditions of exile in the face of the triumph of fascism was the production of the critical theory of society, which was the Institute's attempt to reconstitute Marxism in the face of the crisis of revolutionary possibility.

4.2 Philosophy and critical theory

The term 'critical theory of society' was adopted by the Institute for Social Research in 1937 to describe their distinctive version of Hegelian Marxism.[67] Although the various members of the 'inner circle' – especially Adorno and Horkheimer – would significantly alter their 1930s conception of 'critical theory', they nonetheless continued to use the term to identify their work throughout the next several decades. In the 1930s, critical theory refers to the shared, interdisciplinary programme, projects and orientation of the Institute, which advocates the primacy of an interdisciplinary social theory over individual social sciences or philosophy. Critical theory refers to the synthesis of philosophy and the social sciences in the Institute's work and the project of social critique with an orientation towards radical social change. In effect, critical theory is a code for the Institute's Marxism during its exile period, although later it would describe the distinctive brand of social theory developed by the Institute's core members and covers a variety of types of theory in the 1960s and 1970s after the key members of the inner circle split from the Institute and pursued their own interests and projects.[68]

In a series of essays published in the 1930s, Marcuse and Horkheimer define the programme and philosophical presuppositions of the Institute's critical theory of society, while distinguishing their enterprise from other social theories and philosophies.[69] Marcuse focuses on the relation between philosophy and critical theory, and although he criticizes bourgeois philosophy, he also defends its progressive elements: 'reason, mind, morality, knowledge and happiness are not only categories of bourgeois philosophy, but concerns of humanity. As such they must be preserved, if not derived anew' (*N*, p. 147). Marcuse's position is that philosophy can play a progressive role in social theory by developing concepts that are subversive of the prevailing ideologies and can provide weapons of critique in the struggle for a better society.

In his 1930s essays Marcuse is concerned at once to preserve what he believes are emancipatory elements in the bourgeois tradition, while criticizing tendencies which he believes serve the interests of repression and domination.[70] Often the progressive and conservative elements cannot be separated, and Marcuse's essays move from analysis of conservative-repressive features of, say, bourgeois culture, to depiction of its emancipatory moments. In general, he suggests that the early revolutionary ideals of the rising bourgeoisie contain aspects of a liberated society, and that their theories of freedom, rationalism, critical idealism, human rights, democracy and materialist theories of human needs and potentialities, continue to be of importance to critical social theory. Often he suggests that the bourgeoisie has failed to realize its ideals and that therefore earlier philosophies of, say, democracy and freedom can be used to criticize their present neglect, distortion or suppression. In his view, many of the earlier bourgeois ideals could be used to criticize the current fascist suppression of liberal rights and liberties.

Marcuse is, however, also quite critical of those tendencies in the bourgeois tradition which he claims contribute to the triumph of fascism. Hence his essays contain ideology-critiques of liberalism, existentialism, idealism, rationalism and bourgeois culture which today are still quite compelling. Marcuse thinks that these philosophies and ideals tend to become every more abstract and formal ideologies which the bourgeoisie uses to legitimate and mystify social conditions. In fact, Marcuse believes that there are conservative-concilatory tendencies in bourgeoisie philosophy from the beginning which primarily function to conserve the bourgeois order of private property, possessive individualism, the unrestricted market and the right to accumulate unlimited capital. But – and Marcuse's essays are full of these dialectical twists and turns – even some of the most ideological concepts of equality, freedom, happiness, etc. provide a 'refuge' which preserves certain rational and human ideals of an emancipated humanity. Thus the conservative and emancipatory motives are often tightly interconnected, requiring careful analysis and critique.[71]

In this conception – shared by Marcuse and the Institute 'inner circle' – there are two traditions in bourgeois culture: a progressive heritage of humanist-emancipatory elements, and a reactionary heritage of conservative, mystifying and repressive elements. In their view, the later phase of bourgeois culture is more irrational and regressive than the earlier, more progressive phase. For instance, in his 1936 essay, 'The Concept of Essence', he writes:

According to the view characteristic of the dawning bourgeois era, the critical autonomy of rational subjectivity is to establish and justify the ultimate essential truths on which all theoretical and practical truth depends. The essence of man and of things is contained in the freedom of the thinking individual, the *ego cogito*. At the close of this era, knowledge of essence has the function primarily of binding the critical freedom of the individual to pre-given, unconditionally valid necessities. It is no longer the spontaneity of the concept but the receptivity of intuition that serves as the organon of the doctrine of essence. Cognition culminates in recognition, where it remains fixated. (*N*, p. 44)[72]

In the early days of the bourgeois era, Marcuse claims, the concept of essence is a critical concept which presupposes the rational autonomy of the subject, its accessibility to universal truths and standards, and its utilizing these standards to criticize and transform social conditions which fail to realize 'essential' needs and potentialities of the individual and society. Later, in the bourgeois era, with the phenomenological theory of essence, the individual is to submit to ideal essences which are usually of an abstract sort, divorced from human practice (Husserl), or which bind the subject to existing ideals, hierarchies and conditions that serve the interests of domination.[73] Others in the Institute for Social Research share this orientation, believing that the earlier ideas of the progressive bourgeoisie correspond to human and social needs and ideals, whereas the later bourgeois philosophies surrender the progressive ideals of the revolutionary bourgeoisie and fall into irrationalism and cynical opportunism, which serve the interest of preservation of the status quo.[74]

We encounter here the Institute's method of 'immanent critique', which confronts ideology with social reality, criticizes a social order – or theory – according to its own self-professed ideals, and shows how bourgeois ideals are contradicted by the socio-economic conditions of existence and thus serve as ideology in the dual sense of 'mystification' and 'legitimation'. This procedure is used by Marcuse to affirm certain bourgeois ideals – such as self-determination, human rights, democracy, etc – which could be used to criticize their suppression in fascist society. During this period Marcuse also subscribes to a rather orthodox version of Marxism.[75] Reversing his earlier evaluation of philosophy as superordinate to the sciences,[76] he now places the critique of political economy in the centre of social theory, and argues that the crucial problems of the individual and society are 'to be approached from the standpoint of economics' (*N*, p. 134). Since critical theory 'recognizes the responsibility of economic conditions for the totality of the established world', and comprehends the 'social framework in which reality is organized' from the standpoint of political economy, the notion that philosophy is a special, superior discipline is rejected (*N*, pp. 134f). However, philosophy is not to be abandoned, for critical theory is to operate with a special synthesis of philosophy and the sciences, utilizing philosophical construction in conjunction with empirical research. Although Marcuse and his colleagues would accept the Marxian position that the economy is the crucial determining factor for all social life, they reject all forms of economic reductionism and attempt to describe the complex set of mediations connecting the economy, social and political institutions, culture and consciousness as parts of a reciprocally interacting social totality.

Critical theory's claim 'to explain the totality of human existence and its world in terms of social being' (*N*, pp. 134–5) contains a theory and programme of social research. Critical theory argues that isolated phenomena can only be comprehended as parts of a whole; hence a crucial task of social theory is to describe the structures and dynamics of the social totality. In effect, it is committed to the theses of historical materialism and the Marxian critique of political economy. The crucial presupposition that both Marcuse and Horkheimer stress is the recognition that social and human existence are constituted by 'the totality of the relations of production' (*N*, p. 82). As Marcuse argues in 'The Concept of Essence', since the economy is the 'essence' of the society, critical theory must describe the workings of the economy and how it is interconnected with and affects other forms of social life.[77]

The critical theory is, Marcuse states, 'linked with materialism' in accord with the 'conviction of its founders' (*N*, p. 135). Following the Institute's strategy of not calling attention to their Marxism, Marcuse does not mention Marx once in 'Philosophy and Critical Theory', although it is clear that Marx is the founder of the critical theory referred to and that the positions enunciated in the essay are the basic tenets of Marxism. Marcuse does, however, propose his own interpretation of Marxian materialism: 'there are two basic elements linking materialism to correct social theory: concern with human happiness and the conviction that it can be obtained only through a transformation of the material conditions of existence' (*N*, p. 135). Consequently, for Marcuse, 'materialism' refers to a social practice and concern with human needs and happiness and not to a philosophical thesis which claims that 'matter' is the primary ontological reality.

Marcuse elucidates the commitment of the critical theory to human needs and their satisfaction in his essay 'On Hedonism',[78] the first detailed statement of his concern with needs, sensuality and happiness, which was to be a major focus of his later philosophy. He defends the claims of the individual to pleasure and sensuous gratification against those ascetic philosophies and systems that would repress needs and passion as being dangerous or immoral. But he also attacks those subjectivist hedonists who claim that pleasure is a purely internal affair and has no objective conditions or criteria of higher and lower, true and false pleasures. Here Marcuse shows how happiness is intimately connected with social conditions which either make possible or impossible human happiness and define its sphere and content. For example, he shows how both for the Greeks and under capitalism the labour system is essentially antagonistic to human happiness and creates two classes, one of which has many more possibilities for gratification than the exploited working classes, whose production makes possible the gratification of the privileged class (*N*, p. 183). Under capitalism, happiness is a class phenomenon and is for the most part restricted to the sphere of consumption (*N*, p. 173). It is limited by the requirements of a labour system where work is for the most part boring and painful. The requirements for submission to the labour system have produced a work ethic that devalues pleasure and produces objective conditions that render happiness transitory or impossible.

Crucial to Marcuse's conception is his connection of freedom with happiness: 'Happiness, as the fulfilment of all potentialities of the individual, presupposes freedom: at root, it is freedom' (*N*, p. 180). In Marcuse's view, without the freedom to satisfy one's needs and to act in self-fulfilling ways, true happiness is impossible. If freedom does not prevail in the material conditions of the existing system, then new social conditions must be created to make possible increased happiness and freedom. Marcuse argues that only in an association of free producers in which the economy is geared towards the satisfaction of human needs (and not profit), and in which each individual receives social goods according to their needs can individuals be truly free and happy: 'Here reappears the old hedonistic definition that seeks happiness in the comprehensive gratification of needs and wants. The needs and wants to be gratified should become the regulating principle of the labour process' (*N*, p. 182).

The potentialities for making a fuller gratification of needs possible reside in modern technology, which could reduce alienated labour through automation and could produce the goods necessary to satisfy one's basic needs (*N*, p. 184). Here, for the first time, Marcuse suggests that technology could produce an environment that could provide aesthetic pleasure and sensual gratification.[79] The fact that technology is not geared towards the satisfaction of human needs is the fault of a social system geared to profit-maximization, which is the source of untold unhappiness and suffering. This theme, adumbrated in his essay on hedonism, will increasingly concern Marcuse and will be a major focus of his later work.

In Marcuse's view, it is impossible for most people to be truly happy in the present society, not only because of the obstacles to freedom and happiness in the labour system, but because the system's dominant pleasures are false and restrictive of true happiness and freedom. From the 1930s until his death, Marcuse was convinced that *reason* can judge between true and false needs, pseudo- and real happiness. Hence, for him, 'happiness is linked to knowledge and taken out of the dimension of mere feeling' (*N*, p. 181). He believes that reason is 'the fundamental category of human thought, the only one by means of which it has bound itself to the fate of humanity' (*N*, p. 135). Reason is the 'critical tribunal' which puts into question the entirety of existence; it has the task of criticizing the irrationality of the social order and defining the highest human potentialities. In the materialist concept, reason is supposed to create a rational society that would liberate the individual from irrational fetters and bonds which restrict freedom, happiness and the development of individual potentialities. Reason must define true needs and the real interests of the individual and society, and must attack the prevailing false needs and repressive interests that should be abolished in the interests of the individual's happiness.[80]

Happiness and unhappiness are thus in part social affairs that can be influenced by social practice. The enforced prolongation of the working day, the maintenance of inhuman working conditions, class division and exploitation, repressive morality, and crisis-ridden economy: all of these social conditions are objective fetters on freedom and happiness and can only be removed

through an economic and political process encompassing the disposal of the means of production by the community, the reorientation of the productive process towards the needs and wants of the whole society, the shortening of the working day, and

the active participation of the individuals in the administration of
the whole. (*N*, p. 193)

Hence, in Marcuse's conception, individual freedom and happiness
can only be secured in a project of radical social reconstruction (*N*,
pp. 192–200).

Marcuse makes clear his commitment here, albeit in muted
language, to the Marxian concept of social revolution. But he does
not subscribe to the restricted orthodox concept of socialism which
equates socialization with nationalization of the means of production regulated by a central plan:

> Not that the labour process is regulated in accordance with a plan,
> but the interest determining the regulation becomes important: it
> is rational only if this interest is the freedom and happiness of the
> masses. Neglect of this element despoils the theory of one of its
> essential characteristics. It eradicates from the image of liberated
> mankind the idea of happiness that was to distinguish it from all
> previous mankind. Without freedom and happiness in the social
> relations of human beings, even the greatest increase in produc-
> tion and the abolition of private property in the means of produc-
> tion remain infected with the old injustice. (*N*, pp. 144–5)

Marcuse here links his concept of socialism with the potentialities
for freedom and happiness that are being repressed or restricted in
the existing societies. He believes that this concern with the condition of human beings and their potentialities links critical theory
with the great philosophies which elucidate the conditions and
characteristics of human freedom, happiness and individuality. The
critical theory is to define the highest human potentialities and to
criticize society in terms of whether it furthers the development and
realization of these potentialities, or their constriction and repression. The ultimate goal and fundamental interest of critical theory is
a free and happy humanity in a rational society. What is at stake is
the liberation of human beings and the development of their
potentialities (*N*, pp. 145f).

This project requires radical social change; consequently all of
critical theory's concepts are geared towards social practice. From a
methodological point of view, critical theory is at once to *comprehend* the given society, *criticize* its contradictions and failures,

and to *construct* alternatives. Its concepts are thus both descriptive and normative and aim at the new society. They are 'constructive concepts, which comprehend not only the given reality, but simultaneously its abolition and the new reality that is to follow' (*N*, p. 145). The concepts of critical theory describe the structure of the given society and 'already contain their own negation and transcendence – the image of a social organization without surplus value. All materialist concepts contain an accusation and an imperative' (*N*, p. 86). The concepts are thus *multidimensional* in simultaneously describing, criticizing and projecting an alternative to the given state of affairs. The paradigm of critical theory for Marcuse is Marx's project, which at once describes the alienation, exploitation, appropriation of surplus value, and capital accumulation in capitalist society, criticizes that society in sharp critical concepts, and projects the image of a society free from the oppressive features of capitalism. Since critical theory is to speak 'against the facts and confront bad facticity with its better potentialities' (*N*, p. 143), it rejects sharp distinctions between fact and value, or descriptive and normative statements, while providing a theory which is at once descriptive, critical and geared towards social change.

In appraising the rationality or irrationality of a social order, the existing society is to be compared with its higher and better potentialities. In Marcuse's view, contradictions between 'what is' and 'what could be' provide an impetus for social change. For example, Marcuse continually compares the potentialities in modern technology and the accumulated social wealth with its current restrictive use, and condemns the society for its failure to use technology in more emancipatory and human ways. Critical theory is thus *future-oriented* (*N*, pp. 145, 153) and has a *utopian* quality. Its future projections are not to be idle daydreams, but an imaginative programme of social reconstruction based on an analysis of tendencies in the present society which could be developed to construct a rational society that would increase human freedom and happiness. This project requires *phantasy* to bridge 'the abyss between rational thought and present reality' (*N*, p. 154). This emphasis on the role of imagination in social theory is a constant theme of Marcuse's later works and purports to reinstate the importance of imagination that was present in such philosophers as Aristotle and Kant, but which has fallen into neglect or disrepute in modern philosophy (*N*, pp. 154–5). For Marcuse believes that, 'Without fantasy, all philosophical knowledge remains in the grip of the present or the past and severed from the future, which is the only link between philosophy and the real history of mankind' (*N*, p. 155).

Further, critical theory is self-critical and critical of the practice to which it connects itself. Marcuse writes: 'Critical theory is, last but not least, critical of itself and of the social forces that make up its own basis. The philosophical element in the theory is a form of protest against the new "Economism", which would isolate the economic struggle and separate the economic from the political sphere' (*N*, pp. 156–7). Here Marcuse is stating in a coded expression that critical theory should be critical of orthodox Marxism, rejecting economic reductionism (the 'new Economism') and should be critical of the working-class movement as well. Within Marxism, critical theory defends the political sphere against the economic, and urges that political decisions and relations be geared to social and human goals: 'the organization of the administration of social wealth in the interest of a liberated humanity' (*N*, p. 157). Critical theory wants to be free of illusions, and is not afraid to put its own theory and Marxism into radical question: 'What . . . if the development outlined by the theory does not occur? What if the forces that were to bring about the transformation are suppressed and appear to be defeated?' (*N*, p. 142). Here Marcuse raises the haunting possibility that if the social forces in the working-class movement are defeated, critical theory is without a social base to realize the theory. It was precisely this predicament that would animate much of Marcuse's later writings, especially *One-Dimensional Man*, and Horkheimer's and Adorno's later work. But in the 1930s Marcuse argues that critical theory should remain faithful to its truths, despite the historical circumstances, for 'critical theory preserves obstinacy as a genuine quality of philosophical thought' (*N*, p. 143).

In Marcuse's conception, critical theory is both to preserve philosophy's highest truths and to unfold a social practice that will make possible their realization. Marx's stress on the unity of theory and practice is thus the foundation of Marcuse's conception of critical theory. Unlike his earlier pre-Institute work, Marcuse now seems to believe that critical social theory does not require any sort of philosophical foundation. During his work with the Institute, Marcuse seems to ground his critical theory in Marxism, which in turn he believes – following, among others, Marx, Lukács and Horkheimer – is grounded in history; more precisely in working-class struggles, and the movement towards socialism. He seems to assume that Marxism is the correct theory of history and society which is in turn being confirmed by (and is thus grounded in) the historical process.

The problem of securing a foundation for social theory begins to arise for Marxism and critical theory when history does not confirm the Marxian theory. The Institute began to see this problem during the late 1930s and early 1940s; but, at least in their published work, they did not formulate the problem and assumed that Marxism and critical theory were grounded in history and therefore did not need a philosophical foundation. During the 1940s and 1950s most of the Institute's 'inner circle' abandoned this position and were then forced to deal with the problem of foundations. However, they took different positions on the issue and, with the exception of Habermas, never systematically or satisfactorily dealt with the problem (and one can question whether Habermas' admittedly systematic and sustained inquiries into this problem are satisfactory). Marcuse, in his post-1950s work, never really addresses or works out the issue of the foundation of critical theory; I shall raise the problem throughout Chapters 6–10, where I shall show that he uses different strategies and positions in various post-Second World War writings to ground his critical theory.

In any case, I do not think that the question of a foundation for critical theory was a central problem for Marcuse in his 1930s critical theory work, as he seemed to assume that (1) Marxism provided conceptual-methodological foundations for critical theory; and (2) that Marxism was confirmed by and grounded in history. Horkheimer seemed to take this position also in the 1930s, while Adorno probably never subscribed to this position and thus always had a 'negative dialectics which maintained that critical theory did not need any sort of 'foundation'. I shall now conclude this chapter with some general reflections on critical theory and Marxism before turning to Marcuse's most sustained attempt to work out the historical and theoretical foundations of critical theory in Marx and Hegel in his first major work, *Reason and Revolution*.

4.3 Critical theory and the crisis of Marxism

'Critical theory' expressed and was developed during an intensified crisis of Marxism within a period in which fascism was a dominant socio-political force and the working-class movement appeared to be defeated on a world-wide scale. This meant that critical theory was cut off from a political movement and audience. In effect, critical theory, although influenced by Lukács's early 1920s Hegelian Marxism, signalled the end of the Lukácsian problematic within 'critical Marxism', which had conceived of revolutionary theory as expressing the consciousness of the proletariat and which rooted radical social theory in proletarian struggle.[81] Not only was there no 'class consciousness' of a revolutionary class which could serve as the subject of history and basis for revolutionary theory, but the defeats of the working-class movement put in question both the Marxian theories of revolution and history.

Nonetheless, from about 1937–40, the Institute continued to use Marxian language, albeit coded, and to conceive of their project in terms of the unity of theory and practice.[82] Such a theoretical project became increasingly tenuous, however, in view of the constant string of defeats of the working-class movements in the fascist countries, in the Spanish Civil War, and in the Soviet Union itself.[83] During this period, revelation of the Stalinist trials and labour camps, and the Soviet Union's pact with Hitler, alienated many former supporters of Marxism, thus intensifying the crisis of Marxism. The outbreak of the Second World War displaced 'class struggle' and the 'construction of socialism' from the contemporary Marxian agenda, and the efforts of many Marxian militants – including the Institute members – were directed towards the war effort and the defeat of fascism. As a result of this historical situation, some members of the Institute recoiled from their previous Marxian stances and commitments and, around 1940, critical theory began to distance itself from Marxism. Adorno and Horkheimer's break with classical Marxism was evident in *Dialectic of Enlightenment*, and a series of Horkheimer's articles provide the transition to this work.[84]

In this historical situation Marxism seemed to have lost its dual grounding in the movement of history and in the consciousness and struggles of the working class. History was not following the Marxian scenario of inexorable evolutionary advance towards socialism, and the working class was no longer a 'revolutionary class'. Thus the Marxian theories of history and revolution appeared increasingly problematical to many former adherents. Consequently, Adorno, Horkheimer, Fromm and others abandoned many of their former

Marxian concepts and presuppositions and reconstructed their 'critical theories' in the 1940s.[85]

In reappraising the Institute's contributions to philosophy and social theory during the 1930s and early 1940s, I would suggest that they at once responded to and expressed the crisis of Marxism and yet contributed to developing an independent non-dogmatic Marxian social theory. Whereas, in the early 1920s, Korsch and Lukács had challenged the ossifying interpretations of the Social Democratic and Communist Parties and aroused a concern to revitalize Marxism by returning to the works of Marx and reconstructing Marxism in relation to the contemporary situation and problems, Lukács's political orthodoxy and move to the Soviet Union forced him to disclaim his innovative Marxian work, *History and Class Consciousness*, while Korsch's expulsion from the Communist Party and his later isolation in America put a damper on his creative efforts to rethink and critically develop the Marxian theory. Although Trotsky and his followers struggled to keep alive the revolutionary core of Marxism, to provide an assessment of contemporary history in Marxian terms, and to repoliticize Marxism in a difficult historical situation, Trotsky's Marxism was extremely orthodox and never really questioned or reconstructed the Marxian theory in the face of the relatively new social orders of fascism, advanced capitalism and Stalinist Russia.[86] In this context the distinguishing feature of the neo-Marxist theory of the Institute was both to preserve the Marxian theory from degenerating into a stale orthodoxy and to develop the theory creatively by applying it to many different social, political and cultural issues. The Institute members analysed the forms of the 'authoritarian state' and sketched out a theory of the emerging advanced capitalist society with analyses of state capitalism, the increased importance of technology in contemporary society, new forms of administration and social control, a planned economy with new corporate and managerial forms, the culture industries, and the integration of the working class – themes that were to occupy the centre of radical social theory for the next several decades. In addition, they developed the Hegelian-Marxian dialectical method and applied it to a wide variety of areas of social and cultural life, while criticizing positivistic empiricism. Rarely, if ever, has such a talented group of interdisciplinary workers come together under the auspices of one research institute, whose members shared common interests and philosophical and methodological presuppositions, and which undertook group projects while developing a critical theory of society.

Within the Institute, Marcuse became one of its most important members. He was, in my view, a more sophisticated philosopher than Horkheimer and had a more solid and detailed knowledge of Marx.[87] Marcuse participated in the Institute's collective projects, helped formulate the concept of critical theory, produced powerful critiques of bourgeois ideology, and wrote many book reviews for the Institute's journal on topics in philosophy, sociology, history and psychology.[88] Marcuse worked especially closely with Horkheimer during the mid- to late 1930s, and their project of critical theory at the time could be differentiated from that of Adorno and Benjamin.[89] Neither Horkheimer nor Marcuse shared Adorno's project of the 'liquidation of idealism', and both shared a version of Hegelian Marxism at odds with Aodorno's early (and later!) works.[90] With the entrance of Adorno into the group's 'inner circle' in the late 1930s, Horkheimer tended to work ever more closely with Adorno, and in the 1940s their version of critical theory began to distance itself from their 1930s programme.[91]

Marcuse did have some political and theoretical differences with the Institute during the 1930s. He told Phil Slater in 1974 that he had political disputes with Horkheimer and believed too that the Institute's work and publications were 'too psychological' and lacked an adequate economic and political dimension.[92] Since Horkheimer rigidly controlled Institute publications, political differences and debate among the members were not allowed to surface in public. Horkheimer felt that the tenuous conditions of exile required the Institute to be extremely careful in their political pronouncements, and Marcuse told me that he had no choice but to 'submit to this discipline'.[93]

There were relatively few shifts in Marcuse's work with the Institute from 1932–42. His writings during this period are quite coherent, and throughout they are consistent with the Institute's version of Hegelian Marxism. He was deeply influenced by his association with the Institute and throughout his life identified his project as 'critical theory'. There is a 'rationalist' turn in his thought during this period where he affirms the heritage of critical rationalism and distances himself from Heidegger, existentialism, *Lebensphilosophie* and phenomenology. Later Marcuse would respond to Adorno and Horkheimer's critique of technology and instrumental reason, and in *Eros and Civilization* and other works would reformulate the concept of reason and reconstruct critical theory.

Marcuse contributed to developing the historical and theoretical foundations of critical theory in his first book in English, *Reason and Revolution*. Here he sympathetically presents Hegel's philosophy and its continuation by Marx, attempting to defend the rational core in Hegel against those who would identify it with fascism. He also contrasts dialectical social theory with positivism, defining the specificity of critical theory by showing its historical roots and the nature of the social theory it opposes. Marcuse paid his respects to the Institute by dedicating *Reason and Revolution* to 'Max Horkheimer and the Institute of Social Research', and remained close to the members of the Institute throughout his life, despite many philosophical and political differences. Let us now examine the book that was in effect the introduction of critical theory into the English-speaking world – *Reason and Revolution*, a book that many consider one of Marcuse's best works and one that would introduce many in the English-speaking world, including myself, to Hegel, Marx and critical social theory.

5

Hegel, Marx and Social Theory: *Reason and Revolution*

Reason and Revolution (hereafter *R&R*) contains Marcuse's most detailed analysis of the Hegelian and Marxian philosophies, and provides, in effect, a historical-theoretical foundation for critical theory by tracing the rise of critical social theory in the nineteenth century and by articulating its basic presuppositions. The book was received as an important interpretation of Hegel, Marx, and the rise of social theory, and it remains today one of the best works on the topic.[1] Marcuse emphasizes the critical-revolutionary elements in Hegel taken over by Marx, arguing that the Marxian theory is the authentic continuation and development of Hegel's philosophy. He also attempts to show that Hegel's thought is incompatible with the contemporary fascist ideas and theories of the authoritarian state which many associated with Hegel. Marcuse combats the interpretations of Hegel as a proto-fascist thinker by positing the Hegelian and Marxian theories as 'negative philosophy' which is rational, critical and subversive of conformist thinking and contrasting it with the 'positive philosophy' that arose after Hegel's death and which 'undertook to subordinate reason to the authority of established fact' (*R&R*, p. xv).

There are striking differences between the presentation of Hegel in *R&R* and that in his earlier book on *Hegel's Ontology*; this shift provides clues to the method and philosophy operative in Marcuse's critical theory in his work with the Institute, and suggests differences between his work in his pre-Institute writings. *Hegel's Ontology* (discussed in Chapter 3) focuses on explicating the central categories of Hegel's ontology. Marcuse takes the concept of 'life' as the key concept, developing an interpretation of Hegel which stresses his continuity with Dilthey's *Lebensphilosophie.* The method of interpretation is a philosophical-hermeneutical approach, close to that of Heidegger, which through a close reading attempts to draw out the text's meaning. The first Hegel book roots his interpretation in Hegel's *Logic* and neglects the socio-political writings and aspects of Hegel's theory, as well as his relation to Marx.

The Hegel of *R&R,* however, is the critical rationalist who is Marx's predecessor. The central concepts presented are precisely those of the book's title, 'reason' and 'revolution'. Reason distinguishes between existence and essence through conceptualizing unrealized potentialities, norms and ideals that are to be realized in social practice. If social conditions prevent their realization, reason calls for revolution. Here Marcuse stresses the 'rationalist' Hegel, whom he wants to defend against interpretations of Hegel as an irrationalist who was a precursor of fascism. For the rest of his life, Marcuse would defend critical rationalism as a progressive heritage of bourgeois thought which received its highest formulations in Hegel and Marx. Although Marcuse would later share the Frankfurt School's critique of 'repressive reason', there is always a strong critical rationalist component in Marcuse's thought.

Marcuse also presents a socio-historical Hegel in *R&R,* who, as a philosopher of the *Zeitgeist,* reflects socio-economic and political developments in his philosophy. His method in *R&R* is that of critical theory, which situates a thinker socio-historically, analyses the theoretical and political content of a work, and provides an ideology-critique of its conservative, or mystifying, features. Let us now examine in some detail Marcuse's reading of Hegel in *R&R.*

5.1 Towards a theory of critical reason and critique of positivism

Marcuse claims that the best ideas of the French Revolution profoundly influenced Hegel's thought (*R&R,* pp. 3ff)[2] and helped him develop a concept of critical reason which is the central concept in Marcuse's interpretation of Hegel. In Marcuse's view, Hegel appropriated the radical principle of the French Revolution in his claim that 'thought ought to govern reality', and in his contrast between a critical employment of reason and 'an uncritical compliance with the prevailing conditions of life' (*R&R*, p. 6). Critical reason is a subversive principle that puts into question the existing state of affairs. Reason demands a rational order of life and criticizes prevailing irrational conditions that fail to satisfy its demands. The ability of reason to guide human life and social practice presupposes that the mind has access to norms and concepts which provide the standards to criticize existing states of affairs, as well as to ideals that should be realized in social life. Critical reason presupposes an autonomy of the subject and an ability to discover truths that transcend and negate the given society in order to alter 'unreasonable' reality until it comes into accord with the demands of reason. Critical theory adheres to this version of revolutionary rationalism, and throughout *R&R* Marcuse finds anticipations of the basic concepts of critical theory in Hegel.

Marcuse points out that the central concepts of Hegel's philosophy – freedom, subject, *Geist*, priority of the universal over the particular, etc. – can be derived from this concept of reason (*R&R*, pp. 5f and 253ff). *Freedom* results from the ability of reason to rise above nature and the realm of causality. Reason constitutes an autonomous *subject* that is able to make its own choices and to perceive and strive to fulfil its needs and potentialities. The subject, in this theory, possesses the quality of *Geist* (mind, spirit) by virtue of which it is able to transcend nature and society, and to gain the 'comprehending knowledge' which constitutes its 'real subjectivity' (*R&R*, p. 9). Moreover, Marcuse asserts that 'critical reason' can become a social force that will help break all fetters which keep the individual in a state of bondage and help create a society which conforms to demands for freedom and happiness: 'the life of reason appears in man's continuous struggle to comprehend what exists and to transform it in accordance with the truth comprehended' (*R&R*, p. 10). In this way, reason can help constitute history and realize human freedom. Reason is thus an integral part of Revolution (*R&R*, pp. 9ff, 253ff).

Contrary to the right-wing Hegelians, then, Marcuse interprets Hegel's categories as categories of emancipation. Reason is a 'critical and oppositional' principle, and 'the spirit of contradiction' stands at the centre of Hegel's thought (*R&R*, p. 11). Marcuse does point out that Hegel's idealism became increasingly conservative, aiming at reconciliation with existing reality, rather than its criticism and negation. But the thrust of Marcuse's interpretation is to valorize the radical components in Hegel, who he believes develops a powerful critique of empiricism and positivism and, especially in his early writings, provides penetrating insights into capitalist development and its effects on human beings.

5.1.1 *Hegel's critique of empiricism*

Marcuse sets out to show that the Hegelian concept of critical reason provides the basis for a powerful critique of empiricism. This is for Marcuse one of the most valuable legacies of Hegel's thought, since empiricism, in Marcuse's view, tends towards scepticism and conformity, and thus is socially conservative. Marcuse asserts that the empiricist attack on universals restricts theoretical knowledge to 'the given', and restricts practical directives to custom, thus submitting the individual to the facts and norms of the existing order. In Marcuse's interpretation, empiricism is an 'abdication of reason' (*R&R*, p. 20), whereas Hegel insists that reason can discover norms and ideals which transcend the given order and can foster social change. Marcuse thus argues that empiricist philosophy, which submits to the existing order of facts and values, is 'conservative and affirmative' (*R&R*, p. 27), whereas Hegel's rationalist philosophy is critical and revolutionary.

In Marcuse's interpretation, critical reason distinguishes between the existence and essence of an entity. Empiricism, on the other hand, naively accepts things as they are, failing to see that the highest potentialities of entities and their fully realized essence perhaps do not yet exist. The 'essence' of an entity refers to a stage of full realization of its potentialities and provides standards which can be used to criticize deficient forms of human behaviour or society. For example, if a society fails to satisfy its potentialities for material well-being, freedom or justice, its existence is seen to be deficient in relation to its higher potentialities, and reason should call for social change, condemning the existing society as 'a "bad" form of reality, a realm of limitation and bondage' (*R&R*, p. 47). Consequently, reason articulates the antagonism between things as they are and as they could be, thus providing an impetus for change. 'True existence begins only when the immediate state is recognized as negative' (*R&R*, pp. 66ff), when beings strive to overcome their deficiencies and develop their potentialities.

Critical reason is thus a vehicle of liberation and, in accordance with the dialectical view of reality, all reality is seen as a process of change and development (*R&R*, pp. 100f, 130ff). Here Marcuse identifies an important Hegelian concept that influenced Marx, who applied Hegelian dialectics to the study of society, arguing that capitalist society was a system of antagonisms and contradictions which was bound to perish and give way to a higher form of social organization that would realize the unactualized potentialities in the existing social order. Far from seeing Hegel's philosophy as the wild metaphysical fantasies of a German professor, Marcuse believes that Hegel's critical philosophical method and concepts provide revolutionary tools that are embodied in Marx's historical materialism and in his own critical theory of society.

Hegel's dialectics presupposes that reality is a process of development in which things constantly turn into their opposites and strive to realize their higher potentialities. Development is a result of contradictions between lower and higher states of being in which the more restricted, partial and incomplete lower state is negated in order to realize higher potentialities. In the well known example, a flower progresses through growth from a seed to a stem, to a bud, to a blooming plant, driven throughout by tensions between its various stages of development, in which lower stages are overcome. Likewise, individuals pass from foetus to unsocialized child, incapable of speech or action, to socialized child, to youth, to adult; in this process of development there are contradictions between the various stages which are overcome by negation of earlier states of being in order to realize their higher potentialities. Thus, in Marcuse's words, 'Dialectic in its entirety is linked to the conception that all forms of being are permeated by an essential negativity, and that this negativity determines their content and movement' (*R&R*, p. 27). Marcuse believes that this dialectical view 'represents the counterthrust to any form of positivism' which accepts the 'ultimate authority of fact' and makes 'observing the immediate given . . . the ultimate method of verification' (*R&R*, p. 27). This 'positive philosophy' is opposed, Marcuse claims, by a 'negative philosophy' which criticizes the given facts in view of their unrealized potentialities.

For Hegelian-Marxian dialectics, contradiction is the essence of reality and is not simply a principle of thought (*R&R*, pp. 100ff, 131ff, 146ff, 158ff). Dialectics is thus rooted in the actual movement of things, and reality is perceived as being permeated with contradictions between fact and potentialities, existence and essence, and between higher and lower states of being. For dialectics, reality is sundered into dynamically oppositional elements, like Being and Nothing in Hegel's *Logic*, or Capital and Labour in Marx's social theory. Reality is conceived as a historical process of development (*R&R*, pp. 238ff) in which change takes place through overcoming contradictions and through the negation of restrictions, limitations or obsolete conditions. Reason is to provide an 'exhaustive analysis of existing contradictions', to discern the higher potentialities in a given situation, and to discover the practice which can negate the bonds or fetters in order to realize the potentialities. Dialectical theory thus requires practice, and the dialectical theory of history and society requires a theory of social change which became for Marx the theory of socialist revolution.

5.1.2 *Critical theory* v. *positivism*

In the last third of *R&R*, Marcuse extends his Hegelian critique of empiricism to a more historical-theoretical critique of positivism, a theme which would be a dominant concern of his later work. Marcuse's strategy in *R&R* is to delineate differences between the two main currents of social theory which developed in Europe. In the decade after Hegel's death, there arose several systems of 'positive philosophy' which, Marcuse claims, provide the foundation of modern positivism. The French philosopher Comte grounds his positivism in 'the matters of fact of observation' within the physical sciences, believing that all truth comes from observation and is to be formulated in scientific laws (*R&R*, pp. 324ff). Positivism for Marcuse, however, is not simply a 'positive' attitude towards science, which assumes that science alone provides the canons of inquiry and truth, but, more generally, 'positivism' refers, in Marcuse's interpretation, to an uncritical conformist attitude toward the 'facts of experience'.[3] A 'common tendency among the various currents of positivism' is, Marcuse claims, the desire 'to counter the sway of apriorism and to restore the authority of experience' (*R&R*, p. 324). Further, 'Positive philosophy was a conscious reaction against the critical and destructive tendencies of French and German rationalism' (*R&R*, p. 324).

Marcuse argues that critical social theories, on the other hand, provide 'instruments for transforming and not for stabilizing or

justifying the given order' (*R&R*, p. 329). The early French socialists, for example, turned their attention to understanding and
overcoming the conflicts of class society produced by capitalist
development. Marcuse points out how the school of Saint-Simon
proposed concrete solutions to the problems of industrial society,
and how the Saint-Simonian Bazard attacked the exploitation of the
working class under capitalism, calling for revolution to do away
with exploitation. There are critical aspects as well, he suggests, in
the theories of Sismondi and Proudhon. Consequently, in Marcuse's words:

> The new political economy was quite different from the classical
> objective science of Adam Smith and Ricardo. It differed from
> them in that it showed the economy to be contradictory and
> irrational throughout its structure, with crisis as its natural state
> and revolution as its natural end. Sismondi's work, the first
> thoroughgoing immanent critique of capitalism, amply illustrates
> the contrast. It held to the criterion of a truly critical theory of
> society. 'We shall take society in its actual organization, with its
> workers deprived of property, their wages fixed by competition,
> their labour dismissed by their masters as soon as they no longer
> have need of it – for it is to this very social organization that we
> object'. (*R&R*, p. 338)[4]

Marcuse stresses that whereas positive social theory views society as
a natural organism which can be studied by the methods of natural
science, critical social theory, on the other hand, sees society as the
product of human activity, which requires different methods of
research and different criteria (i.e. freedom, reason, justice, etc.) to
judge its adequacy to human and social potential. He argues that
'Hegel had considered society and the state to be the historical work
of man and interpreted them under the aspect of freedom; in
contrast, positive philosophy studied the social realities after the
pattern of nature and under the aspect of objective necessity'
(*R&R*, p. 326). Further,

> Marx considered society to be irrational and hence evil, so long as
> it continued to be governed by inexorable objective laws. Prog-
> ress to him was equivalent to upsetting these laws, an act that was
> to be consummated by man in his free development. The positiv-

ist theory of society followed the opposite tendency: the laws of society increasingly received the form of natural objective laws ... The deification of progress into an independent natural law was completed in Comte's positive philosophy. (*R&R*, p. 332)

Hence, critical social theory rejects claims that there are natural, objective laws of social progress, and believes that the law-like aspects of social life were often tyrannical and irrational forces that could be eliminated in a free society (i.e. the laws of capitalist accumulation, surplus-value, crisis tendencies, etc.).

Marcuse's characterization of positivism was attacked by Sidney Hook, who, in a critical review of *R&R*, argues that Marcuse provides a completely misleading account of positivism and an illicit attack on it:

According to him, Hegel's 'liberalism' provoked the counter-revolutionary philosophic doctrines of positivism, which in turn gave rise to modern sociology. Among these positivists Mr Marcuse lists not only thinkers like St. Simon and Comte but the black reactionary Stahl and connects their basic approach with that of contemporary positivism. This is the nearest thing to a political amalgam that has appeared in a book on philosophy. The least common denominator of this inclusive positivism is apparently the refusal to accept the idealist principle 'that the matters of fact of experience have to be justified before the court of reason'. The refusal to accept this principle means to Mr Marcuse either accommodation to the status quo or mere reformism. To link Comte, the continuator of the French Enlightenment, with Stahl, who would have liked to be its executioner, is arbitrary enough. But more arbitrary are the social positions which Mr Marcuse allegedly derives from the denial of the idealist principle. It shows that he does not come within hailing distance of understanding positivism. Positivism in social thought does not take its point of departure from ready-made facts but seeks to discover by scientific, not dialectical, methods what the facts are. It is only by testing our ideals and principles by available facts that we can tell whether our choice of them has been intelligent. As for Mr Marcuse's dissatisfaction with positivist reformism, 'reform' is just as much an ideal as 'revolution', and positivists can be and have been revolutionists just as dialecticians can be and have been reformists, and even stand-patters.[5]

Marcuse did not directly answer Hook, but much of his later work provides criticisms of the sort of empiricism which Hook advocates.[6] Although, in *R&R*, Marcuse did not develop the connections between nineteenth-century positivism and its later varieties, he did write critical book reviews in the *Zeitschrift für Sozialforschung* on the works of logical positivism, Dewey's pragmatism, and other empiricist theories that anticipate his critique of one-dimensional thought in *One-Dimensional Man*.[7] Interestingly, he tends to criticize 'one-dimensional thought' from the standpoint of Hegel's logic, identity theory and concept of truth. In a critique of Carnap's notion of formal logic, Marcuse argues that 'Logic has to do with the universal conditions of truth, and truth is raised and preserved (*aufgehoben*) in the thinking and action of human beings; hence these conditions are not to be separated from the content of thinking and acting'.[8] Polemicizing against the formal concept of logical judgment in the unity of science programme advocated by Carnap and other 'logical positivists', Marcuse argues that judgment and truth 'are bound together with the identity of thinking and being. Thinking and being come together in truth: thinking makes being accessible and thought realizes itself (*verwirklicht sich*)'.[9] Against the formal-logical notion of correctness, Marcuse argues that this notion sunders thought and being; thus the formalized concept of judgment 'conceptualizes nothing; it does not maintain itself in the conceptualized possibilities of things critically against their given existence; it only establishes what already exists. It does not move in the two-dimensionality of essence and fact, which is the authentic locus of truth, but only in the one-dimensionality of facts'.[10]

Marcuse is contemptuous of the attempts to formulate theories of truth in formal logic which he believes produces an 'empty language' and manipulation of signs.[11] In a review of Russell and von Mises he writes:

The debasement of cognition that is so clearly reflected in these formulations distinguishes all the general methodological utterances of modern positivism. Unable to fulfil its quest for certainty and security, positivist thought seeks refuge in tautological definitions and the fixed conventions of everyday language. It orients knowledge to the ideal of providing an adequate description of that which is . . . In its quest for certainty and security, positivism is compelled to formalize all propositions to such an extent that they either state nothing about reality (see R. v. Mises' thesis above) or state only things in which nobody is interested and which everybody knows anyway. The propositions cannot be disputed because all controversial content has been removed. The problem of meaning and truth, on the other hand, should begin only where there is a controversial matter, one on which no agreement can possibly be arrived at by going back to the 'basic propositions' of the 'object language'. The problems of freedom, reason, justice cannot be discussed within a conceptual framework that centres around 'basic propositions' because disagreement and the transcendence of sense-perception belong to their very essence. If meaning and truth are to be derived from statements such as 'I am hot' or 'this is red', then all philosophic statements are *a priori* meaningless and false.[12]

In a provocative review of Dewey's *Theory of Validation*, Marcuse notes the early critical tendencies in positivism (Locke, Montesquieu and the French Enlightenment), the tendencies in Hume to combine critique of religion and metaphysics with submission to custom and habit, and Comte's subordination of reason and truth 'to the observation of facts, and "facts as they are"'.[13] He notes liberating tendencies within the early stages of positivism: 'freedom to investigate, to observe, to experiment, to refrain from premature judgment and decision – even the liberty to contradict'.[14] The problem is that positivism limits freedom 'to the realm of science, and a scientific behaviour is the condition of positivistic freedom'.[15] This means that positivism is forced to submit to what establishes itself as a verifiable reality (fascism in Marcuse's example), and is thus forced to submit to the facts in the last instance. Although positivism can propose experiments and test results,

positivism is unable to state anything 'scientific' about the desirability of the ends themselves. The positivist can weigh the ends against the means necessary to achieve them, he can investigate the conditions of their realization and ask whether it is 'reasonable' to realize certain ends, he can show the consequences that are implied in this realization. But this is about all he can do. His analysis stops short at the prevailing desires and interests of men, which are the given facts, and therefore stops short at the multitude of ends prevalent in these desires and interests.[16]

Although Marcuse believes that Dewey's theory of valuation, which places value-inquiry at the centre of social theory, is preferable to the positivist attempt to eliminate values from social science, he still finds Dewey's perspective limited, specifically Dewey's optimism that the individual possesses the autonomy and independence to engage in a continual process of valuation and revaluation. Here Marcuse argues that the desires and interests of those in contemporary society have been so shaped by the prevailing order that they are incapable of choosing and realizing their own values. Further, those with a real desire for freedom and creativity will clash with the established authorities and will be unable to 'validate' their values:

> they cannot test and 'verify' their values because in order to do so, they must have already won. And despite their failure to verify their values the forces of freedom are 'good', 'right', and 'valuable' beyond test and verification, and if their cause loses, the world, and not their values, will have been refuted.[17]

Against Dewey and the positivists, Marcuse argues that critical theory defends certain values which transcend the given order and facts, providing the criteria within which 'the facts' can be evaluated. Above all, critical theory is committed to freedom:

> In the present situation of material and intellectual culture, the problem of values is, in the last analysis, identical with the problem of freedom. The conditions of matters of fact have become so unified that the one idea, freedom, covers all that is good, right and admirable in the world. And all efforts to place the value of freedom on the same scientific level with other current valuations is an affront to freedom. For science is essentially in itself freedom, and cannot verify freedom through anything other than freedom. Freedom – and this is the profound result of Kant's analysis – is the only 'fact' that 'is' only in its creation; it cannot be verified except by being exercised.[18]

5.2 Hegel and Marx

Throughout *R&R* Marcuse is concerned to elucidate the central categories of dialectics found in Hegel and Marx. In this way he provides a revealing account of the categories and method of his own critical theory. His sympathetic presentation of Hegel's dialectics, which focuses on the emancipatory elements of his thought and method, rather than on the dubious and reactionary elements of Hegel's idealism, reveals a deep commitment to Hegelian-Marxian dialectics. Marcuse's 1960 preface, 'A Note on Dialectic' shows how his own emphasis on 'the power of negative thinking' and the 'great refusal' is rooted in the Hegelian-Marxian concept of dialectics:

> Dialectic thought thus becomes negative in itself. Its function is to break down the self-assurance and self-contentment of common sense, to undermine the sinister confidence in the power and language of facts, to demonstrate that unfreedom is so much at the core of things that the development of their internal contradictions leads necessarily to qualitative change: the explosion and catastrophe of the established state of affairs' (*R&R*, p. ix).

Although Marcuse, in his post-Second World War critical theory rarely discusses Hegel's philosophy, his entire project exemplifies the spirit and method of dialectics which *R&R* is concerned to develop.

Throughout *R&R* Marcuse finds anticipations of Marx in Hegel, Hegelian elements in Marx, and frequent similarities of doctrine. He claims, for example, that Hegel's early theological writings (1790–1800) are motivated by the political problem of the relation between the individual and society, analysing for the first time the alienation of the individual from the emerging capitalist order (*R&R*, pp. 34ff). In an original interpretation of the early Hegel, Marcuse discusses how Hegel's insights into social antagonisms, the bourgeois property order, the anarchy of the capitalist market, and the need for the state regulation of the economy anticipate some of Marx's central conceptions (*R&R*, pp. 56–61, 73–90, *passim*).

Marcuse also argues that Hegel's *Phenomenology of Spirit* provides insights into the role of labour in the constitution of the self and the social world, and that Hegel grasps the specific 'mode of labour characteristic of modern commodity production' (*R&R*, p. 77).[19] He explicitly states that Hegel 'comes close to' Marx's doctrine of abstract labour and the 'function of labour in integrating the various individual activities into a totality of exchange relationships' and thus 'clearly foreshadows Marx's critical approach' (*R&R*, p. 78). Marcuse also tries to show that Hegel's political philosophy is not really compatible with fascism, since Hegel develops a rational theory of the state and stresses the importance of rule by law.[20] He does, however, point out its conservative features as well, and attempts to provide a balanced account of Hegel's theory of the state that neither falls into the extremities of simply dismissing Hegel as a proto-fascist,[21] nor provides an apologetic defence of Hegel.[22]

Despite the often uncanny similarities between Hegel and Marx which Marcuse works out, he stresses that the transition from Hegel to Marx is 'in all respects a transition to an essentially different order of truth, not to be interpreted in terms of philosophy' (*R&R*, p. 258). In Marcuse's interpretation the passage is from philosophy to social theory: 'all the philosophical categories of Marxian theory are social and economic categories, whereas Hegel's social and economic categories are all philosophical concepts' (*R&R*, p. 258). Marcuse claims that 'even Marx's early writings are not philosophical', but express the 'negation of philosophy' (*R&R*, p. 258). He is suggesting that the transition from Hegel to Marx should not be interpreted within philosophy simply as a break with Hegel, but should rather be seen as a break with traditional philosophy which reconstitutes philosophy as a moment in social theory, grounded in political economy, and which provides an instrument of social practice. We see here that Marcuse reverses his previous hierarchy in the relation between philosophy and social theory: where previously (see 3.1) he claimed that philosophy was superordinate to social theory, he now sees philosophy as but a part of social theory.

On Marcuse's interpretation, the existence of the proletariat for Marx contradicts the alleged reality of reason in bourgeois society and consequently falsifies Hegel's theory (pp. 260ff). Since, for Hegel and Marx, labour is the activity through which the human being realizes itself, then if the labour system is destructive of its members, the entire social order is condemned. From Hegel's concept of reason and Marx's analysis of alienated labour, Marcuse derives the Marxian theory of revolution:

> if the existence of the proletariat, then, bears witness to 'the complete loss of man', and this loss results from the mode of labour on which civil society is founded, the society is vicious in its

entirety and the proletariat expresses a total negativity: 'universal suffering' and 'universal injustice' . . . The critique of society cannot be carried through by philosophical doctrine, but becomes the task of socio-historical practice. (*R&R*, p. 261)

We see here that Marcuse makes the oppression of the proletariat the foundation of the Marxian theory of revolution. His later questioning of the Marxian theory of the proletariat will require him radically to rethink and reconstruct the Marxian theory, while at this point we note again that Marcuse is remarkably 'orthodox'.

Marcuse criticizes the individualistic approaches to liberation of Kierkegaard and Feuerbach; he argues that although Hegel demonstrates the social nature of human life, it is Marx, among all post-Hegelian thinkers, [23] who penetrated to the social origins of human bondage and suffering in the capitalist labour process, arguing that the abolition of alienated labour was necessary for human liberation and the rational reconstruction of society. In his discussion of Marx's project of the abolition of alienated labour (*R&R*, pp. 273–95) Marcuse stresses typical themes on his own appropriation of Marx, namely the elements of communistic individualism, the repudiation of any fetishism concerning the socialization of the means of production or the growth of the productive forces, and the subordination of all these factors to the idea of the free realization of the individual (*R&R*, pp. 294–5). Marcuse claims that these elements of the Marxian project have been 'attentuated in the post-Marxian development of his critique of society', and he wishes to provide a corrective for bureaucratic communism, which puts development of productive forces before development of human beings. Marcuse also stresses the commitment of Marxian materialism to the idea of happiness, which he believes differentiates it from Hegelian rationalism.

Marcuse's interpretation of Hegel and Marx discloses his strong commitment to Hegelian Marxism. It also shows the groundlessness of Alasdair MacIntyre's claim that Marcuse is a 'pre-Marxian thinker'.[24] Rather, in the preceding chapters, I hope to have demonstrated Marcuse's adherence to the Marxian theory, methodology and revolutionary project. In *Reason and Revolution* Marcuse makes clear his commitment to Hegelian-Marxian dialectics and acceptance of the Marxian theory of the proletariat (*R&R*, pp. 261ff), the Marxian anthropology and analysis of the labour process (*R&R*, pp. 273ff), the critique of capitalism, the theory of capitalist collapse (*R&R*, pp. 310ff), and the theory of socialist revolution (*R&R*, pp. 318f). He attacks 'revisionism' (*R&R*, pp. 398ff) and refers favourably to Lenin (*R&R*, pp. 314, 401). Marcuse's Marxism at this point is rather orthodox, and although he will later develop many criticisms of orthodox Marxism, it is ludicrous to call him a 'pre-Marxian thinker'.

Nonetheless, it is clear that Marcuse is deeply committed to elements of Hegel's philosophy, and I would suggest that just as the theoretical problems in his first stage of work (1928–32) derived from a too uncritical appropriation of Heidegger's philosopy, likewise Marcuse's appropriation of Hegel's ontology and epistemology is too uncritical in his work with the Institute. In fact, in *R&R* Marcuse never really criticizes Hegel's philosophy as such, but focuses criticism on Hegel's political doctrines, which he portrays as a 'betrayal' of Hegel's philosophical ideals. His analysis therefore suggests that there is only an accidental relation between Hegel's philosophy and politics. I would argue, however, that Hegel's political positions are compatible with, and often follow from, his philosophy, and that consequently there are serious philosophical problems in Hegel that are the source of his conservative politics. In the following discussion I shall argue that Marcuse's attempts to make Hegel the basis for revolutionary social theory is problematical in several respects.

First, I would argue that it is precisely Hegel's basic philosophical positions that are the origin of the political problems in Hegel that Marcuse criticizes. For example, Hegel's 'hypostatization of universals' (*R&R*, pp. 71) and priority of the universal over the particular – which Hegel maintained throughout his writings – has its analogue in Hegel's subordination of the individual to the state (=universal), for the state is a prime example of a Hegelian 'concrete universal' which absorbs and transcends individuals. Moreover, it should be noted that Hegel's thoroughgoing panrationalism and his concept of the Absolute lend themselves to apologetic distortion and misuse. To claim that the driving force of history is reason implies that all states, social forms of life and philosophies are more or less perfect embodiments of reason, from which one can find the realization of reason in the existing order. Such an idealistic theory of history also covers over the role of material interests as causal factors in history. The concept of an Absolute contains mystifying overtones of finality, completeness and perfection, inflated by Hegel into the audacious claims that philosophy was completed in his system and that reason was realized in the Prussian state. Marcuse does not sufficiently criticize this philosophical hubris or the philosophical assumptions which led Hegel to these views.

Furthermore, Marcuse seems to believe that Hegel's logic and ontology explicate the structures of reality and contain the canons of philosophical truth. Marcuse writes, uncritically, that Hegel's *Logic* 'expounds the structure of being-as-such, that is, the most general forms of being' (*R&R*, p. 62). He interprets the *Logic* as an ontological treatise: it is no mere conceptual analysis or inventory of philosophical categories, for, Marcuse points out, Hegel postulates a unity of thought and being, logic and metaphysics (*R&R*, p. 63), while arguing for a material logic (*R&R*, p. 122): '*The Science of Logic* deals with the general ontological structure these entities have'; consequently, the process of thought grasps the 'objective structure of being' (*R&R*, p. 127).

Despite the critique of speculative metaphysics found in Kant, Marx, Nietzsche and Heidegger (four of Marcuse's philosophical mentors), he nonetheless seem to accept Hegel's ontology, for he can write without any irony or critical overtones: 'the foundation of the absolute knowledge that the *Phenomenology of Mind* presents as the truth of the world are given in Hegel's *Science of Logic*' (*R&R*, p. 120).

Marcuse seems to believe that the Hegelian philosophy is critical, radical and subversive: 'negative philosophy'. This evaluation of Hegel comes out in Marcuse's argument that Marxism is the only authentic continuation of the Hegelian philosophy (*R&R*, pp. 252ff); in the evaluation of Hegel's philosophy by his opponents after his death as subversive and hostile to the status quo (*R&R*, pp. 321ff, 364f); and by Nazi opponents of Hegel, who saw his philosophy as incompatible with the New Order (*R&R*, pp. 409–19). But in view of Hegel's reactionary apologetics, submission to the Prussian state, and surrender of the critical function of philosophy – all recognized in Marcuse's own interpretation – the notion of Hegel's radicalism and 'negative dialectics' cannot be unambiguously maintained. Although Hegel's early work did contain a critical method and radical impulses, Hegel's critical dialectic came to a standstill with the concept of Absolute Knowledge in the *Phenomenology*. Hegel's system then gave the impression of finality and completeness in which the dialectic comes to rest in a haven of philosophical truth. Accordingly, we need to make distinctions between the radicalism of the early Hegel – appreciated in different ways by Dilthey, Marcuse, Lukács and Habermas[25] – and the conservative and idealist theodicy in the later Hegel. In his later work, Hegel actually denied the critical function of philosophy, as when he maintained in the *Philosophy of Right* that philosophy is its time apprehended in thought.[26]

In fact Marx himself made sharper criticisms of Hegel's philosophy than Marcuse. Marx's early unpublished manuscript on Hegel's *Philosophy of Right* criticizes in detail Hegel's theory of the absolute state, monarchy and bureaucracy, while arguing for radical democracy.[27] Marx's commentary on Hegel's *Phenomenology of Mind* in his 1844 Paris *Manuscripts* contains a powerful criticism of Hegel's idealism and idealist dialectics which could be compared with Marcuse's tendency to play down critical discussion of Hegel's idealism.[28] Although Marcuse provides a striking interpretation of those elements in Hegel that were later taken up by Marx and critical theory, he fails to criticize adequately Hegel's philosophy. The problem, I believe, is that Marcuse was too heavily under the influence of Hegel's philosophy; moreover he thought that it was politically important to stress the Hegelian and dialectical roots of the Marxian philosophy, and the continuity between Hegel and Marx, in view of Social Democratic and other 'revisionist' attempts to sever Marxism and dialectics.[29] Hence in *R&R* Marcuse takes great pains to demonstrate the continuity between Hegel and Marx, and to disclose the Hegelian roots of the Marxian theory.

In sum, both of Marcuse's Hegel books are remarkably uncritical of Hegel's philosophy. *Hegel's Ontology* presents Hegel's ontological thought as the culmination and high point of Western philosophy, while *R&R* focuses on Hegel's crucial importance for critical social theory. Whereas *Hegel's Ontology* focuses solely on Hegel's theoretical texts, and *R&R* adds some material on Hegel's socio-historical context, both books ignore Hegel's biography, which mediates the texts, the historical context and the intellectual milieu. In this respect, Marcuse's interpretation of Hegel shows a tendency to ignore biography almost completely when discussing philosophy or intellectual history; this is perhaps an inheritance from Heidegger's interpretive techniques, which scrupulously ignore biographical factors when discussing philosophy.

Another problem with Marcuse's presentation of Hegel's thought in *R&R* is that he gives too little attention to the complex dialectics of German Idealism, minimizing Hegel's interaction with the philosophies of Kant, Fichte and Schelling in developing his views. Moreover, Marcuse rarely discusses other interpretations of Hegel or the ferocious debates concerning Hegel's philosophy, with the exception of the critiques of Hegel's philosophy after his death by Schelling, F. J. Stahl and others. In *R&R*, he seems primarily interested in showing the radical elements of Hegel's philosophy, which made it the target of conservative critiques, with the aim of showing the incompatibility between Hegel's philosophy and fascism. Except for this issue, Marcuse does not deal with the heated debates over the meaning and significance of Hegel's philosophy, choosing instead to present Hegel's basic ideas and the connections with Marx and critical theory.

Marcuse's procedure might be compared with Lukács's *The Young Hegel*, which was written about the same time as *R&R*, but was delayed in its publication by the war.[30] Lukács provides a provocative presentation of the evolution of Hegel's philosophy, rooting it in its social conditions in Germany and within the context of the vicissitudes of German Idealism. Like Marcuse, Lukács presents Hegel's early work as a dual response to the French Revolution and capitalism, but Lukács's study contains much more detailed discussions of Hegel's early writings and connects the texts with the conditions of Hegel's life and the socio-cultural context of the time more impressively than Marcuse. Lukács also spends much energy combatting the dominant interpretations of Hegel by various German Hegelians and Neo-Hegelians. Lukács is, as usual over zealous in attacking 'imperialist' and 'idealist' interpretations of Hegel, and is obsessed with vindicating Marx, Engels, Lenin and Stalin as the only correct interpreters and critics of Hegel, who provide the canon of philosophical truth. This procedure does produce some provocative Marxist-Leninist criticisms of Kant, Hegel and German Idealism, as well as some fiery polemics that make for exciting reading. Marcuse is much more careful and restrained than Lukács and does not open himself as much to wholesale dismissal by non-marxist Hegel scholars.

Marcuse, however, intends to do more than simply develop a Marxist philology of the early Hegel and, unlike Lukács, covers the entirety of Hegel's philosophy, its appropriation by Marx and its impact on the rise of social theory. Indeed, Marcuse provides in *R&R* the first Marxists analysis of the entirety of Hegel's work as a primary source of Marxism. In this context, Marcuse stresses the importance for Marxism of both the method and the substantive concepts of Hegel's philosophy.

Reason and Revolution is thus one of the key texts in developing an Hegelian Marxism. Sympathizers of Hegelian Marxism regularly praise the book, whereas critics like Colletti sharply criticize it.[31] Marcuse systematically presents the continuities between Marx and Hegel, and those critical-emancipatory elements in Hegel which he believes should be taken up in critical theory. The book is of more than philological interest in interpreting Hegel as it reveals those Hegelian-Marxian elements which shaped his own thought. Thus although in his post-Second World War work he would not take such aggressively Hegelian positions, he would continue to defend dialectics, critical reason and the emancipatory moments in Hegelian idealism.

5.3 Radical despair and the struggle against fascism

Marcuse's theoretical work was interrupted for almost a decade by America's entry into the Second World War. Marcuse, along with several Institute colleagues, decided that the fight against fascism was the top priority on the historical agenda, and that he could best contribute to the struggle while working for the US intelligence and information service. As he put it in a 1972 interview: 'I went to Washington so I could work during the war – that is, speaking plainly, to do everything that was in my power to help defeat the Nazi regime'.[32]

Marcuse, along with Institute members Franz Neumann and Otto Kirchheimer, first went to the Office of War Information (OWI), which was a sort of government propaganda agency. The OWI was an offshoot of the Office of the Coordination of Information (COI), which was set up by Roosevelt in 1941 under William Donovan, known since his youth as 'Wild Bill'.[33] Its function was to set up an international secret service for the United States that could counter the fascist menace and deal with espionage, anti-American and isolationist propaganda, and the dreaded 'fifth column' which had aided fascist success in the Balkans.

Describing his OSS activities, Marcuse notes: 'I was a political analyst. The division of the OSS that I was working in was a sort of research institute that was supposed to examine political developments in the countries involved in the war. I was responsible for central western Europe'.[34] Marcuse's Communist critics sometimes use his work with American intelligence services to taint him with CIA affiliations, since the OSS was the forerunner of the CIA.[35] Marcuse answers: 'If critics reproach me for that, it only shows the complete ignorance of these people, who seem to have forgotton that the war then was a war against fascism and that, consequently, I haven't the slightest reason for being ashamed of having assisted in it'.[36]

By the end of the war, Marcuse's OSS unit was transferred to the State Department and he was in charge of their Central European Division. In his words:

My main task was to identify groups in Germany with which one could work towards reconstruction after the war; and to identify groups which were to be taken to task as Nazis. There was a major de-Nazification programme at the time. Based on exact research, reports, newspaper reading and whatever, lists were made up of those Nazis who were supposed to assume responsibility for their activity. Later it was said that I was a CIA agent.

HABERMAS: Yes, yes.

MARCUSE: Which is ridiculous, since the OSS wasn't even allowed near the CIA. They fought each other like enemies.

HABERMAS: My question is aimed, not only at disposing of this absurdity, but also at clarifying, politically, what actually came of your suggestions. Are you of the impression that what you did then was of any consequence?

MARCUSE: On the contrary. Those whom we had listed first as 'economic war criminals' were very quickly back in the decisive positions of responsibility in the German economy. It would be very easy to name names here.[37]

After the war, Marcuse and his colleagues attempted to counter the trend towards cold war anti-Communism which began to spread. In Henry Pachter's words: 'Franz Neumann and Herbert Marcuse bombarded Secretary of War Stimson with plans for a post-war Germany that would give democratic socialism a chance; they probably prevented the worst stupidities an occupation regime is capable of'.[38] Communist witchhunts had begun in the State Department and Marcuse's position became increasingly precarious. H. Stuart Hughes notes: 'it has seemed deliciously incongruous that at the end of the 1940s, with an official purge of real or suspected leftists in full swing, the State Department's leading authority on Central Europe should have been a revolutionary socialist who hated the cold war and all its works'.[39]

The 1940s and early 1950s were a difficult period for Marcuse. He was forced to grind away in government bureaucracies and had to remain in Washington due to his wife, Sophie's, illness, when pressure from right-wing repression in the anti-Communist crusade began. Moreover, he was unable to get a suitable university post, and was isolated from his Institute colleagues after some returned to Germany and Neumann accepted a post at Columbia.[40]

In the long period between the publication of *Reason and Revolution* and *Eros and Civilization*, Marcuse's only major publication was a long review of Jean-Paul Sartre's *Being and Nothingness*.[41] Marcuse begins with a description of the existentialist analysis of the absurdity of human existence and the existentialist response: '"consciousness and revolt", and defiance is its only truth'.[42] Given Marcuse's situation, he must have felt an affinity for this doctrine. He then writes:

Camus's *Mythe de Sisyphe* recaptures the climate of Nietzsche's philosophy: 'Absurd man envisages a burning and icy universe, transparent and limited, where nothing is possible but everything is given, beyond which is extinction and the void'. Thought moves in the night, but it is night 'of desperation which remains lucid, polar night, eve of the mind out of which will perhaps rise that white and integral clarity which designs every object in the light of the intellect'.[43]

Marcuse notes that the existentialist 'experience of the "absurd world" gives rise to a new and extreme rationalism' that takes two forms: Camus' rejection of systematic philosophy in favour of 'living the absurd life' and 'artistic creation', contrasted with Sartre's attempt 'to develop the new experience into a philosophy of the concrete human existence: to elaborate the structure of "being in an absurd world" and the ethics of "living without appeal"'.[44]

Marcuse then provides a detailed account of Sartre's analysis of freedom, human conflict, alienation and the other failures of the human project which led Sartre to conclude that 'man is a useless passion'.[45] Marcuse, however, refuses to accept the existentialist individualism and ontology to which he was once attracted and sharply attacks Sartre's existentialism as he analyses its intellectual roots, its contradictions and its deficiencies. He concludes: 'In so far as existentialism is a philosophical doctrine, it remains an idealistic doctrine: it hypostatizes specific historical conditions of human existence into ontological and metaphysical characteristics. Existentialism thus becomes part of the very ideology which it attacks and its radicalism is illusory'.[46]

In retrospect, the other great philosophical treatise of the 1940s which especially interested, and deeply influenced, Marcuse was a production of his colleagues Adorno and Horkheimer, *Dialectic of Enlightenment*.[47] Their account of the reifications of consciousness and human life from primitive magic to modern science is even more despairing than Sartre's work. The thrust of the book is the failure of the Enlightenment, which has degenerated into modern positivism, the culture industry, science and technology as ideology and domination, and the destruction of the individual in the administered society. Adorno and Horkheimer attempt to lay out 'the discovery of why mankind, instead of entering into a truly human condition, is sinking into a new kind of barbarism'.[48] They later described their work as an 'assessment of the transition to the world of the administered life', and believed the 'sinister trend' was accelerating.[49] Implicitly, Marxism too is part of the 'dialectic of Enlightenment' and serves as a new instrument of domination, rather than as a vehicle for emancipation. Many critics have seen Adorno and Horkheimer's joint work as an abandonment of their previous commitments to Marxism and as a capitulation to extreme pessimism.[50]

Marcuse, by contrast, never abandoned his commitment to Marxism, and throughout the post-war period to the end of his life remained loyal to the 1930s critical theory project. Like Adorno and Horkheimer, however, Marcuse would question the Marxian faith in the productive forces, technology and the proletariat. Whereas Marx and most Marxists of the Second and Third International assume that progress in the development of the productive forces – especially technology – will lead to contradictions with obsolete capitalist relations of production, Marcuse and his colleagues saw that the productive forces themselves were serving as instruments of domination that strengthened even obsolete and oppressive capitalist relations of production. The critique of science, technology and instrumental reason separated Marcuse and his colleagues from more 'scientific Marxists', and hostile debates continue to take place between these opposed currents of Marxism.

During a difficult historical period, Marcuse refused to capitulate to radical despair, and while he began questioning Marxian theories of the proletariat as the revolutionary class and the inevitability of capitalist crisis and collapse, he remained firmly committed to Marxian socialism. Instead of abandoning Marxism, he chose to reconstruct it. Consequently, in the mid-1950s he sought a new foundation for critical theory in Freud's anthropology, and during the next several decades would develop new perspectives on revolution and socialism. Things picked up for him in his personal life as well. He received a suitable professorship at Brandeis university in 1954, where he became a popular and respected teacher, and eventually a well known scholar. He married a remarkable woman, Inge Neumann, the widow of his close friend Franz Neumann, after Neumann's tragic death in a car accident.

In retrospect, the rather extreme Marxian orthodoxy of Marcuse's work with the Institute for Social Research represents something of a break in Marcuse's development. After abandoning the ultra-radical, individualistic and extremely philosophical works of his youth during his work with the Institute, Marcuse returned to these positions in his third, post-Second World War, period. After Adorno, Horkheimer and the Institute for Social Research returned to Germany, Marcuse remained in the USA, because, as he told me, 'my work and my friends were in this country'.[51] It is as if, having cut his ties with his Institute associates, Marcuse could return to his earlier concern with Schiller, art, play, fantasy, utopia and the other themes that would distinguish his post-Second World War work.

In the following chapters, I wish to stress theoretical-political developments in Marcuse's post-1950 works that have been frequently overlooked. Marcuse is often described as the theorist of 'one-dimensional society' and criticized for his 'pessimism' and 'rupture between theory and practice'.[52] This characterization fails to describe the complex developments in Marcuse's post-Second

World War writings and their interaction with the vicissitudes of a tumultuous historical epoch. Although Marcuse's works through *ODM* emerged from the historical situation defined by the cold war, the McCarthy era and the 'Great American celebration' (C. Wright Mills) – generally reflecting the relative stabilization of American capitalism during this period – his post-1965 writings respond to a new era of struggle and capitalist crisis. Here Marcuse again re-politicizes critical theory and goes further than any of his Institute colleagues in making critical theory an element of political practice, attempting repeatedly the integration of politics and philosophy once yearned for, but never achieved, by his colleagues. At the same time, Marcuse's works continue to respond to the 'crisis of Marxism' and seek to reconstruct the Marxian critique of capitalism and to discover new forces of radical social change in an era in which it appears that the proletariat in the advanced capitalism countries is no longer a force of revolution. In the following chapters, I shall examine closely Marcuse's major post-Second World War writings and his attempts to at once develop critical theory and reconstruct Marxism.

6

Repression and Liberation: *Eros and Civilization*

During the 1950s, in one of his most obstinately creative periods, Marcuse confronted the theoretical challenges posed by the pessimism of works like Sarte's *Being and Nothingness* and Adorno's and Horkheimer's *Dialectic of Enlightenment.* The series of defeats of the Left suffered by Marcuse since the failure of the German Revolution of 1918, the intensification of the cold war and arms race, the emergence of a form of consumer capitalism which he despised, the anti-Communist witchhunts of the McCarthy era, and his own difficult personal circumstances made Marcuse vulnerable to the pessimistic philosophical doctrines that were in the air. He did not surrender to despair, however, but set out instead to work on developing his own critical theory of contemporary society and vision of liberation through an intensive study of Freud, classical and modern literature, philosophy and aesthetics.

This project began to take shape in a series of lectures given at the Washington School of Psychiatry in 1950–1, and it eventually found expression in *Eros and Civilization* (hereafter *EC*).[1] In a 1978 interview Marcuse told me that he turned to intensive study of Freud because he was aware of the absence in Marxism of emphasis on individual liberation and the psychological dimension.[2] Marcuse claimed that he wanted to produce a theory that would explain why revolutionary consciousness had failed to develop and which could identify the subjective conditions which led individuals to conform to fascism, Stalinism and consumer capitalism. He stated that he had read Freud in the 1920s, and had also studied the Marx-Freud debates at that time, recalling articles by Siegfried Bernfeld and others. He believed that the first of Wilhelm Reich's works that he read was the *Mass Psychology of Fascism*, but did not remember reading Reich's earlier work until later. Marcuse said that he and other members of the Institute for Social Research believed that Reich 'moved too fast from subjective conditions to objective conditions' and 'vastly oversimplified' fascism in claiming that sexual repression created personalities who were susceptible to fascism, and in explaining fascism's success through its ability to manipulate repressed personalities and provide sexual surrogates. Marcuse claimed that he and his Institute colleagues thought that more adequate socio-economic analysis was needed to explain fascism, and that a more thoroughgoing mediation between subjective and objective conditions were also necessary.

Marcuse also recalled Institute debates on Freud in the 1930s, a period during which Freudian themes began to appear in his work for the first time. In 'On Hedonism', for instance, he writes:

The unpurified, unrationalized release of sexual relationships would be the strongest release of enjoyment as such and the total devaluation of labour for its own sake. No human being could tolerate the tension between labour as valuable in itself and the freedom of enjoyment. The dreariness and injustice of work conditions would penetrate explosively the consciousness of individuals and make impossible their peaceful subordination to the social system of the bourgeois world.[3]

The subversive potential of sexual desire would become a major theme in *EC* and Marcuse's subsequent work.

In the 1950s Marcuse returned to his early interests in literature and aesthetics, taking up once again the study of Schiller, the aesthetics of German Idealism, and modernist *avant-garde* literature.[4] At the same time, he began studying Fourier and utopian socialism. Marcuse sought to investigate the relation between cultural radicalism and political change, and the relation between art and liberation. He felt that Marx had neglected these themes and failed to describe the emancipatory political potential in art. Marcuse emphasized to me the continuity in these concerns with his early interest in literature and aesthetics, but insisted that he now wanted to develop these themes in the context of the Marxian revolutionary theory.[5]

Marcuse's work in *EC* responds to the crisis of revolutionary possibility in the depths of the cold war period. American capitalism was experiencing an era of expansion described by phrases like the 'affluent society' (Galbraith), the 'end of ideology' (Bell), 'the great American celebration' (Mills), and 'the consumer society'. The dominant social theories were both 'positivistic', limiting themselves for the most part to describing the 'facts', and 'affirmative', celebrating and legitimating the existing social order. Marxism too was in a rather sterile and dogmatic phase, controlled by Marxist-Leninist orthodoxy, while Social Democracy was repudiating its Marxist heritage. Possibilities for socialist revolution in the advanced capitalist countries, especially the United States where Marcuse now lived, appeared to be at a nadir. Capitalist affluence combined with anti-Communist propaganda – reinforced by McCarthyist witchhunts – were stabilizing the capitalist system to an unprecedented degree. History and the Marxian scenario for revolution no longer seemed to guarantee revolutionary possibility, and in this situation Marcuse turned to develop new perspectives on liberation and utopia. His achievement in *EC* was a resolute attempt to keep the space of emancipation open during a period that did not promise the sort of radical change envisaged earlier by Marcuse and most classical Marxists.

In the following pages I shall show how Marcuse reconstructs Freudian and Marxian theories in order to develop a critical theory of contemporary society, combined with a sketch of a non-repressive society which draws on Marx, Freud, utopian socialism, German Idealism and various poets and philosophers. We shall see how Marcuse's project went beyond Marx to envisage new possibilities for liberation in an era when revolutionary action and even critical thinking were threatened by oppressive social forces and conformist ideologies. In his resolutely utopian work, Marcuse articulates the vision of human emancipation that was to distinguish his version of critical theory. Whereas Adorno, Horkheimer and most other Institute members were reluctant to develop any detailed utopian concepts, or outlines, of an alternative society,[6] Marcuse attempted to develop a theory of emancipation and to sketch out alternatives to the present way of life. The addition of eros, art and emancipation to his Hegelian Marxist theory provided new substance to Marcuse's thought and was eventually to attract a large audience for his critical theory. He summarized the thrust of the new stage in his work in the 1964 Introduction to *Negations*: 'thought in contradiction must become more negative and more utopian in opposition to the status quo' (N, p. xx).

In the first part of *EC,* Marcuse attempts to explain why repression prevails in advanced industrial societies and to analyse the obstacles to liberation. In the second half of the book he begins developing his theory of liberation and the outlines of a non-repressive society. *EC* is arguably the seminal work of Marcuse's critical theory and establishes the foundation for much of his later work. The book contributed to serious philosophical study of Freud, showed links between Freud and Marx which had been, for the most part, previously overlooked, and introduced Marcuse to a wide academic audience. *EC* also had some impact on the counter-culture that emerged in the 1960s.[7] Although *EC* is an original and provocative book, it is often obscure and poses its social critique in the 'Aesopian' language typical of critical theory during its exile phase. Hence it requires interpretation that makes explicit what is implied or left unsaid, and which clarifies its theoretical and political importance while pointing to its shortcomings.

6.1 Civilization and its discontents: towards a critical theory of socialization and anthropology of liberation

The opening chapters of *EC* contain a critical dialogue with Freud's theory of civilization, above all *Civilization and its Discontents.*[8] Marcuse wishes to answer Freud's pessimism concerning the possibility of attaining happiness in civilization and to refute Freud's argument that a non-repressive society is impossible. For Freud, progress in civilization requires imposed labour and instinctual repression. Freud argues that unimpeded sexual gratification is incompatible with the discipline necessary in the struggle for existence, and that renunciation and delay in satisfaction is a prerequisite for progress. Happiness and sexual pleasure, Freud claims, have no cultural value and are to be subordinated to work, monogamous reproduction, moral rectitude and social restraint. On Freud's theory, culture is thus a methodical sacrifice of pleasure and is the social equivalent to repression (*EC,* pp. 3f).

Freud's analysis implies that a non-repressive civilization is impossible both because the fact of scarcity requires hard labour to ensure survival, and because human nature requires coercive law and order to keep aggressive and destructive impulses in line.[9] To counter Freud, Marcuse argues that Freud's own theory shows that socialization and repression are historically specific and subject to social transformation. Then Marcuse argues that a reading of the 'hidden trend of psychoanalysis', in conjunction with reflection on the technical-economic potential of the current society, shows that a non-repressive civilization *is* possible. In this encounter with Freud, Marcuse both uses Freud against Freud and reconstructs some of Freud's ideas to develop his own anthropology and critical theory.

Freud's distinction between the 'pleasure principle' and 'reality principle' is, in Marcuse's view, the crucial concept in Freud's metapsychology. For Freud, the instincts are originally governed by the pleasure principle: they aim solely at 'gaining pleasure; from any operation which might arouse unpleasantness ("pain") mental activity draws back' (*EC*, p. 13). From early on, however, the pleasure principle comes into conflict with a harsh environment, and after a series of disciplinary experiences, 'the individual comes to the traumatic realization that full and painless gratification of his needs is impossible' (*EC*, p. 13). Under the tutelage of the reality principle, the person learns what is useful and approved behaviour, and what is harmful and forbidden. In this way one develops one's rational faculties, becoming 'a conscious, thinking *subject*, geared to a rationality which is imposed on him from outside' (*EC*, p. 14).

Whereas, for Freud, the reality principle is represented by the ego, and the superego occupies an intermediate position between the id and external world, for Marcuse the reality principle seems to play the role of both the ego and superego in Freud's theory.[10] For Marcuse, the reality principle enforces the totality of society's requirements, norms and prohibitions which are imposed upon the individual from 'outside'. This process constitutes for him a thoroughgoing domination of the individual by society which shapes thought and behaviour, desires and needs, language and consciousness. In Marcuse's words: 'neither his desires nor his alteration of reality are henceforth his own: they are now "organized" by his society. And this "organization" represses and trans-substantiates his original instinctual needs' (*EC*, pp. 14–15).

Marcuse thus reconstructs Freud's theory in order to provide an account of how society comes to dominate the individual, how social control is internalized, and how conformity ensues. He concludes that 'Freud's individual psychology is in its very essence social psychology' (*EC*, p. 16) and repeatedly emphasizes that Freud's psychological categories are historical and political in nature.[11]

Marcuse boldly fleshes out the 'political and sociological substance of Freud's theory' to develop what I would call a *critical theory of socialization.* Whereas most theories of socialization stress its humanizing aspects by claiming that socialization makes individuals more 'human' – and thus legitimate dominant social institutions and practices[12] – Freud exposes the repressive content of Western civilization and the heavy price paid for its 'progress'. Although industrialization has resulted in material progress, Freud's analysis of the instinctual renunciations and unhappiness produced raises the question of whether our form of civilization is worth the suffering and misery (*EC*, pp. 3ff). In Marcuse's view, Freud's account of civilization and its discontents puts in question the whole ideology of progress, productivity and the work ethic, as well as religion and morality, by 'showing up the repressive content of the highest values and achievements of culture' (*EC*, p. 17).

Furthermore, Marcuse believes that there is a 'hidden trend in psychoanalysis' which discloses those aspects of human nature that oppose the dominant ethic of labour and renunciation, while upholding 'the tabooed aspirations of humanity': the demands of the pleasure principle for gratification and absence of restraint (*EC*, p. 18). He argues that Freud's instinct theory contains a 'depth dimension' which shows that our instincts strive for a condition in which freedom and happiness converge, in which we fulfil all our needs. For Marcuse, *memory* contains images of gratification and can play a cognitive and therapeutic role in mental life: 'Its truth value lies in the specific function of memory to preserve promises and potentialities which are betrayed and even outlawed by the mature, civilized individual, but which had once been fulfilled in the dim past and which are never entirely forgotten' (*EC*, pp. 18–19).[13]

Marcuse subtly reformulates the therapeutic role of memory stressed in psychoanalysis. In Freud's theory, the suppression of memory takes place through the repression of unpleasant or traumatic experiences, which are usually concerned with sexuality or aggression; the task of psychoanalysis is to free the patient from the burden of repressed, traumatic memories – whose repression often produces neurosis – by providing understanding and insight that would dissolve neurotic behaviour. Although Marcuse preserves the psychoanalytic linkage between forgetting and repression, he stresses the liberating potentialities of memory and recollection of pleasurable or euphoric experiences rather than the unpleasant or traumatic experiences stressed by Freud. In his reconstruction of Freud, Marcuse suggests that remembrance of past experiences of freedom and happiness could put in question the painful performances of alienated labour and manifold oppressions of everyday life. Marcuse's analysis implies that society trains the individual for the systematic repression of those emancipatory memories, and devalues experiences guided solely by the pleasure principle. Following Nietzsche in the *Genealogy of Morals*, Marcuse criticizes 'the one-sidedness of memory-training in civilization: the faculty was chiefly directed towards remembering duties rather than pleasures; memory was linked with bad conscience, guilt and sin. Unhappiness and the threat of punishment, not happiness and the promise of freedom, linger in the memory' (*EC*, p. 232).

Along with memory, Marcuse suggests that *phantasy* provides images of a better life by speaking the language of the pleasure principle and its demands for gratification.[14] He stresses the importance of great art for liberation because it embodies the emancipatory contents of phantasy through producing images of happiness and a life without anxiety. In Marcuse's view, the phantasies in our daydreams and hopes anticipate a better life and embody the eruption of desires for increased freedom and gratification. Marcuse concludes that Freud's theory of the unconscious provides testimony for his own earlier claim of the identity of freedom and happiness:[15]

> the unconscious, the deepest and oldest layer of the mental personality, *is* the drive for integral gratification, which is absence of want and repression. As such it is the immediate identity of necessity and freedom. According to Freud's conception, the equation of freedom and happiness tabooed by the conscious is upheld by the unconscious. (*EC*, p. 18).

The unconscious, on this account, contains the memory of integral gratification experienced in the womb or childhood, peak experiences during one's life, or, more obscurely, in the archaic memories of a historical condition without repression or fear. Marcuse holds that the 'psychoanalytic liberation of memory' and 'restoration of phantasy' provide access to memories and phantasies of happiness and freedom which are subversive of the present life. He suggests that Freud's theory of human nature, far from refuting the possibility of a non-repressive civilization, shows that there are aspects of human nature that are striving for happiness and liberation. In defending the claims of the pleasure principle, Marcuse believes that he is remaining true to a materialism which takes seriously material needs and their satisfaction, and the biological 'depth-dimension' of human nature.[16] In his view, defence of the validity of the claims of the pleasure principle has critical-revolutionary import in that, for Marcuse, Freud's analysis implies that the human being can only tolerate so much repression and unhappiness, and when this point is passed, the individual will rebel against the conditions of repression. Freud's theory thus contains elements of an *anthropology of liberation* which analyses those aspects of human nature that provide potentiality for radical opposition to the prevailing society.

Marcuse concludes that Freud's theory contains radical implications that have been covered over, or neglected, and which he wishes to restore in their most provocative form. He argues that this requires a restoration of Freud's instinct theory, preserving his emphasis on the importance of sexuality and acknowledgement of its vital and explosive claims. Neo-Freudians who deny the primacy of sexuality have, in Marcuse's view, repressed Freud's deep insights into human sexual being by relegating sexual instincts to a secondary place in their theory (*EC*, pp. 238ff). Marcuse believes that Freud's theory discloses the depth and power of instinctual energies which contain untapped emancipatory potential. He describes these instinctual energies which seek pleasure and gratification as 'Eros'.[17] A liberated Eros, Marcuse claims, would release energies that would not only seek sexual gratification, but would flow over into expanded human relations and more abundant creativity. The released Eros would desire, he suggests, a pleasurable aesthetic-erotic environment requiring a total restructuring of human life and the material conditions of existence.

Marcuse not only appropriates Freud's theory of sexuality, but takes over his theory that human nature is constituted by a conflict between the life instincts, Eros, and the destructive instincts, Thanatos. Marcuse thus accepts the most tabooed and frightening of Freud's notions: his postulation of an instinctual tendency towards destruction and aggression.[18] Although the death instinct serves to provide Freud with an explanation of such phenomena as sadism, violence and war – as well as repetition compulsions, masochism and suicide – the concept was rejected by most of

Freud's followers, including Reich, Roheim, Fromm and most neo-Freudians.[19] Furthermore, Marcuse accepts Freud's notion of the 'political economy of the instincts', which postulates a fixed quantum of psychic energy and maintains that strengthening the life instincts would increase their mastery of the death instincts. On the other hand this analysis implies that the weakening of the life instincts would diminish their power over the death instincts and would thus release destructive energies: 'Civilization plunges into a destructive dialectic: the perpetual restrictions on Eros ultimately weaken the life instincts and thus strengthen and release the very forces against which they were "called up" – those of destruction' (*EC*, p. 44; see also *EC*, p. 139). Marcuse thus suggests that a dangerous consequence of repression is that weakening the life instincts would increase aggression and violence. This analysis implies that the very survival of civilization requires reduction of repression, and strengthening the life instincts so that released instinctual energy could master and tame the death instincts.[20]

Although *EC* offers an imaginative reconstruction of Freud's metapsychology, Marcuse seems to accept aspects of the energy-instinct model that Freud took over from nineteenth-century science.[21] It is surprising to many that Marcuse accepts the biological and mechanistic elements of Freud's instinct theory, which presupposes a constant amount of instinctual energy that strives to maintain an equilibrium, as if the human organism was a thermodynamic, hydraulic system governed by the laws of the conservation of energy and inertia. Marcuse's acceptance of the biologistic elements of Freud's instinct theory was motivated, I believe, not only by the intention of supplementing the Marxian theory, but by the aim of reconstructing the Marxian anthropology to provide a new foundation for revolutionary hope in an anthropology of liberation. Since history had not provided a guarantee of revolution, Marcuse turned to *nature* to provide a foundation for revolutionary possibility. In his reading of Freud, human nature contained rebellious and creative energies which will not tolerate excessive oppression and, if liberated, could generate revolutionary struggle. In a sense, Marcuse is returning to the revolutionary perspectives of his first period, where a contradiction between human nature and capitalist society elicited 'radical action'. He also returns to his reflections on human nature and takes up again his attempt to develop a revolutionary anthropology which undercuts philosophical dichotomies between essentialism and historicism (see 3.3 above).

Although Marcuse has been criticized for essentializing human nature in *EC* and for uncritically appropriating Freud's ahistorical theory of human nature, in fact Marcuse historicizes Freud, arguing that his categories encourage socio-political development.[22] Freud's theory, as noted, enables Marcuse to explain how human beings become dominated by society and how their social character becomes a 'second nature'. This theory helps Marcuse to explain why revolutions have often failed and to criticize contemporary society by showing the price paid in freedom and happiness in becoming 'civilized' or 'socialised'. Marcuse believes that Freud's anthropology, if adequately reconstructed, can be useful for critical theory, and is therefore more 'affirmative' towards Freud than his Institute colleagues (Adorno, Fromm and Horkheimer) who began making use of Freud in their critical theories long before Marcuse.

Although Marcuse accepts Freud's instinct theory, he criticizes Freud's theory of the necessity of repression and reconstructs Freud to argue that a non-repressive society *is* possible. Marcuse sharply criticizes Freud's claim that repression is necessitated by scarcity and fixed, ahistorical instincts, resulting in an eternal conflict between the pleasure principle and the reality principle.[23] Against Freud, Marcuse argues that the reality principle takes historically specific forms, and that repression is thus a historical product of a given society. Although all societies have a reality principle and practice repression, a particular society with its own institutions and prohibitions plays the crucial role in domination and repression. In order to call attention to the specific social-historical components of repression and the reality principle in advanced industrial society, Marcuse introduces two concepts:

(a) *Surplus-repression:* the restrictions necessitated by social domination. This is distinguished from (basic) *repression*: the 'modifications' of the instincts necessary for the perpetuation of the human race in civilization.
(b) *Performance principle:* the prevailing historical form of the *reality principle.* (*EC*, p. 35)

Although Marcuse claims that these concepts are an 'extrapolation' from Freud's theory (*EC*, p. 35), they really provide a Marxian modification of Freud. For the concept 'surplus repression' was inspired by, and functions analogously to, Marx's concept of 'surplus-value', and the perfomance principle is connected with Marx's critique of capitalism and alienated labour.

Although Marx is not mentioned once in *Eros and Civilization*, many of his ideas are present, and the book can be seen as an attempt to use Freud's theory to carry through a Marxian critique of contemporary capitalism and a transvaluation of values which could be used in a project of social reconstruction. For example, rather than using the standard Marxian categories of exploitation, he uses the concepts of surplus repression and the performance principle to function as concepts critical of capitalist society. Yet Marcuse also goes beyond orthodox Marxism and uses Freud and others to add a psychological and a cultural dimension to radical social theory that is missing in orthodox Marxism. Crucially, whereas the usual interpretations of Marx and Freud at the time juxtaposed them as incompatible and contradictory to each other, Marcuse attempts to show how Freudian ideas can be used in a Marxian theory of social critique and social reconstruction. Thus Marcuse shows both how a Marxian critique can correct and radicalize Freud, and how Freud can in turn be used in developing a radical psychology, theory of socialization, and anthropology of liberation – all of which Marcuse believes a critical theory of society needed and could not discover in Marx.

6.2 Civilization and domination: Marx, Freud and critical theory

Marcuse argues that repression is not a consequence of an eternal condition of scarcity, but of 'a specific organization of scarcity, and of a specific existential attitude enforced by this organization' (*EC*, p. 35). He writes:

> The prevalent scarcity has, throughout civilization (although in very different modes) been organized in such a way that it has not been distributed collectively in accordance with individual needs, nor has the procurement of goods for the satisfaction of needs been organized with the objective of best satisfying the developing needs of the individuals. Instead, the *distribution* of scarcity as

well as the effort of overcoming it, the mode of work, have been *imposed* upon individuals – first by mere violence, subsequently by a more rational utilization of power. However, no matter how useful this rationality was for the progress of the whole, it remained the rationality of *domination*, and the gradual conquest of scarcity was inextricably bound up with and shaped by the interest of domination. (*EC*, p. 35).

Underlying this conception is Marx's notion of history as class struggle, in which a ruling class has expropriated the wealth and has forced poverty and alienated labour upon the exploited working class. Opposed to a distribution of scarcity in the interests of the dominating class is a social organization (socialism) that produces with the objective of satisfying human needs, and which distributes in accordance with individual needs (in Marx's formula, 'from each according to their abilities, to each according to their needs'). Marcuse notes that an increasing rationality has been employed in the 'distribution of scarcity', but that 'progress' is controlled by groups wishing to maintain their economic power, which has produced, in effect, 'progress in domination' (*EC*, p. 89).

A key category for Marcuse and critical theory is that of *domination*, which combines Max Weber's theory of rationalization with Marx's critique of capitalism and a Freudo-Marxist notion of repression.[24] Marcuse defines the term in 'Freedom and Freud's Theory of the Instincts': 'Domination is in effect whenever the individual's goals and purposes and the means of striving for and attaining them are prescribed to him and performed by him as something prescribed. Domination can be exercised by men, by nature, by things – it can also be internal, exercised by the individual on himself'.[25] Domination is thus a process in which society comes to control and even constitute the individual, taking both internal and external forms. Externally, domination takes place through force, social repression and institutional-systemic restraint (i.e. like police brutality, or wage-labour, through which one is forced to sell oneself on the labour market and to submit to exploitation and a repressive organization of labour in order to survive). Marcuse stresses that domination also has an internal dimension, for it involves the internalization of prohibitions, values and social demands through which the individual disciplines him- or herself, acting out internalized social roles and behaviour. Although Marcuse claims to explicate a 'depth-dimension' of appression, neglected by many Marxists, he also overcomes the overly psychological theories of repression held by many Freudians.[26] Rather, Marcuse's theory combines external and internal aspects of domination. This is evident in his description of repression, which is an important sub-category of domination. '"Repression", and "repressive" are used in the non-technical sense to designate both conscious and unconscious, external and internal processes of restraint, constraint and suppression' (*EC*, p. 8).

In Marcuse's view domination has its origins – and here he follows Marx and Weber – in the organization of labour and technology.[27] He argues that the machine-like regularities and motions in the labour process habituate individuals in advanced industrial society to submission to social authority. In this way, domination takes the form of internalizing technical imperatives and mechanical behaviour. Domination also takes place within the *administration* of social life through the mass media and entertainment industries, advertising, increased management and fragmentation of the labour process, growing socio-political control mechanisms and mobilization, and new commodities and technologies which have produced new forms of social control and a new apparatus of domination.[28] Hence domination is operative in a multitude of regions of everyday and social life. The magnitude of social domination – and the obstacles it provides to radical social change – justifies, he believes, concern with a Freudian social psychology, which would explain the internalization of domination and provide insights that could lead to its subversion and diminution, thus reversing the trends of contemporary society.

In sum, domination is a new, improved mode of social control distinguished by 'voluntary servitude' and 'happy submission', in which the individuals themselves carry out prescribed patterns of thought and behaviour. Domination constitutes the very 'second nature' of human beings who assimilate prescribed thoughts, values and forms of behaviour in which they desire, feel and think what the social powers and institutions require.[29] Domination is thus related to psychological phenomena like self-deception, mystification and false consciousness, as well as to class oppression, exploitation, and administrative control. The category 'domination' thus provides a bridge between psychological and social theory through an account of the mediations between individual and social life which socialize and control the individual. For Marcuse domination is a crucial totalizing concept that combines ideology and institutions, norms, values and social practice; culture, socioeconomic and political phenomena; social and individual psychology; and an entire technical apparatus and social system.[30]

In *EC*, Marcuse argues that the specific mode of domination and organization of labour create different social forms and institutions – even a different reality principle:

> For example, a society in which all members normally work for a living requires other modes of repression than a society in which labour is the exclusive province of one specific group. Similarly, repression will be different in scope and degree according to whether social production is oriented on individual consumption or on profit; whether a market economy prevails or a planned economy; whether private or collective property. (*EC*, p. 37)

Although Marcuse does not make this explicit, he is in effect contrasting capitalism with socialism. Moreover, he argues that while every social organization requires some repression to provide the necessities of life, certain

> specific historical institutions of the reality principle and the specific interests of domination introduce *additional* controls over and above those indispensable for civilized human association. These additional controls arising from the specific institutions of domination are what we denote as *surplus repression*. (*EC*, p. 37)

Hence, against Freud, Marcuse argues that a specific reality principle and institutions in our society demand repression over and above what is rationally needed to provide for social and individual needs.[31]

As examples of surplus repression, Marcuse suggests 'the modifications and deflections of instinctual energy necessitated by the perpetuation of the monogamic-patriarchal family, or by a hierarchical division of labour, or by public control over the individual's private existence' (*EC*, pp. 37–8). Marcuse suggests that in order to ensure conformity to the requirements of the labour system, there was a desexualization of the body and a 'subduing of the proximity senses' (*EC*, pp. 38–9). Restrictions were put on sexuality, and sexual activity was put in the service of reproduction. Certain sexual acts, like oral or anal sex and homosexuality, which did not serve reproduction, were tabooed. Further, sex was channelled into 'monogamic reproduction' within the structure of the family. Pre- and extra-marital sex were also prohibited.

This organization results in a quantitative and qualitative restriction of sexuality: the unification of the partial instincts and their subjugation under the procreative function alter the very nature of sexuality: from an autonomous 'principle' governing the entire organism it is turned into a specialized temporary function, into a means for an end. In terms of the pleasure principle governing the 'unorganized' sex instincts, reproduction is merely a 'by- product'. The primary content of sexuality is 'the function of obtaining pleasure from zones of the body'; this function is only 'subsequently brought into the service of that of reproduction'. (*EC*, p. 41)

Under a repressive organization of sexuality, gratification as such, pleasure for the sake of pleasure, is taboo and 'remains the ill- reputed privilege of whores, degenerates and perverts' (*EC*, p. 201). For this reason, Marcuse thinks the so-called 'perversions' express rebellion and 'uphold sexuality as an end in itself' (*EC*, p. 50).

The specific reality principle that governs behaviour and creates surplus repression in contemporary society is the *performance principle:* 'under its rule society is stratified according to the competitive economic performances of its members' (*EC*, p. 44). The performance principle 'is that of an acquisitive and antagonistic society' (*EC*, p. 45) in which domination is perpetuated by a ruling class. It is related to what Max Weber called the 'spirit of capitalism', or what is today called the 'work ethic'.[32] It also suggests a role-stratified society in which one performs according to pre-established norms and rules, thus conforming to social roles and behaviour. In a society of increasing social control, all aspects of life – labour, leisure, even sexuality – are directed by the dictates of the performance principle. But the realm in which it inflicts its heaviest damage and makes its severest demands is the realm of *labour*:

For the vast majority of the population, the scope and mode of satisfaction are determined by their own labour; but their labour is work for an apparatus which they do not control, which operates as an independent power to which individuals must submit if they want to live. And it becomes the more alien the more specialized the division of labour becomes. Men do not live their own lives but perform pre-established functions. While they work, they do not fulfil their own needs and faculties but work in *alienation.* Work has now become *general,* and so have the restrictions placed upon the libido: labour time, which is the largest part of the individual's life time, is painful time, for alienated labour is absence of gratification, negation of the pleasure principle. Libido is diverted for socially useful performances in which the individual works for himself only in so far as he works for the apparatus, engaged in activities that mostly do not coincide with his own faculties and desires. (*EC,* p. 45)

In Marcuse's account, 'alienation' is rooted in the organization of labour which he describes in terms of Marx's concept of alienated labour and Freud's theory of repression. In addition to the inhumanity and exploitation in labour relations stressed by Marx, Marcuse points to the pain, the restriction on erotic energies and the absence of gratification in alienated labour. This analysis suggests that alienated labour, demanded by a historically specific performance principle, is an important constituent of surplus repression. Marcuse adds a psychological dimension to Marx's analysis by arguing that under the rule of the performance principle, alienation enters consciousness and permeates body and mind, actions and thought (*EC,* p. 45). In this way, the alienated labour of capitalist society becomes a duty that the individual willingly performs, since it has introjected alien prescriptions which require certain labour performances and instinctual renunciation, thus subjecting the individual to discipline from without and within. The superego stands ready to punish anyone who transgresses the performance principle.

The result of this subjection of the pleasure principle to the reality principle in a system of alienated labour is disastrous for the individual. As Marcuse ironically puts it, the human being under the rule of the performance principle exists part-time. During the working day one is an instrument of alienated labour; at home one is 'free'. But since the pleasure principle's demand for gratification is so powerful, a society governed by the performance principle must even manipulate one's free time. People must be conditioned to 'forget the claim for timeless and useless gratification, for the "eternity of pleasure"' (*EC*, p. 47). For if individuals are allowed to experience too much pleasure outside work, or have too much time to question their alienated existence, they might perhaps revolt and cause trouble, or drop out of the system. The hours of the working day are therefore long and exhausting to ensure that leisure time will be 'a passive relaxation and a re-creation of energy for work' (*EC*, p. 48). Furthermore, leisure time is subjected to the manipulation of the mass media and entertainment industries, which directly control free time and socialize the individual into accepting the society's institutions, ideology and way of life. Marcuse refers here to the function of the media to reduce individuals to captive passivity and indoctrinate them with the dominant ideology.[33] Thus at home and at work the system enforces its domination of the individual.

Surplus repression, we have seen, is present in factories and offices, bedrooms and living rooms, and the public and private spheres. Marcuse's concept of surplus repression provides aspects of a critical theory of socialization that rejects the existing labour system, social institutions and values, while also calling for a socio-economic organization that would abolish surplus repression. Since repression in Marcuse's interpretation is a product of particular historical institutions and a specific social-economic system and reality principle, Marcuse believes that it can be diminished by social-economic-ideological changes that abolish the sources of surplus repression. Consequently, against Freud, Marcuse believes that a non-repressive civilization is possible.

The more viable the possibility of eliminating alienated labour and surplus repression, the more rigid, Marcuse believes, is the opposition of the system to radical social-economic change. To contain the possibility of emancipation and to maintain the status quo, the society becomes increasingly totalitarian, establishing new forms of social control. Marcuse's analysis of the totalitarianism of a system of domination and administration, the manipulation of consciousness and desire, and the alienation and destruction of the individual, are only foreshadowed in *EC*, pp. 89–105; they are developed in his later writings.

Although Marcuse's indictment of advanced industrial society is total, the situation is not (yet) hopeless in his diagnosis. The most salient feature of the present society, he claims, is the 'discrepancy between potential liberation and actual repression' (*EC*, p. 101). He believes that enough social wealth and available resources are on hand to overcome scarcity in the distribution of recourses, and that the conditions are present which would permit society to reduce repression and abolish alienated labour. In his view, technology makes possible a reduction of alienated labour and at the same time renders repression superfluous by mechanizing labour and minimizing the time necessary to perform painful toil and routine tasks. But prevailing interests of domination militate against a rational use of technology and use it instead as a means for improved social control and domination, rather than as an instrument of liberation (*EC*, pp. 93f).

6.3 The roads to liberation

After analysis of the obstacles to liberation in his theory of civilization and domination, in the second half of *EC* Marcuse discusses prospects for liberation. Marcuse is responding here to cultural pessimism generated by theories of Freud, Weber and his critical theory colleagues, and the failure of the Marxian theory of revolution and socialism to produce what he took to be an emancipated society. *EC* appeared during a decade when pessimistic cultural philosophies were widespread in intellectual circles, and when social scientists declared the end of ideology, which meant the end of utopian-revolutionary projects of social reconstruction. In this climate of cultural despair among Left intellectuals and conformity among dominant social theorists, Marcuse turned to study and defend the most radical ideas in the Western cultural heritage. The second half of *EC* contains sketches of Marcuse's utopian philosphy and outlines of his notion of a non-repressive civilization, which directly counter theories that were rejecting such radical and utopian projects.

   Looking at *EC* as a whole, Marcuse uses Marx, Freud and critical theory in the first half of the book to analyse obstacles to liberation and to show the price paid in human happiness for the 'benefits' of contemporary civilization. It is as if only by confronting the forces of domination and repression without illusion does the necessity for liberation and radical social change emerge. Freud is especially useful for this project, for not only does he point to the depths of pain and suffering in human existence, but he also reveals the deep-rooted psychic and somatic possibilities for liberation. It is as if in the depths of suffering, Marcuse finds new hope for overcoming pain and misery through creating new forms of happiness and freedom.

Marcuse finds testimony to the hope of liberation not only in Freud's instinct theory, but in great art, utopian social theory, and philosophy. Refusing to capitulate to repressive social forces, Marcuse sketches out a concept of a non-repressive civilization. The utopian element, which finds its first sustained expression in *EC*, was influenced by Marcuse's reading of the utopian Marxist, Ernst Bloch.[34] To realize the promises of the technological society, Marcuse argues that repression and alienation, which he sees as a product of the current forms of socio-economic organization, can only be overcome through abolishing the present society and creating a new one. To carry through the project of liberation, such a non-repressive civilzation requires a new reality principle, liberated human beings and radical social reconstruction. The following pages will elucidate these components of Marcuse's theory.

6.3.1 *The new reality principle*

In a 'Philosophical Interlude' (*EC*, pp. 106ff) Marcuse carries out a philosophical analysis of the presuppositions of Western rationality. He claims that the prevalent reality principle of Western civilization presupposes an antagonism between subject and object, reason and the passions, and the individual and society. Nature is experienced on this basis as raw material to be mastered, as an object of domination, as provocation or resistance to be overpowered (*EC*, p. 110). The ego in Western thought is thus conceptualized as an aggressive, offensive subject, fighting and striving to conquer the resistant world. Through labour, the subject seeks continually to extend its power and control over nature. The Logos of this reality principle is, Marcuse argues, a logic of domination that finds its culmination in the reality principle of advanced industrial society, the performance principle. The performance principle is hostile to the senses and receptive faculties that strive for gratification and fulfilment. In contains a concept of repressive reason which seeks to tame instinctual drives for pleasure and enjoyment. Its values, which are the governing values of capitalist societies and bureaucratic Communist societies, include:

> profitable productivity, assertiveness, efficiency, competitiveness; in other words, the Performance Principle, the rule of functional rationality discriminating against emotions, a dual morality, the 'work ethic', which means for the vast majority of the population condemnation to alienated and inhuman labour, and the will to power, the display of strength, virility.[35]

This hegemonic version of the reality principle has been challenged, Marcuse argues, from the beginning of Western philosphy. Against the antagonistic struggle between subject and object, an opposing ideal of reconciliation and harmony has been formulated, in which the subject strives for fulfilment and gratification. This 'Logos of gratification', Marcuse suggests, is found in Aristotle's concept of the *nous theos* (*EC*, p. 112) and Hegel's ideal of the subject coming to fruition in absolute knowledge. In these philosphical conceptions, the subject is to attain a condition of reconciliation after a process of struggle, suffering and labour, in which alienation is finally overcome. Schopenhauer advocates a similar idea of the restless, ever-striving will seeking peaceful Nirvana (*EC*, p. 119). Marcuse also finds the logic of gratification in Nietzsche's stress on the body, the passions, joy and liberation from time and guilt (*EC*, pp. 119–24). These conceptions have in common an ideal of gratification as the highest state of being which Marcuse argues is a 'total affirmation of the life instincts', and an 'erotic attitude towards being' (*EC*, p. 112). The values affirmed in this reality principle would be the antithesis of the repressive performance principle and would stress 'receptivity, sensitivity, non-violence, tenderness, and so on. These characteristics appear indeed as opposites of domination and exploitation. On the primary psychological level, they would pertain to the domain of Eros, they would express the energy of the life instincts, against the death instinct and destructive energy'.[36]

   This alternative reality principle also finds expression in Freud's notion of the Nirvana principle, which holds that all instincts aim at rest, quiescence and the absence of pain (cf. *EC*, pp. 25ff, 124ff). In fact, Marcuse wishes to use the Nirvana principle to help produce a new reality principle that would overcome the conflict between the pleasure principle and reality principle by eliminating the antagonisms which have caused so much suffering and misery in Western civilization. Marcuse believes that this new reality principle would serve the interests of individual gratification and fulfilment and not repression and domination. The new reality principle would aim at reconciliation between nature, society and humanity.[37] By its allegiance to the logic of gratification, it would realize the hidden ideal of Western civilization found in certain philosphers and poets in the tradition that were especially cherished by Marcuse.

6.3.2 *Phantasy, art and play*

Marcuse believes that the outlines of a new reality principle are found in the images of phantasy and its aesthetic embodiments, and in turn he grounds his high evaluation of phantasy and art in Freud's instinct theory. For Freud, phantasy is the one mental activity that is free from domination by the reality principle, and thus is in intimate contact with the unconscious.[38] Phantasy 'speaks the language of the pleasure principle', and preserves and expresses the 'tabooed images of freedom' and gratification (*EC*, pp. 141ff). Art is thus the 'most visible "return of the repressed"' (*EC*, p. 144). All authentic art for Marcuse aims at 'the negation of unfreedom' (*EC*, p. 144) and expresses a demand for liberation. The truth value of its images relate not only to the past, but to the future, for authentic art refuses to accept the 'limitations imposed upon freedom and happiness by the reality principle' (*EC*, p. 149). Such art is thus a vehicle of the Great Refusal: 'This Great Refusal is the protest against unnecessary repression, the struggle for the ultimate form of freedom – "to live without anxiety"'.[39]

Phantasy and emancipatory art aim at surmounting an antagonistic reality and overcoming repression: 'Imagination envisions the reconciliation of the individual with the whole, of desire with realization, of happiness with reason' (*EC*, p. 143). Moreover, Marcuse argues that phantasy 'aims at an "erotic reality where the life instincts would come to rest in fulfilment without repression"' (*EC*, p. 146). Thus art in its highest potentialities, like critical theory, is a protest against the existing order, a refusal to conform to its repression and domination, a projection of alternatives and, at least in the case of the surrealists (*EC*, p. 145), a demand that they be realized.

Examples of the archetypal images of liberation which Marcuse interprets as symbols of the new reality principle are Orpheus and Narcissus. These poetic figures express an experience of being which embodies an alternative reality principle.[40]

> Phantasy is cognitive in so far as it preserves the truth of the Great Refusal, or positively, in so far as it protects, against all reason, the aspirations for the integral fulfilment of man and nature that are repressed by reason. In the realm of phantasy, the unreasonable images of freedom become rational, and the 'lower depth' of instinctual gratification assumes a new dignity. The culture of the performance principle makes its bow before the strange truths which imgaination keeps alive in folklore and fairy tale, in literature and art'. (*EC*, p. 160)

Marcuse opposes Orpheus and Narcissus, archetypes of the Nirvana principle, to Prometheus, the hero of the performance principle (*EC*, p. 161).[41] He argues that they stand for a reality principle opposed to Promethean productivity, toil and progress through repression. Orpheus and Narcissus are the 'image of joy and fulfilment; the voice which does not command but sings; the gesture which offers and receives; the deed which is peace and ends the labour of conquest; the liberation from time which unites man with god, man with nature' (*EC*, p. 162). Citing poets such as Hesiod, Rilke, Gide and Valéry, Marcuse shows how these archetypes of gratification symbolize a new reality principle through their 'revolt against culture based on toil, domination and renunciation' (*EC*, p. 164). They symbolize an ideal of released (and not repressed) Eros, a state of peace and beauty, a redemption of pleasure and halt of time: 'silence, sleep, night, paradise – the Nirvana principle not as death but as life' (*EC*, p. 164). In Baudelaire's words,

> 'There all is order and beauty
> Luxury, calm, and sensuousness.' (*EC*, p. 164)

Such a reality principle would demand 'the order of gratification' and previews Marcuse's later view that reality should be aesthetically transformed, that a new merger of technology and art would create an aestheticized environment. Marcuse's vision of a non-repressive civilization reveals him as a romantic revolutionary.[42] His ideal of a non-repressive civilization finds its most sustained and poignant expression in *EC* in the image of a life without toil, anxiety and misery. His revolutionary romanticism is expressed in his account of Orpheus and Narcissus as the symbolical bearers of a new reality principle.

Narcissus for Marcuse symbolizes a non-repressive sublimation, a diffusion of sexuality throughout one's activites. The 'narcissism' symbolized is not the autoeroticism that withdraws from reality, but what Freud described as '"a feeling which embraced the universe and expressed an inseparable connection of the ego with the external world"' (*EC*, p. 168). The liberation of Eros symbolized here makes possible a 'oneness with the universe', a 'refusal to accept separation from the libidinous object (or subject)' that 'aims at liberation – at the reunion of what has become separated' (*EC*, p. 170). There are echoes here of the Hegelian notion that the liberated subject finds itself in the world, seeking a fusion of self and other in order to overcome alienation and to achieve reconciliation with the world.

Orpheus, on the other hand, symbolizes a non-repressive creativity. He is the 'archetype of the poet as liberator and creator' (*EC*, p. 170), whose songs and music represent the values of pacification, gratification and harmony. Orpheus, like Narcissus, 'protests against the repressive order of procreative sexuality' (*EC*, p. 171), and through his songs produces images of liberation and a non-repressive civilization: 'The Orphic Eros transforms being: he masters cruelty and death through liberation. His language is *song*, and his work is *play*. Narcissus's life is that of *beauty* and his existence is contemplation' (*EC*, p. 171).

Marcuse defends this utopian conception by arguing that the implementation of its ideals have become increasingly realistic. He hints that a 'turning point' in civilization is at hand where, building on the accomplishments of past civilizations, the human species can for the first time create a reality that overcomes scarcity, repression and alienated labour. Marcuse argues that such a state is hypothetically possible, and that the present civilization based on the performance principle is in fact obsolescent (*EC*, pp. 150ff), given the present level of technological development and amount of social wealth, which could make possible a good life for everyone if it was more rationally utilized and equably distributed.

Although in order to realize this ideal some material comforts might have to be sacrificed, the reconciliation between pleasure and reality principle does not depend on the existence of abundance for all. The only pertinent question is whether a state of civilization can be reasonably envisaged in which human needs are fulfilled in such a manner and to such an extent that surplus repression can be eliminated. (*EC*, p. 151)

Marcuse argues that such a non-repressive civilization *can* be envisaged, based on a 'non-oppressive distribution of scarcity' and a 'rational organization of fully developed industrial society after the conquest of scarcity' (*EC*, p. 152). These pre-conditions (which presuppose radical social-economic transformation) would make possible 'the prevalent satisfaction of basic human needs' by overcoming surplus repression and by abolishing alienated labour: 'This satisfaction would be (and this is the important point) *without toil* – that is, without the rule of alienated labour over human existence' (*EC*, p. 152). The crucial point is that the conditions are in fact present to abolish alienated labour: 'Under the "ideal" conditions of mature industrial civilization, alienation would be completed by general automatization of labour, reduction of labour time to a minimum, and exchangeability of functions' (*EC*, p. 152). Marcuse concludes that the very technical-industrial condtions which helped produce alienation have developed the forces of production to the point where alienated labour and social repression could conceivably be reduced and eventually eliminated.

The beginning of the reduction of surplus repression and alienated labour would be the reduction of the length of the working day (persistently demanded by Marx in the same context). This might mean a decrease in the standard of living for some, but the good life would be measured by other criteria than the amassment of consumer goods: 'the universal gratification of basic human needs, and the freedom from guilt and fear' (*EC*, p. 153). In Baudelaire's words: 'True civilization does not lie in gas, nor in steam, nor in conveyer belts. It lies in the reduction of the traces of original sin' (*EC*, p. 153), i.e. in the reduction of guilt brought about by a harsh superego which has internalized the demands of surplus repression and instinctual renunciation and punishes itself with guilt when it transgresses the demands. In a non-repressive civilization, a minimum of time and energy would be spent upon 'necessary labour', and the amount of free time would be expanded to fulfil human needs: 'Eros, the life instincts, would be released to an

unprecedented degree' (*EC*, p. 154). Marcuse claims that the released Eros would evolve 'new and durable work relations', new
social relations and a new erotic reality. This non-repressive civilization would transform

> the human existence in its entirety, including the work world and
> the struggle with nature . . . The struggle for existence then
> proceeds on new grounds and with new objectives: it turns into
> the concerted struggle against any constraint on the free play of
> human faculties, against toil, disease and death. (*EC*, p. 157)

This transformation presupposes a reversal between working time
and free time, or labour and play. Today's reality principle (the
performance principle) is derived from the sphere of alienated
labour and urges productivity, hard work, efficiency, profitable and
competitive performance as its ideal. In this way, the working day
dominates both one's life and leisure and renders one a slave of
alienated labour. The new reality principle is derived from free-
time activity and advocates the release of 'time and energy for the
free play of human faculties *outside* the realm of alienated labour'
(*EC*, p. 156). The basis of the non-repressive civilization would thus
be the free satisfaction of human needs and the development of
human potentialities – as Marx envisaged in his *Economic and
Philosophical Manuscripts*.

The notion of aesthetic education and the transformation of work
into play as the basis of a new civilization was the cultural ideal of
Schiller (*EC*, pp. 180ff).[43] After initial enthusiasm for the French
Revolution, Schiller was horrified by the Reign of Terror and
sketched the outlines of an aesthetic culture in his *Letters on the
Aesthetic Education of Man*.[44] In a non-repressive civilization, the
conflict between reason and the senses would be overcome, so that
'reason is sensuous and sensuousness rational' (*EC*, p. 180).
Operating through the play impulse, 'the aesthetic function would
"abolish compulsion, and place man, both morally and physically,
in freedom". It would harmonize the feelings and affections with
the ideas of reason, deprive the "laws of reason of their moral
compulsion" and "reconcile them with the interest of the senses"'
(*EC*, p. 182). This concept of the aesthetic function preserves the
connotation of *Sinnlichkeit* as pertaining to sensuality, sense-

cognition and art, and defends its important role in human life, redeeming the senses against the tryanny of repressive reason.

In Marcuse's reading, Schiller calls, for a new aesthetic culture that could be a formative influence in reshaping civilization. Schiller connected the aesthetic function with the play impulse which, in turn, would mediate between the passive, receptive 'sensuous impulse' and the active, creative 'form impulse', thus reconciling reason and the senses. The objective of the play impulse is beauty, and its goal is freedom (*EC*, p. 187). The play impulse aspires to a condition of freedom from restraint and anxiety, involving 'freedom from the established reality: man is free when the "reality loses its seriousness" and when its necessity "becomes light" ' (*EC*, p. 187). This 'freedom to play' and to create an 'aesthetic reality' requires liberation of the senses and a ' "total revolution in the mode of perception and feeling" ' (*EC*, p. 189).

In his discussion of Schiller, Marcuse proposes a new concept of reason which he describes as 'libidinal rationality' (*EC*, pp. 223ff). In this conception, reason is not repressive of the senses but acts in harmony with them, helping to find objects of gratification and to cultivate and enhance sensuality.[45] Marcuse rejects the dominant philosophical paradigm, which sees reason as the distinctly human faculty and the senses as disorderly, animalic, and inferior. The concept of reason operative in this model, Marcuse suggests, is repressive and totalitarian and does not adequately allow for aesthetic-erotic gratification and development (*EC*, pp. 119ff). Marcuse's ideal is a form of human life in which reason becomes sensuous, protecting and enriching the life instincts, and whereby the senses help create a 'sensuous order' (*EC*, pp. 223ff). He assumes that as more restrictions are taken away from the instincts and as they freely evolve, they will seek '*lasting* gratification' and will structure relations that will make continual gratification possible. In this way, 'Eros redefines reason in his own terms. Reasonable is what sustains the order of gratification' (*EC*, p. 224). This could make possible freer, more fulfilling human relations and could create a social order and community based on freedom, gratification, co-operation and rational authority. Then, 'repressive reason gives way to a new *rationality of gratification* in which reason and happinesss converge' (*EC*, p. 224).

Just as Marcuse now grounds revolutionary possibility in human nature, so too does he reconstruct reason and root rationality in nature. Previously, reason for Marcuse was the principle of bourgeois enlightenment and individual autonomy that *transcended* nature, creating a sphere of freedom that was the highest refuge of truth and selfhood. Perhaps Marcuse was persuaded by the arguments of *Dialectic of Enlightenment* that reason had turned into an instrument of oppression and that the rationalist project had been rendered ineffective by the technological rationality (and reality!) that absorbed reason into the rationality of domination. Marcuse could not accept, however, the political dead-end that Adorno and Horkheimer had reached, nor could he accept either traditional forms of rationalism or irrationalism. Thus, he sought a new ontological foundation for reason and revolution in nature that would obliterate ontological dualisms between nature and history, the individual and society, and the 'rational' and 'irrational'. Such a foundation he discovered in Freud's instinct theory and in Schiller's merging of the senses and reason which overcame the antagonism postulated by Kant and others. This project would lead to new perspectives on liberation that would stress the primary importance of human needs and gratification. Such an ideal of liberation would supplement traditional Marxian calls to end exploitation and injustice, and could lead to a more emancipatory concept of socialism as a new way of life – ideas which Marcuse developed further in the 1960s and which will be the focus of Chapter 10.

Ending the conflict between reason and gratification could only be possible, Marcuse believed, in a non-repressive society with a new reality principle. Although some conflict between reason and instinct will remain – if only because sexual desire is non-reciprocal and some may refuse sexual advances of desiring subjects – Marcuse suggests that truly free individuals would be capable of self-regulation and harmonious relations with others (*EC*, pp. 226ff). He even suggests that there might be elements within instinctual life itself which would defer and postpone immediate gratification, if only in the interests of more intense and enhanced pleasure later (*EC*, pp. 226–7). In such a situation, free individuals choose and determine their own pleasures, and 'really exist as individuals, each shaping his own life; they would face each other with truly different needs and truly different modes of satisfaction – with their own refusals and their own selection' (*EC*, pp. 227–8).

Marcuse's concept of 'libidinal rationality' presupposes that human beings instinctively seek pleasure, and assumes a creative

potential to seek self-fulfilment and build a non-repressive civilization. Schiller's merger of the senses and reason is combined in this
ideal with a Hegelian drive to reconcile opposites and to overcome
oppositions. Marcuse believes that 'the idealistic and the materialis-
tic critiques of culture meet' in the dual emphasis on creating an
order of abundance and freedom while eliminating surplus repression and alienated labour. (*EC*, p. 194). Further, 'Both agree that
non-repressive order becomes possible only at the highest maturity
of civilization, when all basic needs can be satisfied with a minimum
expenditure of physical and mental energy in a minimum of time.
Rejecting the notion of freedom which pertains to the rule of the
performance principle, they reserve freedom for the new mode of
existence that would emerge on the basis of universally gratified
existence-needs' (*EC*, pp. 194–5).

6.3.3 *Eros released*

Marcuse argues that a shortening of the working day and minimizing the need for repressive labour would release erotic energies that
would render obsolete restrictions on sexuality. He argues that
surplus repression could be abolished if the division of labour were
'reoriented on the gratification of freely developing individual
needs' (*EC*, p. 201). Since the body would no longer be merely an
instrument of labour, it could be resexualized. This liberation of
Eros would

> first manifest itself in a resurgence of pre-genital polymorphous
> sexuality and in a decline of genital supremacy. The body in its
> entirety would become an object of cathexis, a thing to be
> enjoyed – an instrument of pleasure. This change in the value and
> scope of libidinal relations would lead to a disintegration of the
> institutions in which the private interpersonal relations have been
> organized, particularly the monogamic and patriarchal family.
> (*EC*, p. 201)

The suggestion that polymorphic sexuality would lead to a disintegration of the bourgeois family is a radical one, but Marcuse does not
develop this suggestion; he argues that such a release of sexuality
will not lead to a 'society of sex maniacs', but to a '*transformation* of
the libido: from sexuality constrained under genital supremacy to

eroticization of the entire personality' (*EC*, p. 201). He stresses that this transformation of sexuality would be a result of radical social change (*EC*, pp. 202f), and would lead to a defusion of sexuality rather than an explosion. Within a repressive society, a sudden release of suppressed sexuality might lead to an orgy of sex mania, but in a non-repressive society, Marcuse argues, sexual energy could be channelled into creating eroticized personalities, non-repressive institutions, and an aesthetic-erotic environment. Moreover,

> In contrast, the free development of transformed libido within transformed institutions, while eroticizing previously tabooed zones, time and relations, would *minimize* the manifestations of *mere* sexuality by integrating them into a far larger order, including the order of work. In this context, sexuality tends to its own sublimation: the libido would not simply reactivate pre-civilized and infantile stages but would also transform the perverted content of these stages. (*EC*, p. 202).

Alasdair MacIntyre complains that it is not clear what, if any, transformations of sexual practice Marcuse is advocating.[46] MacIntyre is not sure whether Marcuse is arguing that 'perversions' would be allowed or whether they would disappear in a non-repressive civilization. Marcuse mentions coprophilia and homosexuality, but rather than endorsing or condemning these practices, he suggests that in a non-repressive civilization they may well take 'other forms compatible with normality in high civilization' (*EC*, p. 203). When discussing the reactivation of 'childhood wishes' and polymorphic sexuality, Marcuse asks if this would include the Oedipal wish for intercourse with one's parents, and quickly concludes that such a desire 'naturally' passes away and would probably not be operative in mature sexuality (*EC*, p. 204).

While Marcuse seems to argue that the 'perversions' would 'pass away' or 'not be operative', Wilhelm Reich argues that in a non-repressive civilization all the so-called 'perversions' would simply disappear:

> The healthy individual has no compulsive morality because he has no impulses which call for moral inhibition ... Intercourse with a prostitute becomes impossible. Sadistic phantasies disappear. To expect love as a right or even to rape the sexual partner

becomes inconceivable, as do ideas of seducing children. Anal, exhibitionistic or other perversions disappear, and with these the social anxiety and guilt feelings. The incestuous fixation to parents and siblings loses its interest; this liberates the energy which was bound up in such fixations. In brief, all these phenomena point to the fact that the organism is capable of *self-regulation*.[47]

Reich championed sexual revolution and increased orgasmic potency as the key to human happiness and health. Both Marcuse and Reich believe that reducing sexual restrictions would release energies that would make possible increased happiness, culture and creative work. But Reich focused on the primacy of genital sex, believing that orgasm was the supreme good. Reich's programme of sexual liberation was criticized by Marcuse as a 'mere release of sexuality', which would indicate that Marcuse is not advocating more and better orgasms, but rather a liberated Eros that would express itself in a variety of ways. Marcuse argues: 'sexual liberation per se becomes for Reich a panacea for individual and social ill. The problem of sublimation is minimized; no essential distinction is made between repressive and non-repressive sublimation, and progress in freedom appears as a mere release of sexuality' (*EC*, p. 239).[48] Against Reich, Marcuse argues that in a non-repressive civilization sexuality would take other forms besides sexual intercourse. He claims that although sublimation deflects sexual energy into non-sexual ends in a repressive society, in a liberated society sublimation could be a non-repressive activity that could eroticize one's social relations and work relations, suggesting the possibility of a *non-repressive sublimation*.[49] Against Freud, Marcuse believes that instinctual liberation would not cause chaos or disorder but could create a libidinal order that would enhance and gratify human life. A released Eros would not only resexualize the body, but would also eroticize reason.[50] Hence, rather than suppressing the passions, reason could seek their gratification and could produce a libidinal order wherein erotic-aesthetic needs could be fulfilled. Although Freud, Reich and Marcuse agree in urging that we change our concept of sex from an activity 'in the service of reproduction to sexuality in the "function of obtaining pleasure from zones of the body"' (*EC*, p. 205), Marcuse proposes an enlargement of the sphere of sexuality such that sexual energies be channelled into social relations, work and creating culture.

While Reich's theory can be interpreted as a programme of

sexual therapy to increase sexual pleasure within the existing society, Marcuse is proposing thoroughgoing social change, and argues
that the full potentiality of Eros can only be released as part of a
process of social transformation. As an isolated individual act,
released polymorphic sexuality might lead to merely individualistic
pleasure that strengthens the existing repressive society; consequently, an emancipatory release of Eros 'must be a supraindividual
process on common ground' (*EC*, p. 209). For Marcuse:

> Libido can take the road of self-sublimation only as a *social*
> phenomenon: as an unrepressed force, it can promote the forma-
> tion of culture only under conditions which relate associated
> individuals to each other in the cultivation of the environment for
> their developing needs and faculties. Reactivation of polymorph-
> ous and narcissistic sexuality ceases to be a threat to culture and
> can itself lead to culture-building if the organism exists not as an
> instrument of alienated labour but as a subject of self-realization
> – in other words, if socially useful work is at the same time the
> transparent satisfaction of an individual need. In primitive society
> this organization of work may be immediate and 'natural': in
> mature civilization it can be envisaged only as the result of
> liberation. Under such conditions, the impulse to 'obtain pleasure
> from the zones of the body' may extend to seek its objective in
> lasting and expanding libidinal relations because this expansion
> increases and intensifies the instinct's gratification. (*EC*,
> pp. 209–10).

Marcuse proposes releasing Eros in a non-repressive civilization in
which all erotic energies would freely flow into a non-antagonistic
continuum of sexual gratification, affectionate interpersonal relationships, play and creative work. The point to be stressed is the
interconnection of instinctual and socio-cultural transformation
that Marcuse is projecting. He is clearly not simply calling for a
merely sexual or solely anthropological revolution, for he argues
that such a non-repressive transformation of sexuality into Eros,
and total individual emancipation can only take place in a transformed society. But he also argues that an effective revolution in the
economic, social and political sphere presupposes, and must be
accompanied by, a transformation of values, consciousness and
culture. Thus Marcuse is calling for a continual total revolution that

would simultaneously alter work and social relations, and would involve a new experience of the world based on a new reality principle. Marcuse's synthesis of Marx, Freud and German Idealism comes out in the following passage:

> In the light of the idea of non-repressive sublimation, Freud's definition of Eros as striving to 'form substance into ever greater unities, so that life may be prolonged and brought to higher development', takes on added significance. The biological drive becomes a cultural drive. The pleasure principle reveals its own dialectic. The erotic aim of sustaining the entire body as a subject-object of pleasure calls for the continual refinement of the organism, the intensification of its receptivity, the growth of its sensuousness. The aim generates its own projects of realization: the abolition of toil, the amelioration of the environment, the conquest of disease and decay, the creation of luxury. All these activities flow directly from the pleasure principle, and, at the same time, they constitute *work*, which associates individuals to 'greater unities'; no longer confined within the mutilating domain of the performance principle, they modify the impulse without deflecting it from its aim. There is sublimation and, consequently, culture: but this sublimation proceeds in a system of expanding and enduring libidinal relations, which are in themselves work relations. (*EC*, pp. 211–12).

Marcuse suggests that 'libidinal work relations' and non-alienated labour are possible only as a result of social revolution by evoking the witness of the utopian socialist, Fourier:[51] 'Fourier insists that this transformation requires a complete change in the social institutions: distribution of the social product according to need, assignment of functions according to individual faculties and inclinations, constant mutation of functions, short work periods, and so on' (*EC*, p. 217). Marcuse is obviously attracted to a non-ascetic socialism which would go far beyond solely redistributing wealth and setting up a 'dictatorship of the proletariat'. For he envisages the development of a non-repressive, aesthetic-social order that would satisfy all the individual's needs for food, shelter, beauty, love, friendship, security and happiness. He quotes approvingly Fourier's objectives: 'the creation of "luxury, or the pleasure of the five senses"; the formation of libidinal groups (of friendship and love); and the establishment of a harmonious order, organizing these groups for work in accordance with the development of the individual "passions" (internal and external "play" of faculties)' (*EC*, pp. 217–18). But he then criticizes Fourier's handing over of the administration of this social organization to a 'giant organization', since this perpetuates repressive elements of the previous social order. Marcuse's opposition to bureaucratic socialism discloses itself in his critique of Fourier's administrative apparatus:

> Fourier comes closer than any other utopian socialist to elucidating the dependence of freedom on non-repressive sublimation. However, in his detailed blueprint for the realization of this idea, he hands it over to a giant organization and administration and thus retains the repressive elements. The working communities of the *phalanstère* anticipate 'strength through joy' rather than freedom, the beautification of mass culture rather than its abolition. Work as free play cannot be subject to administration: only alienated labour can be organized and administered by rational routine. (*EC*, p. 218)

In the concluding chapter on 'Eros and Thanatos', Marcuse notes some objections to the concept of a non-repressive civilization. His theory, he believes, provides answers to the arguments Freud proposed against the possibility of a non-repressive civilization. First, where Freud argues that scarcity necessitated repressive labour, Marcuse claims that the distribution of scarcity has been imposed in the interests of domination, and that our current social wealth and technology make possible a decent life for all with a minimum of socially necessary labour.[52] Second, while Freud argues that powerful sexual instincts have to be repressed to ensure the time and energy for labour and to avoid sexual chaos, Marcuse claims that a liberated Eros will flow to the realms of labour and culture, that sexual conflict and obstacles to satisfaction may serve to enhance the value of the activity (*EC*, pp. 226f), and that the nature of human sexuality does not refute the possibility of non-repressive sexual gratification.

Marcuse also suggests that Eros contains its own morality (*EC*, pp. 228f) which would guide the individual to maximize pleasure and minimize destructive effects.[53] In so far as 'libidinal morality' aims at instinctual liberation, it differs radically from traditional morality, which, in Marcuse's view tends towards repression of the life instincts. Thus Marcuse constantly criticizes 'idealist' or 'humanist' ethics as repressive and conformist (see, for example, *EC*, pp. 248ff). He never really develops an ethical theory or detailed critique of traditional ethics, although I believe that his writing contains notions of the 'good life' that are implicit in much of his thought but are never systematically worked out (see Chapter 10). Marcuse seems to have been suspicious of ethical theory and, like Marx, was reluctant to develop his own 'ethics'.

Finally, Marcuse argues that release and enhancement of the life instincts will tame and control the destructive instinct, Thanatos (*EC*, pp. 22ff, 139, 231ff). Although he accepts Freud's notion of a death instinct, he thinks that in a non-repressive civilization the life instincts will control aggressive instincts and use the aggressive instincts for the purposes of enhancing life (*EC*, pp. 234f). Moreover, he suggests that although 'joy wants eternity' and time and death negate this wish, one can increase one's joy in life by holding on to past pleasures and anticipating future ones:

> From the myth of Orpheus to the novel of Proust, happiness and freedom have been linked with the idea of the recapture of time: the *temps retrouvé*. Remembrance retrieves the *temps perdu*, which was the time of gratification and fulfilment. Eros, penetrating into consciousness, is moved by remembrance; with it he protests against the order of renunciation; he uses memory in his effort to defeat time in a world dominated by time. (*EC*, pp. 232–3)

The recollection of past sufferings can ally the life instincts against those forces that caused suffering, thus enlisting time-consciousness in the cause of liberation.[54] Moreover, in the non-repressive civilization,

> Death would cease to be an instinctual goal. It remains a fact, perhaps even an ultimate necessity – but a necessity against which the unrepressed energy of mankind will protest, against which it will wage its greatest struggle. It this struggle, reason and instinct could unite. Under conditions of a truly human existence, the difference between succumbing to disease at the age of ten, thirty, fifty or seventy, and dying a 'natural' death after a fulfilled life,

may well be a difference worth fighting for with all instinctual energy. Not those who die, but those who die before they must and want to die, those who die in agony and pain, are the great indictment against civilization. (*EC*, p. 235)

Marcuse champions Life against Death and claims that although the struggle for life cannot defeat the fact of death, it can at least allow one to die with a good conscience that one has fought to produce a society that will protect and enhance life. Marcuse's emphasis throughout *EC* is to face reality, to confront the brutal facts of pain, disease, suffering and death and to struggle against these phenomena in the interests of liberation and the good life. In this view, death and suffering are an ineradicable part of reality – but so is the drive for freedom, happiness and lasting gratification. In Marcuse's imaginative Freudo-Marxist scenario, life (Eros) is engaged in a titanic battle against death (Thanatos) which rages within each individual and within the larger socio-historical environment. Through the Great Refusal, each individual can refuse repression and suffering in the interests of liberation and happiness, and within society each individual must choose to submit to the forces of repression and destruction, or to struggle for increased happiness and freedom. Consequently, each individual must not only fight for liberation against a repressive society, but must struggle against the society lodged within one's own psyche. Marcuse's theory of liberation therefore depicts a war of the psyche and body parallel to Marxian class war.

The categories of *EC*, however, displace Marxian class struggle with the struggle between Eros and Thanatos. Marcuse has not really successfully synthesized Freud and Marx, but has developed in *EC* a theory of civilization and philosophy of history that is more Freudian than Marxian. In his later writings, Marcuse would return to the more socio-economic Marxian framework and would attempt to integrate more dialectically the Marxian and Freudian theories. His temporary displacement of the primacy of Marxian theory represents his response to a historical situation which required both a more socio-psychological explanation of the depth of psychic-social integration and a new foundation for the hopes of liberation. Although it is easy to criticize Marcuse for his partial abandonment of orthodox Marxism, one should note how *EC* provides a potential enrichment and expansion of the Marxian theory. Although Marcuse never abandoned his commitment to Freud's instinct theory, in his later writings his Marxian theory plays a far greater role than Freudian theory. With this in mind, let us conclude with a discussion of Marcuse's motivations for undertaking his synthesis of Marx and Freud, and an assessment of its contributions and shortcomings.

6.4 Critique of *Eros and Civilization*

Eros and Civilization is one of Marcuse's most original and provocative books. Although Marx is never mentioned, the book provides a synthesis of Marx and Freud which militantly espouses Freud's instinct theory, while advocating ideals of play, polymorphic sexuality and instinctual gratification. *EC* also contains, however, a powerful critique of alienated labour and the values and ideology of capitalist society, as well as a call for the reduction of sexual repression. The book reveals Marcuse's profound concern with human needs and happiness and his deep commitment to human liberation. There are, however, problems with *EC*; in concluding this chapter, I want to evaluate, first, Marcuse's ideal of liberation and then his use of Freud.

6.4.1 *Eros, play and liberation*

The impact of Schiller and the aesthetics of German Idealism on Marcuse's ideal of liberation can hardly be exaggerated. For Marcuse, great art contains images of liberation, and aesthetic education cultivates personalities whose harmonious fusion of the senses and reason can no longer tolerate alienated labour and surplus repression. This conception yields a new concept of reason and carries through a modification of Marcuse's previous Hegelian-Marxian rationalism. Such a project places crucial importance on the aesthetic-erotic components of experience and eventually led Marcuse to develop a new concept of socialism in his later writings. Both Schiller and Marcuse advocate concepts of play, phantasy and art which see them as expressive of emancipatory human qualities. Both assume a positive notion of childhood and see human beings as the vessels of an abundance of potentially gratifying energies and faculties. Marcuse combines Schiller's concepts of play and aesthetic education with Freudian notions of the liberation of sexuality to develop new perspectives on liberation which aim at the absence of surplus repression and the full satisfaction of human needs and development of human potentialities. This vision of liberation is close to that of the early Marx (also influenced by German Idealism and Romanticism!) and provides the model of a non-repressive civilization which he believes captures the emancipatory features of socialism in both Marx and the utopian socialists.

It should be stressed that Marcuse's appropriation of Schiller – like his appropriation of Freud – is selective and rather uncritical. He incorporates the more radical side of Schiller, leaving aside the more conservative aspects which emphasize inwardness, individual cultivation and withdrawal from immediate political concerns – aspects which Marcuse sharply criticized earlier in Heidegger, but does not mention in his discussion of Schiller. Moreover, Marcuse, like both Schiller and Kant, does not really sketch out the political institutions and details of the social transformation that would make a non-repressive civilization possible. In both Schiller and Marcuse there is a neglect of democracy and a relative neglect of the material-historical conditions necessary for radical social transformation. Schiller's social ideal was modelled on a simple rural democracy in the Swiss city-states, and it is not clear how Marcuse's conception differs, despite his call for the development of technology and industrialization. Moreover, Schiller foresaw direction of his aesthetic state by a 'new class' of a spiritual-intellectual elite guided by ideals of 'beauty and harmony'.[55] Such a concept might work for small artistic circles, as it was actually practised by various Romantics and Expressionists, but it is not clear how this could work as the model for a social organization of complex industrial-technological societies.

Furthermore, there are problems with Marcuse's ideal of liberation and play. Adorno sharply criticizes Schiller on the grounds that play often partakes of the archaic reproduction of the compulsions of childhood and animals.[56] He belives that surrender to the 'rhythm of blood and body' surrenders the individual to archaic 'mythic remains' which a free humanity should overcome.[57] Previously a similar criticism was made by Freudian critics against Marcuse's use of Freud; they claimed that Marcuse's interpretation of memory and phantasy put a positive value on what constituted for Freud regressive return to childhood compulsions.[58]

It has also been argued that Marcuse exaggerates the role of play and display in his concept of a non-repressive civilization and underplays the importance of the liberation of labour.[59] Here it should be noted that Marcuse is reacting against an overemphasis on labour and production by both contemporary Marxists and the bourgeois work ethic,[60] and is engaging in a polemic against Erich Fromm, who advocates an ideal of the 'productive man'.[61] Marcuse seems to believe that making 'productivity' the end of life reinforces the capitalist work ethic and performance principle, thus strengthening the ideological basis of the system which requires intense competitive labour, productive control over the environment and people, and the sacrifice of pleasure and freedom for the sake of augmenting production. He is insistent in his demand that socially necessary labour time be reduced to a minimum, so that 'the system of societal labour would be organized rather with a veiw to saving time and space for the development of individuality outside the inevitably repressive work world' (*EC,* p. 195). But Marcuse also argues that while ideals of productivity serve to strengthen existing repressive societies, 'freed from this enslavement, productivity loses its repressive power and impels the free development of individual needs' (*EC,* p. 156). Thus he implies that in a non-repressive society, productivity would again, as with the Greeks, be connected with 'making' and that non-repressive labour is possible that would provide for the satisfaction of needs and the development of potentialities (*EC,* pp. 47, 212ff).

Marcuse also suggests that in a non-repressive civilization, the sharp dichotomy between work and play would be overcome and all activity would be geared towards fulfilling needs and developing potentialities. Liberated labour would in a sense 'play' with technology, tools, ideas and aesthetic forms, realizing new possibilities of human creativity and interaction, allowing freedom and gratification to enter the work world. Marcuse indicates this possibility in a 1967 lecture, and comes back to the theme in several of his later works: 'I believe that one of the new possibilities, which gives an indication of the qualitative difference between the free and unfree society, is that of letting the realm of freedom appear within the realm of necessity – in labour and not only beyond labour'.[62] Hence I belive that despite some of the passages in *EC,* it would be a mistake to read Marcuse simply as a hedonist espousing play and rejecting labour. For it becomes clear in his later work that he is proposing a way of existence that is not divided into a sharp dichotomy between labour and play which would make possible 'non-alienated libidinal work' and 'play and display'.[63]

Another problem is that Marcuse fails to make gender distinctions in *EC*, and does not analyse the specificity of women's oppression. He does not address the problem of domestic labour, or the overcoming of oppressive sex roles and divisions of labour in the new society he envisages. For instance, although automation may liberate human beings from some types of economic bondage, this does not necessarily entail the liberation of women from domestic labour, unless the specificities of labour in the home are dealt with. Although labour time could be significantly reduced by atuomation and free time could be increased, under the system of patriarchy that coexists with capitalism, male free time might very well be increased at the expense of women. Thus Marcuse's ideal of liberation and a non-repressive society – for all its emphasis on sexual emancipation – lacks adequate analysis of the specificity of women's oppression and the forms that women's emancipation would take. We shall return, however, to this issue in Chapter 10, where I discuss Marcuse's turn towards feminism and his reflections on women's liberation in the 1970s.

Marcuse's choice of Narcissus and Orpheus as his mythic-poetic symbols for a non-repressive civilization has also been criticized, along with his citing of Prometheus – Marx's cultural hero – as a symbolic figure of a repressive performance principle.[64] It is claimed that Marcuse's cultural ideals here are individualistic types, solitary aesthetes who belong to no community, have no political involvement and no essential relations to other people. In fact, Narcissus is often interpreted as a prototype of 'narcissistic' self-love. And Orpheus's famous relation with Eurydice ended in disaster, making him a symbol of the destructiveness of failed love.[65] For Marcuse, these strange cultural heroes signify, on the contrary, an ideal of wholeness, of a fully integrated psyche and body that is harmoniously reconciled with the world. In Marcuse's view, 'The Orphic-Narcissistic images are those of the Great Refusal: refusal to accept separation from the libidinous object (or subject). The refusal aims at liberation – at the reunion of what has become separated' (*EC*, p. 170).

In Marcuse's interpretation, Orpheus refuses repressive sexuality and seeks union with the object of desire, despite all obstacles, while Narcissus's Eros is suffused through his entire personality, making him independent and self-contained. Both seek a 'fuller Eros' and a new erotic reality that will provide total gratification. Marcuse's Narcissus looks into nature, sees himself and loves what he sees.

While the Narcissus in the Greek myth sorrows because he cannot possess or become one with his image, and in a more modern version drowns in the pool trying to embrace his image, Marcuse's Narcissus sees himself as a part of nature and himself as a source of pleasure and meaning. Although his cultural heroes have mystical and quietistic overtones, Marcuse's debate with Norman O. Brown over *Love's Body* indicates that he conceives the aesthetic-erotic 'great refusal' as part of a political struggle aimed at transforming reality and eliminating surplus repression.[66]

Marcuse's ideal of liberation is rooted in Freud's instinct theory and concept of the 'Nirvana principle' which holds, in Marcuse's interpretation, that release of instinctual-erotic energies will lead to a condition of gratification and harmony. His mythic-poetic formulations suggest that instinctual gratification, peace, harmony, creativity, song, dance and love are features of a liberated society neglected in most Marxian theories of socialism. While only the most prosaic philistine could reject such ideals, it remains a difficult question whether such an ideal of liberation should ground itself in Freud's instinct theory, or whether another anthropological theory would better serve to ground Marcuse's ideal of liberation and an emancipated society. This issue leads to a discussion of the use and abuse of Freud in radical social theory, which will conclude this chapter.

6.4.2 *Freud and critical theory*

Many serious objections have been levelled against Marcuse's interpretation and use of Freud.[67] His appropriation of Freud is indeed selective and has been frequently criticized by more orthodox Freudians. Sometimes Marcuse reinterprets Freud to support his own position when orthodox Freudian ideas are at odds with the position that Marcuse is advocating.[68] On the other hand, Marcuse neglects other Freudian ideas that critical theory could utilize in developing a social psychology, anthropology and theory of a non-repressive society.[69] Most criticisms centre on what is claimed to be Marcuse's uncritical acceptance of Freud's energy instinct model and his theory of the 'political economy of the instincts'.[70] It is claimed that although Marcuse wants to incorporate Freudian ideas into an anthropology of liberation, the Freudian model that he adopts contains some darkly deterministic implications that Marcuse does not fully consider. If, it is claimed, human behaviour is constituted by biological instincts which are in turn shaped by childhood experiences and socialization, and if our behaviour is determined by an explosive Id, a destructive Thanatos, a mysterious archaic heritage, the birth trauma and separation anxiety, as well as a powerful Oedipus complex, then human freedom becomes rather problematical.[71] Do not these notions posit a biological-psychic Thermidor to liberation within the human organism itself? In fact, Marcuse even accepts Freud's theory of the archaic heritage and primal father. This is puzzling, for most critics argue that Freud's notion provides a mystified view of history which makes it appear that the very material of history is instinctual repression and the struggle against repression, and presents a historical scenario of an eternal drama of repression, revolt and the re-institution of repression.[72] Marcuse also seems to accept uncritically Freud's concept of the Oedipus complex as the crucial event in personality formation – a notion that has come under sharp attack in recent years.[73]

In the view of many, Marcuse is not sufficiently critical of Freud and does not see that the emancipatory elements in 'the hidden trend in psychoanalysis' require a different psychological-anthropological foundation. Anthony Wilden, for instance, argues that Marcuse fails to recognize the regressive role of phantasy in Freud, for whom 'fantasy, phantasy-making, and daydreaming are controlled by the retropressive timelessness, the entropic inertia' of infantile fixation.[74] This criticism suggests that to utilize phantasy, memory and the aesthetic dimension in an anthropology of liberation, as Marcuse intends, requires freeing these concepts from their Freudian significations and developing them in another anthropological-psychological framework – as Ernst Bloch does in *The Principle of Hope*.[75]

Along these lines, it is claimed that the very notions of Eros and Thanatos – and their symbiotic interaction – are fraught with obscurities.[76] Marcuse makes rather extreme – and, in the view of some critics, unsubstantiated – claims for Eros, the liberation of which will create a new reality, human and social. There are overtones of the Platonic Eros in Marcuse's motion that sublimation of bodily energies will tame aggressive instincts and unify the personality in a higher mode of being, but it is claimed that there is no evidence or argument that this will indeed occur.[77]

There have also been many criticisms of Marcuse's use of

'Thanatos', and positing a death instinct. The death instinct for Freud covers both external manifestations, such as aggression, and internal manifestations, such as the 'repetition compulsion'. Whereas there is evidence that aggression can be reduced through increased gratification and reduction of frustration, it is not clear that repetition compulsions (which were Freud's chief emphasis in formulating the concept of the death instinct) would be reduced simply through strengthening the life instincts – indeed, Freud thought that a difficult and long psychoanalytic therapy was necessary to cure such neurosis.[78] In fact, it is not apparent to what extent Eros and Thanatos are more than conceptual myths. I believe that Freud provides important contributions to developing a critical theory of socialization and anthropology of liberation, but rather than using Freud's concepts of Eros and Thanatos, I would propose using the Marxian categories of needs and powers, the emancipation of the senses, the development of many-sided human beings, and social and individual praxis as the fundamental anthropological categories for critical theory.[79] Consequently I believe that Marcuse has not adequately mediated the Marxian and Freudian anthropologies in his critical theory and is too uncritical of Freud.

Moreover, Marcuse presents a truncated version of Freud. He minimizes Freud's theory of the unconscious, and the symbolic interaction that takes place in the communication between consciousness and the unconscious (or between the patient and the analyst), in which desires attempt to express themselves, in which symbols are used to elucidate the depths of the human situation, and in which communication sheds light on the dark recesses of the psyche, lightening the burden of oppression forced upon individuals through repressive socialization. Although Marcuse claims that he is interested in contributing to the philosophy of psychoanalysis, rather than therapy, philosophers like Habermas and Ricoeur have shown the importance of the Freudian hermeneutic of experience for increasing understanding of human nature and contributing to the process of self-formation.[80] There is also a failure in Marcuse's anthropology to take account of the role of communication in human experience and to see the realm of symbolic interaction as more and other than the projections of desire and phantasy. The problem, I maintain, is too heavy reliance on Freud's instinct theory as revealing the core of human nature.

There are, however, many attractive features to Marcuse's anthropological perspectives and theory of domination and liberation.

Marcuse uses Freud's categories to provide a psychological explanation of the failures of revolutionary consciousness to develop in the West and in the Soviet Union, which would also account for the workers' submission to fascism, Stalinism and corporate capitalism.[81] In so doing, he at once uses Freud as a front for a Marxian critique of capitalism and to revise Marxian theories of human nature and socialism, bringing elements of play, sexuality and aesthetic sensibility into the Marxian theory – elements neglected or suppressed by most Marxist theorists of revolution. Thus, Marcuse could both enlarge the Freudian concept of repression to include what Marx discussed under the rubrics of alienation and exploitation, and could emphasize the importance of elements of a non-repressive civilization and liberated humanity that were neglected in the Marxian anthropology and theory of revolution which focused on the alienation of labour and its liberation.[82]

Moreover, Marcuse's theory of Eros contains an admirable defence of the life-affirming, creative characteristics of human nature. Previous philosophers – from Plato, Augustine and Kant to the present day – have tended to emphasize the destructive and asocial features of the derivatives of Eros (sex, passion, etc.)[83] Against this ascetic tradition, Marcuse defends erotic energies as the very principle of life and creativity. His linking of aesthetic and erotic dimensions of human experience is also important in both explicating features of an emancipated individual and a non-repressive society. Despite the problems in Marcuse's theory, he forces us to rethink the problematics of liberation and revolution and to think through the implications for critical theory of Freud's metapsychology, theory of society, culture and history. Thus, *Eros and Civilization* continues to be a valuable and provocative work that should be read and rethought – and supplemented by the anthropology of Marx, Bloch, Sartre, Habermas and other theoretical labours in this area. Developing a critical anthropology and psychology that combine theories of labour, sex and communication within a critical theory of society aiming at social critique and human liberation remain important theoretical tasks. While Marcuse makes important contributions to this project, *Eros and Civilization* does not provide an adequate synthesis; continued reflections and theoretical work are needed.

7
Marcuse's Critique of Bureaucratic Communism: *Soviet Marxism*

Marcuse's *Soviet Marxism* (hereafter *SM*) is an interpretation of both the political phenomenon of Communism in the Soviet Union and its ideological doctrine and departures from classical Marxism. His study combines Marxian ideology critique with political analysis of the Soviet Union, using as sources documents, speeches and party pronouncements, as well as the classical texts of Marxism-Leninism. The interconnection of philosophical and political factors makes Marcuse's study a complicated and often difficult presentation of a complex and controversial phenomenon; consequently, *SM* demands a detailed analysis and criticism of Marcuse's interpretation – a task neglected in most previous discussions of Marcuse's thought.

Soviet Marxism is, I believe, a widely misunderstood book. Most interpreters, or critics, have failed either to discern its dialectical analysis of both liberating and oppressive features, or Marcuse's interpretation of possible liberalizing trends, in conjunction with continued repression. Consequently, previous discussions have been one-sided; no one has analysed Marcuse's ambivalent approach to the subject, which in turn has resulted in contradictory responses to his study. In general, New Left critics, who take a mostly critical position towards the Soviet Union, praise the book as a critique of Stalinism, the Soviet bureaucracy and the Soviet state.[1] Communists who attack the book claim that Marcuse's interpretation is wholly negative and argue that he takes the position of a cold war, anti-Soviet propagandist.[2] Some anti-Soviet left-liberals claim that Marcuse provides apologetics for the Soviet Union, while

Western anti-Communist ideologues claim that Marcuse's book is pro-Soviet![3]

In my view, Communists who attack Marcuse for his defamation of the Soviet Union, anti-Communists who criticize him for his alleged defence of Soviet Marxism, and those critics who praise him for his critique of Stalinism, all miss the point that Marcuse's interpretation is not a clear-cut 'for' or 'against', but instead portrays the contradictory tendencies within a highly complex phenomenon. Thus I would argue that *SM* quite appropriately moves from analysis of the structure and tendencies of development of Soviet Marxism to sharp criticism and a sympathetic portrayal of liberalizing tendencies.

SM occupies a problematical place within Marcuse's writings. He rarely refers back to it in later works, and has told an interviewer that he sees it as an 'interruption' in his work which is not central to his major concerns – a position that I shall contest in this chapter.[4] I shall argue that premature dismissal of the book, or ignoring it as many previous studies have done, would be a mistake. *SM* has an interesting place within critical theory, since it is one of the first attempts by a critical theorist to analyse and criticize the Soviet Union in any detail.[3] *SM* also begins efforts by Western Marxists to overcome sectarian discourse about the Soviet Union with critical and analytical discussion. Many previous representatives of Western Marxism tended to defend uncritically the Soviet Union or to attack it harshly – or, as with Sartre and Merleau-Ponty, to swing sharply from one attitude to another.[6] Benjamin, Brecht, Bloch and others, whatever their private doubts, refused to criticize the Soviet Union openly. Even Karl Korsch, who had developed one of the first independent Marxist critiques of the Soviet Union in the 1920s, reluctantly concluded in the post-war period that it was reactionary to attack the Soviet Union since the only significant political choice, he believed, was between American capitalism and Soviet Communism.[7] Leftists of Trotskyist, anarchist and later Maoist tendencies, on the other hand, frequently attack the Soviet Union as the incarnation of evil, often outdoing professional anti-Communist cold warriors in their polemical diatribes. The Frankfurt School generally maintained a discrete silence on the issue in the 1930s and 1940s, although some of its members, like Wittfogel and Horkheimer, eventually became bitter anti-Communists.[8] Marcuse spoke out in the 1950s, but did so in cautiously critical tones.

Consequently, his study of Soviet Communism is important for its contributions to developing a critical Marxist discourse on the Soviet Union that avoids the sectarian polemics of Communist apologists, anti-Communist ideologues, or Marxian sects.

SM is also important for interpreting Marcuse's thought because it reveals parallels between his theories and critiques of the Soviet Union and advanced capitalist societies. These similarities raise the question of the extent to which Marcuse's theory of 'advanced industrial society' and 'one-dimensional society' are versions of 'post-industrial convergence theory', which maintains similarities between capitalist and Communist societies by virtue of a similar technological base and a similar mode of social organization and control. *SM* helps to show to what extent Marcuse *does* utilize post-industrial 'convergence' theories, and to what extent his analysis differs. His study of the Soviet Union thus provides insight into both his method of social analysis and his theory of contemporary society. In this sense, the book can help us to depict characteristic and central features of Marcuse's thought. Consequently, to interpret *SM* adequately, we must discuss his writing strategy and method of analysis, examine his analysis of Soviet Communism, situate the book within Marcuse's post-Second World War writings, and interpret the book and its strategy within its historical context. In this way, we can adequately appriase his study of Soviet Marxism, note its ambivalences, and perceive its strengths and shortcomings.

7.1 Marcuse and Soviet Communism

Although Marcuse was a student of Marxism from around 1918, he became a specialist in Communism and the Soviet Union during the Second World War in his work with the OSS and then the State Department. After the Second World War he became the chief political analyst for the central European section of the State Department and helped prepare a lengthy classified intelligence report on 'The Potentials of World Communism'.[9] After his Institute colleagues left government service for academic posts, Marcuse was forced to stay in Washington because of his wife Sophie's illness. Marcuse thus witnessed the beginnings of the cold war and the repression of radicals and liberals in government service during the McCarthy era, although he told me that he was not directly subject to a witch-hunt himself.[10] Rather, he was tired of being a government bureaucrat and eager to return to writing and teaching. Consequently, at the time of his wife's death in 1951, he left his State Department job and sought an academic position. His first appointments were with the Russian Institute of Columbia University and the Russian Research Center at Harvard. In the Acknowledgements in *SM*, he notes that his work on the political tenets of Soviet Marxism, which forms the first half of the book, was carried out in 1952–3 at Columbia, while the second half of the book on the ethical tenets of Soviet Marxism was prepared at Harvard in 1954–5.

Although both the Columbia and Harvard research institutes were centres of cold war anti-Communism, Marcuse openly taught Marxism at Columbia and was known as 'Marxist-in-residence' at Harvard.[11] His published book on Soviet Marxism indicates that Marcuse was neither an orthodox Communist, nor a cold warrior. He himself claims that his ambivalent attitude towards his subject reflects the ambivalence of Soviet Marxism as both a realization and distortion of Marxism. In his words, the 'fundamental ambivalence' in Soviet development consists in the fact that 'the means for liberation and humanization operate for preserving domination and submission, and the theory that destroyed all ideology is used for the establishment of a new ideology' (*SM*, p. xiv).

Marcuse's writing strategy in *SM* is to confront Soviet 'ideology' with 'reality' so as to provide an 'immanent critique' of both Soviet ideology and society by exposing its distortions of Marxism and its failure to realize Marxian socialist ideals in practice. In an Introduction to the original 1958 Columbia University Press edition – which was omitted without explanation from the 1961 Vintage edition – Marcuse claims that his 'immanent critique'

> starts from the theoretical premises of Soviet Marxism, develops their ideological and sociological consequences, and re-examines the premises in the light of these consequences. The critique thus employs the conceptual instruments of its object, namely Marxism, in order to clarify the actual function of Marxism in Soviet society and its historical direction.[12]

In the Introduction to the 1958 edition, Marcuse explicitly sets forth a Marxian method of historical analysis which relates ideology to its social reality; identifies 'objective trends' and 'tendencies' of Soviet society; and conceptualizes Soviet development 'in terms of the interaction between Soviet and Western society'.[13] Throughout the book, he shows how trends of international geopolitics and the capitalist world market influenced Soviet development. He also assumes that although Soviet society 'is not socialist in the sense envisaged by Marx and Engels', it has nonetheless institutionalized Lenin's version of Marxism, and thus study of the ideology of Soviet Marxism will reveal certain characteristics and tendencies of Soviet society.[14]

Although Marcuse provides a frequently penetrating critique of the degeneration of Marxism in the Soviet Union into what Oskar Negt has called a 'science of legitimation',[15] his statements about Soviet 'reality' are often curiously uncritical, as our examination of Marcuse's discussion of the Soviet bureaucracy, state and the 'new rationality' will show. It seems that Marcuse intended to promote a thaw in cold war anti-Communist attitudes by providing a more favourable picture of the Soviet Union than in the virulently anti-Communist propaganda dominant at the time. He did this by emphasizing 'liberalizing trends' that might produce progressive changes in the Soviet system in the future.

His analysis was a response to what he perceived as liberalizing trends emerging from Soviet society during Khrushchev's regime.[16] Although *SM* contains no explicit analysis of changes brought about by Khrushchev's ascent to power, the 1961 preface to the Vintage paperback edition and the 1963 preface to the French translation appraise Khrushchev's government postively as carrying through liberalizing policies. While Marcuse told me that he never had any 'illusions' that Khrushchev would personally carry through significant reforms, he did see the basic 'tendencies' of Soviet Communism moving towards liberalization (see 7.2 below).[17] Later he became more critical of the post-Khrushchev regime, especially after the invasion of Czechoslovakia in 1968. Thus Marcuse's views on the Soviet Union were responses to a changing and fluid histori- cal situation, and he modified his analysis in response to changing historical circumstances.

7.1.1 *Domination and the new rationality*

Marcuse focuses his critique of Soviet society on what he perceives as new forms of domination, which are parallel to tendencies towards domination and new forms of social control in capitalist societies. Domination in Soviet Communist society is constituted both by what Marcuse calls 'the new rationality' and by the Soviet bureaucracy. The 'new rationality' utilizes technological rationality to organize both industry and society. The rationality of modern machine industry demands 'attitudes of standardized conformity and precise submission to the machine which requires adjustment and reaction rather than autonomy and spontaneity' (*SM*, p. 69). If nationalization and centralization are co-ordinated so as to erect a gigantic apparatus that dictates to and controls its citizens and workers in all spheres of life, then

> progress in industrialization is tantamount to progress in domination: attendance to the machine, the scientific work process, becomes totalitarian, affecting all spheres of life. The technological perfection of the productive apparatus dominates the rulers and the ruled while sustaining the distinction between them. (*SM*, p. 69)

In Marcuse's view, the rationality of the Soviet industrial system demands submission to the machine process, surrender of individual intiative to 'efficiency and performance within the established pattern' (*SM*, p. 69). Hence the Soviet organization of labour and society is aimed towards domination and serves to subjugate the labourers to the machine apparatus rather than aiming at their liberation and the development of their potentialities.

This analysis is remarkably similar to Marcuse's earlier critique of 'technological rationality' in American capitalism and German fascism. In a 1941 essay, 'Some Social Implications of Modern Technology', he describes how technology and technological rationality are becoming instruments for 'control and domination'.[18] He analyses how the organization of modern industry requires subordination to dictates of efficiency and standardized performance, concluding:

> There is no personal escape from the apparatus which has mechanized and standardized the world ... in manipulating the machine, man learns that obedience to the directions is the only way to obtain desired results. Getting along is identical with adjustment to the apparatus. There is no room for autonomy. Individualistic rationality has developed into efficient com-

pliance with the pre-given continuum of means and ends. The latter absorbs the liberating efforts of thought, and the various functions of reason converge upon the unconditional maintenance of the apparatus.[19]

Likewise, Soviet ideology claims that reason is realized in the Soviet state so that, in Marcuse's words, 'dissent is not only a political crime but also technical stupidity, sabotage, mistreatment of the machine' (*SM*, p. 69). Whereas technological rationality allegedly serves as an instrument of class domination in capitalist society, Soviet ideology claims to have created a 'conformity' between productive forces and productive relations that provides the foundation for a rational society. It also claims to have overcome the conflict between the individual and society, and between private interests and the general interest by abolishing class divisions and class exploitation. The official Soviet ideology claims that since Soviet society has institutionalized the actual interests of individuals and has created a thoroughly rational society, it is the duty of the individuals to submit to the social order.

Marcuse notes that outside the context of Soviet Marxism, 'the equation of the Soviet state with a free and rational society is not accepted', and comments: 'Since in actuality the individual interest is still antagonistic to the interest of the whole, since nationalization is not socialization, the rationality of Soviet Realism appears as utterly irrational, as terroristic conformity' (*SM*, p. 70). To overcome the discrepancy between ideology and reality, *Soviet ideology* assumes a ritualistic and magical character. The propositions are learned mechanically, are endlessly repeated, and are performed like a ritual which is magically supposed to bring about the desired results. He claims:

Soviet Marxism here shares in the decline of language and communication in the age of mass societies. It is senseless to treat the propositions of the official ideology at the cognitive level: they are a matter of practical, not of theoretical, reason. If propositions lose their cognitive value to their capacity of bringing about a desired effect, that is to say, if they are to be understood as directives for a specific behaviour, then *magical* elements gain ascendancy over comprehending thought and action. (*SM*, p. 72)

Marcuse's analysis of Soviet ideology is similar to his critiques of language and ideology in advanced capitalist society.[20] However, in *SM* he claims that the progressive feature of Soviet ideology is that it preserves the promises of Marxian theory which continues to be the official ideology in the Soviet bloc. Marxism, in Marcuse's view, plays a contradictory role in the world today. On the one hand, it serves as a revolutionary ideology which 'moves large under-privileged masses on an international scale' who are 'whipped into political action, contesting and challenging advanced industrial civilization' (*SM*, pp. 73–4). But the Marxist ideology also becomes a powerful tool of domination in the hands of Soviet administrators: 'Through the means of mass communication, they transmit the objectives of the administration, and the underlying population responds with the expected behaviour' (*SM*, p. 76).

Marcuse would develop a similar theory of the function of mass communications in capitalist society in *One-Dimensional Man*. We have noted several key similarities in Marcuse's analysis of Communist and capitalist societies. He concludes that:

> The fundamental difference between Western and Soviet society is paralleled by a strong trend towards assimilation. Both systems show the common features of late industrial civilization – central-ization and regimentation supersede individual enterprise and autonomy; competition is organized and 'rationalized'; there is joint rule of economic and political bureaucracies; the people are co-ordinated through the 'mass media' of communication, enter-tainment industry, education . . . Nationalization, the abolition of private property in the means of production, does not, by itself, constitute an essential distinction as long as production is central-ized and controlled over and above the population. Without initiative and control 'from below' by the 'immediate producers', nationalization is but a technological-political device for increas-ing the productivity of labour, for accelerating the development of the productive forces and for their control from above (central planning) – a change in the mode of domination, streamlining of domination, rather than prerequisite for its abolition. (*SM*, p. 66)[21]

Marcuse implies here that without *workers' control* of industry and society, nationalization does not constitute a qualitative improvement in the lot of the working class. He criticizes the tendency of bureaucratic Communism to fail to develop socialist democracy, and implies that genuine socialist socialization requires a democratization of society. This means that the workers make the decisions that determine their labour activity, controlling the organization of labour, pay and working conditions without a bureaucracy directing them from above. Marcuse explains the lack of full workers' control in Soviet society from the situation of the Russian economic base in its historical context, citing its industrial backwardness and need to industrialize rapidly, its isolation and encirclement by a hostile capitalist world – thus repeating the standard Communist explanation for the failure of the Soviet Union to realize more adequately the Marxian ideal of socialism. Marcuse's critique of the Soviet state, however, suggests that the Russian Revolution has not resulted in liberation, but rather in a 'change in the mode of domination' (*SM*, pp. 66f).

Yet in the 1961 preface to the Vintage edition, Marcuse states:

It remains to clarify a point that has caused much misunderstanding, due, in fact, to my inadequate treatment. The book recurrently stresses certain tendencies that make for assimilation, and perhaps even convergence of Western and Soviet society ... I would like to dissociate myself from this position, while maintaining my emphasis on the all-embracing political character of the machine process in advanced industrial society. It is precisely this 'total' character of the machine process which *limits* the tendencies towards assimilation and convergence between Western and Soviet society (in terms of time as well as structure) and generates very different potentialities of development. (*SM*, pp. xi–xii)

Marcuse then stresses how 'basically different social institutions' in the Soviet Union 'are designed to make for a different development' (*SM*, p. xii). He argues that competition with the West will fuel technological progress, automation and the reduction of labour in the Soviet Union, and also 'militates against the planned production of wasteful and destructive goods and services and thus against the planned perpetuation and even augmentation of labour' (*SM*, p. xv). He also believes that the 'nationalized economy offers no internal resistance to a rationalization of technical progress which would accelerate the reduction of the working day in the realm of necessary labour' (*SM*, p. xv). Thus Marcuse sees greater potential for liberation through automation and technology in the Soviet Union than in the West.

7.1.2 *Bureaucracy and the new class*

Marcuse argues that control of the labour process and society functions through fundamentally different social institutions in capitalist and Communist societies, yet it also shows certain parallels and similarities. Against the ideological conception advanced by Communist ideologues that the socialist state is 'withering away' and performs 'simple administrative functions' (*SM*, pp. 87–8), Marcuse claims that:

> the Soviet state exercises throughout political and governmental functions against the proletariat itself: domination remains a specialized function in the division of labour and is as such the monopoly of a political, economic and military bureaucracy. This function is perpetuated by the centralized authoritarian organization of the productive process, directed by groups which determine the needs of society (the social product and its distribution) independent of the collective control of the ruled population. (*SM*, p. 69)

The significant power of domination and administration in the Soviet Union and control over the means of production rests in the hands of the *bureaucracy*. Similar to capitalist societies, the state assumes administrative functions over and against the people, thus perpetuating the 'separation of the "immediate producers" from collective control over the process of production' (*SM*, p. 89). Marcuse concludes: 'The Soviet state thus takes shape exactly as that structure which Engels described as characteristic of class society: the "common societal functions" become a "new branch of the division of labour" and thereby constitute *particular* interests separate from those of the population. The state is again a reified, hypostatized power' (*SM*, p. 89).

The question of whether the Soviet bureaucracy is a 'new class' in the Marxian sense is, Marcuse suggests, a 'problem of Marxist exegesis' (*SM*, p. 89). Marcuse argues that if 'class' is defined in terms of *ownership* of the means of production, then the Soviet bureaucracy is *not* a class. However, if *control* over the means of production is the criterion, and control is purely in the hands of the bureaucracy and is denied the 'immediate producers', then it would appear that the bureaucracy has assumed features of a new class (*SM*, p. 89).[22]

It should be noted that Marcuse's discussion of the Soviet bureaucracy on pp. 91–100 is really not as critical as one might expect. He attempts to define the bureaucracy, its function and the 'basis and scope of its power', asking if the bureaucracy is limited in the exercise of its power and if it constitutes a potential liberating aspect capable of 'exploding and changing the structure of Soviet society' (*SM*, p. 92). In defining the bureaucracy he asks 'who or what is that Soviet state?', and answers that 'neither the rise of the Soviet intelligentsia as a new ruling group, nor its composition and its privileges are any longer disputed facts' (*SM*, p. 91). But is the 'intelligentsia' the new ruling group? Is the Soviet Union the first technocratic society? No doubt the technocrats have high status, privileges and even power in Soviet society, but most Soviet specialists argue that the ruling bureaucracy is constituted almost entirely by the Communist *Party members* and not the intelligentsia.[23] Marcuse's omission of the role of the Party in constituting the bureaucracy is striking. He does mention that 'In Soviet doctrine, it is the Party which exercises the social control overriding all technical-administrative control' (*SM*, p. 94), but does not clarify the relation between the bureaucracy and the Party or discuss how Party membership is essential for real power within the bureaucracy. Thus, against Marcuse's position, one could argue that the real basis of the power of the bureaucracy would seem to be one's position in the Party and not necessarily one's intellect, technical training or economic function and position.

Marcuse raises the question of whether, with the development of Soviet society towards the 'transition from socialism to Communism', the bureaucracy will lose its 'class character' (I would say 'Party character') and 'would be "open" and lose its "political" content to the degree to which, with the wealth of the material and intellectual productive forces, the general societal function would become exchangeable among the individuals' (*SM*, p. 93). The belief that the division of labour will be abolished and that the bureaucracy will be 'open' and will lose its political Party content seems to be a rather utopian speculation and assumes a potentiality for radical change in Soviet society. Is such a possibility, Marcuse asks, 'even theoretically consistent with the actual structure of the Soviet state'? (*SM*, p. 93).

Although Marcuse does not deny that the bureaucracy has a highly privileged position and therefore a vital interest in maintaining its special position and the status quo, he believes that 'bureaucracy, by itself, no matter how huge it is, does not generate self-perpetuating power unless it has an economic base of its own from which its position is derived' (*SM*, p. 93). He claims that since the 'traditional sources of economic power are not available to the Soviet bureaucracy' (i.e. private ownership), then 'control therefore and not ownership must be the decisive factor' (*SM*, p. 93). Further, he believes that the 'control' exercised by the bureaucracy is limited and is 'subject to overriding laws and forces' (*SM*, p. 94). The weight of Marcuse's interpretation of the Soviet bureaucracy seems to stress the limits to the power and the built-in liberalization trend in the bureaucracy, and not its repressive, self-perpetuating features, antagonistic to socialist democracy. Marcuse argues that:

> the monopolization of power is counteracted by two forces: on the one side, the Central Plan, in spite of its vagaries, loopholes and corrections, ultimately supersedes and integrates the special interests; on the other side, the entire bureaucracy, up to the highest level, is subject to the competitive terror, or, after the relaxation of the terror, to the highly incalculable application of political or punitive measures, leading to the loss of power. (*SM*, p. 95).

Although the Central Plan is the creation of the Party bureaucracy, once formulated it sets limits to the bureaucracy's power and provides the framework within which policy is formulated and carried out.[24] 'Once institutionalized, they have their own momentum and their own objective requirements, the vested interests themselves depend on the observance of these requirements' (*SM*, p. 95). Since the bureaucracy is highly competitive, inefficiency and nonconformity are severely punished. The Central Plan sets the production goals which must be met if the bureaucrats are to hold or enhance their positions, and thus provides boundaries which are not to be transgressed or questioned. As examples of absolute guiding principles and goals to which the bureaucracy must submit, Marcuse cites the industrialization policy to sustain the priority of heavy industry, the collectivization-agricultural policy and the foreign policy of peaceful coexistence: these policies, despite very different historical conditions, were all formulated by Lenin, adhered to by Stalin, and define the framework for the development of Soviet society (*SM*, pp. 98–9). Marcuse concludes:

> The Soviet bureaucracy thus does not seem to possess a basis for the effective perpetuation of special interests against the overriding general requirements of the social system on which it lives. The bureaucracy constitutes a separate class which controls the underlying population through control of the economic, political and military establishments, and exercise of this control engenders a variety of special interests which assert themselves in the control; however, they must compromise and ultimately succumb to the general policy which none of the special interests can change by virtue of its special power. (*SM*, p. 100)

Marcuse's generosity towards the Soviet bureaucracy is odd, given his dislike of bureaucratic socialism and his general critique of bureaucracy as domination. To understand his position, we should put his analysis in its historical context and see that his discussions are geared to counteract the prevailing Western cold war propaganda, which portrayed the Soviet bureaucracy as a totalitarian police organization controlled by the diabolical Communist Party. However, Marcuse does not provide an ideological whitewash for the Soviet bureaucracy, for although he stresses the limits to its power and its potential liberalizing tendencies, he also frequently deflates the claims of Soviet ideologists and provides many sharp criticisms of the Soviet Union. For example, later in *SM* he suddenly escalates his criticism of the Soviet state: 'The totalitarian administration strengthens itself *and* the very forces against which it acts' (i.e. capitalism) and 'in doing so, it perpetuates the repressive economic and political features of the Soviet system' (*SM*, p. 155). Earlier he had pledged *not* to use the pejorative term 'totalitarianism' in his discussion of Soviet society (*SM*, p. 63), but in *SM*, pp. 154 and 155, he refers to the 'totalitarian administration'. Moreover, he stresses that the Soviet state has consistently diverted a large sector of its productive forces to militarization and that 'The maintenance of a vast military establishment (armed forces and secret police) with its educational, political and psychological controls perpetuates authoritarian institutions, attitudes and behaviour patterns which counteract a qualitative change in the repressive production relations' (*SM*, p. 156). But after calling attention to the repressive features of militarism and a bureaucracy with its own vested interest in self-perpetuation and, consequently, in perpetuating repressive production (and political) relations', Marcuse argues that 'repressive economic and political relations' increasingly contradict 'the more fundamental and general interests and objectives in the development of the Soviet state' (*SM*, p. 156). Furthermore, he sees a trend towards 'liberalizing the Stalinist bureaucracy' (*SM*, p. 157) and a softening of hard-line foreign policy as the 'fundamental trend' (*SM*, p. 159) of Soviet Marxism.

By now it should be clear that Marcuse's *Soviet Marxism* is not solely a critique of Stalinism or the present Soviet bureaucracy. Marcuse's analysis implies that Stalinism is being surpassed and that the bureaucracy contains built-in trends towards liberalization which run counter to arbitrary, militaristic or dictatorial policies. He believes that the terroristic features of Soviet Marxism are disappearing, arguing that 'terror tends to become predominantly technological, and, in the USSR itself, strictly political terror seems to be the exception rather than the rule' (*SM*, p. 96).

The subsequent policy of placing dissenters in mental hospitals, the political persecution of Soviet Jews and the repressive measures taken against dissenting members of Ukrainian, Lithuanian and other nationalist groups seems to render Marcuse's evaluation questionable. Thus, Marcuse's belief in the de-Stalinization taking place in the Soviet Union seems to contain an underestimation of the repressive-authoritarian features of Soviet society that still prevail. An example of Marcuse's failure to see the continuation of Stalinism in Soviet Marxism is his interpretation of the 1956 revolts in Eastern Europe. He writes: 'It was this de-Stalinization which stimulated the events in Poland and Hungary' (*SM*, p. 158). This may be partially true, but the 1956 Eastern Europe uprisings were also a genuine demand for freedom, democracy and an improved economic position that was denied by a Stalinist bureaucracy which would not allow liberalization that challenged its vested interests and which consequently responded with force and repression.[25] Whereas Marcuse interprets the revolts and demand for liberalization in Eastern European countries as an outburst following a de-Stalinization programme, they are also a reaction against continuing, repressive Stalinism that was crushed by a continuation of Stalinism – a point not adequately stressed by Marcuse. To suggest, as Marcuse does, that Stalinism is historically surpassed is perhaps as much wishful thinking as the Soviet pronouncement that capitalism is in its final crisis.

Hence I maintain that Marcuse's *SM* lacks a serious and sustained critique of Stalinism, the Soviet bureaucracy and Soviet political repression. Marcuse could well have appropriated the critiques of Soviet Marxism by Trotsky, Souverine, and others into his interpretation, as they call attention to phenomena neglected or played down in *SM*.[26] Part of the deficiency of Marcuse's interpretation is its lack of historical analysis. It is customary to divide Soviet history into an account of Lenin and the 'heroic period' of the revolution (in which the promise of the revolution flowered); the Stalinist period (often portrayed as the betrayal of the revolution: i.e. by Trotsky, Deutscher, etc.); and today's post Stalinist leadership, which manifests both a continuity and discontinuity in relation to Stalinism. Marcuse, however, has concentrated his analysis for the most part on post-1950 trends, making historically unsystematic references back to the Lenin and Stalin eras. He does recognize a 'break between Leninism and Stalinism' (*SM*, p. 58), but does not explicate the central features of Leninism and Stalinism; he neither elucidates the break in a detailed fashion, not does he explicate the continuities systematically. Since he believes a de-Stalinization trend is underway, he presupposes a discontinuity between Stalinism and post-Stalin Soviet Marxism, but lacking a detailed theory and critique of Stalinism, he cannot really develop the differences.[27]

One of the difficulties in Marcuse's interpretation of Soviet Marxism is that he seems to take Soviet Marxism as a single block. He does not analyse the revolutionary innovations of the heroic period, the regressive changes instituted by Stalin, nor does he explicate the views of the left-wing opposition that projected alternative models to repressive, bureaucratic socialism. Particularly striking is his almost total neglect of Trotsky (mentioned only once in the whole book!), whose critique of Stalinism and bureaucratic socialism surely should be taken into account and critically discussed. Perhaps Marcuse's belief that Stalinism was being abolished explains his omission of Trotsky's critique of Soviet Marxism, which could be said to be bound up with a historically surpassed stage of

Russian history and no longer relevant to today's situation – but this would assume that Stalinism has been surpassed! Marcuse also does not handle, in any detail, the questions raised by Trotsky, and continued by Marxists of many tendencies, as to whether the Soviet Union is truly a socialist society and to what extent it shares features of both capitalist and socialist economic models. He does not analyse the sense in which, and extent to which, capitalist institutions and practices still exist in the Soviet Union, nor does he discern any attractive socialist features of the society, or the sense in which capitalism has been abolished. He remarks offhandedly at a couple of points that Soviet Marxism is not socialism ((*SM*, pp. 70, 138), but does not specify *why* it is not socialism,[28] and therefore does not carry out adequately an 'immanent critique' which measures Soviet Marxism against Marxian socialism.

7.1.3 *Critique of Soviet ideology*

Marcuse's critique of Soviet ideology is more detailed, penetrating and successful than his critique of the Soviet political system. This is not surprising, since Marcuse's forte since the 1930s has been critique of ideology. In *Soviet Marxism* he turns the Marxian critique of ideology against Soviet Marxism itself in the last several chapters of Part 1 and throughout Part II, on the 'Ethical Tenets' of Soviet Marxism. For Marcuse, the most striking and paradoxical feature of Soviet Marxism is that a blatant revisionism masquerades as a relentless orthodoxy in which the function of the dialectic 'has undergone a significant change' (*SM*, p. 122).[29] Marcuse argues that whereas the Marxian dialectic is a tool of critical and revolutionary thought that analyses the contradictions and antagonisms of a social order, Soviet Marxism surrenders the critical dialectic and uses it to justify the existing regime, by codifying it into a philosophical system which contains categories, laws and principles that are used to legitimize the rationality of the established Soviet society. In this formalization of the Marxian dialectic, there is a pre-eminent emphasis on the dialectics of nature. Engels's text on this subject is the canonical classic.[30]

Marcuse criticizes the notion of a dialectic of nature, arguing that generalizing dialectical materialism into a philosophical world-view pre-eminently exemplified in a dialectics of nature leads to a 'de-emphasis of history' (*SM*, p. 129). For Soviet 'dialectical materialism', formulation of universal, atemporal laws is given priority over understanding the dynamics of a given social-economic formation and its dialectical transition to a higher stage. The devaluation of history is revealed in the division of the Marxist theory into dialectical and historical materialism, a division that Marcuse argues 'would have been meaningless to Marx, for whom dialectical materialism was synonymous with historical materialism' (*SM*, p. 124). Historical materialism for Soviet Marxism is an 'extension' and 'application' to the study of society and history of the basic laws and principles of dialectical materialism. Hence, historical materialism is but one branch of a particular scientific-philosophical system for Soviet Marxism, whereas for Marx one could argue that the theory of historical materialism was the foundation of Marxism.

The Soviet interpretation of historical materialism exhibits a petrification of the dialectic: 'history is reified into a second nature' (*SM*, p. 129) and is described by deterministic laws. Historical materialism is thus reduced to a set of 'objective laws of social development', which 'codified into an ideology and interpreted by the officials of the Party, justifies policy and practice' (*SM*, p. 129). Soviet development is said to be the outcome of necessary social laws and thus the present Soviet state is sanctioned by the Marxist ideology. The Party which comprehends, interprets and applies these laws is the sole repository of truth, whose action is claimed to be in accord with the objective laws of history (*SM*, pp. 129–30, 134f). In Marcuse's view, Soviet Marxism therefore contains a crude, mechanistic and deterministic theory of history that is used to justify state politics and ensure Party domination.

Within the ideological sphere, since philosophy has been denied its critical, oppositional status in Soviet Marxism and serves as an instrument of domination, the centre of (potential) opposition and criticism, Marcuse claims, has shifted from philosophy to literature and art. Marcuse detects a duality in the realm of ideology that is intrinsic to the higher ideological creations, such as philosophy and art. On the orthodox Marxist analysis of the relations between the economic base and ideological superstructure, all ideology is an 'illusion' (*Schein*): mere ideas which reflect one set of class interests that exclude all conflicting or dissenting ideas. As a 'reflection' of the base, ideology represents real realities but in a false form – false because they are one-sided – the ideas of the ruling class which claim universal validity. Consequently, ideology 'serves as a prop for a specific social system' (*SM*, p. 110). However, the stabilizing, apologetic function of ideology does not exhaust its content or function:

> the function of ideology goes far beyond such service. Into the ideology has entered material which – transmitted from generation to generation – contains the perpetual hopes, aspirations and sufferings of man, his suppressed potentialities, the images of integral justice, happiness and freedom. They find their ideological expressions chiefly in religion, philosophy and art, but also in the juristic and political concepts of liberty, equality and security. (*SM*, p. 110).

This dual function of ideology corresponds to Marcuse's analysis of the dual function of art.[31] Marcuse claims that art and philosophy are those aspects of the superstructure that are the furthest removed from the economic base. Further, 'the more the base encroaches upon the ideology, manipulating and co-ordinating it with the established order, the more the ideological sphere which is remotest from the reality (art, philosophy), precisely because of its remoteness, becomes the last refuge for the opposition to this order' (*SM*, p. 110).

Traditionally, philosophy was the ideological sphere most remote from the material base and was the centre of opposition to the existing order. For Marx, philosophy was to be translated into reality and thus lose its merely ideological character through the revolutionary action of the proletariat and its realization in the socialist society, thus bringing philosophy from heaven to earth. This realization of philosophy would consequently negate its rarified ideological nature as mere ideas on the top of the superstructure. Soviet Marxism claims to have carried out this realization of philosophy, thus achieving 'the negation of philosophy' (i.e. as ideology). Against this conception, Marcuse argues that if the social-historical reality prevents the realization of philosophy, then theory becomes the refuge of truth, preserving emancipatory ideas from their suppression or distortion in the historical reality (*SM*, p. 111). Therefore, philosophy 'not only anticipates political practice, runs ahead of it, but also upholds the objectives of liberation in the face of a failing practice' (*SM*, p. 111). Hence philosophy becomes 'ideology', not as 'illusion' or 'false consciousness', but as 'conscious distance or disassociation from, even opposition to, the repressive reality' (*SM*, p. 111). Moreover, Marcuse now claims that 'Marxian theory is in its very substance philosophy', in the sense that it projects practical measures for changing the world and preserves the promise and hope for liberation and the abolition of oppression. In this analysis authentic philosophy cannot be negated, surpassed or overcome, for philosophy has an inherent critical, oppositional status. This conception of philosophy as opposition is operative throughout Marcuse's later writings and repeats his earlier concept of philosophy as a crucial part of social theory and radical practice (see Chapters 2–5).

Since Soviet Marxism has abolished the oppositional status of philosophy and has integrated philosophy into its ideological apparatus of domination, philosophy cannot be used as an instrument of social critique or a means of expressing oppositional ideas, alternatives to the status quo, or dissent from the prevailing ideology. But if there is a conflict between the individual interests and the general interest, if individual needs are not fulfilled and are 'repelled by reality, they strive for ideological expression' (*SM*, p. 112). And to the extent that the promises of liberation are not fulfilled, ideological opposition is potentially explosive.

In Marcuse's view, the centre of opposition has shifted in the Soviet Union from philosophy to literature and art, thus the Soviet state must attempt to coerce art and the cultural apparatus to serve the interests of the state. The tool for transforming art into an instrument of social control is *Soviet realism*. Marcuse sharply distinguishes between realism and Soviet realism:

> Realism can be – and has been – a highly critical and progressive form of art; confronting reality 'as it is' with its ideological and idealized representations, realism upholds the truth against concealment and falsification. In this sense realism shows the ideal of human freedom in its actual negation and betrayal and thus preserves the transcendence without which art itself is cancelled. In contrast, Soviet realism conforms to the pattern of a repressive state. (*SM*, pp. 113–14)

Soviet realism emasculates art by robbing it of its critical-cognitive function. Marcuse repeats his earlier analysis of the subversive-liberating potentialities of art, arguing that its images 'preserved the determinate negation of the established reality – ultimate freedom' (*SM*, p. 114). Furthermore:

> art reveals and at the same time consecrates the (subjectively and objectively) unmastered forces in man and his world, the 'danger zones' beneath and beyond social control. Viewed from the position of a repressive society, ultimate freedom resides in these danger zones. On its deepest level, art is a protest against that which is. By that very token, art is a 'political' matter: if left to itself, it may endanger law and order. Plato's treatment of art and his system of rigid censorship which fuses aesthetic, political and epistemological criteria, does more justice to the nature and function of art than does its evaluation as 'free' intellectual, emotional, or educational entertainment. (*SM*, p. 117)

When society is the negation of freedom, art preserves the images of liberation. It can do this only by 'total refusal, that is, by not succumbing to the standards of the unfree reality, either in style, or in form, or in substance' (*SM*, p. 117). To counteract this subversive potential of art, 'The Soviet state by administrative decree prohibits the transcendence of art: it thus eliminates even the ideological reflex of freedom in an unfree society. Soviet realistic art, complying with the decree, becomes an instrument of social control in the last still nonconformist dimension of the human existence' (*SM*, p. 118). Soviet art is to 'reflect' the ideal images of Soviet society (the ideal worker, soldier, farmer, etc.) bringing about a strange convergence of realism and romanticism (*SM*, p. 116).

Fundamentally, Soviet art has an educative role: '"Art teaches . . . a definite relation to reality"' (*SM*, p. 118), writes a Soviet ideologue. Marcuse notes that art shares the 'magical character' of Soviet ideology: it is to create and establish certain effects, a certain type of person, certain attitudes: i.e., it is to create good, obedient, patriotic citizens, hard-working labourers, heroic soldiers, orthodox socialist thought. To be strictly avoided in Soviet realism are images portraying the dark, tragic side of human life. Even 'formalism' is rejected, as are all dissonance, discord, surrealism or 'bourgeois decadence'. Marcuse's critique can be summed up briefly: Soviet Marxism 'wants art that is not art and it gets what it asks for' (*SM*, p. 116).[32]

Soviet ethics, too, Marcuse argues, robs ethics of its emancipatory-humanist features, reducing ethics to legitimation of norms of Soviet practice. Marcuse analyses acutely how the heretical-oppositional status of Marx's critique of capitalism, concept of socialism and ethic of liberation is muted in Soviet Marxism, which more and more comes to resemble bourgeois ethics with its work ethic, puritan sexual morality and exhortations to conformity, all of which 'converge on the subordination of pleasure to duty – the duty to put everything one has into service for the state, the Party and society' (*SM*, p. 217). This means, practically, monogamic sexual relations directed towards child-rearing, disciplined labour geared towards higher productivity, leisure as relaxation from work and recreation of energy for more work – in a word, conformity to values very similar to bourgeois values. Marcuse notes that the Soviet ethic 'is in every respect a *competitive work morality*, proclaimed with a rigidity surpassing that of bourgeois morality' (*SM*, p. 217). 'Love for one's work' is the highest principle of Communist morality, and all the exhortations incessantly propagandized focus on work morale (*SM*, p. 218). 'All work, under socialism, has a creative character ... and work per se is declared to be one of the most important factors in the building of moral qualities' (*SM*, p. 218).

Marcuse's commitment to individual freedom and happiness leads him to reject the repressive Soviet work ethic against which he urges a consideration of the Marxist distinction 'between work as the realization of human potentialities and work as "alienated labour"' (*SM*, p. 218). He argues that the Soviet work ethic obliterates the Marxist distinction between alienated and non-alienated labour: 'the individual is supposed to invest all his energy and all his aspirations in whatever function he finds himself or is put by the authorities' (*SM*, p. 219). For Marcuse, the 'all-round, many-sided individual' in the Marxist theory becomes the 'all-round labourer' in the Soviet concept who invests all his or her energy into labour. He disputes the Soviets' claim to have abolished alienated labour with nationalization and insists that socialism and liberation require the development of the individual and the extension of democracy and freedom throughout all spheres of life. Marcuse thus finds the Soviet ideology and ethics at odds with genuine Marxian socialism, as is the Soviet political system.

Although Marcuse's critique of Soviet ideology is sharp, there are some deficiencies in his analysis. Similar to his treatment of Soviet Marxism as a political-historical phenomenon, he treats Soviet Marxist philosophy as a bloc and does not distinguish between the versions of Soviet Marxism developed by Lenin, Trotsky, Stalin, the Left opposition and later Soviet systematizers. Moreover, Marcuse's treatment reflects the Soviet attempt to present Marxism as a piece: one, finished, non-antagonistic system. But a serious critique of Soviet Marxism should show how the current orthodoxy is a revision of both Marxism and Leninism. In fact there is no really satisfactory discussion of Lenin's role in transmitting Soviet Marxism, his relation to Marx and Engels, his own philosophical contribution, or how his political praxis modified Marxism. Marcuse's one reference to Lenin's philosophical writings is a swipe at him.[33] But he ignores Lenin's many explications of the dialectical method, his theory of the state, his late *Philosophical Notebooks*, which correct some of the views in *Materialism and Empirio-criticism*, and his constant stress on the revolutionary import of Marxism. Similarly, Marcuse does not discuss the debates within Soviet Marxism and the differences between the versions of Soviet Marxism by various Soviet Marxist thinkers whose debates had ideological as well as political significance. Thus Marcuse recognizes no dialectic of Soviet philosophy: he does not clarify the tension between Marx and Lenin, between Leninism and Stalinism, between Marxism-Leninism (or Trotskyism) and the current Soviet orthodoxy – as if Soviet Marxism were one unified doctrine from Lenin to the present day.

On a philosophical level, there is no detailed exposition and critique of the Soviet codification of Marxism. One explanation is that Marcuse was not writing for philosophers (although probably only professional philosophers or Sovietologists could understand much of his book), but was primarily interested in the political dimension of Soviet Marxist ideology. Moreover, Marcuse published his *Soviet Marxism* in a period of Soviet ideological vacuum. Whereas during Stalin's life several of his essays had been canonical, after his death they were increasingly ignored, and comprehensive texts explicating the current Soviet Marxist ideology were not published until 1958–9, after the publication of *Soviet Marxism*.[34] Hence Marcuse did not have the material at hand to make a comprehensive, detailed critique of the current Soviet ideology – indeed, a serious philosophical and political critique of Soviet

Marxism is a task that still remains to be performed by critical Marxists today.

Although Marcuse sharply criticizes Soviet Communist society and ideology, he does believe that there are trends both within the Soviet political system and its ideology that may lead to liberalization.

7.2 Towards a possible liberalization?

Early in *Soviet Marxism*, Marcuse asks if there is an 'inner dynamic' in Soviet society 'which may counteract the repressive tendencies and transform the structure of Soviet society' (*SM*, p. 78). The repressive policy operative in Soviet society was explained during Stalin's time by the doctrine of 'socialism in one country', i.e. the struggle for survival against a hostile capitalist environment necessitating a crash programme of industrialization and re-armament. In fact, up until today, 'the initial isolation of the Bolshevik Revolution, the confinement of socialism to backward areas, and the reconsolidation of capitalism on an intercontinental scale are held responsible for the internal as well as external contradictions which plague Soviet society' (*SM*, pp. 78–9). The doctrine of 'socialism in one country', and the ensuing development of Soviet society, shows the extent to which Soviet Marxism was influenced by its relation to the capitalist orbit and how its policies were determined by configurations in the international arena.

This situation has led some political analysts to postulate a vicious circle of a self-perpetuating continuum of repression: capitalist encirclement necessitates a high degree of industrialization, militarization and repression in the Soviet Union; the strengthening of Soviet society in turn is a stabilizing and unifying factor in the capitalist world; hence a steady escalation of industrial competition, militarization, international rivalry and hostilities in the cold war, which perpetuates repression and militates against progressive social change in both camps. Marcuse is aware of this analysis, but sees a series of factors and trends that would indicate both a move towards possible liberalization in Soviet society and a relaxation of tension on the international scene. Indeed, Marcuse claims that liberalization in the Soviet Union (de-Stalinization) and peaceful coexistence are profoundly interrelated. I shall summarize briefly

Marcuse's case for an improved situation in Soviet society, which in turn would ease international tensions and increase the chances for peaceful coexistence.

(1) On the international scene, a cooling off of the cold war could make it possible to ease repression in the Soviet Union. A reduction in defence expenditure could increase consumer expenditure and create a better life for the Russian people, which might secure mass loyalty and reduce the need for repression. Reduction in military expenditure in the West would further reduce international tensions and would shift competition between capitalist and Communist societies from the military arena to political, economic and cultural fields. Marcuse conjectures that a concerted programme to improve Soviet society (made possible by a re-allocation of expenditures and the relaxation of repression) and to create a model socialism could serve to demonstrate the superiority of socialism, which would spread 'by contagion' (*SM*, pp. 82–3), thus improving the position of socialism in the struggle between the two world systems. On these grounds, Marcuse seems to believe that the Soviet Union has objective reasons in its own interest to practice a foreign policy of peaceful coexistence and to reduce internal repression.

(2) Within Soviet society, increased productivity and social wealth would 'overflow' (*SM*, pp. 155, 161) from heavy industrialization and militarization into consumer goods that will make possible a more egalitarian society in which each citizen can be provided for according to his or her needs (*SM*, pp. 151–2). Marcuse argues that the Soviet bureaucracy is 'linked to intensified development of productive forces' and will not oppose an 'overflow' of productivity into consumer goods, which would provide a satisfaction of consumer needs that might 'effectuate a gradual but qualitative change in the circumstances of the underprivileged population and, correspondingly, in the political institutions' (*SM*, p. 155). Moreover, Soviet Marxism's drive to overtake and surpass capitalism could serve to improve the quality of Soviet society: 'The attainment of the international objectives – chiefly the weakening of Western society from within – ultimately depends on the attainment of a higher level of Soviet society (in Marxist language, the second stage of socialism)' (*SM*, p. 150).

(3) There are also ideological reasons for liberalization summed up in the formula 'the transition from socialism to Communism'. From

the beginning of Soviet Marxism, the official goal has been to 'transform the system itself into the "higher" second phase' (*SM*, p. 151). Since the industrial base has been created which is strong enough to provide resources for heavy industry, defence and consumer goods (*SM*, p. 161), failure to provide for individual needs (for material goods, freedom, etc.) would lead to a contradiction with the Marxist-Leninist ideology. Marcuse argues that an increasing contradiction between increased material comforts, higher productivity, growing social wealth and continued repression could create an 'explosive' situation that could lead to the liberalization of Soviet society. These changes would be propelled by an ideology that projected the ideal of a rational society without exploitation, repression or social contradictions contained in the concept of the transition from socialism to Communism. This argument assumes that Marxism-Leninism *is* a progressive ideology, which, if genuinely appropriated and practised, could act as a progressive force of social change in the Soviet Union.

(4) Marcuse also argues that, freed from repressive use as an instrument of social control, 'technological rationality may be a powerful vehicle of liberation' (*SM*, p. 240). In the Soviet Union, Marcuse argues, 'there seems to be no *inherent* forces which resist accelerated and extensive automation – either on the part of management or on the part of labour' (*SM*, p. 240). In most capitalist countries, by comparison, management will only introduce automation if they can realize a substantial profit, while organized labour resists automation that results in the loss of jobs. In contrast, Marcuse sees no obstacles in the Soviet Union to replacing 'socially necessary and unpleasant labour' by machine work. This elimination of alienated labour would make possible the elimination of the repressive work ethic. But Marcuse argues that the liberating use of technology requires radical social change. By itself, technological progress can be 'dehumanizing and destructive': assembly-line work, speed-ups, longer working days, production of waste, etc. (*SM*, p. 241). Therefore, 'the truly liberating effects of technology are not implied in technological progress per se; they presuppose social change, involving the basic economic institutions and relationships' (*SM*, p. 241). Thus Marcuse does not subscribe to the 'technocratic' thesis that technology in itself is a vehicle of social progress, which of its own dynamic will create a better society.

The truly liberating use of technology, Marcuse claims, involves the 'transfer of control from above to below while retaining the same social base (nationalization)' (*SM*, p. 241). If the workers truly control their technology and labour activity, they can develop their individuality while utilizing technology both as an exercise in their creativity and inventiveness, and in freeing them from mechanical, routine work. This liberating use of technology would aim at 'growth in the consciousness and enjoyment of freedom' (*SM*, p. 242), and could make possible the 'all-round individual', which is the human ideal of the Marxian theory. Marcuse's speculations on the potential liberating or enslaving possibilities of technology, introduced here, are developed in his later work.

Marcuse concludes that the 'new rationality' in Soviet Marxism and the Marxist ideology assume a dynamic that portends a possible liberalizing trend. He believes that the Soviet technological education promotes standards of rationality which will lead its citizens to see the irrational features of the Soviet system, and to deplore the contradiction between increased productivity and undiminished repression. He also believes that the citizens will become increasingly aware of the contradiction between the ideal of the Marxist-Leninist ideology and reality of the Soviet system:

> Whether the working day is reduced to five hours and less or not, whether the individual's free time is really his or not, whether he must 'earn his living' by procuring the necessities of life or not, whether he can freely choose his occupation or not – all these can be verified by the individuals themselves. No matter how regimented and manipulated the latter may be, they will know whether Communism thus defined is a fact or not. (*SM*, p. 249)

Anticipating Bahro's concept of 'surplus consciousness' (see 9.51), Marcuse suggests that individuals can see for themselves whether the ideological promises have been fulfilled and that they will become increasingly disenchanted if the contradictions between the ideal and the real, the rationality fostered by technology and education and the irrationality of the system, grow and become increasingly detected and abhorred. Thus Marcuse believes that Marxism-Leninism is a generally critical and progressive ideology which could develop a momentum, forcing the Soviet ruling clique to relax repression, and that 'the continued promulgation and indoctrination in Marxism may still turn out to be a dangerous weapon for the Soviet rulers' (*SM*, p. 250). He concludes: 'Ideological pressure thus seems to tend in the same direction as technical-economic pressure, namely towards the relaxation of repression' (*SM*, p. 251).

Although Marcuse sees a liberalization trend in Soviet Marxism rooted in its historical situation, its material base, relations of production and its ideology, he believes that 'total mobilization', and thus domination, will continue:

Improvement and liberalization will be conditional upon the relentless struggle for higher productivity of labour, upon socialist competition, and upon total mobilization of the people for work and for training ... it is rooted in the objective conditions under which the Soviet state operates, in the 'anomaly' of capitalist and socialist coexistence which Lenin's political testament epitomized. The notion of socialism in a 'capitalist environment' precludes abandonment of the total mobilization of the people; it also precludes a fundamental change in the value system which subordinates socialist freedom to toil and discipline. (*SM*, p. 163)

Consequently Marcuse does not see Soviet Marxism realizing in the foreseeable future Marx's ideal of 'freedom and initiative "from below", in handing over control to the "immediate producers"' (*SM*, pp. 63f). Progress and liberalization will, he believes, come from above: 'administered liberalization'. Marcuse does not therefore claim that the power of the bureaucracy will significantly diminish, that the state will wither away, or that significant democratization and increase of freedom will take place: 'the continued strengthening of the state and of the party agencies remains on the agenda' (*SM*, p. 164). His point is that liberalization will be the result of a conscious political decision on the part of the bureaucracy and that therefore the transition to Communism will neither be a consequence of mass struggle, nor the mechanical result of a pre-determined technical-economic development. Since he does not perceive any significant trend towards workers' democracy, he is uncertain as to whether the Soviet Union will achieve genuine socialist democracy: 'Whether or not the growth of the welfare state will ultimately bring the administration under direct popular control, that is to say, whether or not the Soviet state will develop into a socialist or Communist democracy, is a question for which the prevailing facts and tendencies do not provide a workable hypothesis' (*SM*, p. 172). In fact, Marcuse concludes on a pessimistic note:

> There is no prospect that this fusion of economic and political controls in a self-perpetuating state will dissolve: it is doubly grounded, in the nationalized but not socialized Soviet economy, and in the international situation of large-scale industry ... the direction is towards a growing welfare state. Rising standards of living up to a practically free distribution of basic goods and services, steadily extending mechanization of labour, exchangeability of technical functions, expanding popular culture – these developments constitute the probable trend ... But these changes themselves will take place within the framework of universal control, universal administration. (*SM*, pp. 171–2)

7.3 Marcuse and Soviet Marxism

A possible explanation for Marcuse's appraisal of the liberalizing trends in Soviet Communism might be the 'thaw' which Khrushchev's denunciation of Stalin produced after the Twentieth Congress of the Communist Party in 1956.[35] Communists and others all over the world were animated by the hope that Khrushchev's speech would mark the end of Stalinism and the beginning of a new period of Communist liberalization. They hoped that Khrushchev's regime would break with Stalinism and create a new type of Communism. Did Marcuse share these hopes? A clear answer is difficult to provide. Marcuse's only references to Khrushchev in the text of *SM* analyse those features in Khrushchev's Twentieth Congress speech which denote continuity with the objectives of the Stalinist regime (*SM*, p. 154), followed by citation of Khrushchev's proclamation that 'the continued strengthening of the state and of the party agencies remain on the agenda' (*SM*, p. 164). Thus, in 1958, Marcuse did not seem to believe that the change in political leadership was a decisive force of de-Stalinization.

Rather, Marcuse derived his analysis of the existence of liberalizing tendencies from study of the socio-economic situation and other trends in the Soviet Union (see especially *SM*, pp. 154–75). He argues that the 'industrial base' has been created to produce a higher form of Communism and that there are structural imperatives in the bureaucracy, ideology, technology and world political constellation that may drive these tendencies to a higher stage of civilization. Hence Marcuse shows himself again to be committed to the Marxian method of social analysis, focusing on the base of Soviet society to discern its essential features, rather than being guided in his analysis by the superstructure of the new Soviet leaders.

In the 1961 preface to the Vintage edition of *SM*, Marcuse claims that the 'trend towards reform and liberalization within the Soviet Union has continued' (*SM*, p. vi). He also seems much more sympathetic towards Khrushchev, accepting Deutscher's analysis of the modifications on Soviet policy, internal and external, in the current Soviet regime (*SM*, p. vi). Furthermore, Marcuse seems to accept Khrushchev's doctrine of 'peaceful coexistence' (*SM*, pp. viif) and call for disarmament (*SM*, p. x) at face value, as well as Khrushchev's claim that the Soviet Union is moving towards the 'second phase' of Communism (*SM*, p. x). These remarks suggest that Marcuse continued to believe in liberalizing trends in the Soviet Union in the early 1960s and that the Khrushchev administration was the vehicle of liberalization.

In a 1963 preface to the French edition of *Soviet Marxism*, however, Marcuse notes that focus on the issue of whether fundamental changes are taking place in the Soviet Union under Khrushchev deflects attention from the more pressing question of whether fundamental changes are taking place in US politics, 'in particular since the arrival to power of the Kennedy administration'.[36] In Marcuse's view, it seemed that US politics was becoming more aggressive and interventionist in the Third World and was forcing the Soviet Union to focus more on competition with the West and the arms race, thus suspending possibilities of liberalization in an intensified cold war atmosphere. He highlights here his thesis that Soviet Communist parties are more and more the 'historical inheritors of the pre-war Social Democratic parties', but indicates that they now face another Communist movement on their Left, namely the Chinese Communists who 'reclaim the heritage of Marxism-Leninism'. Consequently, in the early 1960s Marcuse perceived a shifting, fluid political situation that made it increasingly difficult to perceive liberalizing tendencies in the Soviet Communist countries.

In historical retrospect, it can be argued that the ousting of Khrushchev in 1964 and controversies over his accomplishments and failures and the extent of his de-Stalinization – combined with the subsequent course of Soviet Communism – put in question whether, or to what extent, genuine liberalization was taking place in the Soviet Union from 1956–64. This is not to deny important changes from the Stalin era, but simply questions whether Marcuse exaggerated the changes and liberalizing trends and underestimated the continuity with the Stalinist period.[37]

It seems that since Marcuse wanted to produce a discourse on the Soviet Union that would contribute to a thaw in the cold war and would promote 'peaceful coexistence', he restrained his criticism of bureaucratic Communism. In view of developments in the Soviet Union since the publication of *Soviet Marxism* in 1958, it is probably Marcuse's most problematical work. As noted, the 'liberalizing trends' that Marcuse analysed as a historical possibility failed to materialize, and there is little evidence that liberalization trends in the Soviet Union will develop in the foreseeable future. Moreover, the nature of Soviet politics domestically and abroad in the two decades since the publication of *SM* does not encourage favourable evaluation or 'balanced' presentation of the Soviet system. Hence, the project of developing a critique of bureaucratic Communism has been carried out by a large number of 'critical Marxists'. Marcuse anticipated this trend, but at the time of the publication of *SM*, he was inhibited, I believe, by the widely shared view of the Left and others at the time that the Soviet Union, for all its faults, was still the only major non-capitalist power in the world and should be supported by all those who sincerely wanted socialism. But with the construction of socialist societies in China and Cuba, and with a proliferation of Third World revolutionary movements throughout the world, people on the Left no longer feel the necessity to identify the cause of world socialism with the Soviet Union. Hence, a conjuncture of the increasingly repressive and bureaucratic features of the Soviet Union with a proliferation of other countries calling themselves socialist, and offfering models of socialism different from the Soviet Union, has led Marxists all over the world to develop a critique of bureaucratic Communism.[38]

Marcuse's *Soviet Marxism* stands in a paradoxical relation to this tendency. Despite the frequently apologetic overtones of his 'liberalization' analysis, Marcuse's study also contains important critiques of Soviet institutions, practice and ideology which could be further developed as aspects of a critique of bureaucratic Communism. For example, in addition to the critical remarks already cited, one finds throughout *SM* declarations that Soviet society is 'an unfree society' (*SM*, p. 118) which is 'utterly irrational' and supported by terroristic conformity (*SM*, p. 70). He suggests that it is not 'a full democracy in which the constitutional rights of all citizens are guaranteed and enforced' (*SM*, p. 71), and even claims it is not a socialist society! (*SM*, pp. 70, 138). Marcuse also makes several references to the 'totalitarian administration' (*SM*, p. 96), noting 'the maintenance of a vast military establishment (armed forces and secret police) with its educational, political and psychological controls' (*SM*, p. 156). He predicts the rise of a Soviet 'welfare state' marked by 'repressive competition and competitive mobilization on a totalitarian scale' (*SM*, p. 173).

Despite its relative historical obsolescence, and despite its apologetic features, which a critical Left should reject, there are still useful sections of *Soviet Marxism* which I have tried to draw out in my interpretation, as I also indicated its ambivalences and its deficiencies. The book is important in Marcuse's corpus as a critique of Soviet Communism that parallels his critique of advanced capitalism in *ODM* and his discussion of an 'advanced industrial society' which conceptualizes allegedly similar features of social control and domination in both capitalist and Communist societies. With regard to Marcuse's tendency to equate different, historically specific trends and institutions under one generic concept of Domination, the more historically specific analyses of *Soviet Marxism* serve as an antidote to some of the more generalizing tendencies of *One-Dimensional Man* and some of his other writings.

Yet Marcuse's relation to theories of 'post-industrial society' and 'convergence theory' remains a difficult issue to resolve. He seems to share the belief held by post-industrial theorists that as the Soviet Union developed its technological base, it would become more like advanced capitalism. But Marcuse differs from those theorists by seeing the negative aspects of the shared technological base as producing new forms of social control – a central theme of *One-*

Dimensional Man, which I shall address in the next chapter; there I shall again take up the issue of to what extent Marcuse does or does not subscribe to convergence theory.

As noted, Marcuse sees important differences in social and economic organization between capitalist and socialist societies and constantly points to these differences (see the discussion earlier in this chapter). Whereas he saw liberalizing tendencies in the Soviet Union as a result, in part, of increased technological rationality, he saw these same tendencies in the capitalist societies as producing a 'one-dimensional society' and 'one-dimensional man'. Thus his relative optimism in *Soviet Marxism* is related to his pessimism in *One-Dimensional Man*.

8

Marcuse's Theory of Advanced Industrial Society: *One-Dimensional Man*

One-Dimensional Man (hereafter *ODM*) articulates the crisis of Marxism in an era which seemed to refute the Marxian theory of history and socialist revolution. Marcuse challenges some of the basic postulates of Marx's theory, while using Marxian categories and method of analysis and critique. The result is a reconstruction of Marxian theory which questions such central features of Marxism as the theory of capitalist crisis and the revolutionary role of the working class in making possible socialist revolution. Marcuse subtitles his book 'Studies in the Ideology of Advanced Industrial Society', but roots his critique of culture and ideology in an analysis of the socio-economic foundation of 'advanced industrial society'. Consequently, the book produces a theory of society that uses the Marxian method of analysis to produce a radical critique of contemporary capitalist and Communist societies, culture and ideology.

ODM contains a synthesis of theories and ideas which Marcuse had been developing for several decades. He combines aspects of the theories of contemporary civilization developed by Hegel, Marx, Freud, Weber, Heidegger and Lukács with theories of advanced industrial society developed by contemporary German and French social theorists and American social scientists and critical journalists. The project of developing a theory of advanced industrial society is essentially indebted to Marcuse's work with the Institute for Social Research.[1] Many of its presuppositions are articulated in his earlier works, or in the texts of other critical theorists, and are not always spelled out in detail in *ODM*. Therefore to unpack the dense problematic of *ODM* requires examining some earlier texts, which do articulate its presuppositions, in order to elucidate the sources and basic concepts of Marcuse's theory.

8.1 Reading *One-Dimensional Man*

Marcuse first published his emerging perspectives on the fate of the individual in industrial society in a 1941 article, 'Some Social Implications of Modern Technology', where he sketches the historical decline of individualism from the time of the bourgeois revolutions to the rise of modern technological society.[2] Individual rationality, he claims, was won in the struggle against regnant superstitions, irrationality and domination, and posed the individual in a critical stance against society. Critical rationality was thus a creative principle which was both the source of the individual's liberation and society's advancement. In the emerging bourgeois ideology of the period, the nascent liberal-democratic society was deemed the social arrangement in which the individual could pursue his or her own self-interest and at the same time contribute to social progress. The development of modern industry and technological rationality, however, undermined the basis of the individual rationality and submitted the individual to increasing domination by the technical-social apparatus (pp. 417ff). As capitalism and technology developed, advanced industrial society demanded increasing adjustment to the economic and social apparatus, and submission to increasingly total domination and administration. Hence, a 'mechanics of conformity' spread throughout the society. The efficiency and power of advanced industrial society overwhelmed the individual, who gradually lost the earlier traits of critical rationality (i.e. autonomy, dissent, the power of negation, etc.), thus producing a 'one-dimensional society' and 'one-dimensional man'.

The characteristic themes of Marcuse's post-Second World War writings build on the Frankfurt School's analyses of the role of technology and technological rationality, administration and bureaucracy, the capitalist state, mass media and consumerism, which in their view produced both a decline in the revolutionary potential of the working class and a decline of individuality, freedom and democracy. In a 1954 epilogue to the second edition of

R&R, Marcuse claims that: 'The defeat of Fascism and National Socialism has not arrested the trend towards totalitarianism. Freedom is on the retreat – in the realm of thought as well as in that of society'.[3] In Marcuse's view, the powers of reason and freedom are declining in 'late industrial society': 'With the increasing concentration and effectiveness of economic, political and cultural controls, the opposition in all these fields has been pacified, co-ordinated, or liquidated' (p. 434). Indeed, reason has become an instrument of domination: 'it helps to organize, administer and anticipate the powers that be, and to liquidate the "power of Negativity". Reason has identified itself with the reality: what is actual is reasonable, although what is reasonable has not yet become actuality' (p. 434).

Not only Hegel's hope that reason would shape and control reality, but Marx's hope that reason would be embodied in a revolutionary class and rational socialist society, had come to naught. The proletariat was not the 'absolute negation of capitalist society presupposed by Marx' (p. 435) and the contradictions of capitalism had not proved as explosive as Marx forecast:

> When Marx envisaged the transition to socialism from the advanced industrial countries, he did so because not only the maturity of the productive forces, but also the irrationality of their use, the maturity of the internal contradictions of capitalism and of the will to their abolition were essential to his idea of socialism. But precisely in the advanced industrial countries, since about the turn of the century, the internal contradictions became subject to increasingly efficient organization, and the negative force of the proletariat was increasingly whittled down. Not only a small 'labour aristocracy' but the larger part of the labouring classes were made into a positive part of the established society. (p. 436)

Anticipating the theory in *ODM*, Marcuse wrote:

> Not just impoverishment, but impoverishment in the face of growing social productivity was supposed to make the proletariat a revolutionary force. Marx's notion of impoverishment implies consciousness of the arrested potentialities of man and of the possibility of their realization – consciousness of alienation and de-humanization. But then the development of capitalist produc-

tivity stopped the development of revolutionary consciousness. Technological progress multiplied the needs and satisfactions, while its utilization made the needs as well as their satisfactions repressive: they themselves sustain submission and domination. Progress in administration reduces the dimension in which individuals can still be 'with themselves' and 'for themselves' and transforms them into total objects of their society. The development of consciousness becomes the dangerous prerogative of outsiders. The sphere in which individual and group transcendence was possible is thus being eliminated – and with it the life element of opposition. (pp. 436–7)

The changed conditions in advanced industrial society made previous forms of class struggle obsolete:

> The tremendous rise in the productivity of labour within the framework of the prevailing social institutions made mass production inevitable – but also mass manipulation. The result was that the standard of living rose with the concentration of economic power to monopolistic proportions. Concurrently, technological progress fundamentally changed the balance of social power. The scope and effectiveness of the instruments of destruction controlled by the government made the classical forms of the social struggle old-fashioned and romantic. The barricade lost its revolutionary value just as the strike lost its revolutionary content. The economic and cultural co-ordination of the labouring classes was accompanied and supplemented by the obsolescence of their traditional weapons. (pp. 438)

Moreover, 'The consolidation of the capitalist system was greatly enhanced by the development of Soviet society' (p. 438). The 'terroristic industrialization' undertaken by the Soviet Union and its 'prevailing unfreedom' 'came to be identified not with a higher but with a lower stage of industrial development and with a hostile foreign power' (pp. 438–9). Against this power, Western society 'answered with total mobilization' which 'completed national and international control over the danger zones of society. The Western world was unified to an extent unknown in its long history' (p. 439). (Compare this passage with *ODM*, p. 21 to see how Marcuse maintained the same basic positions for over a decade prior to the publication of *ODM*.)

Marcuse's theses of capitalist stabilization and integration of the working class were highlighted in a 1957 preface to Raya Dunayevskaya's *Marxism and Freedom:*

> The key for the understanding of Marxism since about the turn of the century is the transformation of 'free' into organized capitalism on an international scale, its economic and political stabilization, and the ensuing increase in the standard of living. This transformation affected the labouring classes of the advanced industrial countries in a decisive way. Under the leadership of their successful bureaucracy, the situation of a major part of these classes changed from one of 'absolute negation' to one of affirmation of the established system. With the reduction of the revolutionary potential in the West, socialism was losing its classical historical agent and area and was subsequently constructed in the backward areas of the East in a way essentially alien to the Marxian conception. The growth of the Communist orbit in turn welded the capitalist countries closer together and created a firmer basis for stabilization and internal unification. Neither wars nor depressions nor inflations nor deflations have arrested this trend. It presents the greatest challenge to Marxist theory and to the Marxist evaluation of contemporary Communism.[4]

Marcuse uses Hilferding's term 'organized capitalism' here to describe the administrative-bureaucratic apparatus which organizes, manages and stabilizes capitalist society.[5] The concept of 'organized capitalism' took on new historical content in the European war economies during the First World War, when the state took over, or managed, various sectors of the economy, and in Friedrich Pollock's concept of 'state capitalism', which theorized Keynesian steering strategies and New Deal reform politics.[6] Pollock's studies of economic planning in the state and the automatization of industry outlined new ways of utilizing technologies as instruments of domination and capitalist stabilization, providing the socio-economic foundation for the Institute's theory of the 'administered society'. Marcuse seemed to assume that 'organized capitalism' *had* stabilized its classical contradictions and averted major crises which were presupposed as necessary conditins for socialist revolution in Marx's theory. Instead, Marcuse saw that the unparalleled aflluence and apparatus of planning and management in advanced capitalism had produced new forms of social control and a 'society without opposition' that closed off possibilities of radical social change.

Marcuse also drew on works from contemporary French thinkers, such as those in the *Arguments* group, and published some articles in French which elucidate his concepts of one-dimensional society and thought. In 'De l'Ontologie à la Technolgie', he proposes the thesis that contemporary society has produced a 'technological world' where '*technology has replaced ontology*'.[7] Marcuse's analysis is based on a conception of the historical rise of a technological world which overpowers and controls its subjects. In this technological world, Marcuse claims that metaphysics is superseded by technology in that the previous metaphysical concepts of subject and object, which postulate an active subject confronting a controllable world of objects, are replaced by a one-dimensional technical world described as 'form without substance' where 'pure instrumentality' and 'efficacy' of arranging means and ends within a pre-established universe is the 'common principle of thought and action' (p. 56). This self-contained and self-perpetuating technological world allows change only within its own institutions and parameters. In this sense, it is 'one-dimensional' and 'has become a universal means of domination' which congeals into a 'second nature, *schlechte Unmittelbarkeit* (bad immediacy) which is perhaps more hostile and more destructive than *primary* nature, the pre-technical nature' (p. 56).

There are two ways to read Marcuse's theory of the one-dimensional technical world and society, which is the primary focus of *ODM*. One can interpret Marcuse's theory as a global, totalizing theory of a new type of society that transcends the contradictions of capitalist society in a new order that eliminates individuality, dissent and opposition. Indeed, there is a recurrent tendency in reading Marcuse to use 'one-dimensionality' as a totalizing concept to describe an era of historical development which supposedly absorbs all opposition into a totalitarian, monolithic system.[8] However, Marcuse himself rarely, if ever, uses the term 'one-dimensionality' (i.e. as a totalizing noun), but instead tends to speak of 'one-dimensional' man, society or thought, applying the term as an adjective describing deficient conditions which he criticizes and contrasts with an alternative state of affairs. Indeed, Marcuse introduces 'one-dimensional' in his earlier writings as an epistemological concept that makes a distinction between one-dimensional and dialectical thought – which is extended in *ODM* to describe social and anthropological phenomena.[9] Since, however, Marcuse criticizes 'one-dimensional' states of affairs with alternatives that are to be fought for and realized, it is wrong to read Marcuse as a theorist of the totally administered society who completely rejects contradiction, conflict, revolt and alternative thought and action. Since there are passages in *ODM* and his later works which put in question this interpretation, it is a mistake to interpret *ODM* simply as the epic of total domination in a quasi-Hegelian attempt to subsume everything into one monolithic totality.

Thus I interpret 'one-dimensional' as a concept describing a state of affairs that conforms to existing thought and behaviour in which there is the lack of a critical dimension and the dimension of alternatives and potentialities which transcend the existing society. In Marcuse's usage the adjective 'one-dimensional' describes an epistemological distinction between signifying practices that conform to pre-existing structures, norms and behaviour in thought and practice, and 'bi-dimensional' thought which appraises values, ideas and behaviour in terms of possibilities that transcend the established state of affairs. This 'bi-dimensional' thought presupposes antagonism between subject and object so that the subject is free to perceive possibilities in the world that do not yet exist but which can be realized through human practice. In the one-dimensional society, the subject is assimilated into the object and follows the dictates of external, objective structures, thus losing its abilities to discern more liberating possibilities and to engage in transformative practice to realize them. Marcuse's theory presupposes the existence of a human subject with traditional features of freedom, creativity and self-determination that stands in opposition to an object-world, perceived as substance, which contains possibilities to be realized and secondary qualities like values, aesthetic traits and ends which can be cultivated to enhance human life.

The distinction between 'one-dimensional' and 'bi-dimensional' thought and practice is rooted in Hegel's subject-object metaphysics.[10] In Hegel's philosophy the subject is at once a being-in-itself and a being-for-itself: 'Something is in itself in so far as it has returned to itself from Being-for-Other' (*R&R*, p. 133). Further, 'the "subject" is the power of an entity to "be itself in its otherness"' (*R&R*, p. 69). The subject has the power of reflection, freedom, comprehending knowledge and transformative (or 'mediating') action (*R&R*, pp. 69ff, 133ff, *passim*). The self-conscious subject, aware of its nature and powers, is a 'being-for-itself' and contains the powers of objectification in which it appropriates and makes its own ideas, forms of behavior, objects and institutions. Essential to its freedom and self-consciousness is the awareness of independence from the object: a free subject controls the object and is able to use its otherness for its own projects; if, however, the object controls the subject, a condition of unfreedom exists. This is precisely the situation in one-dimensional society where the object exercises control and domination over the subject. The tension between subject and object, central to Hegel's (and Marcuse's) thought, dissolves, and the subject assimilates itself to the object and thus loses its subjectivity. In forfeiting its powers of self-determination and self-consciousness, the subject loses its capacity to determine its own development and instead becomes an object of domination.

In Marcuse's analysis, 'one-dimensional man' has lost, or is losing, individuality, freedom and the ability to dissent and to control one's own destiny. The 'private space', the dimension of negation and individuality, in which one may become and remain a self, is being whittled away by a society which shapes aspirations, hopes, fears and values, even manipulating vital needs. In Marcuse's view, the price that one-dimensional man pays for its satisfactions is surrender of its freedom and individuality. The following chart contrasts what Marcuse perceives as traits of authentic individuality with those of one-dimensional man; the contrast suggests which dimensions are lacking in one-dimensional man and elucidates the concept of authentic individuality from which Marcuse criticizes the deficiencies of one-dimensional man:

Authentic Individuality	*One-dimensional Man*
(1) Autonomy/individual capacity to think, choose and act:	(1) Heteronomy/social domination of thought and behaviour:
(a) freedom from domination;	(a) servitude to social control;

(b) freedom for self-determination, choice, dissent and refusal.
(2) Creative self-activity: growth and development.
(3) Reflection and critical awareness of needs, assumptions and one's unique selfhood
(4) Power and will: ability for creative action.

(b) conformity, false needs and consciousness.
(2) Mimesis: mechanical reproduction of conformist behaviour.
(3) Unreflective and non-critical acceptance of prevailing needs, ideas and feelings; no sense of one's own needs and potentialities.
(4) Powerlessness/conditioned behaviour.

In losing its individuality, one-dimensional man also loses its freedom. Freedom involves knowledge, will and power: knowing what you need and want; willing to choose or deny; being able to resist obstacles and having the power to fulfil one's needs and develop one's potentialities. One-dimensional man does not know its true needs because its needs are not its own – they are administered, superimposed and heteronomous; it is not able to resist domination, nor to act autonomously, for it identifies with public behaviour and imitates and submits to the powers that be; lacking the power of authentic self-activity, one-dimensional man submits to increasingly total domination: 'thus emerges a pattern of *one-dimensional thought and behaviour* in which ideas, aspirations and objectives that, by their content, transcend the established universe of discourse and action are either repelled or reduced to terms of this universe' (*ODM*, p. 12).

This analysis shows that Marcuse is a radical individualist who is deeply disturbed by the decline of the traits of authentic individuality which he so highly values. One-dimensional society and one-dimensional man are the results of a long historical development that has led to a continual erosion of individuality which Marcuse has criticized over several decades. *ODM* can thus be interpreted as an extended protest against the decline of individuality in advanced industrial society. The cognitive costs involved include loss of an ability to perceive another dimension of possibilities and alternatives that transcend the one-dimensional thought and society.

Again rooting his conception in Hegel's philosophy, Marcuse insists on the importance of distinguishing between existence and essence, fact and potential, and appearance and reality. One-dimensional thought is not able to make these distinctions and thus submits to the power of the existing society, deriving its view of the world and mode of behaviour from existing realities. Marcuse is again reworking here the Hegelian-Marxian theme of reification and alienation, where the subject loses its power of comprehending and transforming subjectivity as it becomes dominated by alien powers and objects. Alienated from its powers of being-a-self, one-dimensional man becomes an object of administration and conformity.

In a lecture on Freud given in Frankfurt in 1956, shortly after the publication of *EC*, Marcuse analysed two distinguishing features of the contemporary personality: (1) '*the reification and automatization of the ego*', and (2) '*the strengthening of extra-familial authority*'.[11] He suggests that the psychological dynamics of the Freudian conflict between ego, id and superego are being replaced by 'increasing autonomic and rigid behaviour' in which the subject directly assimilates social roles and conformist behaviour. In this world, *mimesis* replaces introjection and individuals are immediately shaped in their behaviour and thought by the 'omnipresent apparatuses of production, distribution and entertainment':

It is as though the free space which the individual has at his disposal for his psychic processes has been greatly narrowed down; it is no longer possible for something like an individual psyche with its own demands and decisions to develop; the space is occupied by public, social forces. This reduction of the relatively autonomous ego is empirically observable in people's frozen gestures, and in the growing passivity of leisure-time activities, which become more and more inescapably de-privatized, centralized, universalized in the bad sense, and as such controlled. This process is the psychic correlate of the social overpowering of the opposition, the impotence of criticism, technical co-ordination, and the permanent mobilization of the collective.[12]

In a 1963 essay, 'Obsolescence of the Freudian Concept of Man', Marcuse provides a historical sketch that describes the transition to a new social order, which requires different personality structures than the previous personality structure described by Freud.[13] The father is no longer a dominant economic figure in the world of 'organized capitalism' and is replaced at home by the authority of the 'mass media, school and sports teams, gangs, etc.' (*5L*, p. 47). The self immediately identifies with social ego-ideals and role-models, and no longer forges its identity through battling its id impulses and superego parent figures: 'The ego shrinks to such an extent that it seems no longer capable of sustaining itself, as a self' (*5L*, p. 47). The result is a 'one-dimensional static identification with the others and with the administered reality principle' (*5L*, p. 47). Social controls are no longer internalized through 'the ingression of society into the mental structure of individuals' (*5L*, p. 52), but are embodied in the societal apparatus and ideology which requires submission to its rules, dictates and institutions (*5L*, pp. 54ff). The result is 'a society of total reification' (ibid.) where the individual's very gratifications, thoughts and behaviour are socially administered.

Marcuse uses his philosophical theory of a one-dimensional technical world and the decline of individuality as the framework for a theory of advanced industrial society. In a preface to 'De l'Ontologie', he indicates that he developed the ideas during a course in 1958–9 at *L'École Pratique des Hautes Études*, describing his emerging social theory as follows:

These tendencies appear to engender a mode of thought and behaviour which represses or rejects all values, aspiration and ideas that do not conform to the dominant rationality. Consequently, an entire dimension of human reality finds itself suppressed: the dimension which permits individuals and classes to develop a theory and a practice of transcendence (*dépassement*) and to envisage the 'determinate negation' of their society. Radical critique and effective opposition (intellectual as well as political) finds itself from now on integrated into the status quo; human existence becomes 'one-dimensional'. Such an integration cannot be explained solely by the emergence of *mass culture*, the *organization man*, or the *Hidden Persuaders*, etc.; these notions belong to a purely ideological interpretation which neglects the analysis of fundamental processes: processes which undermine the base upon which the radical opposition could develop.

Is this atrophying of the very base of historical transcendence, is this neutralization of negative forces, which appears as the supreme achievement of industrial society, rooted in the very structure of technical civilization? Or are they solely the work of repressive institutions? Has technicity itself so profoundly transformed capitalism and socialism that the Marxist and anti-Marxist notions of development find themselves invalidated? Does the atrophy of the process of transcendence announce the possibility of the absorption of negating forces, the mastery of contradictions inherent in this situation through the technological domination of the world, through a standard of living constantly elevated through a universal administration of society? Do these phenomena announce instead the phase in the course of which quantitative change is going to become qualitative? These are the questions that have guided our analysis: they have as point of departure the political-economic transformation of the technological society and examine, on this base, the different forms of atrophy in traditional culture, and in neo-positivist and analytical philosophy.[14]

This is, then, the programme of *One-Dimensional Man* which raises the spectre of the closing-off, or 'atrophying', of the very possibilities of radical social change. Against those criticisms which claim that Marcuse abandons Marxism in this project, I would argue that the method and framework of Marcuse's theory is a fundamentally Marxian critique of capitalism and that Marcuse intends to describe a more advanced form of a social order which still contains many of the features that Marx ascribed to capitalism. In the Introduction to *ODM*, Marcuse writes that in the capitalist world the bourgeoisie and the proletariat 'are still the basic classes. However, the capitalist development has altered the structure and function of these two classes in such a way that they no longer appear to be agents of historical transformation' (*ODM*, pp. xii–xiii). In my reading, Marcuse is carrying out a Marxian analysis in *ODM* of changes in the class structure and the socio-economic foundation in advanced capitalist societies which require a reformulation of the Marxian theory of the proletariat as a revolutionary class and the development of a new theory of advanced capitalism. Although his theory puts in question aspects of the Marxian theory, he carries through, as I shall attempt to show, a powerful Marxian critique of contemporary capitalism.

8.2 *One-Dimensional Man* as a theory of advanced capitalism

There are, however, tensions in *ODM* between the development of a more general theory of 'advanced industrial society' and a more specific critique of contemporary capitalist societies. While Marcuse generally describes his theory in *ODM* as an analysis of 'advanced industrial society', he often refers specifically to 'advanced capitalism', and most of his examples come from analysis of US capitalist society.[15] In fact Marcuse is one of the few Marxists of his day to draw on contemporary American social science and critical journalism to develop a theory of contemporary capitalism. However, against the frequent critique that Marcuse accepted too uncritically the 'ideological' literature of 'bourgeois' social theorists,[16] I would suggest that he draws on this material primarily to support his own conception, emanating from post-1940s critical theory, of the technical world and administered society. His students during this period claim that Marcuse rarely discussed the texts of social scientists, except as illustrations of his own ideas, and therefore primarily used the analyses of C. Wright Mills, Daniel Bell, Vance Packard and others to support his own theory of contemporary society.[17] Nonetheless, I believe that Marcuse provides material that can be used to develop a theory of advanced capitalism, and in the following pages I shall offer a reading of *ODM* which provides such a Marcusean theory.

What is striking about *ODM* is Marcuse's posture of total critique and resolute opposition to capitalist society in its totality. Marcuse perceives destructive tendencies in advanced capitalism's most celebrated achievements and sees irrationality in its self-proclaimed rationality. He maintains that the society's prosperity and growth are based on waste and destruction, its progress is fuelled by exploitation and repression, while its freedom and democracy are based on manipulation. Marcuse slices through this ambiguity and sharply criticizes the dehumanization and alienation in its opulence and affluence, the slavery in its labour system, the ideology and indoctrination in its culture, the fetishism in its consumerism, and the danger and insanity in its military-industrial complex. He concludes that despite its spectacular achievements, 'this society is irrational as a whole. Its productivity is destructive of the free development of humans needs and faculties . . . its growth dependent on the repression of the real possibilities for pacifying the struggle for existence – individual, national and international' (*ODM*, pp. ix–x).

In so sharply criticizing contemporary American society, Marcuse both went against the currents of conformist academic thinking and anticipated the multi-faceted critiques of American society that were to emerge in the 1960s. *ODM* had a curious reception and impact. It angered both orthodox Marxists, who could not accept comprehensive critique of Marxism, and many others who were unable to assent to such radical critiques of contemporary capitalist society.[18] The book was, however, well received by the New Left and a generation dissatisfied with the current social order and the orthodoxies of the dominant Marxist and academic theories. For the New Left, *ODM* provided an articulation of what young radicals felt was wrong with the current society, and the book's dialectic of liberation and domination provided a context for radical politics which struggled against domination and for liberation. Moreover, *ODM* showed that the problems confronting the emerging radical movement were not simply the Vietnam war, racism or inequality, but the system itself, and that solving a wide range of social problems required fundamental social restructuring. In this way, *ODM* played an important role in the political education of a generation of radicals (Marcuse's impact on the New Left will be the topic of Chapter 9).

ODM provides a theory of an historical epoch during which radical opposition was at a low point and capitalist affluence and repression prevailed.[19] In the following pages, I shall depict the basic features of Marcuse's theory of 'advanced industrial society', which I shall present as a theory of advanced capitalism and critique of American society. Then, in 8.3, I shall highlight Marcuse's critiques of classical Marxism and shall offer some critical remarks on Marcuse's theory of advanced capitalism.

8.2.1 *Commodities, false needs and the consumer society*

For Marcuse, advanced capitalism is a commodity-producing society in which the commodity form and consumerism play a role far greater than that envisaged by Marx and most orthodox Marxists. Marcuse was one of the first Marxists to provide a theory of the consumer society through analysing the role of consumerism, advertising, mass culture and ideology in integrating and stabilizing the capitalist mode of production.[20] The seminal ideas of Marcuse's theory are found in the early Marx's *Economic and Philosophical Manuscripts* – not just in the celebrated critique of alienated labour upon which Marcuse focused in the 1930s, but also in those striking passages where Marx discusses the role of commodities, needs and money. Marcuse develops and concretizes these core ideas of the early Marx's critique of capitalism together with Lukács's analysis of the commodity and reification in *History and Class Consciousness*,[21] arguing that in advanced capitalism, commodities and consumerism have transformed the very personality structure – the values, needs and behaviour of the individuals – in a way that binds 'one-dimensional man' to the social order that produces these needs: 'The people recognize themselves in their commodities; they find their soul in their automobile, hi-fi set, split-level home, kitchen equipment. The very mechanism which ties the individual to his society has changed, and social control is anchored in the new needs that it has produced' (*ODM*, p. 9).

In Marcuse's view, the most striking feature of advanced industrial society is its ability to contain all social change and to integrate all potential agents of change into one smoothly running, comfortable and satisfying system of domination. This 'one-dimensional society' is made possible by 'new forms of social control' which help create needs and consciousness that accepts and conforms to the system, thus systematically suffocating the need for radical social change.

New forms of social control, such as mass culture and advertising, produce needs that integrate individuals into the consumer society, but so does the entirety of the system of production and distribution. In an important passage, Marcuse writes:

The productive apparatus and the goods and services which it produces 'sell' or impose the social system as a whole. The means of mass transportation and communication, the commodities of lodging, food and clothing, the irresistible output of the entertainment and information industry carry with them prescribed attitudes and habits, certain intellectual and emotional reactions which bind the consumers more or less pleasantly to the producers and, through the latter, to the whole. The products indoctrinate and manipulate; they promote a false consciousness which is immune against its falsehood. And as these beneficial products become available to more individuals in more social classes, the indoctrination they carry ceases to be publicity; it becomes a way of life ... and as a good way of life, it militates against qualitative changes. (*ODM*, pp. 11–12)

Although Marx argued that capitalism created a world in its own image and analysed bourgeois ideology, needs and commodity fetishism, he did not anticipate the extent to which ideology, mass culture and consumerism would integrate the working class into capitalist society. In his political analyses, Marx always discounted the possibility of the identification of the working class with capitalist society and believed that it would always acquire revolutionary consciousness and be a revolutionary class.[22] Marx always focused his analysis on production and did not believe that consumption would compensate for alienated labour, exploitation and working-class oppression.

Marcuse, by contrast, argues that consumer and conformist *needs* help integrate the working class into capitalist society. Although he claims that all human needs are historical and are preconditioned by the prevailing institutions and interests, Marcuse believes that it is crucial to distinguish between *true needs* that are essential to human survival and well being, and *false needs* that are 'superimposed on the individual by particular societal interests in his repression: the needs which perpetuate toil, aggressiveness, misery and injustice' (*ODM*, p. 5). False needs are for Marcuse artificial and heteronomous: they are imposed upon the individual from outside by manipulative vested interests.[23] For example, consumer needs for money, possessions, property and security are repressive to the extent that they perpetuate conformity and alienated labour. Although these needs and their satisfaction provide momentary pleasure, they perpetuate a system whose continuation impedes the fulfilment of individual and social needs and potentials.

For Marcuse, the satisfactions of the consumer society are 'repressive' and the needs are 'false' because they bind individuals to a social order which actually restricts their freedom and possibilities for happiness, fulfilment and community, while providing commodities and a way of life that impedes development of a more rational social order. The social order is 'false' because its affluence depends on production of waste and destruction, while its wealth rests on exploitation; the productivity is 'repressive' because it forces unnecessary social labour and consumption on its population. Moreover, the needs produced are 'false' because expectations are produced that lead one to believe that their gratification will provide genuine fulfilment. Advertising, for instance, promises commodity solutions to problems or associates the product with the 'good life': advertisements for certain shampoos or mouthwashes, for instance, promise popularity and intensified sex appeal; soft drinks promise fun, youth, community; cars promise power and social prestige; worthless tonics promise health and vitality; mass-produced clothes promise individuality and style; and a bevy of products of dubious worth promise solutions to a variety of problems. These expectations and anticipations are, for the most part, 'false promises'; needs for products based on these expectations are 'false needs'.

Marcuse characterizes 'true needs' as 'vital needs' which 'have an unqualified claim for satisfaction ... [e.g.] nourishment, clothing, lodging at the attainable level of satisfaction' (*ODM*, p. 5). He insists that individual and social needs can be evaluated by objective 'standards of *priority*', which 'refer to the optimal development of the individual, of all individuals, under the optimal utilization of the material and intellectual resources available to man' (*ODM*, p. 6). On a social level, the goal would be maximum satisfaction of the vital needs with a rational use of resources; this could be calculated in the same way as the government calculates the needs of its budget and allocates resources accordingly. On the individual level, 'the question of what are true and false needs must be answered by the individual himself' (*ODM*, p. 6) – but the individuals must be free and autonomous to the extent that they are capable of really discerning what their true needs are, and not merely reproducing a condition of manipulation and indoctrination. That is to say, only I can determine my individual needs but I must be free from the tyranny of the prevailing repressive needs to do so. The dilemma, then, is: 'how can people who have been the object of effective and productive domination by themselves create the conditions of freedom?' (*ODM*, p. 6).

In order to liberate one's self from the universe of prevailing false needs, one must become conscious of one's conditioning and re-condition one's self to be able to discern one's true needs. The process of liberation aims at 'the replacement of false needs by true ones, the abandonment of repressive satisfactions' (*ODM*. p. 7). But 'the distinguishing feature of advanced industrial society is its effective suffocation of those needs which demand liberation – liberation also from that which is tolerable and rewarding and comfortable – while it sustains and absolves the destructive power and repressive function of the affluent society' (*ODM*, p. 7). Hence liberation from false needs involves the rejection and refusal of a whole system of needs and the affirmation of other needs that contradict the established ones.

Marcuse is arguing that in advanced industrial society the needs that support and expand the consumer society have become individual needs to buy, possess and consume, which are powerful factors of stabilization: counterrevolution built into the instinctual structure, as he puts it in *An Essay on Liberation*.[24] Moreover, Marcuse argues that these false needs are shared by all groups and classes of society, indicating an assimilation and integration of potential oppositional forces within the prevailing establishment of needs and satisfactions:

> If the worker and his boss enjoy the same television programme and visit the same resorts, if the typist is as attractively made up as the daughter of her employer, if the negro owns a Cadillac, if they all read the same newspaper, then this assimilation indicates not the disappearance of classes, but the extent to which the needs and satisfactions that serve the preservation of the Establishment are shared by the underlying population. (*ODM*, p. 8)

Marcuse is suggesting that commodities and false needs integrate the working class as well as the middle and upper strata into advanced capitalist society, thus transforming what Marx took to be a force of radical opposition into a stabilizing and conservative force. Not only does this analysis put into question Marx's theory of the revolutionary working class, but it demands, Marcuse suggests, a rethinking of the problematics of alienation. For in the dominant sociological sense of alienation it is questionable to describe the integrated and contented state of 'one-dimensional man' as that of 'alienation'.[25] If the system has satisfied the needs it has created, and delivered the goods, and if the individuals accept and conform to the system, in what sense can we say they are 'alienated'? In Marcuse's words,

> The concept of alienation seems to become questionable when the individuals identify themselves with the existence which is

imposed upon them and have in it their own development and satisfaction. This identification is not illusion but reality. However, the reality constitutes a more progressive state of alienation. The latter has become entirely objective; the subject which is alienated is swallowed up by its alienated existence. There is only one dimension, and it is everywhere and in all forms. (*ODM*, p. 11)

To clarify Marcuse's concept of alienation in *ODM*, I should point out that there are two quite different concepts of alienation operative in the literature today: (1) a philosophical-anthropological concept rooted in Hegel and Marx that is used, often quite differently, by neo-Marxists, existentialists and various other thinkers and disciplines,[26] contrasted with (2) a sociological concept rooted in Durkheim's analysis of anomie and suicide which is used, often differently, by Merton, Parsons and other sociologists.[27] The sociological concept talks of the alienation of the individual from society, other people, popular culture or values in the sense of 'separation'. There is usually a psychological component in which one 'feels alienated', and the condition is usually contrasted with a healthier situation of conformity or adjustment. For those who use a philosophical-anthropological concept of alienation, however, the very condition of conformity, valorized in the sociological literature, is precisely what is deplored as alienation. The philosophical-anthropological concept of alienation thus presupposes a concept of being-human in which one is alienated from one's basic human needs and potentialities through repression, coercion or submission to social domination.

The thrust of Marcuse's analysis is that people are increasingly alienated from their fundamental potentiality for creative individuality. He suggests that alienation is more pervasive than ever before, in that throughout all spheres of life autonomy and freedom are disappearing. Marcuse follows Marx in believing that alienation is prevalent in the sphere of labour, for the labour market demands that one must sell oneself as a labour commodity. One must then conform to the requirements of the organization of labour and submit to the dictates of the interests who control the labour process. Marcuse also believes that commodity fetishism and alienation are far more widespread than in Marx's day, in that alienation spreads into the spheres of consumption and leisure, resulting in the 'complete degradation of man to an object' and 'the progressive brutalization and moronization of man'.[28] One-dimensional man is thus increasingly alienated from basic human potentialities, true needs and the possibility of increased freedom and happiness.

In Marcuse's view, the system's widely championed individualism is a *pseudo-individualism*: prefabricated, synthesized and administered by the advertising agencies, corporations and media manipulators. Further, the individual's freedom is a *pseudo-freedom* that fails to see that bondage to the system is the price of its being able to 'choose' to buy a new car and live a consumer life-style. Although one-dimensional man conceives of itself as free, Marcuse believes this 'freedom' and 'choice' is illusory because the people have been preconditioned to make their choices within a predetermined universe that circumscribes their range of choices to the choice between Ford or General Motors, Wheaties or Cheerioes, Tweedledum or Tweedledumber:[29]

> Thus economic freedom would mean freedom *from* the economy – from being controlled by economic forces and relationships; freedom from the daily struggle for existence, from earning a living. Political freedom would mean individuals' liberation *from* politics over which they have no effective control. Similarly, intellectual freedom would mean the restoration of individual thought now absorbed by mass communication and indoctrination, abolition of 'public opinion' together with its makers. (*ODM*. p. 4)

Marcuse urges liberation from the alienated freedoms that serve as an ideological veil for bondage and domination. He claims that the system's much lauded economic, political and social freedoms, formerly a source of social progress, lose their progressive function and become subtle instruments of domination which serve to keep the individuals in bondage to the system that they strengthen and perpetuate. For example, economic freedom to sell one's labour power in order to compete on the labour market submits the individual to the slavery of an irrational economic system; political freedom to vote for generally indistinguishable representatives of the same system is but a delusive ratification of a non-democratic political system; intellectual freedom of expression is ineffectual when the media either co-opt and defuse, or distort and suppress ideas, and when the image-makers construct the public opinion that is hostile and immune against oppositional thought and action. Marcuse concludes that genuine freedom and well-being depend on liberation from the entire system of one-dimensional needs and satisfactions, and require 'new modes of realization ... corresponding to the new capabilities of society' (*ODM*, p. 4). (These new modes of realization will be discussed in Chapter 10.)

8.2.2 *The integration of labour and recomposition of the working class*

Marcuse's analysis thus challenges Marx's theory of the revolutionary proletariat and his theory that revolutionary consciousness would inevitably develop as the contradictions of capitalism sharpened and the condition of the working class worsened. Whereas Marx argued that exploitation and grinding poverty would create 'radical needs' which represent the negation of capitalist society,[30] Marcuse argues that the working class is coming to share dominant needs with the middle classes, which flattens out class differences and antagonisms and promotes the integration of the working class within the capitalist system. Moreover, he claims that the 'widely discussed "social and cultural integration" of the labouring class with capitalist society ... derives from an integration *in the plant* itself, in the material process of production' (*ODM*, p. 29). Marcuse argues that the working class is being integrated into the sphere of production in advanced capitalism due to a rise in wages and the elimination of the more unpleasant elements of work. He suggests that there is a change in the nature of work and recomposition of the working class in advanced capitalism, transforming what was once a sphere of opposition into a sphere of stabilization.

To support these allegations, Marcuse argues that 'Mechanization is increasingly reducing the quantity and intensity of physical energy expended in labour' (*ODM*, p. 24). This argument claims that automation is eliminating 'the revolting, inhuman aspects of exploitation' and the 'physical pain and misery' which Marx described in his critique of capitalism. Although Marcuse admits that 'arrested partial automation' has prevented the total elimination of exhausting industrial work, he cites passages to the effect that where machine assembly-line work still exists, it is supposedly transformed: 'The machine seems to instill some drugging rhythm in the operators', creating an 'in-group feeling' in each crew, a belief that 'all in all we are in the swing of things' (*ODM*, p. 26).

Next, Marcuse cites a recomposition of the working class such that 'the "blue-collar" workforce declines in relation to the "white-collar element"' and 'the number of non-production workers increases' (*ODM*, p. 27). According to Marcuse, these changes result from the growing mechanization and automation of production which frees workers from industrial labour. These changes put in question Marx's claim that an industrial proletariat is the basic force of production and social change by suggesting that changes in the nature of work and the production process shift production from living labour to machines and from industrial to non-industrial labour, thus 'de-centring' industrial labour by replacing it with modes of labour free from the revolting (and revolt-causing) aspects of industrial labour.

Marcuse also claims that there is an integration of the working class within the factory. He cites studies that suggest that workers are increasingly eager 'to share in the solution of production problems' and to participate in helping run the factory itself (*ODM*, p. 30). He claims that workers are increasingly identifying with the interests of the corporations that are providing them with regularly higher wages, health and retirement insurance, as well as personnel management and unions to help solve their problems and grievances. Moreover, in bureaucratic corporations, there are no bosses or local capitalists to personify greed and exploitation, thus 'hatred and frustration are deprived of their specific target, and the technological veil conceals the reproduction of inequality and enslavement' (*ODM*, p. 31).

Although Marcuse does not carry out a detailed analysis of changes in class structure and the segmentation of the working class under advanced capitalism,[31] he does anticipate the impact that automation would have on the working class and indicates some of the consequences of its application for the Marxian theory.[32] In a revealing letter to Raya Dunayevskaya in 1960 he writes:

I may have told you that my new book, with the tentative title *Studies in the Ideology of Advanced Industrial Society*, is some sort of western counterpart of *Soviet Marxism* – that is to say it will deal, not only with the ideology but also with the corresponding reality. One of my problems will be the transformation of the labouring class under the impact of rationalization, automation and, particularly, the higher standard of living. I am sure you will know what I mean if I refer to the discussion among the French sociologists in *Arguments* and especially Serge Mallet's articles. It is a question of a changing – that is to say – a more affirmative attitude of the labourer not only towards the system as a whole but even to the organization of work in the more highly modernized plants. Mallet's field study of French workers in the Caltex establishment in France points up sharply the rise of a highly cooperative attitude and of a vested interest in the establishment.[33]

Although Marcuse questions the Marxian theory of the revolutionary proletariat by citing the alleged integration of labour and changed nature and position of the working class, he concludes that despite changes in the working class, its composition and its working conditions since the publication of *Capital*, the domination, exploitation and alienated labour inherent in capitalist relations of production still exist:

In reality neither the utilization of administrative rather than physical controls (hunger, personal dependence, force), nor the change in the character of heavy work, nor the assimilation of occupational classes, nor the equalization in the sphere of consumption, compensate for the fact that the decisions over life and death, over personal and national security are made at places over which the individuals have no control. The slaves of developed industrial civilization are sublimated slaves, but they are slaves, for slavery is determined 'neither by obedience nor by hardness of labour but by the status of being a mere instrument, and the reduction of man to the state of a thing' (François Perroux). (*ODM*, pp. 32–3)

Marcuse suggests here that beneath the appearance of satisfaction and well-being lie the reality of exploitation and dehumanization, which is veiled by the omnipotent technical apparatus, corporate structure and social wealth. In this situation, 'Domination is transfigured into administration' (*ODM*, p. 32) and

the organizers and administrators themselves become increasingly dependent on the machinery which they organize and administer. And this mutual dependence is no longer the dialectical relationship between Master and Servant, which has been broken in the struggle for mutual recognition, but rather a vicious circle which encloses both the Master and the Servant. (*ODM*, p. 33)

Thus Marcuse holds on to the Marxian theory of exploitation and alienated labour while describing changes in the capitalist labour process and structural position of the industrial working class. In the next chapter (9.4) we shall examine the political consequences that Marcuse draws from his analysis of the obsolescence of the Marxian proletariat and the changed situation of the working class in advanced capitalism. Next, however, let us examine his views on the merger between business and politics in the capitalist state. Marcuse claims that politics, once a sphere of potential opposition and change, is becoming a conservative sphere in which the state directly serves the interests of business in stabilizing and strengthening the capitalist system.

8.2.3 *The capitalist state and one-dimensional politics*

In 'The Closing of the Political Universe', Marcuse cites the role of the government as a 'stimulating, supporting, and even controlling force' in the economy (*ODM*, pp. 19ff). In this 'new society' (ibid) the capitalist state assumes Keynesian steering functions to manage and regulate the economy.[34] The state and economy are thus increasingly integrated, and business and government become blended into forces serving 'the national purpose' and the 'American way of life'. 'In the political sphere', Marcuse writes, 'this trend manifests itself in a marked unification and convergence of opposites' (*ODM*, p. 19), taking the form of bi-partisanship in foreign policy and a lack of real political alternatives in the domestic sphere 'where the programmes of the big parties become ever more indistinguishable even in the degree of hypocrisy and in the odour of the clichés' (*ODM*, p. 19). Within advanced capitalism, capital and labour are allied under the threat of Communism and as beneficiaries of the spoils of social wealth. Not only is there no major oppositional labour party in the United States, but the socialist and even Communist parties in Europe 'have agreed to work within the framework of the established system', testifying 'to the depth and scope of capitalist integration' (*ODM*, pp. 20–1).[35] In such a situation, the Marxian hopes for proletarian revolution appear illusory;

politics is not the site of class struggle but of class collaboration – which hides the fact that the state is really an instrument of class domination.

The form that political integration takes in advanced capitalist society is the 'welfare-warfare state', which supposedly at once stimulates the economy, mobilizes the citizens against the Enemy, and raises 'the standard of administered living' (*ODM*, p. 48). Marcuse cites the ambivalence of this phenomenon, noting at once that the welfare state perpetuates unfreedom by intensifying administration (*ODM*, pp. 49ff), and yet cannot be rejected out of hand since when it provides 'comprehensive social legislation' or 'adequate government expenditures for services other than those of military defence', it provides useful social services and contributes to social progress (*ODM*, pp. 50f). Yet even its progressive functions block alternatives by providing a system of 'subdued pluralism' and 'countervailing powers' in which 'the competing institutions concur in solidifying the power of the whole over the individual' (*ODM*, pp. 50–1).

The more sinister aspects of the welfare-warfare state reside in the fact that 'the society as a whole becomes a defence society' (*ODM*, p. 51). Here the arms race and cold war stimulate the economy and unite the populace against the Enemy without, and at the same time produce the most deadly and destructive weapons in history, whose massive use would probably constitute the end of the human race. This 'insanity of the whole' excuses 'particular insanities and turns the crimes against humanity into a rational enterprise' (*ODM*, p. 52) – since increased defence spending and the arms race are justified by the need to preserve the society against its Enemy. The result is that the growth and power of the warfare state serves to strengthen the society against the prospects of rational qualitative social change.[36]

Not only does the threat of a Communist enemy unify previously opposing forces to defend the 'national purpose', but to some extent there is a convergence of interests between the capitalist and Communist superpowers. Both systems are structured to avoid qualitative change and both are systems of domination with entrenched bureaucracies (*ODM*, pp. 39–45).[37] Moreover, Marcuse does not see any possibility of 'third force' countries offering significantly different patterns of development or hopes for liberation: 'On the contrary', he writes, it rather seems that the superimposed development of these countries will bring about a period of total administration more violent and more rigid than that traversed by the advanced societies which can build on the achievements of the liberalistic era ... the backward areas are likely to succumb either to one of the various forms of neo-colonialism, or to a more or less terroristic system of primary accumulation. (*ODM*, p. 47)

In Marcuse's view, capitalist and Communist societies are mobilized against the possibilities of liberation and are restrictive of its higher possibilities: the 'pacification of the struggle for existence' and the progressive 'abolition of labour' (*ODM*, p. 53). 'This pacification would mean the emergence of a genuine world economy – the demise of the nation state, the national interest, national business together with their international alliances' (*ODM*, p. 53). But 'this is precisely the possibility against which the present world is mobilized' (*ODM*, p. 54).

Although Marcuse does hold out the possibility that the non-industrialized societies might undergo a different type of industrialization, with different technologies and goals, which would avoid the deformities of capitalist and state socialist industrialization (see *ODM*, pp. 47–8), his analysis fails to anticipate the upsurge of Third World liberation movements. Nor does he anticipate how the success of these revolutions might disrupt the capitalist economic system, intensify rivalries between the capitalist and Communists blocs, and create both new possibilities of liberation and new dangers of nuclear war.[38] In general, Marcuse's political analysis in *ODM* is sketchy and has been frequently criticized (see note 35). His analysis of culture and ideology, however, is much stronger, and is in fact the focal point of his work, which is subtitled 'Studies in the Ideology of Advanced Industrial Society'.

8.2.4 *The containment of Eros and Logos*

Advanced capitalism creates a social order in which culture and ideology replace brute force as new forms of social control. Indeed, Marcuse shows himself in *ODM* to be an outstanding critic of contemporary culture. During his years with the Institute for Social Research, Marcuse excelled as a critic of bourgeois ideology, and he continued to confront and criticize the dominant forms of ideology during the last several decades. There is, however, an ambiguity in Marcuse's use of the term ideology in *ODM* which reproduces the ambivalences and changes within culture and ideology in advanced capitalism. Sometimes Marcuse uses the concept of ideology in the classical Marxian sense, as theories or ideas which mystify social reality and legitimate a given society so as to perpetuate class domination.[39] For example, he speaks of ideologies of positivism, behaviourism, operationalism, analytical philosophy, and so on, providing in addition various analyses of how mass culture, forms of language, social science and empirical research produce hegemonic ideology. In other contexts, however, Marcuse speaks of the 'absorption of ideology in reality ... as today ideology is in the process of production itself' (*ODM*, p. 11). Similarly, he talks of science and technology as ideology (to use Habermas's phrase), as if science and technology themselves, in their structure and functions, had become 'ideological'. He claims that the ideology of the consumer society is contained in the very process of production and consumption and not just in an 'ideological superstructure'. In this conception, ideology resides in the satisfactions and symbolic values consumed through the purchase and use of commodities.[40]

Against the 'end of ideology' theorists, Marcuse argues that advanced capitalism 'is *more* ideological than its predecessors' by virtue of the way in which ideology permeates the process of production, consumption, culture, thought and everyday life (*ODM*, pp. 11ff, *passim*).[41] Since commodities, the mass media, shopping centres and the very facade of the consumer society shape aspirations and needs, 'ideology' is incorporated into the material base of society and should not be seen, Marcuse suggests, solely as a 'superstructure' which has to do with consciousness and ideas alone. 'Culture' thus takes on new forms in advanced capitalism and assumes increasingly important social functions as an instrument of social control and a direct constituent of the structure and social practices in the consumer society.[42]

Moreover, Marcuse argues that culture, once operative in a potentially subversive aesthetic realm, is now part and parcel of the commodity system. He believes that 'high culture' traditionally opposed itself to society and provided a transcendent sphere that contained the desires and truths not permitted or realized in the everyday world. Great art contains, in his view, the negation of unfreedom and in previous times preserved a realm of freedom and promise of happiness denied in the world of labour and everyday affairs. He claims that,

> prior to the advent of this cultural reconciliation, literature and art were essentially alienation, sustaining and protecting the contradiction – the unhappy consciousness of the divided world, the defeated possibilities, the hopes unfulfilled, and the promises betrayed. They were a rational, cognitive force, revealing a dimension of man and nature which was repressed and repelled in reality. (*ODM*, p. 61)

For Marcuse, art 'in its most advanced positions ... is the Great Refusal – the protest against that which is' (*ODM*, p. 63). But today, art's power of transcendence and negation is being dissolved, and art is being integrated into the one-dimensional society. Hence, what was once a subversive force is now 'a cog in the culture machine' and an adornment to the society. Art is transformed into a mass-produced commodity form in paperbacks, LPs, cassettes and cheap reproductions which both entertain and indoctrinate. There is thus a 'flattening out of the antagonism between cultural and social reality through the obliteration of the oppositional, alien and transcendent elements in the higher culture by virtue of which it constitutes *another dimension* of reality' (*ODM*, p. 57). Whereas art once elicited a certain respect which called for attention and critical response, today it is reduced to a familiar commodity/artifact which is part of everyday experience, which adorns and entertains but does not challenge or transcend the given society.

This condition of cultural integration is a serious matter for the cultural revolutionist Marcuse. His hope that art and aesthetic education could be an emancipatory force (see *Eros and Civilization*) appears to be dashed in one-dimensional society. Furthermore, not only has high culture been absorbed into a cultural pluralism, which assimilates all art forms to a harmless unity of artistic tendencies, but culture has become a mode of domination through the hegemony of the culture industries which bombard its audiences with ideologies, images, advertisements and values that reproduce and legitimate the present way of life.[43] Mass culture, in this view, forms a totality which reinforces conventional values and promotes conformist behaviour, thus becoming an increasingly important instrument of socialization.

At stake is the conquest of what Marcuse calls the 'unhappy consciousness'. For Hegel, the 'unhappy consciousness' is torn between its yearning for 'what could be' and its dissatisfaction with 'what is'.[44] The happy consciousness of one-dimensional society, on the other hand, finds its satisfactions in consumerism, mass culture and a less repressive sex life. Since sexual discontent creates an 'unhappy consciousness', earlier, sexually repressive, social orders had a vast reservoir of discontent, potentially explosive libido to deal with. Bourgeois literature overflows with *l'amour fou*, absolute passion and explosive sexuality, which threatened to disrupt the social order (*ODM*, pp. 77–8). Liberalized sex, Marcuse suggests, permits a reduction of frustration and thus helps promote a general satisfaction and acceptance of the established society. Further, the consumer society sells sex and uses sex to sell its commodities and system. Sex is good business and 'is integrated into work and public relations and is thus made more susceptible to (controlled) satisfaction' (*ODM*, pp. 74–5).

In its ability to integrate Art and Eros, one-dimensional society exhibits its power to contain and control those impulses which Marcuse believes are most explosive and subversive: the aesthetic-erotic impulses. Such a triumph over the subversive aspects of sex and culture would provide a heavy blow to the prospects for liberation and constitutes, in Marcuse's view, a deep-rooted anthropological transformation which in turn requires individual liberation and social revolution.

Marcuse's point is that people will accept social domination more readily if they are granted liberalized sexuality for compensation and that increased sexual pleasure can generate submission, thus weakening 'the rationality of protest' (*ODM*, p. 75). The distance between the reality principle and pleasure principle is diminished and thus conflict between the individual and society is lessened. Marcuse claims that manipulative sexual liberalization contains 'repressive modes of desublimation', which 'extends liberty while intensifying domination' (*ODM*, p. 72). Marcuse introduces the paradoxical concept of 'repressive desublimation' to describe sexual liberalization which promotes repression. Whereas Freud sees sublimation as a deflection of sexual energy from orgasmic release to a non-sexual end,[45] Marcuse argues that this release is 'repressive' if sexual energy is contracted into a restrictive model of sexuality, and suggests that the capacity for full sexual satisfaction is reduced in advanced industrial society (*ODM*, pp. 73f). More convincing, perhaps, is the earlier point that desublimation can be repressive because increased permissiveness robs the sphere of protest of vital instinctual energy, thus generating submission to a repressive system: 'The contrast to the pleasures of adjusted desublimation, sublimation preserves the consciousness of the renunciation which the repressive society inflicts upon the individual, and thereby preserves the need for liberation' (*ODM*, p. 75).

In Marcuse's analysis, public and corporate officials, and the mass media, utilize a one-dimensional language to smooth over social contradictions and problems so as to attempt to restrict thought and public discourse to the terms and interests of the established society. Marcuse acutely analyses the methods and tricks through which language shapes public thought and discourse through 'magic-ritual formulas' and 'fixed images' which 'abridge thought' and 'cut off development of meaning' (*ODM*, pp. 84–91). This language attempts to manipulate its audience with authoritarian dicta and to prevent critical thought and discourse. Marcuse cites contemporary examples of 'Orwellian language' in which concepts such as democracy, freedom and equality are used in capitalist countries to perpetuate class society, unfreedom and inequality, while 'socialism' and 'worker's democracy' are used by Communist countries to perpetuate party dictatorship.[46] Marcuse also analyses a logic of manipulation that is almost surrealistic in its unification of opposites. In the 1950s, Marcuse notes discussion of a 'clean bomb' with 'harmless fall-out' and newspapers stating that 'Labour is seeking missile harmony' (*ODM*, pp. 89f). The trend continued, and in the 1970s the counterrevolutionary President Richard Nixon proclaimed a 'New American Revolution', while right-wing groups called themselves 'libertarians' and 'Young Americans for Freedom' and advertisers tried to sell a 'revolutionary new detergent'.

This corruption of language makes it problematical to call for the elimination of nuclear weapons if the bomb is 'clean' and the fall-out is 'harmless', or to militate for radical social change if 'revolution' is taking place everywhere. Moreover, within one-dimensional society, new terms are constantly being coined to provide a functional, operational language which sanitizes the system's failings and dirty deeds. CIA crimes are referred to as 'covert operations'; their assassination team is called a 'health alteration committee'; and they refer to the overthrow of Allende's government in Chile as a 'destabilization program'. In Vietnam, the bombing and destruction of villages is called a 'pacification program', the village refugees are called 'ambient non-combat personnel', and the concentration camps in which they are housed are referred to as 'pacified hamlets'. The number of individuals killed is a 'body count', bombing one's own troops is 'accidental deliverance of ordinance equipment', getting killed by one's own troops is falling prey to 'friendly fire', and unprovoked aggression against an innocent village is a 'pre-emptive defense strike' or 'retaliatory action', while the invasion of Cambodia is described as an 'incursion'. Marcuse's comment is apt: 'People who speak and accept such language seem to be immune to everything – and suspectible to everything' (*ODM*, p. 93).

The use of these images and formulas parallels Orwell's (*Nineteen Eighty-four*) Newspeak, which reverses the meaning of words ('peace is war'); the corrupted language of one-dimensional society not only reverses meanings but completely redefines concepts and debases once honourable language. One-dimensional language suppresses both the dimensions of history and criticism (*ODM*, pp. 97ff) so as to repress the spectre of historical alternatives and the memories of past oppression, struggles and revolutionary hopes. In Marcuse's words: 'Remembrance of the past may give rise to dangerous insights, and the established society seems to be apprehensive of the subversive contents of memory. Remembrance is a mode of dissociation from the given facts. Memory recalls the terror and the hope that passed' (*ODM*, p. 98).[47] Citing Adorno's concept of 'the spectre of man without memory' (*ODM*, p. 99), Marcuse fears that an 'historical amnesia' closes off an understanding of how historical factors produced the current social facts. In Marcuse's view:

recognition and relation to the past as present counteracts the functionalization of thought by and in the established reality. It militates against the closing of the universe of discourse and behaviour; it renders possible the development of concepts which de-stabilize and transcend the closed universe by comprehending it as historical universe. Confronted with the given society as object of its reflection, critical thought becomes historical consciousness; as such, it is essentially judgment. Far from necessitating an indifferent relativism, it searches in the real history of man for the criteria of truth and falsehood, progress and regression. The mediation of the past with the present discovers the factors which made the facts, which determined the way of life, which established the masters and the servants; it projects the limits and the alternatives. (*ODM*, pp. 99–100)

In contrast to historically open-ended, multidimensional critical discourse, one-dimensional thought and language wants to close the universe of discourse and behaviour into its own pre-constructed frame of reference which promotes conformist thought and action. One-dimensional language thus rejects and undermines historical and critical reason; it attempts to suppress memory and does not demonstrate or explain, but 'communicates decision, dictum, command' (*ODM*, p. 101); it identifies person and function and makes 'individuals appear to be mere appendices or properties of their place, their job, their employer, or enterprise' (*ODM*, p. 92); it uses a falsely personalized language ('your congressman', 'your individuality clothes shop', 'your' beer); it revels in clichés and pseudo-concreteness; it pontificates right and wrong and inculcates the accepted values. It tends to imprison its users in a prefabricated universe which attemps to contain thought and behaviour within the established framework. Not only do the media, advertisers and politicians promote one-dimensional thought and behaviour, but, in Marcuse's view, the dominant modes of research and philosophy reinforce these tendencies.

In his analysis of 'The Research of Total Administration' (*ODM*, pp. 104ff) Marcuse argues that the established framework of the existing society is the unquestioned frame of reference for empirical social sciences, industrial sociology and social engineering. These enterprises, Marcuse argues, proclaim the 'existing social reality as its own norm' (*ODM*, p. 119). In his analysis of typical academic descriptions of democracy and politics in the United States, Marcuse shows that the definitions and framework of inquiry are derived from the prevailing institutions and ideology, so that 'democracy', for instance, is defined and evaluated in terms of the functioning of representational democracy in the United States today. 'By virtue of its methodology, this empiricism is ideological' (*ODM*, p. 114). It is ideological in that it represses historical components of democracy, the absence of which in the United States could raise the question as to whether 'American democracy' is really democratic. It is ideological in that it redefines democracy in terms of the present American system and is thus obviously able to conclude with satisfaction that the American political system is democratic (cf. *ODM*, pp. 114–20). Hence, 'committed to this framework, the investigation becomes circular and self-validating' (*ODM*, p. 116).

The framework of empirical research itself in inadequate because (1) it provides a partial, incomplete description of the facts, in which many determining, constitutive facts are outside its frame of reference (cf. *ODM*, p. 119); (2) it is non-critical and ideological in that it provides an idealized reflection of the society. In Marcuse's view, empirical social theory is but 'the recognition of that which is' (*ODM*, p. 119). For a critical theory, however, 'recognition of facts is critique of facts' (*ODM*, p. 118). Finally, (3) the empirical research is a stabilizing factor in the one-dimensional system of repression: 'the descriptive analysis of the facts blocks the apprehension of facts and becomes an element of the ideology that sustains the facts. Proclaiming the existing social reality as its own norm, this sociology fortifies in the individuals the "faithless faith" in the reality whose victims they are' (*ODM*, p. 119). The stabilizing function of positivistic empiricism is well illustrated in Marcuse's critique of industrial sociology, in which the concepts of research become a form of social control and means of mystification which cover over the roots of the real social problems (*ODM*, pp. 107–14). Thus, the 'research of total administration' contributes to help integrate the individual into a system of domination and to create a consciousness which accepts this servitude.[48]

In a similar way, a dominant mode of philosophy in the Anglo-American culture takes as its norms conventional rules of linguistic usage and social practice. Many logical positivists and philosophers in the ordinary language school claim that all philosophical problems involve explicating the correct use of words.[49] In the Wittgensteinian formulation, 'the meaning is the use', and the clarification and description of the correct use of language is supposed to solve all philosophical problems. 'Correct usage' involves conformity to generally accepted usage, to use language correctly means to follow linguistic conventions. Language, Wittgenstein says, is a form of life, and to use language correctly means to follow the rules in the language game one is playing.[50] Thus philosophy, in Wittgenstein's own words, 'leaves everything as it is'. This mode of philosophy is,

Marcuse believes, eminently conservative, taking as its subject matter the 'totalitarian scope of the established universe of discourse' (*ODM*, p. 195) and defending and reinforcing the rules and conventions of this universe.[51]

Secondly, linguistic philosophy in a Wittgensteinian formulation purports to be a 'therapy' aiming at 'correction of abnormal behaviour in thought and speech, removal of obscurities, illusions and oddities, or at least their exposure' (*ODM*, p. 170).[52] The linguistic philosopher wants to remove 'mental cramps', perplexities and dilemmas, exorcizing philosophy of all metaphysical ghosts and existential conundrums. Its therapy, like conservative psychoanalysis, aims at adjustment, removing philosophical or existential worries, finding satisfaction in common usage, common sense and conventional thought and behaviour. The philosophical target of this therapy, Marcuse claims, is to debunk all transcendent concepts and critical thought that oppose or contradict 'the prevailing universe of discourse and behaviour' (*ODM*, p. 171). Against this mode of conformist thought, Marcuse defends dialectical thinking which transcends the established universe, using concepts, norms and values that criticize the established discourse and society and that protect alternatives (*ODM*, pp. 193–9). Marcuse claims that in 'the larger context of experience', which transcends the world of ordinary language and conventional behaviour, there exist multi-dimensional social-historical complexities, ambiguities and unresolved problems and contradictions that do not easily lend themselves to one-dimensional linguistic analysis. Marcuse rejects the 'purged' and 'impoverished' language of ordinary language analysis on the grounds of its reductionism and conservatism (*ODM*, p. 175). He objects also to its style, which moves 'between the two poles of pontificating authority and easy-going chuminess' (*ODM*, p. 174). He defends the 'irreducible difference' between everyday thinking and language compared with philosophical thinking and language (*ODM*, p. 178), concluding that one-dimensional philosophy is 'destructive of philosophic thought and of critical thought' (*ODM*, p. 176).

The result of the co-operation between the universities, media, government, corporations and social institutions to combat nonconformist thought and behaviour is the production of what Marcuse calls 'one-dimensional man'. One-dimensional man is the product of a one-dimensional society that systematically contains and eliminates opposition and dissent. Underlying one-dimensional society is a new configuration of science, technology and mechanized industry which differentiate advanced industrial societies from previous social formations. Let us, then, conclude our examination of Marcuse's theory of advanced capitalism by examining the role of science and technology in the new technological order. First, however, I shall address the question of whether Marcuse is a technological reductionist and determinist.

8.2.5 *Science, technology and capitalism*

It has been argued that Marcuse replaces the emphasis on the primacy of the economy and relations of production in the Marxian theory with a theory of 'advanced industrial society' that places primary emphasis on technology and 'technological rationality'.[53] In fact, critics like Morton Schoolman reduce Marcuse's problematic to a theory of 'technological rationality' which becomes the all-powerful, all-encompassing demi-urge that in Schoolman's reading of Marcuse supposedly constitutes one-dimensional society in its entirety.[54] This analysis fails to see how the system of advanced capitalism itself plays a structuring role in helping to produce science and technology, which it shapes and uses for specific social purposes. In this section I shall suggest that Marcuse provides analyses of how capitalist imperatives structure technological rationality, and I shall suggest that Marcuse offers an account of the reciprocal interaction between the development of capitalism, technology and technological rationality that avoids both technological determinism and reductionism as well as economistic theories that reduce technology simply to an epiphenomenon of the economy.

Halfway through *ODM*, Marcuse writes:

At this stage, it becomes clear that something must be wrong with the rationality of the system itself. What is wrong is the way in which men have organized their societal labour . . . The wrong organization of society demands further explanation in view of the situation of *advanced* industrial society, in which the integration of the formerly negative and transcending social forces with the established system seems to create a new social structure. (*ODM*, pp. 144–5)

This and other passages imply that science and technology are constructed and utilized in advanced capitalism (and some state socialist societies) to provide a technical apparatus of production, administration and domination which provides new forms of social control. In this view, there is a homology and reciprocal interaction between technology and social forms, such that, as Marx writes in a famous passage which Marcuse cites: 'the handmill gives you society with the feudal lord; the steam-mill society with the industrial capitalist' (*ODM*, p. 154). Marcuse adds, 'when technics becomes the universal form of material production, it circumscribes an entire culture; it projects an historical totality – a "world"' (*ODM*, p. 154). In view of the charges that Marcuse is a technological determinist, or theorist of an 'autonomous technology' that is 'out of control', it is crucial to see that he is aware that science and technology are constructed and used by dominant interests in a given society for specific ends which themselves help constitute their forms and functions.

For instance, at the beginning of *ODM*, he claims that the society is 'totalitarian' not by virtue of a technological monolith imposing itself in the totality of life, but rather: 'By virtue of the way it has organized its technological base, contemporary industrial society tends to be totalitarian' (*ODM*, p. 3). That is, the society is totalitarian by virtue of the fact that capitalism permeates every aspect of society and everyday life, while producing a system of increasingly total domination 'which operates through the manipulation of needs by vested interests' (*ODM*, p. 3). Here Marcuse is arguing that 'vested interests' create and use technology to produce, sell and distribute the commodities upon which its profits and power depend, so as to produce a society of consumers who desire items that the ruling elite wants them to want. In this case, it is the types and functions of technology that maintain and reproduce capitalism and not the mere fact of technology that is the basis of a totalitarian societal domination.

Although Marcuse does not describe in detail those vested interests that run the society, his references to C. Wright Mills, Vance Packard, William Whyte and Fred Cook (*ODM*, p. xvii, *passim*) indicate that it is the economic, political and miltary elites, or – in other words – the capitalist ruling classes[55] who utilize technology as an instrument of profitability and social control. Thus the problem in advanced capitalist society is not that people are enslaved by technology, but that it functions in many instances as an instrument of class domination.

Although there are passages in *ODM* which suggest that technology itself is the fundamental constituent of one-dimensional society, in a lecture on 'Industrialization and Capitalism in the Work of Max Weber', delivered during the same year as *ODM*'s publication, Marcuse spells out the reciprocal interaction between scientific-technological rationality and the capitalist economic system in creating advanced industrial society.[56] The study places the relationship between industrialism, capitalism, technology and domination in a more adequate conceptual framework than the analysis in chapter 6 of ODM by describing the role that the specific features of the capitalist economic system play in the creation of advanced industrial society, as well as how the capitalist mode of production helps structure science, technology and technological rationality.

Max Weber, like Marcuse, saw an inner connection between rationality and domination, while investigating and interpreting this relationship within the framework of industrial capitalism. Although, on Weber's account, the Western concept of reason fully realizes itself in industrial capitalism, and develops into a system of total bureaucracy which is the specific form of Western capitalist domination (*N*, p. 203), Marcuse argues that technical rationality is but one of the factors that has constituted industrial society. He stresses that during the development of industrial capitalism, 'formal rationality turns into *capitalist* rationality' (*N*, p. 204), and appears as both the taming of the irrational 'acquisitive drive' and subordination of reason to a 'systematic, methodical calculation, 'capital accounting''' (*N*, p. 205). Capitalist reason 'becomes concrete in the calculable and calculated *domination* of nature and man' (*N*, p. 205). Capitalist reason functions as technological reason, 'as the production and transformation of material (things and men) through the methodical-scientific apparatus ... its rationality organizes and controls things and men, factory and bureaucracy, work and leisure' (*N*, p. 205). But, Marcuse asks, '*to what purpose* does it control them?' (*N*, p. 205). What is the driving force of this apparatus? To what ends is this 'calculable efficiency' directed?

The capitalist rationality, Marcuse points out, is conditioned and controlled by two material conditions, two unique historical facts: (1) the provision of human needs and calculable efficiency takes place within the *private enterprise* system and is geared towards the *profit* of the individual entrepreneur or enterprise; (2) the means of production are private property, and the labourers must sell their wage labour to the owner of the means of production to provide for their own needs (*N*, p. 206). Since the capitalist society is directed by the 'focal reality' of a market-exchange system and private property geared to procure maximum profit, the 'calculable efficiency' of capitalist rationality is directed towards the maximization of profit. Consequently, 'technological rationality' is subordinate to the interests of the dominant powers who control science, technology and the entire apparatus of production and distribution. A contradiction exists, therefore, between calculation directed by the profit motive and the full development of technical resources and social productivity, indicating that the capitalist class restricts rational development of the productive forces and unnecessarily fetters both the economy and society. In this interpretation, science and technology are inextricably bound to the capitalist mode of production and do not exist as autonomous social forces. Thus capitalist rationality becomes *irrational*, subject to domination by the capitalists' 'werewolf thirst for profit' (Marx). Consequently, interests and factors not deducible from a concept of technological rationality help produce the technical apparatus. In this way, material conditions, historical factors and private interests intervene and reciprocally interact with technological rationality in the construction of advanced industrial civilization.

Marcuse's essay on Max Weber thus contains an important clarification of the relationship between capitalism and technology that improves upon the somewhat ahistorical analysis in *ODM* by showing how technological rationality develops within the capitalist system and how the capitalistic development of science and technology produces one-dimensional society. Rather than being 'out of control' or 'autonomous', science and technology are controlled and constituted by specific societal powers and have specific social functions which render advanced capitalism qualitatively different from previous social formations. Thus despite passages that suggest a kinship with theorists of 'autonomous technology' like Ellul or Heidegger, for Marcuse technology is used as an instrument of social control and profitability by the 'vested interests' which control society (*ODM*, pp. 3f). In conversations with me on this topic (December 1978) Marcuse regretted formulations in *ODM* that suggested similarities with theorists of 'autonomous technology', and in succeeding writings he distanced himself from such theories. For example, in *An Essay on Liberation* he writes: 'science and technology are the great vehicles of liberation, and it is only their use and restriction in the repressive society which makes them into vehicles of domination' (*EL*, p. 21). Earlier, in 'Some Social Implications of Modern Technology', he argues: 'Technics by itself promotes authoritarianism as well as liberty, scarcity as well as abundance, the extension as well as the abolution of toil'; he then cites the use of technology by the national socialists as an example of a repressive use of technology (pp. 414ff). I shall discuss Marcuse's proposals for emancipatory uses of technology and his theory of the 'new technology' in Chapter 10, which should make it even clearer that Marcuse is neither a technological reductionist nor a technophobe.

I have presented Marcuse's theory of advanced industrial society in *ODM* as a theory and critique of advanced capitalism. In view of his sharp critique and indictment of advanced capitalism, its defenders bitterly attacked Marcuse's 'negativism',[57] and critics from the Left denounced his 'one-dimensional pessimism'.[58] In the next section, I shall propose some critical perspectives on Marcuse's theory of advanced capitalism that call attention to its insights and shortcomings. At stake is providing critical evaluation of *ODM* that is lacking in the hitherto one-sidedly laudatory or hostile reactions to one of Marcuse's most important and controversial works.

8.3 Critical remarks on Marcuse's theory of advanced capitalism

To understand and evaluate adequately both the achievements and shortcomings of *ODM*, one must consider the historical context in which the book was produced and the poverty of radical social theory during that period. When *ODM* appeared in 1964, there had been few attempts within Marxism to develop a theory of advanced capitalism which seriously questioned Marxian orthodoxy, and both Marxism and 'bourgeois' social science were in the grip of positivistic empiricism and ideological orthodoxies. During the 1950s in the USA conformist social theory proclaiming the 'end of ideology' was in vogue, and there were but a few honourable thinkers, like C. Wright Mills, Erich Fromm, Paul Baran and Paul Sweezy, and some critical journalists like I. F. Stone and Fred Cook, who either used Marxism in a creative way, or sharply criticized

American society.[59] In this context, one of the virtues of Marcuse's project is his ability to combine Marxian theory with critical social science in order to provide aspects of a theory of advanced capitalism that challenges prevailing orthodoxies.

Although Marcuse's theory of capitalist stabilization and the integration of the working class questioned central aspects of the Marxian theory, he continued to identify himself as a Marxist and to defend Marxism against its critics. In a revealing passage in 'The Obsolescence of Marxism', he writes:

> The title of my paper is not supposed to suggest that Marx's analysis of the capitalist system is outdated; on the contrary I think that the most fundamental notions of this analysis have been validated, and they can be summarized in the following propositions.
>
> (1) In capitalism the social relationships among men are governed by the exchange value rather than use value of the goods and services they produce, that is to say their position is governed by their marketability.
>
> (2) In this exchange society, the satisfaction of human needs occurs only as a by-product of profitable production.
>
> (3) In the progress of capitalism, a twofold contradiction develops: between (a) the growing productivity of labour and the ever growing social wealth on the one side, and their repressive and destructive use on the other; and (b) between the social character of the means of production (no longer individual but collective instruments of labour) and their private ownership and control.
>
> (4) Capitalism can solve this contradiction only temporarily through increasing waste, luxury and destruction of productive forces. The competitive drive for armament production profit leads to a vast concentration of economic power, aggressive expansion abroad, conflicts with other imperialist powers and finally to a recurrent cycle of war and depression.
>
> (5) This cycle can be broken only if the labouring classes, who bear the brunt of exploitation, seize the productive apparatus and bring it under the collective control of the producers themselves. I submit that all these propositions with the exception of the last one seem to be corroborated by the factual development. The last proposition refers to the advanced industrial countries where the

transition to socialism was to take place, and precisely in these countries, the labouring classes are in no sense a revolutionary potential.[60]

Marcuse constantly argues that his theory is simply an attempt to update the Marxian theory in relation to changes in contemporary society. In his view, 'a re-examination and even reformulation of Marxian theory cannot simply mean adjusting this theory to new facts but must proceed as an internal development and critique of Marxian concepts'; consequently, Marxism 'is obsolete precisely to the degree to which this obsolescence validates the basic concepts of the theory. In somewhat plainer English: the factors which have led to the passing and obsolescence of some decisive concepts of Marx are anticipated in Marxian theory itself as alternatives and tendencies of the capitalist system'.[61] Marcuse continued to identify his works as a development of the Marxian theory up until his death, while continually questioning those elements of the Marxian theory that he believed were obsolete or were not radical enough for contemporary prospects for social change. Even in *ODM* Marcuse indicates from time to time his preference for socialism over capitalism (see *ODM*, pp. 220f and 252F), and although his advocacy of socialism is rather muted and cryptic in *EC, SM* amd *ODM*, in his post-1965 writings Marcuse once again openly and frequently champions socialism over capitalism (see the discussion in the next two chapters). Thus I would argue that it is wrong to claim, as so many of Marcuse's critics frequently do, that Marcuse is a 'pre-Marxist', 'non-Marxist', or 'anti-Marxist' thinker, for he continued to use the Marxian method and theory while revising those elements which he believed were obsolete or inadequate.

Yet Marcuse *did* contest some of the fundamental postulates of orthodox Marxism, including the Marxian theory of the proletariat as the agent of radical social change. On Marcuse's analysis in *ODM*, not only is the proletariat immunized against political action, indoctrinated with the dominant ideology, and intergrated into the consumer society, but its needs, satisfactions and consciousness are supposedly similar to those of the bourgeois class. Such an integration of the working class on the basis of growing affluence and a flattening out of class differences would create an unparalleled stabilization of capitalism, thus refuting Marx's theory that capitalism was doomed to perpetual crisis with growing impoverishment, class division and conflict, such that the workers would arise in capitalism's final crisis and would seize control of the means of production, expropriate the capitalist exploiters and seize power in the creation of a workers' state and classless society.[62]

Marcuse thus counters Marx's concept of capitalist stagnation with a concept of expansion, Marx's impoverishment thesis with an affluency thesis, and Marx's notion of the growing proletarization and radicalization of the workers with a theory of the increasing integration of the working class. He opposes Marx's theory of increased capitalist crisis and production anarchy with a theory of increased capitalist organizations and co-operation, and replaces Marx's final breakdown theory with a theory of capitalist stabilization. In turn, Marxist critics sharply attacked Marcuse's theory of capitalist stabilization, arguing that he had surrendered the Marxian theory of capitalist crisis, its emphasis on contradictions and class struggle, and its attempt to find disintegrating factors within the society and social forces that would be able to overthrow capitalism and construct socialism.[63]

The orthodox Marxian strategy of critique tended either to quote classical Marxian doctrine against Marcuse, or to present social facts and tendencies which put in question Marcuse's theses.[64] Against Marcuse's theory of an affluent society which 'delivers the goods' and minimizes class differences, it was argued that Marcuse's analysis in *ODM* focuses too exclusively on the post-war boom in the USA and underestimates the deep contradictions and explosive disequilibrium in advanced capitalism.[65] Critics contend that although the reconstruction period after the Second World War created highly advantageous conditions for the expansion of US (and world) capitalism, this period of capitalist expansion and stability is coming to an end, and advanced capitalism is entering a period of crisis and intensified class conflict.[66] It has been alleged that Marcuse shared the Keynesian illusion that capital had finally found a strategy and practice to manage capitalism's crisis tendencies and business cycles, whereas, in fact, during the 1970s and 1980s the global crisis of capitalism put in question theories of capitalist stabilization.[67]

There is no doubt that Marcuse exaggerated in *ODM* the stability of capitalism and failed to analyse adequately its crisis-tendencies and contradictions. Consequently, his theory of 'one-dimensional society' cannot account either for the eruption of social revolt on a global scale in the 1960s, or for the global crisis of capitalism in the 1970s and 1980s. It seems that Marcuse failed to perceive the extent to which his theory articulates a stage of historical development that was soon coming to a close and would give way to a new era marked by world crisis of capitalism, social revolt and revolutionary struggles both within and without capitalist societies. By failing to show adequately how the one-diminsional tendencies that he analysed were a function of specific historical conditions, and by failing to specify in more detail counter-tendencies, Marcuse blurred the distinction between temporary containment of crisis-tendencies, revolt and struggles in contrast to permanent transcendence in a new social order characterized by the intensification of technological rationality and the integration of culture, politics and society into one monolithic system.

Yet it is also the case that Marcuse *does* indicate that he is analysing trends of social development to which there are counter-trends (*ODM*, pp. xv–xvii). In the Introduction to *ODM* he writes that his study 'will vacillate throughout between two contradictory hypotheses: (1) that advanced industrial society is capable of containing qualitative change for the foreseeable future; (2) that forces and tendencies exist which may break this containment and explode the society' (*ODM*, p. xv). Near the end of *ODM* he writes: 'The unification of opposites in the medium of technological rationality must be, *in all its reality*, an illusory unification, which eliminates neither the contradiction between the growing productivity and its repressive use, nor the vital need for solving the contradiction' (*ODM*, p. 256).

Thus Marcuse does recognize that both social conflicts and tendencies towards change continue to exist and that radical social transformation may eventually be possible. Although the focus of his analysis is on the containment of the contradictions of capitalism, he describes it in the passage just cited as a 'forced unity', or 'illusory unification' rather than as an elimination of all contradictions and conflicts.[68] In my view, to interpret properly both *ODM* and Marcuse's project as a whole, *ODM* should be read in relation to *Eros and Civilization* as well as to the works that follow, such as *An Essay on Liberation* and *Counterrevolution and Revolt*. It is precisely the vision of 'what could be' articulated in *EC, EL* and other writings that creates the bleakness of 'what is' in *ODM*. Marcuse continues to believe that contradictions exist between the higher possibilities and the existing system. The problem in *ODM* is that one-dimensional thought cannot perceive this distinction, but Marcuse insists that it continues to exist unabated and, if perceived, could be a vehicle of individual and social transformation.

In his writings after *ODM* Marcuse focuses more on social contradictions, struggles and the disintegrating factors in advanced capitalism. For his post-1965 works to fit intelligibly within his project as a whole, *ODM* must be read as a theory of containment of contradictions, forces of negation, and possibilities of liberation that exist but are suppressed and contained. Even in *ODM* Marcuse continues to point to these forces and possibilities, and to recognize the liberating potential hidden in the oppressive social system. In his discussion of technology, for instance, Marcuse analyses both its repressive aspects in advanced industrial society and its potentially liberating aspects (see my discussion in 8.2.5 and 10.2). As I shall argue in Chapter 10, even in his most 'pessimistic' book, *ODM*, Marcuse is a visionary utopian animated by a sense that life could be like it exists in art and dreams if only a revolution could take place that would eliminate its repressive features. Consequently, the theory of one-dimensional society and domination must be seen in the light of his theory of potentials for liberation, and his analysis of 'what is' should be read against his vision of 'what could be'. Thus I suggest that *ODM* should be read as a theory of the containment of the contradictions of capitalism and possibilities for liberation, which, in turn, erupted in the late 1960s and are seized upon anew in *EL, CR&R* and his later writings. For Marcuse's project as a whole to make sense, 'one-dimensional society' must contain potentially explosive tensions and conflicts, which indeed later become a central focus of his post-1965 writings (see my discussion in the next chapters).

Yet it must also be admitted that the theory of one-dimensional society remains one of Marcuse's distinctive contributions to contemporary social theory, and it is a theory that articulates some of his most fundamental and abiding perceptions. Although Marcuse gave a different account of the situation of advanced capitalism in post-1965 writings such as *EL, CR&R* and many essays and lectures, during an interview with me in December 1978, when I asked him his current opinion of *ODM*, he responded: 'I stick to what I wrote in *One-Dimensional Man*', insisting that his analysis of social trends had been 'confirmed' by recent assaults on the changes that struggles of the 1960s had been producing. Marcuse mentioned attacks on welfare programmes, typified by Proposition 13 in California; government and business demands for cutbacks on social programmes and less government regulation; the *Berufsverbot* in Germany and other repression of radicals throughout the world; conservative attacks on abortion, feminism and the Equal Rights Agreement; the increased strength of major corporations and multinationals; and conservative and neo-conservative offences in many areas of social and political life. He added, however, that the 1960s unleashed new social forces and opened up new space for struggle that was still open and should be utilized by forces of opposition to militate for radical social change.

Despite the problems with Marcuse's theory, it provoked much useful debate about the nature and possibilities for change in advanced capitalism and helped stimulate much excellent historical research and analysis, for after its publication, a number of books appeared which traced the historical processes through which capitalist development produced new forms of social control and domination.[69] Whereas Marcuse's book is sometimes weak on historical analysis and empirical detail, a body of literature was published, inspired at least in part by Marcuse's theory, which provides historical-theoretical support for his imposing synthesis. Marcuse's theory, however, minimizes the continued contradictions in advanced capitalism between the state, economy and culture – and the struggles and contradictions within these regions. Marcuse thus sacrifices – to the detriment of his theory – the traditional Marxian emphasis on social contradictions, tensions and struggles. A problem with Marcuse's theory – shared by many of the studies of capitalism, cited in the above note, that were influenced by him – is that it pictures the development of industrial society as a successful attempt on the part of corporate capitalism to dominate totally its helpless and passive victims. Such a historical synoptic fails to take account of the continuing struggles against corporate capitalism, the fact that many of capital's instruments of social control were defensive manoeuvres against working-class offensives and capitalist crisis tendencies. Theories of one-dimensional society also fail to note continuing struggles and pockets of resistance, individual and cultural revolts, and opposition to advanced capitalism that continue to exist despite decades of capitalist hegemony.[70]

As a reaction against Marcusean theories of capitalist hegemony that were developed by many in the New Left, and against 'capital logic' approaches which are akin in certain ways, new radical approaches to advanced capitalism and its history have arisen which focus on class struggle and resistance to capitalist domination.[71] Against both Marcusean theories of capitalist hegemony and traditional Marxian theories which still appeal to the revolutionary proletariat and the imminent collapse of capitalism, it should be stressed that Marx himself analysed both mechanisms of ruling-class control and power, as well as working-class struggle and resistance, attempting to depict as fully as possible the resources and power of both antagonists. In a period of capitalist offensive and stabilization of capitalist hegemony, Marcusean types of analyses are useful for a Marxism that is more than repetition of dogmatic litany. However, Marcusean themes of one-dimensional society cannot account for capitalist crises or revolutionary struggles and upheavals. Thus radical social theory must analyse *both* instruments of capitalist domination and struggle and resistance, and tendencies toward capitalist stabilization and containment contrasted with tendencies towards contradiction and crisis.[72] Rather than seeing advanced capitalism as a closed, monolithic system, it is preferable to see it as a system of contradictions, tensions and conflicts which capital desperately tries to manage – and profit from – but which oscillates from stasis to change, from oppression and domination to struggle and resistance, and from stability and containment to conflict and crisis.

This is, in fact, the perspective of most of Marcuse's post–1965 writings. Marcuse is a sensitive historical barometer, and when new contradictions, disintegrating factors and crises surfaced in the 1960s, making possible again radical social change, Marcuse quickly championed the new forces of rebellion and turned to reconsider Marxian theses which he had temporarily put in question or rejected. In his writings after *ODM*, Marcuse argues that despite the integration of the working class, the objective conditions for radical social change and the need for the elimination of capitalism still exist. In the late 1960s he turns to focus on various disintegrating tendencies emerging in the streamlined system of advanced capitalist domination, claiming that new forces are appearing which manifest a total break with the system and are potential bearers of radical change and liberation.

It is my contention that in his post-1965 writings, Marcuse

overcomes many of the theoretical deficiencies of *One-Dimensional Man* by analysing the contradictions and possibilities for radical change both within and without the capitalist sphere. He also provides a clearer picture of the global totality by emphasizing differentiations among the socialist countries and the importance of the Third World and its struggles within the global configuration of contemporary capitalism and socialism. Further, he shifts his emphasis from an amorphous 'advanced industrial society' to contemporary capitalism, especially regarding the United States, thus providing a sharper focus on US society. Finally, he specifies in more detail his concept of the alternative society and returns critical theory to political practice geared towards radical social change, thus re-politicizing critical theory. Let us now turn to the vicissitudes of critical theory in Marcuse's later work and examine how he relates his critical theory to radical politics.

9

Marcuse, Radical Politics and the New Left

Marcuse was not the first Marxist to formulate theories of the integration of the working class and capitalist stabilization, but few other avowed Marxists have presented such a theory so bleakly and bluntly. Marcuse's dilemma was that he wanted at the same time to remain a Marxist, be loyal to the project of critical theory developed by the Institute for Social Research, and be an independent thinker. In view of his writings and activity both before and after the publication of *ODM*, it is clear that he revently desired *total revolution*, described as a radical upheaval and overthrow of the previously existing order, bringing about wide-ranging changes that would eliminate capitalism and establish revolutionary socialism. As noted, Marcuse has told me that his experiences in the German Revolution of 1918 gave him a sense that genuine revolution was characterized by a totality of upheaval – a view articulated at the time by Rosa Luxemburg, whom Marcuse greatly admired and who decisively influenced his concept of revolution.[1] Consequently, with such a totalistic concept of revolution, any reforms or social change that did not lead to an overthrow of capitalism only impressed Marcuse as a cosmetic improvement of the existing system.[2]

In situations when such a total and radical social upheaval appears unlikely, Marcuse is bound to become pessimistic about the possibility of radical social change. Nonetheless, he constantly affirms the relevance and importance of the Marxian critique of capitalism, and near the end of *ODM* reaffirms his belief in the superior rationality of socialism:

> the facts are all there which validate the critical theory of this society and of its fatal development: the increasing irrationality of

the whole; waste and restriction of productivity; the need for aggressive expansion; the constant threat of war; intensified exploitation; dehumanization. And they all point to the historical alternative: the planned utilization of resources for the satisfaction of vital needs with a minimum of toil, the transformation of leisure into free time, the pacification of the struggle for existence. (*ODM*, pp. 252–3)

This affirmation of his continued commitment to socialism is followed by a poignant and revealing passage in which Marcuse articulates his anger and regret that there is not in fact a revolutionary situation, or class, to carry through the Marxian theory of revolution:

> the facts and the alternatives are there like fragments which do not connect, or like a world of mute objects without a subject, without the practice which would move these objects in the new direction. Dialectical theory is not refuted, but it cannot offer the remedy. It cannot be positive ... On theoretical as well as empirical grounds, the dialectical concept pronounces its own hopelessness. (*ODM*, p. 253)

Whereas, earlier, the critical theory of society could count on oppositional forces within the society, disintegrating tendencies that would activate these forces, and the 'liberation of *inherent* possibilities' (*ODM*, pp. 254ff), Marcuse no longer saw any possibility for revolutionary forces to explode the society from within, believing that advanced capitalism is so totalitarian and pleasantly repressive that only *absolute refusal* can be sustained as a 'truly revolutionary mode of opposition' (*ODM*, pp. 255ff). Marcuse explicitly renounces here advocacy of any reformism, or piecemeal change, and claims that only non-integrated 'outsiders' can be a truly revolutionary force (*ODM*, pp. 256–7).

9.1 The Great Refusal

In 1964 Marcuse perceived only a slight chance that the most exploited and persecuted outsiders, in alliance with an enlightened intelligentsia, might mark 'the beginning of the end' and signify some hope for social change:

However, underneath the conservative popular base is the substratum of the outcasts and outsiders, the exploited and persecuted of other races and other colours, the unemployed and the unemployable. They exist outside the democratic process; their life is the most immediate and the most real need for ending intolerable conditions and institutions. Thus their opposition is revolutionary even if their consciousness is not. Their opposition hits the system from without and is therefore not deflected by the system; it is an elementary force which violates the rules of the game and, in doing so, reveals it as a rigged game. When they get together and go out into the streets, without arms, without protection, in order to ask for the most primitive civil rights, they know that they face dogs, stones and bombs, jail, concentration camps, even death. Their force is behind every political demonstration for the victims of law and order. The fact that they start refusing to play the game may be the fact which marks the beginning of the end of a period. (*ODM*, pp. 256–7)

This passage bears witness to the hope that the civil rights struggle signalled the beginning of a period of radicalization and change of consciousness which would create new possibilities for qualitative social change. However, this was merely a hope, and Marcuse thought that there was just a 'chance' of a radical coalition forming: 'The chance is that, in this period, the historical extremes may meet again: the most advanced consciousness of humanity and its most exploited force. It is nothing but a chance' (*ODM*, p. 257). Hence Marcuse ended *One-Dimensional Man* on a note of pessimism, bordering on resignation and stoical opposition for the sake of loyalty to humanity's highest hopes and reverence towards those who have died in the struggle for those hopes:

The critical theory of society possesses no concepts which could bridge the gap between the present and its future; holding no promise and showing no success, it remains negative. Thus it wants to remain loyal to those who, without hope, have given and give their life to the *Great Refusal*.

At the beginning of the fascist era, Walter Benjamin wrote: 'It is only for the sake of those without hope that hope is given to us'. (*ODM*, p. 257)[3]

Marcuse's concept of the 'Great Refusal' and his advocacy of the revolutionary potential of those strata, groups and individuals not integrated in advanced industrial society provide the crux of his alleged kinship with anarchism.[4] In my view, however, Marcuse's conception here is really closer to notions of individualistic revolt advocated by the artistic *avant-garde* and bohemia than to anarchism. The term the 'Great Refusal' was inspired by André Breton,[5] who defended the total refusal of the institutions, values and way of life in bourgeois society. It is this notion of individualistic refusal and revolt that characterizes Marcuse's political conception in *ODM* rather than anarchist concepts of mutual aid, revolutionary mass upheaval or collective self-government. Marcuse rarely uses the term 'anarchism' in a favourable way and never discusses in any detail anarchist thinkers or texts. In fact, anarchists like Murray Bookchin attack Marcuse for being too dogmatically Marxist in his political conceptions.[6]

Moreover, throughout the last chapters of *ODM* there are frequent expressions of a stoical and defiant individualism – and occasional quietism – which are at odds with anarchist notions of collective action (see, for example, *ODM*, pp. 242–3). Other passages seem to suggest a type of 'personal withdrawal' (*ODM*, p. 243) quite foreign to anarchist (or Marxist!) activism and to express contempt for the 'masses', which is utterly at odds with anarchist and Marxist humanism (*ODM*, p. 245).[7] Marcuse's radical individualism and emphasis on individual revolt is thus a deeply rooted aspect of his thought. As we have seen in his early writings, he championed the 'radical act' against capitalist society, and although he formulated the concept in Marxian terms, there were elements of Heideggerian individualism in his project which surfaced again in *EC, ODM* and other later writings. Some of Marcuse's critics see concepts like the Great Refusal as ineradicably Heideggerian elements in his thought,[8] but in my view his emphasis on on individual revolt and self-transformation constitute a vital component of his revolutionary theory which maintains that there can be no meaningful talk about social change unless the individuals themselves are liberated from capitalist needs and consciousness and possess 'radical needs' for thoroughgoing social change.

Instead of seeing Marcuse's emphasis on the Great Refusal as a capitulation to 'bourgeois individualism' – or 'one-dimensional pessimism - I see his use of the concept in *ODM* as a revealing indication of the depth and parameters of the crisis of Marxism in an era when a revolutionary theorist could simply not point to any forces of revolution, or revolutionary class, in the advanced capitalist countries. Marcuse is thus honestly questioning the Marxian theory of revolution in an era in which proletarian revolt was for the most part absent and there were no spectacular revolutionary struggles or forces evident in the advanced capitalist countries during a period of almost unprecedented affluence and relative stabilization.

Almost on the eve of *ODM*'s publication, however, the civil rights struggles which Marcuse alluded to at the end of his book intensified, and the New Left and anti-war movement began to grow in response to the accelerating American military intervention in Vietnam. During this period, a generation of radicals turned to study Marcuse's book, which seemed to have denied the possibility of fundamental political change. During the heroic period of the New Left in the 1960s, *ODM* helped to show a generation of political radicals what was wrong with the system they were struggling against, and thus played an important role in the student movement.[9] Marcuse himself quickly rallied to the student activists' cause and in 1965 began modifying some of his theses to take account of the surge of militancy which both surprised and exhilarated him. Yet although the Great Refusal was being acted out on a grand scale, Marcuse's theory had failed to specify in any detail agents of social change or strategies for revolution. Consequently, Marcuse began a desperate search for a radical politics that was to occupy him the rest of his life. This search led him to defend confrontation politics and revolutionary violence and deeply alienated Marcuse from those who advocated more moderate models for social change.[10]

In his post-1965 writings, Marcuse sought a 'revolutionary subject' that would make such change possible, as well as a revolutionary strategy that it could follow. Since the industrial working class (Marx's proletariat = revolutionary subject) was, in his view, integrated into advanced capitalism, Marcuse sought a new revolutionary subject successively in non-integrated outsiders or minorities, students and intellectuals, a 'new sensibility', 'catalyst groups' and in Rudolf Bahro's concept of 'surplus consciousness'. Marcuse supported strategies of militant confrontation politics from about

1965–70, then shifted to the advocacy of political education and the formation of small oppositional groups modelled on workers' councils; during the 1970s he called for a 'United Front' politics and 'the long march through the institutions'. Throughout, Marcuse remained faithful to a radical, Marxist tradition of revolutionary socialism represented by Marx, Luxemburg and Korsch, while he increasingly criticized orthodox Marxist–Leninist conceptions of revolution and socialism.

Marcuse was the only member of the original Frankfurt school who enthusiastically supported political activism in the 1960s, gearing his writing, teaching and political interventions towards New Left struggles. The result was a remarkable series of writings, from 'Repressive Tolerance' in 1965 to a study of Rudolf Bahro's *The Alternative in Eastern Europe* in 1978, which attempted to articulate the theory and practice of the New Left while repoliticizing critical theory. This political involvement won Marcuse notoriety as a guru of the student movement, creating a heated political-intellectual situation that made it extremely difficult to appraise his works dispassionately and to measure his contributions to critical theory. Caught up in the political debates of the day, Marcuse's ideas were subject to fierce polemics and sometimes fervent espousal. Moreover, he himself frequently revised his views, developing new revolutionary perspectives, while his critics were attacking his previous positions. Marcuse's political writings theorized the vicissitudes of the New Left and both reflected and commented on its development. With the passage of time, it is now possible to gain the necessary distance and perspective to evaluate critically all of Marcuse's writings from 1965–79 and to analyse his political positions in relation to their historical context.

9.2 Marcuse's advocacy of confrontation politics: 'Repressive Tolerance'

In 1965, Marcuse staunchly defends confrontation politics in his provocative essay, 'Repressive Tolerance', published in the book *A Critique of Pure Tolerance* (hereafter *CPT*).[11] This politically explosive essay was criticized harshly for its obvious partisanship, violating the academic taboo of neutrality, as it called for 'intolerance toward prevailing policies, attitudes, opinions, and the extension of tolerance to policies, attitudes, and opinions which are outlawed and suppressed' (*CPT*, p. 81). In effect, Marcuse proposed intolerance towards the established society and its racism, militarism and imperialism (the Vietnam war was beginning to be an explosive issue), as well as towards its waste and planned obsolescence, advertising, environmental destruction, pollution and the other 'intolerable' phenomena that Marcuse was criticizing. His stated goal was the elimination of violence and the reduction of repression, which he argued was prevented by 'violence and suppression on a global scale' (*CPT*, p. 82).

Marcuse criticized imperialist violence in Indo-China, Latin America, Africa and Asia and the harsh repression of oppositional minorities in the centres of Western capitalism. These racist and imperialist policies 'should not be tolerated because they are impeding, if not destroying, the chances of creating an existence without fear and misery' (*CPT*, p. 83). Marcuse's essay responds to the contemporary repression of blacks and civil rights workers in the south, the scare of nuclear annihilation in the Cuban missile crisis, the escalation of the Vietnam war, the French atrocities in Algeria, and Goldwater's presidential candidacy, which together stirred up atavistic sentiments on the right and increased repression and destructiveness throughout the capitalist world. Marcuse maintains that if the society is thoroughly irrational and destructive, then it must be militantly opposed and its excesses and negativities must no longer be tolerated.[12]

Marcuse bases his argument on Justice Holmes's position that civil rights could be suspended if society faced a 'clear and present danger'. Marcuse claims that militaristic and repressive policies do constitute a 'clear and present danger', since advocacy of war and calls for the suppression of dissenting radicals constitute threats to civil liberties and even to human survival that could no longer be tolerated (*CPT*, pp. 109ff). Not only free speech and academic freedom *per se* are at stake in 'Repressive Tolerance', but also whether increasing racism, militarism and repression should be tolerated or actively opposed. Marcuse argues that 'pure tolerance' and neutrality only strengthen the system, and impede liberation and the reduction of violence. Since the media are controlled by the establishment, the people are indoctrinated in advance and are immunized against oppositional ideas (*CPT*, pp. 94ff). Hence the need for radical means to break through the distorted universe of thought and to bring the public to an awareness of the dangers of aggressive and brutal policies, which were currently being tolerated. Such an activity of enlightenment aiming at radical change 'could only be envisaged as a result of large-scale pressure which would amount to an upheaval' (*CPT*, p. 101). Refusal of tolerance could be translated into resistance to the war and draft, attacks on the military, strikes and boycotts, civil disobedience, marches on Washington, occupation of universities and factories, and intolerance towards the representatives of the policies opposed.

It is questionable, however, whether it is a correct radical position to advocate an 'intolerance thesis' to justify confrontation politics. The 'clear and present danger' argument (as a justification to repress 'intolerable' ideas) is often used as an excuse to repress radicals. Therefore it seems that radicals should defend free speech and civil liberties, while at the same time urging militant struggle against obviously dangerous and repugnant practices and policies (such as imperialist wars, racism, brutality towards women and children, etc.) 'Intolerance' towards the worst aspects of imperialist capitalism, or bureaucratic communism, may well be justified or necessary, but it should not be formulated in any way that suggests the suppression of free speech, for such arguments often play into the hands of authorities who are all too eager to suppress radicals and tend as well to alienate people from what is often perceived as the 'authoritarian Left'.

Thus radicals should take the position of Rosa Luxemburg, who urged the defence of free speech as the freedom to speak differently, to dissent, thus defending unrestricted communication and the development of an open and lively 'public sphere'.[13] Nonetheless, given the tight control of the means of communication by the established society at the time, Marcuse was probably correct that confrontation politics was the most effective means for radicals to express their dissent from the prevailing policies and their opposition to the dominant institutions.[14] Even more controversial was his position on violence. Put simply, Marcuse opposed the violence of the established society and supported violence to overthrow it. He argues that 'in the advanced centres of civilization violence prevails' (*CPT*, p. 102) in police brutality, in prisons and mental institutions, against racial minorities and women, and in increasingly brutal forms against the people of underdeveloped countries who dare to struggle for their liberation against imperialist domination. Marcuse makes distinctions between the structural violence embedded in the system and the violence that would eliminate systemic violence, between reactionary and revolutionary violence and between violence of the oppressers and the oppressed.[15] In his view, applying standards of pacifism and non-violence to the struggles of the oppressed against their oppressers serves 'the cause of actual violence by weakening the protest against it' (*CPT*, p. 103).

The capstone of his argument is the insistence that we must choose sides between Establishment or Opposition, and we must make every effort to distinguish between true and false, right and wrong, and to oppose militantly what are perceived as false ideas and wrong policies. To a generation of intellectuals nurtured on relativism, ambiguity and neutrality, this was a difficult pill to swallow, and when students drew the line and told their teachers, 'either you're with us or against us', confused academics turned on Marcuse and accused him of corrupting the youth. Marcuse firmly committed himself to the Left, siding with the militants. He supported his position by arguing that historically the Left had furthered progress, that violence emanating from the rebellion of the oppressed had reduced injustice, cruelty and war, while increasing freedom, equality and justice (*CPT*, pp. 99ff). In short, the Left had furthered the cause of 'progress in civilization' (*CPT*, p. 107). As examples Marcuse cited the English civil war, the French Revolution and the Chinese and Cuban Revolutions (but not the American or Russian Revolutions!)[16] He argues that violence that had come from the ruling classes had not aided progress, but had instead created a depressing history of oppression and a long series of dynastic and imperialist wars, culminating in fascism (*CPT*, pp. 108f). Marcuse concludes that the ruling classes have historically 'tightened and streamlined the continuum of repression' (*CPT*, p. 109) and that to perceive this and to motivate people to fight for a different history requires radical re-education and a change of political consciousness to break through the prevailing distorted consciousness and to shift the balance of public opinion from Right to Left.

9.3 In search of the revolutionary subject

Marcuse's critique of pure tolerance, his insistence that we must take a pro or con stance concerning the existing society and its policies, and his advocacy of militant opposition, made his ideas the centre of heated debate. At this point Marcuse also turned to a resolutely revolutionary socialist perspective. This move is recorded in many articles, including his 1967 Berlin lectures published in *Five Lectures* and *An Essay on Liberation*.[17] Marcuse's gloom about the demise of revolutionary opposition is dispelled in these writings, which glow with revolutionary optimism. He now sees new prospects for revolution, since the 'outsiders' and relatively few practitioners of the Great Refusal have expanded to a 'growing opposition to the global domination of corporate capitalism' (*EL*, p. vii). Marcuse now believes that the 'threatening homogeneity has been loosening up and an alternative is beginning to break into the repressive continuum' (*EL*, p. viii). The alternative is liberation: 'an emergence of different goals and values, different aspirations in the men and women who resist and deny the massive exploitative power of corporate capitalism even in its most comfortable and liberal realizations' (*EL*, p. vii).

An Essay on Liberation is a highly charged work that expresses the ambience of revolutionary utopianism in the 1960s. Its close connection with its historical situation constituted the text's relevance and interest, but also accounts for its shortcomings. For Marcuse greatly exaggerates the emancipatory potential of the 1960s struggles, and does not adequately articulate the limitations of the liberation struggles then taking place. At the time of its publication *EL* was enthusiastically read as an affirmation of total revolution; it at once exhilarated radical students and shocked the academic establishment.[18] Marcuse unabashedly affirms the counterculture and student movement as the manifestation of a '*new sensibility*',[19] producing 'a political practice of methodical disengagement from the refusal of the Establishment aiming at a radical transvaluation of values' (*EL*, p. 6).

The new sensibility 'expresses the ascent of the life instincts over aggressiveness and guilt' (*EL*, p. 23), and contains a 'negation of the needs that sustain the present system of domination and the negation of the values on which they are based' (*5L*, p. 67). Instead of the need for repressive performance and competition, the new sensibility posits the need for meaningful work, gratification and community; instead of the need for aggression and destructive productivity, it affirms love and the preservation of the environment; it refuses obscene consumerism, waste and planned obsolescence, and calls for a simpler, more human life; against the horrors and ugliness of capitalist industrialization, it claims a need for beauty and sensuousness. It translates these values into 'a practice that involves a break with the familiar, the routine ways of seeing, hearing, feeling, understanding things so that the organism may become receptive to the potential forms of a non-aggressive, non-exploitative world' (*EL*, p. 6). This total refusal of the dominant societal needs, values and institutions represents a radical break with the entirety of the society's institutions, culture and life-style.

The new sensibility, Marcuse believes, is a radically anti-capitalist political force and a catalyst of revolutionary change. It contains a subversion of the needs on which capitalism depends for its very existence and produces new needs that represent the negation of capitalism. Marcuse totally affirms those bearers of the new sensibility which he finds in the New Left and counterculture as portents of a possible liberation from the capitalist warfare state. Throughout the book, Marcuse champions the student movement and youth culture that was horrifying the established society (see *EL*, pp. 7ff, 34ff, 49ff, and 79ff).

Since the publication of *An Essay on Liberation*, Marcuse has modified his formerly positive evaluation of the counterculture, as well as the political use of obscenity, rock music, guerilla theatre, and 'flower power'.[20] There is no doubt that he was carried away by the enthusiasm generated by the struggles of the 1960s to the extent that he exaggerated the importance of the student movement and diffuse counterculture revolts as agents of revolutionary change. However, it should be noted that even at the height of his militant enthusiasm, Marcuse never said that the counterculture and new sensibility was a *revolutionary* force. He claimed that its emergence is encouraging because (1) 'it signifies a total break with the dominant needs of repressive society' (*5L*, p. 69); (2) it is characteristic of a state of disintegration and thus indicates cracks in the system, a possible breaking through the continuum of domination; and (3) it is a catalyst for change which may play a revolutionary role in connection with other forces, as it is contagious and may spread throughout society. Hence Marcuse's position is that the new sensibility could contribute to producing a new revolutionary movement but is not itself *the* revolutionary subject.[21]

Moreover, Marcuse does not see any substantial mass support for the new radicalism in the working class and continues to stress that a radical upheaval is unlikely unless there is an acute economic crisis to radicalize the masses.[22] Over and over in essays, lectures and interviews Marcuse indicates that in his view there can be no revolution without the working class, and never claims to see evidence that the working class is responsive to the new radicalism.[23] He concludes that we are in a pre-revolutionary situation and that radical change requires intensified work in political education: 'Historically, it is again the period of enlightenment prior to material change – a period of education, but education which turns into praxis: demonstration, confrontation, rebellion' (*EL*, p. 53).

Although Marcuse was attacked by orthodox Marxists for his 'revisionism', he continued during the late 1960s to adhere to the Marxian tenet that the working class is the crucial revolutionary force. He also never abandoned the Hegelian-Marxian search for a 'revolutionary subject'.[24] Far from abandoning the Marxian revolutionary problematic, in retrospect some of the problems of Marcuse's account in the late 1960s derive from a failure to question more radically Marxian concepts of the proletariat as the privileged agent of revolution, the concept of a 'revolutionary subject', and the Marxian concept of revolution as a radical upheaval and overthrow of the existing society leading to the seizure of state power and the establishment of a revolutionary government. The problem is that the Marxian model simply did not fit the process of social change taking place in the 1960s in the USA and other advanced capitalist countries. Although Marcuse is to be lauded for expanding Marxian discourse, opening up its categories to new historical content, and championing progressive social forces, ultimately his view of social transformation was still too deeply immersed in the Marxian theory of revolution, forcing him in the 1970s to revise more radically his views on social change, the working class and the transition to socialism (see my discussion in the next sections).

Contrary to many interpretations of Marcuse's position, his evaluation of the 'subverting forces in transition' in *An Essay on Liberation* does not claim that blacks, students and the counterculture are the new agents of revolution; instead he offers a rather well balanced account of the political potential and limitations of these groups. He saw radical possibilities in ghetto uprisings and the emergence of black power, but he carefully analysed contradictions which were defusing the revolutionary potential of ghetto revolt and the black liberation movement (*EL*, pp. 57ff). Likewise, he was restrained in his evaluation of the radical potential of the student movement (*EL*, pp. 59ff).

From about 1965–72, the student movement in the United States and throughout the world engaged in a series of spectacular actions which made it appear that a new revolutionary force was in the making. Marcuse's *An Essay on Liberation* was written at the peak of this radicalization period and was concluded shortly after workers in France joined with students in a remarkable show of revolutionary zeal and solidarity.[25] At this time, students all over the world were taking over universities, demonstrating and fighting against the Vietnam war and the military machine that was waging it, driving Lyndon Johnson to resign and revitalizing leftist rhetoric while nourishing hopes for socialist revolution. During this tumultuous period, Marcuse was proclaimed guru of the student movement, and he tirelessly defended and advised students and movement radicals.[26]

In *An Essay on Liberation*, Marcuse stresses the strategic role of students and university in society, noting that the student rebellion poses a threat to the system which depends on them to provide administrators, scientists, lawyers, teachers and the like to keep it going (*EL*, pp. 59ff). Their opposition to a university system that produces society's elite, combined with demands for radical reforms, touched on a very vulnerable pillar of the society which would be increasingly dependent on education and intellectual skills. Most frightening to the establishment powers was the total character of the refusal, which was at once political and moral. For the radical students' revulsion was not only aimed at the society's worst imperialist and racist excesses, but attacked the university, middle-class culture, decaying liberalism, abstract parliamentary democracy, and fetishistic consumerism – a total rebellion that struck at the foundations of society. But Marcuse made clear to students in Berlin in 1967 that: 'I have never said that the student opposition today is by itself a revolutionary force, nor have I seen the hippies as the "heir of the proletariat"! Only the national liberation fronts of the developing nations are today in a revolutionary struggle' (*5L*, p. 93).

Marcuse's revolutionary hopes were based on the belief that Third World liberation struggles were weakening the global framework of capitalism and were shifting the balance of power from capitalism to socialism. His argument was that:

> by virtue of the evolution of imperialism, the developments in the Third World pertain to the dynamic of the First World, and the forces of change in the former are not extraneous to the latter . . . The National Liberation Fronts threaten the life line of imperialism; they are not only a material but also an ideological catalyst of change. The Cuban revolution and the Viet Cong have demonstrated: it can be done; there is a morality, a humanity, a will, and a faith which can resist and deter the gigantic technical and economic force of capitalist expansion. More than the 'socialist humanism' of the early Marx, this violent solidarity in defence, this elemental socialism in action, has given form and substance to the radicalism of the New Left; in this ideological respect too, the external revolution has become an essential part of the opposition within the capitalist metropoles. (*EL*, pp. 80, 81–2)[27]

In Marcuse's view, Third World revolutionary movements threaten to cut off markets, sources of raw materials, a cheap labour supply and super profits, and by their successes spur on other revolutionary movements (the core of truth in the domino theory!), including the opposition at home. He now includes the Third World within the Global space and dynamics of capitalism, arguing

> these areas, and these forces are not external to the capitalist system. They are an essential part of its global space of exploitation, they are areas and forces which this system cannot allow to go and shift into that other orbit (of socialism or communism), because it can survive only if its expansion is not blocked by any superior power. The National Liberation movements are expressive of the internal contradictions of the global capitalist system.[28]

Marcuse stresses that the Third World revolutionary movements alone will not destroy advanced capitalism:

> The National Liberation movements in the Third World are not by themselves a revolutionary force strong enough to overthrow advanced capitalism as a system. Such a revolutionary force can

be expected only from a confluence of forces of change in the centres of advanced capitalism with those in the Third World. To bring this about is really a most difficult task. (*5L*, p. 95).

Further, 'the exemplary force, the ideological power of the external revolution, can come to fruition only if the internal structure and cohesion of the capitalist system begins to disintegrate. The chain of exploitation must break at its strongest link' (*EL*, p. 82). The paradoxical inversion of Lenin's claim that the capitalist chain must be broken at its weakest link indicates that the success of the Third World liberation movements is linked to the ability and the will of the capitalist superpower to support counter revolutionary forces throughout the world and to suppress liberation movements. Hence a 'fateful link persists between the prospects of the liberation movements and the prospects of radical change in the metropoles. The "negating" forces abroad must be "*synchronized*" with those at home'.[29]

Marcuse is aware that synchronization between revolutionary struggles in the Third World and the advanced capitalist countries is extremely difficult, but insisted that revolutionaries everywhere had common interests that were eliciting a growing solidarity (see *EL*, 79f). He himself maintained solidarity both with New Left struggles and Third World liberation movements, criticizing the Soviet Union and European Communist parties from the Left, arguing that they were not sufficiently revolutionary.[30] Unlike his analysis in *One-Dimensional Man*, which offered little hope for radical change, Marcuse now argued continually that a crisis was possible, and in essay after essay called attention to the contradictions in capitalism which could erupt into a crisis, thus emphasizing the weaknesses and disintegrating factors in the system that were portents of the possibility of radical change.[31]

Beginning around 1970, however, Marcuse turned the major focus of his attention from the world political constellation and analysis of the prospects for world revolution to an analysis of prospects for radical social transformation in the United States, focusing on strategies for the New Left in the bastion of world capitalism. The results of his inquiry were published in *Counter-revolution and Revolt*. In this book he turns from the militant Third World strategy implicit in his late 1960s writings to a United Front strategy, which he seems to propose at least for US and advanced capitalist societies.[32]

9.3.1 *Towards a 'United Front':* Counterrevolution and Revolt

Counterrevolution and Revolt represents an important development in Marcuse's analysis of capitalist society and strategy for social transformation. Whereas *One-Dimensional Man* portrays a society of total integration grounded in consumer needs, he now argues that the society of happy consumers is disintegrating, and the needs themselves are a source of mounting frustration as the rising expectations of commodity paradise are unfulfilled for the underlying majority. Whereas in *One-Dimensional Man* Marcuse stresses the tendencies towards the integration of the working class into the labour system and place of work (*ODM*, pp. 24–32), he now emphasizes the disintegrating tendencies in the production system itself, and argues that the base of exploitation and reservoir of dissatisfaction is expanding to include the majority of the underlying population. Consequently, whereas in *ODM*, Marcuse only saw potential opposition in non-integrated outsiders, or radical students and intellectuals, he now perceives a greatly expanded potential base for opposition and struggle.

In accord with his new analysis of the social potential for change, he modifies his political strategy. Marcuse seems to assume that if a few militant outsiders face a hostile, integrated majority immune to radical ideas and against change, then the bleak prospects for radical change may well drive the isolated radicals to desperate rebellion. If, however, the entire society is oppressed and the people are ready for change, there is a base for a United Front, and the mobilization of the oppressed majority against the oppressors will be a viable possibility calling for new strategies, organization and goals. Consequently, Marcuse's shift from ultra-Left militancy in *An Essay on Liberation* to an emphasis on political education and organization of a United Front against the capitalist system is grounded in what he perceives as increasing tendencies towards disintegration in advanced capitalist society, which creates new space for radical change.

In *CR&R* and his subsequent 1970s writings, Marcuse significantly modifies his theory of one-dimensional society and abandons his defence of confrontation politics and revolutionary violence. Whereas his perceptions of the integration of the working class and the stabilization of capitalism led him to affirm the New Left as an important new political force and to defend their forms of struggle, his perceptions of limitations of New Left struggles and new possibilities for social change in an era of disintegrating capitalism led Marcuse to re-evaluate both his theory of society and of radical social change. Underpinning the theoretical-political shifts noted here is a shift in his concept of 'negation in the dialectic'. It has been previously argued that Marcuse lacked a concept of dialectical negation, substituting a theory of 'external mediation' for the Marxian concept of the 'determinate negation.'[33] That is, in searching for the forces of negation that would 'negate' capitalist society Marcuse elicited 'external' factors: non-integrated outsiders, radicals and minorities, and then Third World revolutionaries as the agents of social transformation. This theory of negation in the dialectic depends on an external mediator and not internal contradictions that could be developed to transform the society radically. However, in *Counterrevolution and Revolt*, Marcuse shifts his analysis of dialectical negation and transformation, and no longer denies the possibility of negation (i.e. forces of change) developing *within* the system. Consequently in *Counterrevolution and Revolt* he discerns disintegrating tendencies *within* capitalist society, and conceives of social change emerging out of the conflicting tendencies in the society, thus revising his category of dialectical negation, as he revised his earlier analysis of capitalist stabilization. In his 1970s writings, Marcuse stresses disintegrating tendencies and societal *contradictions*, picturing society not as a closed, one-dimensional monolith, but as a system of contradictory, shifting tendencies which contains the possibilities of progressive transformation and/or barbaric regression.

Marcuse claims that although it sometimes appears that the latest stage of capitalism is restabilized and has little potential for radical change, a 'very *different* reality lies behind the appearance' (*CR&R*, p. 5). He argues that the integration of the working class is a surface phenomenon that 'hides the *dis*integrating, centrifugal tendencies of which it is itself an expression' (*CR&R*, p. 6). These disintegrating tendencies are rooted in the very conditions of the consumer society that were the basis of integration and stabilization in his earlier writings. He suggests that 'it is the overwhelming *wealth* of capitalism which will bring about its collapse', and asks, 'Will the consumer society be its last stage, its gravedigger?' (*CR&R*, p. 7). Although Marcuse believes that the mass base created by eighteenth- and nineteenth-century capitalism (the proletariat) no longer exists qua revolutionary force; nonetheless a *new base* is being created by twentieth-century capitalism.

Marcuse argues that the ruling hierarchy, who represent the interests of capitalism as a system, increasingly control the means of production and organize and administer society in accord with their financial and political interests.[34] What this means is that more and more people are losing control over economic and political decision-making power and over their own labour activity, such that 'ever more strata of the formerly independent middle classes become the direct servants of capital, occupied in the creation and realization of surplus value while being separated from control of the means of production' (*CR&R*, p. 9). New working strata in the service industries (the 'tertiary sector') and the scientific-technical intelligentsia (Mallet's 'new working class') are also increasingly subjected to the rule of capital. Marcuse argues that the development of capitalism increases domination as 'technical progress = growing social wealth (the rising GNP!) = extended servitude' (*CR&R*, p. 4). Hence, 'the basis of exploitation is thus enlarged beyond the factories and shops, and far beyond the blue-collar working class' (*CR&R*, p. 10).[35] Consequently, domination of the entire society by the capitalist mode of production, and its rulers and managers, reveals 'the essential contradiction of capitalism in its most extreme concentration: capital versus the mass of the working population as a whole' (*CR&R*, p. 15). Marcuse now proposes that all workers collectively form one working class which is increasingly dominated by monopoly capital, utilizing Marx's distinction between *Gesamtarbeiter* and *Gesamtkapital* (composite labour versus composite capital) (*CR&R*, p. 9f). Although there are many differences among the various segments of the working population, the overwhelming majority share the position of being forced to sell their labour power for a wage, are separated from ownership and control of the means of production, and to not even control their own labour activity:

> 'The extension of exploitation to a larger part of the population, accompanied by a high standard of living, is the reality behind the facade of the *consumer society*; this reality is the unifying force which integrates, behind the back of the individuals, the widely different and conflicting classes of the underlying population. (*CR&R*, pp. 15–16)

Marcuse next argues – and we encounter another radical departure from his earlier position – that the rising standard of living has created new needs and rising expectations which capitalism cannot fulfil; Marcuse suggests that this failure will create growing tensions and hostilities which may explode the system. These needs and expectations fall into two categories. First, in creating *consumer needs*, capitalism creates images of the good life (ease, enjoyment, luxury, sex, etc.) which appear to be within the reach of everyone: streamlined cars, travel and luxury vacations, tempting sexual objects, nifty household goods, entertainment and culture – consumer paradise. But the inability of the great majority to attain this standard of living and life-style, celebrated daily in the mass media and part of the very fabric of the consumer society, causes great frustration and discontent. There is a possibility, Marcuse believes, that the unfulfilled consumer needs and 'rising expectations' for increased consumption may themselves generate dissatisfaction and revolts that will be intensified and potentially explosive in an era of scarcity.[37]

The growing awareness of the society's failures and dissatisfaction with its way of life is being nurtured by a second kind of need being developed in advanced capitalism which Marcuse calls '*transcending needs*'. He suggests that the system implants needs for freedom, individuality and happiness that it cannot fulfil. The ideologies of advanced capitalism that promote personal gratification and fulfilment are becoming, Marcuse believes, increasingly contradictory and subversive of the system itself. For, to the extent that these ideologies cannot be realized, they too promote frustration and revolt. Marcuse believes that these transcending needs can help produce the ability to see through capitalism's ideological veil and to see into its damning contradictions: 'One knows one can live otherwise' (*CR&R*, p. 21). He concludes that capitalism itself, the consumer society at its highest and most affluent stage, may be creating the needs that will bring about its transformation: 'The centrifugal forces which appear in the emergence of transcending needs operate behind the back of the capitalist managers, and they are generated by the mode of production itself ... Capitalism has opened a new dimension, which is at one and the same time the living space of capitalism and its negation' (*CR&R*, pp. 18–19).

Reversing the tendency in *One-Dimensional Man* to call attention to factors of stability and cohesion in advanced capitalism, Marcuse now emphasizes factors which suggest that the system may be breaking down and disintegrating: dissatisfaction with and revolt against work, decline of real wages, permanent inflation and high unemployment, an unstable monetary system, liquidity crisis, ecology and energy crises – all of which, he believes, are producing a new consciousness of the failures of capitalism. This breakdown is documented daily in the media and finds expression in government studies of labour and the economy, as well as in radical critiques.[38] The question, however, is whether the breakdown will make possible a more progressive, rational social order, or a repressive, reactionary solution to the crisis of capitalism. For the threatened breakdown of the consumer society is countered, Marcuse claims, by a new reorganization of capitalism which he dalls the *counterrevolution*: 'The consumer society is the form in which monopoly state capitalism reproduces itself at its most advanced stage. And it is at this stage that repression is reorganized: the "bourgeois-democratic" phase of capitalism terminates in the new counter-revolutionary phase' (*CR&R*, pp. 23–4).

9.3.2 The 'preventive counterrevolution'

In the opening pages of *Counterrevolution and Revolt*, Marcuse claims that, 'The Western world has reached a new stage of development: now, the defence of the capitalist system requires the organization of counterrevolution at home and abroad' (*CR&R*, p. 1). To impose its system and order so as to protect its vested interests, the counterrevolution 'practises the horrors of the Nazi regime' (*CR&R*, p. 1): cruel persecution, torture and even genocide. The counterrevolution strives to prevent not only socialist revolution, but even minimal and long overdue social progress. The bulwark of the counterrevolution is the United States of America. Abroad, this means US support of military dictatorships, police states, reactionary governments who maintain the status quo and protect US interests, counterinsurgency and the suppression of national liberation movements, use of the US military in an attempt to police the world and contain Communism, and imperialist destruction of countries who dare to resist the will of the capitalist superpower.

At home, Marcuse projects the frightening possibility that the discontent and crises which he sees as a possible breaking up of capitalist domination may lead not to progressive radical change, but rather to a new fascism. The people's frustrations and aggressions could provide a mass base for fascism, and Marcuse sees signs of such a proto-fascist syndrome in the United States today (*CR&R*, pp. 24–9).[39] As a refugee from German fascism, Marcuse is extremely sensitive to the dangers of fascistic tendencies. He proposes the term 'preventive counterrevolution' to describe repressive policies that try to prevent even the possibility of a revolution, and he continues to analyse counterrevolutionary tendencies and the dangers of fascism.[40] But Marcuse stresses that the 'preventive counterrevolution' is not yet fascism, which, if it emerged in the USA, would in any case take a different form than German fascism. In a 1971 talk at Berkeley, Marcuse states:

> We are far from a fascist form of government, but some of the possible preconditions are emerging. They are well known and I will just give you a list: the courts, used more and more as political tribunals; the reduction of education and welfare in the richest country in the world; anti-democratic legislation, such as preventive detention and the no-knock laws; economic sanctions if you are politically and otherwise suspect; the intimidation and self censorship of the mass media. These are very frightening signs. You cannot say history repeats itself; it never repeats itself in the same form. The fact that we cannot point to any charismatic leader, the fact that we cannot point to any SS or SA here, simply means that they are not necessary in this country. If necessary, other organizations can perform the job, possibly even more efficiently. I do not have to tell you which organizations I have in mind.[41]

In view of the counterrevolution, 'The only counterforce is the development of an effectively organized radical Left, assuming the vast task of *political education*, dispelling the false and mutilated consciousness of the people so that they themselves experience their condition, and its abolition, as vital need, and apprehend the ways and means of their liberation' (*CR&R*, p. 28). Marcuse warns that if US society does enter a period of acute crisis, and if a fascist solution is attempted to solve capitalism's contradictions, then it is of utmost importance that the radical opposition becomes stronger and offers a viable alternative in order to become an effective political force in a period of disintegration and change.

9.3.3 *The New Left in the 1970s: against misplaced radicalism*

Marcuse maintains that the 'Marxian theory remains the guide of practice, even in a non-revolutionary situation' (*CR&R*, p. 33). He criticizes, however, what he sees as a prevalent tendency among the New Left (as well as the Old Left) to 'the distortion and falsification of Marxian theory through its *ritualization*' (*CR&R*, p. 33). For Marcuse Marxian theory is dialectical and historical: it describes the changes and transitions in the social-historical world. In his view, neo-Marxist theory must describe changes in the economy and society and the effect that these changes have on the totality of life and the prospects for social transformation. Because the Marxian concepts are historical, all of the concepts used to describe eighteenth- and nineteenth-century capitalism cannot obviously be used to describe twentieth-century capitalism; consequently, for Marcuse, Marxist theory and practice require constant reconstruction to keep in touch with the changes in the historical situation (*CR&R*, pp. 33ff). He stresses the need continually to revise the Marxian theory and suggests the relevancy of the New Left's reformulation of Marx's thesis on Feuerbach: 'Philosophers have previously only interpreted Marxism in various ways; the point, however, is to change it'.

The New Left is to be commended, Marcuse believes, for the vision of a free, liberated individual in a non-repressive society.[42] In Marcuse's view, the New Left is an especially advanced political force because it has drawn political struggle into the realm of (1) non-material needs (self-determination, non-alienated human relations, solidarity, autonomy, co-operation and community, women's liberation, etc.); and (2) the physiological dimension (the preservation of nature, aesthetic-erotic satisfaction and happiness, etc.) (*CR&R*, p. 129). The radicalization of the New Left is, at its best, integral, and combines the revolt of reason with the revolt of sensibility and the instincts, and the political revolution with the personal revolution, the gesture of the barricade with the gesture of love (*CR&R*, p. 130). The movement is novel in that it embraces new values, life-styles and alternatives which are a radical refusal of the prevailing values and ideology, and is therefore a subversive threat to the system that has evoked a violent response from the underlying population whose values are being attacked and rejected.

In Marcuse's view, although the majority of the population resists the thought and action of the New Left, it reflects a growing discontent and dissatisfaction with the system and contributes to undermining its power further (*CR&R*, p. 31). The problem is that the 'countervalues, counterbehaviour' and its Marxist-socialist theory and practice are alien to the large majority of the working population, who are not aware of the radical cleavage between what is possible and what is actual, or of the existing possibilities for qualitative change. The New Left's survival and possibilities of becoming a political force for radical change therefore depend on overcoming this hostility, communicating its vision, and changing and raising consciousness. These activities require political education and a demonstration that we are all oppressed and exploited by capitalism to such a degree that radical change is in the overwhelming interest of the society as a whole. Marcuse now proposes that a critical theory of society must show the shared, common condition of oppression and exploitation in the current society in concepts which at once characterize, criticize and project constructive alternatives, in a language that avoids canned vocabulary and clichés. The task is to convince people of the need for radical change and to make socialist ideas acceptable and attractive. Although critical theory should avoid the fetishism of the working class (as the sole or principle agent of social change), it must nonetheless attempt to radicalize all the people by showing how their dissatisfactions and frustrations are a result of the capitalist system. Marcuse's insistence that radical change requires a juncture of the working class and radical opposition seems to indicate a new 'United Front' turn in his thought: 'Radicalism has much to gain from the "legitimate" protest against the war, inflation and unemployment, from the defence of civil rights – even perhaps from a "lesser evil" in local elections. The ground for the building of a united front is shifting and sometimes dirty – but it is there' (*CR&R*, p. 56).[43]

From the mid-1960s to the early 1970s Marcuse made a major effort to repoliticize theory and directed much of his work towards the concerns of the New Left.[44] He travelled widely in Europe and America, speaking at conferences and to New Left audiences, and published many books and articles on the topics of liberation and revolution which became the central focus of his work.[45] In the mid-1960s Marcuse moved from Brandeis University, where he had taught from 1954 to 1965, and began teaching at the University of Calfornia at La Jolla.[46] At this time Marcuse received notoriety as 'Father of the New Left' and regularly received threats on his life which occasionally forced him to go into hiding; at other times, devoted students would stand guard at his house.[47] Marcuse was now achieving renown as one of America's greatest professors, who was unusually revered by his students – if not by all his colleagues. His students included many radicals, and several have written appreciative tributes to his effectiveness as a teacher.[48] Many of Marcuse's students are today teaching at universities and publishing works influenced by him.

During the 1970s Marcuse became involved with the women's movement and in 1974 lectured at Stanford and then in Europe on 'Marxism and Feminism'.[49] Here he enthusiastically embraced the goals of women's liberation and defended women's rights, sexual liberation and the equality of the sexes in terms of his categories in *Eros and Civilization* and more recent works. Marcuse continued to reflect on the update the Marxian theory, and gave a lecture in 1974 on 'Theory and Practice' at the fiftieth anniversary celebration of the Frankfurt Institute.[50] It is appropriate that Marcuse would defend on this occasion the politicizing of critical theory and the continued relevance of Marxism, and analyse the prospects and strategy for social change, as he, of all the original members of the 'inner circle' of the Frankfurt Institute, had gone the furthest in actually relating critical theory to political practice. In the late 1970s Marcuse continued to be active, lecturing to the American and European Left, and to the end of his life in 1979 he continued to write, lecture and discuss theory and politics with colleagues and young radicals.[51]

In a sense, Marcuse's political writings from 1964 until his death articulate successive theories and practices of the New Left. The individualistic 'Great Refusal' advocated at the end of *ODM* corresponds to revolt that was fermenting within advanced capitalist societies, and remarks at the end of *ODM* valorize the civil rights struggles. 'Repressive Tolerance' and his late 1960s essays and lectures justify the confrontation politics that were emerging in the anti-war movement as a response to the Vietnam war. *EL* expresses the moment of revolutionary euphoria during the spectacular struggles of 1968, and *CR&R* articulates the political realism of a movement which saw in the early 1970s that it was facing a long and difficult struggle to transform the existing society.

The extent to which a German-American professor entering his seventh decade involved himself with the New Left is quite remarkable. After decades of deep political pessimism, corresponding to devastating defeats of the Left, Marcuse saw his hopes for socialist revolution enlivened by New Left radicalism. Consequently, one encounters a change in the tone of his writings in the mid-1960s from a stoical pessimism to a more optimistic and utopian perspective. In this way, the New Left rejuvenated Marcuse, intensifying and radicalizing his thinking. In the New Left, Marcuse found concrete referents for his dialectical categories of contradiction, negation and the Great Refusal. In Marcuse, the New Left found a teacher, defender and spokesperson.

Marcuse was, however, somewhat embarrassed by the media image of New Left 'prophet' or 'father'. In a 1978 interview with the BBC, he insisted:

> I was not the mentor of the student activities of the sixties and
> early seventies. What I did was formulate and articulate some
> ideas and goals that were in the air at the time. That's about it.
> The student generation that became active in those years did not
> need a father figure, or grandfather figure, to lead them to protest
> against a society which daily revealed its inequality, injustice,
> cruelty and general destructiveness. They could experience that –
> they saw it before their own eyes.[52]

Marcuse's actual involvement with the New Left was stormy. Although he was revered by many, for others he was a 'revisionist', 'idealist philosopher', or 'elitist'. While, in 1967, Marcuse's defence of socialism and revolutionary violence was jubilantly acclaimed in Berlin, in 1968 his comments on utopian socialism were met with disdain by many of the same students. Many of the New Left were angry, impatient and ready to tear down the 'monster' and slay the 'beast' immediately. Marcuse always cautioned the New Left against 'counter-productive' action which were not part of a well thought-out theoretical strategy for social change. He insists:

> I combatted the anti-intellectualism of the New Left from the
> beginning. The reasons for it are, in my view, the isolation of the
> student movement from the working class, and the apparent
> impossibility of any spectacular political action. This led gradual-

ly so some kind of . . . well, let me say, inferiority complex, some kind of self-inflicted masochism, which found expression in, among other things, contempt for intellectuals because they are only intellectuals and 'don't achieve anything in reality'. This contempt serves well the interests of the powers that be. (Ibid.)

Whereas that faction of the New Left who would become 'Weatherman' wanted to destroy the universities, Marcuse told them that the Universities provided the best refuge for radicals in American society to struggle for socialism. When Progressive Labor wanted to go to the factories and wake up the working class, Marcuse was sceptical and told them it might be better to organize and radicalize the students. The 'action-faction' of the Students for a Democratic Society (SDS) wanted revolutionary action; Marcuse advised theory. Newly born Leninists wanted a party; Marcuse proposed revolutionary affinity groups, based on workers' councils, loosely organized into a mass movement and united by demonstrations, confrontations and, when appropriate, direct action. Consequently, sectarian radicals also developed global critiques of Marcuse's politics, often attacking him as vehemently as did his academic and right-wing critics.

In general, Marcuse represented the non-sectarian, anti-authoritarian wing of the New Left, criticizing the more excessive 'action factions', as well as the authoritarian-sectarian groups which began to spring up in the early 1970s. He was constantly open to new struggles and impulses in the movement and totally identified with the New Left. When asked by Bill Moyers in a 1974 television interview whether the New Left was dead, Marcuse insisted: 'I don't think it's dead and it will resurrect'; and he continued to claim throughout the 1970s that the New Left had not collapsed.[53] Moreover, in the same period, he carried out a sustained critique of orthodox Marxist-Leninist theories of revolution and developed new revolutionary perspectives.

9.4 Towards a new concept of revolution and critique of orthodox Marxism

Marcuse's emerging critique of the orthodox Marxian theory of revolution is evident in a conversation with Hans-Magnus Enzensberger, published in *Kursbuch* in 1970 under the title 'The Question of Organization and the Revolutionary Subject'.[54] Enzensberger continually confronts Marcuse with orthodox Marxist-Leninist positions on capitalism and revolution, while Marcuse radicalizes his critique of orthodox Marxism and moves towards new revolutionary perspectives. After discussing the prospects for fascism in America and other advanced capitalist countries, the following exchange takes place:

> ENZENSBERGER: The contradictions which you indicate must allow themselves to be concretized within American society itself, which means as class-contradictions. Or, do you see no possibility of establishing them within American class struggles?
> MARCUSE: Its really a question of overriding (*übergreifende*) contradictions. Marx never claimed that the contradictions of the capitalist system were concentrated exclusively in the class of industrial workers. Rather, they penetrate the entire society, the infrastructure as well as the superstructure. They naturally realize themselves in very different ways in the social classes, but they are contradictions of the system as a whole.
> ENZENSBERGER: They will not then, in your opinion, explode in the first instance in the contradictions between wage labour and capital?
> MARCUSE: Of course they appear in the contradiction between capital and labour. But when someone claims to be a Marxist, they must beware of fetishizing the class-concept. With the structural transformations of capitalism, classes and their situations also modify themselves. Nothing is more inappropriate and dangerous for a Marxist than to use a reified concept of the working class. (pp. 53–4)

When challenged by Enzensberger as to why he called the Marxian proletariat a 'mythological concept', Marcuse answers:

> The Marxian proletariat carries the features of the English industrial workers of the middle of the 19th century. The rising level of wages, the increasing power of the unions and the workers' parties have transformed that proletariat into a working class which corresponds to late capitalism. The class is oppressed, just as before, but not in the explosive and brutal forms which Marx describes. When today someone talks of a proletariat without

carrying through a precise class analysis, without analysing the changes in social being, they are reifying the Marxian categories. (Ibid.)

Marcuse's position, which he continued to develop in the 1970s, has rather important consequences for radical politics. He continually affirmed that the industrial working class today is no longer equivalent to Marx's proletariat, which is a historically specific concept derived from an earlier stage of capitalist development, and argued that the category of immiseration is no longer the crucial criterion delineating the revolutionary subject. Rather, the mark of potentially revolutionary forces is *oppression*.[55] Those oppressed people who are not totally integrated into the system, who do not identify with the system, may develop needs or consciousness that might provide the subjective conditions for radical social change. These needs are not necessarily born out of poverty, Marcuse stresses. They might grow out of oppression at work, sexual oppression, racial oppression or simply the experience of living in an oppressive society whose way of life is no longer tolerable. Such potentially radical forces of opposition are not solely – or even primarily? – to be found in the industrial working class, but may cut across classes and be found in groups of intellectuals, students, the unemployed, racial minorities, etc.

Marcuse stresses that the concept of the 'proletariat' for Marx is both a socio-economic category and a political one.[56] As a sociological concept, the proletariat describes the industrial working class engaged in manual labour, which is defined by wage-labour sold to capital that is both 'alienated' from the products of labour and the control of labour activity and is exploited through its production of surplus value and consequent appropriation by the capitalist class. As the most alienated and exploited class, the proletariat is for Marx, politically, a 'revolutionary class' whose life-activity represents the absolute negation of capitalist society,[57] and whose intolerable working and living conditions create *needs* to overthrow the existing society and to create a new one. Thus, for Marx, the proletariat is an explosive *political* force, and Marx believed that its position in the process of production and organization in the factory, in trade unions and in political parties made it the central *revolutionary* force. Moreover, Marx believed that it was a *universal* class which represented the general need to eliminate capitalism.

Marcuse stresses again and again that the proletariat is the potentially revolutionary subject for Marx because it does not share the needs of the bourgeois class and because its needs demand the overthrow of capitalism.[58] If the working class is free of capitalist consciousness, values and needs, then it is capable of producing a new society since it is free from the needs and values of the old one. If, however, industrial workers are not free from capitalist needs and values and if they share needs and values with the rest of the 'underlying population', then such workers are not a 'revolutionary subject' in Marx's sense.

Therefore the 'proletariat' for Marx is not simply identical with 'wage-labour' or the 'working class' *per se*, but is pre-eminently a political concept denoting the subject of revolution. In a letter to Lassalle which Marcuse liked to quote, Marx claimed that the 'proletariat is revolutionary or it is nothing at all'.[59] Marcuse insists that today the industrial working class is no longer the radical negation of capitalist society and is therefore no longer *the* revolutionary class. It has no monopoly today, he claims, on oppression and immiseration, and is in fact better organized, better paid and better off than many members of racial minorities, women, and service, clerical and agricultural workers, as well as the unemployed and unemployable.[60] In this case, the industrial working class no longer possesses 'radical needs' to overthrow the system and is thus not a revolutionary proletariat in Marx's sense. Thus Marcuse rejects theories which make the industrial working class the privileged agent of revolution and which operate with a fetishized concept of class. In a conversation with Habermas, he states:

> To say that the proletariat is integrated no longer does justice to the existing state of affairs. Instead, one must go further in one's formulations. In present-day late capitalism, the Marxist proletariat, in so far as it still exists at all, only represents a minority within the working class. The working class, in terms of its consciousness and praxis, has been embourgeoisified to a great extent. Therefore, we cannot apply reified, fixed Marxist concepts directly and rigidly to the present situation. The expanded working class, which today makes up 90 per cent of the population and which includes the great majority of white-collar workers, service workers – in short, everything Marx ever designated under the term productive worker – this working class remains a potential agent or subject of revolution; but the revolution itself

will be an entirely different project than it was for Marx. One will have to contend with groups which were of no significance whatsoever to original Marxist theory; for example, the renowned marginal groups organized by students, oppressed racial and national minorities, women (who comprise no minority but rather the majority), citizens' initiatives, etc. These are not substitute groups who are to become the new revolutionary subjects. They are, as I call them, anticipatory groups that may function as catalysts, and no more than that.[61]

This situation invalidates previous theories of revolution which posited a radical, violent upheaval led by proletarian insurrections, aiming at the conquest of state power and the establishment of a 'dictatorship of the proletariat'. Answering Enzensberger, who was defending the orthodox Marxian scenario, Marcuse argues that the very concept of a 'dictatorship of the proletariat' is no longer an appropriate political concept:

When proletariat signifies 'factory worker', as it did for Marx, then this formulation is completely inadequate. The 'dictatorship of the proletariat' was for Marx – and people forget this too easily – the dictatorship of the overwhelming majority of the people over a minority. Is the 'proletariat' in this sense still an overwhelming majority in the advanced industrial lands? Does it have today a monopoly on being-exploited?[62]

Marcuse was probably the most tenacious and unyielding critic of the Marxian concept of the 'proletariat' as the privileged revolutionary subject. Recent historical scholarship has questioned the cogency of Marx's own concept of the proletariat, which conflates features of the English, French and German working classes into a quasi-Hegelian revolutionary subject.[63] Timothy McCarthy has claimed that philosophical conceptions of the early Marx structured his concept of the proletariat and that Marx's concept of the 'revolutionary proletariat' was put in question by the revolutions of 1848, by the historical situation in Europe in the 1850s and 1860s, the Paris Commune and the later developments of the labour movement.[64] The failure of the proletariat to carry out its revolutionary mission and the changed class composition of the working class in the twentieth century has led André Gorz to write a polemic,

Adieux au Proletariat, which calls – in the spirit of Marcuse – for new perceptions of the working class(es) and new perspectives on social transformation.[65] While incurring the wrath of many orthodox Marxists, Marcuse's critique of traditional Marxism thus forced those interested in radical social change to rethink the dynamics of class composition and social change in advanced capitalism through his constant interrogation of the Marxian theory.

Marcuse's new perspectives on revolution also contest the Marxian theory of capitalist collapse, which postulates a final, apocalyptic breakdown of capitalism accompanied by revolutionary upheaval.[66] Indeed, capitalism has been in 'crisis' for centuries, but has not yet collapsed. Will it ever? Does such a concept of absolute collapse even make sense? Instead of waiting for capitalism to collapse, or fantasizing about revolutionary insurrection, Marcuse proposed throughout the 1970s less dramatic concepts of social transformation, calling for a 'long march through the institutions' and the development of 'counterinstitutions'. In a 1974 address at the fiftieth anniversary of the founding of the Institute for Social Research in Frankfurt, Marcuse championed 'intelligence in opposition' and called for the development of a 'counter-psychology', 'counter-sociology', 'counter-education', and radical therapy.[67] Although he supported radical politics aiming at the structural transformation of society, he argued that he did not think that 'revolutionary violence' is justified in the advanced capitalist countries. In a 1977 article published in Germany during a period of terrorism, Marcuse argues that terrorist violence is counterproductive since it: (1) provokes violence from the society which is destructive for the Left; (2) has little real possibility of gaining mass support or altering the system; and (3) violates revolutionary morality.[68] Hence, in the present situation of advanced capitalism, Marcuse rejects the concept of armed struggle by a conspiratorial party, or terrorist group, as an element of political change.

Marcuse also puts in question the 'myth of October', which posits revolution as a dramatic process of violent upheaval which in an armed uprising overthrows the previous bourgeois-capitalist order and overnight institutes a socialist (or 'transitional') society. As Karl Korsch and others have argued, the Marxian concept of revolution itself was formed by the Jacobin theory in the French Revolution, and the Leninists appropriated this tradition.[69] Consequently, the (at least immediate) success of the October Revolution created a 'myth of October' that the revolutionary process consists of a dramatic insurrection and violent overthrow of a previously existing social order. Since such events have indeed played a role in many Third World revolutions, the myth has a basis in reality. In question, however, is the relevance of this vision of revolution to the transition to socialism in advanced capitalist countries. In his 1970s writings, Marcuse suggests that structural transformation aiming at the elimination of capitalism and the institutionalization of a social-ist democracy will be a long and protracted process, implying that the myth of ten glorious days which will shake away capitalism is misleading and irrelevant to the 'long revolution' at stake.[70]

Marcuse seems to reject his earlier concept of revolution as a 'catastrophic upheaval' which, as we have seen, dominated his theory of social change from the beginning (see 1.1, 3.2 and 9.1). Although he does not disavow confrontation politics, or even violence in some situations, on the whole in his last years he advocated more gradualist, democratic coalition politics that would create the preconditions for socialism. During the 1970s, he tended to sublimate his 'revolutionary romanticism' into theories of a liberated society and humanity, rather than into visions of a re-volutionary apocalypse. Several decades of severe disillusionment after the defeat of the German revolution, the Spanish communes, the triumph of fascism, the strengthening of monopoly capitalism after the Second World War, and the failures of the New Left, finally produced a 'revolutionary realism' in Marcuse that led him to formulate new perspectives on revolution and to criticize both Marxist-Leninist theories and his own former views. Marcuse's openness to new perspectives and ideas and his readiness to revise his theory in the light of new experiences demonstrate a remarkable flexibility and openness in his thinking which has been grossly underestimated due to many critics' perception of him as a victim of 'one-dimensional pessimism' with a 'Mind not to be changed by Place or Time'.[71] On the contrary, Marcuse was remarkably flexible and was until his death always open to new ideas and perspectives.

9.4.1 *Marcuse and Bahro on the new subjective conditions for revolutionary change*

In the late 1970s Marcuse returned to his analysis in *CR&R* that advanced capitalism is producing new subjective conditions for revolution as the objective conditions intensify and the classical contradictions of capitalism become ever more visible as the socio-economic conditions deteriorate. Developing Rudolf Bahro's analysis in *The Alternative in Eastern Europe*,[72] Marcuse argues that a new consciousness is developing within advanced capitalism which can see the discrepancy between 'what is' and 'what could be' and can perceive the need for radical social change. This 'radical consciousness' will not, Marcuse warns, take the form of 'proletarian class consciousness', but is generated in the form of what Bahro calls 'surplus consciousness'.[73]

Applying Bahro's analysis of the production of consciousness in existing socialist societies to the conditions of advanced capitalism, Marcuse states:

> The capitalist mode of production, through the increasing mechanization and intellectualization of labour, accumulates an increasing quantity of general ability, skills, knowledge – a human potential which cannot be developed within the established apparatus of production, because it would conflict with the need for full-time de-humanized labour. A large part of it is channelled into unnecessary work, unnecessary in that it is not required for the construction and preservation of a better society but is necessitated only by the requirements of capitalist production.
>
> Under these circumstances, a 'counter-consciousness' emerges among the dependent population (today about 90% of the total?), an awareness of the ever more blatant obsolescence of the established social division and organization of work. Rudolf Bahro, the militant East German dissident (he was immediately jailed after the publication, in West Germany, of his book *The Alternative*) uses the term *surplus-consciousness* to designate this (still largely vague and diffused) awareness. He defines it as 'the growing quantity of free mental energy which is no longer tied up in necessary labour and hierarchical knowledge'.[74]

'Surplus consciousness' is a product of expanding education, scientific and technical development, and refinement of the forces of production and labour process that at once produce a higher form of consciousness and yet do not absorb or satisfy in the labour process or everyday life the needs and ideals produced. In effect, Bahro and Marcuse are arguing that critical consciousness and emancipatory needs are being developed by the contradictions in the social conditions of advanced industrial society – capitalist and state socialist. Marcuse believes that the relations of production in both systems produce hierarchy in the labour system and society, inefficiency, waste, inequality, alienation and domination, while fostering needs for participation and fulfilment in the labour system and everyday life, increased freedom, equality and opportunities, leading to a higher level of consumption and a more satisfying life. Marcuse argues:

> Blocked in finding satisfying ways of effective realization, it becomes, among the dependent population, consciousness of frustration, humiliation, and waste. At the same time, capitalist mass production constantly stimulates this consciousness by the display of an ever larger offer of commodities over and above the necessities (and even amenities) of life. The system is thus compelled, by the requirements of enlarged competitive accumulation, to create and to renew constantly the *needs* for 'luxuries', which are all but inaccessible to those who lack the necessary purchasing power. Late capitalism invokes the images of an easier, less repressive, less inhuman life, while perpetuating the alienated labour which denies this satisfaction. In short, late capitalism daily demonstrates the fact that the wherewithal for a better society is available, but that the very society which has created these resources of freedom must preclude their use for the enhancement (and today even for the protection) of life.
>
> In this form, the consciousness of the underlying population is penetrated by the inherent contradictions of capitalism. To be sure, their appearance does not correspond to their essence; surplus consciousness does not conceptualize the dynamics of late capitalist production. Nonetheless, surplus consciousness tends to become a material force, not primarily as class consciousness, but rather as the consciousness of an opposition which expresses itself in new (or recaptured) modes of action, initiated not by any specific class, but by a precarious and temporary 'alliance' of groups among the dependent population. Such actions include the 'citizens' initiatives' (e.g., the organized protest against nuclear energy installations, against capitalist urban renewal), the fight against racism and sexism, the students' protest, etc. At the same time, workers' initiatives transcend the merely economic

class struggle in the demands for the self-organization (*autogestion*) of work.[75]

Bahro and Marcuse are aware that 'surplus consciousness' can take many forms and that, in Marcuse's words,

> In the subjectivity of surplus consciousness, compensatory and emancipatory interests are forced together into a unity. Compensatory interests concern mainly the sphere of material goods: bigger and better consumption, carriers, competition, profit, 'status symbols', etc. They can (at least for the time being!) be satisfied within the framework of the existing system: they compensate for dehumanization. Thus, they contradict the emancipatory interests.[76]

That is, the surplus consciousness can be 'bought off' by, or 'absorbed in', expanded consumption and other compensations. But a cultural revolution can intensify and develop the emancipatory interests by promoting needs for non-alienated labour, more freedom and happiness, and new social relations and communities (pp. 29ff). This would require liberation and politicizing of the imagination, and takes the form of 'demystifying enlightenment' (p. 34). It would be the product of 'catalyst groups' and would require for its implementation a new 'league of communists' to replace party dictatorship (i.e. in existing socialist countries). Constructing genuine socialism would require also an extension of the workers' councils form throughout economic, social, cultural and political life.[77]

Marcuse suggests that Bahro's analysis of the crucial transformative role of a cultural revolution and a new 'league of communists' calls attention to the need for the process of democratization to be led by intellectuals. He claims that intellectuals' position in the process of production endows them with an increasingly important role in the revolutionary transformation and construction of socialism. Marcuse writes: 'a relatively small number of scientists, technicians, engineers, and indeed even media agents could, if organized, disrupt the reproduction process of the system and perhaps even bring it to a standstill' (p. 31). But Marcuse quickly adds, quoting Brecht, '"that's not the way things are" ("*die Verhältnisse sind nicht so*"). It is precisely their integration (*Einordnung*) into the production process, to say nothing of their privileged income, that works against the radicalization of this group. Nevertheless, the social position of these groups gives them a leading role in the revolution' (pp. 31–2).

Marcuse believes that Bahro's analysis implies that 'intellectuals' – taken as a broad category for scientists, technicians, cultural workers, the 'new working class', etc – are the primary bearers of 'surplus consciousness' which stands against the 'compensatory interests of the masses' (p. 29). That is, whereas the masses may be satisfied with consumerism, mass culture and their subordinate position – which in Bahro's analysis produces 'subordinate consciousness' – 'intellectuals', in the broadest sense, are interested in creative work, participation in social processes, technical-scientific knowledge, rationality, cultural ideals, etc., which provide the possibility for this social group to represent 'emancipatory interests' to the extent to which they oppose repression, inequality, irrationality, hierarchy and class privileges. Marcuse describes this group as a potential 'democratic elite' who would assume certain educational-cultural functions that would articulate emancipatory interests and spread critical consciousness throughout the society, creating the possibilities of democratizing and humanizing society. He claims that Bahro's analysis once more requires consideration of Plato's 'educational dictatorship of the intelligentsia' and Rousseau's dictum that people must be 'forced to be free' (p. 32).

Furthermore, continuing his polemic against 'fetishizing the proletariat', Marcuse claims that, in Bahro's words, 'the proletariat cannot be a ruling (*herrschende*) class (Bahro, p. 196)' (p. 32). In the capitalist lands, is not the industrial working class, Marcuse asks citing Bahro on socialist countries, '"too narrow a basis ... to reconstruct the society? Do not the specific workers' interests even play an increasingly often conservative role?" (Bahro, p. 258)' (p. 33). Marcuse is especially impressed with Bahro's analysis of 'subalternity' which explains tendencies towards a conservative, subordination of the working class to a labour, party or bureaucratic hierarchy.[78] In Marcuse's view, Bahro's concept of 'subalternity' explains why the working class currently exists in both capitalist and socialist countries as a subordinate class and why it is not capable today of revolutionizing society. Hence Bahro's analysis suggests to Marcuse that a new theory of revolution and the transition to socialism is necessary, both in advanced capitalist and state socialist countries. After setting out Bahro's basic ideas, Marcuse concludes with a 'recapitulation of the critique of the Marxist-Leninist model of revolution', summing up the critique that I have been working out in this chapter.[79]

Contradictions in Bahro's book – and in Marcuse's reading of it – reproduce central political contradictions in Marcuse's own theory. On the one hand, Bahro and Marcuse adhere to the tradition of socialist democracy advocated by Marx, Luxemburg, Korsch and others.[80] Bahro's and Marcuse's ideal of socialism includes the reduction of alienated labour by shortening the length of the working day; overcoming divisions of labour, stratification and hierarchy; and carrying out a cultural revolution to educate the people so as to make possible genuine democracy. They connect here with the workers' council tradition, which represents a rejection of orthodox Leninism and bureaucratic Social Democracy. On the other hand, there are authoritarian, even neo-Leninist, tendencies in both Bahro and Marcuse. As Andrew Arato and others have argued, Bahro tends to legitimate socialist development in the Soviet Union as a historically necessary and even progressive stage of industrialization and modernization, and, as I showed earlier, Marcuse tends to focus on the liberalizing tendencies in the Soviet Union in his book on *Soviet Marxism* (see Chapter 7). Moreover, not only are there veiled apologetics for existing Communism side by side with demands for more democratic and non-authoritarian socialism, but both Marcuse's and Bahro's conception of socialism contains a mixture of democratic and elitist tendencies. Marcuse's insistence on the need for socialist transformation to be precipitated by revolutionary intellectuals and outsiders, combined with his belief that the majority of the people are integrated within existing capitalist (and socialist?) societies, make him sceptical of democratic socialist transformation carried out by the working classes themselves. Consequently, like Lenin, he generally believed that revolutionary consciousness must be brought to the workers from 'outside', and while he was always suspicious of Lenin's concept of the Party, he enthusiastically attached his conception of revolutionary transformation and the construction of socialism to Bahro's theory, which he believed provided a genuinely Marxist theory – and which in fact provided a Marxist legitimation of his own deepest beliefs. Unfortunately, however, in some ways Marcuse distorts and really differs from Bahro; moreover, there are some problems with both Bahro's and Marcuse's positions which I shall discuss in the conclusion to this chapter.

9.4.2 *Critique of Marcuse's new revolutionary perspectives*

Marcuse's critique of the orthodox Marxist theory of revolution is provocative, but on some issues I believe that more reflection is needed and that some of his positions should probably be rejected. For instance, I think that Marcuse clearly exaggerates the role of the intellectual as a revolutionary *avant-garde* and leader of the revolution.[81] Marcuse constantly argues that radical change is initiated by *avant-garde* intelligentsia, and he has even been attracted to the notion of an 'intellectual dictatorship'.[82] He enthusiastically appropriates Bahro's analysis that since intellectuals are playing an increasingly important role in the process of production, they will assume increased importance as catalysts and leaders of radical change (i.e. due to their education and role in the production process, intellectuals possess 'surplus consciousness' which makes possible an 'otherness of consciousness' and an instinctual structure which tends to rebel against oppression and leads to a practice of refusal). Marcuse concludes that Bahro's analysis of the role of intellectuals in the production process and the transition process to socialism leads to the 'position, tabooed by Marxism as well as liberalism, of Plato's educational dictatorship of the most intelligent' and Rousseau's position that 'the people must be forced to be free'.[38] It is curious and distressing that Marcuse would return to these notions which he seemed to reject in a conversation with Habermas a year earlier: 'Today I wouldn't have talked about educational dictatorship. The passage you cited was intentionally written for purposes of provocation. Perhaps educational dictatorship within democracy but not simply educational dictatorship'.[84]

The notion of an 'educational dictatorship' is a questionable one, but I do not think that Bahro's analysis entails the notion of a revolutionary elite, *avant-garde* or dictatorship in the sense advocated by Plato, Rousseau, Lenin and – sometimes – Marcuse. Rather, Bahro talks of the necessity of a far-reaching cultural revolution and the development of a 'collective intellectual through which is mediated the whole society's awareness of the problems of its development'.[85] Bahro then indicates that the notion of the 'collective intellectual' is a legacy from Antonio Gramsci and his notion of cultural workers developing a 'counter-hegemony'.[86] The Gramsci-Bahro concept does not presuppose an intellectual elite or notion of the traditional intellectual, which Marcuse identifies with, but rather presupposes a new kind of intellectual.[87] Bahro describes this as

> what Gramsci called a collective intellectual, creating and exer- cising majority consensus for change, in democratic communica- tion with all interests in society. The main function of this league of communists will consist in so introducing society into the cultural revolution that it passes through a planned – and yet not imposed – practical change; a change, therefore, which is brought about by overwhelmingly positive needs.[88]

Marcuse, by comparison, is operating with the traditional concept of the intellectual defined as someone who possesses special know- ledge by virtue of their education, high level of culture and cognitive talents.[89] The Gramsci-Bahro notion of the 'collective intellectual', on the other hand, defines the intellectual in terms of her/his abilities to interact politically, to struggle with the people, to articulate their needs and interests and to help translate theory into practice.[90] Sociologically, this type of political intellectual is rooted within political organization and struggle, while Marcuse's classical intellectual finds its locus within academia and the cultural ap- paratus. It is not at all clear whether or how 'classical intellectuals' will be in the vanguard of social change during the coming years, and there are good reasons to doubt that intellectuals in the broadest sense – or in any sense – should be designated as the privileged vehicle of social change.

   In effect, both Marcuse and Bahro are advocating *change from above*. Bahro's critique of 'existing socialist society' is reminiscent of Trotsky's critique of Stalinism and demand for revolutionary vanguardism which would carry through a genuinely socialist re- volution against counterrevolutionary bureaucratic deformations (i.e. Stalinism).[91] Although Bahro urges a democratization of the revolutionary process and a cultural revolution which will create the pre-conditions for socialist democracy, some critics have detected neo-Leninist, or Trotskyist, elements in his theory which would perpetuate features of Party domination and elitism in his 'league of communists' and 'collective intellectual'.[92] Both Bahro and Marcuse dismiss working-class initiatives and struggles as significant elements of social change. The events in Czechoslovakia during and following 1968 and struggles in Poland in the 1970s and 1980s indicate, however, that working-class struggles continue to play a major role in social change.[93] In this regard, Bahro, Marcuse and others fail to recognize the continued militancy and potential for emancipatory struggle in the working classes.

Significant forces of social change in the last decades have often taken place through an *alliance* of intellectuals, workers and others, and not simply through intellectual vanguardism alone. It is therefore wrong to make intellectuals a privileged vehicle of social change. Moreover, as Alvin Gouldner has argued, intellectuals are becoming a 'new class' with its own interests and drive for power which make intellectuals, at best, a 'flawed universal class'.[94] In my view, it is a mistake to ascribe to *any* class or group a privileged role as conveyor of revolutionary consciousness, force or leadership. Social and historical situations are too complex and varied to allow us to designate *a priori* any one group or class a privileged role in the revolutionary process. Further, the working class and intelligentsia, as well as women, minorities, students and every other group or class, are fragmented by contradictory tendencies. Hence there are radical and conservative elements within both the intelligentsia and working class. It seems impossible in this situation to discern which is more 'revolutionary' or even which has more 'revolutionary potential'.

Marcuse is too eager to dismiss the working class as a potential agent of social change and too quick to champion the radical potential of intellectuals, students and non-integrated groups. This is an understandable reaction against those who would limit forces of change and bearers of radical consciousness to the industrial working class, but the fact is that many radical struggles cut across class, social group, race and sex, and make it difficult to discern a privileged 'revolutionary subject'. For example, revolts against work are taking place in factories, offices and schools, as well as in the home (by radicalized women). Anti-nuclear, anti-war, feminist, environmental and other struggles today include women and men of all social classes, radicals from the Old and New Left, members of church groups and labour unions, and even conservatives concerned with the 'quality of life'. Earlier, the anti-war movement in the Vietnam era contained a coalition of diverse individuals and groups whose struggles affected the course of the Vietnam war by limiting the option for military intervention of the capitalist super-powers. Consequently, it seems a mistake to maintain a privileged revolutionary subject when social change in fact comes from a variety of groups and struggles.

Since struggle and change in advanced capitalism take such contradictory and amorphous forms, it seems impossible to discern any revolutionary subject, and perhaps the entire concept should be abandoned. Marcuse's conclusion that the industrial working class is not *the* revolutionary subject led him to deep pessimism over the possibility of radical social change in the advanced industrial countries. Then Marcuse eagerly embraced the 'new sensibility' in the 1960s as a potential revolutionary subject, but when the New Left and counterculture failed to fulfil his expectations, he later turned to Rudolf Bahro's concept of surplus consciousness to serve as a potential revolutionary subject for the future.

The problem with Marcuse's theory of revolution is that despite his sharp critique and modification of orthodox Marxism, his theory is still too tied up with the Hegelian-Marxian problematic of the revolutionary subject, which presupposes a unitary revolutionary class as the subject of revolution.[95] In this concept, the features explicated by Marx in his early analysis of the proletariat are ascribed to whatever group, class or tendency the revolutionary theorist believes is the key to the revolution. This concept reached its logical conclusion – and *reductio ad absurdum* – in Lukács' notion of the proletariat as the identical subject-object of history.[96] Lukács's contrived construction and the subsequent critique that it elicited should have shown the dangers of a Hegelian-Marxian concept of the revolutionary subject and the need for another approach to revolutionary theory.

Reflection on the history and sociology of revolution puts in question whether revolutionary transformation comes from a revolutionary subject or rather, as I would argue, from classes (or sectors of a class), groups, organizations and individuals in struggle. It seems idealist and obtuse to ascribe revolutionary change to *a* (or to *the*) revolutionary subject, since social change comes from complex conjunctures and alliances between different social groups and forces. Therefore it is wrong to identify in advance the revolutionary subject with any particular social class, group or tendency. Indeed, it is extremely difficult to specify in advance, especially in advanced capitalist societies, 'revolutionary forces'. As Marcuse puts it: 'The social agents of revolution – and this is orthodox Marx – are formed only in the process of the transformation itself, and one cannot count on a situation in which the revolutionary forces are there ready-made, so to speak, when the revolutionary movement begins' (*5L*, p. 64).

In this conception, the role of revolutionary theory is to analyse existing social forces and groups in struggle and to indicate which groups are bearers of universal interests, emancipation or radical social change. The problem for revolutionary theory today is the thorny issue of how to *fuse* groups-in-struggle into a revolutionary *movement*. Although there has been a proliferation of new social movements and struggles in recent years, many of these groups are fighting for specific interests or goals (i.e. peace, nuclear disarmament, women's rights, black or brown power, etc.). Whereas many of these struggles are worthy and worth supporting in their own right, the challenge to the Left is to build *linkages* between the various groups-in-struggle to provide the basis for an anti-capitalist, anti-imperialist movement. Although Marcuse calls for a 'United Front' against capitalism and for coalitions between different groups and struggles, he does not really provide much analysis of how groups-in-struggle are to be fused into a revolutionary movement, or what forms that movement should take.[97]

Although Marcuse continued to advocate socialism, his last writings do not really contain a socialist programme, or an explicitly socialist organizing base and strategy, despite his frequent appeals to 'revolution' and 'socialism'. Moreover, Marcuse never clearly specifies how the immediate political struggles he cites will lead to the realization of the revolutionary goals that he projects. To create a revolutionary socialist movement requires development of an explicitly anti-capitalist and pro-socialist organizing strategy which must make clear that capitalism is the source of a variety of problems and that socialism offers the solution. This requires demonstration that capitalism should indeed be eliminated and the development of revolutionary socialist consciousness.

Although I question whether there is a 'revolutionary subject' defined as a universal revolutionary class, I do think it is important to specify the nature and conditions of revolutionary *subjectivity*, defined as a *universalizing consciousness* which formulates and translates society's needs into political action and prefigures alternative institutions, values and practices which will create a better life for all. The strength of Marcuse's type of 'critical', or 'Hegelian', Marxism is its stress on the subjective conditions of (and obstacles to) revolutionary change and formulations of alternatives to the given society. This subjective and speculative emphasis is a necessary component of the revolutionary project that structuralist Marxism – which also rejects notions of a revolutionary subject – lacks. Radical social change requires taking seriously existing consciousness and needs, criticizing mystifications and distortions, and formulating needs, values and ideas which will aid in the process of human liberation. This requires a universalizing consciousness of normative ideals against which existing consciousness and practice can be criticized and transformed. Revolutionary theory should formulate this universalizing subjectivity and communicate it to the members of a society, or groups, to try to create a consensus around ideas and actions that can realize progressive social change. Universalizing subjectivity may in some cases involve simply translating into theory and practice existing needs and ideals arising from people's consciousness and struggles, although it may also require an anticipatory dimension that prefigures a liberated society and humanity. Thus, although the concept of the revolutionary subject seems an impediment to developing revolutionary theory today, concepts of *revolutionary subjectivity* remain essential components of the revolutionary project.

Although Marcuse sharply polemicizes against identification of the revolutionary subject with Marx's proletariat, he does not question the concept of the revolutionary subject itself. Indeed, his protracted search for a revolutionary subject was the source of his pessimism in *One-Dimensional Man*, his overemphasis on students, intellectuals, the new sensibility and finally 'surplus consciousness' as revolutionary agents. The concept of the revolutionary subject is also responsible for his tendency to dismiss working-class struggles as 'non-revolutionary' because they do not meet the exalted criterion of the 'revolutionary subject'. Thus I conclude that the concept of the revolutionary subject is a spectre that has haunted Marcuse's project from the beginning, and that it should be exorcized in the interests of developing new concepts to describe the conditions, prospects and goals of emancipatory social change.

Marcuse is still to be lauded for his many provocative critiques of the Marxian theory of revolution and for his sustained attempts to develop new revolutionary perspectives adequate to the social conditions of advanced capitalism. But perhaps Marcuse's most important contributions to radical social theory are his projections of aspects of a new society and demands that we develop new visions of human life in our struggles for a better society. Let us then conclude our study of Marcuse's work with an examination of his concepts of an alternative society, visions of liberation, and defence of utopian socialism.

10

Liberation and Utopia

As the possibilities for radical social change dramatically accelerated in the 1960s, Marcuse began renewed reflection on liberation and revolution which he concluded required utopian concepts of an alternative society and a new concept of socialism. He constantly argued that since the problems in the existing society could not be solved by piecemeal reform, a new society is needed to provide maximum human freedom and well-being.[1] He remained an intransigent revolutionist who believed that it was necessary to have in view the goals of liberation to produce political theory and action which would not simply reproduce the oppressive features of the existing society. Since 'the whole is not true', a radically new social order is necessary to provide liberated human beings with a good life.[2] Although Marcuse came to appreciate the benefits of more gradual social change, he maintained constantly that the changes and reforms should strive for human liberation and social revolution if they are not to be merely cosmetic improvements of the existing society. In this sense, whatever political positions Marcuse may have defended at a given time and place, the goal of a new society and liberated humanity remained central to his thought.

Marcuse is not, however, a naive Manichean who fails to see any positive aspects in existing society, as some critics contend.[3] Instead, he argues that the 'positive' and 'negative' aspects are inextricably intertwined, so that an 'objective ambiguity' adheres to all social phenomena that contain an 'inseparable unity of opposites'.[4] Emancipatory social transformation will – in the spirit of Hegelian *Aufhebung* – raise those elements in the old society which promote human freedom and happiness to a higher level, by eliminating all repressive features and by creating a society which in its totality aims at human well-being (and not production, profit and social control). Such a society would be so radically different from the present one that

> the new possibilities for a human society and its environment can no longer be thought of as continuations of the old, nor even as existing in the same historical continuum with them. Rather, they presuppose a break with the historical continuum; they presuppose the qualitative difference between a free society and societies that are still unfree, which, according to Marx, makes all previous history only the pre-history of mankind. (*5L*, p. 62).

The totalistic character of Marcuse's critique of the existing society attracted a generation of radicals to his thought, and the total character of the young militants' revolt attracted Marcuse to them.[5] Describing the opposition of radical youth to their society, Marcuse states:

> it is sexual, moral, intellectual and political rebellion all in one. In this sense it is total, directed against the system as a whole; it is disgust at the 'affluent society', it is the vital need to break the rules of a deceitful and bloody game – to stop co-operating any more.[6]

He eulogized the complete rejection of the existing society in the May 1968 revolt in France as 'the great, real, transcending force, the "*idée neuve*". in the first powerful rebellion against the whole of the existing society, the rebellion for the total transvaluation of values, for qualitatively different ways of life' (*EC*, p. 22).[7] For Marcuse, the liberation struggles in Southeast Asia, Cuba, China and Latin America, combined with revolts by students, minorities, workers and women in the advanced capitalist countries 'confront the critical theory of society with the task of re-examining the prospects for the emergence of a socialist society qualitatively different from existing societies, the task of redefining socialism and its preconditions' (*EL*, p. ix).

Marcuse decided that since existing socialist countries fail to provide attractive emancipatory alternatives to capitalist societies, a new concept of *socialism* needs to be articulated (*5L*, p. 62). He concluded that Marx himself was not radical enough in his formulations of socialism and asked 'whether decisive elements of the Marxian concept of socialism do not belong to a now obsolete stage in the development of the forces of production?'. In Marcuse's view, the social wealth, technologies, and knowledge exist to create a freer and happier social order than Marx envisaged. Consequently, Marcuse called for new perspectives on socialism that would help people see the differences between the present reality and its higher possibilities and see the restrictive uses of the present social wealth in contrast to possibilities of another society and way of life.[8]

Marcuse perceives socialism as 'a qualitatively different society, in which the relations of human beings to each other, as well as between humans and nature, are fundamentally revolutionized'.[9] For Marcuse, 'the alternative is socialism. But socialism neither of the Stalinist brand nor of the post-Stalinist brand, but that *libertarian socialism* which has always been the integral concept of socialism, but only too easily repressed and suppressed'.[10] Such a concept of socialism, in contrast to existing socialism, radically differs so that it is necessary to break the Marxian taboo on utopian speculation in order to project its emancipatory features. In 'Liberation from the Affluent Society', Marcuse states:

> we have been too ashamed, understandably ashamed, to insist on the integral, radical features of a socialist society, its qualitative difference from all the established societies: the qualitative difference by virtue of which socialism is indeed the negation of the established systems, no matter how productive, no matter how powerful they are or they may appear.[11]

It might be noted that the utopian impulse is a deep one in Marcuse and has been a constituent element in his appropriation of Marxism from the beginning. In 'Philosophy and Critical Theory', he writes that critical theory

> always derives its goals only from present tendencies of the social process. Therefore it has no fear of the utopia that the new order is denounced as being. When truth cannot be realized within the established social order, it always appears to the latter as utopia. This transcendence speaks not against, but for, its truth. The utopian element was long the only progressive element in

philosophy, as in the constructions of the best states and the highest pleasure, of perfect happiness and perpetual peace.[12]

10.1 Towards a new concept of socialism

Marcuse's move to a militantly utopian position is cryptically indicated in the title of his 1967 Berlin lecture, 'The End of Utopia' (published in *Five Lectures*). This phrase could be interpreted in two ways, and in fact these two different interpretations illuminate different phases of Marcuse's post-1950s work. In *ODM*, Marcuse's analysis signified the end of utopia in Mannheim's sense: the stabilization of advanced industrial society invalidated utopian thinking, ending its relevance for social theory and political practice. However, in the mid-1960s Marcuse spoke for the end of the taboo against utopian thinking precisely on the grounds that utopian ideas are so relevant and viable that they cannot be dismissed as 'merely utopian' in the pejorative, etymological sense of 'utopia' as 'nowhere' (*EL*, pp. 3ff). The very forces of production, Marcuse believes, are 'utopian', for the technical-material capabilities present at hand make possible the creation of a society without poverty, repression and exploitation.[13]

For these reasons, Marcuse proposes lifting the Marxian taboo against utopian thinking, for such a

> revision is suggested, and even necessitated, by the actual evolution of contemporary societies. The dynamic of their productivity deprives 'utopia' of its traditional unreal content: what is denounced as 'utopian' is no longer that which has 'no place' and cannot have any place in the historical universe, but rather that which is blocked from coming about by the power of the established societies. (*EL*, pp. 3–4)

Marcuse counters a frequent criticism that Marxism is a hopelessly 'utopian' conception which realistic people should not accept. He states that:

> I will not be deterred by one of the most vicious ideologies of today, namely, the ideology which derogates, denounces and

ridicules the most decisive concepts and images of a free society as merely 'utopian' and 'only' speculative. It may well be that precisely in those aspects of socialism which are today ridiculed as utopian, lies the decisive difference, the contrast between an authentic socialist society and the established societies, even the most advanced industrial societies.[14]

These reflections led Marcuse to utilize more aggressively the term 'concrete utopia' to describe the alternative society envisaged.[15] He insists that democratic and emancipatory socialism is indeed a possibility today. The problem is that although 'the material and intellectual forces for the transformation are technically at hand', 'their rational application is prevented by the existing organization of the forces of production' (*EL*, p. 64). This signifies that utopian transformation is possible, but it can only take place as a radical break with the present society (*5L*, p. 62). Marxian socialism, Marcuse suggests, should not, on the one hand, be dismissed as 'utopian' because there is no revolutionary class, because its demands for the abolition of poverty, misery and alienated labour in the creation of a free society are eminently rational and represent the real need for and goal of liberation. On the other hand, Marcuse suggests, Marxism is not utopian enough, for the technical-material possibilities at hand make possible even more radical and emancipatory social transformation than Marx envisaged.

In describing the most advanced and emancipatory possibilities of a new society, Marcuse now rejects the previous ontological dualism in his thought between the realms of necessity and freedom, and work and play. He formulates his critique of these dichotomies as a critique of the Marxian concept which conceives of the realm of freedom only beyond the realm of necessity, which remains a realm of alienated labour, as if one could be free only in a realm beyond labour.[16] Marcuse now writes: 'I believe that one of the new possibilities, which gives an indication of the qualitative difference between the free and unfree society, is that of letting the realm of freedom appear within the realm of necessity – in labour and not only beyond labour' (*5L*, p. 63). This is a change of the utmost importance in Marcuse's theory, for he now posits the possibility of non-alienated labour which can be genuinely self-fulfilling, and thus eliminates the sharp division in his theory between labour and play, as well as overcoming the excessively negative concept of labour as inevitable necessity, unfreedom (see sections 3.4 and 6.4).

Marcuse struggled with the concept of the relation between the realms of freedom and necessity in the Marxian project in a series of essays which provide a transition between his earlier position that freedom cannot enter the realm of necessary labour and his later notion that radical transformation of the labour process and technical apparatus could make possible free activity in the realm of labour. In the 1964 foreword to *Negations*, Marcuse cites the famous passage in Marx's *Grundrisse* on automation,[17] which stresses the liberating possibilities in automation through (1) reducing socially necessary labour-time; (2) giving humans control over their entire labour apparatus; thus (3) making possible a thoroughgoing organization of the labour process and the construction of a labour apparatus that will make possible non-alienated labour. Marcuse now argues that automation makes possible experimentation with the labour apparatus as a whole and creative restructuring of the labour process which could increase the realm of freedom while minimizing alienated labour. In Marcuse's view:

> In totalitarian technological society, freedom remains thinkable only as autonomy over the entirety of the apparatus. This includes the freedom to reduce it or to reconstruct it in its entirety with regard to the pacification of the struggle for existence and to the rediscovery of quiet and of happiness. The abolition of material poverty is a possibility within the status quo; peace, joy, and the abolition of labour are not. And yet only in and through them can the established order be overcome. Totalitarian society brings the realm of freedom beyond the realm of necessity under its administration and fashions it after its own image. In complete contradiction to this future, autonomy over the technological apparatus is freedom *in* the realm of necessity. This means, however, that freedom is only possible as the realization of what today is called utopia.[18]

Marcuse is no naive technocrat or futurist who thinks that increased automation and technological progress will automatically increase human freedom. He argues that the development of technology also increases the possibility of servitude and domination,[19] in which individuals could become cogs in the social-technical machine, servants of the apparatus. For Marcuse the danger exists that freedom and individuality will diminish in both the realms of labour and leisure. In 1966 he wrote:

> it seems to me that contemporary industrial society has all but closed this realm of freedom, and closed it not only by virtue of its ingression into all spheres of the individual existence (thus pre-conditioning the free time), but also by virtue of technical progress and mass democracy. What is left to individual creativity outside the technical work process is in the way of hobbies, do-it-yourself stuff, games. There is, of course, the authentic creative expression in art, literature, music, philosophy, science – but it is hardly imaginable that this authentic creativity will, even in the best of all societies, become a general capability. The rest is sport, fun, fad.[20]

For Marcuse automation and technological progress might lead to increased liberation and free time, or to increased slavery, in which the features of creativity and individuality will diminish in both the work world and leisure world. Human liberation thus requires: collective control over the entire apparatus of labour and socialization of the means of production in a 'free association' of workers and citizens; reconstruction of the labour apparatus to produce objects of consumption necessary to fulfil human needs that would simultaneously allow development of human potentialities within the labour process; reduction of socially necessary labour time and expansion of free time; and the education of individuals to obtain the capacity for creativity, autonomy and individuality in both labour and free time.[21]

> Then, the 'realm of freedom' may perhaps appear in the work process itself, in the performance of socially necessary labour. The technical apparatus could then serve to create a new social and natural environment: human beings could then have their own cities, their own houses, their own spaces of tranquillity and joy: they could become free and learn how to live in freedom with the others. Only with the creation of such an entirely different environment (which is well within the capabilities of technology and well beyond the capabilities of the vested interests which

control technology), would the words 'beauty', 'creativity', 'community', etc. designate meaningful goals; the creation of such an environment would indeed be non-alienated labour.[22]

By the late 1960s these reflections led Marcuse to criticize the concept in Marx's *Capital III* which maintains that 'Human freedom in a true sense is possible only beyond the realm of necessity'.[23] Marcuse now argues that Marx's distinction between the realm of freedom and necessity

> epitomizes the division of the human existence into labour time and free time, the division between reason, rationality on the one hand, and pleasure, joy, fulfilment on the other hand, the division between alienated and non-alienated labour. . . According to this classical Marxian concept, the realm of necessity would remain a realm of alienation, no matter how much the working day is reduced. Moreover this conception seems to imply that free human activity is essentially different, and must remain essentially different from socially necessary work.[24]

Marcuse then argues that there is another Marxian conception in the *Grundrisse* which posits the possibility of freedom and creative activity within the realm of necessary labour, thus overcoming the dichotomy between free. creative activity and socially necessary labour in *Capital III*: 'This concept', Marcuse writes,

> envisages conditions of full automation, where the immediate producer is indeed 'dissociated' from the material process of production and becomes a free 'Subject' in the sense that he can play with, experiment with the technical material, with the possibilities of the machine and of the things produced and transformed by the machines. But as far as I know this most advanced vision of a free society was apparently dropped by Marx himself and no longer appears in the *Capital* and in the later writings.[25]

Thinking through the consequences of this notion of non-alienated labour led Marcuse to rethink also the concepts of socialism and to sharpen his criticism of existing socialist societies. Throughout his writings, Marcuse polemicized against the tendency in socialist theory and practice to fetishize the unfettered development of the forces of production at the expense of developing new relations of production and human potentialities.[26] He argues both for a new technology (to be discussed in the next section) and against the development of current technology without radical reconstruction of the labour process and technical apparatus. Here Marcuse corrects tendencies in existing socialism to take over both capitalist technologies (assembly line and Fordism, nuclear energy and weapons, etc.) and capitalist relations of production (Taylorism, labour stratification and hierarchy, wage differentials, etc.)[27] Emancipatory socialism, by contrast, requires completely new institutions, relations of production, technologies and labour apparatus. Such radical transformation would make possible the sort of non-alienated labour, erotic relations and harmonious community envisaged by Fourier (*EL*, pp. 21 – 2).[28] In this conception, socialism is 'first of all , a new form of human existence' in which 'self-determination' and freedom would at last be a real possibility for the majority of the population:[29] 'What is at stake is the idea of a new theory of human existence, not only as theory but also as a way of existence: the genesis and development of a vital need for freedom and of the vital needs of freedom' (*5L*, p. 65). Human beings in this society would have 'a different sensitivity as well as consciousness: men and women who would speak a different language, have different gestures, follow different impulses; men and women who have developed an instinctual barrier against cruelty, brutality, ugliness' (*EL*, p. 21). Consequently, in order to produce this type of socialism, there must be 'the emergence and education of a new type of human being free from the aggressive and repressive needs and aspirations and attitudes of class society, human beings created, in solidarity and on their own initiative, their own environment, their own *Lebenswelt*, their own "property" '.[30] Such a revolution in needs and values would help overcome a central dilemma in Marcuse's theory – sharply formulated in *ODM* – that continued to haunt him: 'how can the administered individuals – who have made their mutilation into their own liberties and satisfactions . . . liberate themselves from themselves as well as from their masters? How is it even thinkable that the vicious circle be broken?' (*ODM*, pp. 250 – 1).[31]

In order to break through this vicious circle, individuals must transform their present needs and consciousness and develop new needs and consciousness so as to create the necessary conditions for social transformation (*5L*, p. 67). In the 1970s Marcuse argued – as I stressed in the last chapter and will continue to demonstrate throughout the present one – that emancipatory needs were developing within contemporary society. Those who fault Marcuse for an allegedly extreme utopianism – which totally rejects this world for dreams of another world – fail to note that in his 1970s writings Marcuse does not posit such a radical rupture between the present historical situation and need-structure and his proposed new human being and liberated society. Throughout the 1970s he specifies social conditions which may begin to produce radical social transformation and valorizes struggles which may lead to radical structural transformation.[32] Moreover, he continued to speculate on the new forms and organization of labour, new technologies, new institutions, new culture, new values and new types of human beings necessary to produce a society that would eliminate the repugnant features of the existing society that have been the target of Marcuse's critical project. Although Marcuse never systematically develops these ideas, there are many indications scattered throughout his later writings as to what kind of individual and social transformation could generate new needs and liberate individuals from what Marcuse calls 'repressive' or 'false needs'.

In this chapter I shall show how Marcuse's theory of liberation is connected to his substantive vision of the 'good life' and a new concept of socialism, and, against many of his critics, will argue that these notions are among his most vital contributions to contemporary social theory. Concepts of liberation and utopia are, Marcuse deeply believes, integral parts of the revolutionary project which must offer a vision of a better way of life to attract people to radical politics and the struggle for radical social change. Moreover, the new needs, values and consciousness must be present during the struggle itself to help prevent new forms of hierarchy and domination from emerging.[33]

Marcuse develops his concepts of liberation and utopia in such works as 'The End of Utopia?' (*5L*), *EL*, *CR&R*, and his lectures and essays of the 1970s. Important components of his analysis are found in *EC* and *ODM*, and although certain core ideas remain constant, there are, as I have tried to show, interesting and significant developments. Marcuse's analyses of liberation and utopia contain three sets of themes that will be the subject of the following pages: (1) the convergence of art and technology in the concept of a new technology; (2) the emancipation of the senses aiming at a 'new sensibility'; and (3) the cultivation of the aesthetic dimension and production of a new culture. These three components are intimately combined in Marcuse's theory, for the new technology will aim at creating an environment and way of life expressive of needs for joy, happiness and beauty. The new culture and sensibility will create a technology of liberation and a social environment which in turn will continue to gratify and enhance human needs and personalities.

10.2 The new technology

Radical social reconstruction requires, in Marcuse's view, 'a total technical reorganization of the concrete world of human life' (*5L*, p. 67). He makes it clear that when he speaks of 'the abolition of the terrors of capitalist industrialization', he is not harking back to an idyllic pre-industrial world, but insists on utilizing to the fullest the best productions of science and technology. However, 'the potential liberating blessings of technology and industrialization will not even begin to be real and visible until capitalist industrialization and capitalist technology have been done away with' (*5L*, p. 68).

Marcuse's concept of liberation rests on the premise that technology contains tremendous potential which, if released, could create a free society. In *ODM*, Marcuse suggests that full automation could make possible the elimination of the system of alienated labour and release the individual for a life of freedom: 'The very structure of human existence would be altered; the individual would be liberated from the work world's imposing upon him alien needs and alien possibilities. The individual would be free to exert autonomy over a life that would be his own' (*ODM*, p. 2). To the extent that the labour process is mechanized and automated, it creates a 'potential basis of a new freedom' (*ODM*, pp. 3ff) by reducing alienated labour and making possible new kinds of labour activity. The current society is 'irrational' *vis-à-vis* its technical capabilities, however, because it tends to introduce technologies that increase the ruling strata's profits and power, and does not construct technologies that would eliminate alienated labour and social domination (*ODM*, pp. 2ff).[39] Consequently, in Marcuse's view, the ultimate absurdity of advanced industrial society is that it mobilizes itself against its most advanced possiblities.[35]

Marcuse does not, however, have faith in the emancipatory

potentialities of the forces of production alone, as if their unfettered development would automatically bring about social progress and would rebel against – and eventually explode – restrictive relations of production. Far from being the technological determinist – or technocrat – he is sometimes accused of being, [36] Marcuse is aware that forces of production are themselves shaped, structured and even constituted by relations of production. He separates himself from technocrats who believe in unlimited progress through technology by arguing that both the forces and relations of production in advanced industrial societies serve as instruments of domination, and that in order to utilize science and technology in the interests of liberation requires a *radical break* with current science and technology, as well as the construction of a *new science* and *new technology* (*ODM*, pp. 227ff). Moreover, he connects the development of a new science and technology with anthropological and political transformation, so he is clearly no technocrat or technological determinist. Marcuse argues that, for the most part technological progress has meant increased domination (*ODM*, pp. xvff and 144ff), but we now face a choice of whether we wish to use technology as an instrument of domination or liberation. The current technical-material possibilities contain tremendous emancipatory potential; social choices must be made to decide whether we wish to develop this potential, or whether we should let our technology be used inefficiently or in the interests of domination.

Since current technology is bound up – in its structure and function – with domination and oppression, breaking with the continuum of domination requires a new technology of liberation. Constructing such a new technology would require an alteration of the current direction of technological progress, new ends and goals for technology, and new kinds of technology. In this light, Habermas's critique that Marcuse's concept of a new science and technology is a romantic hangover of German idealism that seeks the 'resurrection of fallen nature' is questionable.[37] Whereas it is true that Marcuse wants to rehabilitate metaphysics and utopian speculation, I see nothing illogical or irrational about his project and find no appeal to 'the resurrection of fallen nature" – although there is an implicit suggestion that human beings cannot be 'resurrected' (i.e. returned to their humanity) without a new technology.

Habermas claims that Marcuse's concept of a new science and technology is logically flawed in that the very logic of technology is that of instrumental rationality. It seems to me, however, that

Habermas's argument rests on dubious metaphysical grounds, for he builds his critique on Gehlens notion that 'there is an immanent connection between the technology known to us and the structure of purposive-rational action' (Habermas, p. 81). In other words, Habermas claims that technology inherently follows the structure of 'instrumental action' or labour. As such, its structure is rooted in the human organism and thus cannot be fundamentally altered. Although Habermas's critique has been widely accepted, I do not see how it invalidates Marcuse's argument that technology can be radically reconstructed.[38] In my view, Habermas and others who defame the notion of a 'new technology' are in effect capitulating to current forms of technology and labour as inevitable and inalterable. For Marcuse, on the other hand, the project of liberation requires a liberation of labour *and* technology – 'that the liberation of science and technology must *accompany* the liberation of labour' as Ben Agger puts it.[39] This is surely revolutionary, but not irrational or logically impossible. We see here that Marcuse emerges once again as the most radical critic of the Frankfurt School, this time in his penetrating critique of science and technology and his radical call for their reconstruction.

Marcuse's projected technological revolution would demand a reversal from the construction of technology as an instrument of domination and destruction to its construction as an instrument of pacification and liberation. This would entail a shift from 'war technology' to 'peace technology' and social transformation from a 'warfare state' to a 'welfare state'.[40] Presently technology is produced to create ever more deadly and destructive weapons, and under capitalism creates waste, planned obsolescence, superfluous luxury items and poisonous chemicals which pollute the environment and destroy human beings. In addition, technology is used to create ever more efficient instruments of social control and an apparatus of social domination. To eliminate the evils of the current forms and uses of technology would require, Marcuse claims, a reversal of both the ends of technological progress and the very forms of technology. For example, achieving the liberation of labour would necessitate a radical subversion of capitalist organization and technologies of labour such as the assembly line, fragmentation and stratification, and those elements which primarily serve the ends of profit and social control and provide obstacles to the full development of human potentialities.[41]

In non-alienated labour, on the other hand, the productive imagination could enter the labour process and workers could experiment with new technical possibilities and uses of technology. For example, new vehicles of transportation could be produced by work teams who design, develop and build the entire vehicle. New technologies of entertainment and communication could be devised; a reconstruction of our cities and homes could take place; new sources of energy could be sought and developed; new devices to do housework could be invented; new organizations of education could be developed which would combine technical and humanistic training.[42] Such a development and use of technology would eliminate the negative features of current technology and could make possible radical social reconstruction and the development of many-sided human beings.

Once toil and scarcity were reduced, technology could be directed towards new ends which would represent a qualitative advance beyond previously existing civilization. Marcuse envisages a *science of liberation* (*ODM*, pp. 230ff) which would combine reflections on liberation with thought about how to reconstruct our technology, environment and human relations to increase dramatically human freedom and well-being. Reversing Comte's theory of the three stages of thought (religious, metaphysical, scientific) Marcuse argues that metaphysical concepts could project and define the possible reality of a pacified existence (*ODM*, pp. 224f). Since the limits of the historically possible are continually extended with the development of technology, 'speculations about the Good Life, the Good Society, Permanent Peace obtain an increasingly realistic content; on technological grounds, the metaphysical tends to become physical' (*ODM*, p. 230). In such a 'science of liberation',

> The free play of thought and imagination assumes a rational and directing function in the realization of a pacified existence of man and nature. And the ideas of justice, freedom, and humanity then obtain their truth and good conscience on the sole ground on which they could ever have truth and good conscience – the satisfaction of man's material needs, the rational organization of the realm of necessity. (*ODM*, pp. 234–5)

In this conception, science and technology are to be reconstructed to serve the interests of human freedom and happiness. For Marcuse, 'Science itself has rendered it possible to make final causes the proper domain of science . . . the transformation of values into needs, of final causes into technical possibilities is a new stage in the conquest of oppressive, unmastered forces in society as well as in nature . . . Technology thus may provide the historical correction of the premature identification of Reason and Freedom' (*ODM,* pp. 232-4). Although during the past centuries the human species has tended to view nature as an object of domination and has perceived science and technology as instruments of domination, Marcuse envisages a 'post-technological rationality, in which technics is itself the instrumentality of pacification, organon of the "art of life". The function of Reason then converges with the function of Art' (*ODM,* p. 238). The new technology would recapture the affinity between art and technique stressed by the Greeks and would create an art of life (*ODM,* pp. 238-9). Marcuse's synthesis of technology and art can be elucidated by unpacking his notion of an *aesthetic reduction* (*ODM,* pp. 239ff) – an extremely provocative and progressive notion that has been little appreciated in the many superficial discussions of Marcuse's concepts of aesthetics and technology.

For Hegel, Marcuse suggests, great art reduces reality to its essentials and shows the fundamental constitutes of spirit and freedom. The aesthetic reduction frees its object from all that is contingent and oppressive, and produces works of art that contain images of freedom and gratification (*ODM,* pp. 239-40). For example, an architect projects an image of a house which will be efficient, comfortable and aesthetically pleasing; the 'aesthetic reduction' here eliminates what is not useful and desirable in current houses and develops new designs to increase human well-being. New emancipatory technologies would embody such an aesthetic reduction, shaping and forming objects to liberate their natural potentialities, aiming to enhance human life. Marcuse argues:

> The rationality of art, its ability to 'project' existence, to define yet unrealized possibilities could then be envisaged as *validated by and functioning in the scientific-technological transformation of the world.* Rather than being the handmaiden of the established apparatus, beautifying its business and its misery, art would become a technique for destroying this business and this misery. (*PDM,* p. 239).

The aesthetic reduction would embody a *reduction of the ferocity of nature* (*ODM*, pp. 235–40). The goal of the pacification of existence would determine the structure and end of the new technology; 'Pacification presupposes mastery of nature, which is and remains the object opposed to the developing subject' (*ODM*, p. 236). A liberating mastery of nature 'involves the reduction of misery, violence, and cruelty' (*ODM*, p. 236). Marcuse's analysis of a liberating mastery of nature and the doctrine that an emancipatory technology must reduce the violence in nature show that he is not a 'nature mystic' or Rousseauean glorifier of nature who urges submission to nature, or to the natural'.[43] Marcuse writes:

> Glorification of the natural is part of the ideology which protects an unnatural society in its struggle against liberation. The defamation of birth control is a striking example. In some backward areas of the world, it is also 'natural' that black races are inferior to white, and that the dogs get the hindmost, and that business must be. It is also natural that big fish eat little fish – though it may not seem natural to the little fish. Civilization produces the means for freeing Nature from its own brutality, its own insufficiency, its own blindness, by virtue of the cognitive and transforming power of Reason. (*ODM*, p. 238)

But while an emancipatory technology reduces the blindness and ferocity of nature against humans, it also reduces 'the ferocity of man against Nature. Cultivation of the soil is qualitatively different from destruction of the soil, extraction of natural resources from wasteful exploitation, clearing of forests from wholesale deforestation. Poverty, disease, and cancerous growth are natural as well as human ills – their reduction and removal is liberation of life' (*ODM*, p. 240). The *reduction of human ferocity against nature* would involve an ecologically beneficial reduction of pollution, of a destructive wrenching of its resources from nature (i.e. strip-mining), and of wanton destruction of nature's preserves for capitalist development. Marcuse anticipates here the central thrust of the environmental and ecology movement.[44] He also suggests reduction of the unrestrained drive towards the domination of nature, and proposes seeing nature as a source of gratification and not as an enemy to be conquered or a mere object of use and domination. At stake here is a new relation between human beings and nature in which nature is respected and cultivated as the field of human life.

This would involve a recovery of nature's life-enhancing forces and cultivation of the sensuous-aesthetic qualities of both one's human nature and outer nature. In order to preserve and enhance nature, it is necessary to end its pollution and destruction in the interests of capitalist profit and domination.[45]

The aesthetic reduction also involves a *reduction in power*. Marcuse claims that ' "pacification of existence" does not suggest an accumulation of power but rather its opposite. Peace and power, freedom and power, Eros and power may well be contraries' (*ODM*, p. 235). The reduction in power means first of all changing relationships from domination of nature to seeking gratification in nature. But it also involves subversion of the dominant power relationships and attitudes towards power in the existing society. In advanced industrial society, excessive concentration of power and excessive will to power among individuals requires, Marcuse believes, creating institutions that are more decentralized and more democratic, as well as personalities that are more co-operative and loving, and less competititive and manipulative.

The 'aesthetic reduction' also envisages a *reduction in repressive productivity*. In order to expand productivity and maximize profit, much waste is created, and superfluous and obsolescent goods abound. Such superfluous and shoddy production wastes resources and labour time, creating an 'artificial scarcity' that squanders basic resources and energy sources, or manipulates their supply to drive up their price. Repressive productivity also engages in the creation of ever new consumer needs and produces wasteful expenditure in parasitical industries to create these needs (i.e. advertising). These needs in turn drive the consumers to purchase a heap of goods and services in order to satiate their ever multiplying commodity needs. This requires hard work to make the money to buy the products, as well as intense competition and conformity to a repressive performance principle. Marcuse accordingly calls for a *reduction of false needs* which are 'repressive precisely to the degree to which it promotes the satisfaction of needs which require continuing the rat race of catching up with one's peers and with planned obsolescence' (*ODM*, p. 241).[46]

To begin eliminating false needs and repressive productivity requires a *reduction in overdevelopment*.[47] Although this might involve a reduction in the standard of living for some, in Marcuse's view it would be in the interest of liberation, by carrying through a reduction of socially necessary labour time and repressive needs. To obtain a pacified existence also requires, Marcuse believes, a 'reduction in the future population' (*ODM*, p. 243). This reduction is called for not only by the Malthusian problem of providing food and goods for the future population, but also by the need to cut back the sheer number of future inhabitants, who threaten to occupy so much living space that the individual will be hard pressed to be able to enjoy solitude or privacy, or to find a pleasant spot where he/she can be alone and enjoy an unpolluted and uncrowded natural environment.

Marcuse anticipates here the 'limits to growth' and 'population control' movements which became increasingly influential in the late 1960s.[48] He opposes the ideology of production and growth as unquestioned goods and critcizes an uncritical acceptance of technology as the basis of progress that has ruled both the capitalist and Communist worlds. Unlike many of the limits to growth and population control advocates, Marcuse proposes radical social reconstruction to solve the problems of industrial society, guided by a substantive vision of liberation which, among other things, includes concepts of a new technology and new values and forms of human existence. In this project, aesthetics plays a fundamental role, both in constructing the forms and types of technology (the merger of art and technology) and in the goals in which technology and social reconstruction are to serve (the aesthetic reduction, aiming at the pacification of existence).

It is important to perceive the centrality of the notion of a new technology in Marcuse's utopian project and the seriousness with which he advances these ideas. He believes that technology can be radically reconstructed and used as an instrument of liberation that will make possible the construction of a new society. Thus Marcuse clearly does not capitulate to 'one-dimensionality', nor does he see it as inevitable or necessary that technology must play an intrinsic role of domination (as do, for example, Max Weber, Jacques Ellul, Heidegger and others).[40] Moreover, Marcuse is in no way fetishizing technology *per se* as certain earlier advocates of a merger of art and technology did, who either aestheticized existing technology (the Futurists) or redefined art in technical terms (the Bauhaus).[50] Marcuse calls for a 'new technology' that will serve human needs and enhance the aesthetic-erotic aspects of existence by providing technologies of liberation.

When Marcuse first sketched out these ideas in *ODM*, he foresaw no human agents who could radically transform technology, and since he did not believe that technology would transform itself into an instrument of liberation, his theory faced a dilemma, for he could not envisage emancipatory social change without a reconstruction of technology. And he could not envisage the production of a new technology without anthropological and political transformation. However, in the 1960s, with the emergence of the 'new sensibility' and many liberation struggles, Marcuse believed that his utopian ideas now attained a historical grounding which made them more relevant and realistic than ever. Crucially, he saw the 'new sensibility' producing a consciousness and values which could create a new technology and new society:

> The liberated consciousness would promote the development of a science and technology free to discover and realize the possibilities of things and men in the protection and gratification of life, playing with the potentialities of form and matter for the attainment of this goal. Technique would then tend to become art, and art would tend to form reality: the opposition between imagination and reason, higher and lower faculties, poetic and scientific thought, would be invalidated. Emergence of a new Reality Principle: under which a new sensibility and a desublimated scientific intelligence would combine in the creation of an *aesthetic ethos*. (*EL*, p. 24)

In this passage, Marcuse indicates the interconnection between the new technology, new sensibility and new culture. To flesh out these ideas let us now examine his concept of the new sensibility and attempt to discern the sort of anthropological transformation that he believes is necessary to create a new technology and society, after which we shall examine more closely the connection between art and liberation.

10.3 The new sensibility and emancipation of the senses

We discussed Marcuse's political evaluation of the new sensibility incarnated in the counterculture, student movement and New Left in the last chapter.[51] As a normative-anthropological principle, the new sensibility develops and historically grounds, Marcuse's notion of a new reality principle and transvaluation of values projected in *Eros and Civilization*. In *An Essay on Liberation*, Marcuse goes back to many ideas first formulated in his earlier seminal work. In the 1966 preface to a new edition of *EC*, Marcuse writes:

> It was the thesis of *Eros and Civilization*, more fully developed in my *One-Dimensional Man*, that man could avoid the fate of a Welfare-Through-Warfare State only by achieving a new starting point where he could reconstruct the productive apparatus without that 'innerworldly asceticism' which provided the mental basis for domination and exploitation. This image of man was the determinate negation of Nietzsche's superman: man intelligent enough and healthy enough to dispense with all heros and heroic virtues, man without the impulse to live dangerously, to meet the challenge; man with the good conscience to make life an end-in-itself, to live in joy a life without fear.[52]

The image of liberation that Marcuse projects involves a 'transvaluation of values' from the existing society and a 'revolution in values'.[53] In Marcuse's words, the transvaluation of values presupposes a new type of human being

> who rejects the performance principles governing the established societies; a type of man who has rid himself of the aggressiveness and brutality that are inherent in the organization of established society, and in their hypocritical, puritan morality; a type of man who is biologically incapable of fighting wars and creating suffering; a type of man who has a good conscience of joy and pleasure, and who works collectively and individually for a social and natural environment in which such an existence becomes possible.[54]

The 'new human being' with new values possesses a 'new reality principle' which is the determinate negation of the performance principle and its values. Marcuse stresses the connection between one's reality principle, values, needs and behaviour. An individual's vision of reality and values become one's 'second nature' and provide norms and aspirations which motivate thought and behaviour.[55] Hence the importance of a new reality principle and transvaluation of values which will literally change one's being. *Dialectics of liberation:* a new reality principle and values will subvert present repressive-conformist thought and action, making possible 'the emergence of new needs, qualitatively different and even opposed to the prevailing aggressive and repressive needs: the emergence of a new type of man, with a vital, biological drive for liberation, and with a consciousness capable of breaking through the material as well as ideological veil of the affluent society'.[56]

As noted, Marcuse argues that the very social conditions of advanced capitalism are producing these new needs and values and that, moreover, the new reality principle, transvaluation of values and radical needs are incarnated in socialist feminism and the more radical elements of the women's liberation movement.[57] In 'Marxism and Feminism', Marcuse argues that 'feminine' values and qualities represent a determinate negation of the values of capitalism, patriarchy and the performance principle, furthermore, 'Socialism, as a qualitatively different society, must embody the antithesis, the definite negation of aggressive and repressive needs and values of capitalism as a form of male-dominated culture'.[58] He states:

> Formulated as the antithesis of the dominating masculine qualities, such feminine qualities would be receptivity, sensitivity, non-violence, tenderness, and so on. These characteristics appear indeed as opposite of domination and exploitation. On the primary psychological level, they would pertain to the domain of Eros, they would express the energy of the life instincts, against the death instinct and destructive energy.[59]

Marcuse returns here to the Freudian instinct theory and argues that 'feminine' values incarnate erotic life-energies which counterpose the destructive qualities of macho aggression, competition and repression. Women, he believes, possess a 'feminine' nature qualitatively different from men, because they have been frequently freed from repression in the work sphere, brutality in the military sphere, and competition in the social-public sphere. Hence they developed characteristics which for Marcuse are the marks of an emancipated humanity. He summarizes the difference between aggressive masculine and capitalist values as against feminist values as the contrast between 'repressive productivity' and 'creative receptivity', suggesting that the increased 'emancipation of female and feminine energy, physical and intellectual, in the established society' will thus subvert the dominant masculine values and the capitalist performance principle.[60]

Marcuse claims that the conditions that are producing the women's movement, combined with the conditions producing new material needs and 'transcending values', will make possible radical social change. The 'cultural revolution' that Marcuse envisages

> involves a transformation of values which strikes at the entirety of the established culture, material as well as intellectual. This attack on the entire traditional system of values finds its peak in the rejection of the Performance Principle. According to this principle, everyone has to earn his living in alienating but socially necessary performances, and one's reward, one's status in society will be determined by this performance (the work-income rela-tion). The rejection of the Performance Principle also rejects the notion of progress which has up to now characterized the de-velopment of western civilization, namely, progress as increas-ingly productive exploitation and mastery of nature, external and human, a progress which has turned out to be self-propelling destruction and domination. Note that this rejection of the Performance Principle does not only strike at the principle gov-erning the existing capitalist society, but at any society which maintains the subjection of man to the instruments of his labour. Now as against this Performance Principle, the cultural revolu-tion calls for an end to this domination, for freedom and solidarity as a quality of human existence, for the abolition of a society which condemns the vast majority of its members to live their lives as a means for earning a living rather than as an end in itself.[61]

In *EL*, Marcuse argues that the cultural subversion contained in the new sensibility manifests an instinctual, moral and aesthetic revolt against the established society, leading to political rebellion that 'envisages a new culture which fulfils the humanistic promises betrayed by the old culture' (*EL*, p. 10). The revolt is generated by new needs and values which represent a break with the needs and consciousness of the consumer society, thus indicating that capital-ist engineering of needs and consciousness may have its limits and is vulnerable to subversion and change. The transformation of needs would constitute the instinctual basis for freedom which the long history of class society has blocked. Freedom would become the environment of an organism which is no longer capable of adapting to the competitive performances required for well-being under domination, no longer capable of tolerating the aggressiveness, brutality, and ugliness of the established way of life. The rebellion would then have taken root in the very nature, the 'biology' of the individual; and on these new grounds, the rebels would redefine the objectives and the strategy of the political struggle, in which alone the concrete goals of liberation can be determined. (*EL*, pp. 3–4)[62]

The new sensibility, Marcuse believes, contains *aesthetic-erotic* aspects which constitute a qualitative difference from personality structures in the existing society. In place of consumer needs, there would be aesthetic needs for beauty and erotic needs for gratification and happiness. The aesthetic-erotic needs would be in the service of the life-instincts and would seek to cultivate and enhance life and counter aggression and destruction. Nietzsche defines the beautiful as life-enhancing, and Marcuse stresses the connection of beauty with sensuousness and pleasure, thus calling attention to the inner connection between the aesthetic and erotic components of the sensibility.[63] The aesthetic-erotic needs would manifest themselves in the drive to create a beautiful and pleasing environment that would eliminate the horrors of capitalist industrialization, terminating in a new society that would eliminate surplus repression. Marcuse concludes that 'The aesthetic universe is the *Lebenswelt* on which the needs and faculties of freedom depend for their liberation' (*EL*, p. 31). In his view, 'Aesthetic qualities are essentially non-violent, non-domineering'; they enable one 'to see things in their own right, to experience the joy enclosed in them, the erotic energy of nature' *CR&R*, p. 74).

Marcuse uses the term 'aesthetic' in its dual sense of 'pertaining to the senses' and 'pertaining to art' (*EL*, p. 24). He believes that without a change in the sensibility, there can be no real social change, and that art can help cultivate the conditions for a new sensibility. Underlying the theory of the new sensibility is a concept of the active role of the senses in the constitution of experience which rejects the Kantian and other philosophical devaluations of the senses as passive, merely receptive.[64] For Marcuse, our senses are shaped and moulded by society, yet constitute in turn our primary experience of the world and provide both imagination and reason with its material. He believes that the senses are currently socially constrained and mutilated and argues that only an emancipation of the senses and a new sensibility can produce liberating social change (*EL*, pp. 24ff and *CR&R*, pp. 62ff).

In *CR&R*, Marcuse roots his concept of the new sensibility in Marx's conception of 'the complete emancipation of all human senses and qualities' (*CR&R*, p. 64).[65] Marx dropped his early anthropological-aesthetic speculations, which played a prominent role in his *Economic and Philosophical Manuscripts of 1844*, but Marcuse believes that they elucidate essential insights into human liberation and important goals for revolutionary change. Art would play an important role in this process, cultivating a new sensibility and becoming a material force in social reconstruction.

Throughout his writings, Marcuse stresses the subversive quality of the aesthetic needs: 'The aesthetic needs have their own social content: they are the claims of the human organism, mind and body, for a dimension of fulfilment which can be created only in the struggle against the institutions which, by their very functioning, deny and violate these claims' (*EL*, p. 27). Fighting for the gratification of aesthetic needs has a very concrete and subversive social content:

> The radical social content of the aesthetic needs becomes evident as the demand for their most elementary satisfaction is translated into group action on an enlarged scale. From the harmless drive for better zoning regulations and a modicum of protection from noise and dirt to the pressure for closing of whole city areas to automobiles, prohibition of transistor radios in all public places, decommercialization of nature, total urban reconstruction, control of the birth rate – such action would become increasingly subversive of the institutions of capitalism and of their morality. (*EL*, pp. 27–8)

In the process of social reconstruction, the *imagination* would mediate between reason and sensibility and would be given free reign in 'the collective *practice of creating an environment*: level by level, step by step – in the material and intellectual production, an environment in which the non-aggressive, erotic, receptive faculties of man, in harmony with the consciousness of freedom strive for the pacification of man and nature' (*EL*, p. 31). This would involve 'affirmation of the right to build a society in which the abolition of poverty and toil terminates in a universe where the sensuous, the playful, the calm, and the beautiful become forms of existence and thereby the *Form* of the society itself' (*EL*, p. 25). In such a world,

> Released from the bondage to exploitation, the imagination, sustained by the achievements of science, could turn its productive power to the radical reconstruction of experience and the universe of experience. In this reconstruction, the historical *topos* of the aesthetic would change: it would find expression in the transformation of the *Lebenswelt* – society as a work of art' (*EL*, p. 45)[66]

The collective practice of creating a new society, culture and sensibility would be a veritable *cultural revolution*, which would express itself in a new language, a new art, a new life-style and new modes of experience and expression (*EL*, pp. 31ff). Marcuse reveals himself here as a theorist of cultural revolution as an indispensible component of radical social change. His ideal of liberation is grounded in the concepts articulated above all in *EC*, aiming at a new reality principle, transvaluation of values and new modes of being. Whereas in *ODM* Marcuse saw few possibilities for actualizing these ideals, he suggests in *EL* that certain 'catalyst groups' are producing a 'new sensibility' which will be the vanguard and vehicle of cultural revolution; and in *CR&R* he argues that the social conditions of advanced capitalism are producing the 'transcending needs' which would go beyond the dominant consumer-competitive needs (see 9.3.2). In his last writings, Marcuse was trying to move out of the political cul-de-sac into which his analysis of 'false needs' and one-dimensional society had led. His 1970s writings, therefore, attempt to articulate how the current society is producing conditions that lead to radical social change. Marcuse does not dismiss as 'reformist' all values, institutions and struggles that do not promise here and now a radical overthrow of the current society. Consequently, critiques like those of Haug, Fry or Kolakowski of Marcuse as an extreme and ineffectual utopian are obsolescent through their failure to take account of the last stages of Marcuse's life-work.

There are, however, both socio-historical and political deficits in Marcuse's perspectives on socialism and liberation. He comes dangerously close to 'post-scarcity' thinking in *Eros and Civilization* and in later writings, where he seems to assume that the material conditions are present to abolish poverty and that abundance for all is a real historical possibility (see especially 6.1 and 10.1). When I pressed Marcuse on this point in an interview in December 1978, he reaffirmed his belief that only the capitalist system and its world-wide system of 'unequal exchange' prevented the end of scarcity. This may be true in some sense, but Marcuse's published writings on utopia and abundance fail to note in any detail that it is exploitation of the Third World that is responsible for the relative overcoming of scarcity in some advanced capitalist countries. Indeed, would the sort of full abundance envisaged by Marcuse be possible in a world of diminishing resources and rising expectations, except at the expense of the exploitation of Third World countries? Does Marcuse's understanding of emancipatory socialism fail to account for the real obstacles to creating post-scarcity societies?

Likewise, Marcuse's reflections on how automation would end alienated labour and make possible the realm of freedom fail to make clear how automation and computerization of the labour process today is increasing the alienation and exploitation of segments of the labour force while driving other segments out of relatively high paid industrial labour into permanent unemployment, or less well paid jobs. He does not discuss the emerging international division of labour which relegates some areas of the world to chronic underdevelopment while other areas gain from the benefits of technological advances. Part of the problem is that Marcuse does not specify the range or site of the liberated society he envisages. It seems to me that the sort of post-scarcity society that Marcuse calls for is only conceivable in highly industrialized societies; even then it is not clear that the abundance would exist which could make possible the elimination of socially necessary labour time to produce a completely free society without exploitation of the Third World.

Moreover, despite Marcuse's attempts to bring feminism into his theory and to discuss the liberation of women, there is not much concrete analysis of the specificity of women's oppression or what forms the liberation of women would take (see discussion in 6.4.1 and 10.2). Thus although Marcuse has directed much more energy than most Marxists to envisaging new forms of socialism and liberation, there are still some deficiencies in his projections of socialist alternatives.

There are also some ambiguities and omissions in Marcuse's post-1970s theories of social transformation. Although Marcuse affirms contemporary struggles that are not overtly 'revolutionary' (such as the women's liberation movement, the anti-nuclear movement, etc.) as reforms that may help produce radical social transformation, he does not show *how* they would produce the radical change he envisages. Thus his political analysis suffers from inadequate linkage and mediation of the political tendencies which he affirms (see the criticism in 9.3.3). Moreover, Marcuse does not provide much analysis of what sort of institutions and practices might help create the needs and struggles that he envisages. Although he does discuss – in much more detail than most of his critics allow – what sorts of values, goals and reality principle could guide the process of social reconstruction, he does not really specify the sociological and political mediations that would make possible liberation and the construction of genuine socialism.

Marcuse might answer that the practices and institutions of revolutionary transformation and a free society are the product of those engaged in the struggle itself, and that a revolutionary theorist has no right to legislate the forms of struggle in advance (*EL*, p. 42). In this case, all the revolutionary theorist can do is to specify the goals of liberation and to indicate which existing struggles embody – at least to some extent – those goals. Marcuse claims that precisely the reason that Marx did not develop more detailed blue-prints of a free society and social transformation is his commitment to the self-activity of the working class and belief that liberation could only be carried out and realized by those engaged in revolutionary struggles. Nonetheless, Marcuse feels that classical Marxism left underdeveloped its cultural-philosophical dimensions; to compensate, he speculates on the goals, values and practice of liberation. Extrapolating from existing social tendencies, he projects a vision of an alternative society which he believes is not adequately developed in classical Marxism.

Throughout this study I have stressed how Marcuse has appropriated the core ideas of a philosophical tradition in which liberation is a central concern, and has applied selected ideas from German Idealism and classical and *avant garde* art to a rethinking of

Marxism. Despite the changes in his 1970s analyses of needs, liberalism and reformism, and socialism and politics, Marcuse never compromises his vision of liberation: socialism for him is always a totally different, humanly liberating social organization, and he insists that one must have such an attractive ideal and goal before one's eyes to avoid compromises, co-optation, and reproducing the repressive features of the society one is struggling against. It is the total and uncompromising insistence that social thought and political struggle must aim at a qualitatively different society to make possible meaningful discussion of 'liberation', 'democracy' and socialism which give Marcuse's thought its characteristic cast and appeal.

Marcuse's refusal to compromise his vision of liberation endowed him with a rare quality of integrity in a tumultuous and difficult political era. He inspired thought of what was possible, and contempt and disgust for what was existent. His view of the discrepency between 'what is' and 'what could be' no doubt led many to radical despair, but convinced others that only thoroughgoing radical change can produce a decent and livable society. At times, however, his vision of liberation was so rarified and sublime in view of a banal or nasty present that only the 'aesthetic dimension' could really sustain and provide refuge for his vision of liberation. Marcuse's interest in the aesthetic dimension was a distinctive feature of his thought from the beginning – although it was displaced from the centre of his theoretical work during the periods of work with Heidegger and then the Institute for Social Research. However, in his post-1955 writings, the emancipatory potential of art plays an increasingly important role in his thought. It is fitting, therefore, to conclude our examination of Marcuse's concepts of utopia and liberation with some general reflections on Marcuse's analyses of the emancipatory potential of art and to evaluate his aesthetic theory as it develops in his various writings.

10.4 Art and emancipation

Art and aesthetic theory have been central to the development of the critical theories of Adorno, Benjamin, Horkheimer, Lowenthal, Marcuse and others who have devoted much of their writing to analysing the cultural sphere and its range of expression and social functions.[67] As we have seen, Marcuse chose to write his doctoral dissertation on the German artist-novel, and there is a distinct continuity in his concern for art and its role in his social theory throughout his writings.[68] In his early work with the Institute for Social Research, Marcuse analysed the nature and social function of art in bourgeois society, and since *EC* Marcuse stated his intentions to write a treatise on aesthetics.[69] In fact, all of his major post-1955 works have contained provocative reflections on the nature and functions of art in the modern world, and his last published book was *The Aesthetic Dimension*.[70]

Why should reflections on art play such a major role in radical social theory? Part of the answer has to do with what Marcuse discerns as the radical-emancipatory potential of the aesthetic dimension. Marcuse is convinced – this theme becomes pronounced in the 1970s – that great art indicts and protests against the existing society and its ideology, values and reality-principle. Authentic art, for Marcuse, contains a vision of liberation that preserves images of freedom and happiness denied in the everyday world. Furthermore, in a world in which language, philosophy and the sciences are incorporated into an apparatus of domination, in which one-dimensional thought prevails, art remains a refuge of critical truths. That is, by its very nature, art pertains to another world and can thus speak truths other than the conventional wisdom. Furthermore, although the dominant intellectual mentality may be obsessed with facts and may scorn emotions and cultural values, art can cultivate a consciousness and subjectivity which requires liberation and radical social change.

In a sense, art shares a vocation with dialectical language within critical theory. The concepts and images of both critical theory and art seek 'an "authentic language" – the language of negation as the Great Refusal to accept the rules of a game in which the dice are loaded. The absent must be made present because the greater part of the truth is in that which is absent'.[71] Marcuse believes that poetry contains 'the power "de nier les choses" (*to deny the things*) – the power which Hegel claims paradoxically for all authentic thought'.[72] Marcuse cites Mallarmé and Valéry to suggest the common thrust of great poetry and dialectical language. He concludes:

As the power of the given facts tends to become totalitarian, to absorb all opposition, and to define the entire universe of discourse, the effort to speak the language of contradiction appears increasingly irrational, obscure, artificial. The question is not that of a direct or indirect influence of Hegel on the genuine avant-garde, though this is evident in Mallarmé, and Villiers de l'Isle-Adam, in surrealism, in Brecht. Dialectic and poetic language meet, rather, on common ground.[73]

The common ground is that of the Great Refusal.

Marcuse is aware of the ambivalence of art which both opposes and protests against the given society, and yet affirms, embellishes and sometimes even celebrates it. Moreover, the art work is inherently 'unreal', appearance, illusion. As such, its indictment is often harmless and ineffectual. The aesthetic experience, its cultivation of emotion, or release of pity and terror, may aid reconciliation and submission to the existing society, even if its truths denounce it. Further, art, like all forms of radical protest, is subject to commodification and co-operation. Critical and ever anti-capitalist, art may be best-sellers and classics (i.e. Brecht), thus falling prey to a harmless cultural pluralism which is able to absorb and defuse the most contradictory truths. And since much great art tends to be complex and difficult, accessible only to the few, it is irrelevant to the exigencies of political struggle.

Marcuse frequently stresses the contradictory tendencies within art and its ambivalent role in everyday life and political revolution. In my view, Marcuse's most coherent position argues: 'As part of the *established* culture, Art is *affirmative*, sustaining this culture; as *alienation* from the established reality, Art is a *negating* force. The *history of Art* can be understood as the *harmonization of this antagonism*'.[74] For Marcuse, there is an 'internal ambivalence of art: to indict that which is, and to "cancel" the indictment in the aesthetic form, redeeming the suffering, the crime. This "redeeming", reconciling power seems inherent in art, by virtue of its being art, by virtue of its form-giving power' (*EL*, p. 43).

A problem with Marcuse's reflections on art and aesthetic theory is his tendency in various writings to overemphasize either the radical or conservative elements of art and thus to neglect the other side of the dialectics of art. For example, in *Eros and Civilization*, Marcuse focuses on the utopian and subversive function of art, arguing that art is the language of the pleasure principle, the expression of humanity's true needs and desires, 'the return of the repressed'. As such, the images of the creative imagination reveal a new reality principle and vision of life without fear, toil and misery that could serve as a vehicle and goal of liberation. All great art is seen as the negation of unfreedom and the embodiment of the Great Refusal. Art contains the collective memory of the species and preserves its archetypal memories of happiness and hopes for liberation. In this conception, Marcuse stresses the oppositional and subversive elements of art which he believes are the bearer of a new reality principle and vehicle of cultural revolution (see chapter 6 for details).[75]

There is a shift in Marcuse's focus in *One-Dimensional Man*, where he sinks into deep cultural pessimism and stresses the conservative, stabilizing function of art, arguing that art has become integrated into the commodity world and is a cog in the one-dimensional cultural machine. He argues that mass culture absorbs and transforms the high culture, robbing it of its subversive potential, so that art is at best an adornment, or a mild diversion. Art thus loses its oppositional features and its emancipatory potential is defused. The *avant-garde* is aware of this problem, he suggests, but its attempt to create new aesthetic techniques, forms and language is doomed to failure, for

> the total mobilization of all media for the defence of the established reality has coordinated the means of expression to the point where communication of transcending contents becomes technically impossible. The spectre that has haunted the artistic consciousness since Mallarmé – the impossibility of speaking a non-reified language, of communicating the negative – has ceased to be a spectre. It has materialized. (*ODM*, p. 68)

The most radical attempts to break with previous art forms and create new ones 'suffer the fate of being absorbed by what they refute. As modern classics, the avant-garde and the beatniks share in the function of entertaining without endangering the good conscience of men of good will' (*ODM*, p. 70).

In the concluding parts of *ODM*, however, Marcuse could not tolerate such hopeless cultural pessimism; there he posits the merger of art and technology, and the notion of the aesthetic reduction, the importance of which I have stressed. Furthermore, in the conclusion to *ODM*, there are some veiled appeals to art and cultural revolution that preview the central role aesthetics will play in his subsequent works. There he writes:

> If the established society manages all normal communication, validating or invalidating it in accordance with social requirements, then the values alien to these requirements may perhaps have no other medium of communication than the abnormal one of fiction. The aesthetic dimension still retains a freedom of expression which enables the writer and artist to call men and things by their name – to name the otherwise unnameable (*ODM*, p. 247)

He then suggests that 'the real face of our time' is shown in Beckett's novels and Hochhuth's plays, arguing that art is a preserve of critical truths which cannot be otherwise expressed and thus has an important revelatory function for critical theory.

In *An Essay on Liberation*, Marcuse swings to the art-as-subversive pole of the dialectics of art, arguing that the new sensibility and radical art forms are playing an indispensible role in the practice of liberation. He now stresses the primary of the aesthetic-erotic components in his vision of a free society and assigns to aesthetics a fundamental role in its construction. He argues that the cultural revolution is a crucial part of the struggle for liberation, thus affirming rock and protest music, soul music and blues, slang and obscenity, the living theatre and guerilla street theatre, as well as surrealism, Russian formalism and other movements of the *avant-garde*. He seems here to champion all the most radical breaks with bourgeois culture and to affirm these aesthetic experiments as revolutionary *per se*, as part of the movement of liberation that postulates a radical break with the existing society.

In *Counterrevolution and Revolt* and *The Aesthetic Dimension*, Marcuse shies away from his seeming rejection of bourgeois art for contemporary and modernist artistic revolts. He argues in *CR&R* that although there is a need for effective communication to indict the established society, and to express the goals of liberation, a new language cannot be 'invented' *ab novum* but must depend on the political use of traditional culture and its forms. Marcuse now criticizes the 'systematic desublimination of culture' and the undoing of aesthetic form as a self-defeating attempt to merge art with reality, as a sacrifice of art's higher dimension by virtue of which it could project and preserve a higher alternative reality (*CR&R*, pp. 81ff). Since it is the aesthetic form that preserves the higher truth and alternative vision, Marcuse champions *form* as essential to art's revolutionary powers. He insists that art must remain 'alienated' from the established society and attacks 'anti-art' as capitulating to the words, sights and sounds of the very reality it wishes to overthrow. Throughout the 1970s Marcuse defends anew the classical high culture that the artistic revolutions of the twentieth century sought to break with, claiming that great eighteenth- and nineteenth-century art is thoroughly anti-bourgeois and 'indicts, rejects, withdraws from the material culture of the bourgeoisie' (*CR&R*, p. 86). The aesthetic universe of great bourgeois art '*contradicts* reality – a "methodical", intentional contradiction' (*CR&R*, p. 86). This negation is contained and preserved in its form, hence Marcuse rejects anti-art, which wants to obliterate aesthetic form to merge directly with reality, as sacrificing precisely the subversive, oppositional features of art. Art, he now suggests, is not equivalent *per se* to revolution, but stands in a relation of tension with political struggles. Art and political revolution are united in wanting to change the world, but they contain a 'unity of opposites' which must preserve their own autonomy and distinct practice of liberation and transformation.(*CR&R*, pp. 103ff).

Hence it appears that there is a conflict between Marcuse's theory in *EL* and his 1970s writings on art. No longer does Marcuse advocate the 'desublimation of art', contemporary artistic rebellion, or the superseding (*Aufhebung*) of art in reality. There is no more celebration of dissident art, slang, obscenity, or the politicalization of art. No longer are certain forms of contemporary political art celebrated as revolutionary *per se*, as part and parcel of the revolution. Instead, the tension between art and revolution is stressed, as are its necessary distance from the otherness to revolutionary practice.[76] Marcuse now defends the form of art as the vehicle of the aesthetic liberation and argues that the forms of the great classical and modernist bourgeois art are exemplary. It seems therefore that a disjunction emerges in Marcuse's theory of the emancipatory potential of art.

When I asked Marcuse why there was such a seemingly abrupt divergence between his theories of emancipatory art from the 1960s to the 1970s, he stressed instead the continuities in his aesthetic theory.[77] He simply thought that counterculture art, dissident artistic revolts, and the political uses of art in the 1960s were better than in the 1970s. He claimed that 1960s folk and protest music, the songs of Bob Dylan, radical theatre and other forms of movement art successfully combined aesthetic form with political messages, and by contributing to a large-scale radicalizing process were playing an important part in a political movement.[78] In the 1970s, Marcuse claims, the dissident cultures were losing, for the most part, both their aesthetic and political quality, sacrificing both concern with the formal qualities which he ascribes to authentic art and political content and effects. Hence, in this situation, Marcuse perceived the need to go back and defend the aesthetic values and works of the classical bourgeois heritage which he believed contained important emancipatory and political potential that was being neglected by the concern with the cultural fads of the moment.[79]

Marcuse's turn to defend the values of high art has both sociological roots and sources in his own intellectual temperment and trajectory. There is a tendency in Marcuse to turn to the consolations of aesthetics after particularly disappointing political interventions. After his experiences in the defeated German revolution, Marcuse turned to a study of literature; he left Berlin for Freiburg, where he wrote a dissertation on the German artist-novel. After his theoretical work with the Institute for Social Research in the 1930s and his work with the American government in the 1940s as part of his political fight against fascism, Marcuse returned to a study of Freud, Schiller and high bourgeois culture which informed *Eros and Civilization*. Similarly, after his involvment in the struggles of the New Left in the 1960s, Marcuse turned to renewed work on aesthetics, producing a slim book which contains his last reflections on art, *The Aesthetic Dimension*.

10.4.1 The Aesthetic Dimension

In retrospect, this poetical work is Marcuse's last testament to his vision of liberation, and sums up and reveals both the contributions and limitations of his thought, as he continues his defence of high bourgeois culture and reflections on the emancipatory potential of aesthetic form. In challenging the prevailing Marxist aesthetic orthodoxy, Marcuse provides criticisms of almost all Marxist theoreticans of revolutionary art, including Lukács, Brecht and

Benjamin. The work is deeply influenced by Adorno and contains a distillation of Frankfurt School aesthetic theory.[80] Marcuse argues:

> In contrast to orthodox Marxist aesthetics I see the political potential of art in art itself, in the aesthetic form as such. Furthermore, I argue that by virtue of its aesthetic form, art is largely autonomous vis à vis the given social relations. In its autonomy art both protests these relations, and at the same time transcends them. Thereby art subverts the dominant consciousness, the ordinary experience. (*AD*, p. ix)

Marcuse argues that all 'authentic art' or 'autonomous art' is emancipatory *per se* because it 'breaks with everyday reality' and 'does not obey the norms of the existing reality principle, but has instead its own set of rules. This autonomy of art comes long before bourgeois society. Medieval cathedrals, for example, represent such a break with the everyday world. Whoever enters it enters a sphere which is not that of the everyday world'.[81] 'A work may be called revolutionary', in Marcuse's view,

> if, by virtue of the aesthetic transformation, it represents, in the exemplary fate of individuals, the prevailing unfreedom and the rebelling forces, thus breaking through the mystified (and petrified) social reality, and opening the horizon of change (liberation). In this sense, every authentic work of art would be revolutionary, i.e. subversive of perception and understanding, an indictment of the established reality, the appearance of the image of liberation. This would hold true of the classical drama as well as Brecht's plays, of Goethe's *Wahlverwandtschaften* as well as Günter Grass's *Hundejahre*, of William Blake as well as Rimbaud. (*AD*, pp. x–xi)

These passages make clear the extent to which Marcuse now defends the political potential of art because 'the world really is as it appears in the work of art' (*AD*, p. xii) and because great art projects another world which stands in opposition to the existing world. Marcuse continues his reflections on the oppositional role of art, his defence of aesthetic form, sublimation, catharsis and of beauty as a crucial normative aesthetic criterion, along the lines sketched out in *EC*, *EL* and *CR&R*. There is, in fact, a continuity that runs through Marcuse's post-1950s aesthetics in his defence of 'authentic art', which projects another world, speaks the language of the instincts and pleasure principle, and projects images of liberation. There is a renewed emphasis on the Freudian anthropology which he draws upon throughout the book (see *AD*, pp. 20–1, 24f, 44, 64f, 69 and 72). In *AD*, however, Marcuse no longer defends the power of art to redeem and 'cancel' evil,[82] and he no longer posits the goal of an ultimate harmony between art and reality, and the human being and its world (see *AD*, pp. 28–9), taking over instead Adorno's principle of the 'permanent non-identity between subject and object, between individual and individual' (*AD*, p. 29), thus affirming Adorno's 'non-identity thesis' over Hegel's 'identity thesis'.[83] Moreover, he no longer sees any possibility of the end of art, of art being sublated into reality (*AD*, pp. 68–9, 71–2); here he takes his aesthetic theory into a more pessimistic direction by denying the possibility of the reconciliation of instincts and society which he posited as an ideal in *EC*, suggesting instead that there can never be a condition of perfect social harmony that will not require art as the bearer of those truths, desires and hopes not realized in the existing world (*AD*, pp. 56ff). These reflections culminate in a powerful passage where Marcuse writes:

> Art declares its *caveat* to the thesis according to which the time has come to change the world. While art bears witness to the necessity of liberation, it also testifies to its limits. What has been done cannot be undone; what has passed cannot be recaptured. History is guilt but not redemption. Eros and Thanatos are lovers as well as adversaries. Destructive energy may be brought into the service of life to an ever higher degree – Eros itself lives under the sign of finitude, of pain. The 'eternity of joy' constitutes itself through the death of individuals. For them, this eternity is an abstract universal. And, perhaps, the eternity does not last very long. The world was not made for the sake of the human being and it has not become more human. (*AD*, pp. 68–9)

In this passage, Marcuse rejects Walter Benjamin's redemptive-messianic view of history and starkly stresses human finitude and embeddedness in nature. He argues that Eros is always subject to limitations and the ingression of destructive energies, making pure and lasting joy impossible. The aesthetic dimension can offer consolation in the face of the impossibility of attaining lasting happiness, but it cannot realize absolute freedom and happiness. Through the 'artistic catharsis', we can come to terms with human suffering, but cannot ultimately transcend it. Although happiness and liberation can be obtained in the aesthetic dimension, they cannot be fully realized in the real world. The realization of our deepest hopes, needs and fantasies can take place in art and dreams but not in everyday life. Reconciliation with nature, of the sort envisaged in *EC*, can therefore only take place in the aesthetic dimension and not in reality. Although the hope which art represents 'ought not to remain ideal' (*AD*, p. 57), it cannot in fact be fully realized. The aesthetic transcendence can affirm its own transitoriness and in doing so reveals the transitoriness of human life: 'Es war doch so schön' (*AD*, p. 59) is the final and ultimate expression of the demand for happiness that art can represent but cannot extend and secure in reality.

In *AD*, Marcuse therefore seems to modify his earlier ideal that liberation requires 'reconciliation with nature' and stresses the limits to the hopes for utopia and liberation. He also suggests that death constitutes the final limit of human joy and striving and is an ineradicable otherness which renders the human being limited and finite. In a powerful passage, Marcuse expresses his final simultaneous acceptance and defiance of death:

> Though the universe of art is permeated with death, art spurns the temptation to give death a meaning. For art, death is a constant hazard, misfortune, a constant threat even in moments of happiness, triumph, fulfilment. (Even in *Tristan*, death remains an accident, a double accident of the love potion and of the wound. The hymn on death is a hymn on love.) All suffering becomes sickness unto death – though the disease itself may be cured. *La Mort des Pauvres* may well be liberation; poverty can be abolished. Still, death remains the negation inherent in society, in history. It is the final remembrance of things past – last remembrance of all possibilities forsaken, of all that which could have been said and was not, of every gesture, every tenderness not shown. (*AD*, p. 68)

It is hard not to read this passage – and several other beautifully lyrical passages – as an acceptance of his own impending death and as a fond farewell to friends and readers.[84] *The Aesthetic Dimension* is one of Marcuse's most evocative, compressed and expressive works. It is, however, controversial in its break with traditional Marxist aesthetics and defence of the 'permanence of art'. Although an adequate appraisal of Marcuse's aesthetics and the role of art in critical theory would require another book, I shall conclude this chapter with some final critical remarks on Marcuse's theory of art and liberation.

10.4.2 *Critique of Marcuse's aesthetics*

Whereas at times Marcuse's writings on art seem to be a replay of the tendency of Romanticism and some versions of artistic modernism to celebrate the artist as the true revolutionary and art as the true revolution, in fact Marcuse posits art more modestly as the helpmate of revolution.[85] For Marcuse, emancipatory art can help produce revolutionary consciousness, or the subjective conditions of revolution, but there is an unresolvable tension between art and politics, the artistic revolution and the political revolution. Although Marcuse insists on the importance of political struggle as the means to realize revolutionary hopes and imperatives, he likewise insists on the autonomy of art, claiming that the most revolutionary art may well be the most removed from the demands of political struggle:

> This thesis implies that literature is not revolutionary because it is written for the working class or for 'the revolution'. Literature can be called revolutionary in a meaningful sense only with reference to itself, as content having become form. The political potential of art lies only in its own aesthetic dimension. Its relation to praxis is inexorably indirect, mediated and frustrating. The more immediately political the work of art, the more it reduces the power of estrangement and the radical, transcendent goals of change. In this sense, there may be more subversive potential in the poetry of Baudelaire and Rimbaud than in the didactic plays of Brecht. (*AD*, pp. xii–xiii)

There are several problems here which deserve commentary. Whereas Marcuse is right that there are subversive elements in classical and modernist art, there are also ideological elements which in turn may undermine the political potential that he valorizes. Marcuse seems to underemphasize here those conservative-ideological elements in high culture in his eagerness to defend its subversive moments. Thus, whereas he correctly polemicizes against those Marxist theories of ideology which reduce it to lies, distorted expressions of class interests and false consciousness, by arguing that ideology also often contains progressive and utopian moments (*AD*, pp. 13ff) he seems to minimize those stabilizing and mystifying elements of ideology in his preferred classics.[86] By defining 'authentic art' as art that most diligently cultivates aesthetic form and preserves the image of liberation, he neglects analysing the role of art within revolutionary movements and underestimates the political potentiality of art which is part of a process of cultural revolution, or is operative in oppositional cultures.

In a sense, Marcuse's analysis falls behind the powerful sociological-aesthetic analysis of modern art by Adorno.[87] In his posthumously published *Aesthetische Theorie*, Adorno argues that modernist, *avant-garde* art responds to the transformations in art and the aesthetic tendencies in the culture industry by divesting itself of traditional aura, harmonious forms and unitary, coherent narrative structures. 'Autonomous art' for Adorno undergoes a 'de-aestheticization' (*Ent-Kunstung*) to free it from traditional aesthetics, bourgeois ideology and the demands of the commercial market. Adorno is referring to such *avant-garde* movements as Dadaism, Surrealism, Expressionism and other tendencies and artists who reject 'affirmative art' and refuse to conform to artistic conventions and the demands of the art market. Such art utilizes fragmentary artistic structures, shock techniques and ugliness, eroticism, brute suffering, violence and destruction as techniques of artistic and sometimes social rebellion. This leads to radical subversion of traditional art forms and artistic rebellions that cannot be easily co-opted by the existing taste and fashions.

Adorno provides a sociological explanation of modernist revolts in terms of the dynamics of advanced capitalism, and valorizes modern art precisely because it refuses to be integrated in the contemporary society. Marcuse by contrast lacks historical specificity in his claim that 'authentic art' is emancipatory *per se* because of its aesthetic form. Eschewing sociological analysis, Marcuse is once again engaging in ontological analysis and is preoccupied with the universal features and permanence of art. Hence he stresses the shared features of all 'authentic art' and believes that all great art from Shakespeare through to Beckett is 'autonomous' by virtue of its aesthetic form. Thus whereas Adorno limits the term 'autonomous art' to describe those *avant-garde* tendencies that are radically non conformist, Marcuse extends it to all his favoured classics which contain the universal features of aesthetic form.

Furthermore, Marcuse roots his concept of authentic art in his theory of the human essence. His Freudian anthropology once again overpowers history in his aesthetic reflections. On this theory, authentic art is expressive of a universal 'species being', and the appeal of great art throughout history seems to be its articulation of universal humanity and artistic value (*AD*, pp. 18ff, 29ff, and 54ff). Universal art is a vehicle for 'the ingression of the primary erotic-destructive forces which explode the normal universe of communication and behaviour' (*AD*, p. 20). Art is thus by nature subversive and oppositional through its expression of erotic and instinctual energies which are stifled by social repression. Art thus expresses primary needs and desires, the 'return of the repressed', and contains the memory of integral gratification and fulfilment by evoking memory of past gratification and happiness (*AD*, p. 56).

Marcuse's emphasis on the permanent, transhistorical qualities of 'authentic art' ultimately takes *beauty* as a universal criterion of aesthetic value. He stresses 'the performance of certain qualities of art through all changes of style and historical periods (transcendence, estrangement, aesthetic order, manifestations of the beautiful)' (*AD*, p. 16), and defends beauty as the privileged quality of aesthetic universality (*AD*, pp. 6, 46ff, 62ff, *passim*). Marcuse abandons here a type of Marxist aesthetics which would stress the historicity of art and would focus on its functions within a given historical society. It has often been argued that 'beauty' is itself a pre-eminently historical category, and that not only are concepts of beauty different in various cultures and historical periods, but the elevation of 'beauty' to a privileged aesthetic role is itself a historical phenomenon. Marcuse is once again returning here to central tenets of idealist aesthetics which have so profoundly shaped his entire work.[88]

Similarly, it seems a mistake to claim that *all* great art must be subversive, oppositional and project images of liberation.[89] In 'On Affirmative Culture', Marcuse indicated the possibility that in a free society, art could 'express reality and joy in reality. A foretaste of such potentialities can be had in experiencing the unassuming display of Greek statues or the music of Mozart or late Beethoven' (*N*, p. 131). But are there not already types of art, such as the ones Marcuse cites here, which express joy in reality here and now? Is this not a genuine part of authentic art? In a conversation with Habermas, Marcuse concedes that he has modified his concept of art and now puts more emphasis on art's 'critical-communicative character'.[90] I would suggest, however, that in Marcuse's later writings on aesthetics, he fails to analyse adequately the dialectics of the 'affirmative character of art' – the focus of his 1937 essay – both as a reproduction of hegemonic ideology and as a genuine expression of 'joy in reality' and human hopes and desires.

Part of the problem with Marcuse's aesthetics is his tendency to ontologize art, combined with a tendency to swing his analysis between two poles of positing art as affirmative or negative, subversive or stabilizing. There is a certain rhythm, or logic, in the weight he ascribes in various works to one pole or another, which moves from exaggerating either the subversive-emancipatory elements of art or its conservative aspects. In works like *EC* and *SM*, Marcuse posits extremely high hopes on the subversiveness of high culture and great art, which, disappointed, lead to the cultural pessimism of *ODM*. Then with the eruption of manifold artistic revolts in the 1960s, Marcuse turns to celebrate again the revolutionary potential of oppositional art, which, disappointed, leads to his critique of 'anti-art' and swings back to a defence of high bourgeois culture in *CR&R* and *AD*. To overcome such one-sidedness, one must hold on to the dialectics of art as at once affirmative and negative, stabilizing and subversive, and must grasp that this is the very nature of art.[91]

I would also argue that one should avoid characterizing some forms of art as revolutionary *per se* and other forms as counter-revolutionary. Making this move led Marcuse to shift from favourably appraising high bourgeois art as preserving oppositional and subversive realms of being in *EC*, to a position where he championed the most radical breaks with bourgeois art in *EL*. Then he sommersaulted back in *CR&R* and *AD* to champion eighteenth- and nineteenth-century bourgeois art and criticized 'anti-art' that lacks the rigour of aesthetic form. To avoid these vacillations, one should keep in mind the complicated dialectic of form and content in appraising the revolutionary or conservative potential of art. In my view, it is a mistake to categorize any specific form of art as in itself, in its formal qualities, revolutionary or conservative. Most forms of art like Expressionism or Realism – or artists like Flaubert or Dostoyevsky – contain contradictory elements which make it impossible simply to affirm a form, or school, or author as revolutionary *per se*.[92] Only a complex analysis of the dialectic of form and content and its relation to its society and political context can show what political potentialities and tendencies a work or author contain. To make form alone the bearer of art's subversive and emancipatory potentialities seems particularly wrong. For example, Brecht's 'alienation effects' and 'separation of the elements' can be used in fascist or Christian art, and Eisenstein's montage can be used for a variety of aesthetic tendencies. What was once subversive art (say Flaubert's *Madame Bovary*) may now be conservative, and even art intending to be subversive or progressive may turn out to have stabilizing or conservative effects in its reception.[93] Most works in fact contain at once subversive and stabilizing, conformist and oppositional, tendencies which require detailed analysis to explicate their ideological and emancipatory content and possible effects. Thus Marcuse's universalizing aesthetic form neglects analysing the social function of art in a given society, and suppresses the dialectic of form and content, artifact and context, and production and reception that is essential in analysing and evaluating works of art from a materialist standpoint.

Despite its problems, Marcuse's continual reflections on utopia and liberation and the role of art in aiding social change contain many important insights. Much great art does have emancipatory potential, and Marcuse's works help us reflect on how cultural revolution can help promote social change. In a difficult historical period, Marcuse had the courage and vision to project alternative possibilities in which a happier and freer life can be envisaged. In his vision of cultural revolution and social reconstruction, art

would then be creativity, a creation in the material as well as intellectual sense, a juncture of technique and the arts in the total reconstruction of the environment, a juncture of town and country, industry and nature, after all have been freed from the horrors of commercial exploitation and beautification, so that Art can no longer serve as a stimulus of business. Evidently, the very possibility of creating such an environment depends on the total transformation of the existing society: a new mode and new goals of production, a new type of human being as producer, the end of role-playing, of the established division of labour, of work and pleasure.[94]

In this passage, Marcuse's utopia finds integral expression. Only the union of art, technique and the new sensibility in a process of revolution and social reconstruction can provide the preconditions for a free society. Marcuse's vision of utopian socialism presupposes anthropological, technical and cultural transformation, integrated into a process of total revolution. He emphasizes aspects of liberation neglected by most traditional Marxists, and remains an important corrective to the deficiencies of traditional Marxist and bourgeois thought.

Throughout his life, Marcuse preserved and cultivated the most radical thought in Western culture, and was devoted both to relentless critique of the present society and culture, and to the construction of an alternative society and culture. Marcuse has much to teach us, and his works remain a fertile source of provocative and radical ideas. The writings of Herbert Marcuse therefore deserve our careful and critical study, for he has transmitted to us the best aspects of radical philosophy and social theory, while making us aware of those features of our society and culture that should be changed or abolished. It is now up to us to develop these ideas and to translate them into practice within the project of constructing a new society and a better world.

Conclusion: Marcuse's Unfinished Legacy

Marcuse's work is frequently presented as falling into three distinct stages: (1) his early 'Heideggerian Marxist' stage from 1928 to 1933; (2) his orthodox 'critical theory' stage from 1933 to 1941, which adhered to the version of Hegelian Marxism developed by the Institute for Social Research in exile; and (3) his post-Second World War writings, in which his work took on a distinctly 'Marcusean' cast.[1] There are some problems, however, with this conventional way of interpreting Marcuse. Although the first two stages are relatively unified and constitute a coherent programme of social theory with political intent, the post-Second World War writings contain a series of ruptures and novel departures. Consequently, depiction of the post-1950 writings as a unified stage attributes a false unity to what is really a heterogeneous body of work.

Marcuse's post-Second World War writings return to the emphasis on the individual as an agent of human liberation and political action central to his early writings and creatively reconstruct the relatively orthodox Marxism, class politics and Hegelian rationalism of his second stage. By bringing Freud, psychology and nature into his theory, he develops a new concept of reason which he calls libidinal rationality (see Chapter 6). He is also more affirmative towards art and culture as a vehicle of human liberation, returning here to the cultural concerns of his youth (see Chapters 1 and 10). Most significantly, he adds a utopian dimension to his theory, rehabilitating and developing the most emancipatory perspectives on socialism found in Marx and the tradition of utopian socialism.

Despite some unifying themes and positions, Marcuse frequently revises his social theory and political analysis during this period.

There is, for instance, a significant rupture between the militant optimism of *Eros and Civilization* and the affirmative stress on 'liberalizing tendencies' in *Soviet Marxism*, in contrast to the bleak pessimism of *One-Dimensional Man*. Starting around 1966 he returns, however, to more utopian and optimistic perspectives on human liberation and social change, and in addition returns to a more orthodox Marxian focus on social contradictions, political struggle and prospects for radical social change (see Chapter 9). From about 1965 until his death, he continually modified his social and political analysis, shifting, for example, from grim affirmation of revolutionary violence in 'Repressive Tolerance' to restrained and then jubilant celebration of existing 'liberation struggles' in 'The End of Utopia' (1967) and *An Essay on Liberation* (1969). His thought takes a 'United Front' turn in 1972 with *Counterrevolution and Revolt*, which backs away from defending revolutionary violence and confrontation politics to advocacy of radical social change *within* the system through undertaking a 'long march through the institutions'.

While some interpreters have failed to see significant developments in Marcuse's post-Second World War writings, others consider his changes and modifications of his positions as signs of confusion or vacillation.[2] There is, however, a certain logic in Marcuse's changes in his theoretical and political positions. First, his theory of advanced capitalism and the contemporary historical situation and his political analysis are usually internally coherent, and he claims that his shifts are justified in response to changing historical conditions. During the period of affluent McCarthyism in the 1950s, it was obviously untenable to find any revolutionary forces in advanced capitalist society, especially in the United States where Marcuse was living. In the early 1960s, the most visible forces of opposition and social revolt were the non-integrated outsiders, students and intellectuals involved in the civil rights movement which Marcuse alluded to at the end of *ODM*. With the beginning of the anti-war movement and the New Left, however, Marcuse discovered new political forces that led him to modify his theory. Their failure to carry through a socialist revolution in the advanced capitalist countries by the 1970s – and doubts about whether this was even remotely possible – led Marcuse to posit more modest political strategies in *CR&R*.

In defence of these shifts, Marcuse could counter that he was orienting his political theory to what he perceived as the most advanced political struggles of the moment – or lack of them – and was thus articulating historical possibilities in contemporary society rather than setting forth his own blueprint for social change. In 1969 he wrote: 'The search for specific historical agents of revolutionary change in the advanced capitalist countries is indeed meaningless. Revolutionary forces emerge in the process of change itself; the translation of the potential into the actual is the work of political practice' (*EL*, p. 79). This would suggest that a revolutionary theorist's task is to articulate goals and strategies existent in actual political struggles and not to legislate in advance forms or forces of struggle. Marcuse also suggested, however, that relatively constant goals and visions of liberation can play a useful role in the struggle – as an anticipatory moment in political practice which can be translated into 'prefigurative politics' in 'catalyst groups' that anticipate liberation and a new society already in existing practice.[3] In this sense Marcuse was both a defender of what he considered the most advanced existing political struggles and was an early advocate of 'prefigurative politics', which urged that existing groups and struggles develop more radical and emancipatory goals and strategies.

In addition to the shifts and developments in Marcuse's thought which I have made a major focus of this study, there are also some constants and continuities in his theory which run through his writings from beginning to end. Marcuse was always a champion of human liberation and grounded his theory in a normative theory of human nature, explicating those human needs and potentials that were being denied, or distorted, in existing society and which required a new society for their gratification and development. Throughout his writings there is a dialectic of the individual versus society, in which society is criticized for repressing and alienating human beings. From the beginning, Marcuse saw capitalism as the fundamental source of human oppression and suffering and thus was sternly anti-capitalist his entire life.

Although Marcuse challenged traditional Marxism on many points, throughout his life he accepted Marxian historical materialism as the most adequate theory of history and society and advocated Hegelian-Marxian dialectics as the best method of socio-historical and political analysis. He applied both to a wide variety of phenomena and often turned Marxian dialectics against Marxian theory, challenging radical social theory to rethink the Marxian project in the light of changes in historical reality since Marx's day and in view of new possibilities for social change and human liberation. Whereas many critics have claimed that Marcuse surrendered the Marxian mode of social analysis and revolutionary political perspectives, I have argued that even in works which challenge Marxism most radically, like *EC* and *ODM,* Marcuse uses the Marxian theory and method of social analysis.

Another theoretical constant in Marcuse's work is thus his commitment to Hegelian-Marxian dialectics. His advocacy of critical and dialectical thinking against reigning philosophical and scientific orthodoxies has been a central feature of his thought since his first essays. Marcuse's defence of the logic and rationality of dialectical thinking in the face of the dominance of positivist and empiricist traditions won him the wrath not only of the academic establishment, but of positivist and structuralist Marxists who saw dialectics as a species of irrationalism. Against these attacks from contemporary versions of Marxism, Marcuse continued to affirm the centrality of dialectical thinking to the Marxian project, arguing that it was the dialectical interplay of description, critique and projecting alternatives to be realized by social practice that constitutes the revolutionary core of Marxism. Against all criticism of dialectics, Marcuse argued that it provides concepts and ways of thinking that best grasp the complexity and multi-dimensionality of social and human reality. For Marcuse, dialectics is the most appropriate method to conceptualize historical change and socio-economic transformation; in his view, only this approach grasps the potentialities in existing realities and discloses both liberating negations and obstacles to the realization of higher potentialities. In this way, dialectics is essential to social critique and political practice. Marcuse is the theorist and practitioner of Hegelian-Marxian dialectics *par excellence* in post-Second World War America, and his preservation of dialectical thinking constitutes an enduring legacy for contemporary thought. Marcuse thus emerges from this study as a paradigm of a 'critical Marxist' whose thought exemplifies the 'spirit of critical thinking' and 'power of negation' while striving to criticize and transform existing realities.

Throughout his life, Marcuse also preserved the classical role of the philosopher as someone who is concerned with what is important in human life and who aims to conceptualize what is essential to human liberation. Marcuse's forte as a philosopher was his ability to synthesize philosophy with critical social theory and political analysis in order to discern the fundamental features of contemporary society, its higher potentialities and the ways that society could be transformed to realize them. In the age of triviality in philosophy, Marcuse remained committed to what was of importance and of essential interest to human beings in his historical epoch. At times, however, his speculative fancy or passionate involvement in the political concerns of the day made him too impatient to engage in the sort of careful analysis of particulars which, for instance, characterized Walter Benjamin's thought. Marcuse was instead a 'generalist' who was able to abstract and articulate what was essential to an issue or thinker without losing the thrust of his critical insights in a morass of details. This trait constitutes both one of his greatest strengths – the ability to grasp the essential – and one of his weaknesses – the lack of adequate concern for detail and particularity.

I have suggested that Herbert Marcuse's responses to what has been called the 'crisis of Marxism' is a key to his thought and writings. However, in conclusion, I want to propose that we view the 'crisis of Marxism' not so much as a sign of weakness but rather as a typical situation for a social theory that faces anomalies or events which challenge its theories. The term 'crisis' in Marxian discourse suggests cataclysmic collapse and, as Habermas suggests, a terminal illness that could bring death to its patient. The concept of 'crisis' within Marxian theory has its origins in theories of the 'crisis of capitalism', which were generally linked to notions of the collapse of capitalism and triumph of socialism. The term crisis was then applied to Marxism itself by Sorel, Korsch and others. In recent years, references to the 'crisis of Marxism' have proliferated, and have been used to cover a variety of phenomena.[4]

However, just as capitalism has survived many crises, so has Marxism. Moreover, just as various crises of capitalism have elicited new survival strategies which in certain ways have strengthened the capitalist system (i.e. imperialism, state capitalism, neo-imperialism, multi-national capitalism, etc.), so too 'crises of Marxism have periodically led to the development and improvement of Marxian theory. Of course, crises of a social theory, or system, may point to, and lead to, their obsolescence and demise, but they may enable the theory or system to modify itself, adapt, and thus survive. A 'crisis' thus brings about a challenge to a social system or theory which may lead to its weakening and collapse, or may lead to its improvement and strengthening. Crises of Marxism are thus rather normal, periodic events which global socio-history theories continually undergo when events belie forecasts, or historical changes appear which force development or revision of the theory. When theories like Marxism are questioned during a 'crisis', debates ensue which frequently improve the theory. Consequently, crises of Marxism do not necessarily refer to failures of Marxism but rather to challenges to the theory to develop and overcome temporary problems.

Herbert Marcuse's work, for the most part, consists of a series of reconstructions of the Marxian theory in the light of historical changes and challenges which required revision and development. Marcuse himself constantly argued that the Marxian theory periodically demands revision and development since the categories are historical categories that are necessarily open to change and transformation. He believed that Marxism was not yet obsolescent, or *passé*, despite the vicissitudes of advanced capitalist development which put in question certain of its theories. Rather than abandoning Marxism, Marcuse sought to update and transform it. Despite his many criticisms of Marxian orthodoxy, Marcuse's attempts to revise and reconstruct the Marxian theory from the beginning to the end of his intellectual career thus emerges from my study as the fundamental determinant of his life and work. His experiences in the First World War and the German revolution introduced him to Marxism via historical experience, and his first published essay reveals a thorough immersion in the Marxian theory. While his early 1928–33 writings contain an idiosyncratic mixture of Marxism, phenomenology, existentialism, philosophy of life and German Idealism, in his work with the Institute of Social Research his Marxism was rather orthodox – indeed, Karl Korsch believed that Marcuse was the most orthodox Marxist among the Institute members.[5] After a decade of government activity in the 1940s, Marcuse continued to remain committed to Marxism when many other former radicals were renouncing their earlier Marxism. Arthur Mitzman told me that after a seminar on social change at Columbia in the 1950s at the height of McCarthyism, when professors, among others, were being scrutinized and judged for their political beliefs, he approached Marcuse and asked him directly if he was a Marxist. Marcuse coolly looked Mitzman in the eyes and answered, 'Yes. And what is your question?'[6]

In the 1960s Marcuse turned to explicit affirmation of Marxian revolutionary perspectives after having put in question certain Marxian positions in his 1950s and early 1960s writings. Almost alone among his critical theory colleagues, Marcuse continued to identify himself as a Marxist throughout an historical epoch that raised serious doubts about the Marxian theory and politics. In a sense, Marcuse remained more faithful to the original 1930s project of critical theory than his Institute colleagues (see Chapter 4). In 1978, in a revealing address, entitled 'Theory and Practice', on the fiftieth anniversary of the formation of the Institute for Social Research in Frankfurt, Marcuse pointedly situates his theory within classical Marxism.[7] He begins by explicating the fundamental tendencies and countertendencies of advanced capitalism and outlines theories of capitalist crisis, socialist revolution and the 'preventive counterrevolution' firmly within a Marxian framework. It is striking that he would so explicitly utilize traditional Marxian categories and situate his own 1970s positions within the Marxian theory in view of the rejection of Marxism by many of the 'inner circle' of the Institute.[8] At the same time, he continues to defend his specifically 'Marcusean' positions of 'concrete utopia', counter-institutions, and the broadening base for social change within advanced capitalism.

Marcuse was, however, in no way a dogmatic or orthodox Marxist. In fact, among Marcuse's most valuable contributions in contemporary social theory are his provocative immanent criticisms of Marxism. Although Marxism was always the theory against which Marcuse measured other theories and historical events, it was for him a theory-in-process which he believed must be constantly revised, updated and reconstructed. Although he never believed that Marxism provided a body of finished truths or absolute knowledge, he did believe that it was the theory which gave the most comprehensive analysis of historical development and provided the best explanation of socio-political, and even cultural, trends while also containing a compelling vision of a better future. But Marcuse never hesitated to criticize or reconstruct Marxism, and I have argued that his writings – and the various stages of his work – can best be seen in retrospect as responses to the continuing crisis of Marxism. His early works respond to the failure of the revolutionary movements of the West to provide revolutionary socialism, and they combat the weaknesses in the theory and practice of institutional Marxism. To compensate for tendencies within Marxism towards abstract and dogmatic ideology, Marcuse called for a 'concrete philosophy'. In criticizing tendencies within Marxism towards economic reductionism and scientific determinism, Marcuse stressed the reciprocal interaction of economics, politics, culture, science and technology, and other constitutive elements within a dialectic of the social totality. Unlike dogmatic Marxists, Marcuse neither reduced socio-economic realities to epi-phenomena of economics, nor did he seek 'laws' of historical development. In view of frequent rigid Marxian class politics and 'reification of the proletariat', Marcuse called for emphasis on the importance of individual rebellion and 'catalyst groups' as factors of social change, as well as providing socialist perspectives on individual and social liberation.

Not only did Marcuse question Marxian doctrines of the proletariat as the agent of socialist revolution and capitalist collapse as its necessary condition, but he expanded significantly the Marxian problematic to take account of problems and phenomena slighted by traditional Marxism. Neglect of the individual in many versions of Marxism led Marcuse to focus on both individual needs and potentialities and to conceive of individuals as political agents of social change. He found dominant versions of Marxism lacking a cultural dimension and appropriated elements of the cultural theories of German Idealism, Romanticism and *avant-garde* modernism into his theory. In addition, he reconstructed the theories of Schiller and Nietzsche into Marxian theories of cultural revolution and the 'transvaluation of values'. His belief that classical Marxism lacked an adequate psychological theory and theory of sexuality drove him to use Freud to develop a Marxian social psychology. The lack of adequate theories of technology in contemporary Marxism led him to use theories of Max Weber and other contemporary critics of technology to analyse the role of 'technological rationality' in constituting contemporary society. His perceptions of changing working conditions and transformations in the status and composition of the working class in an increasingly mechanized and automated labour process showed him the need to develop new theories of industrial society and advanced capitalism. He also perceived changed conditions of everyday life and leisure, and analysed in detail the important role of consumerism and mass culture in generating needs and consciousness which reproduce advanced capitalism. Neglect within classical Marxism of the problems of women led him to feminism and the development of what he called 'socialist feminism'.

In sum, Marcuse injects a vital transfusion of imagination and creative thinking into the Marxian project. He adds a cultural dimension lacking in many versions of Marxism and a philosophical-speculative dimension that dares to conceive of and posit radical alternatives. Marcuse has thus renewed the Marxian project with ideas and speculation from traditions of progressive thought closed off to many versions of 'scientific' or 'orthodox' Marxism. His forte in theory construction was his ability to combine the themes listed above into a revitalized Marxism in original and illuminating ways. He avoided scholasticism and abstract system-building and instead constantly developed new theories of the changing conditions of contemporary society, socialist revolution, and human liberation.

Marcuse was one of the few Marxist philosophers who attempted both to unite philosophy and politics and to restore the utopian dimension of socialist thought. Most Marxists who aim at the union of theory and practice mould revolutionary theory into an instrument of practical political action. Within Marxism, Marcuse sought to resurrect the utopian moment in Marx covered over by the tradition of scientific Marxism and ignored by most orthodox Marxists. In fact, part of the crisis of Marxism has been its lack of utopian thinking and underdeveloped perspectives on socialism and liberation. For most people today in the West, existing socialist societies fail to provide an attractive form of democratic and emancipatory socialism which could be used as a model for advanced industrial societies. Unfortunately, Marxism has been dominated by uncreative and dogmatic thinking which all too frequently either reproduces the litany of the founders or engages in scientistic-empirical research, or sterile 'theoretical practice'.

It is precisely the utopian and speculative dimension of Marcuse's project that has aroused the ire of dogmatic Marxists, prosaic liberals and timid conservatives.[9] In my view, those who dismiss Marcuse's 'utopianism', or 'romanticism', not only fail to appreciate some of the more attractive features of his thought, but in addition they miss the fundamental tensions and ambiguities. Marcuse synthesizes currents within Marxism that view human liberation as the by-product of the advance of science and technology with romantic-idealist currents that portray liberation as the develop-

ment of human potentialities and the realization of individuality in a
'realm of freedom'. It is thus absurd to dismiss Marcuse as 'anti-
scientific', or a 'technophobe', since he bases his theory of liberation
on developments of science and technology which produce, he says
again and again, the material base of freedom.[10] On the other hand,
he believes that current forms of science and technology are producing obstacles to liberation and in some cases are becoming forms
of domination (see 10.2).

In a sense, Marcuse's theory can be seen as the latest phase of
'romantic anti-capitalism'.[11] Throughout his life, Marcuse's critique
of capitalism has been relentless and, however, flawed, remains one
of the most compelling aspects of his thought. But Marcuse is almost
as severe a critic of 'actually existing socialism'. Although he had
been critical of Soviet Marxism for decades, the Soviet invasion of
Czechoslovakia in 1968 and other events caused him to sharpen his
critique of Soviet Communism and of orthodox Marxism-Leninism.
Against both 'bureaucratic communism' and 'scientific Marxism',
Marcuse cites elements of Marx's own utopian and critical-
dialectical thinking. In this way he develops a contemporary form of
critical, humanistic and dialectical Marxism appropriate to the
problems and demands of the contemporary era.

There are, however, a series of tensions in Marcuse's thought
which I have attempted to analyse in this study. Although Marcuse
retains elements of quite orthodox Marxism, in other ways he is
heterodox, even heretical. Thus his thought is at once within and yet
beyond classical Marxism. Indeed, it is extremely difficult to
categorize Marcuse's thought within conventional categories, for,
as I have been arguing, he attempts to undercut traditional
dichotomies between, for instance, essentialism and historicism in
both his earlier existentialist-Marxian anthropology and later
Freudian-Marxian anthropology (see Chapters 3 and 6). These
attempts, however, are not always explicit or successful, and therefore are tensions between historicist and essentialist aspects of his
thought.

There are similar tensions in Marcuse between rationalist and
anti-rationalist, and materialist and idealist elements. At times,
Marcuse is a complete Hegelian-Marxian rationalist (see Chapters
3–5) while at other times he attempts to develop a 'new rationality'
and attacks 'repressive reason' (see Chapter 6 and 10.3). Although
he constantly defines his theory as 'materialist', he also affirms

'idealist' elements in Marx's theory and in his own version of Marxism as of vital importance for critical theory. At his best, he undercuts dichotomies between traditional rationalism and anti-rationalism, and materialism and idealism; but admittedly at times he emphasizes one element against the other, which might confuse readers trying to pin Marcuse down to traditional positions.

These theoretical ambiguities are reproduced in his ideal of liberation and in his various political perspectives on social change. Whereas there are strongly individualist elements in his ideal of liberation, there are also collectivist aspects in his emphasis on species-being, solidarity and collective praxis. Whereas Marcuse often promotes a goal of subject-object identity in his theory of liberation (e.g. *EC*, which posits liberation in terms of reconciliation of subject and object), at other times (e.g. *The Aesthetic Dimension*) he affirms the ineradicable non-identity of subject and object (see 10.4.1). Although 'authentic praxis' for Marcuse sometimes appears to be, as for Marx, non-alienated labour, in other texts Marcuse seems to advocate an ideal of gratification exemplified in sexual pleasure or play – although occasionally his ideal of liberation affirms free activity as an ideal that is beyond the dichotomies of work and play, labour and leisure (see 6.3.1). Marcuse often champions individual rebellion and the 'Great Refusal' as the road to liberation, but he also advocates more conventional political practice (e.g. revolutionary violence, mass strikes, or coalition politics), often calling for the fusion of individual-personal politics with collective action (see Chapter 9). Sometimes Marcuse's political perspectives are quite elitist, while at other times they are extremely democratic (see 9.4.2). And whereas Marcuse frequently sees technology as providing a great obstacle to liberation (e.g. *ODM*), he also sees it as a vehicle of liberation (e.g. automation, the 'new technology', etc.; see 10.2).

In this study I have attempted to elucidate these tensions and ambiguities in Marcuse's writings by showing how his positions are responses to certain historical conditions and cultural or political tendencies. I have emphasized changes and developments of his thinking in relation to the vicissitudes of contemporary history and thought. In summing up, however, it must be admitted that the tensions cited in the previous paragraphs produce a very uneasy mixture of tendencies which defy simple summary or clear-cut evaluation. Most of Marcuse's critics have erred, I believe, by failing to perceive these antinomies and have consequently presented (or dismissed!) Marcuse as, for example, a historicist or essentialist, a bleak pessimist or a starry-eyed utopian, an elitist individualist or a dogmatic Marxist, a stubborn rationalist or a blatant irrationalist. All these one-sided characterizations and criticisms fail to grasp the complex, protean nature of Marcuse's thought and the difficulties in conceptualizing it in traditional categories. This fact alone leads many to dismiss Marcuse as obscure, while others find him deep and original. Whatever one's final attitude towards Marcuse, I think that his temporary rise to the pinnacle of intellectual controversy can partly be explained by the multi-dimensionality of his thought, which provides something for everyone either to embrace enthusiastically or to criticize sharply. Thus Marcuse's widespread and contradictory attraction and repulsion can be partly attributed to the tensions and ambiguities in his thought and one-sided receptions of his work. If this is the case, then many previous superficial or failed criticisms of his work can be seen to derive from one-sided interpretations of his multi-dimensional project.

Despite the problems in his work, I believe that Marcuse is among the most important thinkers of our era. In my view, Marcuse's critique of Marxism contains the most sustained and provocative attempt in our times to rethink Marxism. His radical questioning of Marxism from within Marxism, his appropriation of the most progressive elements of the Western tradition, and his relentless criticism of the dominant forms of ideology, culture and society constitute an important legacy. Whatever the deficiencies of his thought and the problems with his revisions, Marcuse forces his readers to think, to criticize and to move beyond conventional wisdom within both dominant Marxist and anti-Marxist establishments. Many Marxists made telling criticisms of Marcuse's revisions of Marxism, and many more critics have exposed problems with his theory. But Marcuse's life-work is impressive and inspiring, as is his loyalty to the most radical elements in the Western tradition. His work, however, offers no closed system or final truths. His thought was constantly open, responsive to changing historical conditions and new historical developments. There are many, sometimes startling, transformations in his thought which are usually responses to historical changes and novelties. In conclusion, therefore, I want to suggest that it is the openness and non-dogmatic radicalism of Marcuse's project, the richness and complexity of his ideas, and the absence of any finished system, or body of clearly defined truths that can be accepted or rejected at ease, which constitute both the fascination and continuing importance of Marcuse's work; we are left with what Ernst Bloch calls an 'unfinished legacy' that demands both assimilation and transcendence.[12] Consequently, critical theory today must appropriate Marcuse's legacy and go beyond his positions, just as Marcuse himself appropriated and went beyond Marxism. For liberation and utopia are not yet.

Notes and References

Introduction

1. Reflecting on Marcuse's role in the New Left after his death, Ronald Aronson writes: 'In the 1960's Marcuse legitimized us. As we broke with the conventional authorities – the parents – all around us, no matter how minimally we understood his words, we found a message of confirmation from this caring but severe figure. *One-Dimensional Man* expressed how negative, how oppressive was this society that seemed so positive. It broke with the American end-of-ideology smugness intellectually as the Civil Rights movement broke with it politically. Marcuse gave philosophical and historical validation to our inarticulate yet explosive demand for a totally different vision. He made available to us a genuinely alternative intellectual culture, style of thought, and reservoir of ideas and writings' (from 'Herbert Marcuse. A Heritage to Build on', *Moving on* (Fall 1979) p. 10).
2. Herbert Gold, 'California Left. Mao, Marx et Marcuse!', *Saturday Evening Post*, 19 October, 1968 p. 59.
3. Paul Breines, in *Critical Interruptions*, ed. Paul Breines (New York: Herder & Herder, 1970) p. ix.
4. Marshall Berman, *Partisan Review*, XXXI (Fall 1964) p. 617.
5. On 'Marcuse as Teacher', see William Leiss, John David Ober and Erica Sherover in *The Critical Spirit*, ed. Kurt H. Wolff and Barrington Moore, Jr (Boston: Beacon Press, 1967) pp. 421–6.
6. Aptly describing Marcuse's absorption into the 1960s culture, Martin Jay writes: 'Through what the French, in a delightful phrase, call 'la drug-storisation de Marcuse', he has himself become something of a commodity. No article on the New Left is complete without a ritual mention of his name; no discussion of the 'counter culture' dares ignore his message of liberation'. See 'The Metapolitics of Utopianism', *Dissent*, vol. XVII, 4 (1970) p. 342.
7. The 'crisis of Marxism' has been analysed by various Marxist (and non-Marxist) thinkers throughout the century. See the discussion by Karl Korsch in *Karl Korsch: Revolutionary Theory*, ed. Douglas Kellner (Austin: The University of Texas Press, 1977) and the discussion of various theories of the crisis of Marxism in Alvin W. Gouldner, *The Two Marxisms* (New York: Seabury Press, 1980).

8. Alasdair MacIntyre calls Marcuse a 'pre-Marxist' thinker, while various Soviet critics, Maurice Cranston, Hans Holz and others call Marcuse 'anti-Marxist' or 'anarchist'. See Alasdair MacIntyre, *Herbert Marcuse: An Exposition and a Polemic* (New York: Viking, 1970); Robert Steigerwald, *Herbert Marcuses Dritter Weg* (Cologne: Pahl-Rugenstein, 1969); Maurice Cranston, 'Herbert Marcuse', *Encounter* 32, 3 (1969) pp. 38–50; and Hans Heinz Holz, *Utopie und Anarchismus. Zur Kritik der kritischen Theorie Herbert Marcuses* (Cologne: Pahl-Rugenstein, 1968). Morton Schoolman claims that 'Max Weber has certainly made the greatest single contribution to Marcuse's effort', claiming that Weber's works, and not Marx, were the decisive theoretical influence on Marcuse. See *The Imaginary Witness* (New York: Free Press, 1980) pp. 137 and 179ff. Throughout this work, I shall criticize such interpretations by making clear the Marxian roots, methodology, framework and political intentions of Marcuse's enterprise.

9. See Carl Schorske, *German Social Democracy 1905–1917* (New York: Harper and Row, 1972). On the Second International's schisms in the First World War, see Hartfield Krause, *USPD. Zur Geschichte der Unabhängigen Sozialdemokratische Partei Deutschlands* (Frankfurt: Suhrkamp, 1975).

10. Interview with Herbert Marcuse, 28 December 1978 in La Jolla, California.

11. Marcuse, *5L*, pp. 102–3.

12. For a similar criticism, see Jean-Paul Sartre, *Critique of Dialectical Reason* (London: New Left Books, 1975). By 'orthodox Marxism' I mean the version of Marxism dominant in the Social Democratic and later Communist parties. Orthodox Marxism, in this usage, is a political-sociological concept which refers to the version of Marxism institutionalized in a political movement, or organization, which dominates its party journals, speeches and textbooks. Such official Marxism is usually dogmatic and rigid, although orthodoxy may change in response to political exigencies. The orthodox Marxism dominant in Marcuse's early period was that of Social Democrats like Bernstein, Kautsky and Hilferding, and then Bolsheviks like Lenin and Trotsky. As Karl Korsch pointed out in 1930, these versions of Marxism shared certain premises concerning Marxism as a theory of the laws of society and history ('scientific socialism'), which often took the form of historical determinism. Moreover, orthodox Marxism generally takes the base-superstructure distinction as the key to historical materialism, often leading to economic reductionism. It places a primary emphasis on politics and economics while playing down the importance of culture, philosophy and the subjective dimension, and contains, with some exceptions, hostility towards Hegel and dialectics. See Karl Korsch, *Marxism and Philosophy* (London: New Left Books, 1970) pp. 98ff. On the critiques of orthodox Marxism by Lukács and Korsch, see, Maurice Merleau-Ponty, *Adventures of the Dialectic* (Evanston, Illinois: Northwestern University Press, 1973).

13. Herbert Marcuse, in *Men of Ideas*, ed. Bryan Magee (London: BBC Publications, 1978). The end of the interview returns to this theme:

MAGEE: I'd like to end our discussion by putting to you one or two of the criticisms most commonly made of your work. The most important of all is one that I've put to you already: that you are clinging to the thought-categories of a theory which has been falsified, namely Marxism, and that you consequently persist in seeing and describing everything as other than it is. The world you talk about simply is not the one we see around us. It exists only in your thought-structures. Is there anything more you would like to say in answer to that criticism?

MARCUSE: I do not believe that Marxian theory has been falsified. The deviation of facts from theory can be explained by the latter itself – by the internal development of its concepts.

MAGEE: If all the defects you acknowledge in Marxism do not cause you to abandon it, what would?

MARCUSE: Marxian theory would be falsified when the conflict between our ever-increasing social wealth and its destructive use were to be solved within the framework of Capitalism; when the poisoning of the life environment were to be eliminated; when capital could expand in a peaceful way; when the gap between rich and poor were being continuously reduced; when technical progress were to be made to serve the growth of human freedom – and all this, I repeat, within the framework of Capitalism.

For a similar defence of what is still valid in Marxism, see Marcuse's 'The Obsolescence of Marxism', in *Marx and the Western World*, ed. Nicholas Lobkowics (Notre Dame: University of Notre Dame Press, 1967) pp. 409–18, discussed below in 8.3.

14. The first studies of Marcuse either grossly oversimplify his thought, reduce it to an easily digestible cultural commodity, or, on the other hand, abruptly dismiss it in polemics that are often politically motivated. They include Robert Marks, *The Meaning of Marcuse* (New York: Ballantine, 1970); MacIntyre, *Herbert Marcuse: An Exposition*; and the right-wing polemic by Eliseo Vivas, *Critique of Marcuse* (New York: Delta, 1972). See the impassioned critiques of these and other early books on Marcuse by Paul Piccone in *Telos*, 3 (Spring 1969) pp. 150–8; Russell Jacoby in *Telos*, 5 (Spring 1970) pp. 188–90; and Robin Blackburn in *Telos*, 6 (Fall 1970) pp. 348–51.

15. This is true of the best late 1960s/early 1970s studies of Marcuse, such as the articles collected in Jürgen Habermas (ed.) *Antworten auf Herbert Marcuse* (Frankfurt: Suhrkamp, 1968); Holz, *Utopie und Anarchismus*; and John Fry, *Marcuse – Dilemma and Liberation* (New Jersey: Humanities Press, 1974). These works – and most of the early articles on Marcuse – focused on *One-Dimensional Man* or his defence of revolutionary violence just when Marcuse was altering his perspectives on advanced capitalism and social change. See the discussion in Chapter 9.

16. The best studies of Marcuse have focused on his relation to Freud and include Sidney Lipshires, *Herbert Marcuse: From Marx to Freud and*

Beyond (Cambridge, Massachusetts: Schenkman, 1974) and Gad Horowitz, *Repression. Basic and Surplus Repression in Psychoanalytic Theory: Freud, Reich and Marcuse* (Toronto and Buffalo: University of Toronto Press, 1977). See my annotated bibliography for further comments on the Marcuse literature.

1 Origins: Politics, Art and Philosophy

1. Herbert Marcuse, 'Lebenslauf', appended to his doctoral dissertation, *Der deutsche Kunstlerroman* (Freiburg i. Br., 1922); reprinted in *Schriften 1* (Frankfurt: Suhrkamp, 1978) p. 344 (hereafter *S1*).
2. Conversation with Herbert Marcuse, 28 December 1978, La Jolla, California; see also Sidney Lipshires, *Herbert Marcuse: From Marx to Freud and Beyond* (Cambridge, Mass.: Schenkman, 1974) p. 1. We shall see that Marcuse's interviews on his early experiences often contain contradictions and that he simply was not concerned to be overly precise because he did not think that the experiences of his youth were particularly important. Accordingly, my discussions with him concerning his early life focused on his 'road to Marx', which he agreed was of utmost importance in appraising his life and thought.
3. Conversation with Marcuse, 28 December 1978. Marcuse also told Helmut Dubiel that he had rarely actively experienced anti-semitism in Germany. See Helmut Dubiel and Leo Lowenthal, *Mitmachen wollte ich nie* (Frankfurt: Suhrkamp, 1980) pp. 27ff. Consequently, like Marx, Marcuse was never especially interested in the 'Jewish question', as were other Jewish Marxists like Max Horkheimer, Walter Benjamin and Ernst Bloch. Nonetheless, Marcuse's Jewish origins may have helped produce alienation from bourgeois society, which may help explain his sharp critiques of bourgeois society and search for an alternative model of society and culture. For a suggestive analysis of Jewish opposition to bourgeois society, see John Murray Cuddihy, *The Ordeal of Civility* (New York: Basic Books, 1974).
4. Herbert Marcuse, *The Aesthetic Dimension* (Boston: Beacon Press, 1977) p. 19.
5. Conversation with Herbert Marcuse, 26 March 1978, San Francisco, California. See also Marcuse's statements in *Revolution or Reform*, ed. and trans. A. T. Ferguson (Chicago: New University Press, 1976) pp. 57–8.
6. Conversation with Marcuse, 26 March 1978.
7. Conversation with Marcuse, 28 December 1978. On the workers' councils movement and the political situation at the time, see A. J. Ryder, *The German Revolution of 1918: A Study of German Socialism in War and Revolt* (Cambridge: Cambridge University Press, 1967) and Peter von Oertzen, *Betriebsräte in der Novemberrevolution* (Düsselfdorf: Droste, 1963). Documents describing the council's ideas and actions are found in Charles Burdick and Ralph Lutz, *The Political*

Institutions of the German Revolution (New York: Praeger, 1966); *Die Rätebewegung*, ed. Günter Hillman (Reinbeck bei Hamberg: Rowohlt, 1971); and Dieter Schneider and Rudolph Kuda, *Arbeiterräte in der Novemberrevolution* (Frankfurt: Suhrkamp, 1973). I discuss Karl Korsch and the German Revolution in my book *Karl Korsch: Revolutionary Theory.*

8. Conversation with Marcuse, 28 December 1978.

9. Although some commentators have claimed that Marcuse was a member of the Spartacus group, he explicitly denied it in a conversation with me (28 December 1978) affirming that he had indeed joined the SPD. He also denies the claim that he had joined the Independent Social Democrats (the USPD) advanced by Perry Anderson, *Considerations on Western Marxism* (London: New Left Books, 1976) p. 27, and Göran Therborn, 'The Frankfurt School', in *Western Marxism: A Critical Reader* (London: New Left Books, 1977) p. 84. On the differences between the Social Democrats (SPD), the Independent Social Democrats (USPD) and the Spartacus League, see the history of the USPD by Hartfield Krause, *USPD, Zur Geschichte der Unabhängigen Sozialdemokratische Partei Deutschlands*, On the Spartacus programme, see Rosa Luxemburg, *Selected Writings*, ed. Dick Howard (New York: Monthly Review Press, 1972).

10. See the sources in note 7.

11. Ibid., and Arthur Rosenberg, *The Birth of the German Republic* (London: Russell & Russell, 1931). On the Baverian Soviets, see Rosenberg and the documents in Hillman (ed.), *Die Rätebewegung*, pp. 54ff. and 134ff.

12. See Ryder, *The German Revolution of 1918*, and Rosenberg, *The Birth of the German Republic.*

13. Marcuse, in *Revolution or Reform?*, p. 57, and a conversation with Habermas and others, 'Theory and Politics', *Telos*, 38 (Winter 1978–9) p. 126.

14. Conversation with Henry Pachter, 11 July 1978, New York City.

15. Conversation with Marcuse, 28 December 1978. See also 'Die Salecina Gespräche', in *Gespräche mit Herbert Marcuse*, Jurgen Habermas, Silvia Bovenschen and others (Frankfurt: Surhkamp, 1978) pp. 98f.

16. Although the statement of Marcuse cited in note 18 indicates that he quit the SPD after the deaths of Luxemburg and Leibknecht in the abortive Spartacus uprising, he told me in an interview at La Jolla, California, in December 1978, that he quit the SPD before the suppression of the Spartacus uprising as a protest against the SPD policies described in the above paragraph.

17. Arthur Rosenberg, *A History of the German Republic* (New York: Russell & Russell, 1965); Ryder, *The German Revolution of 1918*; and Michael Balfour, *The Kaiser and His Times* (New York: Norton, 1972).

18. Marcuse, *Five Lectures* (Boston: Beacon Press, 1970) pp. 102–3. See note 16.

19. Conversation with Marcuse, March 1978.

20. Ibid.

21. Conversation with Marcuse, December 1978, Marcuse told me that he and his radical friends were extremely excited by the Russian Revolution and avidly followed its developments. Compare Georg Lukács, *History and Class Consciousness* (Cambridge: MIT Press, 1971) pp. xi.
22. Marcuse, *Revolution or Reform?*, pp. 57–8. It should be noted that Marcuse went to Freiburg in 1921, not in 1919 as he states in this interview; compare 'Lebenslauf' in note 1.
23. Before the recent Suhrkamp publication of his dissertation in *Schriften* 1, the only original copy was in the library at the University of Freiburg. Leo Lowenthal told me that as far as he knew, Marcuse's associates in the Institute for Social Research had never seen it and that Marcuse never really discussed it with them (conversation with Lowenthal, 22 March 1978, Berkeley, California). None of Marcuse's friends in San Diego whom I interviewed in March 1978 knew anything about it. Hence, Marcuse's dissertation, *Der deutsche Künstlerroman*, is a relatively unknown source of many of his later positions. The following discussion of the importance of Marcuse's doctoral dissertation to his later philosophy is indebted to conversations with Marcuse and Stanley Aronowitz, and to correspondence with Barry Katz and Josef Chytry.
24. Conversation with Marcuse, December 1978.
25. Marcuse cites Witkop's works throughout his dissertation. Henry Pachter remembers Witkop as a somewhat bohemian type, but rather academic, who loved neo-romantic literature (conversation in New York, 30 December 1979). Pachter also remembers that Witkop advised Jewish students not to seek academic careers because of anti-semitism. This might explain, in part, why Marcuse did not seek an academic career immediately after receiving his PhD.
26. Marcuse's dissertation was part of the revival of Hegel in Germany, whose philosophy was used to criticize and provide an alternative to the neo-Kantian and other academic philosophies dominant in Germany at the time. The 'cultural sciences' (*Geisteswissenschaften*) approach was developed by Wilhelm Dilthey, Georg Simmel, the early Lukács, and others (see note 46). On the Hegel revival of the 1920s, see Heinrich Levy, *Die Hegel-Renaissance in der deutschen Philosophie* (Charlottenburg: Heise, 1927).
27. Georg Lukács, *Soul and Form* (Cambridge: MIT Press, 1974) and *Theory of the Novel* (Cambridge: MIT Press, 1971). Lukács's importance for Marcuse and other radicalized intellectuals of his generation can hardly be exaggerated. Leo Lowenthal told me in a conversation during March 1978 how he had memorized passages of *The Theory of the Novel*, stressing its importance for himself and the 'inner circle' of the Frankfurt School. I shall analyse Lukács's influence on Marcuse throughout this study. On Lukács's importance for critical Marxism, see the articles in *Telos*, 10 (Winter 1971) and *Telos*, 11 (Spring 1972) as well as the studies by Andrew Arato and Paul Breines, *The Young Lukács and the Origins of Western Marxism* (New York: Seabury, 1979) and Andrew Feenberg, *Lukács, Marx and the Sources of Critical Theory* (Totowa, NJ: Rowman and Littlefield, 1981).
28. Lukács, *The Theory of the Novel*, pp. 41, *passim*. This experience of

alienation and the need for its overcoming was a shared theme of existentialism and Western Marxism that was central to the work of Lukács, Heidegger, Marcuse, Sartre and others.

29. Compare Marcuse *S1*, pp. 9ff, and Lukács, *The Theory of the Novel*, pp. 29–69. Both are indebted to Part III of Hegel's aesthetics (see source in note 30 and in Marcuse, *S1*, pp. 9ff).

30. Lukács, *The Theory of the Novel* and G. W. F. Hegel, *Aesthetics: Lectures on Fine Art* (New York: Oxford, 1975).

31. The theme of an authentic existence would be one of the features of Heidegger's philosophy that would attract Marcuse. See Martin Heidegger, *Being and Time* (New York: Harper and Row, 1962), discussed in the next section of this chapter and in Chapter 2.

32. Compare Hegel, *Aesthetics*; Friedrich Nietzsche, *The Birth of Tragedy* (Garden City, NY: Doubleday, 1967); and Lukács, *The Theory of the Novel*.

33. Curiously, whereas Lukács, following Hegel, posits medieval Christendom as an integrated culture (*The Theory of the Novel*, pp. 37ff), Marcuse chooses instead the Norse Viking culture, whose heroic deeds and ballads he praises in almost Nietzschean terms, *S1*, pp. 10ff.

34. Compare Lukács, *The Theory of the Novel*, pp. 40ff.

35. The word '*Befreiung*' (liberation) appears throughout *The German Artist-Novel* and is one of its main themes. Marcuse expresses great sympathy for 'liberation movements' such as *Sturm und Drang*, literary Bohemia, romanticism and other literary subcultures, previewing his later sympathy for the 'new sensibility'.

36. For those interested in German literature, I might note that Marcuse's study contains chapters covering: 'The Beginnings of the Artist-Novel' in Moritz and Heinse; Goethe; the early romantic artist-novel (Bretano, E. T. A. Hoffmann and Eichendorff); the offspring of the romantic artist-novel; the transformation of the artist-novel into the 'social tendency' novel; Gottfried Keller's *Der grüne Heinrich*; the recent turning away from historical time in the artist-novel; contemporary artist-novels analysed from the standpoint of the problem of art and life; and, in conclusion, a study of the artist-novels of Thomas Mann.

37. On the *Sturm und Drang* movement and the cultural-historical background to the period, see Hans Kohn, *The Mind of Germany* (New York: Harper & Row, 1960) and Jost Hermand, *Von Mainz nach Weimar* (Stuttgart: Metzler, 1969).

38. Marcuse, *S1*, pp. 85ff. On Romanticism, compare Lukács, 'The Romantic Philosophy of Life', *Soul and Form*, pp. 42ff; Kohn, *The Mind of Germany*; and Hermand, *Von Mainz nach Weimar*.

39. Marcuse, *S1*, pp. 174ff. On the 'Young Germany' movement, see Kohn, *The Mind of Germany*, and Hermand, *Von Mainz nach Weimar*.

40. Michael Lowy, for instance, suggests that Marcuse and Benjamin root their respective doctoral dissertations in German Romanticism; see 'Marcuse and Benjamin: The Romantic Dimension', *Telos*, 44 (Sum-

mer 1980) pp. 25–34. Lowy claims that what Benjamin and Marcuse have in common 'is not so much Jewish messianism as German Romanticism, with its nostalgia for pre-capitalist communities and its counterposing of artistic *Kultur* to prosaic bourgeois society' (p. 25). Not only is there little nostalgia for pre-capitalist communities in Marcuse's dissertation but he does not counterpose 'artistic Kultur' to 'prosaic bourgeois society'; rather, as will be shown, he calls for the integration of art and society. Moreover, Marcuse tends to be quite critical of Romanticism and is more affirmative toward German 'classicist' realist literature in his dissertation, singling out for praise Goethe, Keller and Mann. Later, a synthesis between 'Romanticism' and 'critical Marxism' will constitute a distinctive feature of Marcuse's post-1955 work and he includes both 'realist' and 'romantic' works of art in his aesthetic pantheon of 'authentic art' in his discussions of the aesthetic dimension from the 1950s to the 1970s.

41. Barry Katz is mistaken to claim that for Marcuse the artist-novel is a 'sub-type of the German *Bildungsroman*, the novel of "education" or "inner development", wherein a central character passes from innocence to mature self-consciousness as the story unfolds'. See 'New Sources of Marcuse's Aesthetics' in *New German Critique*, 17 (Spring 1979) p. 177. In fact Marcuse contrasts the *Künstlerroman* and *Bildungsroman* throughout his dissertation, arguing that the *Bildungsroman* represents an overcoming of the problematic of the *Künstlerroman* and is thus a distinct artistic type. See *S1*, pp. 12, 50, 75–8, 83–4, 217 and 230–1. On the *Bildungsroman*, see Lukács, *Theory of the Novel*. Katz's review is full of errors, mistranslations and illicit readings of Marcuse's dissertation in the language of his later work. For instance, Katz writes:

Even in a time of universal suffering and oppression, the lost values of a world at one with itself, of the immediate unity of the artistic life and the fully human life, are preserved – if in an attenuated form – in the shape of artistic subjectivity. With its evocation of the fully developed artistic personality and self-consciousness, the *Künstlerroman* thus represents both a symptom of the devaluation of the world, of a reality estranged from its own potentialities, and a concrete anticipation of the negation and transcendence of this estrangement. The alienation of the artist from an artless world, which is embodied in the *'Zwischen-zwei-Welten-stehen'* (standing between two worlds) of literary characters from Werther to Tonio Kröger, guarantees a refuge of transcendent ideals against the bad facticity of the present ... The true artist – far from the unwitting affirmations of the bourgeois artisan or the scholar-poet, both of whom are remote from the conflicts and chaos of lived experience – emerges for the first time as a specific human type, an embodiment of negation, straining against the oppressive restraints of a one-dimensional society (pp. 178 and 180).

In fact, Marcuse nowhere makes these claims in his dissertation, and rather than advocating a theory of the 'aesthetic dimension' which preserves 'lost values' and 'transcendental ideals' that contain a 'concrete anticipation of negation and transcendence of estrangement', Marcuse most favourably presents art which expresses joy in reality, which is integrated with life and is 'affirmative'. Consequently, Marcuse's 'true artist' is not the voice of negation but of affirmation in his dissertation. There is also no attempt by Marcuse to 'map out a refuge of ontological stability, resistant to the variegations of everyday existence' (Katz, pp. 187–8). If anything, Marcuse is celebrating 'variegations' and finding joy in everyday reality. Katz's errors and misreadings are too numerous to list here. Suffice it to say that although there are often uncanny anticipations of the later Marcuse in his dissertation, there are also discontinuities and tensions between the concept of art in his dissertation and his later aesthetic theory which should not be overlooked. See my review of Katz's book *Herbert Marcuse and the Art of Liberation* (London: New Left Books, 1982), in *Telos*, 56 (Summer 1983).

42. Marcuse told me in an interview in March 1978 that Keller's *Der grüne Heinrich* was his favourite artist-novel.

43. Marcuse will later see intellectuals as harbingers and catalyists of social change; see the discussion in Chapter 9.

44. Marcuse cites Feuerbach's influence on Gottfried Keller, claiming that Feuerbach's materialism liberated Keller from his previous religious views and that, thanks in part to Feuerbach, henceforth Keller possessed a 'glowing and powerful earthiness (*Diesseitigkeit*) which saw in the living reality the singular, the highest and the most beautiful, recognizing irreplaceable value in every single being ... seizing everything past and present in its wonder-full (*wundervollen*) necessity' (*S1*, p. 214). Later Marcuse would stress Feuerbach's importance for Marx, a theme discussed in Chapter 3.

45. Compare *S1*, pp. 87ff with *Reason and Revolution*, pp. 6ff. In both texts Marcuse describes attempts to restructure reality according to higher ideals and to transform into reality the ideals of the Enlightenment and progressive philosophy. In his dissertation Marcuse notes elements in the philosophies of Kant and Fichte that emphasize the ability to constitute the world and praises the French Revolution as an attempt to realize the ideals of progressive philosophies. In *Reason and Revolution*, Marcuse discusses the philosophy of Hegel and German idealism as philosophical expression of the ideals of the French Revolution (discussed in Chapter 5 below).

46. See Wilhelm Dilthey, *Das Erlebnis und die Dichtung*; the enlarged second edition (Leipzig, 1907) is cited by Marcuse. On Dilthey and his method, see Rudolf A. Makkreel, *Dilthey, Philosopher of the Human Studies* (Princeton: Princeton University Press, 1975). See also Lukács's discussion of the 'cultural sciences' methodology in his 1962 preface to *Theory of the Novel*, pp. 11ff.

47. Marcuse draws on Lukács's discussion of 'The Bourgeois Way of Life and Art for Art's Sake', in *Soul and Form*, pp. 58ff, as well as on Thomas Mann's *Reflections of an Unpolitical Person* and other sociopolitical writings.

48. This is evident in Marcuse's first published essay, 'Contributions to a Phenomenology of Historical Materialism', discussed in Chapter 2.
49. See Lukács, 'Preface', *The Theory of the Novel*, pp. 12ff.
50. Lukács, *Soul and Form*. See the studies in the anthology *Die Seele und das Leben* (Frankfurt: Suhrkamp, 1977) and Dennis Crow, 'Form and the Unification of Aesthetics and Ethics in Lukács' *Soul and Form*', *New German Critique*, 15 (Fall 1978) pp. 159ff.
51. Lukács, *History and Class Consciousness*. I shall discuss the decisive impact of this work on Marcuse's first published essays in Chapter 2.
52. Lukács, 1967 Preface, *History and Class Consciousness*, p. xxxi.
53. Interview with Marcuse, 28 December 1978.
54. Herbert Marcuse, *Schiller-Bibliographie unter Benutzung der Trämlschen Schiller Bibliothek* (Berlin: S. Martin Fraenkel, 1925). Marcuse expressed his evaluation of the Schiller bibliography to me in an interview on 26 March 1978.
55. 'Heidegger's Politics: An Interview with Herbert Marcuse by Frederich Olafson', *Graduate Faculty Philosophy Journal*, vol. 6, no. 1 (Winter 1977) p. 28.
56. Martin Heidegger, *Sein und Zeit* (Tübingen: Niemeyer, 1953); English translation, *Being and Time* (New York: Harper & Row, 1962).
57. Conversation with Marcuse, 28 December 1978.
58. See Edmund Husserl, *Ideas* (New York: Collier, 1962). Husserl's and Heidegger's philosophy and its appropriation and criticism by the young Marcuse will be discussed in Chapter 2.
59. Husserl, *Ideas*.
60. Heidegger, *Sein und Zeit*.
61. The reception of Heidegger's philosophy is discussed in my doctoral dissertation *Heidegger's Concept of Authenticity* (Columbia University, 1973). Debates over Heidegger's philosophy will be discussed in Chapter 2.
62. Herbert Marcuse, letter to Maximillian Beck and his wife, 9 May 1929. Beck was the editor of *Philosophische Hefte*, the journal that published Marcuse's first essay, which we shall examine in the next chapter. The Becks were personal friends of Marcuse and also of his wife Sophie. I would like to thank Professors Herbert Spiegelberg and William McBride for making a copy of this letter available to me.
63. Marcuse interview, 'Heidegger's Politics', pp. 28–9.
64. Walter Benjamin, letter to Scholem, 25 April 1930. Cited in *Brecht Chronicle*, compiled by Klaus Volker (New York: Seabury, 1975) p. 56. Henry Pachter told me that P. Dubislaw, a friend of Karl Korsch, referred to Heidegger's philosophy at the time as 'Quatschosophie' and that the term was frequently used to label Heidegger's philosophy in Korsch's circle (conversation in New York, 11 July 1978).
65. For some contemporary interpretations and controversies see *Heidegger and Modern Philosophy*, ed. Michael Murray (New Haven: Yale University Press, 1978).
66. See Marcuse's conversation with Habermas and others, 'Theory and Politics', pp. 125ff for discussion of this issue, which will be a major theme in the next two chapters.
67. Marcuse, 'Heidegger's Politics', p. 28.
68. Ibid.

69. On the elevated concepts of art in Benjamin, Bloch and the early Lukács, see Richard Wolin, 'Notes on the Early Aesthetics of Lukács, Bloch and Benjamin', *Berkeley Journal of Sociology*, vol. XXVI (1981) pp. 89–110. Wolin shows that these thinkers responded to the 'crisis of modernity' with programmes of cultural renewal which ascribed important roles to art. The three thinkers all developed epistemologies, Wolin argues, which would privilege art as a source of critical truth. Later, in *Eros and Civilization*, Marcuse would himself take up this position in his own way, but for several decades he tended to present philosophy and social theory as fundamental sources of critical knowledge. Thus Marcuse has a more affirmative relation to philosophy and social theory than other neo-Marxists at the time.

2 Phenomenological Marxism?

1. Marcuse's article, 'Beiträge zu einer Phänomenologie des Historischen Materialismus', appeared in *Philosophische Hefte*, I (Berlin: 1928) pp. 43–68 – a journal edited by his friend Maximillian Beck which was oriented toward phenomenology and German Idealism, but which occasionally published articles on Marxism. The article has been reprinted in the first volume of Marcuse's collected works, *Schriften* I (Frankfurt: Suhrkamp, 1978) pp. 347–84. Page references will refer first to the *Philosophische Hefte* original publication and then to the *Schriften* edition (hereafter *S1*); translations are my own. A translation appeared in *Telos*, 4 (Fall 1969), but it is so bad – especially in its bizarre rendering of Heidegger's terminology – that I cannot recommend its use.
2. On 'critical Marxism' and its differences from 'scientific Marxism', see Alvin W. Gouldner, *The Two Marxisms* (New York: Seabury, 1980) and my review in *Theory and Society*, vol. 10, no. 2 (March 1981) pp. 265–78. 'Existential' and 'phenomenological' Marxisms were developed by Sartre and Merleau-Ponty in France after the Second World War. The project was influenced by French interpretations of Hegel and the early Marx shaped by Heideggerian and Sartrean existentialism. See Paul Piccone, 'Phenomenological Marxism', *Telos*, 9 (Fall 1971) and Mark Poster, *Existential Marxism in Postwar France* (Princeton: Princeton University Press, 1975). Whether existentialism, phenomenology and Marxism are or are not compatible is debated in the anthology *Existentialism versus Marxism*, ed. George Novack (New York: Delta, 1966).
3. Johann Arnason, *Von Marcuse zu Marx* (Neuwied: Luchterhand, 1971) p. 7.
4. Piccone, 'Phenomenological Marxism', p. 11.
5. Pier Rovatti, 'Critical Theory and Phenomenology', *Telos*, 15 (Spring 1973) p. 36.

6. Marcuse, 'Contributions', p. 45 (*S1*, p. 347). This definition of Marxism is taken almost verbatim from Lukács's book on *Lenin* (Cambridge: MIT Press, 1969).
7. In 1923 Lukács, in *History and Class Consciousness* (Cambridge: MIT Press, 1971) and Korsch, in *Marxism and Philosophy* (London: New Left Books, 1970) published works that stressed the importance of subjective factors in the Marxian theory of revolution against dominant objectivistic-economistic versions of Marxism, which saw the role of Marxian theory as formulating 'objective' scientific laws rooted in the economy that would inevitably lead to the triumph of socialism. Against 'scientific socialism', Lukács and Korsch rehabilitated Hegelian dialectics, stressing subject-object interaction, contradictions and mediations, and the role of the subject. Marcuse was to share their evaluation of the importance of the Hegelian roots of Marxism and their radical-activistic interpretation, believing at the time that Lukács and Korsch were the foremost interpreters of the radical and progressive elements of the Marxian theory (interview with Marcuse, 28 December 1978). Marcuse notes the importance of Lukács's *History and Class Consciousness* in a 1930 essay, 'Zum Problem der Dialetik', first published in *Die Gesellschaft*, vol. VII, 1930; reprinted in *S1*, pp. 407ff and translated in *Telos*, 27 (Spring 1976) pp. 12ff. He reviews Korsch's *Marxism and Philosophy* in 'Das Problem der geschichtlichen Wirklichkeit' (*Die Gesellschaft*, vol. 8, 1931, reprinted in *S1*, pp. 469ff. On Lukács, see the books cited in Chapter 1, note 27 and note 16 below. On Korsch, see the articles in *Telos*, 26 (Winter 1975–6) and my book *Karl Korsch*.
8. Marcuse, 'Contributions', p. 45; *S1*, p. 347.
9. Ibid.
10. Lukács, *History and Class Consciousness*. At this point in his career, Marcuse has not yet begun his critique of science and technology, a concern he will later share with the early Lukács, the late Husserl, Heidegger, Adorno and Horkheimer, and others – a critique that is a defining characteristic of the current of 'critical Marxism' (see Gouldner, *The Two Marxisms*). On the tendency in the early Lukács to equate science with reification, see Gareth Stedman Jones, 'The Marxism of the Early Lukács', *New Left Review*, 70 (November–December, 1971) and the critique of Jones in Feenberg, *Lukács, Marx and the Sources of Critical Theory*, pp. 208ff and 274ff.
11. Marcuse, 'Contributions', p. 47; *S1*, p. 350.
12. Marcuse, 'Contributions', p. 47; *S1*, p. 350. Marcuse is quoting Marx in *The German Ideology* here.
13. Ibid.
14. Ibid.
15. Lukács, *History and Class Consciousness*. During a conversion in La Jolla, California, 28 December 1978, Marcuse stressed the importance of *History and Class Consciousness* for developing Marxism and noted its impact in his own thought. Marcuse also said that he believed that Lukács and Korsch were the 'most intelligent' Marxists to write after the deaths of Luxemburg and Leibknecht, and that in his 1930s work

with the Frankfurt Institute for Social Research, he took a more favourable position toward *History and Class Consciousness* than Horkheimer and his other colleagues. Morton Schoolman's claim that Lukács's theory of reification had no impact on Marcuse's thought at the time, and his suggestion that Marcuse was consciously combating the Lukácsian theory of reification is without foundation. See *The Imaginary Witness*, pp. 5ff and 134ff. I shall cite some central Lukácsian passages in Marcuse's second published essay in section 2.3, and my discussion of *One-Dimensional Man* in Chapter 9 will indicate how Marcuse returns to Lukács's problematic in his later works.

16. Lukács, *History and Class Consciousness*, especially the chapter 'Reification and the Consciousness of the Proletariat'. On Lukács's theory of reification see Arato and Breines, *The Young Lukács*; Stefan Breuer, *Die Krise der Revolutionstheorie* (Frankfurt: Syndikat, 1977); Feenberg, *Lukács, Marx*; and Lucien Goldman, *Lukács and Heidegger*.

17. See T. W. Adorno and Max Horkheimer, *Dialectic of Enlightenment* (New York: Seabury, 1972); Max Horkheimer, *Eclipse of Reason* (New York: Seabury, 1974); Marcuse, *One-Dimensional Man* (Boston: Beacon Press, 1974); and Jürgen Habermas, *Knowledge and Human Interests* (Boston: Beacon Press, 1971), and 'Science and Technology as "Ideology"', in *Toward a Rational Society* (Boston: Beacon Press, 1970).

18. Marcuse, 'Contributions', pp. 47ff; *S1*, pp. 350ff.

19. Marcuse, conversation in La Jolla, 28 December 1978.

20. Marcuse criticizes Lukács's theory of class-consciousness as the weak point in his analysis, within the context of a defence of the importance of Lukács's work, in 'On the Problem of the Dialectic', *Telos*, 27, p. 24. The translation, though, falsely reads that the significance of *History and Class Consciousness* is 'not to be overestimated', whereas instead Marcuse's German text suggests that its importance 'cannot be overestimated'.

21. Marcuse, 'Contributions', p. 47; *S1*, p. 351. The Marx quote is from his early 'Introduction to the Critique of Hegel's Philosophy of Right' in Marx and Engels, *Collected Works*, vol. 3 (New York: International Publishers, 1975) p. 182.

22. Marcuse, 'Contributions', p. 48; *S1*, p. 351. The Marx quote here is from *Theses on Feuerbach*, Number 7, which Marx repeats in *The German Ideology* in his definition of revolutionary practice. This notion is crucial to Marcuse's position that radical action alters at once social conditions and human nature.

23. Marcuse, 'Contributions', p. 48; *S1*, p. 351.

24. The question can be raised concerning whether this etymological play on *Not-wendig* is tenable in view of the aura of mechanical determinism around the concept of historical necessity. I note, however, Marcuse's critique of 'objectivistic Marxism' below.

25. See the critiques of Marxian 'objectivism' and 'determinism' by Karl Korsch in *Marxism and Philosophy*, and *Karl Korsch*, as well as the discussion by Russell Jacoby, 'Toward a Critique of Automatic Marxism', *Telos*, 10.

26. Marcuse, 'Contributions', p. 48; *S1*, pp. 352ff.
27. Marcuse, 'Transcendental Marxism', *Die Gellschaft*, VIII (1931) reprinted in *Schriften* 1, p. 467.
28. Marcuse, 'Contributions', p. 51; *S1*, pp. 356–7.
29. Although there are tensions in Marcuse's early writings between Heideggerian individualist perspectives and Marxian class perspectives, I would argue, against Morton Schoolman, that Marcuse does not in his early essays abandon notions of class struggle for emphasis on the 'discontented, doubting, disaffected and ambivalent individual' as the subject of revolutionary action (see Schoolman, The Imaginary Witness, pp. 10ff, 79, *passim*). Instead, I believe that Marcuse tries to merge notions of individual and class struggle in his concept of radical action. The passage just cited indicates that Marcuse accepts at this point Marxian theories of the proletariat as the authentic subject of radical action, but is already beginning to doubt whether the proletariat will carry through its mission in view of the 'botched-up revolutionary situations' of the recent past. Later, of course, the distinctive feature of Marcuse's revision of Marxian will be his radical questioning of the proletariat as the subject of revolution.
30. Marcuse, 'Contributions', p. 51; *S1*, pp. 356–7.
31. Marcuse's critics have argued that Marcuse is actually much closer to Heidegger at this point than to Marx, and that the deficiencies in his early work are due to a domination of his thinking by a Heideggerian anthropological-ontological perspective – a perspective that some critics claim is basic to his later work as well. The orthodox Marxist-Leninist Robert Steigerwald, in his highly critical *Herbert Marcuses 'dritter Weg'*, argues that Marcuse's early writings constitute a dialogue with Marx from the standpoint of Heideggerian existentialism 'which has nothing to do' with genuine Marxism (p. 49) and that 'Marcuse's system is through and through subjective idealism' (p. 111). This claim contradicts Steigerwald's own argument that Marcuse's philosophical project is an attempt to discover a 'third way' between Marxism and bourgeois philosophy and fails to articulate the Marxian elements operative in Marcuse's early philosophy.

Alfred Schmidt, in an essay on Heidegger and Marcuse, argues that Marcuse's writings from 1929–3 'appropriated the Marxist teaching within the horizon of Heidegger's *Being and Time*'; See 'Existential-Ontologie und historischer Materialismus bei Herbert Marcuse', in *Antworten auf Herbet Marcuse*, ed. Jürgen Habermas (Frankfurt: Surhrkamp, 1968) p. 19. This picture of Marcuse as a Heideggerian appropriating Marxism into an 'existentialist' perspective is quite dubious for, as I shall try to show in the following pages, Marcuse carries out a Marxist appropriation and critique of Heidegger's *Being and Time*; thus Habermas's remark that Marcuse was the first Heideggerian Marxist comes closer to characterizing accurately Marcuse's blend of Marx and Heidegger in his early writings. See Jürgen Habermas, *Theorie und Praxis* (Berlin und Neuwied: Luchterhand, 1963) p. 330. In an article on 'Herbert Marcuse's Heideggerian Marxism', *Telos*, 6 (Fall 1970), Paul Piccone and Alex Delfini argue that 'Marcuse in 1928 ... is fundamentally the same Marcuse of 1970' (p. 39) and that his 'late work is fundamentally Heideggerian in character' (p. 44). I shall try in this chapter to show that even Marcuse's early work is fundamentally Marxist, and not 'Heideggerian', and shall argue later that although Heideggerian elements appear in some of Marcuse's later works, his fundamental project is the reconstruction of Marxism – a project that takes a variety of forms in a corpus marked by a series of vicissitudes and ruptures.

32. Marcuse, 'Contributions', p. 52; *S1*, p. 358.

33. On the importance of overcoming the subject–object dichotomy and the similarity between Heidegger and Lukács, see Goldman, *Heidegger and Lukács*, and for Marx's and Lukács' attempt to shatter the subject–object conceptual framework, see Feenberg, *Lukács, Marx and the Sources of Critical Theory*. This rejection of the dominant philosophical framework in the Western philosophical tradition is a distinguishing feature of 'critical Marxism', or the 'philosophy of praxis'.

34. Martin Heidegger, *Being and Time*, pp. 126–30 and pp. 175–90. Heidegger's concept of authenticity, which is the crucial concept for Marcuse's appropriation of Heidegger, see my 1973 PhD dissertation, *Heidegger's Concept of Authenticity*. Heidegger's analysis of fallenness and inauthenticity can be compared with Lukács's analysis of alienation and reification in *History and Class Consciousness*, pp. 83–110. Both deplored tendencies that 'reified' human beings into 'things'. Lucien Goldmann sees *Sein und Zeit* as 'a confrontation with Lukács' work: the answer is polemic with it from a standpoint of anxiety and death', accomplished by transposing Lukács's analysis 'on a metaphysical level by modifying the terminology, without ever mentioning Lukács'. *Mensch, Gemeinschaft und Welt in der Philosophie Immanual Kants* (Zurich: 1945) p. 244, and his posthumously published *Lukács and Heidegger*. Marcuse is sceptical on this point, believing that Heidegger had not read either Marx or Lukács at the time (see 1.3) and in fact Heidegger usually puts the term 'reification' in quotation marks, as if he was not happy with the term and preferred his own concepts of inauthenticity, fallenness and *das Man*. Moreover, the crucial difference is that whereas Heidegger sees reification and alienation as ontological constituents of human beings in all societies, Lukács see them as historically specific features of a capitalist society that can be removed by social practice. Although Marcuse would generally take this view, there are overtones in his early essays of Heidegger's ontologizing of alienation (see my discussion of his essay on labour in the last part of Chapter 3).

35. See the second part of my PhD dissertation, *Heidegger's Concept of Authenticity*, dealing with 'Extrication and Individuation' for a discussion of Heidegger's doctrine. For a critique of Heidegger's doctrine of authentic existence see my review of Adorno's *Jargon of Authenticity*, in *Telos*, 19 (Spring 1974) pp. 184–92.

36. Marcuse, 'Contributions', p. 54; *S1*, p. 361. This dialectical negation is twofold in that the disavowal (*Widerruf*) applies not only to past

possibilities for authentic action which are creatively re-covered and repeated, but also applies to past possibilities (ideas, institutions, social-economic-political forms of life) which repressively and irrationally dominate today and so should be negated to make possible historical development and to liberate authentic historical possibilities from the chains of the past. On this basis I believe that Steigerwald makes a grave error when he identifies the Heideggerian-Marcusian notion of *Widerruf* with the attitude of total rejection of the past, as if *Widerruf* signified a total negation or annulment, 'in which the past is to be obliterated, annihilated, cancelled out' (Steigerwald, *Herbet Marcuses 'dritter Weg'*, p. 60). It is essential to see that for Heidegger and Marcuse *Widerruf* and *Erwiderung* are part of a project of *Wiederholung*, which signifies a recovering, retrieving and repeating of past possibilities for authentic existence chosen from the heritage, and thus in no way signifies a total rejection of the heritage, as some Nazi philosophers proclaimed in their notion of *Widerruf*, which Steigerwald tries erroneously to identify with Marcuse's concept. Rather, *Widerruf* is the moment of negation in the project of repetition in which one criticizes and rejects that which in one's tradition and historical situation is obsolete and constrictive of more liberating possibilities.

37. Sartre, *Critique*.
38. Marcuse, 'Contributions', p. 58; *S1*, p. 367.
39. A set of similarities between Heidegger and Marx was worked out by Maxmillian Beck in an article just preceding Marcuse's 'Contributions' in the same philosophical journal. See 'Referat und Kritik von Martin Heidegger's "Sein und Zeit"', *Philosophische Hefte* I (Berlin: 1928) pp. 9–10. Interestingly, Beck was one of the philosphers later supported by the Frankfurt School during their exile period. Both Marcuse and Beck, however, were mistaken in seeing any profound similarities between Marx and Heidegger, a point Marcuse would later clearly see and constantly emphasize. He stressed this to me in conversation in San Francisco on 26 March 1978, and I heard him make the same point in discussion with philosophy students at Columbia University in 1968 and 1972, where he took the position that there was little in Heidegger's philosophy that was not conformist.
40. Marcuse, 'Contributions', p. 55; *S1*, pp. 362–3.
41. Ibid., pp. 55–6; *S1*, pp. 363–4.
42. Ibid., p. 56; *S1*, p. 364.
43. Ibid.
44. These remarks of Heidegger are quoted by Karl Löwith, who published excerpts from letters by Heidegger to him, which he received in the 1920s when Heidegger was working on *Sein und Zeit*, in an article, 'Les implications politiques de la philosophie de l'existence chez Heidegger', *Les Temps Modernes* (November 1946). Löwith's article is valuable in its discussion of the intellectual milieu around Heidegger, and provides some hitherto unrevealed views of Heidegger on a variety of topics.
45. Löwith, 'Political Implications of Heidegger', p. 346.

46. Ibid., pp. 345–8.
47. In *Being and Time,* p. 298, Heidegger writes, 'On what is one to resolve? Only the resolution itself can give the answer . . . To resoluteness, the *indefiniteness* characteristic of every potentiality-for-being into which *Dasein* has been factically thrown, is something that necessarily *belongs.* Only in a resolution is resoluteness sure of itself'.
48. The story of Heidegger's support for Hitler and the Nazis in 1932–3, his assumption of the Rectorship of the University of Freiburg in 1933, his resignation in 1934, and his muted criticism of National Socialism during the rest of the war is told by Löwith in the article referred to in note 44 and in an unpublished PhD dissertation by Karl Moehling, *Martin Heidegger and the Nazi Party* (Northern Illinois University, 1972), some of which is summarized in his article 'Heidegger and the Nazis', *Listening,* 12 (1977) pp. 92–105. The issue of Heidegger's relation to the Nazis, and the relationship between Heidegger's philosophy and fascism, has elicited spirited discussion. After Löwith's rather harsh critique of Heidegger in *Les Temps Modernes* in 1947, and his claims concerning the affinity of Heidegger's philosophy and personality with fascism, defences of Heidegger appeared in the November 1947 issue of *Les Temps Modernes.* In Germany, the issue of Heidegger's politics was subject to much bitter polemic, discussed in the French journal *Critique* (November 1966), in an article by Beda Alleman in *Heidegger,* ed. Otto Pöggeler (Köln: 1969) and in Pöggeler's book *Philosophie und Politik bei Heidegger* (Freiburg: Karl Alber, 1972). In the USA Heidegger was severely criticized by, among others, Walter Kaufmann, in *From Shakespeare to Existentialism* (Garden City: Doubleday, 1960) and was defended by, among others, Hannah Arendt, who was a Heidegger student when Marcuse was working with Heidegger. Arendt minimized Heidegger's complicity with Nazism, stressing his criticism of the regime from 1934 until the collapse of fascism (see 'Martin Heidegger at Eighty', in *Heidegger and Modern Philosphy*). Two recent studies which stress the affinity between Heidegger's philosophy and his support of fascism are Karsten Harries, 'Heidegger as a Political Thinker', in *Heidegger and Modern Philosophy*, and Stephen Eric Bronner, 'Martin Heidegger: The Consequences of Political Mystification', *Salmagundi* 38/9 (Summer/Fall 1977). For Marcuse's position on Heidegger and fascism, see the interview with Frederick Olafson, 'Heidegger's Politics'.
49. On Heidegger's nihilism see the article by Bronner, 'Martin Heidegger', and Stanley Rosen, *Nihilism* (New Haven: Yale, 1973).
50. Marcuse, 'Contributions', p. 61; *S1*, p. 373.
51. Ibid., p. 65; *S1*, pp. 378–9. 'Historicity' in Heidegger's theory refers to the basic structures of historical existence; see *Being and Time,* pp. 424ff. Both Heidegger and Marcuse conceive of 'historicity' as a fundamental structure of human existence: all human activities and creations are 'historical' and are therefore constituted by 'historicity'. Historicity is the central category of Marcuse's early 1928–33 essays, and as the passage just quoted indicates, he takes the Heideggerian

ontological category of 'historicity' and gives it a Marxian foundation with categories such as mode of production, needs, class struggle, etc. Morton Schoolman is wrong, however, in explicating 'historicity' in terms of 'factors that predispose the individual to action . . . Historicity pertains to factors that determine radical action', in *The Imaginary Witness*, pp. 8–9. Strictly speaking, historicity encompasses all features of human being – radical or not – and Schoolman seems to collapse the concept of historicity into Heidegger's concept of authenticity which does, in Marcuse's view, indicate factors that dispose the individual to radical action (anxiety, being towards death, the call of conscience, etc.). Hence historicity is an ontological category that refers to the historical constitutents of existence, encompassing all human behaviour and productions, and is not a privileged signifier for the conditions that produce 'authentic individuality' as it is for Schoolman (see his discussion, pp. 27 and 35). I shall discuss Marcuse's concept of historicity further in section 3.2, and will indicate in section 4.1 why he dropped the term in his work with the Institute for Social Research.

52. Ibid. A Marxist reinterpretation of Heideggerian notions of care (*Sorge*) and practical concern (*Besorgen*) is carried out by Karel Kosik in *Dialectics of the Concrete* (Boston: Reidel, 1976).

53. For a later development of this claim, see Gunther Stern, 'The Pseudo-concreteness of Heidegger's Philosophy', *Philosophy and Phenomenological Research*, VIII, no. 3 (March 1948) pp. 337–71.

54. On 'existential' and 'phenomenological' Marxism, see the sources in note 2 of this chapter. A more strictly theoretical, de-existentialized attempt to combine phenomenology and Marxism is found in Tran Duc Thao's *Phenomenologie et Materialisme Dialectique* (Paris: Vrin, 1951). Thao was allegedly on the central committee of the Vietnamese Communist Party in the 1970s and is probably free of his infatuation with Husserl. An Italian effort to bind together phenomenology and Marxism is found in Enzo Paci's *The Function of the Human Sciences and the Meaning of Man* (Evanston: Northwestern, 1972). Since Marcuse's early essays were generally unknown, I should stress that he anticipated this trend rather than directly influenced it. Later he would reject attempts to synthesize phenomenology and dialectics, or existentialism and Marxism – a position he would take from his work with the Institute for Social Research to the end of his life. It is possible that conversations with Adorno might have cured him of his fondness for phenomenology; indeed, Adorno has written what to this day remains the most withering attack on phenomenology – see T. W. Adorno, *Zur Metakritik der Erkenntnistheorie* (Frankfurt: Suhrkamp, 1970).

55. Marcuse, 'Contributions', p. 57; *S1*, p. 366.

56. Engels, 'Ludwig Feuerbach', cited in 'Contributions', p. 57; *S1*, pp. 366–7.

57. Lenin, 'The fight for social revolution', cited in 'Contributions', p. 57–8; *S1*, p. 367.

58. Marcuse, 'Contributions', p. 58; *S1*, p. 368.

59. Ibid. A classical presentation of the phenomenological method is found in Edmund Husserl, *Ideas* (New York: Collier Books, 1962).
60. Ibid., p. 59; *S1*, p. 369.
61. Ibid.
62. Ibid.
63. Ibid.
64. Marcuse carries out a similar critique of the phenomenological reduction in 'Über konkrete Philosophie'. *Archiv fur Sozialwissenschaft*, 62 (1929) pp. 115–16 (reprinted in *Scriften 1*, pp. 385–406), and criticizes the limitations of the phenomenological method in 'On the Problem of Dialectics', pp. 19ff; 'The Concept of Essence' in *Negations*; and a later essay 'On Science and Phenomenology', in Robert Cohen and Marx W. Wartofsky, eds, *Boston Studies in the Philosphy of Science*, II (1965) pp. 279–91.
65. The relations and differences between Husserl, Heidegger and other phenomenologists are analysed in Herbert Spiegelberg, *The Phenomenological Movement* (The Hague: Martinus Nijhoff, 1960).
66. This is clear in Husserl's treatment of values as eternal essences and in Max Scheler's phenomenological theory of the intuition of values. On Husserl's phenomenological ethics, see A. Roth, *Edmund Husserls ethische Untersuchungen* (The Hague: Martinus Nijhoff, 1960) and Marvin Farber, *Phenomenology and Existence* (New York: Harper & Row, 1967). There may be other ways for a phenomenologist to handle the problems of ethics, but the most important representatives of the phenomenological tendency have yet to deal satisfactorily with ethical thematics. Heidegger and Sartre, for example, have programmatically excluded the problems of ethics from their major phenomenological works, although ethical concerns are found throughout and call for clarification and development. See my dissertation, *Heidegger's Concept of Authenticity*, on this topic.
67. Marcuse, 'Contributions', p. 59; *S1*, p. 370.
68. Ibid.
69. Marcuse, 'Contributions', p. 60; *S1*, p. 370.
70. Ibid.
71. Ibid.
72. Ibid.
73. Marcuse was one of the first to use material in the recently published *German Ideology* in a philosophical problematic that conceptualizes the basic structures of history, society and human nature. His appropriation of historical materialism provided him with a philosophical apparatus that would eventually enable him to reject phenomenology and existentialism and to develop his philosophy and social theory within Marxism. This transition takes place in Marcuse's work with the Institute for Social Research, which we shall examine in Chapter 4.
74. Interview with Marcuse, 28 December 1978.
75. See the references in notes 7 and 26.
76. Some of Max Adler's texts have been translated in *Austro-Marxism*,

ed. and trans. Tom Bottomore and Patrick Goode (New York: Oxford, 1978).

77. Many members of the Vienna Circle considered themselves both socialists and positivists, and discerned a compatibility with Marxism. For a recent attempt to defend positivist-materialist elements of Marxism, see Sebastiano Timpanaro, *On Materialism* (London: New Left Books, 1976).

78. I should mention that Marx's 1844 *Economic-Philosophical Manuscripts* had not been published when Marcuse wrote his first essays. In fact, he wrote one of the first and best reviews of the *Manuscripts* when they were first published in 1932, and henceforth would utilize the early Marx to secure the basic presuppositions of his theory, and would no longer rely on Heidegger's anthropology or phenomenology. The importance of Marx's 1844 *Manuscripts* for Marcuse's project and his review of them will be discussed in Chapter 3, section 3.3.

79. Marcuse, 'Zur Wahrheitsproblematik der soziologischen Methode', *Die Gesellschaft*, VI (1929); reprinted in Adorno, Horkheimer, Marcuse, *Kritische Theorie der Gesellschaft*, Bd IV, (no date) pp. 338–9.

80. Karl Mannheim, *Ideology and Utopia* (New York: Harcourt, Brace & World, 1936). On the reception of Mannheim's book, see Volker Meja, 'The Controversy about the Sociology of Knowledge in Germany', *Cultural Hermeneutics*, 3 (1975). On Mannheim and the Frankfurt School, see Martin Jay, 'The Frankfurt Critique of Mannheim', *Telos*, 20 (Summer 1974) and exchanges between James Schmidt in *Telos*, 21 (Fall 1974) and Jay in *Telos*, 22 (Winter 1974–5).

81. Marcuse, 'Contributions', pp. 63–4; *S1*, p. 376.

82. That Marx did not advocate this crude materialism, which has dominated Soviet Marxism to the present day and was maintained by Kautsky and other leading Marxists at the time of Marcuse's early writing, is clear from an examination of Marx's early writings, which will be discussed in Chapter 3. See also Alfred Schmidt, *Marx's Concept of Nature* (London: New Left Books, 1976).

83. Marcuse, 'Contributions', p. 65; *S1*, p. 379.

84. Lukács was later to repudiate his rejection of materialism; see the 1967 preface to the re-edition of *History and Class Consciousness*. Sartre's critique of philosophical materialism is found in the essay, 'Materialism and Revolution', and his later quasi-Marxian work, *The Critique of Dialectical Reason.*

85. Engels maintained in his 'Lugwig Feuerbach' essay, quoted by Marcuse, that the 'basic question of all philosophy' concerned the relation between thought and being – hence the choice between idealism and materialism – claiming that Marxism resolutely opted for philosophical materialism, and holding that being and nature were primary and that spirit and thought were secondary and derivative; thus consciousness, on this analysis, is a 'product, function and derivation of matter'. Lenin, Bukharin, Stalin, Kautsky and other prominent Marxists followed this line, which became a pillar of orthodox Marxism. See Karl Korsch, *Marxism and Philosophy.*

86. See Gustav Wetter, *Sowjet Ideologie Heute* (Frankfurt: Fisher, 1962) pp. 24–67; the collective work *Marxist Philosophy* (Moscow: Progress Publishers, 1968) pp. 9–13, 53–83; and R. O. Gropp, *Grundlagen des dialektischen Materialismus* (Berlin: VEB Verlag, 1970) pp. 17–21, 35–78. The orthodox Marxist Steigerwald follows this line in attacking Marcuse for his 'deviation' from philosophical materialism, *Herbert Marcuses 'dritter Weg'*, pp. 62–75.

87. Marx stressed, especially in his early writings, the development of the many-sided individual as the goal of socialism; see the discussion in Chapter 3. Once Marcuse broke with Heidegger, he was increasingly to stress the importance of the *Marxian* theme of the emancipation and development of the individual.

88. Marcuse, 'Über konkrete Philosophie'. Page references will refer first to the original *Archiv* pagination and then to the *Schriften 1* reprint.

89. This is the young Marx's sense of 'radical'; see Marx and Engels, *Collected Works*, vol. 3 (New York: International Publishers, 1975) p. 182. I might note that a major theme of twentieth-century philosphy is a dissatisfaction with the abstractions of the traditional philosophers, which had degenerated into 'school philosophies', rigid and academic systems of categories. Against these scholasticisms, Dilthey and *Lebensphilosophie* sought the concrete in a 'philosophy of life' based on Nietzsche's 'will to power' and Bergson's theory of *élan vital* and *durée*. Husserl sought a new concrete philosophy in his phenomenological turn to the things themselves; Heidegger sought concreteness in his turn to 'being-in-the-world' as the starting point of philosophy and in his concern for everyday life, the individual, death, anxiety and the like; Sartre and Merleau-Ponty would seek the concrete in the realm of consciousness and experience, in art, in the body, sexuality, revolt, struggle and history. American philosophers, like James and Dewey, would seek the concrete in experience, nature, art and religion. English philosophers, dissatisfied with the abstractions of the old Idealism, as well as logical atomism and positivism, would turn to a study of ordinary language and common experience. Hence, every major school of philosophy had its own concept of the 'concrete', which has come to signal a claim to primordiality, authenticity, the really real, etc. in its different usages. Marcuse's lust for the concrete was thus rooted in a fundamental drive of twentieth-century philosphy for a new philosophy that would finally satisfy the drive for concrete reality prevalent in those who were dissatisfied with the moribund systems of the classical philosophers, in which once living philosophies had degenerated into abstractions to be memorized, rehearsed and reproduced in class-rooms and journals. On the search for the concrete, compare Stefan Breuer, *Die Krise der Revolutionstheorie* (Frankfurt: Syndikat, 1977) pp. 20ff, and the amusing anticipation of this problematic by Hegel, 'Who Thinks Abstractly?' in Walter Kaufmann, *Hegel* (Garden City: Doubleday, 1968).

90. Marcuse, *Über konkrete Philosphie*, p. 119; *S1*, p. 395.

91. Ibid.

92. Ibid., pp. 118–19; *S1*, p. 344.
93. Ibid., p. 123; *S1*, p. 400.
94. See Walter Lowrie, *Kierkegaard* (London: Oxford University Press, 1938) and Josiah Thompson, *The Lonely Labyrinth* (Carbondale: Southern Illinois University Press, 1967).
95. Marcuse, *Über konkrete Philosophie*, p. 124; *S1*, pp. 401–2.
96. Ibid., p. 125; *S1*, p. 403.
97. Ibid., p. 126; *S1*, p. 403.
98. Ibid., p. 127; *S1*, p. 405.

3 Studies in the Marxian Philosophy

1. It is necessary to write a *'Habilitations-Dissertation'* in Germany, which must be accepted by the philosophy faculty and must then be published, in order to be promoted to a tenured position at a German university. Marcuse chose to work under Heidegger and published his dissertation on completing it, although it was never formally accepted by Heidegger. See Herbert Marcuse, *Hegels Ontologie und die Grundlegung einer Theorie der Geschichtlichkeit* (Frankfurt: Klostermann, 1932; new edition 1968, to which pagination will refer; hereafter, *Hegel's Ontology*). Seyla Benhabib is working on a translation of the text for the MIT series on German philosophy and social theory.

2. In *Being and Time*, Heidegger talks of the 'ontological mystery of movement' and the difficulty in characterizing movement, change and development with the categories of ontology. Marcuse probably felt that the more dynamic and historical categories of Hegel and Marx could contribute to developing a better theory of social change and historical development than that found in Heidegger, or any phenomenological or existential ontology. For example, in a review of a book on sociology by Hans Freyer, Marcuse identifies the actual movement of history with revolution, as if revolution were part of the dynamics of history itself. See 'Zur Auseinandersetzung mit Hans Freyers "Soziologie als Wirklicheitswissenschaft"', *Philosophische Hefte*, III, 1/2 (1931) pp. 89–90. Marcuse concluded 'Contributions to a Phenomenology of Historical Materialism' on a similar note, writing, 'Organic historical development and revolution are not simply a contradiction; rather, revolution appears as the necessary form of historical movement. Further, revolution alone can transform the *existence* (*Existenz*) of the historical human being (*Dasein*)' (*S1*, pp. 383–4). In both essays cited, Hegel was praised for his dynamic historical ontology, which provided the basis for Marx's historical materialism.

3. Heidegger was giving seminars and lectures on Hegel during the early 1930s which produced, among other texts, 'Hegel's Concept of Experience', later published in *Holzwege* (Frankfurt: Klostermann, 1950) and translated into English by Kenley Dove (New York: Harper & Row, 1970).

4. Since it was probably impossible to work with Heidegger on a study of

Marx, Marcuse chose Hegel as the thinker who was at once of crucial importance to Marxism and to traditional ontological problematics of the sort one could write about in a German academic philosophy faculty. Moreover, Marcuse saw Marx as the culmination of German Idealism and thus believed that it was important to study the roots of German Idealism to understand Marxism properly. He concluded his first published essay by presenting Marx as both the heir to German Idealism and its corrective ('Contributions', *S1*, p. 384) and took this position throughout his life.

5. Conversation with Marcuse, 28 December 1978.

6. See Chapter 2 for discussion of the impact of *History and Class Consciousness* on Marcuse.

7. For Marcuse's discussions of Lukács in the period under investigation, see 'Zum Problem der Dialektik', Parts I and II, *Die Gesellschaft*, VII, 1 (1930) pp. 15–30, and VIII (1931) pp. 541–57, trans. Morton Schoolman and friends in *Telos*, 27 (Spring 1976) pp. 12–39.

8. Heidegger, *Being and Time*.

9. Although 'academic socialism' (*Katherdersozialismus*) was in vogue after the 1918 German Revolution, there were few university professors involved with Marxist philosophy. See Korsch, *Marxism and Philosophy*, pp. 29ff, and Perry Anderson, *Considerations on Western Marxism* (London: New Left Books, 1976) for discussion of how concern with culture and philosphy would later be a defining characteristic of the emerging current of 'critical Marxism'.

10. Marcuse, 'Transzendentaler Marxismus?', p. 445.

11. In 'On the Philosophical Foundation of the Concept of Labour in Economics', Marcuse writes: 'every genuine economic theory is explicitly or inexplicitly connected with an ontology of man that transcends it. Furthermore, exonomic theory has at least a rough concept of historical human existence as such, which directs its development'. Throughout the essay, he claims that labour cannot be correctly conceptualized simply as economic activity, but rather its function within human life as a whole must be determined by an ontological analysis of labour, requiring 'a fundamental philosophical discussion of the concept of labour'. Marcuse, 'Über die philosophischen Grundlagen des wirtschaftlichen Arbeitsbegriff', *Archiv fur Sozialwissenschaft und Sozialpolitik*, 69, 3 (1933) pp. 257–92, trans. Douglas Kellner, *Telos*, 16 (Summer 1973) pp. 9–37. This essay will be discussed in section 3.3

12. Marcuse, 'Transzendentaler Marxismus?', p. 445.

13. There is tension between this concept of philosophy as opposition and the ontological concept of philosophy as a discipline discerning and explicating the basic structures of being – a tension that would characterize Marcuse's philosophical enterprise from beginning to end.

14. Marcuse, *Hegel's Ontology*, pp. 9ff; Marcuse repeats this notion in *Reason and Revolution*, pp. 30ff.

15. Marcuse, 'Das Problem der Geschichtlichen Wirklichkeit', *Die Gesellschaft*, VIII (1931) pp. 350–67; reprinted in *Schriften 1*,

pp. 469ff.; page references are to *Schriften 1* source. For Korsch's critique of current Marxian orthodoxies hostile to philosophy, see his *Marxism and Philosophy*, and *Die materialistische Geschichtsauffassung und andere Schriften* (Frankfurt: Europäische Verlagsanstalt, 1971).

16. Marcuse, 'Das Problem der Geschichtlichen Wirklichkeit', *S1*, p. 470.
17. Ibid., *S1*, pp. 470–1. Compare Marx's 'Contribution to a Critique of Hegel's Philosophy of Law', *Collected Works*, vol. 3, pp. 183ff.
18. Marcuse, Das Problem der Geschichtlichen Wirklichkeit', *S1*, pp. 471ff.
19. Marcuse, 'Zur Wahrheistsproblemik der soziologischen Methode'.
20. Marcuse, 'Transzendentaler Marxismus?'
21. Marcuse, 'On the Problem of the Dialectic'.
22. Marcuse, 'Zur Kritik der Soziologie', *Die Gesellschaft*, VIII, 9 (1931) pp. 270–80, and his reviews of Noack and Freyer in *Philosophische Hefte*, II (1930) pp. 91–6.
23. Marcuse, 'On the Problem of the Dialectic'. Compare Siegfried Marck, *The Dialectic in Contemporary Philosophy* (Tübingen: Mohr, 1929 and 1931, two volumes). Marck was a neo-Kantian and Social Democratic philosopher who later was supported by the Institute for Social Research and wrote book reviews for their journal.
24. Marcuse, 'On the Problem of Dialectic', pp. 22f.
25. Compare Marcuse, *Hegel's Ontology* and 'On the Problem of Dialectic', pp. 17–22 and 25–38.
26. Marcuse, 'On the Problem of the Dialectic', pp. 25ff.
27. Ibid. p. 27. In fact, Marcuse was more sympathetic to Dilthey's ontology than Heidegger's during this period – another theoretical difference which might have caused Heidegger displeasure, leading to his rejection of Marcuse's Habitationsschrift on Hegel; see the discussion in Chapter 4.
28. Ibid., pp. 35ff.
29. Ibid., p. 35. Further, 'It is already evident . . . that Hegel here means the process of reification (*Verdinglichung*) and its transcendence (*Durchbrechung*) as a basic occurrence of human life, which Marx represented as the basic law of historical development' (p. 36).
30. Ibid., p. 36.
31. Ibid., p. 38.
32. Ibid., p. 22.
33. Marcuse, *Hegel's Ontology*, p. 1. The term 'historicity' appears in almost all of Marcuse's 1928–1932 essays; the use of this term indicates that he has not yet liberated himself from the ontological perspectives of German Idealism for a more materialist approach to history.
34. Ibid.
35. Ibid., pp. 2–3.
36. Ibid., pp. 3ff, *passim*.
37. Ibid., p. 8.
38. Ibid., pp. 1–2, 363–8, *passim*.

39. See Georg Lukács, *Die Zerstörung der Vernunft* (Neuwied und Berlin: Luchterhand, 1962) pp. 491–2.
40. This judgment was frequently expresssed to me by philosophers in Germany. See also Richard Bernstein, 'Herbert Marcuse: An Immanent Critique', *Social Theory and Practice*, vol. 1, no. 4 (Fall 1977) who calls *Hegel's Ontology* Marcuse's 'most serious and brilliant work' (p. 97).
41. Marcuse, *Hegel's Ontology*, pp. 79ff. Compare Chapters 5 and 8 of this book.
42. T. W. Adorno, *Zeitschrift für Sozialforschung* I, 2 (1932) pp. 409–10.
43. Ibid., p. 410.
44. Ibid. See also another Adorno review which indicates his high regard for Marcuse's book on *Hegel's Ontology*. *Zeitschrift für Sozialforschuung*, II, 1 (1933) pp. 107–8.
45. On Adorno's early critique of Idealism, see Susan Buck-Morss, *The Origins of Negative Dialectics* (New York: The Free Press, 1977). Adorno's PhD dissertation was a critique of Husserl, and he had just finished writing a long critique of Kierkegaard. Adorno and Marcuse did not really know each other well until the late 1930s, when they were together with the Institute for Social Research in New York and later in California. I shall later discuss Adorno's impact on Marcuse's post-Second World War theory.
46. The differences between Marcuse's two Hegel books are discussed by Jean-Michel Palmier, *Herbert Marcuse et la nouvelle gauche* (Paris: Belfond, 1973) pp. 42–98.
47. See my discussion in Chapter 5.
48. Marcuse, 'Neue Quellen zur Grundlegung des Historischen Materialismus', *Die Gesellschaft*, IX, 8 (1932) pp. 136–74; trans. Joris de Bres in *Studies in Critical Philosophy* (hereafter *SCP*); page references will be to the English publication, but the translations will often be my own. I might note that Marcuse's review of Marx's *Economic and Philosophical Manuscripts of 1844* brought his name to the attention of a broader public, especially on the Left, than he had earlier enjoyed. Henry Pachter told me of the admiration that he and others in Korsch's circle had for Marcuse's review when it was first published and that this was the first time they had taken notice of Marcuse (conversation with Pachter, 11 July 1978, New York).
49. Istvan Meszaros, *Marx's Theory of Alienation* (London: Merlin, 1970) p. 11. See Karl Marx, *Economic and Philosophical Manuscripts of 1944, Collected Works*, vol. 3, pp. 231ff.
50. Marcuse, Conversation with Habermas and others, 'Theory and Politics', p. 25.
51. Marcuse's essay was both an anticipation of, and direct influence on, this trend to assign a fundamental importance to the writings of the early Marx in interpreting the Marxist corpus as a whole. The Marxist-Leninist Steigerwald claims that Marcuse's article is 'actually the mine of almost all attempts up until now to revise Marxism on the basis of the early Marx', and 'contains all the stereotypes of bourgeois and re-

visionist Marx-critiques that start with the early Marx, and which are today still influential', *Herbert Marcuse 'dritter Weg'*, p. 87. Iring Fetscher gives Korsch, Lukács and Marcuse credit for inaugurating 'the current interpretation (dominant in the West) from the early writings of Marx', in *Marx and Marxism* (New York: Seabury, 1971) p. 46.

The project of revising the accepted picture of Marxism on the basis of the new material found in the early writings of Marx was also formulated, but differently, by two Social Democrats, Landshut and Mayer, who edited and wrote an introduction to the first German edition of the *Manuscripts, Die Frühschriften* (Leipzig: 1932). They argued that Marxism was 'fundamentally an ethical doctrine', and developed an interpretation that influenced later ethico-humanist trends of Marx interpretation that emphasized the philosophical character of Marxism, playing down the importance of its critique of political economy and revolutionary social theory. See, for example, Karl Löwith, *From Hegel to Nietzsche* (Garden City, NY: Doubleday, 1967); Jean-Yves Calvez, *La Pensée de Karl Marx* (Paris: Seuil, 1956); and Erich Fromm, *Marx's Concept of Man* (New York: Grove Press, 1963). The *Manuscripts* also had a strong influence in France and helped produce a succession of syntheses of Marx, Hegel and existentialism in the works of Sartre, Merleau-Ponty, Kojeve, Hippolyte and to some extent Lefevbre and Garaudy. On the impact of the early Marx on the French scene, see Poster, *Existential Marxism*.

52. Steigerwald summarizes this Marxist-Leninist devaluation of Marx's *Manuscripts* in *Herbert Marcuses 'dritter Weg'*, pp. 86–91, and on p. 116 lists several 'Marxist' commentaries which 'correct' 'bourgeois' Marx-interpretations. See also Louis Althusser, *For Marx* (New York: Vintage, 1968) who claims that there is an 'epistemological break' between the philosophical (= 'ideological' = 'non-scientific') early works and the 'scientific' later works of Marx.

53. Marx's early writings have been frequently used by Eastern European Marxists in the interests of developing a 'humanistic' version of Marxism used to criticize the orthodox 'Stalinist' versions. See the articles in *Socialist Humanism*, ed. Erich Fromm (Garden City, NY: Doubleday, 1966) and the works of Kosik, Schaff, Kolakowski, Markovic, Petrovic, Stojanovic and others.

54. A fuller documentation of the various interpretations of Marx's *Manuscripts* and their wide-ranging effects can be found in Erich Thier, 'Etappen der Marxinterpretation, *Marxismusstudien*, I (Tübingen: 1954); Jürgen Habermas, 'Zur philosophischen Diskussion um Marx und den Marxismus', *Theorie und Praxis* (Berlin und Neuwied: Luchterhand, 1963) pp. 261–335 – an important discussion left out of the English translation of *Theory and Practice*; and Emilo Bottigelli, Introduction, *Manuscripts de 1844* (Paris: 1969) pp. *viiff.*

55. Marcuse makes this even more explicit in his discussion of the relation between Marx and Hegel at the end of his article; see *SCP*, pp. 40–8.

56. Marcuse, *SCP*, pp. 5ff, 31f, *passim*. On this theme, see my article 'Karl

Marx and Adam Smith on Human Nature and Capitalism' in The *Subtle Anatomy of Capitalism*, ed. Jesse Schwartz (Santa Monica, Cal.: Goodyear, 1977).

57. For Marx's celebrated discussion of the alienation of labour, see *Economic and Philosophical Manuscripts of 1844*, and the commentary by Meszaros, *Marx's Theory of Alienation*.

58. The relationship between the concepts of objectification (*Vergegenständlichung*), externalization (*Entäusserung*) and alienation (*Entfremdung*) in Hegel and Marx has been a central issue of debate since the publication of Marx's *Manuscripts*. Marx ends his *Manuscripts* with a discussion of Hegel, where he objects to a 'double error' (pp. 331ff): (1) Hegel's idealism reduces concrete history to a thought-process and illicitly tries to grasp history through 'abstract philosophical thinking' (p. 331); and (2) Hegel presents alienation as the externalization and objectification of spirit, and thus fails to grasp the historically specific material conditions of alienation which revolutionary practice is to eliminate (pp. 332ff). Both Marx and Marcuse claim that Hegel collapses objectification, externalization and alienation into one ontological process which fails to distinguish between the necessary features of externalization and objectification in all human activity and the contingent features of alienation, removal of which is necessary for human liberation. This point is highlighted in a study by George Lukács, *The Young Hegel* (London: Merlin, 1975). Lukács compares Hegel's theory of 'externalization' (*Entäusserung*) with Marx's theory of alienation, providing a detailed historical and conceptual analysis of these terms (pp. 537–49); he then contrasts Hegel and Marx on the concept of 'objectification' (pp. 549ff). See also the commentary and critique by Jean Hippolite, 'Alienation and Objectification: Commentary on G. Lukács' *The Young Hegel*', in *Studies on Marx and Hegel* (New York: Harper & Row, 1969). Hippolite in turn defends Hegel by re-ontologizing both alienation and objectification and criticizing Marx's 'optimistic' view that alienation could be overcome (pp. 87ff).

59. Many critics claim that Marx's anthropology in the *Manuscripts* is primarily Feuerbachian and is utilized as a polemical model against Hegel's idealist anthropology. See Lloyd Easton and Kurt Guddat, *Writings of the Young Marx on Philosophy and Society* (Garden City, NY: Doubleday, 1967); Schlomo Avineri, *The Social and Political Writings of Karl Marx* (New York: Cambridge, 1968); and Althusser, *For Marx*, pp. 45ff. The interpretation of the early Marx as a Feuerbachian critic of Hegel is wrong in that Marx is neither a Hegelian nor a Feuerbachian in his early writings but is instead creating his own synthesis of Feuerbach *and* other young Hegelians, Hegel and British political economy. Although Marx frequently champions Feuerbach's naturalism against Hegelian Idealism, he counteracts the passive aspects of Feuerbach's theory of human nature with emphasis on the active, creative aspects of the human being and concepts of labour and *Geist* of Hegel. On the heterogeneous origins of Marx's theory of

labour, see the article by R. N. Berki, 'On the Nature and Origins of Marx's Concept of Labor', *Political Theory*, vol. 7, no. I (February 1979) pp. 35–56).

60. Marcuse is one of the first to stress explicitly that Marx's anthropology conceives of human beings in terms of *needs* and *powers*. On this theme, see Bertell Ollman, *Alienation* (New York: Cambridge, 1971) and Agnes Heller, *The Theory of Need in Marx* (London: Allison & Busby, 1976).

61. We see here that Marcuse historicizes the concept of essence in the context of historical materialism. For other attempts to rethink the problematics of human history and essence, see György Markus, 'Human Essence and History', *International Journal of Sociology*, vol. IV, no. 1 (Spring 1974) pp. 82ff, and Erich Fromm, *Marx's Concept of Man*. It is still to me an open question whether a concept of 'essence' is necessary to talk about alienation, or whether materialist concepts of needs and powers would not serve better as anthropological concepts critical of capitalist society which enable us to criticize the capitalist mode of production, its dominant needs, values and consciousness, and its effects on human beings. To avoid philosophical mystification, it is necessary to conceptualize a theory of human nature that does not adopt an idealist concept of human essence, explicated in terms of a fixed species characterized by simplicity, identify, unchangeability, etc. On this issue I think that Breuer, *Die Krise der Revolutionstheorie*, is wrong to claim that Marcuse remains trapped in an idealist theory of essence, for Marcuse rejects idealist doctrines of essence and is groping for a historicist-materialist concept. That is, although there are features of the idealist problematic in Marcuse, he is struggling, with the help of Dilthey's historicism and Marx's materialism, to overcome the presuppositions of German Idealism and to develop a new philosophical theory of human nature and history. In his work with the Institute for Social Research, it is clear that he has made progress in this direction; see the essay, 'The Concept of Essence', *Negations*, pp. 96ff. where he criticizes the Platonic, Christian and idealist theories of essence and advocates a Marxian materialist conception. A mark of Marcuse's project henceforth will be reformulation of a materialist theory of human nature – a problematic that will surface in his work with the Institute, his appropriation of Freud and his later anthropology of false needs – which will be discussed in the next several chapters. For another critique of Breuer's reduction of Marcuse's theory to the problematic of German Idealism, see the penetrating review by James A. Ogilvy, *Telos*, 35 (Spring 1978) pp. 219–26.

62. On the allegedly 'idealist' and 'historicist' nature of Marcuse and critical theory, see Göran Therborn, 'The Frankfurt School', in *Western Marxism: A Critical Reader* (London: New Left Books, 1977); and for a critique of Marcuse's falling prey to a reductionistic Marxian materialism, see Jean Baudrillard, *The Mirror of Production* (St Louis: Telos Press, 1975).

63. The term the 'metaphysics of labour' was introduced by Adorno as a critique of an alleged reduction of essential human nature to labour by Marx. See T. W. Adorno, *Gesammelte Schriften*, vol. 5 (Frankfurt: Suhrkamp, 1971) p. 270. Habermas and his colleagues criticized the reductionistic anthropology of labour in Marx, which failed to conceptualize adequately symbolic interaction and pointed to a 'secret positivism' in Marx. See Jürgen Habermas, *Human Knowledge and Interests* (Boston: Beacon Press, 1971); Albrecht Wellmer, *Critical Theory of Society* (New York: Seabury, 1974); and Jóhann Páll Árnson, *Von Marcuse zu Marx*, who criticizes Marcuse for his reductionistic anthropology of labour (pp. 28ff). Stefan Breuer takes a similar line in *Die Krise der Revolutionstheorie*, pp. 45ff and 111ff.

64. Jean Baudrillard claims in *The Mirror of Production* that the presuppositions of capitalist political economy remain operative in the Marxian-Marcusian theories of labour, production, use-value, etc. He believes that radical social theory must break with the presuppositions of political economy to conceptualize human emancipation in terms of play, sexuality, symbolic exchange and other cultural activities (pp. 17ff, *passim*). But Baudrillard's critique is also misplaced, because Marx includes aesthetic, erotic and even 'spiritual' activity in his discussion of emancipation and talks of the 'play' of human senses, imagination and body-power in non-alienated labour. Marcuse analyses in detail emancipatory aesthetic and erotic activity in his later writing; thus it is nonsensical to claim that he remains strait-jacketed by the presuppositions of political economy. Further, in his critique of 'the ethic of labour' and 'aesthetic of non-labour', Baudrillard misinterprets the thrust of Marx and Marcuse's theory of labour, falsely claiming that they 'exalt labour as value, as end in itself, as categorical imperative. Labour loses its negativity and is raised to an absolute value'. Against this view, it is clear that both Marx and Marcuse described oppressive features of socially necessary labour and call for an emancipation of labour that will raise labour to a form of creative and fulfilling activity.

    Baudrillard contrasts the Marxian emphasis on labour with an ideal of 'symbolic exchange' described as a 'discharge with a pure waste, a symbolic discharge in Bataille's sense (pulsating, libidinal) . . . a gratuitous and festive energizing of the body's powers, a game with death, or the acting out of a desire' (p. 43). But does not the paradigm of Baudrillard's ideal of human activity seem to be masturbation ('a discharge with a pure waste . . . pulsating, libidinal') or gratuitous violence and destruction ('a game with death')? Thus, whereas some of Baudrillard's criticisms are justified (i.e. that there is a tendency in Marxism to overestimate the role of labour in human life and to impose its categories on primitive and non-capitalist societies), his own ideal of 'symbolic exchange' is extremely vague and tinged with irrationalism. See my critique of Baudrillard in *Theory, Culture and Society* (1984, forthcoming).

65. Marcuse told me that Rosa Luxemburg's theory of revolution and the events of the Russian and German Revolutions decisively influenced

his early concept of revolution, which he perceived as a 'catastrophic upheaval' and total restructuring of social life (conversation, 28 December 1978). We shall see how this concept continued to be operative in Marcuse's 1960s understanding of revolution and that only in the 1970s did Marcuse reformulate his concept of revolution (see Chapter 9).

66. See Marx, *Manuscripts*, especially pp. 293–326 and *SCP*, pp. 30ff.

67. Ibid., pp. 300ff and 322ff. This is the utopian notion of socialism explicated in the *Critique of the Gotha Program* by the formula, 'From each according to his abilities, to each according to his needs'. On the origins and history of this formula, see the book by Marcuse's friends, Frank E. Manuel and Fritzie P. Manuel, *Utopian Thought in the Western World* (Cambridge: Harvard University Press, 1979) pp. 697ff.

68. Steigerwald, *Herbert Marcuses 'dritter Weg'*, p. 102.

69. Marcuse, *Reason and Revolution*, p. 295.

70. Marcuse, 'On the Philosophical Concept of Labour.'

71. Ibid., p. 11.

72. Ibid., pp. 12ff.

73. Ibid., pp. 29ff.

74. Ibid., p. 25. See the discussion in note 63. The notion that labour is a burden goes back to 'Jehovah's curse' in the Bible, and was repeated by Adam Smith, who saw labour as a 'sacrifice'. In insisting that all labour is a burden, Marcuse is transposing Heidegger's notion that 'life is a burden', *Being and Time*, p. 173, to the labour process.

75. Marcuse, 'On the Philosophical Concept of Labour', pp. 14ff, 23ff, and 29ff.

76. Breuer, *Die Krise der Revolutionstheorie*, p. 111. Breuer's critique of Marcuse's alleged hypostatizing conditions of labour under capitalism into an ontological concept is interesting, but his claim that 'Capital, as the Substance become Subject, has incorporated labour into itself', reproduces the worst features of Adorno's paranoia over the disappearance of subjectivity in the 'totally administered society'. Compare Ogilvy's review, *Telos*, 35. What I call 'the fallacy of ontological generalization' criticizes the illicit projection of historically specific conditions onto a universal Concept.

77. Compare Baudrillard, *The Mirror of Production*. Breuer never mentions Baudrillard – although he cites Foucault, Derrida and other French thinkers – but many of his criticisms of Marx and Marcuse are quite similar to Baudrillard's anti-Marxist polemic.

78. Karl Marx, *Capital III* (New York: International Publishers, 1966). See also the *Marx-Engels Reader*, pp. 440–1. Marcuse ends his essay on labour with the famous quotation on the realms of freedom and necessity. We shall see that one of the most significant developments in Marcuse's later thinking is his reformulations of the relation between the realms of freedom and necessity and his notion of the possibility of freedom entering the realm of necessity through non-alienated labour (see Chapter 10). Marcuse would discover passages in Marx's *Grundrisse* (first published in 1939) which contained notions of

non-alienated labour within the realm of necessity that would lead him to rethink these issues.

79. The desire to preserve a realm of unconditioned freedom of the self also helps explain tendencies in the essay on labour towards a dualism between the self and the world, as in the passages where Marcuse claims that the self is other than its body and is not subject to the same forces and laws as historical processes. Such passages in the essay on labour suggest an uncharacteristic dualism which Marcuse is usually careful to avoid in his early essays. See, for example, 'Zur Kritik der Soziologie', where he stresses the indissolvable unity of the human being and its world and claims that this dialectical unity is an essential condition of the possibility of social-historical transformation (pp. 276ff).

80. Marcuse, 'On the Philosophical Concept of Labour', pp. 31ff.

81. See Albrecht Wellmer, 'Communications and Emancipation: Reflections on the Linguistic Turn in Critical Theory', in *On Critical Theory*, ed. John O'Neill (New York: Seabury, 1976).

82. Curiously, the issue does not explicitly come up in Marcuse's discussion with Habermas, 'Theory and Politics', although there is detailed debate over other aspects of their rather different anthropologies. See especially pp. 132–40.

83. Marcuse, *Reason and Revolution*, pp. 273–312.

4 Critical Theory and the Critique of Fascism

1. Marcuse, 'Theory and Politics', p. 126. Although Barry Katz claims that, 'To the best of Marcuse's knowledge, Heidegger never read the *Habilitationschrift* on *Hegel's Ontology*' ('Praxis and Poiesis', *New German Critique*, no. 18 (Fall 1979) p. 16), Jürgen Habermas told me that Marcuse had told him that Heidegger had rejected his dissertation, but was never clear about why Heidegger had rejected it (conversation with Habermas, Starnberg, Germany, December 1980).

2. Conversation with Leo Lowenthal, April 1978 and Marcuse, December 1978; see also, 'Theory and Politics', p. 126f.

3. See Martin Heidegger, *Die Selbstbehauptung der deutschen Universität* (Freiburg-im-Breslau: Korn, 1933). For texts of other speeches by Heidegger and documents pertaining to his activity with the Nazis, see Guido Schneeberger, ed., *Nachlese zu Heidegger, Dokumente zu seinem Leben und Denken* (Bern: Buchdruckerei AG Suhr, 1962); some of this material has been translated in *German Existentialism*. See note 54 in Chapter 2 for a list of books and articles on Heidegger and Nazism. According to Katz, Marcuse found Heidegger's entry into the Nazi Party 'a great shock' ('Praxis and Poiesis', p. 16). Henry Pachter, who was a student in Freiburg at the time, said that it would be strange if Marcuse found Heidegger's involvement with National Socialism surprising because: (1) Nazi students filled Heidegger's

classes and enthusiastically clamoured around him; (2) Heidegger's wife was an outspoken member of the party and supporter of national socialism; (3) at the Davon debate with Ernst Cassier in 1929, Nazi students supported Heidegger and shouted down Cassier with slogans and insults; and (4) Heidegger's life-style and thinking were sympathetic to fascist *völkisch* ideology: he wore Bavarian peasant clothes and affected peasant manners; he spent as much time as possible in his mountain retreat in Todtnauberg; and he was becoming increasingly nationalistic and political in the 1930s (conversation with Henry Pachter, New York, June 1980). Jürgen Habermas concurred in this analysis (discussion in Starnberg, December 1980).

4. Martin Jay, *The Dialectical Imagination* (Boston: Little, Brown & Co., 1973) p. 28. Compare Marcuse, 'Theory and Politics', pp. 126ff, which provides more information on Marcuse's entry into the Institute. He reports that he was especially impressed by the Institute's critical study of Marxism, political analysis of fascism, and serious reflections on psychoanalysis (p. 126). Marcuse would, of course, make important contributions in all these areas. On the history of the Institute, see Jay's pioneering study; my critical review 'The Frankfurt School Revisited', *New German Critique*, 4 (Winter 1975) pp. 131–52, which disputes some of Jay's interpretations; Helmut Dubiel, *Wissenschaftsorganisation und politische Erfahrung* (Frankfurt: Suhrkamp, 1978); and Kellner and Roderick, 'Recent Literature on Critical Theory', *New German Critique* 23 (Spring-Summer 1981) pp. 141–70.

5. See T. W. Adorno, *Kierkegaard* (Frankfurt: Surhkamp, 1974; reprint of 1933 text) and *Zur Metakritik der Erkenntnistheorie* (Frankfurt: Suhrkamp, 1972) which contains a revised version of the text Adorno was working on in the 1930s that criticized phenomenology. Adorno's critiques of Heidegger were eventually published in *Jargon of Authenticity* and *Negative Dialectics*. For some of Horkheimer's criticisms of Heidegger, see 'Zum Rationalismusstreit in der gegenwärtigen Philosophie', in *Kritische Theorie I* (Frankfurt: Suhrkamp, 1968) pp. 134ff.

6. Morton Schoolman's claim that Marcuse continued to develop a historicist ontology as a foundation for critical theory is mistaken, for he fails to see the changes in Marcuse's work with the Institute for Social Research. See his 'Introduction to Marcuse', pp. 3ff. Schoolman does not realize that Marcuse's post-1934 work, at least until the 1950s, assumed that the Marxian critique of political economy and historical materialism provided the foundation for critical theory. Consequently, Marcuse abandoned his earlier search for an ontological foundation – although ontological themes continue to reappear in his work during this period. However, in his post-Second World War work, when Marcuse began to doubt aspects of the Marxian theory, he returned to search for an ontological foundation for his theory, as we shall see in Chapter 6.

7. Jay, *The Dialectical Imagination*, pp. 24ff.

8. Ibid., Helmut Dubiel, in *Wissenschaftsorganisation und politische Er-*

fahrung, stresses the central role that Horkheimer played as Director, although Marcuse himself claims that Dubiel unduly exaggerates Horkheimer's role and influence. See 'Theory and Politics', pp. 128ff.

9. Alfred Schmidt, *Zur Idee der kritischen Theorie* (München: Hanser, 1974) pp. 37ff.

10. Ibid., p. 41.

11. Ibid., p. 42. The first statement cited by Marx is found in the Introduction to the *Critique of Political Economy* and the latter in the Introduction to *Capital.*

12. On the Institute's project of merging philosophy and the social sciences in an interdisciplinary social theory, see Max Horkheimer, 'Die gegenwärtige Lage der Sozialphilosophie und die Aufgaben eines Instituts für Sozialforschung', *Sozialphilosophische Studien* (Frankfurt: Fisher, 1972); discussed in my *New German Critique* review of Jay, *The Dialectical Imagination,* and in Dubiel, *Wissenschaftsorganisation.*

13. Korsch, *Marxism and Philosophy.*

14. The *Zeitschrift für Sozialforschung* (hereafter *ZfS*) was reprinted in 1970 by Kösel Press with a foreword by Alfred Schmidt (reprinted in *Zur Idee*) and was republished again in an inexpensive paperback edition by Deutsche Taschenbuch Verlag in 1980 with an introduction by Jürgen Habermas, translated in *Telos,* 45 (Fall 1980) pp. 114–21.

15. Horkheimer, 'Vorwort', *ZfS,* vol. 1, no. 1 (1932) p. 1.

16. Ibid., pp. 1–111.

17. This theoretical project will be the subject of section 4.2.

18. Most of the essays that will be discussed in this chapter are translated in *Negations* (hereafter referred to as *N*) (Boston: Beacon Press, 1968). Page references will be to this edition, although occasionally I shall modify the translations.

19. For discussion of the Institute's critique of fascism, see Jay, *The Dialectical Imagination,* and the texts in *The Essential Frankfurt School Reader,* ed. Andrew Arato and Eike Gebhardt (New York: Urizen, 1978), especially pp. 3–162. On the capitalist roots of fascism, see Franz Neumann, *Behemoth* (New York: Oxford University Press, 1940). On the Institute's studies of family and authority, see the Institute for Social Research, ed. Max Horkheimer, *Autorität und Familie* (Paris: Alcan, 1936) and Erich Fromm, *Escape from Freedom* (New York: Holt, Rinehart & Winston, 1970).

20. Marcuse, 'Theory and Politics', p. 128. For Hitler's speech, see *My New Order,* (New York: Reynal and Hitchcock, 1941) pp. 93ff.

21. This is, in fact, the orthodox Marxian line advocated by the Comintern, where George Dimitrov at the Seventh World Congress of the Communist International stated that 'fascism is the open, terrorist dictatorship of the most reactionary, most chauvinistic, and most imperialist elements of finance capital', in *The United Front* (San Francisco: Proletarian Publishers, 1975). I shall argue that Marcuse takes a rather orthodox Marxian line on most crucial issues throughout the 1930s. For an analysis of the differences between monopoly capitalism and the earlier competitive capitalism, see Paul Baran and Paul Sweezy's *Monopoly Capital* (New York: Monthly Review, 1965).

22. To avoid confusion, I should note that the essay was written in 1934 and that the term 'existentialism' here loosely refers to some of the philosophical tendencies of Heidegger and his followers. But by extending the term from its philosophical to a political form (*N*, p. 31) Marcuse uses it as a label for characterizing a broad spectrum of writers; thus not all of the positions stated refer to Heidegger's philosophy. Indeed, some of the positions analysed are at odds with Heidegger's *Sein und Zeit* and the 'existentialism' of people like Kierkegaard, Nietzsche and Jaspers, and refer more specifically to the doctrines of Carl Schmitt and a group of Nazi ideologues whom Marcuse cites. Marcuse attempts to justify his procedure in note 68 of his essay: 'The possible reproach that we are playing off philosophical against political existentialism has been refuted by philosophical existentialism itself, which, as Heidegger's most recent publications show, has politicized itself. The original opposition is thus cancelled' (*N*, p. 274). Such an undifferentiated critique of Heidegger, however, fails to analyse the complicated relations between Heidegger's philosophy and Nazism, and simply brushes Heidegger with guilt by association with Nazi ideologues. Although there are passages in Heidegger's infamous 1933 address, *Die Selbstbehauptung der deutschen Universität*, where Heidegger supports Nazism and claims that 'earthy and bloody forces' are the real forces of history (*N*, p. 35), Heidegger's 'irrationalism' and 'activism' are of a quite different sort than national socialism. Thus, whereas there are continuities between Heidegger and fascism, there are also differences which Marcuse's discussion fails to distinguish. See the sources in Chapter 2, note 54, which debate the complicated issue of the relation of Heidegger's philosophy to fascism.

23. Marcuse is probably referring here to Heidegger's assumption of the Rectorship of the University of Freiburg in 1933, and his speeches using his ontological-existentialist terminology in support of the Nazis. See Schneeberger, *Nachlese zu Heidegger*, for the documents.

24. See my discussion in Chapter 2 of the sharp criticisms of Heidegger's philosophy that Marcuse develops in his early writings, and my discussion in Chapter 3, where I depict the philosophical differences between Marcuse's work and Heidegger, even when they were working together. Hence, whereas there is clearly a sharpened critique of Heidegger in his work with the Institute, this is grounded to some extent in his pre-Institute work; consequently, one should see both the continuities and discontinuities between Marcuse's pre- and post-1934 work.

25. One might compare Marcuse's position here with that of Adorno, who from the beginning was concerned to attack idealist and subjectivist philosophies, of which existentialism and phenomenology were prime targets. See the works cited in note 5 of this chapter. In general, Adorno takes a far more critical approach to bourgeois philosophy than Marcuse and Horkheimer. See Breuer, *Die Krisis der Revolutionstheorie*, pp. 130ff and 264ff, and Buck-Morss, *The Origin of Negative Dialectics*, who provides a fine discussion of the differences between Adorno's and Marcuse-Horkheimer's 1930s versions of critical theory, rooted in Adorno's early association with Walter Benjamin

and development of his own well defined philosophical project by 1930, before he came to work with the Institute.

26. Marcuse, 'Philosophie des Scheiterns: Karl Jaspers Werk', *Unterhaltungsblatt der Vossichen Zeitung* (14 December 1933; reprinted in an anthology *Karl Jaspers in der Diskussion* (München: Piper, 1973); (hereafter, 'Jaspers' – page references to the *Karl Jaspers* anthology). Marcuse wrote this review essay for a Swiss newspaper while working at the Institute branch in Geneva, but before his close collaboration with Horkheimer. Hence it should not be considered part of his Institute work, although it is revealing of his attitude towards existentialism at the time, distinguishing between a 'good' and 'bad' version.

27. Marcuse, 'Jaspers', p. 125. In effect, Jaspers is proposing a rejection of Heidegger's philosophical enterprise directed towards the Question of Being, suggesting that Heidegger is a traditional metaphysican and is not really an 'existential' philosopher at all.

28. Ibid., p. 126. Jaspers's concept of selfhood and freedom is remarkably similar to the concepts operative in Marcuse's essay 'On the Philosophical Concept of Labour', compare pp. 30ff. See also Heidegger's *On the Essence of Reason* (Evanston: Northwestern University Press, 1969) for a similar notion of absolute freedom. There is a certain pathos in the fact that all these doctrines of absolute freedom of the self appeared in Germany precisely when freedom was being so strictly curtailed.

29. Marcuse, 'Jaspers', p. 126. It is interesting that Marcuse was never impressed by Jaspers's call for a theory of communication as a fundamental mode of self-development – a theme central to German existentialism. Compare here Habermas, who would later develop a communication-oriented critical theory of society. See *Human Knowledge and Interests*, and many of Habermas's post-1970s works.

30. Marcuse, 'Jaspers', pp. 127ff.

31. Ibid., p. 130. Marcuse's attraction to the ethical elements of existentialism suggests a deep ethical impulse at the origins of his thought which would constantly reappear in his later work but is never fully developed to the extent to which his anthropological and aesthetic interests were. Concerning Jaspers: although some of his programme is suggestive and his concepts are provocative, unfortunately his prose is incredibly dull and cumbersome; hence his writings do not really fulfil the promise of his enterprise. Marcuse, in fact, is remarkably uncritical of Jaspers. Compare Stephen Eric Bronner's critique of Jaspers in *Authenticity and Potentiality: A Marxian Inquiry into the Role of the Subject* (PhD dissertation, Political Science, the University of California, Berkeley, 1975). Jaspers's major work, which Marcuse was reviewing, has been translated into English, although it is virtually unreadable. See Karl Jaspers, *Philosophy* (in three volumes) (Chicago: University of Chicago Press, 1961).

32. Marcuse, 'Jaspers', pp. 130–1. This essay is the last one, to my knowledge, in which 'historicity' plays a major role; hence I believe that the passage cited represents Marcuse's break with the existentialist con-

cept of historicity – a critique that reappears in the essay on liberalism and fascism (*N*, pp. 32f).

33. It is curious that elements of the universalism, naturalism and existentialism which Marcuse criticizes in the essay on fascism (*N*, pp. 5ff) would reappear in his own later work, although, of course, in a different form.

34. In his earlier work, Marcuse rarely, if ever, had anything particularly positive to say about Kant or rationalism. See, for instance, the critical references to Kant in his article criticizing Max Adler's Kantian-Marxism, 'Transzendentaler Marxismus?'.

35. I think Marcuse is using Kant here against Heidegger and fascism. Heidegger taught many courses on Kant during the period in which Marcuse studied in Freiburg and seemed to be one of Heidegger's favourite philosophers. Hence, jabbing his former teacher with a philosophical needle, Marcuse cited Kant against Heidegger's current positions, which could quite rightly be seen as a betrayal of Kant's rationalist heritage. See Heidegger's 1929 book on Kant, *Kant and the Problem of Metaphysics* (Bloomington: Indiana University Press, 1969).

36. The concept of reason would play a central role in the philosophical enterprises of Marcuse and his colleagues. During the 1930s they tended to contrast the substantive and critical concept of reason in Hegel and Marx with various forms of irrationalism and positivism (see, for example, *Reason and Revolution*). Later, they would sharpen their critiques of 'reason', taking the forms of a critique of instrumental reason in Adorno and Horkheimer (see *Dialectic of Enlightenment* and *Eclipse of Reason*) and an attempt by Marcuse to develop an overcoming of repressive reason through a synthesis of reason and passion, resulting in a 'libidinal rationality', and 'rationality of gratification' (see Marcuse's *Eros and Civilization*, which will be discussed in Chapter 6).

37. Marcuse's remarks here apply most directly to German idealist-romanticist culture. He cites Spengler as expressing the other-worldliness of the 'soul-culture': ' "The word 'soul' gives the higher man a feeling of his inner existence, separated from all that is real or has evolved, a very definite feeling of the most secret and genuine potentialities of his life, his destiny, his history. In the early stages of the languages of all cultures, the word 'soul' is a sign that encompasses everything that is not world" ' (Spengler, *N*, p. 108).

38. Institute for Social Research, *Studien über Autorität und Familie.*

39. Marcuse, 'A Study on Authority', in *SCP*, pp. 49–156.

40. Marcuse, 'Authority and the Family in German Sociology to 1933', in *Autorität und Familie*, p. 738.

41. Ibid., p. 738.

42. Ibid., p. 739.

43. Ibid., p. 740.

44. Ibid.

45. Ibid., p. 749.

46. Max Horkheimer, 'Authority and the Family', in *Critical Theory*,

pp. 127 and 128. For a critique of Horkheimer's analysis, see Mark Poster, *Critical Theory of the Family* (New York: Seabury, 1978) pp. 53ff. Poster fails to note Marcuse's article on sociologies of the family, claiming that 'Marcuse's contribution to *Studies on Authority and the Family* was an intellectual history of the idea of authority' (p. 58).

47. Horkheimer, 'Authority and the Family', p. 98.
48. Conversation with Marcuse, March 1978.
49. Wilhelm Reich, *The Mass Psychology of Fascism* (New York: Farrar, Strauss & Giroux, 1970) p. 30.
50. Ibid., p. 32.
51. Ibid., chapters 7–13.
52. Fromm, *Escape from Freedom*. Fromm was more optimistic than other Institute members that the trends towards fascism could be reversed through the creation of more 'productive' and 'loving' personalities. Marcuse claimed that the Institute criticized *Escape from Freedom* 'very severely' (conversation with Habermas and others, 'Theory and Politics', p. 127). The bitter debate between Fromm and Marcuse will be discussed in Chapter 6. On Fromm's relationships with the Institute, see Jay, *The Dialectical Imagination*.
53. Fromm, *Escape from Freedom*.
54. See my discussions of ideology, popular culture and the ideological apparatus in 'Ideology, Marxism, and Advanced Capitalism', *Socialist Review*, 42 (November–December 1978) pp. 37–66, and 'TV, Ideology, and Emancipatory Popular Culture', *Socialist Review*, 45 (May–June 1979) pp. 13–54.
55. On the fascist public sphere, see Reinhard Kuehnl, 'Problems of a Theory of German Fascism', *New German Critique*, 4 (Winter 1975) pp. 26–50; the articles in *New German Critique*, 11 (Spring 1977) pp. 3–150; and Rainer Stollmann, 'Fascist Politics as a Total Work of Art', *New German Critique*, 14 (Spring 1978) pp. 41–60. On the fascists' use of radio see the provocative discussion by Marshall McLuhan in *Understanding Media* (New York: Signet, 1964), and for a discussion of fascist theatre, see Henning Eichberg, 'The Nazi Thingspiel', *New German Critique*, 11 (Spring 1977).
56. On fascism as a cultural synthesis see the articles in *New German Critique*, 11 (Spring 1977). The following analysis is much indebted to material published in *New German Critique*.
57. See Anson Rabinbach, 'Ernst Bloch's *Heritage of Our Times* and Fascism', *New German Critique*, 11, and Ernst Bloch, 'Nonsynchronism and Dialectics', *New German Critique*, 11.
58. Ernst Bloch, *Erbschaft dieser Zeit* (Frankfurt: Suhrkamp, 1962).
59. Wilhelm Reich, *Mass Psychology*, and 'What is Class Consciousness', in *Sex-Pol*, ed. Lee Baxandall (New York: Vintage, 1972).
60. See the articles on the fascist public sphere, cited in note 55.
61. See the articles in *The Frankfurt School Reader*, and the discussion in Jay, *The Dialectical Imagination*, chapter 5.
62. Walter Benjamin, 'The Work of Art in the Age of Mechanical Reproduction', in *Illuminations* (New York: Schocken, 1968).

63. Siegfried Kracauer, 'The Mass Ornament', *New German Critique*, 5 (Spring 1975).

64. Marcuse, *Negations*, pp. ix–x.

65. Max Horkheimer, 'Die Juden und Europa', *Zeitschrift für Sozialforschung*, VIII, 1/1 (1939) p. 115. This essay was one of the last overtly Marxist essays that Horkheimer wrote and was excluded from publication in the two volumes of his collected essays from the period *Kritische Theorie*, ed. Alfred Schmidt (Frankfurt: Suhrkamp, 1969).

66. Neumann, *Behemoth*, and Pollock, 'State Capitalism: Its Possibilities and Limitations', *Studies in Philosophy and the Social Sciences*, IX, 2 (1941) and 'Is National Socialism a New Order', *Studies in Philosophy and the Social Sciences*, IX, 3 (1941). There is debate over whether Marcuse sided with Neumann or Pollock. Jay claims that 'Marcuse, who was personally much closer to Neumann, adopted a position nearer to Neumann's in *Reason and Revolution*, where he wrote, "The most powerful industrial groups tended to assume direct political control in order to organize monopolistic production, to destroy the socialist opposition, and to resume imperialist expansion!"', quoted in Jay, *The Dialectical Imagination*, p. 155. Slater, however, claims: 'Marcuse too seems to have sided, implicitly, with Pollock; in his last contribution to the *Zeitschrift*, he wrote: "The Third Reich is indeed a form of 'technocracy'. The technical considerations of imperialistic efficiency and rationality supersede the traditional standards of profitability and general welfare!"', Slater, *Origin and Significance of the Frankfurt School*, p. 21. These quotes indicate that Marcuse consistently took neither Neumann's nor Pollack's position, although he was certainly personally closer to Neumann. See H. Stuart Hughes, *The Sea Change* (New York: McGraw-Hill, 1977) p. 174. Helmut Dubiel and Alfons Söllner claim that Marcuse's position 'mediated' between the Neumann and Pollock camps. See 'Die Nationalsozialismusforschung des Instituts für Sozialforschung', the introduction to their anthology of Institute writings on National Socialism, *Wirtschaft, Recht und Staat in Nationalsozialismus* (Frankfurt: Europäische Verlagsanstalt, 1981) pp. 7–32. They claim that Marcuse's analysis of 'technological rationality' in 'Some Social Implications of Technology' (*Studies in Philosophy and Social Science*, vol. 9, no. 3, 1941, pp. 414–39) provides a theory of the new technocratic features of national socialism – shared by other advanced industrial societies – but that Marcuse sees 'technological rationality' rooted in the development of the capitalist economy and thus implicitly defends the 'primacy of the economic' advocated by Neumann. In this way, Marcuse can, with Pollock, claim that national socialism is a new order with a technocratic state apparatus, but with Neumann can continue to stress its role in stabilizing and reproducing capitalism. Moreover, Dubiel and Söllner claim that the high level of abstraction in Marcuse's analysis allows him to 'transcend' the alternatives of state versus monopoly capitalism. There is a parallel here with Marcuse's theory of advanced industrial society, which is anticipated in this essay (see my discussion in 8.1).

67. As Helmut Dubiel points out, in the early 1930s the Institute used the

code words 'materialism' and 'materialist', or 'economic theory of society', to describe their Marxian programme, while only around 1936–7 did they adopt the term 'critical theory'. Dubiel's book *Wissenschaftsorganisation und politische Erfahrung* is valuable in documenting and analysing the shifts in the Institute for Social Research's work from (1) an early 'materialist' stage (1930–1936/7) to (2) a 'critical theory' stage (1937–40) and (3) a later 'critique of instrumental reason' stage, where they transform 'critical theory' and distance themselves from Marxism. I would suggest, however, that Marcuse's work in this period resists these shifts and is quite coherent and unified from his entry into the Institute in late 1932 to his departure for government service in 1942 (see the discussion in 4.3).

68. 'Critical theory' in the 1930s was a relatively unified and collective project, while after the 1940s Adorno and Horkheimer, Marcuse, Fromm, Neumann and others developed quite different social theories and had quite different political orientations. See Dubiel, *Wissenschaftsorganisation*, on the 1930s critical theory programme. An adequate comparative analysis of the different versions of post-1940s critical theory has yet to be published, although there is some material in David Held, *Introduction to Critical Theory* (Berkeley: University of California Press, 1980).

69. See especially Max Horkheimer, 'Traditionelle und kritische Theorie'. *Zeitschrift für Sozialforschung*, VI/2 (1937) and the articles by Horkheimer and Marcuse on the theme 'Philosophy and Critical Theory' in *Zeitschrift für Sozialforschung*, VI/3 (1937). Horkheimer's 1930s essays are collected in *Kritische Theorie*, two volumes (Frankfurt: Suhrkamp, 1968) and Marcuse's are found in *Negations*. Horkheimer analyses the concept of critical theory and the programme of interdisciplinary research and differentiates it from traditional social theory. See my discussion in 'Frankfurt School Revisited', and Dubiel, Wissenschaftsorganisation.

70. See *Negations*, and Stefan Breuer's provocative discussion of Marcuse's 1930s essays in *Die Krise der Revolutionstheorie*, pp. 118ff.

71. See Marcuse, 'Philosophy and Critical Theory' (*N*, pp. 134–58) for an example of the sort of careful ideological analysis that I am suggesting characterizes Marcuse's work in this period.

72. Marcuse. 'The Concept of Essence'; the essay first appeared in *Zeitschrift für Sozialforschung*, V/1 (1936). See also 'The Struggle against Liberalism in Totalitarianism', where Marcuse discusses the 'unbridgeable abyss' between Kant's rationalism and defence of human rights and the philosophy of Heidegger, which 'turns traitor to the great philosophy that it formerly celebrated as the culmination of Western thought' (*N*, pp. 40–2). Compare my article 'Ideology, Marxism, and Advanced Capitalism', where I argue that the historical trajectory of ideology in the modern era has tended to take the form of degeneration from once rational-emancipatory programmes of social reconstruction (ideology-as-ism) to apologetic rationalizations and idealizations of the existing society (ideology-as-hegemony).

73. Marcuse claims that this was the function of Max Scheler's notion of a 'material eidetics' (*N*, pp. 61ff.) which is related to fascist submission to authority and irrationalism (see note 40, *N*, p. 277).

74. Compare Horkheimer, who from his first major work, *Anfängen der bürgerlichen Geschichtsphilosophie* (Frankfurt: Suhrkamp, 1971), distinguishes between apologetic-ideological and progressive-utopian moments in bourgeois culture and generally sees more progressive elements in the philosophies of Kant, Hegel and Schopenhauer than in later philosophies such as existentialism, positivism, pragmatism, etc., which he interprets as the collapse and betrayal of earlier ideals.

75. In a sense, Marcuse's shift towards defending the progressive bourgeois heritage against fascism reflects the turn in the Comintern and Social Democracy towards a 'united front'. Thus, during the 1930s, not only is Marcuse's theory close in certain respects to the dominant Marxian orthodoxy, but so are his politics. For further discussion, see 4.1.2 and 4.3.

76. See my discussion of Marcuse's earlier concept of philosophy in 3.1.

77. In 'The Concept of Essence', Marcuse translates the traditional concept of essence into Marxian terms and argues that what is essential in the theory of society is the system of production which produces the totality of social relations and facts (*N*, p. 70).

78. The essay 'On Hedonism' first appeared in *Zeitschrift für Sozialforschung*, VII/1 (1938) and is important both as a defence of critical theory's commitment to bodily gratification and as an anticipation of Marcuse's later incorporation of Freudian elements into his anthropology; it is reprinted in *Negations*.

79. Marcuse writes: 'industrial society has differentiated and intensified the objective world in such a manner that only an extremely differentiated and intensified sensuality can respond adequately to it. Modern technology contains all the means necessary to extract from things and bodies their mobility, beauty and softness in order to bring them closer and make them available. Both the wants corresponding to these potentialities and the sensual organs through which they can be assimilated have been developed. What man can perceive, feel and do in the midst of advanced civilization correspond to the newly opened-up wealth of the world. But only those groups with the greatest purchasing power can take advantage of the expanded capacities and their gratification' (*N*, p. 184). Marcuse will later argue for a 'new technology' (see *One-Dimensional Man*, chapter 9, discussed in 10.2), whereas here he shares the Marxian belief that the development of technology itself will lead to a dramatic increase in human well-being. After the critiques of 'instrumental reason' and 'science and technology as domination' by the Institute in the 1940s, Marcuse concluded that only a 'new technology' could realize technologies' emancipatory potential because the structure and organization of current technologies served as instruments of domination.

80. Marcuse provides some examples of what he means by false needs and pseudo-happiness: 'Pleasure in the abasement of another as well as

self-abasement under a stronger will, pleasure in the manifold surrogates for sexuality, in meaningless sacrifices, in the heroism of war are
false pleasures because the drives and needs that fulfil themselves in
them make men less free, blinder, and more wretched than they have to
be. They are the drives and needs of individuals who were raised in an
antagonistic society' (*N*, p. 194). I shall discuss the concept of false
needs later in my analysis of *One-Dimensional Man*, in which Marcuse
makes the concept a crucial aspect of his critique of contemporary
society (8.2.1).

81. Lukács, *History and Class Consciousness*.
82. See Horkheimer, 'Traditional and Critical Theory', and my discussion
in 'Frankfurt School Revisited'.
83. In his intellectual biography *qua* interview/conversation, Leo Lowenthal tells of a lunch at the Tip-Toe Inn in New York around 1937,
where he, Horkheimer, Marcuse and Wittfogel were discussing the
current political situation and Horkheimer ventured the remark that it
wouldn't be surprising if Hitler and Stalin signed a pact. Lowenthal
recounts that Wittfogel jumped up from the table, angrily threw down
his napkin, cursed, and left the restaurant in a great rage. Lowenthal
says that this incident reflects the heated debates over the Soviet Union
in the Institute during the 1930s and the increasingly critical stance of
many of the Institute members. See Leo Lowenthal, *Mitmachen wollte
ich nie. Ein autobiographisches Gespräch mit Helmut Dubiel* (Frankfurt: Suhrkamp, 1980) pp. 86–7. The discussion of fascism in this book
sheds light on the debate over fascism within the Institute (pp. 101ff,
passim).
84. See T. W. Adorno and Max Horkheimer, *Dialectic of Enlightenment*
(New York: Seabury, 1972) and Horkheimer's essays, 'The End of
Reason') reprinted in *The Essential Frankfurt School Reader* and
'Authoritarian State', translated in *Telos*, 15 (Spring 1973). On the
shifts in Adorno's and Horkheimer's 1940s critical theory from the
earlier Institute project, see Jay, *The Dialectical Imagination*; Kellner,
Karl Korsch: and Dubiel, *Wissenschaftsorganisation*.
85. Horkheimer went furthest in abandoning Marxism, see Kellner, *Karl
Korsch*. Marcuse told Phil Slater in 1974 that he felt that Horkheimer's
last interviews and articles were 'beneath criticism' and talked of
Horkheimer's 'betrayal of critical theory' and 'theoretical collapse',
while Jürgen Habermas described the late Horkheimer's work to me in
similarly bitter terms, denouncing him as an 'outright reactionary' in
his later years. See Phil Slater, *Origin and Significance of the Frankfurt
School* (London: Routledge & Kegan Paul, 1977) pp. 89 and 165;
conversation with Jürgen Habermas, November 1976, Austin, Texas.
86. On Trotsky's orthodoxy, see Peter Beilharz, 'Trotsky's Marxism –
Permanent Involution?', in *Telos*, 39 (Spring 1979) pp. 137–52.
87. Throughout the following chapters, I shall discuss Marcuse's relationship to Marxism, attempting to discern which elements of the Marxian
theory he attempted to affirm, or reconstruct, and which elements he
criticized or rejected. My interpretation of the depth and orthodoxy of

Marcuse's commitment to Marxism at the time is supported by Karl Korsch, who had precisely this impression when he visited the Institute in New York in 1938. After characterizing other members of the Institute in a letter to Paul Mattick, Korsch writes: '*Marcuse* is a sort of orthodox Marxist who might even still be a Stalinist, and is bureaucratically authoritarian in matters of bourgeois philosophy and Marxism (which today have become one and the same). Theoretically, he has somewhat more character and solidity than the others, whose greater "freedom" consists only in a greater fluctuation and uncertainty', quoted in Kellner, *Karl Korsch*, p. 284. Korsch's letters provide some fascinating insights into the activities, politics and personalities in the Institute during their American exile. See the selection, edited and annotated by Michael Buckmiller, in *Marxistische Revolutionstheorien*, ed. Claudio Pozzoli (Frankfurt, Fisher, 1974), especially pp. 182ff, which I review in *Telos*, 27 (Spring 1976) pp. 212ff.

88. Marcuse's book reviews begin modestly with a short review of a book on 'family politics' in *ZfS*, II, 1, p. 134. By the next issue he was writing most of the reviews for the philosophy section and continued to contribute many book reviews to every issue up to 1941, when the *Zeitschrift* ceased publication. The broad range of topics he covered reveal Marcuse's wide range of interests. Although most of Marcuse's reviews are rather sparse summaries of the book's contents, there is some interesting material that make his reviews a hitherto overlooked source of his ideas in the 1930s. I shall draw on his criticisms of logical positivism and (pragmatism) in his reviews in 5.2. A complete list of his book reviews in the *Zeitschrift* appears in the bibliography.

89. On the differences between Horkheimer-Marcuse's and Adorno-Benjamin's version of critical theory in the 1930s, see Susan Buck-Morss, *The Origin of Negative Dialectics* (New York: Free Press, 1977) pp. 65–9.

90. On Adorno's programme of the 'liquidation of idealism', see Buck-Morss, *The Origin of Negative Dialectics*, pp. 111ff, *passim*.

91. See Jay, *The Dialectical Imagination*, Dubiel, *Wissenschaftsorganisation*, and Buck-Morss, *The Origin of Negative Dialectics*. The collaboration of Adorno and Horkheimer was facilitated by their living close to each other in California, whereas Marcuse, Lowenthal, Pollock and others had gone to Washington, DC to work in government agencies as part of the struggle against fascism.

92. Slater, *Origin and Significance*, pp. 89 and 165.

93. Conversation with Marcuse, 28 December 1978.

5 Hegel, Marx and Social Theory: *Reason and Revolution*

1. Herbert Marcuse, *Reason and Revolution* (New York: Oxford University Press, 1941). Pagination is similar in the Oxford edition, the 1954 Humanities Press edition, and the 1960 Beacon Paperback edition.

When *R&R* was published in 1941, it received somewhat mixed reviews. Writing in the Institute's journal, Paul Tillich stated: 'This book is an extremely valuable interpretation of Hegel's philosophy in its social and political significance and consequences, and constitutes a monumental introduction to the method of socio-historical criticism, to the method of "critical theory" as developed by Max Horkheimer and the Institute of Social Research', *Studies in Philosophy and Social Science*, vol. IX, no. 3 (1941) pp. 476–8. Tillich presents a sympathetic account of the book and regrets only that *R&R* does not contain a fuller account of Hegel's philosophy of religion and aesthetics, claiming that 'Even a critical social theory cannot avoid an "ulitmate" in which its criticism is rooted because reason itself is rooted therein' (p. 478). Tillich also raises the provocative question, 'Is positivism as such or only a special type of positivism reactionary?' (p. 478).

Although Karl Löwith admired Marcuse's scholarship and his 'excellent analysis of the foundations of Hegel's philosophy', he believes that Marcuse is mistaken in interpreting Hegel primarily in terms of those elements of his philosophy taken over by Marx. Löwith stresses the importance of the religious elements in Hegel, the concept of recognition as a key anthropological principle not adequately stressed by Marcuse, and argues that 'reconciliation' is the goal of the Hegelian system (*Philosophy and Phenomenological Research*, vol. II, no. 4 (1942) pp. 560–2). In the same issue, Marcuse wrote a rejoinder to Löwith's criticisms, who replied to Marcuse's remarks (pp. 564–6). The most pointedly critical reviews of Marcuse's book were written by Sidney Hook in *The New Republic*, vol. 105 (21 July, 1941) pp. 90–1, and *The Living Age*, vol. 360 (August 1941) pp. 594–5. In *The New Republic*, Hook berates Marcuse's book as 'a kind of apologetic defence, before the event, against the charge that Hegel was a forerunner of fascism' (p. 90). Hook claims that Marcuse's interpretation of Hegel's philosophy as a response to the French Revolution and his defence of the liberal elements in Hegel's philosophy are 'highly dubious and on basic questions definitely wrong' (p. 91). What especially angers Hook is Marcuse's broadside polemic against positivism – a critique that I shall discuss later in this chapter. In *The Living Age*, Hook complains that Marcuse 'obscures the essential fact that Hegel was an outspoken conservative' and dismisses the books as a 'tendentious apologetic' (pp. 594, 595). Other book reviews were more favourable and include: Hans Kohn, *The Annals of the American Academy of Political and Social Science*, vol. 217 (September 1941) pp. 178–9; Herbert Rosinski, *The Nation*, vol. 153 (13 September 1941) pp. 231–2; Benjamin E. Lippincott, *American Political Science Review*, vol. XXXVI, no. 2 (April, 1942) pp. 386–7; J. Glenn Gray. *Political Science Quarterly*, vol. LVII, no. 2 (June, 1942) pp. 292–3; and John H. Hertz, *American Historical Review*, vol. XLVII, no. 3 (April, 1942) p. 591.

2. For other accounts of Hegel and the French Revolution, see Georg Lukács, *The Young Hegel* (London: Merlin Press, 1975); Joachim

Ritter, *Hegel und die Französische Revolution* (Frankfurt: Suhrkamp, 1965); and Jean Hippolite, 'The Significance of the French Revolution in Hegel's *Phenomenology*', in *Studies on Marx and Hegel* (New York: Harper & Row, 1973).

3. Marcuse had defined 'positivism' earlier in *R&R* as 'a general term for the philosophy of "common sense" experience' (*R&R*, p. 112). It is typical for Marcuse's characterization of the history of philosophy that England is usually excluded from important philosophical developments. Accounts of positivism generally root the movement in Locke, Hume and British empiricism and their rejection of speculative metaphysics. Marcuse, however, roots the rise of positivism in continental Europe, in the reaction against critical rationalism. Thus, on his account, positivism is not so much a healthy reaction against the excesses of speculative metaphysics as it is a rejection of the critical method and tendencies of continental rationalism. It should be noted that 'positive philosophy' is a perjorative term for Marcuse, denoting a conformist attitude, whereas 'negative philosophy' is favourably evaluated for being critical, radical and subversive.

4. I might note that these thinkers were major influences on Marx, whose thought and politics were shaped by his study of these precursors of critical theory. However, Marcuse does not adequately indicate their connection with Marx and critical theory. In fact, his discussion of the transition from Hegel to Marx pictures Marx as emerging fully developed from Hegel, as if Zeus were to have sprung fully grown from the head of Minerva! A more balanced interpretation would have indicated the influences on Marxism of French socialism and British political economy, perhaps discussing in turn how Hegel influenced his appropriation of these tendencies.

5. Sidney Hook, review in *The New Republic*, p. 91.

6. The following discussion lays out Marcuse's understanding and critique of contemporary positivism. His detailed book reviews, cited in note 7 below, show how he thought that earlier positivism was linked to its contemporary versions, and indicate the continuities and discontinuities involved. Marcuse would elaborate on his concept of positivism in *One-Dimensional Man*, and a series of articles which precede that work: discussed in Chapter 8. Lucio Colletti has taken up attacking Marcuse's criticisms of scientific positivism and empiricism; see *From Rousseau to Lenin* (London: New Left Books, 1972) and *Marxism and Hegel* (London: New Left Books, 1973). The critiques of Marcuse are more or less the same in both books, which sometimes overlap. Colletti is concerned to purge all dialectics from Marxist materialism and provides an 'ideal type' of Hegelian idealism and dialectics to which he assigns Marcuse, as well as Lukács, Heidegger, Bergson and others! Such an undifferentiated 'critique' fails to see where Marcuse differs from Hegel and covers over the differences between Marcuse, Lukács, Heidegger, *et al.* as well. Colletti even takes on the difficult task of ignoring, suppressing or sometimes criticizing those hated elements of Hegelian dialectics and philosophy in Marx,

Engels, Lenin and the other Marxian thinkers whom he otherwise seems to admire.

7. See Marcuse's critique of Dewey's *Logic of Inquiry* and the positivists' *International Encyclopedia of Unified Sciences* in *Zeitschrift für Sozialforschung*, VIII, 1/2 (1940) pp. 221–32; his critique of Dewey's *Theory of Valuation* in *Zeitschrift für Sozialforschung*, IX, 1 (1941) pp. 144–8; and the critique of von Mises and Russell in *Zeitschrift für Sozialforschung*, IX, 3 (1941) pp. 483–90.

8. Marcuse, 'Critique of Positivist Encyclopedia', p. 23.

9. Ibid.

10. Ibid.

11. Ibid., p. 232.

12. Marcuse, 'Critique of Russell and von Mises', pp. 483 and 485.

13. Marcuse, 'Critique of Dewey', p. 144. In this example, Marcuse refers back to the early, more radical period of positivism and concedes that the positivist critique of metaphysics previously had a relatively progressive function.

14. Ibid., p. 145.

15. Ibid.

16. Ibid., p. 146. This review, in effect, provides an answer to Hook's criticism cited in note 5.

17. Ibid., p. 147.

18. Ibid., pp. 147–8. In a remarkable essay, 'Some Social Implications of Modern Technology', in the same volume as the Dewey Review, *ZfS*, IX, 3 (1941), Marcuse examines some of the forces that were restricting freedom in contemporary society. Here Marcuse previews some of his later analyses of the role of technology as an instrument of domination, the decline of the individual in technological society, and the emerging new forces of social control. Against the tendencies towards conformity, Marcuse champions an ideal of autonomous individuality and critical rationality. This study forms the matrix from which his later critical theory of contemporary society was to develop, and I shall refer back to the essay in the discussion of *One-Dimensional Man* (see 8.1).

19. See Karl Marx, *Economic and Philosophic Notebooks of 1844*, pp. 329ff. For other interpretations of *The Phenomenology of Spirit*, see Jean Hippolite, *Genesis and Structure of the Phenomenology of Mind* (Evanston: Northwestern, 1975); Alexandre Kojeve, *Introduction to the Reading of Hegel* (New York: Basic Books, 1969); and Charles Taylor, *Hegel* (New York: Cambridge, 1975).

20. For other interpretations of Hegel's political philosophy, see Franz Rosenzweig, *Hegel und der Staat* (Aalen: Scientia, 1962; republication of 1920 edn); Eric Weil, *Hegel et l'Etat* (Paris: Vrin, 1950); Walter Kaufmann, ed., *Hegel's Political Philosophy* (New York: Atherton, 1970); Z. A. Pelczynski, ed., *Hegel's Political Philosophy* (New York: Cambridge, 1971); Scholomo Avineri, *Hegel's Theory of the Modern State* (New York: Cambrdige, 1972); Charles Taylor, *Hegel and Modern Society* (New York: Cambridge, 1978; and Raymond Plant, 'Hegel and Political Economy', *New Left Review* 103 and 104 (1977).

21. A much harsher critique of Hegel's *Philosophy of Right* is found in Karl Popper, *The Open Society and Its Enemies* (New York: Harper & Row, 1963). Although Marcuse's grasp of Hegel is far superior to Popper's often superficial and incorrect readings, some of Popper's virulent critique of Hegel's philosophy of the state is justified, laying out some of the more excessive apologetics and paean to German nationalism which Marcuse plays down. For a critique of Popper's methodology and inadequate source material, see Walter Kaufmann's 'The Hegel Myth and Its Method', in *From Shakespeare to Existentialism* (Garden City: Doubleday, 1960).

22. Avineri, *The Social and Political Writings of Karl Marx*, argues that Hegel's political philosophy was progressive for its period, and that both capitalism and a strong state were necessary to bring Germany into the industrial era. Avineri's interpretation may be historically correct, but his attempt to paint Hegel as a progressive liberal tends to suppress the undeniably reactionary traits of Hegel's philosophy. For debate on this topic, see the anthologies edited by Kaufmann and Pelczynski cited in note 20.

23. For a more detailed analysis of post-Hegelian philosophy, see Karl Löwith, *From Hegel to Nietzsche* (Garden City: Doubleday, 1967); Sidney Hook, *From Hegel to Marx* (Ann Arbor: Michigan, 1962); and *Vormarxistishcer Sozialismus*, ed. Manfred Hahn (Frankfurt: Fisher, 1974).

24. Alasdair MacIntyre, *Marcuse* (London: Fontana, 1970). MacIntyre totally ignores Marcuse's early writings and deep immersion in Marx during his formative period, emphasizing instead his study with Heidegger (for whom, he falsely claims, Marcuse wrote his doctoral dissertation). MacIntyre's account of critical theory is extremely superficial, and his 'summaries' of Marcuse's books are simple-minded, reductionistic and uniformed. Most of the book is an attempted hatchet-job on Marcuse, and whatever valid criticisms MacIntyre may have are lost in hyperbole ('almost all of Marcuse's key positions are false', p. 7), supercilious attacks on Marcuse (see, for example, p. 61, where he claims that Marcuse's critique of Soviet Marxism is 'senile'), or idiotic counter-examples (see his astounding attempt to 'refute' Marcuse's theses on technological rationality by citing the 'accidental' character of the Vietnam war and the 'myth of American imperialism', pp. 70ff). Throughout his 'faithful . . . exposition' (?!) (p. 7), MacIntyre obsessively remarks that Marcuse is 'pre-Marxist' (pp. 22, 40, 54, 61). I hope that my study discloses the perverseness of MacIntyre's 'interpretation', which shares the worst features of Soviet tirades against Marcuse's 'non-Marxism'. For a sharp attack on MacIntyre's book, see Robin Blackburn's review in *Telos*, 6 (Fall 1970) pp. 348–51.

25. On the early Hegel, see Wilhelm Dilthey, *Die Jugendgeschichte Hegels* (Leipzig: Teubner, 1921); Georg Lukács, *The Young Hegel*; and Jürgen Habermas, 'Labour and Interaction', in *Theory and Practice* (Boston: Beacon Press, 1974).

26. Hegel, *Philosophy of Right* (New York: Oxford, 1942) pp. 10ff.

27. Marx, *Contribution to the Critique of Hegel's Philosophy of Law, Col-*

lected Works, vol. 3, pp. 5ff. This manuscript is especially important because it records Marx's commitment to a form of radical democracy and sharp criticism of absolute state sovereignty, monarchy, bureaucracy and features of political absolutism that have plagued 'actually existing socialist' societies. Marx's early commentary on Hegel's political philosophy can thus be used to develop criticisms of existing socialist societies.

28. Marx, *Economic and Philosophic Manuscripts of 1844*, pp. 331ff.
29. Marcuse writes: 'The schools of Marxism that abandoned the revolutionary foundations of the Marxian theory were the same that outspokenly repudiated the Hegelian aspects of the Marxian theory, especially the dialectic' (*R&R*, p. 398). In this section Marcuse again distances himself from Marxian 'revisionism' and sees its errors rooted in its abandonment of the Hegelian dialectic.
30. Lukács, *The Young Hegel*. In a 1954 preface, Lukács provides information on the book's genesis, revision and eventual publication (pp. xiff).
31. For a sympathetic account of Hegelian Marxism and Marcuse's contribution, see Iring Fetscher, *Marx and Marxism*. For critiques of Hegelian Marxism that explicitly focus on Marcuse, see Lucio Colletti, *Marxism and Hegel*; Neil McInnes, *The Western Marxists* (New York: Library Press, 1972); and Steigerwald, *Herbert Marcuses 'dritter Weg'*.
32. Marcuse, in *Revolution or Reform?*, ed. by A. T. Ferguson (Chicago: New University Press, 1976) p. 58.
33. On the Office of War Information, see Frank W. Fox, *Madison Avenue Goes to War* (Provo, Utah: Brigham Young University Press, 1975) and R. Harris Smith, *OSS* (Berkeley: University of California Press, 1972). Donovan would become head of the OSS, the government intelligence agency for which Marcuse later worked during the war. See Smith, *OSS*, pp. 2ff.
34. Marcuse, *Revolution or Reform?*, p. 59.
35. See the anonymous 'Progressive Labour' article, 'Marcuse: Cop-out or Cop?', *Progressive Labor*, vol. 6, no. 6 (February, 1969) pp. 61–6. Smith's book, *OSS*, provides important background on the OSS and its relation to the CIA. Smith points out that there were both pro- and anti-communist members in the OSS, which included Marcuse, Franz Neumann, Norman O. Brown, William Bundy, Clark Clifford, John Galbraith, Arthur Goldberg, Walt Rostow and Arthur Schlesinger, to name but a few of the well known people of various political persuasions who worked in America's intelligence service during the war. Smith stresses the anti-colonialism and 'tradition of dissent' in the OSS and their support for Asian nationalism in their struggles against Western colonialism (including support for the Viet Minh and Ho Chi Minh). Whereas Smith's interpretation of the CIA, which emerged from the OSS, is rather uncritical, it seems that the OSS was different in origin, composition, purpose and function from the CIA, and that OSS activity does not make Marcuse and his colleagues 'agents of American imperialism'.

36. Marcuse, *Revolution or Reform?*, p. 59.
37. Marcuse, Conversation with Habermas and others, 'Theory and Politics', *Telos*, 38 (Winter 1978–9) pp. 130–1.
38. Henry Pachter, 'On Being an Exile', *The Legacy of the German Refugee Intellectuals*, p. 36. Describing his friend Franz Neumann's activity, Marcuse writes: 'He devoted most of his efforts to plans for a democratization of Germany which would avoid the failures of the Weimar Republic; he tried to demonstrate that denazification, in order to be effective, must be more than a purge of personnel and an abolition of Nazi legislation – that it must strike at the roots of German fascism by eliminating the economic foundations of the anti-democratic policy of German big industry. Neumann saw that the efforts to attain this objective failed, but he continued to work for strengthening the genuinely democratic forces in Germany in the narrow field still open for such efforts'; 'Preface' to Franz Neumann, *The Democratic and the Authoritarian State*, ed. Herbert Marcuse (New York: The Free Press, 1957) p. viii.
39. H. Stuart Hughes, *The Sea Change* (New York: McGraw-Hill, 1975) p. 175.
40. Ibid.
41. Marcuse, 'Existentialism: remarks on Jean-Paul Sartre's *L'Être et le néant*', *Philosophy and Phenomenological Research*, VIII, 3 (March 1949), reprinted as 'Sarte's Existentialism' in *Studies in Critical Philosophy*, with a brief postscript. Sartre, *Being and Nothingness* (New York: Philosophical Library, 1956).
42. Marcuse, 'Sartre's Existentialism', *SCP*, 160.
43. Ibid.
44. Ibid., p. 161.
45. Sartre, *Being and Nothingness*, p. 615.
46. Marcuse, 'Sartre's Existentialism', p. 161.
47. T. W. Adorno and Max Horkheimer, *Dialectic of Enlightenment* (New York: Herder & Herder, 1972). The book was first published in Amsterdam in German in 1947. Marcuse participated in the discussions in New York and California that provided the background to the book and described it to me as 'one of the most authentic expressions of critical theory' (La Jolla, California, 28 December 1979).
48. Adorno and Horkheimer, *Dialectic of Enlightenment*, p. xi.
49. Ibid. p. ix.
50. Jay, *The Dialectical Imagination*, pp. 253ff.
51. Conversation with Marcuse, 28 December 1978.
52. Perry Anderson, for instance, writes: 'Marcuse in America came to theorize a structural "integration" of the working class into advanced capitalism, and thus the insurmountability of the gulf between socialist thought – now inevitably become "utopian" once again – and proletarian action in contemporary history. The rupture between theory and practice that had silently started in practice in Germany in the later twenties was clamantly consecrated in theory in the mid sixties, with the publication of *One-Dimensional Man*', *Considerations on Western*

Marxism, p. 34. Anderson does not discuss, however, Marcuse's post-*One-Dimensional Man* attempts to repoliticize critical theory, thus freezing his sketch of Marcuse at an earlier stage of his complicated development.

6 Repression and Liberation: *Eros and Civilization*

1. On Marcuse's invitation to the Washington School of Psychiatry and the organization of the school, see Katz, 'Praxis and Poeisis', p. 145. I might add that Marcuse was listed as a 'Guest Lecturer' in the school's 1950–1 course bulletin, and his course was described as follows:

   B-3 Philosophical and Political Aspects of Psychoanalysis, *Marcuse*, Time and dates to be announced, 4 sessions.
      The course attempts to explore the underlying philosophy of psychoanalysis. Psychoanalytical theory and practice imply a specific attitude toward the established forms of society, and the development of psychoanalysis indicates a change in this attitude from critical materialism to conservative idealism. This will be illustrated by a philosophical discussion of the concepts of personality, sanity, neurosis, anxiety, frustration, and repression.
      The course will also examine the role which psychoanalysis plays in the conflicting political philosophies of our time. It will include a discussion of the relationship between psychoanalysis and Marxism, and an analysis of Existentialism.
      Open to all students at the discretion of the Admissions Committee. $10.

   The bulletin indicates that the faculty included during the 1950–1 school year Erich Fromm, Frieda Fromm-Reichmann, Ernest Schachtel, Clara Thompson and Patrick Mullahy. Thus Marcuse had the opportunity to make contact with some of the top Freudian and 'revisionist' psychoanalyists of the period.
2. Conversation with Marcuse, March 1978.
3. Marcuse, 'On Hedonism', *N*, p. 187.
4. In a conversation with me in March 1978, Marcuse stressed the continuity in his aesthetic concerns and theory between his post-1950s work and his studies in the 1920s (discussed in Chapter 1). He insisted, however, that his decisive study of Schiller began in the 1950s and that his earlier work on a Schiller bibliography was 'just a job' and did not have an important influence on his thought.
5. Conversation with Marcuse, March 1978.
6. It has been claimed that Adorno and Horkheimer were influenced by the Jewish prohibition on creating images of God or paradise which inhibited them from projecting political alternatives. See Jay, *The Dialectical Imagination*, p. 56, and Jürgen Habermas, 'Der deutsche Idealismus der Jüdischen Philosophen'. *Philosophisch-politische Profile* (Frankfurt: Suhrkamp, 1971) p. 41. It seems to me that Adorno and

Horkheimer simply were not as interested in politics or socialism as Marcuse, and hence were not as concerned to project social-political alternatives or to posit any specific political practice. See Chapter 9, 'Critical theory and radical politics' for further discussion of this issue.

7. *EC* has had a complicated and interesting history. The publication of its epilogue in *Dissent* sparked a bitter controversy with Erich Fromm; see *Dissent*, II, 4 (Fall 1955) pp. 342–9, and *Dissent*, III, 1 (Spring 1956) pp. 79–83. The book received a mixed reception from the psychoanalytic establishment and Freud scholars. See the favourable review by Martin Grotjahn, *Psychoanalytic Quarterly*, XXV (1956) and the critical reviews by Herbert Fingarette, *Review of Metaphysics*, X (June 1957) pp. 660–5, and Sidney Axelrad, 'On Some Uses of Psychoanalysis'. *Journal of the American Psychoanalytic Association*, VIII (January 1960) pp. 175–218. Several studies have criticized Marcuse for his distortions of Freud. See Anthony Wilden, 'Marcuse and the Freudian Model'. *The Legacy of the German Refugee Intellectuals, Salmagundi*, 10/11 (Fall 1969–Winter 1969) pp. 196–245; Jean Laplanche, 'Notes sur Marcuse et al Psychanalyse', *Marcuse Cet Inconnu, La Nef*, 36 (Janvier–Mars 1969); Erich Fromm, *The Crisis of Psychoanalysis* (New York: Holt, Rinehart & Winston, 1970); Sidney Lipshires, *Herbert Marcuse: From Marx to Freud and Beyond* (Cambridge, Mass.: Schenkman, 1974); and Schoolman, *Imaginary Witness*. In the 1960s, *EC* was seen as a major influence on the emerging counterculture. See Theodore Roszak, *The Making of a Counter Culture* (Garden City, NY: Doubleday Anchor Books, 1969) and Morris Dickstein, *Gates of Eden* (New York: Basic Books, 1977). *EC* also made a deep impression on a current of Western Marxism and what would become known as Freudo-Marxism. Early translations of its chapters were published in the French journals *La Table Round* and *Arguments* (see Bibliography) and the book influenced a generation of French thinkers. See Jean-Michel Palmier, *Herbert Marcuse et la Nouvelle Gauche*, and Alain J. Cohen, *Marcuse: Le Scenario Freudo-Marsien* (Paris: Editions Universitaires, 1974). Orthodox Marxists, and those influenced by Habermas's version of critical theory, criticized Marcuse's too uncritical acceptance of Freud's instinct theory. See Steigerwald, *Herbert Marcuses 'dritter Weg'*, and Arnson, *Von Marcuse zu Marx*. New Left rebellions against orthodox Marxism found *EC*'s emphasis on sexuality, culture and liberation a refreshing supplement to an often overly 'economistic' or 'objectivistic' Marxian orthodoxy. See the often contradictory receptions by French Freudo-Marxists like Baudrillard, Deleuze, Guattari, Lyotard and others, as well as the Freudo-Marxian syntheses in Bruce Brown, *Marx, Freud, and the Critique of Everyday Life* (New York: Monthly Review Press, 1973); Russell Jacoby, *Social Amnesia* (Boston: Beacon Press, 1975); and Gad Horowitz, *Repression* (Toronto: University of Toronto Press, 1977). As this sketch indicates, *EC* has had extremely varied and contradictory effects and continues to be one of Marcuse's most provocative and controversial works.

8. Sigmund Freud, *Civilization and its Discontents, The Standard Edition of the Collected Works of Sigmund Freud*, XXI, pp. 57–145 (London: The Hogarth Press, 1953–66).

9. See Freud's *Civilization and its Discontents*, where he argues that repression is necessary to check the unruly and aggressive instincts in human nature that make 'man a wolf to man'; *Standard Edition*, pp. 57ff, and especially section V; and *The Future of an Illusion, Standard Edition*, XXI, pp. 1–56, where Freud argues that humans are lazy by nature and must be forced to work.

10. *EC*, pp. 12ff and 'Freedom and Freud's Theory of Instincts', *5L*, pp. 5ff. Compare Freud, 'Formulations Concerning the Two Principles in Mental Functioning', *Collected Papers*, IV (London: The Hogarth Press, 1950) pp. 14ff.

11. See also 'Freedom and Freud's Theory of Instincts', where Marcuse writes: 'The structure of Freud's theory is open to and in fact *encourages* consideration in political terms ... this theory which appears to be purely biological, is fundamentally social and historical', p. 1.

12. See George Herbert Mead, *Mind, Self and Society* (Chicago: University Press, 1934) and many theories discussed in Kurt Danziger, *Socialization* (London and Baltimore: Penguin Books, 1971). For critical remarks on dominant theories of socialization, see Marcuse, 'Progress and Freud's Theory of Instincts', *Five Lectures*, pp. 28–43.

13. Marcuse cites Ernest Schachtel's paper, 'On Memory and Childhood Amnesia' as an important analysis of 'the explosive force of memory and its control and conventionalization by society' (*EC*, p. 19). Marcuse's concept of the importance of memory for liberation was shaped by the ideas of Adorno and Benjamin. See Benjamin, *Illuminations*, and Martin Jay, *The Dialectical Imagination*, pp. 267–8.

14. On the emancipatory role of daydreams, phantasy and hope, see Ernst Bloch, *Das Prinzip Hoffnung* (Frankfurt: Suhrkamp, 1959), especially Part II on 'The Anticipatory Consciousness'.

15. Marcuse, 'On Hedonism', *Negations*.

16. Marcuse, *EC* and 'Freedom and Freud's Theory of Instincts'. Marcuse continued this defence of Freud to the end of his life. See his conversations with Habermas and others, *Gespräche mit Herbert Marcuse* (Frankfurt: Suhrkamp, 1978).

17. 'Eros' for Marcuse signifies instinctual energies that contain the creative life-affirming and social aspects of human nature. See *EC*, pp. 26f, 40ff, 83ff, and 204ff.

18. Freud never used the term Thanatos, although it is widely used in psychoanalytic literature as a synonym for the death instinct. Freud's biographer, Ernest Jones, writes: 'Freud himself, never, except in conversation, used for the death instinct the term Thanatos, one which has become so popular since ... Stekel had in 1909 used the word Thanatos to signify a death-wish, but it was Federn who introduced it in the present context'. Ernest Jones, *The Life and Work of Sigmund Freud*, vol. III (New York: Basic Books, 1952) p. 252. See also Paul Federn, *Ego Psychology and the Psychoses* (New York: Basic Books, 1952) p. 272.

19. For critiques of Freud's concept of the death instinct see Wilhelm Reich, *Sex-Pol*, pp. 17f and 85, and *The Function of the Orgasm* (New York: Farrar, Straus & Giroux, 1973) pp. 154ff; Otto Fenichel, *Collected Papers* (New York: Norton, 1962) pp. 366ff; and Erich Fromm, *The Anatomy of Human Destructiveness* (New York: Holt, Rinehart & Winston, 1973).

20. Marcuse develops this theme in a later article, 'Aggressiveness in Advanced Industrial Society', *Negations*, writing: 'in the Freudian conception, destructive energy cannot become stronger without reducing erotic energy: the balance between the two primary impulses is a quantitative one; the instinctual energy is mechanistic, distributing an available quantum of energy between the two antagonists', pp. 257–8. Marcuse stuck to this model of Freud's instinct theory to the end of his life; see the discussion in Chapter 10.

21. For a critique of the Freudian energy-instinct model, see Wilden, 'Marcuse and the Freudian Model'; Richard Wollheim, *Freud* (New York: Viking, 1971); and William Barrett and Daniel Yankelovich, *Ego and Instinct* (New York: Harper & Row, 1971). Marcuse's use of Freud's instinct theory will be critically discussed in 6.4.2 below.

22. See section 6.1 and note 11 above. Earlier, Marcuse tried to historicize and concretize the anthropologies of Heidegger and Hegel, bringing them into the Marxian project (see discussion in Chapters 2 and 3). In a sense, he is now attempting a similar project with Freud.

23. Against Horowitz, *Repression*, I would suggest that both Freud, and what Horowitz calls 'Marcuse's Freud', do not limit obstacles to a non-repressive civilization to exogenous factors, like scarcity, but also stress the internal obstacles of human instincts. Marcuse reinterprets and reconstructs Freud's instinct theory to show that what Freud believed were insurmountable elements to a non-repressive society *within* human nature misunderstood the nature, function and goal of human instincts. See section 6.3 for Marcuse's reconstruction of Freud and theory of liberation.

24. Max Weber's influence of Marcuse's theory of domination will be discussed in more detail in the next two chapters. Weber's theory of domination was taken over by critical theory and applied in different ways, without citing Weber, in its two epics of domination, *Dialectic of Enlightenment* and *One-Dimensional Man*. The concept in turn became a central concept in contemporary critical theory. See William Leiss, *Domination of Nature* (Boston: Beacon Press, 1974) and the collection of essays edited by Alkis Kontos, *Domination* (Toronto: University Press, 1975). I shall argue below that many of Marcuse's interpreters misunderstand his concept of domination, and am grateful to Bob Antonio for insisting on the similarities between the critical theory concept of domination and that of Max Weber.

25. Marcuse, 'Freedom and Freud's Theory of Instincts', *SL*, 1. There are conceptual problems in clarifying and relating such terms as domination, repression and alienation in Marcuse's critical theory. He uses both 'domination' and 'repression' as broad, generic terms which include external-social oppression as well as Freudian notions of

psychological repression, introjection, etc. Alkis Kontos suggests making a distinction between 'force' and 'hegemony' as instruments of social control (without noting the parallel to Gramsci), defining 'oppression' as 'a condition of overt, visible, forceful restriction of another's life-activity'. 'Domination', on the other hand 'refers to a totally distinct condition. The dominated are denied the fulfilment of their ontological capacities ... Unlike slaves, the dominated appear in the guise of free, self-determined agents, but it does not mean that they are so. The process of internalization of the external structures of domination can be identified and exposed'. See Alkis Kontos, 'Through a Glass Darkly: Ontology and False Needs', *Canadian Journal of Political and Social Theory*, vol. 3, no. 1 (Winter 1979) pp. 38ff. Although it often makes sense to make the Gramscian distinction between force and hegemony, I believe that domination and repression for Marcuse combine overt force/oppression and internal control mechanisms. This is clear in Marcuse's definition of repression (*EC*, pp. 8, 276) and I believe that it is also true of domination, which I am suggesting is a comprehensive totalizing concept of social control in his theory.

26. Marcuse has been harshly criticized for distorting Freud's theory of repression, which refers generally to unconscious suppression of illicit desires and painful or traumatic experiences. See Fingarette, Wilden, Laplanche, Fromm and Lipshires (bibliographical references in note 7). These criticisms, however, fail to note that Marcuse is consciously modifying the Freudian category to include external and internal phenomena, thus rejecting the – in his view – too internal-psychological theory of repression in Freud. This is clear in Marcuse's definition of repression in *EC*, p. 8 (cited below) and in the index to *EC*, where next to the category 'repression' he lists '(suppression, oppression)' (*EC*, p. 276).

27. See, especially, Marcuse's essay 'Some Implications of Modern Technology', *Studies in Philosophy and Social Science*, IX (1941), *Soviet Marxism* and *One-Dimensional Man*. I shall elaborate on this theme in the following chapters.

28. Marcuse, 'Some Implications of Modern Technology'. For a discussion of Marcuse's theory of the apparatus of domination which combines administration and violence, see Wolfgang Lipp, 'Apparat und Gewalt', *Soziale Welt*, Jahrg. 20, Heft 3 (1970) pp. 274–303.

29. Marcuse, 'Some Implications'. Compare Fromm, *The Sane Society*, and Jacoby, *Social Amnesia*.

30. In an otherwise useful article, 'Marcuse and the Problem of Happiness', *Canadian Journal of Political and Social Theory*, vol. 2, no. 1 (Winter 1978), Charles Rachlis writes: 'As a form of ideology, domination consists in the falsification of reality by particular social interests, and the substitution of this falsehood for reality via the surplus-repressive controls embodied in the performance principle' (p. 73). I do not believe that domination is simply 'a form of ideology', but believe that domination is a much more comprehensive category which

links such things as ideologies, institutions, social practice and individual behaviour. See the Lipp article cited in note 28 for a suggestive collection of quotes from Marcuse's text which indicate that he links discussion of a social apparatus of administration, force and coercion with ideology in his theory of domination.

31. Marcuse's theory of 'surplus repression' has been criticized in *Francois Perroux interroge Herbert Marcuse* (Paris: Aubier-Montaigne, 1969) and by many other people, for being too vague to calculate. This criticism is not entirely convincing to me for it does seem possible to be able to calculate the amount of socially necessary labour-time and to subtract that from actual labour-time, and hence to provide an estimate of the current amount of surplus repression due to socially imposed but unnecessary labour-time. It is more difficult, however, to calculate sexual repression, although one can criticize a society's too severe sexual prohibitions, values and institutions as examples of surplus repression that impose sexual deprivation on individuals and impede sexual gratification. Horowitz, *Repression*, shows that Freud also makes a distinction between 'basic' and 'surplus' repression and attempts to provide a grounding of Marcuse's concept of surplus repression in Freudian theory.

32. See Max Weber, *The Protestant Ethic and the Spirit of Capitalism* (New York: Scribner, 1958). Marcuse would argue that the 'performance principle' also applies to Soviet Communist societies and that its function as the dominant reality principle is an indication of domination and repression in the Soviet Union. See *Soviet Marxism*, discussed in the next chapter.

33. On the topic compare T. W. Adorno and Max Horkheimer, 'The Culture Industry', *Dialectic of Enlightenment*, with Douglas Kellner, 'Ideology, Marxism, and Advanced Capitalism' and 'TV, Ideology, and Emancipatory Popular Culture', in *Socialist Review*, 42 (November–December 1978) and *SR*, 45 (May–June 1979).

34. In an essay, 'The Realm of Freedom and the Realm of Necessity. A Reconsideration', *Praxis*, V, no. 1–2 (1969) Marcuse writes: 'I am happy and honoured to talk to you in the presence of Ernst Bloch today, whose work *Geist der Utopie*, published more than forty years ago, has influenced at least my generation, and has shown how realistic utopian concepts can be, how close to action, how close to practice' (p. 20).

35. Marcuse, 'Marxism and Feminism'. This lecture was delivered at Stanford on 7 March 1974 and printed in *Women's Studies*, vol. 2, no. 3 (1974) and various underground newspapers, like the Austin *rag* where I first encountered it. Marcuse utilizes here the concepts in *EC* that we are discussing, and concretizes his contrast between the two reality principles in terms of current struggles for liberation in the women's movement.

36. Marcuse, 'Marxism and Feminism'.

37. This passage is reminiscent of the early Marx's concept of Communism in the *Economic-Philosophical Manuscripts*. We see again the strong

hold that the ideas of the early Marx exerted over Marcuse (see Chapters 1–3).

38. See Freud's papers, 'Formulations Concerning the Two Principles in Mental Functioning', in *Collected Papers*, IV, and 'The Relation of the Poet to Daydreaming', *Character and Culture, Collected Papers*. For a criticism of Marcuse's use of Freud's theory of phantasy, see Wilden, 'Marcuse and the Freudian Model'.

39. It is one of the ironies of modern philosophy that Marcuse introduces his concept of the 'Great Refusal' with a passage by the speculative metaphysician Whitehead, who wrote in *Science and the Modern World*: 'The truth that some proposition respecting an actual occasion is untrue may express the vital truth as to the aesthetic achievement. It expresses the "great refusal" which is its primary characteristic' (quoted in *EC*, p. 149). The origins of the concept, however, are probably with Breton and surrealism, where there was also talk of the 'great refusal'.

40. Statements that a 'new basic experience of being would change the human existence in its entirety' (*EC*, p. 158) disclose the subterranean Heideggerian influence on Marcuse. The later Heidegger opposes a 'new experience of being' (*Seinslassen*: letting Being be) to the predominant experience of a technological society that strives to dominate nature, to subject nature, humans and other beings to the will to power. See Martin Heidegger, *The Question of Technology* (New York: Harper & Row, 1976).

41. I criticize Marcuse's choice of Orpheus and Narcissus as cultural ideals in the conclusion to this chapter.

42. Marcuse confesses in 'The End of Utopia': 'I am an absolutely incurable romantic', *SL*, p. 82.

43. Marcuse compiled a bibliography on Schiller in 1925, and his early immersion in German literature and aesthetics often emerges in his later writings.

44. Friedrich Schiller, *The Aesthetic Letters, Essays, and the Philosophical Letters* (Boston: Little, Brown, 1845).

45. A constant theme in Marcuse's writing is criticism of repressive reason – a position that links him with Norman O. Brown in *Life Against Death* (New York: Vintage, 1959). Marcuse's stress on the need to develop a concept of 'sensuous reason' and his sharp critique of Brown's *Love's Body* (see *Negations*) shows that Marcuse is not proposing abandoning reason, however, as some uninformed critics charge. See Vivas; Marcuse never advocates any form of 'irrationalism' which rejects reason, but he does offer a rather different concept of reason than more classical rationalists, or even representatives of critical theory. See his revealing exchange with Habermas, 'Theory and Politics', pp. 132ff. *Vis-à-vis* the concept of reason, one discerns a rather sharp break from Marcuse's Hegelian rationalism in his 1930s 'critical theory' essays and *R&R* in contrast to *EC* and his later writings.

46. MacIntyre, *Marcuse*, pp. 46ff. Against MacIntyre, Fromm and others,

Gar Horowitz argues in *Repression* that Marcuse does not reject genital sexuality, but does reject a repressive genitality that suppresses all elements of sexual activity that do not contribute to genital intercourse. According to Horowitz, Marcuse maintains that renunciation of desire for gratification of non-genital zones and 'containment' of partial sexual impulses is repressive and totalitarian as well if it leads to limiting 'sexual expression to heterosexual genital (procreative) intercourse between a single, dominant "husband", and a single, subordinate "wife", legally married for life, and to prohibit, in varying degrees, all other manifestations of sexuality' (p. 67). In Horowitz's view, rather than displacing genital sexuality by pre-genital sexuality, Marcuse is advocating activation and intensification of '*all* erotogenetic zones' (*EC*, p. 201). Horowitz claims that this ideal of sexuality is close to Freud's, and suggests the term 'polymorphic genitality' (p. 75) to describe the ideal of sexuality as at once genital and non-genital. Rather than strait-jacketing Marcuse into an either/or model of sexual advocacy (i.e. either non-genital 'polymorphic perversity', or straight genital sex), Horowitz sugrests that Marcuse's ideal advocates *both* enlarged and intensified sexuality. Marcuse's further point, explicated in the following pages, is that partial expressions of sexuality (i.e. 'perversions') will lose their neurotic or destructive traits in a liberated Eros which will, furthermore, spread erotic energies to other relations and activities, rather than to confine them to the bedroom or brothel.

47. Wilhelm Reich, *The Sexual Revolution* (New York: Vision Press, 1969) pp. 6–7.

48. I do not think that Marcuse fully does justice to Reich, who was one of the first to attempt to synthesize Marxian and Freudian ideas. During the 1920s and 1930s Reich made important contributions in theory and practice to both the Marxian and psychoanalytic movements, which Marcuse does not adequately appraise in his rather superficial dismissal of Reich. To be sure, after Reich was expelled from both the Marxian and psychoanalytic movements, he wasted his creative energies during a difficult exile period in the sort of occult science that Marcuse complains about. But this should not keep us from studying Reich's important works, such as the essays collected in *Sex-Pol*; *The Mass Psychology of Fascism*, or *The Function of the Orgasm*. For sympathetic readings of Reich's Freudo-Marxism, see Bertell Ollman's introduction to the *Sex-Pol* essays, and 'The Marxism of Wilhelm Reich', in *The Unknown Dimension*, ed. Dick Howard and Karl Klare (New York: Basic Books, 1972). For a more critical view of Reich's merger of Marx and Freud, see Michael Schneider, *Neurosis and Class Struggle* (New York: Seabury Press, 1976) and Horowitz, *Repression*.

49. Many of Marcuse's Freudian critics are quick to point out that the notion of a 'non-repressive sublimation' is a logical impossibility in Freud's theory, as sublimation is always for Freud a 'repressive' deflection of erotic energies. See Lipshires, *Herbert Marcuse*, pp. 38–47. Marcuse could answer that he is rejecting here the or-

thodox psychoanalytic position and is suggesting a provocative conceptual reformulation that explicates features of liberation.

50. See section 6.3.2 and note 45 above.
51. In *An Essay on Liberation*, Marcuse suggests 'passing from Marx to Fourier' (*EL*, p. 22). For Fourier's ideas, see Mark Poster's anthology, *Harmonian Man* (New York: Doubleday, 1970) and the discussion in Manuel, *Utopia*.
52. *EC*, pp. 35ff, 132ff, and 222ff. Marcuse's ideal obviously presupposes a 'post-scarcity' society of abundance. Whether we are or not in such a situation is a topic of current debate. Marcuse continued to argue that we are in a post-scarcity situation already, and that it is only the capitalist mode of production and consequent unequal distribution of wealth and imposition of scarcity that prevents development of a genuine society of abundance for all. Conversation with Marcuse, La Jolla, California, 28 December 1978.
53. The notion of a 'libidinal' or erotic morality is one that tantalizes Marcuse and denotes his distance from idealist and rationalist morality which he claims is repressive. The concept is hotly debated within Freudian circles. See Lipshires, *Herbert Marcuse*, pp. 50ff.
54. Time and time again Marcuse cites the importance of the liberation of memory. See section 6.1 and the concluding paragraph of *The Aesthetic Dimension*, p. 73.
55. On Schiller's concept of the aesthetic state, see the forthcoming book by Josef Chytry. I am indebted to Chytry's work for insights into the relation between Schiller, German Idealism and Marcuse.
56. T. W. Adorno, *Ästhetische Theorie* (Frankfurt: Suhrkamp, 1970) pp. 469–72.
57. Ibid.
58. Wilden, 'Marcuse and the Freudian model'. See the next section for details of this criticism.
59. See Steigerwald, *Herbert Marcuses 'dritter Weg'*, and Erich Fromm, *The Crisis of Psychoanalysis* (New York: Fawcett, 1970).
60. Marcuse's critique of the work ethic and production here shows the groundlessness of Baudrillard's critique discussed in 3.3.
61. Fromm's books *Man for Himself* (New York: Holt, Rinehart & Winston, 1947), *The Sane Society* and other writings make the 'productive personality' an ideal character type. Marcuse thinks that Fromm falls prey here to the capitalist work ethic and bourgeois humanism. For a discussion of the split and the continuing debate between Marcuse and Fromm, see Martin Jay, *The Dialectical Imagination*, chapter 3.
62. Marcuse, 'The End of Utopia', *SL*, p. 63.
63. See Chapter 10 for further discussion of this issue.
64. Morton Schoolman claims that Marcuse 'disregards' the 'melancholic and pathological traits of Orpheus and Narcissus'; see 'Marcuse's "Second Dimension"', *Telos*, 23 (Spring 1975) pp. 104ff. Schoolman concludes that this constitutes a 'definitive nihilism' in Marcuse (p. 108). I would instead argue that Marcuse's selective interpretation of the Orpheus and Narcissus myths reveals some of his deepest values;

hence adequate interpretation should make clear these values and question whether Marcuse's values are adequate to the achievement of liberation.

65. On the mythological sources of the Narcissus and Orpheus myths, see Robert Graves, *The Greek Myths* (Baltimore and London: Penguin, 1965). The myth of Narcissus was the basis for Freud's theory of narcissism. See Freud, 'On Narcissism', *Standard Edition, XIV*, pp. 67–102 and Otto Kernberg, *Borderline Conditions and Pathological Narcissism* (New York: Aronson, 1975). The popularity of Christopher Lasch's *The Culture of Narcissism* (New York: Norton, 1979) has occasioned a heated debate over the nature and significance of narcissism in contemporary society. Against Lasch, who relentlessly flagellates the 'narcissistic personality', Stanley Aronowitz, basing his analysis on Marcuse's concept of narcissism as the 'great refusal', argues that there is an emancipatory moment in narcissism which refuses submission to alienated labour, repressive sexuality and the demands of a bureaucratic society. See Aronowitz, 'On Narcissism' in *Telos*, 44 (Summer 1980), as well as the other articles on narcissism in a 'Symposium on Narcissism' in the same issue. See also the debate on Lasch's work in *Salmagundi*, 46 (Fall 1979).

Orpheus, too, is a controversial and mysterious figure in the mythological tradition. In one tradition, Orpheus is said to have been killed by the Maenads for teaching sacred mysteries opposed to the cult of Dionysus (Aristophanes: *Frogs*, p. 1032; Ovid: *Metamorphoses* xi, pp. 1–85). Another account claims that Orpheus was Dionysus in disguise (Proclus: Commentary on Plato's *Politics*, p. 398). Yet another account claims that Orpheus had condemned the sexual promiscuity of the Maenads, rejected their sexual advances, and preached and practised homosexuality. In this tradition, he was seen as a misogynistic foe of women (embittered because of his disaster with Eurydice?) and both Aphrodite and Dionysus wanted his death (Ovid, *Metamorphoses*); Plutarch: *On the Slowness of Divine Vengeance*, p. 12). Finally, another tradition holds that Orpheus was a Shaman who had access to ancient wisdom and was killed by Zeus for divulging divine secrets (Pausanias: ix, 30.3). See Graves, pp. 111–15.

66. See Marcuse's exchange with Brown in *Negations*, where he makes clear that he is advocating the political fight as the way to liberation.

67. See the references in note 7. The most extensive studies of Marcuse's use and abuse of Freud, based on a detailed study of psychoanalytic literature, are Horowitz, *Repression*, and Sidney Lipshires, *Herbert Marcuse: From Marx to Freud and Beyond*. Lipshires's study is valuable for his constant juxtaposition of Freudian and Marcusean positions, and their comparison with other positions in psychoanalytic literature. Lipshires is often justified in criticizing Marcuse's use of Freud and other Freudians to support his own position, but Lipshires is generally uncritical towards Freud and believes he has refuted Marcuse's positions merely by showing how orthodox Freudian positions are at odds with Marcuse. Schoolman takes the same tact in *Imaginary Witness*.

68. See Lipshires, *Herbert Marcuse*, for many examples.
69. For example, Marcuse makes minimal use of Freud's theory of the unconscious, the symbolic dimension of experience, and communication stressed by Lacan, Baudrillard, Ricoeur, Habermas and others. Compare Marcuse's use of Freud with Jacques Lacan, *Ecrits: A Selection* (New York: Norton, 1978); Jean Baudrillard, *The Mirror of Production*; Paul Ricoeur, *Freud and Philosophy* (New Haven: Yale University Press, 1971); and Jürgen Habermas, *Knowledge and Human Interests* (Boston: Beacon Press, 1971). Moreover, he rejects Freud's theory of character which is essential to Erich Fromm's synthesis of Marx and Freud.
70. See the sources in note 21 above.
71. Marcuse himself describes these obstacles to freedom as real factors denied by idealist theories of freedom in 'Freedom and Freud's Theory of Instincts'.
72. For an early critique of Freud's theory of civilization and concept of the primal father, see Wilhelm Reich, 'The Imposition of Sexual Morality'. *Sex-Pol*. Discussions of Freud's theory from anthropological and psychoanalytic perspectives can be found in *The Psychoanalytic Study of Society*, IV, ed. Warner Muensterberger and Sidney Axelrad (New York: International Universities Press, 1967).
73. Marcuse periodically refers to the Oedipus complex throughout his writings on Freud but neither discusses it in any detail, nor does he criticize it. Freudians maintain that he does not adequately utilize the Oedipus concept in his theory; see Laplanche, 'Notes sur Marcuse', pp. 131ff, and Lipshires, *Herbert Marcuse*, passim. Axelrad claims that Marcuse misinterprets the Oedipus concept, 'On Some Uses of Psychoanalysis', pp. 182ff. For a through assault on the concept of the Oedipus complex, see Gilles Deleuze and Felix Guattari, *Anti-Oedipus* (New York: Viking, 1977).
74. Wilden, 'Marcuse and the Freudian Model', pp. 236ff.
75. Bloch, *Das Prinzip Hoffnung*.
76. See the sources in note 21; Lipshires, *Herbert Marcuse* and MacIntyre, *Marcuse*.
77. Marcuse, *EC*, pp. 210ff. It could be argued that Marcuse's concept of Eros is more Platonic than Freudian.
78. See Fromm, *The Anatomy of Human Destructiveness*.
79. For a discussion of Marx's anthropology and its usefulness for contemporary theory, see my article 'Karl Marx and Adam Smith'.
80. Habermas, *Knowledge and Human Interests*, and Ricoeur, *Freud and Philosophy*.
81. See Jacoby, *Social Amnesia*, and Robinson, for defences of Marcuse's use of Freud along these lines.
82. In a sense, Marcuse anticipates the critiques of the over-emphasis within Marxism of labour and productivity later argued by Habermas, Wellmer, Baudrillard and others. His reconstruction of Marxian theories of liberation and socialism will be the focus of Chapter 10, where we shall return to these themes.
83. See Robert Solomon, *The Passions* (New York: Doubleday, 1976).

7 Marcuse's Critique of Bureaucratic Communism: *Soviet Marxism*

1. For example, Arnson, *Von Marcuse zu Marx*, titles his chapter on *Soviet Marxism*, 'Marcuses Kritik des Stalinismus' and argues that 'Marcuse is the only theorist of the Frankfurt School who has made the attempt of a systematic confrontation with Stalinism' (p. 177). Palmier, in his *Sur Marcuse*, describes *SM* as a 'passionate polemic against the Stalinist bureaucracy . . . an analysis without doubt pessimistic of Soviet Marxism and its cruel contradictions' (pp. 24, 34).

2. Marcuse writes in the 1961 Vintage Preface: 'In the Soviet Union, critics accused me of endeavouring "to depreciate and distort communist morality", to consider "capitalist society as the triumph of individual freedom" and to repeat "the old bourgeois lie about socialism being a rigorous totalitarian system based on universal oppression"' (*SM*, p. v). Steigerwald, *Herbert Marcuses 'dritter Weg'*, titles his chapter, 'The book against Soviet Marxism' and claims that Marcuse's interpretation is a form of anti-Soviet cold war propaganda that serves the interests of Western capitalistic-imperialism.

3. Marcuse writes in the 1961 Vintage Preface: 'In the United States, I am said to treat "Soviet Marxism as a stage in mankind's struggle toward freedom and socialism", and to be more unambiguous in my "critical analysis of Western life and society" than in my analysis of the Soviet Union' (*SM*, p. v). Marcuse takes these 'contradictions' as an indication of his success in freeing himself 'from Cold War propaganda and in presenting a relatively objective analysis, but I would suggest that these contradictory appraisals of his book mirror the real ambivalences that Marcuse's interpretation contains. Left-liberal critiques of *Soviet Marxism*'s apologetic features include a review by L. Stern in *Dissent*, vol. V, no. 1 (Winter 1958) pp. 88–93, and George Lichtheim's review in *Survey* (January-March 1959) reprinted in *Collective Essays* (New York: The Viking Press, 1974) pp. 337–47. *SM* received its sharpest critique from the Left from Marcuse's friend Raya Dunayevskaya, in her review 'Intellectuals in the Age of State Capitalism', *News and Letters* (June-July and August-September 1961). Dunayevskaya claims that Marcuse exaggerates the continuity between Marxism and Stalinism and fails to point out that the 'Soviets' – originally organs of workers' democracy – had been suppressed by a bureaucratic and repressive state that had nothing in common with Marxian socialism. Dunayevskaya deplores Marcuse's failure to indicate more clearly the differences between Marxism, Leninism and Stalinism and to criticize Stalinism more sharply as a total perversion of revolutionary Marxism. Although Dunayevskaya fails to take note of the critical moments in Marcuse's analysis – which I shall bring out in this chapter – she quite rightly calls attention to Marcuse's atypically restrained use of the 'power of negation' in his analysis of Soviet Marxism. Throughout this chapter I shall speculate as to why Marcuse's analysis of Soviet Marxism was not more critical.

4. Sidney Lipshires, *Herbert Marcuse: From Marx to Freud and Beyond*, p. 27.

5. On the various positions towards the Soviet Union within critical theory during the 1930s and 1940s, see Dubiel, *Wissenschaftsorganization und politische Erfahrung.*

6. After having defended Communism in *The Communists and the Peace* in 1952 (New York: Braziller, 1968), Sarte then attacked Stalinism in *The Ghost of Stalin* after the brutal suppression of the uprisings in Hungary, Poland and East Germany in 1956 (New York; Braziller, 1968). Merleau-Ponty, having defended Communism in *Humanism and Terror* (Boston: Beacon Press, 1969), attacked Stalinism in 1957 in his *Adventures of the Dialectic,* which included a polemic against Sartre and other intellectuals who engaged in apologetics for the Soviet Union. On French debates over Communism, see H. Stuart Hughes, *The Obstructed Path* (New York: Delta, 1968).

7. See Kellner, *Karl Korsch,* especially the section on Lenin and the Soviet Union, and Korsch's letter to Brecht, pp. 289f.

8. On the late Horkheimer's anti-Communism, see my review article, 'The Frankfurt School Revisited'. On Wittfogel's changing stances toward Communism, see G. L. Ulmen, *The Science of Society: Toward an Understanding of the Life and Work of Karl August Wittfogel* (The Hague: Mouton, 1978).

9. On Marcuse's government service, see 5.3 below and Katz, 'Praxis and Poiesis', pp. 111–39.

10. Interview with Marcuse, 28 December 1978.

11. Arthur Mitzman told me that during his classes at Columbia, Marcuse openly taught Marxism and identified himself as a Marxist. At Harvard, his colleagues perceived him as 'Marxist-in-residence'. Interview with Sidney Monas, Austin, Texas.

12. Herbert Marcuse, 'Introduction', *Soviet Marxism* (New York: Columbia University Press, 1958) p. 1.

13. Ibid., pp. 1–5

14. Ibid., pp. 8–12.

15. Oskar Negt, 'Marxismus als Legitimationswissenschaft: Zur Genese der stalinistischen Philosophie', introduction to *Abram Deborin-Nikolai Bucharin: Kontroversen über dialektischen und mechanistischen Materialismus* (Frankfurt: Suhrkamp, 1969).

16. For the text of Khrushchev's speech and his recollections concerning its background, see *Khrushchev Remembers* (Boston: Little, Brown & Co., 1970). For Communist responses to Khrushchev's speech, see Columbia University's Russian Institute, *The Anti-Stalin Campaign and International Communism* (New York: Columbia University Press, 1956). See also Isaac Deutscher's essays, republished in *Ironies and History* (Berkeley: Ramparts Press, 1971), expecially Part One. See Louis Althusser's remarks on French reactions to Khrushchev's speech in *For Marx* (New York: Vintage Books, 1970) pp. 10ff, and *Essays in Self-Criticism* (London: New Left Books, 1976).

17. Interview with Marcuse, 28 December 1978.

18. Marcuse, 'Some Social Implications of Modern Technology', pp. 414ff. Once again, in both the 1941 essay and *SM* Marcuse's analysis of

domination is similar to Max Weber's theory, although Weber is not mentioned in either text – though Marcuse does cite Lewis Mumford, Veblen, Horkheimer and many American sources on the subject of technological rationality in the 1941 article.

19. Marcuse, 'Some Social Implications', p. 419.
20. In *ODM*, Marcuse continues his analysis of the degradation of language and ideology in advanced industrial societies, capitalist and Communist. See *ODM*, pp. 84ff, especially pp. 94 and 101f, where he provides examples of one-dimensional Communist language and ideology. See also the earlier draft of this chapter, 'Language and Technological Society', *Dissent*, vol. VIII, no. 1 (Winter, 1961) pp. 66–74. Marcuse's analysis of the degeneration of Marxism into a legitimating ideology provides a paradigmatic analysis of the shift from ideology-as-ism to ideology-as-hegemony, in which a once relatively rational and subversive programme of social reconstruction becomes a legitimating-stabilizing instrument of social control. See my article, 'Ideology, Marxism, and Advanced Capitalism'.
21. In a 1954 review article Marcuse stresses certain trends towards domination rooted in the industrial-technological features of 'advanced industrial society' which undercut differences between capitalism and communism; see 'Recent Literature on Communism', *World Politics* vol. VI, no. 4 (July 1954) pp. 515–25, where he writes: 'Certain basic trends seem to be dangerously common to both competing systems: the triumph of technological rationality, of large industry over the individual; universal co-ordination; the spread of administration into all spheres of life; and the assimilation of private into public existence' (p. 517).
22. Marcuse's analysis here might be compared with Milovan Djilas's interpretation of *The New Class* (New York: Praeger, 1957). Djilas argues that a new class has arisen in the Communist societies which performs the same dominating, repressive and exploitative functions in Soviet society as the bourgeois class performs in capitalist society. He argues against Marcuse that the new class possesses its privileges and special interest through its *ownership* of collective property and is therefore a 'new owning and exploiting class'; see pp. 44f, and 54ff. Others have argued convincingly that it is not ownership and economic power that is the basis of domination in the Soviet Union, but rather that political power in the party hierarchy and bureaucracy becomes the basis of power and domination. See Claude Lefort, *Elements d'une Théorie de la Bureaucratie* (Paris: Droz, 1971), part of which is translated as 'What is Bureaucracy', *Telos*, 22 (Winter 1974–5) pp. 31–65, and Serge Mallet, 'Bureaucracy and Technocracy in the Socialist Countries', *Essays on the New Working Class*, ed. and Trans. Dick Howard and Dean Savage (Saint Louis: Telos Press, 1975), especially pp. 132ff.
23. Djilas argues in detail for the party character of the bureaucracy in *The New Class*, pp. 39–43 and 'The Party State', pp. 70ff. A typical statement is: 'The Party is the main force of the Communist state and

government. It is the motive force of everything. It unites within itself the new class, the government, ownership, and ideas' (p. 78). See also Lefort, 'What is Democracy?', pp. 45ff. Marcuse's friend Barrington Moore's book, *Terror and Progress – USSR* (Cambridge, Mass.: Harvard University Press, 1954) analyses prospects of a technocratic development in the USSR, in which technical-bureaucratic administration would replace political terror; collective rule would replace personal rule, and a 'larger flow of goods and services would be distributed to the population' (p. 189). Moore indicates in the preface that Marcuse suggested the title to him and discussed the book with him in detail. In fact, Moore and Marcuse worked together closely on several of their books, and no doubt their exchange of views on Soviet Communism influenced the interpretations of both of them. See Marcuse's review of *Terror and Progress* in 'Recent Literature on Communism', pp. 519ff. Although it is possible that Moore and Marcuse may have grasped a long-range trend in the Soviet Union in which power and the constitution and control of the bureaucracy will shift from loyal Party members to technocrats or the intelligentsia, nonetheless, when Marcuse published *SM*, and even today, the bureaucracy and power of the state seem to be concentrated in the hands of the Party. And while technocrats seem to be gaining power, the intelligentsia seems to be suspect; thus there is little evidence that the Soviet Union will indeed be the first technocracy.

24. Marcuse writes: 'This framework leaves much room for personal and clique influences and interests, corruption and profiteering; it also permits one group (and one individual of the group) to come out on top – but it also sets the limits beyond which the mobilization of power cannot go without upsetting the structure on which Soviet power rests' (*SM*, p. 97).

25. For other views of the 1956 Eastern Europe uprisings, see Raya Dunayevskaya, *Marxism and Freedom* (New York: Twayne Publishers, 1958); Marcuse's preface to her book notes his disagreement with Dunayevskaya's interpretation of these events (p. 12). See also Stern's critical remarks on this issue in his review of *SM*, pp. 91f.

26. On the history of the Soviet Union, see Trotsky's many works; Boris Souverine, 'Stalinism', in *Marxism in the Modern World*, ed. Milorad M. Drachkovitch (Stanford: University Press, 1965); E. H. Carr's multi-volume opus, *History of Soviet Russia* (London and Baltimore: Penguin Books, 1964–78); and Charles Bettleheim, *Class Struggles in the USSR: First Period, 1917–23 and Second Period, 1924–29* (Hassocks, England: Harvester, 1977 and 1978).

27. On the discontinuity between Leninism and Stalinism see the articles in the anthology *Stalinism*, ed. Robert C. Tucker (New York: Norton, 1977), especially the studies by Tucker and Stephen F. Cohen, 'Bolshevism and Stalinism'. Curiously, Cohen's comprehensive discussion of the main trends in Soviet studies, which stresses the continuities between Leninism and Stalinism, fails to mention that Marcuse's *SM* did stress a 'break' (*SM*, p. 58), although, as I am indicating, he does

not analyse the issue adequately. Cohen's article, and other historical research he draws upon, put in question the claims of Solzhenitsyn, the 'new philosophers' and other anti-Communists and ex-Communists, like Kolakowski, that there is a direct line of continuity between Marxism, Leninism and Stalinism. Cohen argues, in fact, quite convincingly for sharp discontinuities between Stalinism and Leninism. See his article, 'Bolshevism and Stalinism' and his book *Bukharin and the Bolshevik Revolution* (New York: Knopf, 1973). On Stalinism see Souverine, 'Stalinism'; Roy Medvedev, *Let History Judge* (New York: Vintage, 1971); and Alvin W. Gouldner, 'Stalinism: A Study of Internal Colonialism', *Telos*, 34 (Winter 1977–8). On the role of Marxism in the Stalinist debacle see the article by Kolakowski and the rebuttal by Markovic in Stalinism. For typical works by the 'new philosophers' – who are really neither 'new' nor 'philosophers' – which try to blame the Gulag on Marx, see Andre Glucksmann *Les Maitres Penseurs* (Paris: Grasset, 1976) and Bernard-Henri Levy, *Barbarism with a Human Face* (New York: Harper & Row, 1979).

28. On the debate over the nature of Soviet Communism, see Svetozar Stojanović, *Between Ideals and Reality* (New York: Oxford, 1973); the article by Antonio Carlo, 'The Socio-Economic Nature of the USSR', *Telos*, 21 (Fall 1974); the book edited by Paul Sweezy and Charles Bettleheim, *The Transition to Socialism* (New York: Monthly Review Press, 1972); and the articles in *Critique* by Hillel H. Ticktin, Towards a Political Economy of the USSR', no. 1, 'Political Economy of the Soviet Intellectual', no. 2 'Socialism, the Market and the State', no. 3. 'Soviet Society and Prof. Bettelheim', no. 6 and 'Class structure and the Soviet Elite', no. 9; the two articles by Ernest Mandel in *Critique*, 3; and the various debates in almost every issue.

29. This was noted by Karl Kosch in his 1930 Afterword to *Marxism and Philosophy* (New York: Monthly Review, 1971).

30. *SM*, pp. 127 and 128–9: 'It is the Dialectics of Nature which has become the constantly quoted authoritative source for the exposition of dialectic in Soviet Marxism' (p. 128). Further, Lenin's *Materialism and Empirio-criticism* replaced the dialectial notion of truth by a primitive naturalistic realism, which has become canonical in Soviet Marxism' (*SM*, p. 133).

31. See my discussions of Marcuse's concept of art in 4.3, 6.3, and 10.4.

32. Rudolf Bahro in *The Alternative in Eastern Europe* (London: New Left Books, 1978) discusses literary opposition in the Soviet Union and stresses that Soviet art does not simply follow a model of one-dimensional 'Soviet realism' to the extent that Marcuse claims. The dissident and oppositional currents in Soviet culture were probably not, as visible however, in the 1950s when Marcuse wrote *SM*.

33. Marcuse, *SM*, p. 133. Marcuse never wrote extensively on Lenin, and although he criticized 'Leninism' in the late 1960s and 1970s, he never developed a systematic critique of Lenin or Leninism.

34. Codifications of Soviet Marxism include G. Glezerman and G. Kursanov, *Historical Materialism* (Moscow: Progress Publishers, 1968)

and R. O. Gropp, *Grundlagen des dialektischen Materialismus* (Berlin: VEB Verlag, 1970). See also the critical analyses of Gustav Wetter, *Sowjet-ideologie Heute* (Frankfurt: Fisher, 1962) and Richard T. De George, *Patterns of Soviet Thought* (Ann Arbor: University of Michigan Press, 1970).

35. See sources in note 16.

36. See Marcuse, 'Preface à l'edition française', *Le marxisme sovietique* (Paris: Gallimard, 1963) pp. 7ff.

37. On the relation between Leninism and Stalinism, see the literature cited in note 27. On the continuities and discontinuities between the Stalinist and post-Stalinist regimes in Russia, see the heated debates between Martin Nicolaus, *Restoration of Capitalism in the USSR* (Chicago; Liberator Press, 1975), Michael Goldfield and Melvin Rothenberg, *The Myth of Capitalism Reborn* (San Francisco: Line of March, 1980), and Albert Szymanski *Is the Red Flag Flying?* (New York: Zed Press, 1980).

38. For critiques of bureaucratic Communism see Stojanović, *Between Ideals and Reality*; the aticle by Lefort, 'What is Democracy?'; Andrew Arato, 'Understanding Bureaucratic Centralism', *Telos*, 35 (Spring 1978); Rudi Dutschke, *Versuch Lenin auf die Füsse zu stellen* (Berlin: Rot Verlag, 1974); Cornelius Castoriadis, 'The Social Regime in Russia', *Telos*, 38 (Winter 1978–9); and especially Bahro, *The Alternative in Eastern Europe*.

8 Marcuse's Theory of Advanced Industrial Society: *One-Dimensional Man*

* Since I accept the feminist critique of sexist language, I am extremely uncomfortable with Marcuse's concept of 'one-dimentional man'. However, since this is one of his distinctive concepts, I am forced to use sexist language in explicating it, although I believe that contemporary critical theory should not use such terminology. In Marcuse's defence, it might be noted that he himself became an ardent feminist, and as early as 1962 participated in a dialogue on women's liberation. See 'Emanzipation der Frau in der repressiven Gesellschaft. Ein Gespräch mit Herbert Marcuse and Peter Furth', *Das Argument*, 23 (October–November 1962), pp. 2–12. In the 1970s Marcuse participated in a women's study group and published an essay on 'Feminism and Socialism' which I shall discuss in 10.3. In the light of Marcuse's early sympathies for feminism and later deep commitment, it is ironic that he should use sexist language as the title and central concept in one of his most important works. This phenomenon points to how sexist language was simply taken for granted before the work of the women's movement of the late 1960s and 1970s, to the extent that even a progressive thinker like Marcuse would use the generic 'man' to describe the human species.

1. *ODM* is one of the classical texts of the critical theory developed by the Institute for Social Research, and many of its key ideas were elabo-

rated during his work with the Institute. But since Marcuse's 1941 essay, 'Some Social Implications of Modern Technology', presents themes which Horkheimer and Adorno developed later in *Dialectic of Enlightenment*, one should grasp the convergence of ideas in the thinking of core members of the Institute and the mutual interaction in the development of their basic ideas, rather than simply seeing *ODM* as a replay of Adorno's and Horkheimer's problematic.

2. Marcuse, 'Some Social Implications of Modern Technology'. Page references to this article, and other articles that I shall use, will be cited in the text.

3. Marcuse, 'Epilogue', second edition of *R&R* (New York: Humanities Press, 1954) pp. 433ff (page references will appear in parentheses). See also Marcuse's account of capitalist stabilization in *Soviet Marxism*, pp. 15ff, which I shall discuss below.

4. Marcuse, 'Preface', pp. 11–12. Marcuse begins his preface to *Marxism and Freedom* by stating that 'a re-examination of Marxian theory' is 'one of the most urgent tasks for comprehending the contemporary situation', but the claims that while 'no other theory seems to have so accurately anticipated the basic tendencies' in capitalist society, none apparently had drawn such incorrect conclusions for its analysis. While the economic and political development of twentieth-century capitalism shows many of the features which Marx derived from the inherent contradictions of the system, these contradictions did not explode in the final crisis' (p. 7). It is precisely this dilemma that preoccupied Marcuse during the last decades of his life.

5. See Rudolf Hilferding, *Das Finanzkapital* (Marx-Studien III; Vienna, Wiener Volksbuchhandlung, 1910) and 'Die Aufgabe des Sozialdemokratie in der Republik', *Protokoll Sozialdemokratie Parteitag Kiel 1927* (Berlin: 1927). Marcuse published articles in *Die Gesellschaft* when Hilferding was editor and long admired him. Evidence that Hilferding's theory of capitalist stabilization and 'organized capitalism' influenced Marcuse's conception in *ODM* is found in his sympathetic explication of Hilferding in *Soviet Marxism*: 'In his *Finanzkapital*, published in 1910, Rudolf Hilferding ... pointed out that, under the leadership of finance capital, the entire national economy would be mobilized for expansion, and that this expansion, through the collusion of giant monopolistic and semi-monopolistic enterprises, would tend towards large-scale international integration, economic as well as political. On this new intercontinental market, production and distribution would be to a great extent controlled and regimented by a cartel of the most powerful capitalist interests. In the huge dominion of such a 'general cartel', the contradictions of the capitalist system could be greatly controlled, profits for the ruling groups secured, and a high level of wages for labour within the dominion sustained – at the expense of the intensified exploitation of markets and populations outside the dominion' (*SM*, p. 18).

6. On the German 'war economy', see Karl Korsch, 'Fundamentals of Socialization' in my anthology *Karl Korsch*, pp. 129ff., who cites the

relevant literature on the topic (p. 134). See Friedrich Pollock, 'State Capitalism', *Studies in Philosophy and Social Science*, vol. IX, no. 2 (1941). I believe that Pollock's studies of automation and state capitalism exerted a generally overlooked influence on Marcuse's theory of 'advanced industrial society'. The first edition of Pollock's *The Economic and Social Consequences of Automation* (Oxford: Blackwell, 1957) took a position similar to Marcuse's conception that although automation was now an instrument of domination in the hands of capital, it could be an instrument of liberation by eliminating mechanical labour that would be performed by machines. See Marramo, 'Political Economy and Critical Theory'. The term 'the administered society' is frequently used by Adorno and Horkheimer. Franz Neumann's theory of monopoly capitalism and capitalist domination also influenced Marcuse's conception of advanced industrial society, for Neumann's description of the fascist *Behemoth* pictured a social order that contained features which would appear in Marcuse's theory of the advancing industrial society. For an excellent discussion of Neumann, see Alfons Söllner, *Geschichte und Herrschaft* (Frankfurt: Suhrkamp, 1979). On Pollock and Neumann, see Arato and Gebhardt, *The Essential Frankfurt School Reader*; Held, *op. cit.*; and Jay, *The Dialectical Imagination*.

7. Marcuse, 'De l'Ontologie à la Technologie'. This article was published in the French *Arguments* group's journal. While working on *ODM*, Marcuse taught in France in 1958–9 and 1961–2. There he had contacts with the *Arguments* group, which was engaged in a similar project of re-evaluating and revising Marxism in the light of tendencies in advanced industrial society. On the *Arguments* group – named after their journal – see Mark Poster, *Existential Marxism*, pp. 209ff, *passim*. Members of the group were carrying out studies of changes of labour and industry in advanced capitalism and were beginning to develop new theories of social change. See their special issues on the working class and technology: *Arguments*, no. 12–13 (January–March 1959) and no. 18 (1960), as well as Serge Mallet's collection of essays *La nouvelle class ouvrière* (Paris: Seuill, 1963). Marcuse cites Mallet's work in *ODM* and debated Mallet in conferences and essays until Mallet's untimely death in the early 1970s.

Other *Arguments* thinkers were focusing on the role of technology in the modern world and a variety of French thinkers were developing theories of a technological society. See Kostas Axelos, *Alienation, Praxis and Techne in the Thought of Karl Marx* (Austin, Texas: University of Texas Press, 1976); Jacques Ellul, *The Technological Society* (New York: Knopf, 1964); and Gilbert Simondon, *Du mode d'existence des objects techniques* (Paris: Aubier, 1958). According to William Leiss (conversation in Washington, DC, August 1980), Marcuse was especially impressed by Simondon's work which he cited in *ODM*. Axelos is a member of the *Arguments* group influenced by Heidegger, and Ellul is a Catholic intellectual deeply critical of technology. Marcuse never cites Axelos or Ellul, and Leiss was not sure of

Marcuse had read them; it would be interesting to know to what extent, if any, they influenced his theory of the 'technological world'. Marcuse's involvement with the German Institute for Social Research, the French *Arguments* group, and American critical social science puts in question Perry Anderson's claims that 'Western Marxists' were highly insular and developed their thought in isolation from each other, with little interaction between Marxists of various countries; see *Western Marxism*, p. 69. This claim is surely incorrect in Marcuse's case.

8. See, for example, Jeremy Shapiro, 'One-Dimensionality: The Universal Semiotic of Technological Experience', in *Critical Interruptions*; Paul Piccone, 'The Changing function of Critical Theory', *New German Critique*, 12 (Fall 1977) pp. 34f. and 'The Crisis of One-Dimensionality', *Telos*, 35 (Spring 1978) pp. 45ff; Tim Luke, 'Culture and Politics in the Age of Artificial Negativity', *Telos, 35* (Spring 1978) pp. 55ff; and Stefan Breuer who in *Die Krisis der Revolutionstheorie*, argues that Marcuse's 'one-dimensionality thesis' signifies a total domination of Capital over every aspect of life, as if Capital had assumed the role of Hegel's Absolute Subject. Marcuse never makes such extreme claims, which misunderstand the function of the concept 'one-dimensional' in his theory.

9. Marcuse uses the concept 'two-dimensional' in his essay 'On the Philosophical Foundation of the Concept of Labour in Economics' in order to distinguish between realms of necessity and freedom in human life; see my translation in *Telos*, 16, pp. 35f. In his dissertation on *Hegel's Ontology*, pp. 79ff, and in some of his articles and book reviews in the 1930s, Marcuse makes an epistemological distinction between 'one-dimensional thought' (positivism) and two-dimensional dialectical thinking; see, for example, 'The Concept of Essence' (*N*, p. 65) and his review of the positivist's *International Encyclopedia of Unified Science*, where he contrasts the positivist 'one-dimensionality of fact' with an Hegelian 'two-dimensionality of essence and fact', *Zeitschrift*, vol. VIII (1939) p. 231. In *ODM*, Marcuse extends this distinction to a wide variety of phenomena; in the following pages I shall elucidate the complex set of meanings that the concept encompasses.

10. Rolf Ahlers argues, in an article entitled 'Is Technology Intrinsically Repressive?' (*Continuum*, VIII, Spring-Summer 1970, pp. 111ff), that Marcuse misinterprets the Hegelian concept of subjectivity by exaggerating the components of Fichtean idealism and playing down the Hegelian emphasis on the incorporation of otherness into subjectivity and the claim that subjectivity 'finds its truth' in the recognition of (and submission to) external norms, objects and institutions. Earlier, Karl Löwith made a similar criticism of Marcuse's interpretation of Hegel in his review of *R & R*, discussed in Chapter Five (see note 1 of that chapter). Ahler and Löwith's criticisms suggest that Marcuse has a quite Fichtean-Kantian reading of Hegel which stresses the absolute sovereignty of the subject – whose domination by the object constitutes the core of Marcuse's fears in *ODM*. Thus I would maintain that a version of Hegel's subject-object dialectic constitutes the

metaphysical-epistemological foundation of Marcuse's conception, but that it is a special reading of Hegel that is certainly subject to debate by Hegel scholars.

11. Marcuse's reading of Freud in his 1956 Frankfurt lectures is more pessimistic than his reading in *EC*, and directly anticipates the theses of *ODM* (compare *EC* with *5L*, pp. 1–43). Marcuse now minimizes those elements of what I call an 'anthropology of liberation' in *EC* and the utopian dimension of emancipation for emphasis on what might be called an 'anthropology of domination' and theory of social control which explains how society comes to dominate individuals and to produce easily manipulable objects of administration.

12. Marcuse's analysis comes close to behaviourism and 'role theory' here in his assumption that behaviour is increasingly shaped directly by societal institutions and dictates as individuals adjust to prescribed and prevailing social roles and conformist behaviour without friction or resistance. Although Marcuse describes tendencies towards increased social domination in *EC*, his commitment to a Freudian anthropology of liberation and acceptance of the Freudian concept of the autonomous ego – which developed as a psychological theory the dominant philosophical concept of the subject from Plato through to existentialism – kept him from assuming the possibility of total social control. It is interesting that in 'Progress and Freud's Theory of Instincts' (see *5L*, pp. 28ff), Marcuse uses certain aspects of the Freudian theory to demystify idealist theories of absolute freedom and total autonomy of the ego and begins to anticipate the very obsolescence of the limited freedom postulated in the Freudian theory – consequences that he will explicitly develop in his 1963 lecture, 'The Obsolescence of the Freudian Concept of Man', which provided much of the anthropological foundation of *ODM* (see *5L*, pp. 44ff).

13. Marcuse, 'Obsolescence of the Freudian Concept of Man'. This is a key essay, articulating Marcuse's turn from the anthropology of liberation in *EC* to an anthropology of domination in *ODM*. Given the relative obsolescence of the Freudian theory, Marcuse makes less use of it in his 1960s and 1970s writings than during the period of *EC*. An exception is his return to a more explicit use of Freud's instinct theory in *The Aesthetic Dimension*.

14. Marcuse, 'De l'Ontologie', p. 54.

15. In 'De l'Ontologie', Marcuse claims that his study focuses on 'certain tendencies at the foundation of the most evolved industrial societies, especially the United States' (p. 54). And in 'Socialism in Developed Countries' (pp. 139ff) he claims that 'I am referring only to the most advanced centres of industrial society and to trends which have by no means fully emerged. Even in the United States they are little more than tendencies, but I am convinced that they are, as it were, infectious and will quite swiftly spread through the capitalist atmosphere to less advanced countries' (p. 140). In *ODM*, Marcuse tends to claim that he is analysing tendencies from advanced industrial societies *per se*, but almost all of his examples come from the United States. See the

interesting exchange between Mallet and Marcuse over whether the United States is or is not the most typical 'advanced industrial' country in *Praxis*, vol. 1, nos. 2/3 (1965) pp. 377–87.

To describe the current form of contemporary capitalism, I have not chosen the term 'monopoly capitalism', since I believe that there are significant differences in the current form of ownership and management in today's multinational corporations, conglomerates, interlocking directorates, etc. from earlier stages of monopoly ownership and control. I also reject the standard Marxist term 'late capitalism', which smacks of ideological wish-fulfilment that capitalism is about to pass away and humanity is about to enter the socialist realm of freedom. At different times Marcuse uses the terms 'advanced capitalism', 'late-capitalism', 'monopoly capitalism' and Hilferding's term, 'organized capitalism'.

16. See Steigerwald, Herbert Marcuses 'dritter Weg', and John Fry, *Marcuse: Dilemma and Liberation* (New Jersey: Humanities Press, 1978) p. 100.

17. Conversations with Ron Aronson, Detroit, April 1980. Note in the passage translated from 'De l'Ontologie' that Marcuse claims that the analyses of American social scientists and journalists that he cites are 'purely ideological and neglect the analysis of the fundamental processes' (p. 54); this analysis Marcuse intends to provide in *ODM*. For Marcuse's opinions on a wide variety of American social theories, see his article, 'Der Einfluss der deutschen Emigration auf das amerikanische Geistesleben', in *Jahrbuch fur Amerikastudien*, X (Heidelberg, 1965) pp. 27ff.

18. Sharp criticisms of *ODM* appeared in reviews by George Lichtheim, *New York Review of Books*, 20 February 1964; Ernest van den Haag, *Book Week* (26 April 1964); Marshall Berman, *Partisan Review*, vol. 31 (Fall 1964); Julius Gould, *Encounter* (September 1964) and Alasdair MacIntyre, *Dissent*, vol. XII (Spring 1965). The first explicitly Marxist critiques were by Raya Dunayevskaya, *The Activist* (Fall 1964); Karl Miller, *Monthly Review*, vol. XIX (June 1967); and David Horowitz, *International Socialist Journal*, vol. IV (November–December 1967). Starting around 1968, there was a torrent of predictable and tiresome critiques of Marcuse by Marxist-Leninists. For discussion of the Soviet attacks, see Klaus Mehnert, *Moscow and the New Left* (Berkeley: University of California Press, 1975). The Progressive Labor Party provided a diatribe against 'Herbert Marcuse and his Philosophy of Copout', *Progressive Labor*, vol. 6 (October 1968), which Marcuse answered in an interview in *The Guardian* (16 November 1968). Starting in the late 1960s, representatives of all ideological types began criticizing Marcuse's theories. Social Democratic critiques include Allen Graubard, 'One-Dimensional Pessimism', *Dissent*, vol. XV (May–June 1968) and Irving Howe, 'Herbert Marcuse or Milovan Djilas?', *Harper's* (July 1969). Liberal critiques include George Kateb, 'The Political Thought of Herbert Marcuse', *Commentary* (Jan. 1970) and Richard Goodwin, 'The Social Theory of

Herbert Marcuse', *Atlantic* (July 1971). Right-wing attacks include some articles in *The National Review* (2 July 1968; 19 November 1968; and 21 October 1969) as well as a vicious and repugnant book by Eliseo Vivas, *Contra Marcuse* (Delta: New York, 1972).

More appreciative reviews of *ODM* include Edgar Z. Friedenberg, *Commentary*, vol. 37 (April 1964); Emile Capouya, *Saturday Review*, (28 March 1964); Andrew Gorz, *Nation* (25 May 1964); and R. D. Laing, *New Left Review*, 26 (1964). See also the sympathetic evaluations in the books already cited by Palmier, Holz, Arnason, and Nicholas, as well as Paul Breines, ed., *Critical Interruptions* (New York: Herder & Herder, 1970). More critical studies appear in Jürgen Habermas, ed., *Antworten auf Herbert Marcuse*. Popularizations of Marcuse's thought began to appear in both books and journals in the late 1960s; see J. M. Palmier, *Sur Marcuse* (Paris: 10/18, 1968); Tito Perlini, *Che cosa ha veramente detto Marcuse* (Roma: Ubaldini Editore, 1968); Herbert Gold, 'California Left', *Saturday Evening Post* (19 October 1968) and Robert W. Marks, *The Meaning of Marcuse* (New York: Ballantine Books, 1970). For attacks on the commodification, emasculation and recuperation of Marcuse's thought in these and other 'texts', see Paul Piccone, *Telos*, vol. 2, no. 1 (Spring 1969), pp. 15–18; Russell Jacoby, *Telos*, 5 (Spring 1970) pp. 188–90; and Robin Blackburn, *Telos*, 6 (Fall 1970) pp. 348–51.

19. On the historical background to the period that Marcuse describes in *One-Dimensional Man*, see Marty Jezer, *The Dark Ages. Life in the United States 1945–1960* (Boston: South End Press, 1982) and Godfrey Hodgson, *America in Our Time: From World War II to Nixon* (New York: Random House, 1976). Other works that provide historical background and empirical detail to Marcuse's theory of 'one-dimensional society', many of which were influenced by Marcuse, are cited in note 69.

20. Henri Lefebvre's *Critique de la vie quotidienne* (Paris: L'Arche 1947–62; three volumes) touches on, in a Marxist framework, some of the Marcusean themes of a corner society, but it is not until his book, *Everyday Life in the Modern World* (New York: Harper & Row 1971) that Lefebvre calls contemporary society 'the bureaucratic society of controlled consumption'. In their work, *Monopoly Capital*, Paul Baran and Paul Sweezy focus on advertising, consumption and mass culture as crucial components of the capitalist system. See the critique of their formulations on these topics by Dallas Smythe, 'Communications: The Blind Spot of Western Marxism', *Canadian Journal of Political and Social Theory*, vol. 1, no. 3 (1977) and my article, 'Critical Theory, Commodities and the Consumer Society', *Theory, Culture and Society*, vol. 1, no. 3 (1983).

21. See Karl Marx, *Economic-Philosophical Manuscripts,* and Lukács, *History and Class Consciousness*, Marcuse continually reflected on and utilized the early critiques of capitalism by Karl Marx which he applied to contemporary society.

22. See the study by Carol Johnson, 'The Problem of Reformism and Marx's Theory of Fetishism', *New Left Review*, 119

(January–February 1980) pp. 70ff, which argues that Marx never applies his theories of ideology or commodity fetishism to analysis of working-class consciousness when he is carrying out concrete political analyses, and that he almost always assumes that the working class is *per se* a revolutionary class with revolutionary class consciousness. Johnson fails to note, however, that Marx's theory of fetishism and ideological mystification is rooted in his early writings and not just his 'later economic writings' (p. 70) and that consequently throughout his work Marx failed systematically to apply his analyses of fetishism and ideology to actual configurations of working-class consciousness. It is precisely this application of Marx's categories to the contemporary working class that is the centre of Marcuse's theory.

On commodity fetishism, see the famous section in chapter 1 of Karl Marx, *Capital*, and on reification see Georg Lukács, *History and Class Consciousness* (MIT: Cambridge, 1971). Karl Korsch offers an interesting discussion of the distinction between fetishism and reification in a letter to Paul Partos: 'You still always use the Lukácsian concept of "reification". Now to be sure Marx in fact occasionally speaks of a "thinglike disguise" and a "thingification" (*Versachlichung*) of the social character of production. But the expression "fetishism" is infinitely better for a materialist and sociological conception and description of this form of thought. With Lukács, who extends the use of this concept without measure, it is at bottom a matter of a protest of a "philosophy of life" against the cold, rigid, fixed and factual material world' (quoted in *Jahrbuch Arbeiterbewegung 2* (Fisher: Frankfurt, 1974). By reification Lukács means the process in which human beings become like things, losing their human qualities – a process rooted for him in the capitalist production process, commodity fetishism, bureaucracy, the mass media and positivist science and philosophy. It is in this Lukácsian sense that Marcuse envisages reification, and much of his analysis can be seen as an extension of the Lukácsian problematic which is the model for Marcuse's analysis in *ODM*. See Chapters 1 and 2 for discussions of Lukács's impact on Marcuse.

23. The concept of false needs and the distinction between true and false needs has caused much controversy. The Marxian heretic Hans Magnus Enzensberger has argued that consumer needs express genuine needs for pleasure, gratification and possession, but in an often distorted fashion; see *The Consciousness Industry* (New York: Seabury, 1974). Marcuse's student William Leiss has been undertaking a sustained polemic against the concept of false needs. See his book *The Limits to Satisfaction* (Toronto: University of Toronto Press, 1976) and articles in the *Canadian Journal of Political and Social Theory*: 'Advertising, Needs, and Commodity Fetishism' (with Stephen Kline) vol. 2, no. 1 (Winter 1978) pp. 5ff; 'Needs, Exchanges, and the Fetishism of Objects', vol. 2, no. 3 (Fall 1978) pp. 27ff; and the exchange between Leiss, Kontos, Macpherson and others in vol. 3, no. 1 (Winter 1979). Although Leiss is correct to argue that the terms 'commodity fetishism' and 'false needs' are usually imprecise, I believe that his own

analyses are valuable because they flesh out and give substance to these notions. That is, I believe that Leiss's analyses of how advertising produces 'symbolic expectations' which commodities are to satisfy provide a good framework to specify how advertising produces false expectations which the commodities cannot satisfy and suggest how, in general, the consumer society and consumption produce 'distorted' (a term that Leiss does use) expectations and satisfactions. Thus I believe that Leiss's quarrel with his theoretical father-figure is semantic and that it makes sense to concretize and clarify concepts like 'false needs' or 'commodity fetishism' rather than to discard them prematurely. In general, much more work needs to be done in clarifying the anthropological concept of 'need' and the effects of socialization in manufacturing, manipulating or maintaining needs.

24. Marcuse, *An Essay on Liberation*, p. 11.

25. For a historical discussion of the introduction of the concept of alienation to contemporary social theory, see Walter Kaufmann's introduction, 'The Inevitability of Alienation', to Richard Schacht, *Alienation* (Garden City: Doubleday, 1971). Kaufmann points out that Marcuse's *Reason and Revolution* was the first book in English to make extensive use of the concept of alienation in his discussions of Hegel and Marx (p. xx) and that Marcuse, Erich Fromm and Hannah Arendt constantly used the term in the 1950s, 'naturalizing' alienation for an American public. It was widely picked up and used by a variety of thinkers, theories and disciplines, becoming a popular buzz-word with no coherent unifying meaning. For an excellent discussion of the different – and conflicting – concepts of alienation operative today, see Schacht's book, which discusses in detail the Hegelian, Marxian, existentialist, sociological and other concepts of alienation.

26. See Schacht, *Alienation*; Bertell Ollman, *Alienation*; and *Meszaros, Marx's Theory of Alienation*. In Chapters 1 and 2, I discuss the differences between the Hegelian, Marxian and existentialist concepts of alienation.

27. See Schacht, *Alienation*, pp. 161ff, for a fine discussion of the sociological literature on alienation.

28. Marcuse, 'Liberation from the Affluent Society', in David Cooper, ed., *Dialectics of Liberation* (London: Penguin, 1968). Marcuse's concept of alienation here is quite similar to that of Erich Fromm, with whom he had some sharp disagreements over Freud and other issues (see Chapter 6). See Fromm, *Escape From Freedom* and *The Sane Society* (New York: Holt, Rinehart & Winston, 1955), discussed in Schacht, *Alienation*.

29. *ODM*, pp. 4ff and 'Liberation from the Affluent Society'. For a well documented liberal critique of the 'pseudo-freedoms' and 'pseudo-choice' in advanced capitalism, which illustrates Marcuse's theses, see Jeffrey Schrank, *Snap, Crackle and Popular Taste* (New York: Dell, 1977); and for radical critiques of the consumer society, see my article 'Critical Theory, Commodities and the Consumer Society' and other articles in *Theory, Culture & Society*, vol. 1, no. 3 (1983).

30. Marx, 'Critique of Hegel', discussed in Chapter 2. On the concept of 'radical needs', see Agnes Heller, *The Theory of Need in Marx* (London: Allison Busby, 1976).

31. Marcuse does not discuss in *ODM* the so-called 'new working class' of managerial and technical personnel described by Serge Mallet, *La nouvelle classe ouvrière*, or the 'white-collar' class which was the topic of so much sociological literature at the time, or the emerging service industries. Consequently Marcuse really lacks a theory of the recomposition of the working class. On this theme, compare C. Wright Mills, *White Collar* (New York: Oxford, 1951); Mallet; Stanley Aronowitz, *False Promises* (New York: McGraw-Hill, 1973); Harry Braverman, *Labor and Monopoly Capital* (New York: Monthly Review, 1974); and Pat Walker, ed., *Between Labor and Capital* (Boston: South End Press, 1979).

32. Here Marcuse cites studies of automation and mechanized labour by Charles Walker, Daniel Bell, Ely Chinoy, Floyd Mason and Richard Hoffman, and Serge Mallet's study of the Caltex refinery (*ODM*, pp. 23–31). It seems to me that Marcuse relies too uncritically on this literature and misinterprets Mallet's study of the Caltex refinery, which intends to show new forms of struggle in the more automated enterprises by the 'new working class'. See Mallet, *La nouvelle classe ouvrière*. Marcuse might also have been influenced by Fredrick Pollock's studies of automation; see his book *Automation*, and Giacomo Marramo's study 'Political Economy and Critical Theory', *Telos*, 24 (Summer 1975) pp. 56ff.

33. Herbert Marcuse, letter to Raya Dunayevskaya, 8 August 1960. I am grateful to Dunayevskaya for sending a copy of this and other interesting letters, and hope that the Marcuse-Dunayevskaya correspondence will someday be published. Dunaveyskaya continually produced sharp Marxist-Humanist critiques of Marcuse's theory in the newspaper *News and Letters* and in her correspondence to Marcuse, whose replies were often interesting.

34. Marcuse cites Galbraith's *American Capitalism*, which discusses the role of the state in advanced capitalism, but he also criticizes Galbraith's 'ideological concept' of 'countervailing powers' (*ODM*, p. 51). In *ODM* – and also in his subsequent writings – Marcuse has hardly any analysis of the role of the state in managing the economy.

35. British reviewers attacked Marcuse on this point, claiming that he failed to appreciate the gains won for the working classes by the labour parties and the real differences these parties offered. See George Lichtheim's review in the *New York Review of Books* (20 February 1964) pp. 164ff, and Alasdair MacIntyre, 'Modern Society: An End to Revolt?', *Dissent*, XII (Spring 1965) pp. 239ff. These same critics have criticized Marcuse for a failure to develop an adequate theory of the welfare state.

36. Marcuse cites Fred Cook's book, *The Warfare State* (*ODM*, p. xvii) and later Seymour Melman's *Pentagon Capitalism* (*CR&R*, p. 9) as important critiques of the military-industrial complex.

37. Marcuse's discussion of the Soviet Union in *ODM*, pp. 39ff, adds little to his discussion in *SM*, and although he rejects the thesis which proclaims a 'convergence' in the nature of Soviet socialist and capitalist societies due to a common industrial-technical base and organization of labour, he does see some similarities and a convergence of interests beneath the differences in the systems. In 'Socialism in Developed Countries' he stresses again the similarities between state capitalism and state socialism (pp. 149ff).

38. Marcuse's superficial analysis of the Third World and failure to anticipate the importance of Third World liberation movements were criticized in the reviews by Horowitz and Miller cited in note 18.

39. For conventional Marxian uses of the concept of ideology, see *ODM*, pp. 120, 145, 188, *passim*. In other passages, Marcuse uses 'ideology' in Mannheim's sense of ideas and world views specific to a class and social order, in which all philosophy, or any ideas, would be 'ideology' (see, for example, *ODM*, p. 199). These differing senses of the concept of ideology at once reveal the synthetic-eclectic nature of Marcuse's thought and his view that ideology – in a variety of forms and types – permeates advanced industrial society, which is '*more* ideological than its predecessor' (*ODM*, p. 11).

40. See *ODM*, pp. 11–12, where Marcuse cites Adorno's *Prisms*. Marcuse was extremely impressed with Adorno's studies of culture and ideology and told me that Adorno's work became increasingly important for him in the 1960s and 1970s (conversation with Marcuse, 28 December 1978). On Adorno's theory of ideology, see my articles 'Ideology', and 'Kulturindustrie und Massenkommunikation', in *Sozialforschung als Kritik*, ed. Wolfgang Bonss and Axel Honneth (Frankfurt: Suhrkamp, 1982) pp. 482–515.

41. On the 'end of ideology' theory, see *The End of Ideology Debate*, ed. Chaim Waxman (New York: Simon & Schuster, 1968) and my discussion in 'Ideology'.

42. Marcuse believed that the increased importance of culture and ideology in advanced capitalism in maintaining social stability and in directly shaping thought and behaviour justified an intensified concern with culture by Marxian radicals (conservation with Marcuse, 26 March 1978). The result is that Marcuse and other 'culture radicals' have added a cultural dimension to contemporary Marxism that was lacking in most earlier versions, although many critics claim that it is at the expense of an adequate economic and political analysis.

43. Chapter 3 of *ODM* can be read as an updating and radicalization of Adorno's and Horkheimer's 'culture industry' theses, in which Marcuse almost completely devaluates the emancipatory potential of art in a society governed by the culture industries. See my article 'Kulturindustrie', and the discussion in 10.4 below.

44. On Hegel's concept of the 'unhappy consciousness' see *The Phenenomenology of Mind* (New York: Harper & Row, 1967) pp. 251ff, and Jean Hyppolite, *Genesis and Structure of Hegel's Phenomenology of Mind* (Evanston, Ill.: Northwestern University

Press, 1978) which focuses on the 'unhappy consciousness' as the key to Hegel's theory.

45. See *ODM*, pp. 73ff. For discussion of Marcuse's paradoxical inversion of Freud's concept of sublimation, see Lipshires, *Herbert Marcuse*, and Horowitz, *Repression*.

46. Marcuse's critique of language is influenced by George Orwell and the Austrian Karl Kraus (*ODM*, pp. 177, 196). For a discussion of Marcuse and Orwell, see Ian Slater, 'Orwell, Marcuse and the Language of Politics', *Political Studies*, vol. XXXI, no. 4 (1975). On Kraus, see Werner Kraft, *Das Ja des Neinsagers: Karl Kraus und seine geistige Welt* (München: Text und Kritik, 1974).

47. The emphasis here on historical remembrance and the appeal for preservation of the subversive and emancipatory elements of the cultural heritage are shared by Adorno, Walter Benjamin and Ernst Bloch. See Benjamin, 'Theses on the Philosophy of History', in *Illumination*, and Bloch, *The Principle of Hope*, discussed in Douglas Kellner and Harry O'Hara, 'Utopia and Marxism in Ernst Bloch', *New German Critique*, no. 9 (Fall 1976).

48. Schoolman, in *The Imaginary Witness*, criticizes Marcuse for failing to note progressive and critical elements in the contemporary social science research literature which Marcuse criticizes. Schoolman, in turn, fails to note conservative aspects.

49. Marcuse cites texts in this section by Wittgenstein, Austin and Ryle, and criticizes as well the neo-positivism of Ayer and Quine.

50. Ludwig Wittgenstein, *Philosophical Investigations* (New York: Macmillan, 1960); *ODM*, p. 174 cites the relevant passages.

51. Marcuse's critique here has given rise to a heated debate as to whether ordinary language analysis, especially Wittgenstein's, is really so completely conservative and conformist. See the articles in the British journal *Radical Philosophy*, no. 8 (Summer 1974), no. 10 (Summer 1975), no. 12 (Winter 1975), no. 13 (Summer 1976) and an article by Alan Wertheimer, 'Is Ordinary Language Analysis Conservative?', *Political Theory*, vol. 4, no. 4 (November 1976); and Schoolman, *The Imaginary Witness*.

52. This notion of philosophical therapy was popularized by the Wittgensteinian John Wisdom in *Philosophy and Psychoanalysis* (Berkeley: University of California Press, 1969). Interestingly, Marcuse himself proposes a 'linguistic therapy' in succeeding works (see *An Essay on Liberation*, pp. 8ff). But Marcuse would argue that whereas Wittgensteinian philosophical therapy wants to manipulate individuals into accepting everyday usage and into conforming to dominant patterns of thought and behaviour, he is arguing that precisely those conventional norms and patterns conceal or suppress truths contained in more metaphysical and critical philosophical discourse. In effect, Marcuse is calling for a rehabilitation in philosophy of metaphysics and dialectical thinking in the face of its destruction by dominant tendencies in ordinary language philosophy or positivism. Marcuse defends his concept of philosophy throughout *ODM* and in 'The Relevance of

Reality', a 1969 presidental address to the Pacific Division of the American Philosophical Association; the article is collected in an anthology of articles by contemporary philosophers on their concepts of philosophy – *The Owl of Minerva*, ed. Charles Bontempo and S. Jack Odell (New York: McGraw-Hill, 1975). The contributions by Quine, Ziff, Wisdom and Ayer show the sort of trivialization of philosophy that Marcuse is attacking and indicates why a thinker rooted in classical philosophy would be appalled by dominant tendencies in contemporary philosophy.

53. For critiques of Marcuse as a technological determinist, see Steigerwald, *Herbert Marcuses 'dritter Weg'*; Claus Offe, 'Technik und Eindimensionalität. Eine Version der Technokratiethese?' in *Antworten auf Herbert Marcuse*, pp. 73ff; Langdon Winner, who presents Marcuse as a theorist of 'autonomous technology' and 'technics-out-of-control' in *Autonomous Technology* (Cambridge: MIT, 1977); and Schoolman, *The Imaginary Witness*.

54. Schoolman also goes wrong by claiming that Weber is the decisive theoretical figure in Marcuse's theory (pp. 179ff) and implies that Marx's failure to conceptualize the role of technology kept him from perceiving 'the most serious form of domination latent in capitalism, which could prevent all further *human* progress' (p. 175). In fact, Schoolman fails to see how Marcuse's appropriation of Weber was mediated through Lukács and the Marxism of the Institute for Social Research and that his synthesis of Weber, Marx, Lukács and varieties of critical Marxism provide the foundation for Marcuse's theory. I have been stressing the role of commodities, needs, fetishism, ideology and the state in constituting advanced capitalism – all Marxist themes to which Marcuse gives his distinctive formulations – and I shall emphasize Marcuse's Marxian critique of Weber in this section to try to distinguish the sort of neo-Marxian social theory which Marcuse develops and to show that he is not a technological reductionist or determinist.

55. Strictly speaking, Marcuse does not exactly provide either a ruling-class analysis like Baran and Sweezy in *Monopoly Capital*, or a power elite analysis à la C. Wright Mills of the dominant 'vested interests'. In fact, instead of utilizing the usual Marxian distinction between the ruling class and working class in *ODM*, Marcuse stresses instead distinctions between the 'dominated' and an apparatus of domination. If pushed, Marcuse will answer that, of course, there is a ruling class with distinct class interests behind the technical apparatus; see, for example, 'Reply to Karl Miller', pp. 44 – a position that Marcuse consistently takes in his post-*ODM* writings. On the difference between 'ruling class' and 'power elite' analyses, see Paul Sweezy, 'Power Elite or Ruling Class?', in *C. Wright Mills and the Power Elite* (Boston: Beacon Press, 1968). Alan Wolfe in *The Seamy Side of Democracy* (New York: McKay, 1973) sensibly argues for the usefulness of both approaches in doing social analysis, and this is, I believe, what Marcuse is doing in *ODM*.

56. I discuss in more detail the relationship between Marcuse and Max Weber in a forthcoming article on 'Critical Theory, Max Weber and Rationalization', which will appear in an anthology on Weber edited by Robert Antonio. For Marcuse's discussion of Weber, see his 1964 article, 'Industrialization and Capitalism in the Work of Max Weber', *Negations*. For discussions of the connections between the theories of Marcuse and Weber, see Jean Cohen, 'Max Weber and the Dynamics of Domination', *Telos*, 14 (Winter 1972) pp. 63ff, and Gertraud Korf, *Ausbruch aus dem 'Gehäuse der Hörigkeit'* (Frankfurt: Verlag Marxistische Blätter, 1971).

57. See Vivas's vicious book, *Contra Marcuse*, and the bitter critique by Richard Goodwin, 'The Social Theory of Herbert Marcuse'.

58. Graubard, 'One-Dimensional Pessimism'.

59. For a discussion of Marcuse and other radical thinkers in American social theory during the 1950s, see Peter Clecak, *Radical Paradoxes* (New York: Harper & Row, 1972).

60. Marcuse, 'The Obsolescence of Marxism', in *Marx and the Western World*, ed. Nicholas Lobkowicz (Notre Dame: Notre Dame Press, 1967). Marcuse's affirmative relationship to Marxism, even during the period in which he was writing *ODM*, comes out in a review of George Lichtheim's *Marxism*, published in *Political Science Quarterly*, vol. LXXVIII, no. 1 (1962) pp. 117–19. While Marcuse praises aspects of Lichtheim's study, he criticizes Lichtheim's position that Marxism is now obsolescent and that its concepts 'are no longer quite applicable to current history' (p. 117). Marcuse insists that Marxism's concepts are 'historical categories which try to define tendencies and counter-tendencies within an antagonistic society' and thus demand development in terms of historical change. Marcuse claims that the continuing relevance or obsolescence of Marxism can only be determined by 'an analysis of advanced industrial society and of the structural changes which the development of this society in coexistence with the Communist societies has brought about' (p. 118). The distinguishing feature of Marcuse's relation to Marxism is thus his combined attempt to develop Marxism and to criticize those aspects that are outdated through constantly confronting Marxism with historical developments which often require a reconstruction of Marxism.

61. Marcuse, 'The Obsolescence of Marxism'. In 'Socialism in the Developed Countries', he affirms that 'the concepts which Marx originated should not be rejected but developed; their further development is already contained in the basic theses' (p. 151).

62. See the famous Chapter 32 in Marx's *Capital*. For discussion of Marxist crisis theories, see Karl Korsch, 'Some Fundamental Presuppositions for a Materialist Discussion of Crisis Theory', in *Karl Korsch*, and Russell Jacoby's survey, 'Politics of the Crisis Theory', *Telos*, 23 (Spring 1975).

63. See Paul Mattick's article, 'The Limits of Integration' in *The Critical Spirit: Essays in Honor of Herbert Marcuse*, ed. by Kurt Wolff and Barrington Moore, Jr (Boston: Beacon, 1967) and his book *Critique of*

454   Notes and References

Marcuse (New York: Seabury, 1973), as well as the article by Mitchell Franklin, 'The Irony of the Beautiful Soul of Herbert Marcuse', *Telos*, 6 (Fall 1970). The problem with these and most orthodox Marxian critiques of Marcuse is that they assume the truth and unquestioned continued validity of Marxism; they fail to see the extent to which Marcuse's enterprise is rooted in an attempt to reconstruct Marxism to make it possible to provide a neo-Marxist account of contemporary capitalism and the prospects for radical social change.

64. In his book *Marcuse – Dilemma and Liberation*, John Fry cites tendencies and empirical research which put in question various theses which Marcuse sets forth in *One-Dimensional Man*, as does Mattick in 'The Limits of Integration'.

65. This position is argued by David Horowitz, *Repression*, and John Fry (see note 64.) For a discussion of the capitalist business cycle which articulates the presuppositions of both Horowitz's and Fry's critique, see Baran and Sweezy, *Monopoly Capital*. This critique exemplifies what might be called the 'Monthly Review' case against Marcuse. Harry Cleaver, in *Reading Capital Politically* (Austin, Texas: University of Texas Press, 1979) shows the similarity between Marcuse and the Monthly Review group.

66. Mattick, 'The Limits of Integration', and Fry, *Marcuse – Dilemma and Liberation*.

67. Ibid. In the last decade there has been an upsurge of interest in theories of capitalist crisis which have to some extent displaced Marcusean types of theories of capitalist hegemony from the center of radical social theory. On the Marxian theory of capitalist crisis, see the sources in note 62, and for discussions of the current global crisis of capitalism, see Harry Magdoff and Paul M. Sweezy, *The End of Prosperity: The American Economy in the 1970s* (New York: Monthly Review Press, 1977); the articles in *The Economic Crisis Reader*, ed. David Mermelstein (New York: Vintage Books, 1975) and *The Subtle Anatomy of Capitalism*, ed. Jesse Schwartz (Santa Monica, Cal.: Goodyear, 1977); Stanley Aronowitz, *Food, Shelter and the American Dream* (New York: Seabury Press, 1974); Harry Cleaver, 'Food, Famine, and the International Crisis', *Zerowork*, 3 (Fall 1977); Dick Roberts, *Capitalism in Crisis* (New York: Pathfinder Press, 1975); Jürgen Habermas, *Legitimation Crisis* (Boston: Beacon Press, 1975); the Union for Radical Political Economics, *Radical Perspectives on the Economic Crisis of Monopoly Capitalism* (New York: URPE/PEA, 1975); and *Business Week*, 'The Reindustrialization of America', 30 June 1980.

68. In 'Socialism in the Developed Countries', *International Socialist Journal*, vol. II, no. 8 (April 1965), after citing a 'suspension of antitheses and contradictions within the society, Marcuse writes: 'Of course, the contradictions of capitalism are not transcended; they persist in their classic form; indeed, perhaps they have never been stronger. Certainly, there has never been such an acute contradiction between the social wealth of the capitalist countries and the use to which that wealth is put. Every available force is mustered to disguise such an

antithesis' (pp. 139 and 140). In 'On Changing the World: A Reply to Karl Miller', *Monthly Review*, vol. 19, no. 5 (October 1967), Marcuse writes: 'the reality of capitalist society is its dynamic of antagonistic tendencies at all levels ... these tendencies generate the internal contradictions of the system ... one such contradiction is precisely that between the (precarious and temporary!) containment of radical social change on the one hand, and the ever more pressing alternative of radical social change on the other' (pp. 43–4). In 'The End of Utopia', he states: 'Today the classical contradictions within capitalism are stronger than they have ever been before' (*5L*, p. 70) – a position that Marcuse constantly takes in his post-*ODM* writings. In Chapter 9, I shall focus on how Marcuse modified his analysis of advanced capitalism and how he returns, in many ways, to more conventionally Marxian modes of social analysis.

69. The following books provide historical background and empirical sociological details to Marcuse's theory of one-dimensional society: Harry Braverman, *Labor and Monopoly Capital*; Richard Edwards, *Contested Terrain*; Stanley Aronowitz, *False Promises*; Stuart Ewen, *Captains of Consciousness* (New York: McGraw-Hill, 1976); Richard J. Barnet and Ronald E. Müller, *Global Reach* (New York: Simon & Schuster, 1974); David Noble, *America By Design* (New York: Basic Books, 1977); Samuel Bowles and Herbert Gintis, *Schooling in Capitalist America* (New York: Basic Books, 1976); Christopher Lasch, *The Culture of Narcissism* (New York: Norton, 1978); Ralph Miliband, *The State in Capitalist Society* (New York: Basic Books, 1968); James O'Conner, *The Corporations and the State* (New York: Harper & Row, 1974); Alan Wolfe, *The Limits of Legitimacy* (New York: Free Press, 1977); Mark Poster, *Critical Theory of the Family*; Nancy Chodorow, *The Reproduction of Mothering* (Berkeley: University of California Press, 1978); and the histories cited in note 19.

70. Critiques of the one-dimensional society theory are inspired by the labour history appproach of E. P. Thompson, Herbert Gutman and others, who stress resistance to capitalism and autonomous workers' culture and struggles, as well as theories that continue to affirm the existence of class struggle and a militant working class in advanced capitalism. This approach informs the work of such Left journals as *Socialist Radical America, Politics and Society, Zero Work, Cultural Correspondence*, and the work of the Marho history group. For a cultural revolutionist, it is curious that Marcuse has never discussed in any detail oppositional culture. On oppositional cultures within contemporary capitalist societies, see Aronowitz, *False Promises*; Raymond Williams, *Culture and Society* (New York: Harper & Row, 1966); for material on oppositional culture in America, see the issues of *Radical America*, vol. III, no. 6 (November 1969) and vol. IV, no. 6 (September–October 1970) and Herbert Gintis, 'The New Working Class and Revolutionary Youth', *Socialist Revolution*, vol. I, no. 3 (May–June 1970). On Chicanos, see Thomas Almaguer, 'Class, Race, and Chicano Oppression', *Socialist Revolution*, 25 (July–September

1975) and Stan Steiner, *La Raza* (New York: Harper & Row, 1970); among the many books on black oppositional culture, see *The Black Panthers Speak*, ed. Philip Foner (New York: J. B. Lippincott, 1970). For a discussion of British youth subcultures, which includes some excellent theoretical discussions of class, culture, hegemony and subcultures, see *Working Papers for Cultural Studies* (Autumn 1974).

71. 'Capital logic' theories are associated with the work of Roman Rosdolsky, Paul Mattick, Harry Braverman and others, who posit the logic of capital as the key to historical development. This tendency, like the ideas of Marcuse, seems to conceive of the development of advanced capitalism in terms of the exigencies of capital accumulation and minimizes elements of class struggle and workers' self activity. See the discussion and criticisms of capital logic theories in Stanley Aronowitz, 'The End of Political Economy', *Social Text*, 2 (Summer 1979).

72. For analyses of how contradictions within advanced capitalism provide space for struggle, see Aronowitz, 'The End of Political Economy'; O'Conner, *The Corporation and the State*; Alvin Gouldner, *The Dialectic of Ideology and Technology* (New York: Seabury, 1975): and my study of 'Network Television and American Society'.

9 Marcuse, Radical Politics and the New Left

1. Conversation with Marcuse, 28 December 1978.
2. See also Marcuse, 'Revolutionary Subject and Self-Government', *Praxis* 5 (1969) pp. 327–8.
3. For Marcuse's appraisal of Benjamin, where he elaborates on this notion, see his 'Nachwort' to Walter Benjamin, *Zur Kritik der Gewalt und andere Aufsätze* (Frankfurt: Suhrkamp, 1965) pp. 99–106. Marcuse's increasingly embittered critic, Erich Fromm, jumped on this passage and wrote: 'These quotations show how wrong those are who attack or admire Marcuse as a revolutionary leader: for revolution was never based on hopelessness, nor can it ever be. But Marcuse is not even concerned with politics; for if one is not concerned with steps between the present and the future, one does not deal with politics, radical or otherwise. Marcuse is essentially an example of an alienated intellectual, who presents his personal despair as a theory of radicalism'; Fromm, *The Revolution of Hope* (New York: Bantam, 1968) pp. 8–9. This quote shows how Fromm tends to take a single passage out of Marcuse's complex theory and build a global critique on the basis of it. Marcuse's later activity and theoretical perspectives show the groundlessness of Fromm's 'critique'.
4. Allegations of Marcuse's supposed 'anarchism' are made by, among others, Maurice Cranston in his article 'Herbert Marcuse', in *Prophetic Politics* (New York: Simon & Schuster, 1970) pp. 85ff. Soviet critics make similar charges; see Steigerwald, *Herbert Marcuses 'dritter Weg'*, and Jack Woddis, *new Theories of Revolution* (New York: International Publishers, 1972).

5. On Breton, see *Manifestoes of Surrealism* (Ann Arbor: University of Michigan Press, 1969) and *What is Surrealism?* (New York: Pathfinder Press, 1978). Marcuse makes explicit the connection between Breton, the Great Refusal and the artistic *avant-garde* in the 1960 preface to *R&R*, pp. x–xi.
6. See Murray Bookchin, 'Beyond Neo-Marxism', *Telos,* 36 (Summer 1978) where Bookchin complains that Marcuse falls back on orthodox Marxian political conceptions time and time again after seeming to break with Marxism and 'pave new theoretical ground' (pp. 5ff). Bookchin claims that despite some kinship Marcuse is at odds with anarchism on fundamental issues.
7. See 'Thoughts on the Defense of Gracchus Babeuf' in *The Defense of Gracchus Babeuf Before the High Court of Vendome* (Amherst: The University of Massachusetts Press, 1967) p. 104.
8. See Paul Piccone and Alex Delfini, 'Marcuse's Heideggerian Marxism', I would also disagree here with Morton Schoolman, who in his book, *The Imaginary Witness*, claims that in Marcuse's early works he stressed the 'hidden capacities of individuals for progressive political opposition' and that he abandoned this belief in the wake of fascism, replacing 'the highly politicized individual of his early writings with a one-dimensional subject, incapable of politics or thought . . . where this version of critical theory is adopted, its disciples become new victims of the politics that gave it birth'. This interpretation completely disregards the theory of liberation – which stressed the creative and rebellious capabilities of human beings – in *Eros and Civilization*, a theory which resurfaced in his later works such as *EL* and *CR&R*. It also misreads *ODM*, failing to see that even here Marcuse explicitly calls for individual revolt and refusal, but is pessimistic about the prospects for collective action which would radically modify the existing society.
9. On Marcuse and the New Left, see Paul Breines's articles in *Antworten auf Herbert Marcuse* and *Critical Interruptions.* Jean-Michel Palmier's *Herbert Marcuse et la nouvelle gauche* (Paris: Belfond, 1973) contains an exhaustive study of the relevance of Marcuse's ideas to New Left theory and practice in France and America. For more critical accounts of Marcuse and the New Left, see A. Quattrocchi and T. Nairn, *The Beginning of the End: France, May 1968* (London: Penguin, 1968) and Henri Lefebvre, *The Explosion: Marxism and the French Upheaval* (New York: Monthly Review, 1969). Cohn-Bendit is sceptical of whether Marcuse had much influence on the French student movement: 'Some people try to foist Marcuse upon us as a mentor. This is a joke. None of us have read Marcuse. Some people have read Marx, perhaps Bakunin and when it comes to modern authors – Althusser, Mao, Guevara, Lefebvre. Almost all the rebels have read Sartre'; cited in E. Batalov, *The Philosophy of Revolt* (Moscow: Progress Publishers, 1977) p. 52. Palmier contests this, claiming that many had read Marcuse and that there was a surge of interest in his writings during and after the May events. On this topic, see Palmier's earlier book *Sur*

Marcuse (Paris: Union Générale d'Editions, 1968) and *La Nef*, 36 (Janvier-Mars 1969) on 'Marcuse. Cet Inconnu'.

10. See 'Ethics and Revolution', where Marcuse defines revolution as 'the overthrow of a legally established government and constitution by a social class or movement with the aim of altering the social as well as the political structure ... such a radical and qualitative change implies violence'; in *Ethics and Society*, ed. Richard T. DeGeorge (Garden City, NY: Doubleday, 1966) p. 134. See also Marcuse, 'Re-Examination of the Concept of Revolution', *New Left Review*, 56 (July–August 1969) pp. 27ff.

11. Right-wing critics had a field day with 'Repressive Tolerance', quoting Marcuse out of context and labelling him an 'elitist authoritarian', 'nihilist' and worse. See Vivas, *Contra Marcuse*, pp. 171–7, who calls Marcuse 'the Torquemada of the left' and 'an intellectual termite' with a 'Nazi mind'. For more intelligent critical discussions of the essay, see David Spitz, 'Pure Tolerance', *Dissent*, XIII (September–October 1966) pp. 510–25: Michael Walzer's critique of Spitz and Marcuse, 'On the Nature of Freedom', *Dissent*, XIII (November–December 1966) which contains Spitz's reply (pp. 725–39); see also Batalov's Marxist-Leninist critique of Marcuse's position, *The Philosophy of Revolt*.

12. For an indication of the gravity of the situation to which Marcuse was responding, and the dangers of nuclear extinction, see Robert Kennedy's memoir of the Cuban missile crisis, *Thirteen Days* (New York: Norton, 1969). Other accounts of the period, which render plausible Marcuse's call for intolerance against the policies of the existing society, include Bruce Miroff, *Pragmatic Illusions* (New York: McKay, 1976) and Hodgson, *America in Our Time*.

13. See Rosa Luxemburg, *The Russian Revolution* (Ann Arbor: University of Michigan Press, 1962) for her defence of civil liberties. On the concept of a 'proletarian public sphere', see Oskar Negt and Alexander Kluge, *Öffentlichkeit und Erfahrung* (Frankfurt: Suhrkamp, 1972).

14. On the New Left's relation to the dominant communications media, see Todd Gitlin, *The Whole World's Watching* (Berkeley: University of California Press, 1980).

15. Marcuse cites Fanon and Sartre here (*CPT*, pp. 103–4), whose advocacy of revolutionary violence against violent oppressors no doubt influenced him. See Franz Fanon, *The Wretched of the Earth* (London: Penguin, 1967) with an introduction by Sartre, and Jean-Paul Sartre, *On Genocide* (Boston: Beacon Press, 1971). For critiques of these theories of revolutionary violence, see the articles in Maurice Cranston, ed., *Prophetic Politics*; Woddis, *New Theories of Revolutions*; and Gil Green, *The New Radicalism* (New York: International Publishers, 1971).

16. Marcuse elaborates his defence of revolutionary violence in 'Ethics and Revolution' and in 'The Problem of Violence and the Radical Opposition' (*5L*).

17. In works like *EC*, *SM* and *ODM*, Marcuse's commitment to socialism

is muted and is often expressed elliptically. In his post-1965 writings, however, he articulates his commitment to socialism much more explicitly. He constantly says that the only alternative to capitalism is socialism and openly proclaims himself a socialist and Marxist: see *5L*, pp. 67ff and 80ff; *EL, passim*; and a 1968 lecture given in commemoration of the twentieth anniversary of *The Guardian,* where he says, 'I believe that the alternative is socialism', and affirms his solidarity with the struggle for socialism. In Chapter 10, I shall discuss his concept of socialism in more detail. There is also a tone of revolutionary buoyancy in his post-1966 writings which first appears, appropriately, in the 1966 preface to a new Beacon Press edition of *Eros and Civilization.*

18. I recall vividly the excitement with which the student movement received this book. See Palmier, *Herbert Marcuse et al nouvelle gauche,* and Arnason, *Von Marcuse zu Marx,* for the European reaction. The Right was again outraged by this book, violently attacking it in a spate of vitriolic reviews. See John Sparrow, 'The Gospel of Hate', *National Review* (21 October 1969); Sidney Hook, *The NY Times Book Review* (20 April 1969); Lewis Feuer, *Book World* (23 February 1969); and, of course, Vivas, *Contra Marcuse,* for some choice violent and intemperate attacks that chide Marcuse for being violent and intemperate.

19. On the historical roots of the 'new sensibility' in the beatnik generation, civil rights movement and 1960s counterculture, see Morris Dickstein, *Gates of Eden* (New York: Basic Books, 1977). For an unabashed celebration of the 'new sensibility' as a revolutionary form of consciousness, see Charles Reich, *The Greening of America* (New York: Random House, 1970) and the collection of reviews of this book, including a critical essay by Marcuse, *The Con III Controversy* (New York: Pocket Books, 1971).

20. Compare *EL* with *CR&R* and *AD*. I shall discuss Marcuse's shifts in appraising the radical potential of the counterculture and his modified theory of 'emancipatory art' in Chapter 10.

21. There was some ambivalence as to the status Marcuse assigned to the 'new sensibility' and New Left groups-in-revolt in the revolutionary process. On one hand, he argued: 'The social agents of revolution – and this is orthodox Marx – are formed only in the process of transformation itself, and one cannot count on a situation in which the revolutionary forces are there ready-made, so to speak, when the revolutionary movement begins' (*5L*, p. 64). On the other hand, in his more enthusiastic moments in *EL*, it seemed as if the new sensibility might be a new revolutionary subject, or at least a 'catalyst' producing a new revolutionary subject (*EL*, pp. 23ff, 52f). On the concept of the revolutionary subject which haunts Marcuse's problematic, see section 9.4.2 below.

22. See *EL*, pp. 50–7, 60.

23. *EL*, pp. 16, 53–6. See the interview with Marcuse in *The New York Times Magazine* (27 October 1968) where he discusses spontaneity and organization, students and workers. He concludes: 'in spite of everything that has been said, I still cannot imagine a revolution

without the working class' (p. 89). It is not until the 1970s that Marcuse questions this basic tenet of orthodox Marxism. See section 9.4 below.

24. See Marcuse, 'Revolutionary Subject and Self-Government', and section 9.4.2 below.

25. For Marcuse's reaction to May 1968 in France, see 'The Paris Rebellion', *Peace News* (28 June 1968) pp. 6–7.

26. See the sources in note 9; Marcuse's interviews listed in the bibliography; and Herbert Gold, 'California Left'.

27. Many of the New Left were attracted to the Third World revolutionary theories of Fanon, Mao, Debray, Castro, Guevara and others; Marcuse was often associated with this tendency; see the books already cited in note 15 for critiques of this 'Third Worldism' and Robert E. Wood's comments on 'Rethinking Third World Revolutions', in *Socialist Review*, 45 (May–June 1979) pp. 159ff.

28. Marcuse, 'Re-examination of the Concept of Revolution', p. 31.

29. Ibid.

30. From the late 1960s on, Marcuse significantly accelerated and radicalized his critique of Soviet Marxism and orthodox Communist parties from his more restrained criticism in *Soviet Marxism* (see Chapter 7). No doubt the continuing stifling repression in the Soviet bloc, the Russian invasion of Czechoslovakia, and the reformist nature of Communist parties in the West, together with the emergence of new socialist forces, led him to re-evaluate Soviet Marxism. See *EL*, pp. 54f.

31. *5L*, pp. 70–1, 96, 98; *EL*, pp. vii–x, 3ff, 23ff, 49ff and 79ff.

32. Marcuse shifts from a more abstract model of advanced industrial society in *ODM*, to a focus on 'corporate capitalism' in *EL*, to a focus on the constellation of capitalism and the Left opposition in the United States in *CR&R*, where he explicitly states that he will only 'focus the discussion on the prospects for radical change in the United States' (*CR&R*, p. 5).

33. For critiques of Marcuse's lack of a concept of 'determinate negation', see Franklin's article in *Telos*, 6, and Steigerwald, *Herbert Marcuses 'dritter Weg'*, pp. 317ff, *passim*. In an article, 'The Concept of Negation in the Dialectic', *Telos*, 9 (Summer 1971) pp. 130–2, Marcuse indeed appeals to a principle of external mediation: 'The power of the negative arises outside this repressive totality from forces and movements still not grasped by the aggressive, repressive productivity of the so-called "society of abundance", from forces and movements which have already freed themselves from this development and thus have the historical opportunity to actually modernize and industrialize humanely' (p. 132). In the late 1960s, however, Marcuse abandoned this notion of 'external negation' for a theory of 'determinate negation', in which the forces of negation were actually produced by contradictions and conditions within the existing society, thus rendering Franklin's critique irrelevant.

34. For an account of current capitalist organization and administration,

Marcuse refers the readers to the works of Baran and Sweezy, Kolko, Magdoff and Domhoff in *CR&R*, p. 5, thus showing that he follows both Marxian ruling-class and power elite analyses and does not accept politically neutral theories of technological domination, as some of his critics of *ODM* claimed (i.e. Claus Offe or Morton Schoolman – see the discussion in the last chapter). Marcuse makes his position clear in a critique of Charles Reich's, *The Greening of America*. First, he sets forth Reich's revolutionary fantasy: 'One day in the foreseeable future, men and women, boys and girls from all walks of life will have enough of the old, will quit. And since there is "nobody in control", this will be it'. Marcuse's rejoinder is: 'Nobody in control of the armed forces, the police, the National Guard? Nobody in control of the outer space program, of the budget, the Congressional committees? There is only the machine being tended to? But the machine not only must be tended to, it must be designed, constructed, programmed, directed. And there are very definite, identifiable persons, groups, classes, interests which do this controlling job, which direct the technical, economic, political machine for the society as a whole. They, not their machine, decided on life and death, war and peace – they set the priorities. They have all the power to defend it – and it is not the power of the machine but *over* the machine: human power, political power'; in *The Con III Controversy*, pp. 16–17.

35. On the 'new working class', see Serge Mallet, *Essays on the New Working Class* (St Louis: Telos Press, 1975) and the literature to which Marcuse refers in *CR&R*, pp. 10 and 35.

36. Marcuse cites the appropriate passage in Marx in *CR&R*, pp. 11–13.

37. A special supplement, 'The Debt Economy' in *Business Week*, (12 October 1974) states: 'It is inevitable that the US economy will grow more slowly that it has . . . Some people will obviously have to do with less . . . Yet it will be a hard pill for many Americans to swallow – the idea of doing with less so that big business can have more . . . Nothing that this nation, or any other nation, has done in modern history compares in difficulty with the selling job that must now be done to make people accept the new reality'. This is a dangerous situation for the capitalist class, in that many political theorists have argued that 'rising expectations' that are not met lead to demands for radical change. See Daniel Bell, *The End of Ideology* (New York: The Free Press, 1960) pp. 31 ff.

38. A study put out by the Health, Education and Welfare Department of the US Government, *Work in America*, concluded that 'A changing American work force is becoming pervasively dissatisfied with dull, unchallenging and repetitive jobs, and this discontent is sapping the economic and social strength of the nation', reported in *The New York Times* (22 December 1972) p. 1. Reports show a decline in productivity in the American economy during the 1970s. See the January 1979 *Economic Report of the President*, prepared by Charles Schultze and the Council of Economic Advisors, and the 1979 study by the New York

Stock Exchange, *Reaching a Higher Standard of Living*. These reports were widely discussed by the business press and were analysed in *In These Times* (23–9 May 1979) p. 17.

39. 'For Marcuse's reaction to the publicity that William Calley received after being brought to trial after revelations of the US massacre of Vietnamese in My Lai, see his article in *The New York Times* (13 May 1971) p. 45.

40. In a conversation with Hans-Magnus Enzensberger, Marcuse discusses tendencies towards fascism in the USA. 'USA: Organisations-frage und revolutionäres Subjekt', reprinted in *Zeit-Messungen* (Frankfurt: Suhrkamp, 1975). The conversation was first published in Enzensberger's journal, *Kursbuch*, 22 (1970) which discussed the dangers of fascism and included a collage of material assembled by Marcuse's friend Reinhard Lettau, 'Täglicher Faschismus'. For similar fears that fascism is on its way in advanced capitalist countries, see *Les Temps Modernes*, 'Nouveau fascisme, nouvelle démocratie', no. 310 (1972) and Bertram Gross, *Friendly Fascism* (New York: Basic Books, 1980).

41. Marcuse, 'The Movement in a New Era of Repression: An Assessment', *Berkeley Journal of Sociology*, vol. XVI (1971–2) p. 8.

42. Marcuse's favourite book on the New Left is *A Disrupted History: The New Left and the New Capitalism*, by Greg Calvert and Carol Neiman (New York: Random House, 1971); see *CR&R*, p. 10. See also *The New Left: A Documentary History*, ed. Massimo Teodori (Indianapolis: Bobbs-Merrill, 1969).

43. It might be noted that the term 'United Front' historically signified in Marxian discourse a merger of left-wing parties, both in leadership and base (as with the Mensheviks and Bolsheviks in the Russian Revolution), or at least a unity of action between working-class parties – and not a loose coalition of democratic groups and rebellious individuals. Marcuse's concept is actually closer to what has been called a 'popular front', in which separate parties, or groups, remain autonomous while they struggle for a 'common programme' or for specific goals. It seems that Marcuse's use of the term 'United Front' serves as a rhetorical device which makes it appear that a coalition of democratic-populist groups may be the most promising force for developing a socialist movement in the United States.

44. For details of some of Marcuse's political involvements with the New Left, see the sources listed in note 9.

45. On Marcuse's 1967 trip to Berlin, see the account in *Der Spiegel*, Nr 25 (1967) pp. 103–4, and the lectures that were later published in *5L*. For an account of Marcuse's less successful visit to Berlin in 1968, see Melvin J. Lasky, 'Revolution Diary', *Encounter*, vol. XXXI, no. 2 (August 1968) pp. 6–8. For Marcuse's speech at the 1967 London 'Dialectics of Liberation' conference, see 'Liberation from the Affluent Society.'

46. Marcuse left Brandeis in 1965 when, after a series of disputes with the university President Abram Sacher, his post-retirement contract was not renewed. See *Atlantic Monthly* (June 1971) p. 74.

47. California newspapers regularly attacked Marcuse, and pressures from the California Board of Regents forced Marcuse to give up teaching officially in 1969, although he was allowed to keep his office and to give informal seminars. On the death threats he received, see *The Nation* (28 October 1968) p. 421.
48. See Angela Davis, *An Autobiography* (New York: Random House, 1974) for her account of Marcuse's influence on her. Other evaluations include 'Marcuse as Teacher', William Leiss, John David Ober and Erica Sherover, in *The Critical Spirit*. pp. 421–6, and Ronald Aronson, 'Dear Herbert', *Radical America*, vol. IV, no. 3 (April 1970).
49. Marcuse, 'Marxism and Feminism', lecture delivered at Stanford University (7 March 1974).
50. Marcuse, 'Theorie und Praxis', in *Zeit-Messungen*.
51. Marcuse, 'Scheitern der Neuen Linken?', *Zeit-Messungen*, translated in *New German Critique*, 18 (Fall 1979). For a report on Marcuse's last lecture in Frankfurt, see Jeffrey Herf, 'The Critical Theory of Herbert Marcuse', *New German Critique*, 18 (Fall 1979). During my last interview with Marcuse in December 1978, he was searching for Horkheimer's essay, 'Die Juden in Europa' as material for a Holocaust essay.
52. Marcuse, BBC interview with Brian Magee, published as part of *Men of Ideas* (London: BBC, 1978).
53. 'A Conversation with Herbert Marcuse', *Bill Moyers Journal* (12 March 1974), transcript, p. 1, and 'Scheitern?'.
54. Marcuse and Enzensberger, 'USA', in *Zeit-Messungen*.
55. Marcuse, 'Theory and Politics', p. 150.
56. In a 1957 preface to Raya Dunayevskaya's *Marxism and Freedom*, Marcuse writes: 'Marx's concept of the proletariat as "revolutionary class in-itself (*an sich*)" did not designate a merely occupational group – i.e. the wage earners engaged in the material production – as a truly dialectical concept, it was at one and the same time an economic, political and philosophical category. As such it comprised three main elements – (1) the specific societal mode of production characteristic of "free" capitalism, (2) the existential and political conditions brought about by this mode of production, (3) the political consciousness developed in this situation. Any historical change in even one of these elements (and such a change has certainly occurred) would require a thorough theoretical modification. Without such modification, the Marxian notion of the working class seems to be applicable neither to the majority of the labouring classes in the West nor to that in the communist orbit' (p. 12). Precisely this issue has preoccupied Marcuse throughout the last decades. Compare *CR&R*, pp. 38–9.
57. Marx consistently took this position from his 1843 'Contribution to the Critique of Hegel's Philosophy of Law', until his death. See Carol Johnson, 'Reformism and Commodity Fetishism', for a collection of Marx's descriptions of the proletariat throughout his life.
58. Throughout his 1970s writings, Marcuse emphasizes that the proletariat is the revolutionary subject for Marx by virtue of its needs; see

CR&R, pp. 38–9 and 'Einheitsfront', p. 21.

59. Karl Marx, Letter to Lassalle, cited in a lecture by Marcuse at Columbia University, 11 October 1972.

60. Marcuse constantly argues this position in the 1970s; see Marcuse and Enzensberger, 'USA', pp. 56ff; *CR&R*, pp. 10ff; Marcuse and Habermas, 'Theory and Politics', p. 150; and 'Reification of the Proletariat', p. 20.

61. Marcuse and Habermas, 'Theory and Politics', p. 150.

62. Marcuse and Enzensberger, 'USA', p. 56, and Marcuse and Habermas, 'Theory and Politics', p. 50.

63. Marcuse's friend Heinz Lubasz argued that 'Marx did not *discover* the revolutionary proletariat', he *invented* it'. See 'Marx's Conception of the Revolutionary Proletariat', *Praxis*, 5, 1–2 (1969) p. 288.

64. McCarthy, *Marx and the Proletariat*.

65. André Gorz, *Adieux au Proletariat*, translated as *Farewell to the Working Class* (Boston: South End Press, 1982).

66. Most Marxist theories of capitalist crisis posit a final collapse of capitalism as part of the crisis theory. See the discussions of the crisis theory cited in Chapter 8 note 67. Up until the post-war period, Marcuse seemed to have accepted orthodox Marxian theories of capitalist crisis and collapse, indicating another dogma of orthodox Marxism which Marcuse is now questioning.

67. Marcuse, 'Theory and Practice', pp. 32f; 'Scheitern?', p. 42.

68. Marcuse, 'Murder is no Weapon of Politics', in *Die Zeit* and *New German Critique*.

69. See the material in my book *Karl Korsch*, especially pp. 80–3 and 274–8, and Korsch's article 'Marx' Stellung in der europäischen Revolution von 1848', in *Karl Korsch: Politische Texte* (Frankfurt: Europäische Verlagsanstalt, 1974).

70. For discussions which portray revolution in the advanced capitalist countries as the result of a long historical process, see Raymond Williams, *The Long Revolution* (London: Penguin Books, 1961); Alvin W. Gouldner, *The Dialectic of Ideology and Technology* (New York: Seabury, 1976); and Bahro, *Die Alternative*, whose analysis can be applied as Marcuse suggests, to capitalist countries.

71. In *The Imaginary Witness*, Morton Schoolman opens his discussion of Marcuse's theory of advanced industrial society with a quote from Milton that contains this phrase, which he later uses as a subtitle for a section of his study (pp. 162ff). My analysis here indicates the insulting ludicrousness of such a designation for Marcuse.

72. Marcuse is extremely impressed by Rudolf Bahro's book *Die Alternative: Zur Kritik des real existierenden Sozialismus* (Frankfurt: 1977), translated as *The Alternative in Eastern Europe* (London: New Left Books, 1978). In a review of Bahro's book, 'Proto-socialism and Late Capitalism', Marcuse describes it as 'the most important contribution to Marxist theory and practice to appear in several decades' (p. 25). The similarity between Bahro's and Marcuse's own theory is striking, so it is not surprising that Marcuse would be attracted to Bahro's

theory. Marcuse suggests that Bahro's analysis of 'really existing socialism' is also relevant for advanced capitalism, and applies Bahro's categories to analyse its social conditions and consciousness. The fact that Bahro presents himself as a critical Marxist who is explicitly developing and expanding Marx's categories by applying Marx's method to analyse contemporary conditions, allows Marcuse to claim the same for himself, and to present Bahro and his own work as creative Marxism which both questions and goes beyond an outdated orthodoxy. On Bahro's background and imprisonment after the publication of his explosive book, see David Bathrick, 'The Politics of Culture: Rudolf Bahro and Opposition in the GDR', and Hugh Mosley, 'The New Communist Opposition: Bahro's critique of the 'Really Existing Socialism''', both in *New German Critique*, 15 (Fall 1978), as well as the interviews with Bahro in *Labour Focus on Eastern Europe* (November 1977 to November 1979).

73. Bahro, The *Alternative*, pp. 257ff.
74. Marcuse, 'Reification of the Proletariat', p. 21, compare Bahro's analysis in *The Alternative*, pp. 257ff.
75. Marcuse, 'Reification of the Proletariat', pp. 21–2.
76. Marcuse, 'Proto-socialism and Late Capitalism', p. 27; compare Bahro, *The Alternative*, pp. 272ff, *passim*.
77. Marcuse, 'Proto-socialism', pp. 31ff; Bahro, *The Alternative*, pp. 253ff, discussed in Mosley, 'The New Communist Opposition', pp. 28ff. Bahro outlines a quite specific programme as to how this transformation could be brought about in existing socialist countries. No doubt the real threat to Party dictatorship and socialist bureaucrats in Bahro's 'alternative' led Party officials to imprison him and then to force him into exile.
78. In the *New Left Review* summary of his theses, Bahro writes:
   The entire second part of my book pursues the question of on what general basis the rule of man over man persists in our society, and how our socio-economic structure concretely functions so as to give rise to this oppressive socio-psychological effect. The problem of subalternity is the cornerstone of my alternative conception. For as regards the practical political perspective of the barriers to be attacked, the movement of general emancipation today has precisely the task of liquidating those conditions that produce subaltern individuals, a species of thinking ants, instead of free people. *New Left Review*, 106 (November–December 1977) 111ff.
79. Marcuse, 'Pro-socialism', pp. 36ff. There are striking similarities between Bahro's 'alternative' socialist society and Marcuse's 'new definition of socialism', which will be discussed in the next chapter.
80. For analysis of the tradition of socialist democracy and criticisms of Social Democratic and Leninist traditions that have suppressed the emancipatory core of Marxian socialism, see Stephen Eric Bronner, 'The Socialist Project' and Iring Fetscher, 'The Changing Goals of Socialism in the Twentieth Century', both in *Social Research*, vol. 47, no. 1 (Spring 1980). Some critics, however, stress the neo-Leninist

features of Bahro's analysis: see Andrew Arato and Mihaly Vajda, 'The Limits of the Leninist Opposition', *New German Critique*, 19 (Winter 1980) and Andrew Arato's review of *Rudolf Bahro: Critical Responses*, ed. Ulf Wolter (White Plains, NY: M. E. Sharpe, 1980) in *Telos*, 48 (Summer 1981). See also David Stark's discussion in 'Consciousness in Command', *Socialist Review*, 57 (May–June 1981) pp. 128ff. Other readers stress Bahro's kinship with a non-Leninist 'Western Marxism' tradition; see Raymond Williams, 'Reflections on Bahro', *New Left Review*, 120 (March–April 1980), who points to his own kinship with Bahro; and a study by Peter Ludz, 'The Aesthetic Dimension of the New Revisionism: Rudolf Bahro' in *Social Research*, vol. 47, no. 1 (Spring 1980), who emphasizes the Marcusean-Habermasian themes in Bahro and the importance of the cultural dimension in his theory. In fact, there are contradictions in Bahro's theory between the tradition of democratic socialism in the Luxemburg-Korsch 'workers' councils' tradition and a neo-Leninist tradition, which stresses revolution from above. Further debate over Bahro's work is found in *Rudolf Bahro: Critical Responses*.

81. See the sources in the note 82; for an especially clear formulation of this position, see Marcuse's discussion with Sartre, 'A Propos de Livre'. *On a raison de se révolter* Liberation (7 juin 1974) p. 9. I review Sartre's book in *Telos*, 22 (Winter 1974–5) and translate there the debate between Sartre and Marcuse on the role of intellectuals in promoting social change. See also the comments on this exchange in Ronald Aronson, *Jean-Paul Sartre – Philosophy in the World* (London: New Left Books, 1980) pp. 319ff.

82. The theme of an 'intellectual dictatorship' is a disturbing theme which winds through Marcuse's works. Although he never develops the concept in any detail, he constantly alludes to it as a 'provocation'. See *EC*, p. 225; *ODM*, p. 40; *CPT*, p. 106; *EL*, p. 70; and 'Proto-Socialism', p. 32.

83. Marcuse, 'Proto-Socialism', p. 32.

84. Marcuse and Habermas, 'Theory and Politics', p. 136. In the '1968 Postscript' to the Beacon Press paperback edition of *CPT*, Marcuse writes: 'However, the alternative to the established semi-democratic process is *not* a dictatorship or elite, no matter how intellectual and intelligent, but the struggle for a real democracy' (p. 122). In fact, Marcuse ends up arguing in 'Proto-socialism' that an elite provides the most promising way to lead the people to a 'real democracy'.

85. Bahro explicitly describes his concept of a new Communist organization and the 'collective intellectual' as:
'(1) not a working-class party in the old – and far too narrow sense, but a combination of all those people, from all strata and groups in society, whose consciousness is dominated by emancipatory needs and interests; (2) not a mass party of the sort where a self appointed elite leadership of authoritarian intellectuals manipulates those labelled "members", but a union of individuals who are like-minded, i.e. interested in solving the same problems and all regarded as equally

competent; (3) not a sectarian corporation of "those who know best",
closed off from society, but a revolutionary community open towards
society and which anyone striving in the same direction can join; (4)
not a super-state organization which guides and controls the actual
apparatus of the state and administration from outside and from above,
but the ideal inspirer of an integrated activity of all groups at the base,
which gives people the capacity to control all decision-making procedures from within'; in 'The Alternative', *New Left Review*, pp. 23–4.
86. Ibid.; see Gramsci, *Prison Notebooks*.
87. See Gramsci, *Prison Notebooks*; Sartre's *On a raison de se revolter*
(Paris: Gallimard, 1973); and my review in *Telos*, 22.
88. Bahro, 'The Alternative', NLR, p. 25.
89. See Sartre's distinction between the 'classical intellectual' and 'organic
intellectual' (Gramsci) in his essay 'A Plea for Intellectuals', in *Between Marxism and Existentialism* (New York: Pantheon, 1975). In
On a raison, Sartre and his friends call for an 'intellectual of a new sort'.
I fear that Marcuse is, by contrast, valorizing the classical intellectual,
of which he himself is an outstanding example.
90. See Gramsci, *Prison Notebooks*, and Bahro, 'The Alternative'.
91. Leon Trotsky, *The Revolution Betrayed* (New York: Pathfinder Press,
1965). Bahro's kinship with Trotsky's political position is discussed in
Hermann Weber, 'The Third Way', in *Bahro: Critical Responses*.
Weber does stress that Bahro's conceiving of the Soviet Union as
constituted by a semi-asiatic mode of production is far from Trotsky's
position on the Soviet Union.
92. Arato-Vadja, 'The Limits of the Leninist Opposition', Arato, *Rudolf
Bahro*; and Stark, 'Consciousness in Command'.
93. Stark, 'Consciousness in Command', argues that Bahro misinterprets
the events in Czechoslovakia in 1968, seeing initiatives emerging solely
from above – from intellectuals, liberal politicians and technocrats –
whereas in fact, according to Stark, working-class initiative and struggle played a significant role in radicalizing, democratizing and extending the struggles in Czechoslovakia before and after the Soviet invasion. The struggles of the working class in Poland in the 1970s and
1980s suggests the limitations of Bahro's and Marcuse's analyses. See
the dossier and discussion in *Telos*, 47 (Spring 1981) for documentation of the events in Poland and their significance for the creation of a
democratic and human socialism.
94. See Alvin W. Gouldner, *The New Class Project* (New York: Seabury
Press, 1979) and 'Prologue to a Theory of Revolutionary Intellectuals',
Telos, 26 (Winter 1975–6).
95. See Marx's 1843 article, 'Contribution to the Critique of Hegel's
Philosophy of Law. Introduction'. Too many discussions of Marx's
theory of revolution take the rather metaphysical concept of the
proletariat-as-revolutionary class sketched out in the first essay in
which Marx even mentioned the proletariat as providing the criteria for
the revolutionary subject. Marcuse himself follows this procedure in
Reason and Revolution, pp. 261ff (discussed in Chapter 5). This is a

mistake, for it tends to reduce the complex and contradictory analyses in Marx's work of the working class and revolution to a rather simplistic formula or model. For evidence that the concept of the revolutionary subject is a deeply rooted element of his theory, see Marcuse's 'Revolutionary Subject and Self-Government', and references to the 'subject of revolution' in his Bahro essay 'Proto-Socialism', pp. 32ff. There is, in fact, a contradiction in Marcuse's concept of the 'revolutionary subject'. In 'Revolutionary Subject and Self-Government', he writes: 'I would like to offer a very tentative definition of revolutionary subject by saying: It is that class or group which, by virtue of its function and position in society, is in vital need and is capable of risking what they have and what they can get within the established system in order to replace this system – a radical change which would indeed involve destruction, abolition of the existing system. I repeat, such a class or group must have the vital *need* for revolution, and it must be capable of at least initiating, if not carrying through, such a revolution' (p. 326).

Here the 'revolutionary subject' is defined as a *revolutionary class* (or group) in the Marxian sense. In *EL*, where Marcuse talks of the 'new sensibility', and in 'Proto-socialism', where he uses Bahro's concept of 'surplus consciousness', he talks of the revolutionary subject in terms of *revolutionary subjectivity* which cuts across class divisions. In the following paragraph, I suggest that while the concept of 'revolutionary subject' should be discarded for revolutionary theory, the concept of 'revolutionary subjectivity' is essential in talking about the conditions and forces of radical change.

96. Lukács, *History and Class Consciousness*.
97. For some ideas on how new social movements might be fused into a new revolutionary movement, see the discussions between Jean-Paul Sartre, P. Victor and P. Gavi in *On a raison de se révolter*, which I review in *Telos*, 22.

10 Liberation and Utopia

1. On this topic, see Marcuse's 'debate' with Karl Popper, *Revolution or Reform?*, ed. A. T. Ferguson (Chicago: New University Press, 1976).
2. Marcuse is in effect concretizing Adorno's aphorism, 'the whole is untrue'. See T. W. Adorno, *Minima Moralia*, p. 50, and *ODM*, 0. 120, where Marcuse quotes Adorno: 'that which is cannot be true'.
3. Marcuse's total rejection of the existing society and call for a radically new one is criticized as a 'manicheism' by Bhikhu Parekh, 'Utopianism and Manicheism', *Social Research*, 39 (Winter 1972). Against this view, I would argue that Marcuse's analysis of the interconnection of positive and negative features in the existing society indicates that he is not operating with a simple-minded manichean dualism, as Parekh and others claim. Marcuse's point is that good and bad features of the present society are so welded together that only its radical transformation can eliminate the evil features. See the note 4 for sources.

4. See Marcuse's description of 'objective ambiguity' and the 'absorption of the negative by the positive' in *ODM*, pp. 225ff; of the 'inseparable unity of opposites' in 'Liberation from the Affluent Society', p. 195; and *CR&R*, pp. 129–30, where he writes: 'the repulsive unity of opposites (most concrete and unsublimated manifestation of capitalist dialectic!) has become the life element of the system; the protest against these conditions must become a political weapon. The fight will be won when the obscene symbiosis of opposites is broken – the symbiosis between the erotic play of the sea (its waves rolling in as advancing males, breaking by their own grace, turning female: caressing each other, and licking the rocks) and the booming death industries at its shores, between the flight of the white birds and that of the grey air force jets, between the silence of the night and the vicious farts of the motorcycles'.

5. A young German succinctly explains Marcuse's appeal in a conversation with Melvin Lasky, 'Revolution Diary': 'Marcuse taught us that it was *the System* that was wrong, the whole System, all of it. You just simply couldn't change a bit here and there. *All of it* had to be changed, for it was all of an organic piece. All of it was evil, and there was no reform possible, *only Revolution*' (p. 6).

6. Marcuse, 'The Question of Revolution', *New Left Review* 45 (September–October 1967) pp. 6–7.

7. See *Gespräche mit Herbert Marcuse*, p. 101, for Marcuse's opinion of 1968 as a radical break with the existing continuum of history.

8. Marcuse believes that this contradiction is fundamental and stresses its importance throughout his work. For example, see the discussion with Enzensberger, *Zeit-Messungen*, pp. 53ff.

9. Marcuse, 'Scheitern der Neuen Linke?', p. 37.

10. Marcuse, 'Guardian Anniversary Talk', in Teodori.

11. Marcuse, 'Liberation from the Affluent Society', p. 19.

12. Marcuse, 'Philosophy and Critical Theory', *Negations*, p. 143.

13. Marcuse often expounded on this theme in the 1970s: 'The word "utopian" should not be used by socialists anymore, because what is said to be utopian, really is not anymore. An example: the elimination of poverty, of suffering. Today the social wealth is so great that a rational organization of productive forces actually directed toward the interests of everyone would make possible the overcoming of poverty in the world in a few years. Further, shortening of working time is according to Marx the precondition of a socialist society. No one denies – not even the bourgeois economists – that the socially necessary labour time could be decisively reduced in the developed industrial lands without diminishing the cultural and material level of life. These examples provide indexes which show that the propagandistic caricature of socialism as utopian is really nothing else but its defamation', *Gespräche*, p. 98.

14. Marcuse, 'The Realm of Freedom and the Realm of Necessity. A Reconsideration', *Praxis*, vol. V, no. 1–2 (1969) p. 20.

15. Marcuse uses the term 'concrete utopia' in 'Theory and Praxis', p. 27,

and his Bahro review, 'Proto-socialism', p. 6. In a 1972 interview, Marcuse rejected the term 'concrete utopia': 'In this context, I reject the term utopia. Utopia means, if it has any meaning at all, something that can nowhere be realized', *Neues Forum*, (November 1972) p. 19. Later in his attempt systematically to subvert and reverse meanings, Marcuse decided to utilize the term 'concrete utopia' which signifies utopian possibilities that can be realized; he stressed to me in conversation (La Jolla, 28 December 1978) that he now used Bloch's term 'concrete utopia' as a positive term to signify the realizability-in-principle of possibilities ideologically defamed as 'utopian'. On Bloch's concept of 'concrete utopia', see Douglas Kellner and Harry O'Hara, 'Utopia and Marxism in Ernst Bloch', *New German Critique*, 9 (Fall 1976).

16. This was Marcuse's own position in his 1933 essay 'On the Philosophical Foundation of the Concept of Labor' (discussed in Chapter 3) and *Eros and Civilization* (discussed in Chapter 6). Its rejection represents one of the most significant changes in Marcuse's theory in the 1960s. A series of articles appeared in the early 1970s which attacked – or defended – Marcuse for maintaining an unbridgeable gap between the realms of freedom and necessity, and work and play, which he had already rejected and overcome. See Edward Andrew, 'Work and Freedom in Marcuse and Marx', *Canadian Journal of Political Science*, vol. III, no. 2 (June 1970); William Leiss, 'Technological Rationality: Notes on "Work and Freedom" in Marcuse and Marx', and Edward Andrew, 'A Reply to William Leiss', *Canadian Journal of Political Science*, vol. IV, no. 3 (September 1971); and Morton Schoolman, 'Further Reflections on Marcuse and Marx', *Canadian Journal of Political Science*, vol. VI, no. 2 (June 1973). These essays are symptomatic of a widespread tendency to neglect emancipatory elements in Marcuse's theory and to fail to note some of the most interesting transformations in his thought.

17. Marcuse, 'Foreword', *Negations*, p. xviii. See Karl Marx, *Grundrisse* (London: Penguin, 1973) pp. 690ff. Marx's *Grundrisse* was of utmost importance in helping Marcuse to envisage a Marxian notion of liberated labour and the realm of freedom appearing within the realm of necessity. He refers to the *Grundrisse* model of liberated labour in several essays and in *ODM*, pp. 35ff and *EL*, p. 21. Although the *Grundrisse* was published in a German language version in Russia in two volumes in 1939 and 1941, Rosdolsky claims that 'only three or four copies of the 1939–1941 edition ever reached the "western world"', cited in Martin Nicolaus, 'Forword', *Grundrisse*, p. 7. Marcuse was one of the first 'Western Marxists' to see the significance of the *Grundrisse* for Marxisn theory. On the *Grundrisse*, see Roman Rosdolsky, *The Making of Marx's Capital* (London: Pluto Press, 1975).

18. Marcuse, 'Forword', *Negations* p. xx.

19. See *EC, ODM* and his neglected essay, 'The Individual in the Great Society', which I shall draw upon in the following discussion.

20. Marcuse, 'The Individual in the Great Society', p. 32.

21. Ibid.
22. Ibid.
23. Marx, *Capital III*; Marcuse concluded his 1933 essay on labour by citing this passage. See 'On the Philosophical Foundation of the Concept of Labour', pp. 36–7 (discussed in 3.4).
24. Marcuse, 'The Realm of Freedom', p. 22.
25. Ibid. Actually, throughout Marx's writings there is a distinction between labour as free, creative activity and alienated labour under capitalism; it is present in the section on automation in the *Grundrisse*, pp. 690–712 (discussed below) and appears in the distinction made by Marx, Engels and others between 'work' as 'wage-slavery' (enforced labour under capitalism) and 'labour' as free, creative activity under Communism. See, for example, the passage in Marx's 1864 'Inaugural Address to the Working Men's International Association', where he distinguishes between 'hired labour' and 'associated labour': 'to bear fruit, the means of labour need not be monopolised as a means of dominion over, and of extortion against, the labouring man himself; and that, like slave labour, like serf labour, hired labour is but a transitory and inferior form, destined to disappear before associated labour plying its toil with a willing hand, a ready mind, and a joyous heart'; Marx, in *The Marx-Engels Reader*, p. 518. See also Marx's 'Critique of the Gotha Program', where Marx talks of overcoming the antithesis between mental and physical labour so that 'labour has become not only a means of life but life's prime want', *The Marx-Engels Reader*, p. 531. These passages suggests that the model of labour and liberation which contains possibilities for the liberation of labour is the most widely used model for Marx and that the model in *Capital* III is both secondary in textual importance in the Marxian corpus and in many ways is politically questionable and misleading.
26. For critiques of fetishizing the development of the forces of production in socialist theory and practice, see Frederic and Lou Fleron, 'Administration Theory as Repressive Political Theory', *Telos*, 12 (Summer 1972) and Fleron's Introduction and Afterword to the anthology edited by him, *Technology and Communist Culture* (New York: Praeger, 1977). In the same anthology see Andrew Feenberg, 'Transition or Convergence: Communism and the Paradox of Development'.
27. See the examples in the Fleron articles and anthology (see note 26), and Rainer Traub, 'Lenin and Taylor', *Telos*, 37 (Fall 1978).
28. Earlier, Marcuse tended to accept Marx's critique of Fourier that work could never become play, that freedom could never enter the realm of necessity. See *EC*, pp. 217ff (discussed in Chapter 6) and the articles, 'Socialist Humanism?', p. 113 and 'The Obsolescence of Marxism?'. In the late 1960s, however, Marcuse favourably cited both Fourier's notion of 'attractive work' and the surrealist notion of the union of freedom and necessity in liberated thought and action (*EL*, pp. 21ff).
29. Marcuse, 'The Realm of Freedom', p. 24.
30. Ibid.
31. For other formulations of the 'vicious circle' dilemma, see *5L*, p. 80 and

EL, pp. 17ff. John Fry, in *Marcuse: Dilemma and Liberation*, argues that Marcuse's critical theory faces a double dilemma in that his social analysis discerns the crucial need for revolutionary change but sees no forces or possibilities to carry through the social transformation needed (pp. 25ff). Fry claims that according to Marcuse's theory, for social change to occur, there must already be needs for social change and for the struggle to be genuinely emancipatory: the needs for emancipation must precede the struggles. This second dilemma faces the 'vicious circle' cited above, namely that for new needs to develop, the mechanisms which produced the old needs must be abolished; or, in Marx's terms, social being must be changed to make possible changes in social consciousness. Fry concludes: 'The original socio-economic based dilemma has now become a re-enforced political, psychological, even instinctual/biological dilemma' (p. 47). Fry argues that Marcuse never resolves this dilemma and that therefore his version of critical theory must be seen as a failure (pp. 149ff). Fry, however, wrote his book in the early 1970s and thus could not examine *CR&R* and Marcuse's other 1970s works, which argue that advanced capitalism is itself producing the conditions to generate the new needs, and that these needs can be cultivated today in 'catalyst' groups and in 'the long march through the institutions', so that change of needs and society can take place in the same process. Fry's book is outdated and superseded by Marcuse's 1970s works, which establish a new foundation for critical theory.

32. See *CR&R*, pp. 17ff. and 'Proto-socialism', discussed in the last chapter. I take up this argument again later in this chapter in discussion of Marcuse's interpretation of the radical potential in the women's liberation movement. It is important to note that Marcuse is not calling for a 'new man' to be generated instantly by a radical conversion or transfiguration *à la* Expressionism and some versions of Existentialism. Rather, Marcuse's analysis suggests that a process of development is needed to create liberated individuals, which requires new institutions, new relations, new values, and ways of existing in a process of social transformation.

33. *5L*, pp. 65 and 74, and *EL*, p. 4.

34. In *EC*, Marcuse talked of technology making possible the abolition of alienated labour, but his central focus was on play, aesthetic and erotic gratification, and cultivation of a new reality principle and not on constructing a new technology. It is only with *ODM* that he radicalizes his critique of technology as hitherto domination and demands a 'new technology' (*ODM*, pp. 227ff). Ben Agger, in a generally provocative article, 'Marcuse and Habermas on New Science', *Polity*, vol. 9, no. 2 (Winter 1976) is thus mistaken when he claims that '*One-Dimensional Man* harbors an attack on the "use" of technology. *An Essay on Liberation*, however, charges technical rationality with containing an inherent function of domination, leading Marcuse to speculate about a nonexploitative science and technology', p. 165. We see here that even some of Marcuse's better interpreters have not thoroughly assimilated

the critique of technology in *ODM* and the concepts of a 'new technology' and 'aesthetic reduction' which find their most detailed formulation in Marcuse's seminal work, *ODM*.

35. Marcuse constantly makes this point and believes that the irrationality of the given society justifies total opposition. He also believes that criteria can be formulated to judge the possibilities of utilizing social resources to satisfy needs and develop potentialities, and that societies can be evaluated as to how they realize or fail to realize their own potentialities; see *ODM*, pp. 219ff. These criteria also enable one to judge the higher rationality of a 'transcendent project' (*ODM*, pp. 220f) and can even be used to justify violence to alter a society that miserably fails to meet human needs; see *CPT* and 'Ethics and Revolution'.

36. See the critiques of Marcuse as a technological determinist and reductionist cited in 8.24, and my polemics there against this position. In addition to the critics cited in the earlier discussion, others who sharply criticize Marcuse's alleged attack on science and technology in *ODM* include Peter Sedgwick, 'Natural Science and Human Theory', *Socialist Register* (1966) pp. 182ff; Rolf Ahlers, 'Is Technology Intrinsically Repressive?', *Continuum* VIII (1970) pp. 111–22; Hans-Dieter Bahr, *Kritik der 'Politischen Technologie'* (Frankfurt: Europäische Verlagsanstalt, 1970); and Jürgen Habermas, 'Technology and Science as "Ideology"', *Toward a Rational Society* (Boston: Beacon Press, 1970). I criticize Habermas's polemic against Marcuse's notion of the new science and new technology in the following pages and am attempting throughout this chapter to make clear the importance of Marcuse's critique of the dominant forms of science and technology and the relevance of his call for a new science and a new technology.

37. Habermas, 'Technology', pp. 86ff.

38. Ben Agger, in 'Marcuse and Habermas', argues that Habermas is unduly conservative in failing to grasp the possibility of a radical reconstruction of science, technology and labour which would eliminate the division of labour, hierarchy and certain forms of technology.

39. Agger, 'Marcuse and Habermas', p. 178.

40. Marcuse anticipates here 'economic conversion' projects begun in the late 1970s by the American Friends Service Committee, the Institute for Policy Studies, and other groups which would reconvert the economy from a war economy to a welfare economy.

41. For critiques of capitalist technology, see André Gorz, 'Technical Intelligence and the Capitalist Division of Labor', *Telos*, 12 (Summer 1972); Harry Braverman, *Labor and Monopoly Capital*; and David Noble, *America by Design*. On the connection between post-Second World War technology and the ecological crisis, see Barry Commoner, *The Closing Circle* (New York: Knopf, 1971) and on the microcomputer technologies, see the CSE Microelectronics Group, *Microelectronics: Capitalist Technology and the Working Class* (London: CSE Books, 1980). On the relationships between technology and capitalist relations of production, see the work of the *Radical Science*

Journal, nos 1–12 (London: 1974–1983), especially Bob Young, 'Science *is* social relations', *Radical Science Journal,* no. 5 (1977), as well as Les Levidow and Bob Young, eds, *Science, Technology and the Labour Process* (London: CSE Books, 1981). Young has told me that he believes that Marcuse had the most profound insights into the relationships between science, technology and capitalism of all neo-Marxist thinkers (conversations in Austin and London, November 1980 and December–January 1980–1).

42. For discussions of alternative technologies which could concretize such a theory of liberation, see Murray Bookchin, 'Towards a Liberatory Technology', in *Post-Scarcity Anarchism* (San Francisco: Ramparts Press, 1971); E. F. Schumacher, *Small is Beautiful* (New York: Harper & Row, 1973); Ivan Illich, *Tools for Conviviality* (New York: Harper & Row, 1973); *Radical Technology*, ed. Godfrey Boyle and Peter Harper (New York: Random House, 1976); David Dickson, *Alternative Technology and the Politics of Technical Change* (London: Fontana, 1974); Michael Shamberg, *Guerilla Television* (NY: Holt, 1971); Hans-Magnus Enzensberger, 'Constituents of a Theory of the Media', in *The Consciousness Industry* (New York: Seabury, 1974).

43. It has been argued that Marcuse is a Rousseauean glorifier of nature against civilization by Andre Clair, 'Une Philosophie de la Nature', *Esprit* (Janvier, 1969) pp. 51ff, and by Jean-Marie Benoist, *Marx est Mort* (Paris: Gallimand, 1970).

44. See *CR&R*, chapter 2, 'Nature and Revolution' and 'Ecology and Revolution', *Liberation* (September 1972) pp. 10–12. Marcuse's concept of a new relation to nature is rooted in the theories of Goethe, Schiller, Schelling and Feuerbach, and is similar in many ways to that of Ernst Bloch, who elaborates in detail a concept of nature as a support and ally in the human project. See Ernst Bloch, *Das Materialismus-problem* (Frankfurt: Suhrkamp, 1972) and *Experimentum Mundi* (Frankfurt: Suhrkamp, 1975), as well as the article by Burghart Schmidt, 'Marxismus und Naturbeherrschung bei Bloch', in *Kritik*, 20 (1979).

45. On the centrality of the 'domination of nature' concept in the Western ideology of science, see the book by Marcuse's student William Leiss, *The Domination of Nature* (Boston: Beacon Press, 1974). Strangely, Leiss almost completely ignores Marcuse's brilliant formulations of a new science and technology as alternatives to science-and-technology-as-domination; thus, in effect, Leiss capitulates to the very ideology of science and technology whose shortcomings he has pointed out. One searches in vain for an alternative conception of technology in Leiss's book, which ignores completely Marcuse's concept of the 'aesthetic reduction'. Again, we see here that even the best of Marcuse's students shy away from some of his most radical and provocative ideas.

46. Marcuse's concept of false needs has always elicited heated debate; see the literature cited in Chapter 8, note 23. The debate is vitiated, in my view, by failure to discuss Marcuse's concept of the 'aesthetic reduction' and the 'new technology', for it is these concepts which would

provide criteria to distinguish between true and false needs. Further, Marcuse's distinction rests on a theory of human nature and its liberation that involves theories of the aesthetic-erotic dimension of human nature, the emancipation of the senses, and the construction of a free society along the lines sketched out in this chapter. See Marcuse's discussion of needs in the interview 'For a United Front of the Left'. *Neues Forum* (November 1972) pp. 20ff. for further clarification.

47. Marcuse returns to the theme of the 'reduction of overdevelopment' in his 1966 preface to *EC*, pp. xviiif.

48. See the Club of Rome's Report, *The Limits to Growth* (New York: Signet, 1972). The Left has generally neglected the problem of limits to growth and population control, leaving the field to ideologists like Paul Ehrlich, who makes uncontrolled population *the* problem of modern society, and its control *the* solution. See *The Population Explosion* (New York: Ballantine, 1968). The issues of limiting population and industrial growth have to be thought through by the Left, which has for the most part accepted production and industrial growth as progressive *per se*, and has ignored the problem of population control by simply labelling the existing population policies as genocidal, or cynically believing that excessive population breeds squalor and poverty, which create the conditions and numbers for revolution. Unfortunately, these conditions also make a fertile ground for hopeless poverty and fascism. Marcuse's concept of the 'aesthetic reduction' thus forces radicals to confront some important issues that have been neglected and often misperceived. I elaborate these issues in a paper, 'The Ideology of Growth', in *Growth in Texas: A Conference Report* (Austin: Southwest Center for Public Policy, 1978).

49. See Jacques Ellul, *The Technological Society* (New York: Knopf, 1964); Martin Heidegger, *The Question Concerning Technology*; and the discussion of these and other theories of technology by Langdon Winner, *Autonomous Technology*.

50. For the futurist manifesto and other writings, see F. T. Marninetti, *Selected Writings* (New York: Farrar, Straus & Giroux, 1972). On the Bauhaus merger of art and technology, see Walter Gropius, *The Scope of Total Architecture* (New York: Harper & Row, 1956) and *New Architecture and the Bauhaus* (Cambridge, Mass.: MIT Press, 1935).

51. The concept of the 'new sensibility' functions for Marcuse both as a description of an historical force, depicting changes of subjectivity in contemporary society, and as an anthropological principle which serves as a normative-regulative ideal.

52. Marcuse, '1966 Political Preface', *EC*, p. xiv.

53. Marcuse, 'Liberation from the Affluent Society', and 'A Revolution in Values'.

54. Marcuse, 'Liberation from the Affluent Society', p. 197.

55. Marcuse, *EL*, pp. 10ff, *CR&R*, pp. 16ff, and 'A Revolution in Values', p. 331.

56. Marcuse, 'Liberation from the Affluent Society', pp. 196–7.
57. Marcuse, *CR&R*, pp. 16ff, 'Proto-Socialism', and 'Marxism and Feminism', where Marcuse argues that the social conditions of advanced capitalism are producing the conditions for the liberation of women and the spread of emancipatory feminine values. Quoting Angela Davis, Marcuse claims: 'The emerging conditions of such a development are mainly:
   — the alleviation of heavy physical labour,
   — the reduction of labour time,
   — the production of pleasant and cheap clothing,
   — the liberalization of sexual morality,
   — birth control,
   — general education'.
58. Marcuse, 'Marxism and Feminism'. A German translation is accessible in *Zeit-messungen*, and was widely discussed; see, for example, the discussion with Silvia Bovenschen and others in *Gespräche mit Herbert Marcuse*, which focused criticism on Marcuse's notion of a 'feminine nature'. See also the discussions by Joan Landes and Margaret Cerullo in *Telos*, 41 (Fall 1979).
59. Ibid.
60. Ibid.
61. Marcuse, 'A Revolution in Values', pp. 332–3.
62. Marcuse returns here to his Freudian anthropology to suggest the possibility of 'A Biological Foundation for Socialism? (*EL*, pp. 7ff). The question mark after the chapter title and use of qualifications like 'perhaps' throughout the chapter indicate that Marcuse intends to be more provocative and tentative than assertive in his biological speculations and renewed synthesis of Marx and Freud.
63. Marcuse frequently alludes in his writings to a close relation between Eros, beauty and a harmonious sensibility. Beauty has the power, he suggests, 'to check aggression: it forbids and immobilizes the aggressor' (*EL*, p. 26), a capacity he believes is symbolized by the Medusa myth. Marcuse also frequently cites Stendhal's notion that beauty expresses the 'promise of happiness'. Finally, he builds on Kant's equation of beauty with harmony, fulfilment, and pure 'interestless' pleasure. He then concludes that aesthetic needs for beauty translates itself into the drive to create a joyful, peaceful and harmonious environment which would make possible the gratification of aesthetic-erotic needs.
64. For a discussion of philosophical attacks on the passions and subjectivity, see Robert Solomon, *The Passions*.
65. Marcuse attributes crucial importance to the anthropology in Marx's 1844 (*Economic-Philosophical Manuscripts*. We recall that Marcuse was one of the first to call attention to their significance and to appropriate aspects of the Marxian theory of human nature into his own emerging theory. See Marcuse, 'The Foundations of Historical Materialism', *SCP* (discussed in Chapter 3). He returns to Marx's *Manuscripts* in *CR&R*, disclosing again that the section labelled by the

editors, 'Private Property and Communism', pp. 293–306, is of vital importance for Marcuse's project.

66. See also Marcuse, 'Society as a Work of Art', *Neues Forum* (November–December 1967) and 'Art as a Form of Reality', *New Left Review*, 74 (July–August 1972) pp. 51–8.

67. On Marcuse's aesthetics, see the sympathetic but critical essay by Stephen Eric Bronner, 'Art and Utopia', *Politics and Society* (Winter 1973); Heinz Paetzold's competent but unexciting discussion in *Neo-Marxistische Aesthetik* (Düsseldorf: Swann, 1974); and Morton Schoolman's provocative but flawed study, 'Marcuse's Aesthetics', *New German Critique*, no. 8 (Spring 1976). On art and critical theory, see Martin Jay, *The Dialectical Imagination*, and Fredric Jameson, *Marxism and Form* (Princeton: Princeton University Press, 1971).

68. Marcuse, *Der deutsche Künstlerroman*, discussed in Chapter 1.

69. See the discussions of Marcuse's theory of art in Chapters 1, 4, 7, 8 and 9; in 10.4.2 I shall critically discuss Marcuse's frequently unsystematic and sometimes contradictory analyses of art in his major works.

70. See Marcuse, *EC*, p. xxviii.

71. Marcuse, 'A Note on Dialectic', 1960 preface to *Reason and Revolution*, pp. x–xi.

72. Ibid.

73. Ibid.

74. Marcuse, 'Art as Form of Reality', p. 54. A similar position is taken in 'On Affirmative Culture', *Negations*, discussed in Chapter 3.

75. See also *Soviet Marxism*, discussed in Chapter 7.

76. See Marcuse, *CR&R*, pp. 195ff, and *AD*, p. xff. and 71ff.

77. Conversation with Marcuse, San Francisco, California, 24 March 1978.

78. Ibid.

79. Ibid. Marcuse went so far as to say that rock music today is protofascistic! Compare *CR&R*, pp. 114f. Marcuse does seem to like the music of Bob Dylan – see *CR&R*, pp. 117, 121; I have been told that in the 1960s Marcuse lectured on the emancipatory features of Dylan's 'Bringing It All Back Home' (conversation with Al Martinich, December 1978). Marcuse's turn from celebration of contemporary oppositional art back to his preferred eighteenth- and nineteenth-century novels and poetry did not please all his comrades in the cultural revolution. In a stinging review of *CR&R*, his friend Kingsley Widmer argues that 'Marcuse's apologetics for standard culturism seem not only misfocused but a mystification of radical retreat', 'Marcuse's Mystification', *The Village Voice* (28 September 1972) pp. 23–6. Widmer complains that Marcuse greatly overestimates the radical potential of 'high art' and underestimates the potential of contemporary aesthetic forms and rebellions. Stronger, Widmer accuses Marcuse of 'a left-religiosity of accepted high-art which can only encourage intellectual falsification', finding it odd that one of the most perceptive and thoroughgoing critics of contemporary culture exempts bourgeois art from his negative critique.

80. Marcuse acknowledges his debt to Adorno in *AD*, p. vii, *passim*. See T. W. Adorno, *Ästhetische Theorie* (Frankfurt: Surhrkamp, 1970). *The Aesthetic Dimension* was written with Erika Sherover Marcuse, his third wife and former student, and is dedicated to her: 'my wife, my friend and collaborator' (*AD*, p. vii). The book first appeared in German with the title *Die Permanenz der Kunst: Wider eine bestimmte Marxistische Aesthetik* (Munich: Carl Hanser Verlag, 1977). The German edition is slightly different, omitting, for instance, the concluding sentence in the English preface, discussed below, that 'there may be more subversive potential in the poetry of Baudelaire and Rimbaud than in the didactic plays of Brecht' (*AD*, p. xiii). The book received few reviews and did not elicit much discussion. Although *AD* develops the defence of bourgeois art in *CR&R*, and the critique of 'anti-art' and 'socialist realism', it contains some departures from Marcuse's earlier positions which I emphasize below. My interpretation of *AD* is indebted to conversations with Fred Alford and to his review article in *Telos*, 48 (Summer 1981) pp. 179–88).
81. Marcuse, 'Theory and Politics', p. 142.
82. Compare *EL*, p. 43 and *CR&R*, p. 99 with *AD*, pp. 55, 58–61.
83. Marcuse's final concession that total reconciliation and harmony are impossible puts in question some of his more utopian projections in *EC* concerning a non-repressive civilization.
84. In the passage before this, Marcuse articulates his final reflections on death (*AD*, p. 68). Compare *EC*, pp. 235ff; 'The Ideology of Death'; and Reinhard Lettau's reflections, 'Herbert Marcuse and the Vulgarity of Death', *New German Critique*, 18 (Fall 1979).
85. *AD*, pp. viiff. Marcuse also takes this position in *CR&R*.
86. See Widmer, 'Marcuse's Mystification'. One could argue also that Marcuse fails to see the utopian and oppositional moments in the popular arts of which he is so disdainful. See my article, 'TV'.
87. Adorno, *Ästhetische Theorie*.
88. See Chapter 6.
89. Marcuse constantly adhered to this position; compare Adorno, *Ästhetische Theorie*, p. 55, who does not require that 'authentic art' should project images of liberation and who prefers 'negative' art.
90. Marcuse, 'Theory and Politics', pp. 141–3.
91. Marcuse takes this position in 'On Affirmative Culture' and 'Art as a Form of Reality', but in other works, as mentioned, he slides from overemphasizing one pole or the other.
92. See my studies of Expressionism in *Passion and Rebellion: The Expressionist Heritage*, eds Stephen Eric Bronner and Douglas Kellner (New York: Bergen Press and Universe Books, 1983.
93. Marcuse is aware that no forms of high culture are *per se* revolutionary or reactionary (*AD*, p. 46), but he does not perceive how what he calls 'anti-art' – as well as popular culture – also takes many forms, with varying tendencies and political potential.
94. Marcuse, 'Art as a Form of Reality', p. 58.

Conclusion

1. See Steigerwald, *Herbert Marcuse's 'dritter Weg'*; Lucien Goldmann, 'Understanding Marcuse', *Partisan Review*, 38, 3 (1971) pp. 247–62; and Jürgen Habermas, 'Psychic Thermidor and the Rebirth of Rebellious Subjectivity', *Berkeley Journal of Sociology*, vol. XXV (1980) pp. 1–12.
2. Schoolman claims in *The Imaginary Witness* that Marcuse is a 'Mind Not be Be Changed by Place or Time', pp. 162ff, and various Marxist-Leninists, like Steigerwald, criticize Marcuse for his 'vacillations'.
3. On the concept of 'prefigurative politics', see *Beyond the Fragments*, by Sheila Rowbotham, Lynne Segal and Hilary Wainwright (Boston: Alyson, 1981).
4. On the 'Crisis of Marxism', see note 7 in the Introduction, and on capitalist crisis theories, see note 62 in Chapter 8 and Jürgen Habermas, *Legitimation Crisis*. Stanley Aronowitz suggested looking at the 'crisis of Marxism' as a periodic occurrence in the history of Marxism at a conference at the University of Illinois in July 1983.
5. Karl Korsch, cited in Chapter 4, note 87.
6. Conversation with Arthur Mitzman, Austin, Texas, October 1980.
7. Marcuse, 'Theorie und Praxis', in *Zeit-Messungen*, pp. 21–36.
8. See Kellner, 'Frankfurt School Revisited', on the Institute's later distancing from Marxism.
9. Leszak Kolakowski has joined the ranks of those who denounce Marcuse's utopianism. See *Main Currents of Marxism: The Breakdown*, vol. 3, (New York: Oxford, 1978) where Kolakowski presents a crude and sometimes grotesque caricature of Marcuse's thought as a 'totalitarian Utopia of the New Left', pp. 396ff. He claims that Marcuse is 'a prophet of semi-romantic anarchism in its most irrational form' and dismisses him as 'the ideologist of obscurantism' who promotes a 'totalitarian myth' (pp. 415, 420). It is curious that the anti-Stalinist Kolakowski echoes Stalinist attacks on Marcuse; compare Steigerwald, *Herbert Marcuses 'dritter Weg'*. Global dismissals of Marcuse shift from those who attack him for his pessimism to those who criticize him for his excessive utopianism. Both types of critique are one-sided and fail to explicate the many-sided complexity of Marcuse's thought, which eludes traditional categorization.
10. See 8.2.4 and 10.2 below.
11. The term 'romantic anti-capitalism' is used by Ferenc Feher, among others, to characterize the early Lukács and Bloch. See Feher's 'The Last Phase of Romantic Anti-Capitalism', *New German Critique*, 10 (1977) pp. 139–54. Characterizing the work of Lukács and Bloch as the *last* phase of romantic anti-capitalism fails to anticipate the work of Marcuse and segments of the New Left. 'Romantic anti-capitalism' seems to be, like 'scientific Marxism', a recurrent ideal-type within the history of Marxism. Compare Alvin W. Gouldner, 'Romanticism and Classicism', and Paul Breines, 'Marxism, Romanticism, and the Case of Georg Lukács', *Studies in Romanticism*, 16/4 (Fall 1977) pp. 473ff.
12. On the concept of an 'unfinished legacy', see Ernst Bloch, *Erbschaft dieser Zeit*.

Bibliography

The following bibliography is the most complete to date of Herbert Marcuse's published books, articles, reviews, interviews and various other contributions to books (prefaces, epilogues, etc.). Previous bibliographies have contained many omissions and errors. The first two bibliographies of Marcuse's publications up to 1967 appeared in *The Critical Spirit. Essays in Honor of Herbert Marcuse*, ed. Kurt H. Wolff and Barrington Moore, Jr (Boston: Beacon Press, 1967), pp. 427–33, and in *Antworten auf Herbert Marcuse*, ed. Jürgen Habermas (Frankfurt: Suhrkamp, 1968) pp. 155–61. There are some omissions in these bibliographies: neither lists the many book reviews that Marcuse published in the *Zeitschrift für Sozialforschung* from 1933–41, and I have discovered in addition some other interesting and important publications not listed. Morton Schoolman published an updated bibliography in 1980 in *The Imaginary Witness* (New York: Free Press, 1980) pp. 359–74, which he claims 'is based both upon bibliographies dated October 1968 and March 1972 that I received from Herbert Marcuse and upon my own research. I have listed all works published after 1972 and those published before that date but omitted from the 1968 and 1972 bibliographies prepared by Marcuse. To the best of my knowledge, the bibliography produced here is the most complete that has been published to date' (p. 359). In fact, however, not only does Schoolman fail to overcome the omissions in previous bibliographies but there are many errors as well. Further, his list of works published after 1972 omits more than half of Marcuse's publications from 1972–9.

Since Marcuse's own lists and previous bibliographies are incomplete, and since he published in a variety of sources often not listed in standard bibliographical reference works or accessible to computer searches, I cannot be sure that my list is complete and would appreciate readers sending me any sources that they discover. I list below first Marcuse's major published books, omitting translations of works that first appeared in English, and most foreign language collections of Marcuse's writings. Next I list articles, reviews, interviews, published lectures and contributions of various sorts to books. Here I do list translations of articles that first appeared in foreign languages, including republication in English and other languages of drafts or texts from his books. I then list the major references that I have consulted in my study.

Books

1922: *Der deutsche Künstlerroman*. Doctoral dissertation submitted to the University of Freiburg, 1922. First published in *Schriften 1* (Frankfurt: Suhrkamp, 1978).

1925: *Schiller-Bibliographie unter Benutzung der Trämelschen Schiller-Bibliothek* (Berlin: S. Martin Fraenkel). A lightly annotated bibliography of the various editions of Schiller's published works.

1932: *Hegels Ontologie und die Grundlegung einer Theorie der Geschichtlichkeit* (Frankfurt: V. Klosterman). Second and third editions published as *Hegels Ontologie und Theorie der Geschichtlichkeit* by Klosterman in 1968 and 1975.

1941: *Reason and Revolution* (New York: Oxford University Press). Second edition published in 1954 by Columbia University Press with a new Afterword. A Beacon Press paperback edition appeared in 1960 with a new Preface.

1955: *Eros and Civilization* (Boston: Beacon Press). A Vintage paperback edition appeared in 1961 with a new Preface and a Beacon Press paperback appeared in 1966 with a new 'Political Preface 1966'.

1958: *Soviet Marxism* (New York: Columbia University Press). A Vintage paperback edition appeared in 1961 with a new Preface but without the original Introduction.

1964: *One-Dimensional Man* (Boston: Beacon Press). Beacon has published many paperback editions, but without adding new material.

1965: *A Critique of Pure Tolerance* with Barrington Moore and Robert Paul Wolff (Boston: Beacon Press). A Beacon Press paperback appeared in 1968 with a new 1968 Postscript by Marcuse to his study 'Repressive Tolerance'.

1967: *Das Ende der Utopie* (West Berlin: Maikowski) contains 'Das Ende der Utopie' and 'Das Problem der Gewalt in der Opposition', which Marcuse delivered at the Free University of Berlin in 1967. Translated in *Five Lectures* but with abridged questions and discussion with the German audience. The German edition was republished in 1980 (Frankfurt: Verlag Neue Kritik) with a discussion '13 years later' by many of the original participants and others.

1968: *Negations: Essays in Critical Theory* (Boston: Beacon Press). Translations of several of Marcuse's 1930s Institute articles and some 1960s studies. Available as Beacon Press paperback.

1969: *An Essay on Liberation* (Boston: Beacon Press). Available as Beacon Press paperback.

1970: *Five Lectures* (Boston: Beacon Press). Contains two lectures presented in 1957 at a conference on Freud at the Frankfurt Institute; the lectures delivered in Berlin in 1967 (see above); and 'The Obsolescence of Psychoanalysis', presented to the annual meeting of the American Political Science Association in 1963, first published in German in *Das Ende der Utopie*, 1967. Also available as Beacon Press paperback.

1972: *Counterrevolution and Revolt* (Boston: Beacon Press). Also available as Beacon Press paperback.

Revolution oder Reform? (Munich: Kösel-Verlag). A debate with Karl Popper. English translation *Revolution or Reform?* (Chicago: New University Press, 1976).

1973: *Studies in Critical Philosophy* (Boston: Beacon Press). Collection of various essays, some translated for the first time. Available in Beacon Press paperback.

1975: *Zeit-Messungen* (Frankfurt: Suhrkamp). Collection of several 1970s lectures and interviews.

1978: *The Aesthetic Dimension* (Boston: Beacon Press). Available as Beacon Press paperback. Appeared earlier in German in a slightly different edition as *Die Permanenz der Kunst: Wider eine bestimmte Marxistische Aesthetik* (Munich: Carl Hanser Verlag, 1977).

Gespräche mit Herbert Marcuse (Frankfurt: Suhrkamp). Conversations with Jürgen Habermas, Silvia Bovenschen and others.

Note: Suhrkamp Verlag has been publishing Marcuse's collected works in German since 1978 under the rubric *Schriften*. *Schriften 1* (Frankfurt: Suhrkamp, 1978) contains Marcuse's doctoral dissertation *Der deutsche Künstlerroman* and early essays that are difficult to obtain. The *Schriften* collection is not, however, aiming at Marcuse's complete works and has so far omitted much of Marcuse's early work in the volumes that have so far appeared.

Articles, Reviews, Interviews, Lectures and Prefaces, etc.

1928: 'Beiträge zu einer Phänomenologie des Historischen Materialismus', *Philosophische Hefte*, 1, 1 (Berlin: 1928) pp. 45–68. English translation, 'Contributions to a Phenomenology of Historical Materialism', *Telos*, 4 (St Louis: Fall 1969) pp. 3–34.

1929: Review of Karl Vorländer, *Karl Marx, sein Leben und sein Werk, Die Gesellschaft*, 6 (part 2), 8 (Berlin: 1929) pp. 186–9.

'Über konkrete Philosophie', *Archiv für Sozialwissenschaft und Sozialpolitik*, 62 (Tübingen: 1929) pp. 111–28.

'Zur Wahrheitsproblematik der soziologischen Methode: Karl Mannheim, *Ideologie und Utopie', Die Gesellschaft*, 6 (part 2), 10 (Berlin: 1929) pp. 356–69.

1930: Review of H. Noack, *Geschichte und System der Philosophie*, *Philosophische Hefte* 2, 2 (Berlin: 1930), pp. 91–6.

'Transzendentaler Marxismus?' *Die Gesellschaft*, 7 (part 2), 10 (Berlin: 1930) pp. 304–26.

'Zum Problem der Dialektik' (part 1), *Die Gesellschaft*, 7 (part 1), 1 (Berlin: 1930) pp. 15–30. English translation, 'On the Problem of the Dialectic', *Telos*, 27 (St Louis: 1976) pp. 12–24.

1931: 'Das Problem der geschichtlichen Wirklichkeit: Wilhelm Dilthey', *Die Gesellschaft*, 8 (part 1), 4 (Berlin: 1931) pp. 350–67.

'Zum Problem der Dialektik', (part 2), *Die Gesellschaft*, 8 (part 2), 12 (Berlin: 1931), pp. 541–57. English translation, 'On the Problem of the Dialectic', *Telos*, 27 (St, Louis: 1976) pp. 24–39.

'Zur Auseinandersetzung mit Hans Freyers *Soziologie als Wirklichkeitswissenschaft*', *Philosophische Hefte* 3, 1–2 (Berlin: 1931) pp. 83–91.

'Zur Kritik der Soziologie', *Die Gesellschaft*, 8 (part 2), 9 (Berlin: 1931) pp. 270–80.

1932: Review of Heinz Heimsoeth, *Die Errungenschaften des deutschen Idealismus. Deutsche Literaturzeitung* 53, 43 (Berlin: 1932) pp. 2024–9.

'Neue Quellen zur Grundlegung des Historischen Materialismus', *Die Gesellschaft*, 9 (part 2), 8 (Berlin: 1932) pp. 136–74. English translation, 'The Foundations of Historical Materialism', *Studies in Critical Philosophy*, pp. 1–48.

1933: 'Philosophie des Scheiterns: Karl Jaspers Werk', *Unterhaltungsblatt der Vossischen Zeitung*, 339 (14 December, 1933).

'Über die philosophischen Grundlagen des wirtschaftswissenschaftlichen Arbeitsbegriffs', *Archiv für Sozialwissenschaft und Sozialpolitik*, 69 (Tübingen: 1933) pp. 257–92. English translation, 'On the Philosophical Foundation of the Concept of Labour in Economics', *Telos*, 16 (St Louis: Summer 1973) pp. 9–37.

Reviews in *Zeitschrift für Sozialforschung*, 2 (1933) of: Gertrud Baumer, *Familienpolitik*, p. 134; Roman L. Bach, *Die Entwicklung der französischen Geschichtsauffassung im 18. Jahrhundert*, p. 424; Hans Böhi, *Die religiöse Grundlage der Aufklärung*, p. 424; Walter Buch, *Niedergang und Aufstieg der Deutschen Familie*, p. 314; E. A. von Buggenhagen, *Die Stellung zur Wirklichkeit bei Hegel und Marx*, p. 424; Edgar Dacqué, *Natur und Erlösung*, p. 269; Alfons Degener, *Dilthey und das Problem der Metaphysik*, p. 425; Alfred Döblin, *Unser Dasein*, p. 269; Werner Falk, *Hegels Freiheitsidee in der Marxschen Dialektik*, p. 424; Heinrich Forsthoff, *Das Ende der humanistischen Illusion*, p. 269; Hans Freyer, *Herrschaft und Planung*, p. 269; Max Hammer, *Erziehungsprobleme des grosstädtischen Kleinburgerhauses*, p. 314; Ernst Harms, *Hegel und das 20. Jahrhundert*, p. 424; Der Alte Heim, *Ein Familienbuch*, p. 314; Magdalena Hoffman, *Der Humanitätsbegriff J. J. Rousseaus*, p. 424; Günther Holstein und Karl Larenz, *Staatsphilosophie*, p. 424; Hermann

Muckermann, *Die Familie*, vol. 1–7, p. 314; Alexander Pfänder, *Die Seele des Menschen*, p. 437; Max, S. J. Pribilla, *Die Familie*, p. 314; *Spinoza-Festschrift*, ed. Siegfried Hessing, p. 424; Adam von Trott zu Solz, *Hegels Staatsphilosophie und das Internationale Recht*, p. 424; Eduard Winter, *Bernard Bolzano und sein Kreis*, p. 425; Hans Zbinden, *Technik und Geisteskultur*, p. 269.

1934: Review of Herbert Wacker, *Das Verhältnis des jungen Hegel zu Kant*. *Deutsche Literaturzeitung* 55, 14 (Berlin: 1934), pp. 629–30.

'Der Kampf gegen den Liberalismus in der totalitären Staatsauffassung', *Zeitschrift für Sozialforschung* 3, 2 (Paris: 1934) pp. 161–95. English translation, 'The Struggle against Liberalism in the Totalitarian View of the State', *Negations*, pp. 3–42.

Reviews in *Zeitschrift für Sozialforschung*, 3 (1934) of: Heinrich Barth, *Das Sein in der Zeit*, p. 87; Franz Böhm, *Ontologie der Geschichte*, p. 263; Franz Brentano, *Kategorienlehre*, p. 421; Friedrich Brunstäd, *Logik*, p. 421; Clemens Cüppers, *Die erkenntnistheoretischen Grundgedanken Diltheys*, p. 416; Wilhelm Dilthey, *Pädagogik*, p. 416; Wilhelm Dilthey, *Der junge Hegel*, p. 416; Arnold Gehlen, *Theorie der Willensfreiheit*, p. 87; Gotthard Günther, *Hegels Logik*, p. 421; Johannes Henning, *Lebensbegriff und Lebenskategorie*, p. 416; Gustav Kafka, *Geschichtsphilosophie*, p. 263; Edouard Krakowski, *Contre le fatalisme historique*, p. 263; Arthur Liebert, *Wilhelm Dilthey*, p. 416, Georges Noël, *La Logique de Hegel*, p. 420; Carl Rabl, *Das Problem der Willensfreiheit*, p. 87; Erich Rothacker, *Geschichtsphilosophie*, p. 263; Max Scheler, *Schriften aus dem Nachlass*, p. 89; Hermann Schmalenback, *Das Ethos und die Idee des Erkennens*, p. 87; Henri Sérouya, *Le problème philosophique de la guerre et de la paix*, p. 93; Paul Simon, *Die Geschichte als Weg des Geistes*, p. 263; *Verhandlungen des dritten Hegelkongresses*, p. 420; Hermann Heimpel, *Deutschlands Mittalter*, p. 437; Leonhart von Renthe-Fink, *Magisches und naturwissenschaftliches Denken in der Renaissance*, p. 437; Heinrich Schaller, *Die Weltanschauung des Mittelalters*, p. 437; Lothar Schreyer, *Die Mystik der Deutschen*, p. 437; Wolfram von der Steinen, *Theoderich und Chlodwig*, p. 437; *Die deutsche Thomas-Ausgabe*, p. 437; Thomas von Aquino, *Summeder Theologie*, p. 437; John Cullberg, *Das Du und die Wirklichkeit*, p. 96; Jean Djordjévitsch, *Les rapports entre la notion d'État et la notion de classes sociales*, p. 273; Ernst Manheim, *Die Träger der öffentlichen Meinung*, p. 96; Josef Pieper, *Grundformen sozialer Spielregeln*, p. 96; Karl Pintschovius, *Das Problem des sozialen Raumes*, p. 100; *Probleme deutscher Soziologie Gedächtnisgabe für K. Dunkmann*, p. 96; Alexander von Schelting, *Max Webers Wissenschaftslehre*, p. 422; Carl Schmitt, *Der Begriff des Politischen*, p. 102; Wilhelm Steinberg, *Die seelische Eingliederung in die Gemeinschaft*, p. 96; Hans Steingraber, *Deutsche Gemeinschaftsphilosophie der Gegenwart*, p. 96.

1935: Reviews in *Zeitschrift für Sozialforschung*, 4 (1935) of: Ernst von Aster, *Die Philosophie der Gegenwart*, p. 269; Joachim Bannes, *Platon*.

Die Philosophie des heroischen Vorbildes, p. 437; Werner Betcke, *Luthers Sozialethik*, p. 437; Dietrich Bischoff, *Wilhelm Diltheys geschichtliche Lebensphilosophie*, p. 437; Erich Dinkler, *Die Anthropologie Augustins*, p. 437; Julius Drechsler, *Prinzipien der Aristotelischen Didaktik*, p. 437; Hans Engelland, *Gott und Mensch bei Calvin*, p. 437; Eberhard Fahrenhorst, *Geist und Freiheit im System Hegels*, p. 95; *Hegel heute*, p. 95; Fritz Hippler, *Staat und Gesellschaft bei Mill, Marx, Lagarde*, p. 95; *Idealismus. Jahrbuch für idealistische Philosophie*, ed. Ernst Harms, p. 271; Otto Kühler, *Sinn, Bedeutung und Auslegung der Heiligen Schrift in Hegels Philosophie*, p. 95; Helmut Kuhn, *Sokrates*, p. 437; John Laird, *Hobbes*, p. 437; Karl Mannheim, *Mensch und Gesellschaft im Zeitalter des Umbaus*, p. 269; Artur Mettler, *Max Weber und die philosophische Problematik in unserer Zeit*, p. 437; Hans Pfeil, *Der Psychologismus im englischen Empirismus*, p. 437; Erich Przywara, *Augustinus*, p. 437; Ludwig Reinhard, *Zur Kritik der marxistischen Geschichtsauffassung*, p. 95; Heinrich Rickert, *Grundprobleme der Philosophie*, p. 96; Heinrich Rickert, *Die Heidelberger Tradition und Kants Kritizismus*, p. 271; Emil Utitz, *Die Sendung der Philosophie in unserer Zeit*, p. 269; Walter Verwiebe, *Welt und Zeit bei Augustin*, p. 437; *Zeitschrift für Deutsche Kulturphilosophie*, eds Hermann Glockner and Karl Larenz, p. 96; E. H. Carr, *Karl Marx*, p. 103; Auguste Cornu, *Karl Marx*, p. 103; Auguste Cornu, *Moses Hess et la Gauche Hegelienne*, p. 103; Karl Marx, *Chronik seines Lebens in Einzeldaten*, assembled by the Marx-Engels-Lenin-Institut, p. 103; Karl Marx, Friedrich Engels, *Briefe an A. Bebel, W. Liebknecht, K. Kautsky und Andere*, p. 103; Gustav Mayer, *Friedrich Engels*, p. 103; Walter Nehler, *Arnold Ruge als Politiker und Politischer Schriftsteller*, p. 124.

1936: 'Autorität und Familie in der deutschen Soziologie bis 1933', in *Studien über Authorität und Familie* (Paris: Felix Alcan, 1936) pp. 737–52.

'Theoretische Entwurfe über Autorität und Familie: Ideengeschichtlicher Teil', in *Studien über Autorität und Familie*, pp. 136–228. English translation, 'A Study on Authority', in *Studies in Critical Philosophy*, pp. 49–156.

'Zum Begriff des Wesens', *Zeitschrift für Sozialforschung*, 5, 1 (Paris: 1936) pp. 1–39. English translation, 'The Concept of Essence', *Negations*, pp. 43–87.

Reviews in *Zeitschrift für Sozialforschung*, 5 (1936) of: Anton Antweiler, *Der Begriff der Wissenschaft bei Aristoteles*, p. 411; Otto Bollnow, *Dilthey*, p. 411; Walter Bröcker, *Aristoteles*, p. 411; H. Dingler, *Das Handeln im Sinne des höchsten Zieles*, p. 107; Hans Freyer, *Pallas Athene. Ethik des politischen Volkes*, p. 107; Arnold Gehlen, *Der Staat und die Philosophie*, p. 107; Paul Gohlke, *Die Entstehung der Aristotelischen Logik*, p. 411; Romano Guardini, *Christliches Bewusstsein*, p. 109; Heinrich Lammers, *Luthers Anschauung vom Willen*, p. 411; Theodor Litt, *Philosophie und Zeitgeist*, p. 107; Jacques Maritain, *Humanisme integral*,

p. 421; Erwin Metzke, *Geschichtliche Wirklichkeit*, p. 107; Merritt H. Moore, ed., *George H. Mead*; J. H. Muirhead, ed.: *Bernhard Bosanquet and his Friends;* Käte Oltmanns, *Meister Eckhart*, p. 411; Heinrich Ropohl, *Das Eine und die Welt*, p. 411; Theodor Steinbüchel, *Christliches Mittelalter*, p. 109; Kurt Sternberg, *Das Problem des Ursprungs in der Philosophie des Altertums*, p. 411; M. A. H. Stomps, *Die Anthropologie Martin Luthers*, p. 411; Thomas von Aquin, *Die Summe wider die Heiden in vier Büchern*, foreword by Alois Dempf, p. 109; Max Wundt, *Platons Parmenides*, p. 411; Willy Zippel, *Die Mystiker und die deutsche Gesellschaft des 13. und 14. Jahrhunderts*, p. 411; N. I. Bukharin, A. M. Deborin, Y. M. Uranovsky *et al.*, *Marxism and Modern Thought*, p. 280; J. Huizinga, *Im Schatten von Morgen*, p. 278; *Ganzheit und Struktur. Festschrift zum 60. Geburtstag Felix Kruegers*, eds Otto Klemm, Hans Volkelt, Karlfried Graf von Durckheim-Montmartin, p. 121.

1937: 'Philosophie und kritische Theorie', *Zeitschrift für Sozialforschung* 6, 3 (Parts: 1937) pp. 625–47. English translation, 'Philosophy and Critical Theory', *Negations*, pp. 134–58.

'Über den affirmativen Charakter der Kultur', *Zeitschrift für Sozialforschung* 6, 1 (Paris: 1937) pp. 54–94. English translation, 'The Affirmative Character of Culture', *Negations*, pp. 88–133.

Reviews in *Zeitschrift für Sozialforschung*, 6 (1937) of: Etienne und Philotheus Böhner, *Die Geschichte der Christlichen Philosophie*, Parts I and II, p. 661; Nicolai Hartmann, *Zur Grundlegung der Ontologie*, p. 174; Edmund Husserl, *Die Krisis der europäischen Wissenschaften und die transcendentale Phänomenologie*, in *Philosophia*, ed. A. Liebert; Johann Gustav Droysen, *Historik*, ed. Rudolf Hubner, p. 421; Fr. Meinecke, *Die Entstehung des Historiusmus*, p. 183; Leo Strauss, *The Political Philosophy of Hobbes*, p. 426.

1938: 'Zur Kritik des Hedonismus', *Zeitschrift für Sozialforschung*, 7, 1–2 (Paris: 1938) pp. 55–89. English translation, 'On Hedonism', *Negations*, pp. 159–200.

Reviews in *Zeitschrift für Sozialforschung*, 7 (1938) of: Franz Böhm, *Anti-Cartesianismus. Deutsche Philosophie im Widerstand*, p. 406; Franz Josef Brecht, *Heraklit. Ein Versuch über den Ursprung der Philosophie*, p. 219; Agnes Dürr, *Zum Problem der Hegelschen Dialektik und ihrer Formen*, p. 404; J. G. Fichte, *Nachgelassene Schriften*, Bd. II: *Schriften aus den Jahren 1790–1800*, ed. Hans Jacob, p. 404; Walter Frank, *Historie und Leben*, p. 226; Erich Franz, *Deutsche Klassik und Reformation*, p. 219; Hans Freyer, *Gesellschaft und Geschichte*, p. 225; Hans Freyer, *Über Fichtes Machiavelli-Aufsatz*, p. 404; Ernst-Günther Geyl, *Die Philosophie des sozialen Lebens im deutschen Idealismus*, p. 404; Heinrich Härtle, *Nietzsche und der Nationalsozialismus*, p. 226; Albert Hartmann, *Der Spätidealismus und die Hegelsche Dialektik*, p. 404; Franz Hippler, *Wissenschaft und Leben*, p. 225; Hans Jacob, ed., *J. G. Fichte*; Eva Kellner-Manger, *Mann und Frau im Deutschen Idealismus*, p. 404; J. Körner, ed., *Friedrich Schlegel*; Oskar Kraus, *Die Werttheorien*,

p. 219; Ernst Kriek, *Völkisch-politische Anthropologie*, p. 409; Hans Lipps, *Untersuchungen zu einer hermeneutischen Logik*, p. 229; Kurt Riezler, *Traktat vom Schönen*, p. 231; Friedrich Schlegel, *Neue philosophische Schriften*, ed. J. Körner, p. 219; Georg Siegmund, *Nietzsche, der Atheist und Antichrist*, p. 226; Gerhard Stammler, *Deutsche Logikarbeit seit Hegels Tod als Kampf von Mensch, Ding und Wahrheit*, Bd. 1: *Spekulative Logik*, p. 219; Franz Xaver Arnold, *Zur Frage des Naturrechts bei Martin Luther*, p. 237; Hellmut Bock, *Staat und Gesellschaft bei Francis Bacon*, p. 238; Josef Bohatec, *Calvins Lehre von Staat und Kirsche mit besonderer Berucksichtigung des Organismusgedankens*, p. 237; Wilhelm Dyckmans, *Das mittelälterliche Gemeinschaftsdenken unter dem Gesichtpunkt der Totalität*, p. 237.

1939: Reviews in *Zeitschrift für Sozialforschung*, 8 (1939) of: John Dewey, *Logic: The Theory of Inquiry*, p. 221; *International Encyclopedia of Unified Science*, vol. I, no. 1; Neurath, N. Bohr *et al.*, *Encyclopedia of Unified Science*; no. 2; Ch. W. Morris, *Foundations or the Theory of Signs*; no. 3: R. Carnap, *Foundations of Logic and Mathematics*; no. 5: Victor E. Lanzen, *Procedures of Empirical Science*, p. 228.

1940; 'An Introduction to Hegel's Philosophy', *Studies in Philosophy and Social Science (Zeitschrift für Sozialforschung)* 8, 3 (New York: 1940) pp. 394–412. An early publication of the Introduction to *Reason and Revolution*, pp. 3–29.

1941: 'A Rejoinder to Karl Löwith's Review of *Reason and Revolution*', *Philosophy and Phenomenological Research* 2, 4 (Buffalo: 1941–2) pp. 564–5.

'Some Social Implications of Modern Technology', *Studies in Philosophy and Social Science* 9, 3 (New York: 1941) pp. 414–39.

Reviews in *Studies in Philosophy and Social Science*, 9 (1941) of: John Dewey, *Theory of Valuation*, p. 144; Albert Myrton Frye and Albert William Levi, *Rational Belief, An Introduction to Logic*, p. 487; E. Gilson, *Dante et la philosophie*, p. 512; Richard v. Mises, *Kleines Lehrbuch des Positivismus*, p. 483; Bertrand Russel, *An Inquiry into Meaning and Truth*, p. 483; Charles Edward Trinkaus, *Adversity's Noblemen*, p. 513; Andrew Paul Ushenko, *The Problems of Logic*, p. 487; Ledger Wood, *The Analysis of Knowledge*, p. 487; Stuart Henderson Britt, *Social Psychology of Modern Life*, p. 500; Albert Walton, *The Fundamentals of Industrial Psychology*, p. 500; Ralph Barton Perry, ... *Shall not Perish from the Earth*, p. 531.

1948: 'Existentialism: Remarks on Jean-Paul Sartre's *L'Être et le néant*', *Philosophy and Phenomenological Research*, 8, 3 (Buffalo: March 1948), pp. 309–36. Republished, with a postscript in German, as 'Existentialismus', *Kultur und Gesellschaft*, 2 (Frankfurt: Suhrkamp, 1965) pp. 49–84. Reprinted in English, with the postscript translated as 'Sartre's Existentialism', *Studies in Critical Philosophy*, pp. 159–90; the reprint omits most of the last paragraph of the original English publication which contains interesting comments on Heidegger's and Sartre's philosophy.

1949: 'Lord Acton: Essays on Freedom and Power', *American Historical Review* 54, 3 (Richmond: April 1949) pp. 447–9.

1950: Review of Georg Lukács, *Goethe und seine Zeit. Philosophy and Phenomenological Research*, II, 1 (September 1950) pp. 142–4.

1951: 'Anti-Democratic Popular Movements', in H. J. Morgenthau, ed., *Germany and the Future of Europe* (Chicago: University of Chicago Press, 1951) pp. 108–13.

Review of John U. Nef, *War and Human Progress, American Historical Review* 57, 1 (Richmond: October 1951) pp. 97–100.

1954: 'Recent Literature on Communism', *World Politics*, 6, 4 (New York: July 1954) pp. 515–25.

1955: 'Dialectic and Logic since the War', in *Continuity and Change in Russian and Soviet Thought*, ed. Ernest J. Simmons (Cambridge: Harvard University Press, 1955) pp. 347–58.

'Trieblehre und Freiheit', in *Sociologica: Aufsätze, Max Horkheimer zum 60. Geburtstag gewidmet* (Frankfurt: Europäische Verlagsanstalt, 1955) pp. 47–66 (abridged version of the last chapter of *Eros and Civilization*).

'Eros and Culture', *Cambridge Review*, 1, 3 (Cambridge: Spring 1955) pp. 107–23.

'The Social Implications of Freudian "Revisionism"', *Dissent*, 2, 3 (New York: Summer 1955) pp. 221–40. Reprinted as the Epilogue to *Eros and Civilization*.

1956: 'A Reply to Erich Fromm', *Dissent*, 3, 1 (New York: Winter 1956) pp. 79–81.

'La Theorie des instincts et la socialization', *La Table Ronde*, 108 (Paris: 1956) pp. 97–110. Translation of material from *Eros and Civilization*.

1957: 'Trieblehre und Freiheit', in *Freud in der Gegenwart: Ein Vortragszyklus der Universitäten Frankfurt und Heidelberg zum hundertsten Geburtstag* (Frankfurt: Europäische Verlagsanstalt, 1957) pp. 401–24. First presented as an address at conferences in Frankfurt and Heidelberg commemorating the 100th anniversary of the birth of Freud, July 1956. English translation, 'Freedom and Freud's Theory of the Instincts', *Five Lectures*, pp. 1–27.

'Die Idee des Fortschritts im Lichte der Psychoanalyse', in *Freud in der Gegenwart*, pp. 425–41. English translation, 'Progress and Freud's Theory of the Instincts', *Five Lectures*, pp. 28–43.

'The Indictment of Western Philosophy in Freud's Theory', *Journal of Philosophy*, 54, 6 (New York: 14 March 1957) pp. 154–5. Summary of a paper presented at conference of 'The general Significance of the Work of Freud', New York, 1956.

'Theory and Therapy in Freud', *Nation*, 185 (New York: 28 September 1957) pp. 200–2.

Preface to Franz Neumann, *The Democratic and Authoritarian State*, ed. Herbert Marcuse (New York: Free Press, 1957) pp. vii–x.

1958: Preface to Raya Dunayevskaya, *Marxism and Freedom* (New York: Bookman, 1958) pp. 7–12. Omitted from later editions.

1959: 'Notes on the Problem of Historical Laws', *Partisan Review*, 26, 1 (New York: Winter 1959) pp. 117–29. Reprinted as 'Karl Popper and the Problem of Historical Laws', *Studies in Critical Philosophy*, pp. 193–208.

'Soviet theory and Practice', *Partisan Review*, 26, 1 (New York: Winter 1959), pp. 157–8. A response to criticisms of *Soviet Marxism* published in *Partisan review*, 25, 4 (New York: Fall 1958) by Alex Inkeles.

'The Ideology of Death', in *The Meaning of Death*, ed. Herman Feifel (New York: McGraw-Hill, 1959) pp. 64–76.

1960: 'De l'ontologie à la technologie: les tendences de la société industrielle', *Arguments*, 4, 18 (Paris: 1960) pp. 54–9.

'Actualité de la dialectique', *Diogène*, 31 (Paris: July–September 1960) pp. 89–98. Translation of 1960 preface to *Reason and Revolution*, 'A Note on Dialectic'.

1961: 'Language and Technological Society', *Dissent*, 8, 1 (New York: Winter 1961) pp. 66–74.

'L'Amour et la Mort', *Arguments*, 5, 21 (Paris: 1961) pp. 59–64. Translation of material from *Eros and Civilization*.

1962: 'Emanzipation der Frau in der repressiven Gesellschaft: Ein Gespräch mit Herbert Marcuse und Peter Furth', *Das Argument*, 23 (West Berlin: October–November 1962) pp. 2–12.

'Idéologie et société industrielle avancée', *Meditations*, 5 (Paris: Summer 1962) pp. 57–71. French translation of paper presented at Fifth World Congress of Sociology, Washington, DC, 1962. A German version appeared as 'Über das Ideologieproblem in der hochentwickelten Industriegesellschaft', in *Ideologie*, ed. Kurt Lenk (Neuwied: Luchterhand, 1971) pp. 395–419.

Review of George Lichtheim, *Marxism, An Historical and Critical Study*, *Political Science Quarterly*, 77, 1 (New York: 1962) pp. 117–19.

1963: 'Dynamismes de la société industrielle', *Annales*, 18, 5 (Paris: 1963), pp. 906–33.

'Zur Stellung des Denkens heute', in *Zeugnisse: Theodor W. Adorno zum 60. Geburtstag*, ed. Max Horkheimer (Frankfurt: Europäische Verlagsanstalt, 1963) pp. 45–9.

'Preface à l'edition française', *Le marxisme sovietique* (Paris: Gallimard, 1963).

'Le viellissement de la psychanalyse', *Partisans*, 32–33 (Paris: October–November 1963). A lecture delivered at the annual meeting of the APSA, published in English in *Five Lectures*.

1964: 'World without Logos', *Bulletin of the Atomic Scientists*, 20 (Chicago: January 1964) pp. 25–6.

490   *Bibliography*

1965: 'Industrialisierung und Kapitalismus', in *Max Weber und die Soziologie heute*, ed. Otto Stammer (Tübingen: J. C. B. Mohr [Paul Siebeck] 1965) pp. 161–80. Address presented at 15th German Sociological Congress held to commemorate the centenary of Max Weber's birth. Translated in *Max Weber and Sociology Today* (New York: Harper & Row, 1971) pp. 133–51. Contains discussion by Marcuse of comments on his paper, pp. 184–6. Revised as 'Industrialisierung und Kapitalismus im Werk Max Webers', in *Kultur und Gesellschaft*, 2 (Frankfurt: Suhrkamp, 1965) pp. 107–29. English translation of the revision, 'Industrialization and Capitalism in the Work of Max Weber', *Negations*, pp. 201–26.

'A Tribute to Paul A. Baran', *Monthly Review*, 16, 11 (New York: March 1965) pp. 114–15.

'Comes the Revolution: Reply to Marshall Berman's Review of *One-dimensional Man*', *Partisan Review*, 32, 1 (New Brunswick: Winter 1965) pp. 159–60.

'Der Einfluss der deutschen Emigration auf das amerikanische Geistesleben: Philosophie und Soziologie', *Jahrbuch für Amerikastudien*, 10 (Heidelberg: Carl Winter Universitätsverlag, 1965) pp. 27–33.

Epilogue to Karl Marx, *Der 18. Brumaire des Louis Bonaparte* (Frankfurt: Insel, 1965) pp. 143–50. English translation, 'Epilogue to the New German Edition of Marx's *18th Brumaire of Louis Napoleon*', *Radical America*, 3, 4 (Cambridge: July–August 1969) pp. 55–9.

Epilogue to Walter Benjamin, *Zur Kritik der Gewalt und andere Aufsätze* (Frankfurt: Suhrkamp, 1965) pp. 99–106.

'On Science and Phenomenology', in *Boston Studies in the Philosophy of Science*, 2, ed. Robert Cohen and Marx W. Wartofsky (New York: Humanities Press, 1965) pp. 279–90. Address presented at the Boston Colloquium for the Philosophy of Science, 13 February 1964.

'Perspektiven des Sozialismus in der entwickelten Industriegesellschaft', *Praxis*, 1, 2–3 (Zagreb: 1965) pp. 260–70. Address presented at Korcula, Yugoslavia, Summer 1964. English translation, 'Socialism in the Developed Countries', *International Socialist Journal*, 2, 8 (Rome: April 1965) pp. 139–51.

'Remarks on a Redefinition of Culture', *Daedalus*, 94 1 (Cambridge: Winter 1965) pp. 190–207. Reprinted in *Science and Culture*, ed. Gerald Holton (Boston: Houghton Mifflin, 1965) pp. 218–35. This collection was republished (Boston: Beacon, 1967).

'Socialist Humanism?', in *Socialist Humanism*, ed. Erich Fromm (New York: Doubleday, 1965) pp. 107–17.

'Statement on Vietnam', *Partisan Review*, 32, 4 (New Brunswick: Fall 1965) pp. 646–9.

'Einige Streitfragen', *Praxis*, 1, 2–3 (Zagreb: 1965) pp. 377–9.

'The Problem of Social Change in the Technological Society', in *Le Développement social*, ed. Raymond Aron and Bert F. Hoselitz (Paris:

Mouton, 1965) pp. 139–60. Volume Printed for limited distribution. Address presented to a UNESCO symposium on social development, May 1961.

1966: 'Ethics and Revolution', in *Ethics and Society*, ed. Richard T. De George (New York: Doubleday, Anchor Books, 1966) pp. 133–47. A 1964 lecture delivered at the University of Kansas.

'Role of Conflict in Human Evolution: Discussion', in *Conflict in Society*, eds Anthony de Reuck and Julie Knight (London: Ciba Foundation, 1966) pp. 36–59, *passim*. Participants: Marcuse, Kenneth E. Boulding, Karl W. Deutsch, Anatol Rapoport and others.

'Sommes-nous déjà des hommes?', *Partisans*, 28 (Paris: April 1966) pp. 21–9.

'The Individual in the "Great Society": Rhetoric and Reality' (part 1), *Alternatives* 1, 1 (San Diego: March–April 1966) pp. 14–20.

'The Individual in the "Great Society"' (part 2), *Alternatives* 1, 2 (San Diego: Summer 1966) pp. 29–35. Parts 1 and 2 reprinted in *A Great Society?*, ed. Bertram M. Gross (New York: Basic Books, 1966) pp. 58–80. Originally presented as an address at Syracuse University, 17 November 1965.

'Vietnam: Analyse eines Exemples', *Neues Kritik*, 36–37 (Frankfurt: July–August 1966) pp. 30–40.

'Zur Geschichte der Dialektik', *Sowjetsystem und Demokratische Gesellschaft*, vol. 1 (Freiburg: Herder Verlag, 1966) pp. 1192–1211.

1967: 'Interview', *L'Archibras* (October 1967). Translated in *Cultural Correspondence*, 12–14 (Summer 1981) p. 63.

'Aggressivität in der gegenwärtigen Industriegesellschaft', *Die Neue Rundschau*, 78, 1 (Frankfurt: 1967) pp. 7–21. English translation, 'Aggressiveness in Advanced Industrial Society', *Negations*, pp. 248–68. Revision of a talk given in Chicago in 1956 to a psychiatric society.

'The Inner Logic of American Policy in Vietnam', in *Teach-Ins: USA*, eds Louis Menashe and Ronald Radosh (New York: Praeger, 1967) pp. 64–7. A talk presented at the University of California, Los Angeles, 25 March 1966.

'The Obsolescence of Marxism', in *Marx and the Western World*, ed. Nikolaus Lobkowicz (Notre Dame: University of Notre Dame Press, 1967) pp. 409–17. Talk presented at International Symposium on Marxism at the University of Notre Dame in April 1966.

'The Responsibility of Science', in *The Responsibility of Power: Historical Essays in Honor of Hajo Holborn*, eds L. Krieger and F. Stern (New York: Doubleday, 1967) pp. 439–44. Revised text of a lecture presented at the University of California, Los Angeles in July 1966.

'Thoughts on the Defense of Gracchus Babeuf', in *The Defense of Gracchus Babeuf*, ed. John Anthony Scott (Amherst: University of Massachusetts Press, 1967) pp. 96–105.

'Zum Begriff der Negation in der Dialektik', *Filosoficky casopis*, 15, 3 (Prague: 1967) pp. 375-9. English translation, 'The Concept of Negation in the Dialectic', *Telos*, 8 (St Louis: Summer 1971) pp. 130-2. Address presented at the Prague Hegel Conference, 1966.

'Love Mystified: A Critique of Norman O. Brown', *Commentary*, 43, 2 (New York: February, 1967) pp. 71-5. A review of Brown's *Love's Body*, reprinted in *Negations*, pp. 227-43.

Art in the One-Dimensional Society', *Arts Magazine* (New York: May 1967) pp. 26-31. Based on an address presented at the School of Visual Arts in New York City, 8 March 1967. Reprinted in *Radical Perspectives in the Arts*, ed. Lee Baxandall (Baltimore: Penguin, 1972) pp. 53-67.

'Professoren als Staats-Regenten?', *Der Spiegel*, 35 (Hamburg: 21 August 1967) pp. 112-18. An interview with editors of *Der Spiegel*.

'Ist die Idee der Revolution eine Mystifikation?', *Kursbuch*, 9 (Frankfurt: June 1967) pp. 1-6. English translation, 'The Question of Revolution', *New Left Review*, 45 (London: September-October 1967) pp. 3-7. Reprinted as 'On Revolution: An Interview', in *Student Power*, eds Alexander Cockburn and Robin Blackburn (Baltimore: Penguin, 1969) pp. 367-72.

'On Changing the World: A Reply to Karl Miller', *Monthly Review*, 19, 5 (New York: October 1967) pp. 42-8.

'Ziele, Formen und Aussichten der Studentopposition', *Das Argument* (West Berlin: 1967) pp. 398-408.

'Die Zukunft der Kunst: Die Gesellschaft als Kunstwerk', *Neues Forum* 14, 167-8 (Vienna: November-December 1967) pp. 863-6.

1968: 'Liberation from the Affluent Society', in *To Free a Generation: The Dialectics of Liberation*, ed. David Cooper (Baltimore: Penguin, 1968) pp. 175-92; reprinted (New York: Collier, 1970). Address presented at Dialectics of Liberation Conference, London, July 1967.

'Gespräch mit Peter Merseburger: Herbert Marcuse und die prophetische Tradition', in *Weltfrieden und Revolution*, ed. Hans-Eckehard Bahr (Hamburg: Rowohlt, 1968) pp. 291-307. A discussion broadcast on German radio, Panorama-Sendung des NDR on 23 October 1967.

'Democracy Has/Hasn't a Future . . . A Present', *New York Times Magazine* (New York: 26 May 1968) pp. 30-1, 98-104. Panel discussion with Norman Mailer, Nat Henthoff and Arthur Schlesinger in New York, May 1968.

'Le philosophe Herbert Marcuse', *Le Monde* (Paris: 11 May 1968) pp. i and iii, 'Le Monde des Livres', interview with Pierre Viansson-Ponte.

'Les étudiants se revoltent contre un mode de vie', *Le nouvel Observateur* (20 May 1968), interview with Michel Bosquet.

'The Paris Rebellion', *Peace News* (Los Angeles: 28 June 1968) pp. 6-7.

'Credo nel progresso, nella scienza, nella technologia mas usati al servizio dell'uomo', *Temp* (Milan: 2 July 1968) pp. 16-23.

'Varieties of Humanism', *Center Magazine* 1, 5 (Santa Barbara, California: July 1968) pp. 12–15. A discussion with Harvey Wheeler.

'The People's Choice', *The New York Review of Books* (New York: 22 August 1968) p. 37. A letter from Marcuse, Erich Fromm, Dwight Macdonald and others endorsing Eugene McCarthy as President.

'L'Express va plus loin avec Herbert Marcuse', *L'Express* (Paris: 23 September 1968) pp. 54–62. An interview with Marcuse translated as 'Marcuse Defends His New Left Line', *New York Times Magazine* (New York: 27 October 1968) pp. 29–109.

'The Father of the Student Rebellion? Herbert Marcuse Talks to Robert McKenzie', *The Listener*, 80 (London: 17 October 1968) pp. 498–9.

'Gespräch mit Herbert Marcuse', *Die Weltwoche* (11 October 1968). Interview with Marcuse.

'Marcuse: Turning Point in the Struggle', *The Guardian* (New York: 9, 16 and 23 November). Interview with Robert Allen.

'Friede als Utopie', *Neues Forum*, 15, 180 (Vienna: November–December 1968) pp. 705–7. Address presented at Fourth Salzburg Humanist Conference, 1968.

1969: 'On the New Left', in *The New Left: A Documentary History*, ed. Massimo Teodori (New York: Bobbs-Merrill, 1969) pp. 468–73. An address presented at the twentieth anniversary programme for *The Guardian* (New York: 4 December 1968).

'The Realm of Freedom and the Realm of Necessity: A Reconsideration', *Praxis*, 5, 1–2 (Zagreb: 1969) pp. 20–5. Address presented at the Korcula Summer School on Marx and Revolution, Yugoslavia, June 1968.

'Revolutionary Subject and Self-Government', *Praxis*, 5, 1–2 (Zagreb: 1969) pp. 326–7. Response to issues raised in discussion at 1968 Korcula Summer School.

'Revolution 1969', *Neues Forum*, 16, 181 (Vienna: January 1969) pp. 26–9. An interview with Heinrich von Nussbaum.

'The Relevance of Reality', in *American Philosophical Association: Proceedings and Addresses, 1968–9* (College Park: 1969) pp. 39–50. Expanded version of Marcuse's presidential address at the annual meeting of the Pacific division of the American Philosophical Association, 28 March 1969.

'Réponse d'Herbert Marcuse', in *François Perroux interroge Herbert Marcuse* (Paris: Aubier-Montaigne, 1969) pp. 199–207.

'Student Protest is Nonviolent Next to Society Itself', *New York Times Magazine* (New York: 4 May 1969) p. 137.

'La Liberté et les impératifs de l'histoire', *La Liberté et l'ordre social* (Neuchâtel: la Baconnière, 1969) pp. 129–43. Address presented in English at a conference organized by the Recontres Internationales de Genève in 1969; first published in English in *Studies in Critical Philosophy*, pp. 211–23.

'Re-Examination of the Concept of Revolution', *New Left Review*, 56 (London: July–August 1969) pp. 27–34.

'Revolution aus Ekel', *Der Spiegel*, 31 (Hamburg: 28 July 1969) pp. 103–6. An interview with the editors of *Der Spiegel*, translated into English in *Australian Left Review* (December 1969) pp. 36–47.

'Nicht einfach zerstören', *Neues Forum*, 16, 188–9 (Vienna: August–September 1969) pp. 485–8.

1970: 'The End of Utopia', *Ramparts* (April 1970) pp. 28–34. Translation of part of 1967 Berlin talk.

'Only a Free Arab World Can Co-Exist with a Free Israel', *Israel Horizons* (June–July 1970). Introduction to Hebrew edition of *One-Dimensional Man* and *An Essay on Liberation*.

'Marxism and the New Humanity: An Unfinished Revolution', in *Marxism and Radical Religion: Essays toward a Revolutionary Humanism*, eds John C. Raines and Thomas Dean (Philadelphia: Temple University Press, 1970) pp. 3–10.

'USA: Organisationsfrage und revolutionäres Subjekt', *Kursbuch*, 22 (West Berlin: 1970) pp. 45–60. Reprinted in *Zeit-Messungen*, pp. 51–69. A conversation with Hans-Magnus Enzensberger.

'Der Humanismus in der fortgeschrittenen Industriegesellschaft', in *Die erschreckenende Zivilisation*, ed. Oskar Schatz (Europa Verlag: Vienna, 1970) pp. 15–33. The volume also contains panel discussions with Marcuse, Leo Lowenthal and others from a 1965 conference on Humanism in Salzburg. The above article appeared as 'Humanismus – gibt's den noch?', *Neues Forum*, 17, 196 (Vienna: 1970) pp. 349–53 and in French as 'Sommes-nous déjà des hommes?', 1966.

'Eine Brief', *Neues Forum*, 17, 196 (Vienna: 1970) p. 353. Marcuse responds to charges that he withdrew from public activity after being attacked as a CIA agent.

'Art as a Form of Reality', in *On the Future of Art*, ed. Edward F. Fry (New York: Viking Press, 1970) pp. 123–34. 1969 talk presented at a conference sponsored by the Gugenheim Museum in New York. Reprinted in *New Left Review*, 74 (London: July–August 1972) pp. 51–8.

'Charles Reich – a negative view', *New York Times* (New York: 6 November 1970) p. 41. Reprinted as 'Charles Reich as Revolutionary Ostrich', in *The Con III Controversy*, ed. Philip Nobile (New York: Pocket Books, 1971) pp. 15–17.

Foreword to second edition of Leo Lowenthal and Norman Gutermann, *Prophets of Deceit* (Palo Alto, California: Pacific Books, 1970) pp. v–vii.

1971: 'Conversation with Sam Keen and John Raser', *Psychology Today*, 4, 9 (Del Mar: February 1971) pp. 35–66.

'Dear Angela; letter', *Ramparts*, 9 (Berkely: February 1971) p. 22.

'The Movement in an Era of Repression: An Assessment', *Berkeley Journal of Sociology*, 16 (Berkeley: Winter 1971–2) pp. 1–14. Address presented at the University of California, Berkeley, 3 February 1971.

'Reflections on Calley', *New York Times* (New York: 13 May 1971) p. 45.

'Zeit für Disziplin', *Neues Forum*, 18, 214 (Vienna: August–September 1971) pp. 39–40. A conversation with Dieter Straubert.

'Reflexion zu Theodor W. Adorno – Aus einem Gespräch mit Michaela Seiffe', in *Th. W. Adorno zum Gedächtnis*, ed. Hermann Schweppenhäuser (Frankfurt: Suhrkamp, 1971) pp. 47–51.

'A Reply to Lucien Goldmann', *Partisan Review*, 38, 4 (New Brunswick: Winter 1971–2) pp. 397–400.

1972: 'Can Communism be Liberal? Herbert Marcuse v. Raymond Aron', *New Statesman*, 23 (London: 23 June 1972) pp. 860–1.

'Ecology and Revolution. A symposium', *Liberation*, 17, 6 (New York: September 1972) pp. 10–12. Marcuse's contribution to a French conference on ecology with Sicco Mansholt, Edgar Morin and others, first published in *Le Nouvel Observateur*, 397.

'Art and Revolution', *Partisan Review*, 39, 2 (New Brunswick: Spring 1972) pp. 174–87.

'Für Einsheitsfront der Linken', *Neues Forum*, 19, 225 (Vienna: November 1972) pp. 19–23. A conversation with Rolf Gössner and Paul Hasse in Freiburg, Germany.

1973: 'Interview with Marcel Rioux', *Forces*, 22 (Montreal: 1973). French version pp. 47–63; English original pp. 76–8.

'When Law and Morality Stand in the Way', *New York Times* (New York: 27 June 1973) p. 39. Republished in *Society*, 10, 6 (New Brunswick: 1973) pp. 23–4.

'Some General Remarks on Lucien Goldmann', *Revue de l'institut de sociologie de l'Université Libre de Bruxelles*, 3, 4 (Bruselles, 1973) pp. 543–4. Reprinted in Lucien Goldmann, *Cultural Creation in Modern Society* (St Louis: Telos Press, 1976) pp. 128–30.

'A Revolution in Values', in *Political Ideologies*, eds James A. Gould and Willis Truitt (New York: Macmillan, 1973) pp. 331–6. A lecture delivered at a conference on Science, Technology and Values, February 1972, at the University of South Florida.

1974: 'Marxism and Feminism', *Women's Studies*, 2, 3 (Old Westbury: 1974) pp. 279–88. A lecture presented at Stanford University, 7 March 1974; reprinted by many underground presses.

'A Conversation with Herbert Marcuse', *Bill Moyers' Journal* (New York: Educational Broadcasting Corporation, 12 March 1974). Transcript of PBS television interview, pp. 1–10.

'Remplacer le "travail aliené" par la création: un entretien avec Herbert Marcuse', interview with Pierre Dommergues and Jean-Michel Palmier, *Le Monde*, 10 May 1974, pp. 22–3.

'A propos du livre "On a raison de se révolter"', *Liberation* (Paris: 7 June 1974) p. 9. Conversation with Jean-Paul Sartre and friends.

'Theorie und Praxis', A lecture presented in Frankfurt on 28 June 1974 on the fiftieth anniversary of the founding of the Institute for Social Research. Revised and expanded in *Zeit-Messungen*.

'Bemerkungen über Kunst und Revolution', transcript of a radio lecture on Senden Freies Berlin, 9 July 1974.

1975: 'Zu "Marxismus und Feminismus"'. Gespräch mit Herbert Marcuse', *Links*, 66 (Offenbach: January 1975) pp. 9–10.

'Was ist Weiblichkeit?', *Schwarze Protokolle*, 11 (Berlin: May 1975) pp. 59–61. Discussion with women's group from Munich, Germany about Marcuse's essay 'Marxism and Feminism', in Starnberg, Germany, July 1974.

'Dialogue: Marcuse-Millet', *Off Our Backs*, 5, 7 (Washington, DC: 1975) pp. 20–1. Excerpts and summary of debate between Marcuse, Kate Millet and others.

1976: 'Un nouvel ordre', *Le Monde Diplomatique*, no. 268 (July 1976).

'Ist eine Welt ohne Angst möglich?' *Der Spiegel*, 37 (Hamburg, 6 September 1976) p. 199. Excerpts from a discussion between Marcuse, Mitscherlich and Biederman.

1977: 'Enttäuschung', in Gunther Neske, ed., *Erinnerung an Martin Heidegger* (Pfullingen: 1977) pp. 161–2.

'Heidegger's Politics: An Interview with Frederick Olafson', *Graduate Faculty Philosophy Journal*, 6, 1 (New York: 1977) pp. 28–40. Interview taken from the transcript of a film taken at a conference on the philosophy of Martin Heidegger, sponsored by the Department of Philosophy, University of California at San Diego, La Jolla, California, 4 May 1974.

'Mord darf keine Waffe der Politik sein', *Die Zeit*, 39 (Hamburg: 23 September 1977) pp. 41–2. English translation, 'Murder is Not a Political Weapon', *New German Critique*, 12 (Milwaukee: Fall 1977) pp. 7–8.

1978: 'Interview with Bryan Magee, "Marcuse and the Frankfurt School"', in *Man of Ideas*, ed. Bryan Magee (London: BBC, 1978) pp. 62–73. Published transcript of a BBC television interview.

'Theory and Politics: A Discussion', *Telos*, 38 (St Louis: Winter 1978–9) pp. 124–53. A discussion with Habermas and others, first published in *Gespräche mit Herbert Marcuse*.

'Un pyromane à la retraitre', discussion with Jean Marabini, *Le Monde* (19 November 1978).

1979: 'The Reification of the Proletariat', *Canadian Journal of Philosophy and Social Theory*, 3, 1 (Winnipeg: Winter 1979) pp. 20–3. Talk presented at the American Philosophical Association Convention, San Francisco, 23 March 1978.

'Protosozialismus und Spätkapitalismus. Versuch einer Revolutions-theoretischen Synthese von Bahros Ansatz', *Kritik*, 19 (Berlin: 1979) pp. 5–27. English translation, 'Protosocialism and Late Capitalism: Toward a Theoretical Synthesis Based on Bahro's Analysis', in *Rudolf Bahro: Critical Responses*, ed. Ulf Wolter (White Plains, NY: M. E. Sharpe, 1980) pp. 24–48.

'Failure of the New Left?' *New German Critique*, 18 (Milwaukee: Fall 1979) pp. 3–11. Expanded version of a lecture given in April 1975 at the University of California, Irvine. First published in German in *Zeit-Messungen*.

1981: 'On *The Aesthetic Dimension:* A Conversation with Herbert Marcuse', *Contemporary Literature*, XXII, 4 (Fall 1981) pp. 416–24. A 1978 interview with Larry Hartwick.

References consulted

Adorno, T. W., *Zur Metakritik der Erkenntnistheorie* (Frankfurt: Suhrkamp, 1970).

Adorno, T. W., *Asthetische Theorie* (Frankfurt: Suhrkamp, 1970).

Adorno, T. W. and Horkheimer, Max, *Dialectic of Enlightenment* (New York: Seabury, 1972).

Althusser, Louis, *For Marx* (New York: Vintage, 1968).

Anderson, Perry, *Considerations on Western Marxism* (London: New Left Books, 1976).

Arato, Andrew and Breines, Paul, *The Young Lukács and the Origins of Western Marxism* (New York: Seabury, 1979).

Arato, Andrew and Gebhardt, Eike (eds) *The Essential Frankfurt School Reader* (New York: Urizen, 1978).

Arnason, Johann Pall, *Von Marcuse zu Marx* (Neuwied and Berlin: Luchterhand, 1971).

Aronowitz, Stanley, *False Promises* (New York: McGraw-Hill, 1973).

Aronowitz, Stanley, *The Crisis in Historical Materialism* (New York: Praeger & Bergin Press, 1981).

Aronson, Ronald, *Jean-Paul Sartre – Philosophy in the World* (London: New Left Books, 1980).

Bahro, Rudolf, *The Alternative in Eastern Europe* (London: New Left Books, 1978).

Baran, Paul and Sweezy, Paul, *Monopoly Capital* (New York: Monthly Review, 1965).

Batalov, E., *The Philosophy of Revolt* (Moscow: Progress Publishers, 1977).

Baudrillard, Jean, *The Mirror of Production* (St Louis: Telos Press, 1975).

Benjamin, Walter, *Illuminations* (New York: Schocken, 1968).

Bloch, Ernst, *Das Prinzip Hoffnung* (Frankfurt: Suhrkamp, 1959).

Bloch, Ernst, *Erbschaft dieser Zeit* (Frankfurt: Suhrkamp, 1962).

Breines, Paul (ed) *Critical Interruptions* (New York: Herder & Herder, 1970).

Bronner, Stephen Eric and Kellner, Douglas (eds) *Passion and Rebellion: The Expressionist Heritage* (New York and London: Universe Books, Bergin Press and Croom Helm).

Breuer, Stefan, *Die Krisis der Revolutionstheorie* (Frankfurt: Syndikat, 1977).

Brown, Norman O., *Life Against Death* (New York: Vintage, 1959).

Buck-Morss, Susan, *The Origins of Negative Dialectics* (New York: The Free Press, 1977).

Carr, E. H., *History of Soviet Russia* (London and Baltimore: Penguin, 1964–1978).

Colletti, Lucio, *From Rousseau to Lenin* (London: New Left Books, 1972).

Dubiel, Helmut, *Wissenschaftsorganisation und politische Erfahrung* (Frankfurt: Suhrkamp, 1978).

Dunayevskaya, Raya, *Marxism and Freedom* (New York: Twayne Publishers, 1958).

Dutschke, Rudi, *Versuch Lenin auf die Fusse zu stellen* (Berlin: Rot Verlag, 1974).

Feenberg, Andrew, *Lukacs, Marx and the Sources of Critical Theory* (Totowa, NJ: Rowman & Littlefield, 1981).

Freud, Sigmund, *Standard Edition of the Collected Works of Sigmund Freud* (London: The Hogarth press).

Fromm, Erich, *Escape from Freedom* (New York: Holt, Rinehart & Winston, 1941).

Fromm, E., *The Sane Society* (New York: Holt, Rinehart & Winston, 1955).

Fromm, E. (ed) *Marx's Concept of Man* (New York: Grove Press, 1963).

Fromm, E., (ed) *Socialist Humanism* (Garden City, NY: Doubleday, 1966).

Fry, John, *Marcuse – Dilemma and Liberation* (New Jersey: Humanities Press, 1974).

Geoghegan, Vincent, *Reason and Eros: The Social Theory of Herbert Marcuse* (London: Pluto Press, 1981).

Gorz, Andre, *Farewell to the Working Class* (Boston: South End Press, 1982).

Gouldner, Alvin W., *The Two Marxisms* (New York: Seabury Press, 1980).

Gouldner, A. W., *The Dialectic of Ideology and Technology* (New York: Seabury, 1975).

Habermas, Jürgen (ed) *Antworten auf Herbert Marcuse* (Frankfurt: Suhrkamp, 1968).

Habermas, J., *Theory and Practice* (Boston: Beacon Press, 1974).

Habermas, J., *Toward a Rational Society* (Boston: Beacon Press, 1970).

Habermas, J., *Knowledge and Human Interests* (Boston: Beacon Press, 1971).

Habermas, J., *Legitimation Crisis* (Boston: Beacon Press, 1975).

Habermas, J., 'Psychic Thermidor and the Rebirth of Rebellious Subjectivity', *Berkeley Journal of Sociology*, XXV (1980) pp. 1–12.

Heidegger, Martin, *Being and Time* (New York: Harper & Row, 1962).
Heller, Agnes, *The Theory of Need in Marx* (London: Allison & Busby, 1976).
Holz, Hans Heinz, *Utopie und Anarchismus* (Cologne: Pahl-Rugenstein, 1968).
Horkheimer, Max, *Eclipse of Reason* (New York: Seabury, 1974).
Horkheimer, M., *Critical Theory* (New York: Herder & Herder, 1972).
Horowitz, Gad, *Repression* (Toronto and Buffalo: University of Toronto Press, 1977).
Husserl, Edmund, *Ideas* (New York: Collier Books, 1962).
Husserl, E., *The Crisis of European Sciences and Transcendental Phenomenology* (Evanston: Northwestern University Press, 1970).
Jacoby, Russell, *Social Amnesia* (Boston: Beacon Press, 1975).
Jameson, Fredric, *Marxism and Form* (Princeton: Princeton University Press, 1971).
Jay, Martin, *The Dialectical Imagination* (Boston: Little, Brown, 1973).
Katz, Barry, *Herbert Marcuse and the Art of Liberation* (London: New Left Books, 1982).
Kellner, Douglas 'The Frankfurt School Revisted', *New German Critique*, 4 (Winter 1975) pp. 131–52.
Kellner, D. (ed) *Karl Korsch: Revolutionary Theory* (University of Texas Press, 1977).
Kellner, D. and Roderick, Rick, 'Recent Literature on Critical Theory', *New German Critique*, 23 (Spring–Summer 1981) pp. 141–70.
Kolakowski, Leszak, *Main Currents of Marxism* (New York: Oxford, 1978).
Korsch, Karl, *Marxism and Philosophy* (London: New Left Books, 1970).
Korsch, K., *Karl Marx* (London: Chapman & Hall, 1938).
Lefebvre, Henri, *Everyday Life in the Modern World* (New York: Harper & Row, 1971).
Leiss, William, *The Domination of Nature* (Boston: Beacon Press, 1974).
Leiss, W., *The Limits to Satisfaction* (Toronto: University of Toronto Press, 1976).
Lipshires, Sidney, *Herbert Marcuse: From Marx to Freud and Beyond* (Cambridge, Mass: Schenkman, 1974).
Lowenthal, Leo and Dubiel, Helmut, *Mitmachen wollte ich nie* (Frankfurt: Suhrkamp, 1980).
Löwith, Karl, *From Hegel to Nietzsche* (Garden City: Doubleday, 1967).
Lowy, Michael, 'Marcuse and Benjamin: The Romantic Dimensions', *Telos*, 44 (Summer 1980) pp. 25–34.
Lukacs, Georg, *History and Class Consciousness* (Cambridge: MIT Press, 1971).
Lukacs, G., *Theory of the Novel* (Cambridge: MIT Press, 1971).
Lukacs, G., *Soul and Form* (Cambridge: MIT Press, 1974).
Lukacs, G., *The Young Hegel* (London: Merlin, 1975).
MacIntyre, Alasdair, *Herbert Marcuse: An Exposition and a Polemic* (New York: Viking, 1970).
Marx, Karl and Engels, Friedrich, *Collected Works* (New York: International Publishers, 1975–84).

Mattick, Paul, *Critique of Marcuse* (New York: Seabury, 1973).
Palmier, Jean-Michel, *Herbert Marcuse et la nouvelle gauche* (Paris: Belfond, 1973).
Piccone, Paul, 'Phenomenological Marxism', *Telos*, 9 (Fall 1971) pp. 3–31.
Poster, Mark, *Existential Marxism in Postwar France* (Princeton: Princeton University Press, 1975).
Reich, Wilhelm, *Sex-Pol* (New York: Vintage, 1972).
Sartre, Jean-Paul, *Critique of Dialectical Reason* (London: New Left Books, 1975).
Sartre, J-P., *On a raison de se revolter* (Paris: Gallimand, 1974).
Schoolman, Morton, *The Imaginary Witness* (New York: Free Press, 1970).
Schmidt, Alfred, *Zur Idee der kritschen Theorie* (München: Hanser, 1974).
Schiller, Friedrich, *The Aesthetic Letters, Essays, and the Philosophical Letters* (Boston: Little, Brown, 1845).
Slater, Phil, *Origin and Significance of the Frankfurt School* (London: Routledge & Kegan Paul, 1977).
Steigerwald, Robert, *Herbert Marcuses dritter Weg* (Cologne: Pahl-Rugenstein, 1969).
Weber, Max, *The Protestant Ethic and the Spirit of Capitalism* (New York: Scribner, 1958).
Weber, M., *From Max Weber* (New York: Oxford University Press, 1958).
Wellmer, Albrecht, *Critical Theory of Society* (New York: Seabury, 1974).
Winner, Langdon, *Autonomous Technology* (Cambridge: MIT, 1977).
Wolff, Kurt and Moore, Barrington, Jr (eds) *The Critical Spirit* (Boston: Beacon Press, 1964).

Index